To Martha Saenz

With best and
warm regards.

[illegible]

June 2002

Liber Amicorum Ibrahim F. I. Shihata

Liber Amicorum Ibrahim F.I. Shihata

International Finance and Development Law

edited by

Sabine Schlemmer-Schulte & Ko-Yung Tung

with a Foreword by

James D. Wolfensohn
President, The World Bank Group

KLUWER LAW INTERNATIONAL

The Hague • London

Boston • New York

Published by Kluwer Law International,
P.O. Box 85889, 2508 CN The Hague, The Netherlands.

Sold and distributed in the U.S.A. and Canada
by Kluwer Law International,
101 Philip Drive, Norwell, MA 02061, U.S.A.
tel: (781) 871-6600; fax: (781) 681-9045

In all other countries, sold and distributed
by Kluwer Law International,
P.O. Box 85889, 2508 CN The Hague, The Netherlands
tel: 31 70 308 1562; fax: 31 70 308 1555

ISBN 9041114793

Kluwer Law International incorporates the publishing programs of
Graham & Trotman Ltd, Kluwer Law and Taxation Publishers,
and Martinus Nijhoff Publishers.

Table of Contents

Foreword

In September 2000, Ibrahim F.I. Shihata retired from the World Bank after more than 15 years of service as Vice President (later Senior Vice President) and General Counsel, and almost 17 years as Secretary-General of the International Centre for Settlement of Investment Disputes (ICSID).

A lawyer of distinction with a strong sense of history, a sharp analytic mind, and a deep feeling for the institution, Ibrahim Shihata has been a devoted executive of this Institution, committed to the causes it serves, and to facing head on the challenges of development.

During his tenure as General Counsel of the Bank, he was actively involved in Bank policy discussion and formulation. He issued a series of detailed legal opinions. Based on these opinions, the Bank was able to respond to a host of development needs not envisaged in the Bank's Articles of Agreement but, as times changed, put on the Bank's agenda by my predecessors and myself. All his opinions were endorsed by the Bank's Board of Executive Directors, which has the authority to interpret the Bank's Articles. It was Ibrahim Shihata's integrity and objectivity that made his advice successful and convincing to the decision-makers in our institution. The special imprint of his advice was that it served the purposes of the institution as a whole, rather than any particular organ of the institution or member country.

Ibrahim Shihata was also the architect of the Multilateral Investment Guarantee Agency (MIGA). He contributed to the establishment of the Global Environment Facility (GEF), was responsible for the preparation of the World Bank Guidelines for the Legal Treatement of Foreign Investment, and played a major role in the establishment of the Inspection Panel.

Under his tenure as Secretary-General of ICSID, the Centre witnessed a great expansion of its case-load, with a ten-fold increase from one or two cases registered per year to twelve cases.

His eleven books on matters related to the World Bank's work have made him one of the most prolific in legal circles, and a much quoted legal writer on the Bank.

There is no more appropriate way to honor Ibrahim Shihata's contribution to the Bank and to the law of international finance and development, and to commemorate his retirement from the bank, than to dedicate this *Liber Amicorum* to him. Ibrahim's friends, prominent practitioners and scholars as well as colleagues from within the institution, have contributed essays on current and emerging issues of international finance and development law, in addition to providing insight into some of his achievements. I am proud of this collective initiative dedicated to an exceptional lawyer and *first among equals* by his peers, and his colleagues in the institution. Together with other outstanding lawyers of the world's legal community, we are privileged to thank, and hold in public esteem a great jurist. May this tribute to Ibrahim Shihata contribute to a fruitful discourse on legal issues of the global development process.

James D. Wolfensohn
President
The World Bank Group

Curriculum Vitae

IBRAHIM F.I. SHIHATA

Place and Date of Birth:
Damietta, Egypt, August 19, 1937

Nationality: Egyptian

Education: *Licence en Droit* (a four year degree, study of law, economics and public finance - Cairo University, 1957)
Graduate Diploma in Public Law (Cairo University, 1958)
Graduate Diploma in Private Law (Cairo University, 1959)
LL.M. (Harvard Law School, 1962, waived)
Doctor of Juridical Science (S.J.D.) (A post graduate doctorate degree in international law, Harvard University, 1964)

Recent and Current Positions:

- Senior Vice President and General Counsel, The World Bank (1983-1998), and Secretary-General, International Centre for Settlement of Investment Disputes (1983-2000);
- Chairman, International Development Law Institute, Rome (1983-)

Earlier Positions:

- Director-General, OPEC Fund for International Development, Vienna (1976-83)
- Executive Director (member of the Board), International Fund for Agricultural Development, Rome (1977-83)
- Legal Adviser, Kuwait Fund for Arab Economic Development, Kuwait (1966-70; 1972-76)
- Lecturer, then Associate Professor of International Law, Ain Shams University, Cairo (1964-66; 1970-72) (gave graduate courses in international air law and international economic law)
- Of Counsel, Zaki Hashem & Associates, Cairo (1970-72)
- Member, Technical Bureau of the President, Damascus, United Arab Republic (Egypt and Syria) (1959-60)
- Member, Egyptian *Conseil d'Etat*, Cairo (1957-60), seconded in the third year to the Technical Bureau of the President of the Republic).

Other Responsibilities:

- Participated in the drafting committee of the Constitution of the Union of Arab Republics, 1971 (chaired by the then Vice President of Egypt and consisting of ministers from Egypt, Syria and Libya).
- Prepared, and participated in the negotiation of the first draft of the Agreements establishing the Arab Fund for Economic and Social

Development; the Inter-Arab Investment Guarantee Corporation; the Arab Bank for Economic Development in Africa and the OPEC Fund for International Development.

- Coordinated the positions of OPEC countries in the negotiations related to the establishment of the International Fund for Agricultural Development (IFAD) and chaired the Committee which prepared the Agreement Establishing IFAD (Rome, 1974-76).
- Coordinated OPEC countries' positions in the negotiations related to establishing the Common Fund for Commodities (Geneva, 1980-82).
- Was in charge of the initiative of establishing the Multilateral Investment Guarantee Agency (MIGA), a World Bank affiliate, Washington, 1983-88. Redesigned the proposal, chaired the 20 meetings of the World Bank's Executive Directors' Committee of the Whole on the preparation of the MIGA Convention and led the efforts for launching MIGA, including the preparation of its detailed regulations until the appointment of its first Executive Vice-President in mid-1988.
- Chaired the three-man group which prepared the "World Bank Guidelines on the Legal Treatment of Foreign Investment" and was in charge of the process which led to the adoption of these Guidelines by the World Bank-IMF Joint Committee of Governors, known as the "Development Committee," in September 1992.

- Represented the organizations he worked for in numerous international negotiations and conferences.
- Gave numerous lectures and speeches in Washington (D.C.), New York, Houston, Cambridge (Mass.), San Francisco, Miami, Dallas, Virgin Islands, Rio de Janeiro, Quito, Caracas, Montevideo, Cambridge (UK), Oxford (UK), London, Paris, Rome, Nice, Belgrade, Vienna, Cairo, Beirut, Alexandria, Hurghada (Egypt), Damascus, Tunis, Amman, Jedda, Kuwait, Dubai, Sanaa, Libreville, Singapour, Beijing, Colombo, Bangkok, Tokyo and Melbourne among other cities.

Publications: Books

- The Power of the International Court to Determine Its Own Jurisdiction, (Martinus Nijhoff, Kluwer International), 1965 (in English)
- International Air and Space Law, 1966 (in Arabic)
- International Joint Economic Ventures, 1969 (in Arabic)
- International Guarantee for Foreign Investments, 1971 (in Arabic)
- Treatment of Foreign Investments in Egypt, 1972 (in Arabic)
- Secure and Recognized Boundaries, 1974 (in Arabic)
- The Arab Oil Embargo, 1975 (in Arabic, English and Spanish)
- The Other Face of OPEC, 1982 (Longman, in English, French and Spanish)

- The OPEC Fund for International Development - The Formative Years, 1983 (in English)
- A Program for Tomorrow - Challenges and Prospects of the Egyptian Economy in a Changing World, 1987 (in Arabic)
- MIGA and Foreign Investment: Origins, Operations, Policies and Basic Documents of the Multilateral Investment Guarantee Agency, 1988 (Martinus Nijhoff, in English; translated into Chinese)
- The World Bank and the Arab World, 1990 (in Arabic)
- The European Bank for Reconstruction and Development, 1990 (Martinus Nijhoff, in English)
- The World Bank in a Changing World, 1991 (Martinus Nijhoff, in English, being translated to Russian)
- Towards Comprehensive Reform, 1993 (in Arabic)
- Legal Treatment of Foreign Investment—The World Bank Guidelines, 1993 (Martinus Nijhoff, in English)
- The World Bank Inspection Panel, 1994 (Oxford University Press, in English)
- The World Bank in a Changing World, Volume 2 (Martinus Nijhoff, 1995)
- My Will For My Country, Volume 1, 1995 (in Arabic)
- My Will For My Country, Volume 2, 1995 (in Arabic)
- My Will For My Country, Volume 3, 1996 (in Arabic)

- My Will For My Country, Volume 4, 1997 (in Arabic)
- Complementary Reform - Essays on Legal, Judicial and Other
- Institutional Reforms Supported by the World Bank, 1997 (Martinus Nijhoff, in English, translated to Russian, 1998)
- My Will for My Country - The Complete Text, 1999 (in Arabic)
- The World Bank Inspection Panel: in Practice (Oxford University Press, revised 2nd ed., 2000)
- The World Bank in a Changing World, Vol. 3 (Martinus Nijhoff, 2000)
- The World Bank Legal Papers (Martinus Nijhoff, 2000)

Other Publications

More than two hundred published essays in Arabic and English in different fields of international law, foreign investment, development finance, international organizations, conflict resolution and international arbitration, many of which have been translated into other languages, especially Arabic, French and Spanish).

Honors and Election to Scholarly Associations:

- Babcock Prize for Best Essay in International Law, Duke University, U.S., 1962
- "Grosses Silbernes Ehrenzeichen am Bande für Verdienste um die Republik Österreich," Republic of Austria, 1983
- Kuwait Prize for Scientific Progress (Social Sciences), 1983

- Member, *Institut de Droit International*, Geneva, since 1989
- Doctor of Law, *honoris causa*, University of Dundee, U.K. (July 1995)
- Doctor of Law, *honoris causa*, Université de Paris I - Panthéon - Sorbonne, France (1996)
- Doctor of Law, *honoris causa,* American University in Cairo (2000),
- Honorary Fellow, Institute of Advanced Legal Studies, University of London (1997)
- Harry Leroy Jones Award, Washington Foreign Law Society, Washington, DC (1998)
- Honorary Chairman, The Egyptian Center for Economic Studies (1999 -)
- Honorary Member of the Chilean Academy of Social Science, Santiago (2000)
- Conference and Proceedings in honor of Ibrahim F.I. Shihata, organized by the American Society of International Law, (ASIL) the Georgetown University Law Center and the World Bank, March 1999 (the book has been published (by ASIL) under the title: The World Bank, International Financial Institutions, and the Development of International Law (Edith Brown Weiss, Andres Rigo Sureda & Laurence Boisson de Chazournes eds., 2000)
- Liber Amicorum Ibrahim F.I. Shihata – International Finance and Development Law (Sabine Schlemmer-Schulte & Ko-Yung Tung eds., 2001)

Professional Societies' Offices and Other Positions:

- Chairman of the Board, International Development Law Institute (Rome, 1983 -)
- Member of the Board, Vienna Institute for Development and Coooperation, Vienna, Austria, since 1982
- Editor, ICSID Review - Foreign Investment Law Journal, Washington, DC (1986 -)
- Founding Advisory Director, Institute of Transnational Arbitration, Houston, Texas (1987 -).
- Member, Executive Council, American Society of International Law, Washington, D.C. (1984-87) and Member of the Society since 1960
- Former Member, Advisory Committee, Research Centre for International Law (Cambridge, United Kingdom)
- Former Vice-President, World Association for International Relations, (The Hague)
- Member, Advisory Board, OPEC Review (1979-)
- Former Member of the Board, The International Fertilizer Development Institute, Muscle Shoals, Alabama (1979 - 83)
- Founding Member of the Board of WTO Association, London (1996-)

Special areas of Expertise

International law; development policy; international arbitration

Introductory Remarks by the Editors

This collection of essays from most renowned international law scholars and practitioners in honor of Ibrahim Shihata, as well as Ibrahim Shihata's academic and professional record itself (chronicled in his *curriculum vitae* reproduced on pages xiii *et seq.* in this book), provide a remarkable testimony to the extent and depth of his contributions to and achievements in international finance and development law. As editors of this book, we will not repeat what others have put in better words. We will also remain silent where the facts clearly speak for themselves. However, on behalf of the institutions with which we are affiliated, and in which Ibrahim Shihata has served for seventeen years, we would like to thank him for the inspiration that his work has given to his friends and colleagues, whose papers we are privileged to present in this *Liber Amicorum*.

This *Liber Amicorum* brings together essays of incumbent or former general counsels or heads of the African Development Bank, the Arab Fund for Economic and Social Development, the Asian Development Bank, the European Bank for Reconstruction and Development, the Inter-American Development Bank, the Inter-American Investment Corporation, the Islamic Development Bank, the International Finance Corporation, the International Fund for Agricultural Development, the Multilateral Investment Guarantee Agency, the Nordic Investment Bank, the Organization of Petroleum Exporting Countries Fund, the World Bank, and other international finance and development institutions. Collectively with distinguished academics, jurists and arbitrators in international tribunals such as the International Court of Justice, the World Trade Organization's Appellate Body, and the International Centre for Settlement of Investment Disputes, well-known practitioners, and colleagues of Ibrahim Shihata at the World Bank's

Legal Department, they write about current and emerging issues in international finance and development law. These issues include the various institutions' special development assistance profile, the settlement of international investment disputes, foreign investment law, legal and judicial reform, the environment, the rule of law, anti-corruption reform, liability and immunity of international financial institutions, etc. All contributions illuminate the broad spectrum of a vital body of international law to the progressive development of which Ibrahim Shihata contributed tremendously.

In addition to the variety of substantive issues the essays deal with, they also show the unique character of Ibrahim Shihata as a practitioner and scholar. They finally reveal the passions Ibrahim Shihata and his friends and colleagues share for attaining the goals of global development through law.

Sabine Schlemmer-Schulte ***Ko-Yung Tung***

Washington, D.C.
December 2000

Post Script

The value of Ibrahim Shihata's work as a lawyer, negotiator, arbitrator, mediator, and "statesman" is unquestioned. He had a major impact on the institutions he served, and many saw him as personifying the "rule of law" in the world of international finance and development institutions. Aside from these aspects, I would here like to express my esteem for a less well-known, but equally important, aspect of his personality, complimentary to, and perhaps even *a conditio sine qua non* for, the part of him holding leading positions in the international civil service and making use of these positions for a public cause.

Beyond the integrity, objectivity, and loyalty to the mission of the institution Ibrahim Shihata displayed in his service to the World Bank's consecutive Presidents and Executive Directors in providing legally sound and practically wise advice, he impressed me in his own personal discipline and devotion to hard work. During the time I worked closely with Ibrahim Shihata, he became a model for me in that particular respect. While I did not agree with him on every issue, legal or managerial, I saw that he applied to himself the rigorous and high standards of professional excellence he asked for from those working with him for the benefit of the institution he served, even in the most extreme and most difficult professional and personal situations. I could understand how his long-held attitude towards work and objectives, made Ibrahim Shihata a natural authority in his field, independent from any position he held.

I am grateful to Ibrahim Shihata for having been able to work with him, experience the satisfaction from hard work, and see that, behind his great mind and disciplined manner, he also has a warm heart, sense of humor, and tolerant soul.

I am equally grateful and in great debt to his distinguished, renowned and learned friends, who have not hesitated for a moment to accept the invitation to contribute to this book in Ibrahim

Shihata's honor when asked, despite their heavy schedules and other demanding commitments.

Those of Ibrahim Shihata's friends who had been invited to contribute but were unable to do so due to conflicting commitments or *force majeure* are also in my gratitude.

I thank Ko-Yung Tung, the World Bank's new General Counsel and Ibrahim Shihata's successor, for not hesitating a second and taking on editorship responsibility for this book at a time where the project was no longer in its infancy but had progressed to a degree that implied full trust in its concept from his side.

Finally, I thank James Wolfensohn, President of the World Bank, for contributing the foreword to this book as well as for his kind and generous support of the project.

With my great respect for the honoree, those who honored him with their contributions, those who would have wanted but could not contribute, the Bank's new General Counsel, and the Bank's President.

Sabine Schlemmer-Schulte
Washington, D.C.
December 2000

Acknowledgements

This *Liber Amicorum* was made possible through the faith, enthusiasm, and commitment of several individuals. This project would not have been realized without the endorsement of Annebeth Rosenboom, Kluwer Law International, The Hague, The Netherlands, who supported the idea of putting together a *Liber Amicorum* in honor of Ibrahim Shihata vigorously from the very beginning. John Berger, Kluwer Law International, Boston, Massachusetts, USA, expertly guided us through the printing process, helped us to manage our deadline, and accompanied the completion of this project, even beyond his official tenure at Kluwer. He was assisted by Salena Hastings and Steve Melisi.

A devoted team of editorial assistants, talented junior lawyers from all over the world at various stages of their beginning careers, coming to the World Bank to work on various projects, volunteered their time to this *Liber Amicorum* as their own personal tributes to a great jurist: my senior editorial assistant, Rowena Margaret S. Gorospe (Philippines); and my four editorial assistants, Nara Beginyan (Armenia), Hege Elisabeth Kjos (Norway), Johanna Rinceanu (Germany), and Maria Fernanda Peréz Solla (Argentina). Last, but not least, my profound thanks go to two individuals who have tirelessly helped in various administrative tasks: executive assistant Michelle Lemaire, and senior staff assistant Meena Pillai.

I personally apologize for and take on the responsibility for any mistakes that occurred in the editing of the contributions to this book.

Sabine Schlemmer-Schulte
Washington, D.C.
December 2000

SHIHATA: THE MAN, THE MISSION

Y. Seyyid Abdulai[*]

I. INTRODUCTION

For many professionals whose lives and careers have been dedicated to the cause of the development of the South, the name of Dr. Ibrahim Shihata stands out in sharp relief. Few who have followed the twists and turns of the international development debate over the last three decades can fail to appreciate the contributions of the man who has left an indelible stamp on so many of the world's working institutions, and who to this day continues to steer the conscience of the international community to face the collective challenge that global poverty represents.

To speak of Dr. Shihata's sense of duty and unwavering commitment to the cause of development is to miss the point about one whose practical struggle to win equal rights and opportunities for the marginalized has won friends and influenced people the world over. Throughout a long and illustrious career in development law and finance, Dr. Shihata always insisted on the imperative urgency of poverty reduction, patiently cajoling reluctant donors and deploying his well-tested diplomatic skills to shore up support for new and durable instruments of change.

For Dr. Shihata, simply living with global poverty as a natural by-product of industrial growth could never be a realistic option for an increasingly interdependent community of nations on the threshold of the 21st century. Nobody ever accused Dr. Shihata of fudging his principal objective, that of securing a genuine multilateral consensus to build a better world with all major players

---

[*] The views expressed in this article are those of the author and should not be attributed to the institution he is affiliated with.

submitting their just quota. Moreover, his personal resolve to force the pace of change has been profound.

Despite a raft of academic accomplishments, Dr. Shihata was, and is, no ivory tower intellectual. As Director-General of the OPEC (Organization of the Petroleum Exporting Countries) Fund for International Development, where he served from its inception in 1976 until July 1983, he is remembered by staff and consultants alike for his assiduous hands-on attention to detail, always going the extra mile and expecting others to follow suit. His personal example of hard work and institution-building zeal effectively inspired his colleagues to work towards improving the lot of the world's poor and disadvantaged.

Often battling against the odds, he successfully convinced and then co-opted numerous floating voters within the development community to back his cause. So how did this extraordinary man come to acquire such authority and the self-assurance needed to pursue such a determined course?

Early exposure to the consequences of economic injustice prompted Dr. Shihata to ponder the origins of deprivation and question the historical forces which held more than half the world in a vice-like grip of underdevelopment. Born into the maelstrom of Middle Eastern politics, Dr. Shihata first gathered three degrees in his native Egypt, graduating from Cairo University Law School in 1957 and obtaining a doctorate in juridical science from Harvard in 1964. In the late fifties he sat on the Council of State in Cairo and served on the Technical Bureau of the ill-fated United Arab Republic in Damascus.

Ever eager to make a lasting difference, Dr. Shihata turned to teaching and writing, eventually authoring over twenty books and monographs on various aspects of advanced economic law and finance. For years he taught international law in Cairo, later serving as legal advisor and general counsel to the Kuwait Fund for Arab Economic Development. There he developed the astute management and diplomatic skills which were to stand him in good stead in his exacting role as Director on the Executive Board of the fledgling International Fund for Agricultural Development (IFAD). For years he guided research through his role as trustee of the Washington Institute on International and Foreign Trade Law and of the Oxford-based Center of Research on the New International

Economic Order. His was the driving force behind the inauguration of the Multilateral Investment Guarantee Agency (MIGA) and his unique contributions to the body of international natural resources law was recognized in 1994 when Dr. Shihata was awarded an honorary doctorate by Dundee University's prestigious Center for Petroleum, Mining Law and Policy.

Today, he is a recognized authority on Bretton Woods and international economic law, having served from 1983 to October 1998 as General Counsel for the World Bank and Secretary-General of ICSID at a time of unprecedented institutional reform and policy transformation. Upon retirement as Senior Vice-President and Special Advisor to the Bank's President this year, he will have penned some five volumes of memoranda and legal opinions, according to the institution's present Managing Director Sven Sandstrøm. In recent testimony, Sandstrøm was effusive in praise of Dr. Shihata's shrewdness "in protecting the multilateral and non-political character" of the World Bank, resisting the blandishments of big powers and jealously safeguarding the interests of all its member countries.

And that is how we, too, would choose to characterize his enduring legacy to the OPEC Fund, a body embracing oil producing nations from all continents but which has nonetheless demonstrated a unique purpose in committing no-strings assistance to the very poorest of developing countries. Under Dr. Shihata's stewardship the OPEC Special Fund grew steadily into a strong moral force, acting independently on the world stage and beholden to no single constituency. Its geographic coverage, Dr. Shihata often reminded audiences, is second only to that of the World Bank Group.

II. THE OPEC FUND'S EARLY YEARS

The origins of the Fund lie in OPEC's response to the challenges posed by the monumental shifts in economic power which attended the first oil price adjustment of 1973. Developing nations had been placed under extreme pressure resulting from worsening terms of trade with the developed world and the attendant scapegoating of OPEC members determined to realize an economic rent for the depletion of their national petroleum resources. Dr. Shihata recalls how the historic Algiers Summit of OPEC Sovereigns and Heads of State meeting in March 1975 first mooted the idea of a collective aid facility to strengthen the OPEC group's record of fraternal cooperation with other developing countries. A spontaneous decision was made, he said, to refer the initiative to a joint committee of OPEC finance ministers charged with detailing specific proposals. Those subsequent discussions soon bore fruit.

He recounts how, back in July 1976, he first arrived in Vienna clutching a copy of the Agreement Establishing the OPEC Special Fund, a temporary facility whose status was unclear and whose potential longevity was doubted even by OPEC insiders at that time. Without legal personality, no money of its own nor any office space to occupy, Dr. Shihata quickly understood his new baby would be stillborn if he did not act decisively. Following initial exchanges with OPEC officials it became obvious that the Special Fund was no full-fledged international organization but neither could it hide under the existing OPEC apparatus.

Since there was no room at the OPEC Secretariat headquarters, Dr. Shihata hung his hat in a suite made available in the Vienna Stock Exchange, courtesy of the Austrian bank *Creditanstalt*. Urged by consultants to draw up grand organizational charts and set about constructing an administrative empire in which international bankers recruited to the cause would be proud to serve, Dr. Shihata recoiled, insisting on doing things his way.

"My job was to manage an organization which did not exist; I had no intention of crowding the place with all kinds of people without knowing what they were going to do," he recalls. "I said, 'we'll start the work first and appoint people and make staff regulations as we progress.'" So with three professionals and a secretary, Dr. Shihata started a process of innovation that transformed what the authorizing document described merely as "an international account" into a permanent and highly regarded lending institution.

Underscoring the temporary nature of the original enterprise, the Fund was constrained from the outset to open separate national accounts in the thirteen member countries into which all repayments would be made. Dr. Shihata therefore saw his first task as challenging the reservations of those who viewed the facility as a mere public relations ploy, and who wished to continue to tie aid disbursement to narrow, bilateral policy interests. "Necessity is the mother of invention and that is what I had to prove," he told an audience seven years later.

He wasted no time. His team managed to sign up six loan agreements within the first five months, an astonishing achievement given the group's operating constraints. It was an elaborate program which succeeded largely because Dr. Shihata adamantly refused to be bound by pre-existing structures common to similar institutions and because he was unafraid to jettison the traditional textbook approach. The mission was paramount, the means secondary.

That is not to suggest he blithely dispensed with the need for advance planning. Rather, he constructed a flexible lending program based on a philosophy which placed the poorest segments of needy countries at the very heart of the Fund's orientation. Instead of following the pattern pursued at that time by many national aid agencies, Dr. Shihata turned his back on the "first-come, first-served" model where loan proposals are entertained following a politically motivated definition of which countries will be eligible. Simply taking on the whole world as one's legitimate field of operations would inevitably mean giving more money to the better off countries at the expense of those which lacked the means and manpower to submit clear applications, and Dr. Shihata knew that to deploy this method would mean compromising the cherished ideals he so earnestly sought to promote.

With hindsight, Dr. Shihata acknowledged that the over-arching philosophy he set out during those early months set the tone for the approach taken by the Fund in later years. He started out with a clean sheet, untrammeled by bureaucratic habits and prejudices. As a general rule, he decided that all categories of activity would in principle qualify for Fund attention. These could be project loans or program loans and the Fund would even entertain applications for balance of payments support. In addition to making contributions to other agencies, the Fund would offer a regular, though limited stream of outright grants for technical assistance since he rightly identified this as one critical area where the poorest countries lacked indigenous capability. Most significantly, no one mechanism was held superior to any other since all were directed towards helping the most disadvantaged countries achieve their respective development objectives.

Choosing who should benefit from Fund operations would prove more problematic. Anxious to head off accusations of political partisanship and of "taking sides," Dr. Shihata elected at the time to use the United Nations' definition of Most Seriously Affected Countries (MSAs), later extending the Fund's brief to include all the Least Developed Countries (LDCs). And naturally, the Fund sought to target the most deprived communities within those beneficiary countries when selecting projects.

When OPEC finance ministers met to review initial progress in August 1976, they found themselves confronted with a blueprint for a much sturdier institution than the one into which they had breathed hesitant life just weeks before. Dr. Shihata had in the interim managed to address a raft of vital technical issues affecting the whole gamut of loan activity. For example, should the Fund finance only foreign costs and ignore local costs; under what counterpart conditions should balance of payments support be extended, and whether undue emphasis should be placed on new projects at the expense of otherwise worthy developments in critical need of additional finance?

Observers were amazed to see the Fund's mission take shape so swiftly and acquire a momentum which many in the financial community believed would take long years to achieve. The explanation for this lay partly in the Fund's philosophical foundation — that is, Dr. Shihata was at constant pains to keep things simple. In essence, he wanted to contribute to any and all activities which stood the best chance of meeting the development goals set by the borrower, rather than simply pushing out loans and building grand portfolios which themselves might just as easily run into the sand for lack of effective commitment. He was primarily interested in what worked, not what looked good on the books.

He was refreshingly unafraid to challenge the wisdom of traditional financial practices where these clearly hampered progress towards the development objective. For example, he demanded to know how one might be expected to help a country in the longer term without also attending, albeit selectively, to the legitimate short-term needs of people who lack the capacity to help themselves.

He insisted on a two-way street. Recipient governments would have to deposit equivalent counterpart funds in local currency to meet local costs wherever possible, and make every effort to meet their obligations to the Fund when payments fell due. Indeed, most beneficiaries understood well enough the sacrifices made by fraternal OPEC countries in offering these financial facilities. Cost overruns inevitably occurred during the construction phase of a number of early projects, and one of the most difficult decisions Dr. Shihata made during this period was to agree to finance these. Most agencies refused, for ideological reasons, to handle cost overruns and the Fund won plaudits from responsible recipients for having the courage to break that taboo. It was the first of many such divergent practices which borrowers came to identify with the Fund's philosophy of solidarity and compassion.

As if testifying to Dr. Shihata's firm control and persuasive vision, OPEC finance ministers began without prompting from the management to discuss a fresh infusion of resources, our first replenishment, and in so doing removed suggestions that the Fund would continue as a temporary facility. That simple act paved the way for a series of moves which Dr. Shihata used to reaffirm the independence of the organization and gear its evolution into a stand-alone entity. Most importantly, he proposed amending the Agreement of Establishment to ensure repayments could be made directly to the Fund for use in future operations, and that was accepted. The Fund's continuity was assured and its status confirmed as an international development finance facility.

The word "special" was eventually excised from the name of the Fund and a separate ministerial council was established along with a governing board to monitor day-to-day administration. Under the new accord signed in May 1980, the Fund acceded to full international legal personality and also acquired the authority to administer accounts provided by member countries in addition to its own resources. But perhaps Dr. Shihata's crowning achievement during this critical period of transition was the agreement's stipulation, enshrined in article 2.03, that the Fund be entrusted as the agent of its members in negotiations with other development institutions. Essentially, it would function as a collective instrument of the will of OPEC countries in international financial fora. The Fund had finally come of age.

By 1980 some hundred projects were under administration by only ten professional staffers, a feat best understood by appreciating the unusual management style of a man whose first priority was always to reduce bureaucratic inertia and free human resources for the job at hand. Farming out necessary project appraisal work to other agencies with spare capacity, especially in the early years, was a good way of conserving resources and minimizing delay. In effect, he was able to kill two birds with one stone. Besides, getting the institution known and trusted by the wider development community was a task he took seriously from the outset.

He tells the story of a chance meeting in Kuwait with World Bank President Robert McNamara back in 1976, just prior to taking up his appointment at the Fund. Asked how he was going to set about building the Fund, Dr. Shihata answered that both institutions would share the same objectives. Since that was so, he added, would the World Bank consider helping out by evaluating projects and administering loans for the Fund — free of charge? McNamara agreed, and with the Bank onboard it was not too difficult to persuade other established development finance institutions to follow suit.

By and large, Dr. Shihata dispensed with using a framework agreement to govern cooperation with other agencies. He considered these too complex and time-wasting. First he sought agreement on general principles. Then, once a project had been identified, he went on to draft a standardized "letter of administration" which simply but boldly clarified the obligations of both sides. "This enabled us to move fast," he recalls, "and create the impression that OPEC countries were willing to help without undue delay and costs." Today, as a direct result of Dr. Shihata's early visionary innovation, the Fund enjoys a vast network of cooperative relations with practically every international agency active in the field.

Then, as now, the policy was clear; no razzmatazz, no grandstanding. Dr. Shihata wanted to achieve effective assistance as quickly as possible, even if that meant sacrificing the PR value of ongoing projects and waiving the opportunity to nurture in-house technical capacity. Recipients needed to see their monies put to good use and know that the Fund was serious about its mission. He calculated that although the political impact of OPEC aid might be lost in the initial stages, the trust generated in the longer term would prove invaluable for the Fund. And so it was. With a growing portfolio and the gradual expansion of technical capability came a steady increase in staff numbers, all of them experienced professionals.

In a few short years and without much rhetoric, the Fund had acquired a "solid reputation." A willingness to both simplify and streamline loan appraisal and disbursement procedures had been critical to the early success of the Fund. So much so that others were beginning to subject their own rules to fresh scrutiny in colloquy with sister institutions. Indeed, at Dr. Shihata's insistence, a number of procedural innovations were soon to be implemented by a broad range of development agencies following coordination meetings held among key donors.

Over the last fifteen years, the Fund has continually sought to refine and streamline the workings of its aid delivery procedures. Efficient procedures are vital to ensuring the effectiveness of all aid delivery, and their absence can jeopardize the best of intentions. Most recent testimony to the Fund's policies emerged last year when former US President Jimmy Carter visited us in Vienna: Carter paid homage to the Fund for doing away with the "organizational confusion and paper-work delays" so often associated with low-interest loans and grants.

Despite its modest image, a steady expansion of responsibilities over the years inevitably required the Fund to relocate to new premises. Having grown too big for its base at OPEC headquarters, the Fund moved into offices at the Strudlhof Palais in 1978 and then to the Deutschmeister Palais in 1982 where it operates today. From there, Dr. Shihata moved swiftly to strengthen the institution's role as the voice of OPEC in the unfolding North-South debate. From its inception, the Fund had always looked beyond its borders in pursuit of a wider development agenda.

III. THE OPEC FUND'S CONTRIBUTION TO THE CREATION AND THE WORK OF OTHER DEVELOPMENT INSTITUTIONS

The part played by the OPEC Fund in establishing the International Fund for Agricultural Development (IFAD) cannot be overestimated. Dr. Shihata himself, as the representative of Kuwait, had been involved in preliminary discussions regarding IFAD even before the OPEC Fund existed. Later, as chairman of the drafting committee, he recalls how the entire process was very nearly hijacked by national delegates intent on scoring ideological points quite at odds with the tone of the putative accord. Many delegates were preoccupied with "making history" while he simply wanted to concentrate on the business at hand. He felt too much time was being taken up with long political speeches masking too little substance.

In the event, Dr. Shihata succeeded in transforming the general mood into one of gentle consensus and most now agree, it was his forthright diplomacy which played midwife to the birth of IFAD.[1]

Ultimately, he recalls, it was a matter of credibility. Talks would have continued indefinitely if the Fund had not said: "we will put up US$400 million, provided the industrialized world puts in US$600 million," and it was that single act which lent final credibility to the position of Southern protagonists and made the formation of IFAD possible. The Fund actually committed over US$435 million to IFAD's initial resources. It was envisaged that for each dollar furnished by the Fund, the OECD nations would provide a dollar and a half. Moreover, IFAD broke new ground with a constitution that split voting rights three ways between the industrialized world, OPEC members, and other developing countries.

Efficiency was the watchword. Under Dr. Shihata's stewardship — and he handled the negotiations for all OPEC member states — the new organization was to entrust project appraisal to other international agencies wherever possible and to rely on these for the administration of loans. There was vehement opposition to the plan; many wanted to build a parallel bureaucracy, insisting there could be no decision without unanimity. Challenged by what he called the doctrinaire posturing of several Group of 77 delegates who spoke at length against any compromise, Dr. Shihata brought his oratorical skills to bear on the already protracted proceedings and finally persuaded the parties to accept a majority decision.

The final deal entailed some tough talking but victory seemed assured — almost. Conscious of the need to head off an expected rearguard action, Dr. Shihata the strategist was loath to see the hard graft of colleagues threatened by ideological dissension. He later chaired the drafting committee establishing the basis of IFAD's operating brief, which included a forward-looking caveat

---

1 For a discussion of Dr. Shihata's role in the formation of IFAD, *see* Fawzi H. Al-Sultan, *Ibrahim F.I. Shihata and the Establishment of the International Fund for Agricultural Development,* in this LIBER AMICORUM at 37.

requiring "credible attitudes among those who should ask for a change in the status quo." He just liked to cover all the angles.

In order to safeguard his mission and extend the financial power of OPEC in promoting the development of the poor and dispossessed, Dr. Shihata never hesitated to deploy the formidable intellectual tools at his disposal. His incisive legal mind enabled him to cut through red tape and dogma with equal aplomb. In the vexed quest to extend the Fund's institutional reach he achieved his goal without rancor, but by building a broad-based consensus. It is simply the measure of a man who would never misuse his scholarship to mystify or put down an opponent purely on whim, but only to advance the task at hand and to bring essential issues to the fore. Thus it was Dr. Shihata the visionary who spearheaded the drive of developing countries to present their case to the Western nations for constructive engagement in the cause of development.

Dr. Shihata attended the negotiating conference convened by the United Nations Conference on Trade and Development (UNCTAD) to establish a Common Fund for Commodities (CFC) to finance buffer stocks under the General Assembly's Integrated Program for Commodities. As with IFAD, he sat as an observer representing the OPEC Fund at the request of OPEC ministers. Though not at that time a direct participant in the proceedings, he suggested that UNCTAD's initial proposals be submitted to technical scrutiny by an expert group, principally bankers, in order to determine their feasibility. Since the proposed mechanism would have to rely on the financial markets this would, he suggested be a necessary precondition for intelligent debate on the issue.

Meetings were subsequently held in Geneva and Washington D.C. during the autumn of 1977, but when the conference resumed it was clear that positions had polarized along the North-South divide and that multilateral consensus was a long way off. Dr. Shihata was initially mandated to accept UNCTAD's proposals as forming "a sound basis for negotiation" while offering "special arrangements" to ease the burden of the poorest countries and even mooting the possibility of extending loans to the Common Fund for Commodities "as a sound investment of liquid assets."

It was evident to Dr. Shihata that the yawning chasm between rich and poor countries on this hot topic could not be bridged by confrontational rhetoric. He consequently adopted a Fabian approach to the talks which recommended linking financial resources to operational requirements and building out the institution as the situation allowed. Having gone some way towards defusing the explosive partisanship which increasingly characterized much of the contact between G-77 and OECD officials, Dr. Shihata went on to urge flexibility in drawing up the final agreement, insisting it would be "neither possible nor advisable to try from the outset to find a specific answer to every minute detail." Rather, he said, general rules should first be established, allowing for problems to be handled as they arise. And this was the essential piece of wisdom that paved the way for eventual compromise in July 1980.

Along the way, Dr. Shihata proposed financing a 'second window' to promote research into the workings of primary commodity markets, and also pledged the OPEC Fund to pay the mandatory capital contributions of the LDCs to the Common Fund. Grants were later earmarked for thirty-five countries in accordance with the Fund's strategy to encourage OECD support for better off MSAs, the majority of which were financially ill-positioned to participate.

In retrospect he believed talks would have progressed further, faster if specialists, not diplomats had made the running, and if UNCTAD's decision to set aside grandiose plans for restructuring world trade had been made much earlier in the proceedings. He singled out delegates' propensity for rhetoric and a group tendency to get lost in dogmatic detail as the principal causes of delay. Greater emphasis should have been laid, he was later to write, on the scale of mutual benefits likely accruing to both sides. If UNCTAD and the South had concentrated less on the creation of the Common Fund and allowed more discussion of the "equally, if not more important task" of building new International Commodity Organizations for the Common Fund to function, the outcome would have been more successful.

Dr. Shihata was concerned to make a difference not only in the macro-economic aspects of global development, but also in assisting research that would directly benefit the world's smallholders. The various regional centers of the Consultative Group on International Agricultural Research (CGIAR) have attracted numerous grants from the Fund, resulting from Dr. Shihata's policy recognition of the crucial role played by research in the agricultural development of developing countries. Aid to the CGIAR has since become a cornerstone of the Fund's highly diversified grant program. Yet, as with other key sectors supported by the Fund's grant aid allocation, Dr. Shihata's original analysis of the challenge posed by agricultural development was pragmatic to the core.

He took the unfashionable view that in order to safeguard farm output gains, efforts throughout the South to curb population growth must be redoubled. Rapid population growth will always require a higher rate of investment merely to maintain existing output per person, he argued, and is also likely to depress wages while accelerating rural-urban migration. Mindful of the national and religious sensitivities associated with population policy, he nonetheless felt moved to urge donors to take practical steps to tackle the problem "where its solution is a prerequisite for sustained growth." He believed the need to place immediate and effective controls on continued population growth in the South was paramount to the development effort, but acknowledged the diplomatic initiative to push for change must come from others.

So he turned his attention instead to the abiding issue of world hunger and the quest for self-reliance. Instead of waiting for the IMF to establish its much-vaunted Financial Food Facility, Dr. Shihata persuaded the OPEC Fund's Governing Board to approve the diversion of balance of payments support loans to finance food imports. At the same time, the Fund began extending grants to CGIAR centers occupied with applied research into agriculture and fisheries. CGIAR assistance to national research institutions would further extend indigenous capacity to develop crop varieties suitable to local conditions.

The largest single grant ever approved by the Fund was a US$25 million sum extended to the International Emergency Food Reserve, jointly administered by the World Food Program and the UN Food and Agricultural Organization. (FAO). The allocation was a typical example of the South-South solidarity that Dr. Shihata sought to reflect in the Fund's management. Proceeds covered the cost of food shipped from the developing countries to meet the needs of the poorest developing nations affected by famine.

Breaking the cycle of aid-dependency was a major preoccupation. Dr. Shihata gave much thought to how the Fund could contribute to helping countries strengthen their own institutions and thereby take firmer charge of their own development agenda. To this end the Fund granted money to national development banks for the creation of small-scale enterprises, and financed the establishment of scientific centers throughout the South. Dr. Shihata played a major role in creating the African Fertilizer Development Center and in establishing the Rome-based International Development Law Institute.[2]

IV. CONCLUDING REMARKS

One of the main constraints faced by the South has been the lack of available professionals capable of handling international negotiations with donor groups and private sector industrialists. Developing countries remain in dire need of experienced individuals, trained in the multidisciplinary skills needed to head off exploitation by unscrupulous corporations. Officials from developing nations often lack the hard-headed ability to spot the diplomatic sleight-of-hand threatening to compromise their national interests. As a lawyer, Dr. Shihata appreciated only too clearly the damage that poor nations continued to sustain as a direct result of the dearth of indigenous expertise in development finance negotiations. Building the intellectual capacity of the South to handle its own affairs with greater aptitude and confidence was therefore one of his top priorities. And the Fund has been proud to carry through his many initiatives in this field.

When Dr. Shihata finally left the Fund in 1983 he bequeathed an institution committed to reviving the economic fortunes of millions of the world's underprivileged. Throughout his tenure at the Fund, he worked to realize a just and equitable international division of labor which, he believed, had to be supported by new and enlightened practices in international trade and finance. Burgeoning acrimony between North and South presented the single most threatening obstacle to institutional progress during his seven-year term at the helm, and residual attitudes of confrontation persist to this day. Against this backdrop, his was a voice of conciliation and pragmatism. "It does not matter," he wrote, "if (development)

---

2 For a discussion of Dr. Shihata's role in the formation of IDLI, *see* L. Michael Hager, *IDLI: A New Model for NGO Structure, Sustainability and Growth,* in this LIBER AMICORUM at 353.

is called a new world economic order, or simply a process of integration of the South into a system of global interdependence." The South cannot aspire to a successful dialogue if its countries look only for concessions while introducing no changes in their own attitudes.

Dr. Shihata pulled no punches. He was quick to castigate the industrialized world for winding down foreign aid commitments and channeling development finance to countries which stayed 'in line'. Developing countries, he often reminded audiences, also needed to revise their own domestic economic orders. Consumption and saving patterns in the South must change, he insisted, along with popular perceptions regarding ill-affordable armaments expenditure and exponential population growth. It was this kind of honest candor, expressed without any hidden agenda by a man of impeccable internationalist credentials, that enabled the OPEC Fund to speak and be heard at the high table.

During a time of unprecedented change, the Fund has resolutely sought to maintain and strengthen traditional relations with donor groups and agencies, while reserving the capacity to respond to new challenges. For example, the Fund has just earmarked additional resources to boost the private sector which we believe will emerge as the engine of growth in developing countries over the coming decade. In so doing, we intend thereby to expand the work Dr. Shihata began years ago to targeting small-scale enterprises for soft loans and start-up capital. Consonant with new thinking, the Fund's focus has seen a palpable shift from large-scale projects to smaller, community-oriented schemes, designed to spread knowledge more efficiently and transfer appropriate technology directly to those who are meant to benefit.

With the next century almost upon us the Fund is devising fresh policy initiatives and new strategies which, we believe, will enhance the overall effectiveness of our aid effort, speeding poverty alleviation and empowering the most disadvantaged communities to help themselves. In order to cope with the exigencies of a fast-changing world, the Fund has significantly adjusted its internal administration to demonstrate greater flexibility and adaptability. Indeed, such improvements have already been clearly vindicated on many occasions by the Fund's rapid response to repeated humanitarian crisis, offering disaster relief to refugees in afflicted areas.

Without doubt, the basic blocks which Dr. Ibrahim used to build this unique institution secured for his successors a very solid foundation for growth, and the enviable continuity with which the Fund has since conducted its impressive global spread of operations bears testimony to his original vision. Yet those of us to whom he passed the baton know there is no room for complacency. We salute his inspiration and strive to live up to his legacy.

IBRAHIM SHIHATA, A NATIONAL OF EGYPT

M.I.M. Aboul-Enein

> *". . . Yes, I have spent (more than) thirty years abroad. A period over which I have been observing and contributing to political and economic liberalization programs in the developing countries . . . but never ever have I lost interest in all what is going on in my motherland EGYPT."*[1]

Since 1972, between the geographical boundaries of Kuwait, Rome, Vienna and the United States, Ibrahim Shihata's professional contributions have been sincere and outstanding. However, there has always been an inner affinity that bounds him — heart and soul — to the so-long left but always thought of Homeland, *EGYPT.*

Since that time, I have observed with real appreciation Dr. Shihata's pivotal contributions to the developing countries including Egypt and I have always been able to trace a sense of duty underneath, inspiring his works. Years later, I took over the office of the Director of the Cairo Regional Centre for International Commercial Arbitration, the works of which — serving the ultimate target of promoting investment in the region and the settlement of relevant disputes — helped take me various strides forward toward more recognition and much deeper appraisal of Shihata's thoughts on reform programs, especially the economic programs.

For an economist and a thinker of high caliber, it was necessarily imperative to take his nostalgia from what is merely heartfelt to a more tangible realm. It did not take him long to realize

---

1 IBRAHIM F.I. SHIHATA, A PROGRAM FOR TOMORROW — CHALLENGES AND PROSPECTS OF THE EGYPTIAN ECONOMY IN A CHANGING WORLD 7 (1987) (in Arabic).

that the most suitable way to air his very own *I LOVE YOU EGYPT* was to devote his expertise to advising on a comprehensive reform program which other experts identified as being capable of establishing Egypt's civilization of modern times.

In drawing up his visionary program, Dr. Shihata has most aptly managed to strike a balance between the liberal objectivity of an all-knowing expert observer and the most subjective — though unbiased — feelings of an emigrant, who, despite all distances and crossroads, has always kept a watchful eye fixed homewards. The present paper is meant to briefly highlight the major features of Shihata's vision for a program, to depict some of its most salient aspects and to focus on the characteristics of economic reform.

The conception of the comprehensiveness of reform appeals to me as the most salient aspect of Shihata's reform philosophy; betterment can never be one-angled . . . and if it happened to, it will only be temporary and fragile. "*Nations exist and survive challenges in as much as they put together Programs for Tomorrow . . . and it is the right of a Nation having an undoubted special role to have a comprehensive program for the future in facing the many challenges from all around.*"[2] Out of this conviction, Shihata draws up a comprehensive reform program involving a totally radical and liberal-in-essence turnover of existing systems.

Far from being a merely reflective exposition of the national *status quo,* Shihata's studies present a probation beyond circumstantial and political constraints into a comprehensive ideology, powerful enough to establish a civilization of modern times. His studies address various matters some of which deal with the planning of economic, administrative, judicial, legal as well as educational reform — all deemed as being complementary to one another.

The sort of comprehensiveness Shihata is after expands to include ideological and cultural aspects, revealing a perfect reading into the thinking of peoples as into the pan-circumstances of nations. Remarkably idiosyncratic it is that Shihata was and always remains so much concerned with the *collective sociological cognizance of the anticipated change.* It seems that Shihata is quite

---

2 *Id.* (Translation from Arabic.)

aware that the idea of comprehensive reform in the sense he suggests to introduce appeals mainly — *if not only* — to the "intelligentsia" and therefore is so much alien to the stated ideologies and common sense approaches of the average citizen. This renders it necessary to call for the re-building of a new culture on the ground, one which is comprehensive enough to grasp the multi-dimensional suggested changes. *"Reform ought not to be unless rooted into an environment comprehensive enough to grasp the motifs involved,"*[3] Shihata asserts.

"The environmental comprehensiveness" alluded to is *ideo-cultural*; there was — and maybe still remain reminiscences of — sophisticated beliefs that gradually obliterate the essence of realities. In so far as economic circumstances are concerned, Shihata finds that there has been a dominating delusive perception of reality tending to erroneously consider sources of secondary importance and temporary nature — such as petroleum revenues and foreign aids — as being the backbone of the Egyptian economy, an attitude highly detrimental to future progress as it takes the expectations of the people distances away from the necessity of effecting structural reforms and increasing productivity rates. This delusive perception of economic and factual realities has to be changed and there should be public awareness of reality, i.e. to see things as they really are, or else the reform program suggested will never find its way to completion. The thought Shihata is here introducing is highly challenging; circumstances are more or less man-made and are thus changeable, but to claim changing man himself culturally and ideologically is a rather hard task that will take much time to realize . . . *and here lies the challenge to which Shihata is really apt.*

What is also salient and remarkably characteristic of Shihata's reform program is that it deals with the collective cultural and socio-political character of the nation and calls for reforming what has been long thought of as taboos or has been wrongfully identified as belonging to concepts that should never be changed for the sake of the action. For instance, Shihata discusses the relation between the State and Religion and calls for constitutional reform which is detailed in the third volume of his famous Quaternion

3 *Id.* at 77.

My Will for My Country (1995–1997). In so far as the relation between the State and Religion is concerned, Shihata airs the belief that it is necessary to re-adapt the Islamic teachings of *"Shari'ah"* to the spirit of today without the least violation of divine sanctity. Shihata remains expectant of the controversies his arguments over the incontestables might unrighteously trigger and, therefore, keeps asserting that "*it is my complete faith in the merciful nature of our Holy Religion that makes me believe that it is not religiously binding to apply the political or economic practices of several centuries ago to the circumstances of the 21st century without any attempt to affect doctrinally accepted adaptations.*"[4]

Along similar lines, the 1990's witness Shihata's most unrestricted argument, that is, the one calling for constitutional reform. Also in the third volume of the famous Quaternion *My Will for My Country* (1995–1997) referred to above, Shihata presents a unique and unprecedented study of the constitutional framework of Egypt from a comparative perspective and pragmatically argues for the importance of effecting changes thereto for the national welfare. Despite the controversies this might trigger, for various political and economic reasons, it remains plausible that the early years of the coming century may indeed witness a sort of constitutional change. When this will happen — in a year . . . a couple of years . . . or maybe a little more — it will be remembered that *Ibrahim Shihata* was a pioneer in putting forward a comprehensive program for constitutional reform.

Shihata's comprehensive program devotes quite a considerable portion to *economic reform*. For him, betterment of the national economic strategies implies a necessity of changing the *macro-economic environment* of Egypt. To achieve a well-grounded reform, all the policies affecting the national economy have to be harmoniously modified. As early as 1987, Shihata devoted his studies of and contributions to the concepts of World Bank reform programs to this sort of research and reached accordingly the conclusion that economic reform would not be achieved unless it addressed two basic fundamentals: (1) bringing the unbalanced economic scales back to stability; and (2) reforming the infrastructure of the various productive sectors.

---

4 IBRAHIM F.I. SHIHATA, TOWARDS COMPREHENSIVE REFORM 201 (1993) (in Arabic).

This includes various recommended schemes, some of which deal with the drawing up of new pricing policies, prioritizing governmental expenditures,[5] increasing state resources as well as increasing exports and a complementary policy to decrease imports. Shihata, presenting his program in 1987, calls for increasing banking interests,[6] arguing that this would help decrease the inflation rate by increasing savings in the Egyptian currency and increasing accordingly the general index of national savings. In the year 1991/1992, indeed the national balance of payments scored remarkable improvement, a result — according to economists — partially caused by the proportional increase in the Egyptian Pound banking interests as compared to the US Dollar interest rates. Within the bounds of this discourse, more recent economic policies prove Shihata's economic stream of thinking — expressed as early as 1980 — to have been a farsighted perspective of the future; in its latest 1999 report, the International Monetary Fund prompts the Egyptian Government to increase banking interests, basing its argument on reasons similar to Shihata's.

In the course of his suggested program, Shihata hails the importance of abridging foreign debts to help overcome deficiency in the balance of payment. In 1991, his perspectives were brought to realization when the Egyptian Government started adopting a wide-scaled economic and monetary reform program having much of the spirit of what was called-for long-before by Shihata. This includes without limitation various agreements entered into

---

5 Since the Ganzoory Government took over in 1996, there has been a trend to reduce governmental expenditures in various fields and many ministerial decrees were issued to this effect.

6 In addressing this issue, Shihata actually adresses a matter of controversial nature and is able to powerfully back his viewpoint. This relates to the legitimacy of enforcing interests; responding to the opinion that bringing the debtor to accept payment of banking interests is an act of injustice (*"Ghabn"* in the Qu'rânic terminology) against the debtor and that it is accordingly an illegitimate and prohibited doing, Shihata opined that the era of paper money and the concurrent growing concept of the temporary value of money make it rational enough to believe that asking the creditor to accept the sum of money lent some time ago without increase implies an obligation to accept a sum less in value than that lent before, which is in itself an act of injustice against the creditor.

7 In the light of the agreement concluded between the Egyptian Government and the International Monetary Fund in 1991, known as "the *Letter of Intention,"* seventeen crediting states held a meeting in Paris in May 1991 and decided to reduce the total value of Egypt's debts by 50 percent and to restructure the remaining sum.

with the International Monetary Fund within the bounds of the *Paris Club Agreement*[7] of 1991. Added to this, all debts payable to the Gulf States as well as the American military debts were waived, constituting altogether up to the year 1993 a total amount of thirteen billion US Dollars.

As early as the 1960's, Dr. Shihata has been well cognizant of the importance of investments in the Arab World and he has developed since that time onwards special interest in this concern that was later ripened by his so many various contributions to and observations in the World Bank and other international development schemes. Later, this helps develop an integral element to his economic reform program, i.e. the assertion of the importance of *encouraging private sector investments.* According to Shihata, it is and will remain of growing significance to free the built-up of the national economy from circumstantial and constantly changing impetuses, such as foreign loans and oil prices — the latter being in constant fluctuation — and to increase instead reliance on more stable and less politically-dependent factors. In admission of the presupposition and in view of the problems facing the progress of the public sector, Shihata states that it is necessary to encourage the contribution of the private sectors in national investments. In his paper "Encouraging Arab and Foreign Investments . . . General Remarks" (1989) (in Arabic), Shihata draws up a comprehensive scheme to encourage private sector investments in Egypt. According to him, it is highly important to help investors develop confidence in the probabilities of the national economic growth. The main influential factor in this concern, as estimated by Shihata, is to bring *the responsiveness of national macro-economic policies to changing circumstances up to a satisfactory level.* Similarly important is the necessity of stabilizing the role of the State and determining the fields of the governmental interference. Further, Shihata believes that there should be a national policy targeting the establishment of an efficient monetary sector powerful enough to withstand changing economic needs and to compete with foreign financial corporations. He prompts with regard to this particular concern the Egyptian Government to establish a large social fund with the contribution of international financial organizations. Only three years later, Shihata's suggestion is reflected in the establishment of the first Egyptian Fund of this kind with the contribution of the World Bank and other sources.

In this discourse, it should be recognized that Shihata's early speculations on the importance of private sector investments — expressed as early as in the 1970s and maybe earlier[8] — are now echoed in Egypt's recent trend to encourage private investments. Statistically, the early 1980's witnessed the participation of the private sector by twenty per cent of the total investments, a percentage that remarkably hiked to sixty-four per cent in 1998. Those who have traced Shihata's writings recognize how far-sighted he was in his concepts for a reform program.

In conclusion, it should be asserted that Shihata's reform programs — particularly those related to the economic reform — are being gradually implemented and there seems to be a sort of acknowledgement — explicit or implicit — that it is the liberal methodology Shihata has followed since the 1960s that is capable of building the Egypt of this new millennium. It is worth noting herein that Shihata's achievements, in so far as his homeland is concerned, is not by any means confined to the programs he drew up on the national level; his contributions to the establishment of various Arab and international financial corporations were of direct benefit to Egypt as well as to the different countries of the region. Shihata has really smoothened the path for future betterment and has expressed a "*will for his country*" that will remain of guidance for long. His call to every Egyptian to "*walk hand in hand and climb up the pinnacle of comprehensive reform for the benefit of many generations to come*"[9] will keep infusing courage and persistence in the collective Egyptian Being.

---

8 *See* IBRAHIM F. I. SHIHATA, TREATMENT OF FOREIGN INVESTMENT IN EGYPT (1971) (in Arabic).

9 IBRAHIM F. I. SHIHATA, TOWARDS COMPREHENSIVE REFORM 13 (1993) (in Arabic).

IBRAHIM F.I. SHIHATA: THE LAWYER AS A DEDICATED PRACTITIONER OF DEVELOPMENT

*Abdlatif Y. Al-Hamad**

It is with great pleasure that I take part, with other writers to this collection of essays, in paying tribute to the many contributions of Ibrahim F.I. Shihata to the cause of economic development in the world. I am grateful to the editors of this publication for giving me this opportunity. My acquaintance with Ibrahim Shihata dates back to 1960 when we were both graduate students at Harvard University, pursuing different disciplines. His admirable personal qualities and brilliant intellect were immediately recognized when we first met. In 1961, I started working for the Kuwait Fund for Arab Economic Development as it was being set up. By 1966 the Kuwait Fund had been in existence for only five years, and to a large extent, it was in its formative years, when Ibrahim Shihata agreed to join the staff of the Fund as a legal advisor, contributing to the shaping and expansion of the activities of the Fund.

At this point it may be of some value to introduce that institution to the reader, who may not be familiar with it. The Kuwait Fund was created in 1961, the very year in which Kuwait became independent. The purposes of the Fund were to assist the Arab States in developing their economies by providing soft loans for their development programs.[1] The Fund was established as an

---

* The views expressed in this paper are the personal views of the author and should not be attributed to the organization he is affiliated with.

1 For an exposition of the role and evolution of the policies of the Kuwait Fund, *see* ABDLATIF Y. AL-HAMAD, FINANCING ARAB ECONOMIC DEVELOPMENT: THE EXPERIENCE OF KUWAIT FUND, (Kuwait Fund Publication, May 1972), paper delivered before a regional meeting organized by UNESOB in 1972.

autonomous body with an independent legal personality. The Kuwait Fund originally operated only in the Arab States; but by 1974 its mandate was expanded to serve all developing countries at large. Its authorized capital was increased from Kuwaiti Dinars 200 million (equivalent to US$720 million) to Kuwaiti Dinars 2000 million (equivalent to US$7200 million) by 1981.

Until 1970, the Kuwait Fund was the only development finance institution of its kind in the Arab region[2] and was, indeed, unique as an agency established by a developing country dedicated exclusively to the task of providing development assistance to other developing countries. Thus, the Fund was in one sense breaking new ground and this made its task all the more challenging.

When Ibrahim Shihata joined the Kuwait Fund, it had a small staff with a limited number of professionals in different disciplines. The modest size of staff of the Fund was turned into an advantage. The organization was closely knit, with few formal barriers between different departments. Everyone was driven by a deep sense of mission. All projects were assessed by a team of professionals who worked closely together throughout the project cycle, and all problems were identified and addressed in an integrated manner.

In this unique situation, the lawyer's role transcended the traditional role of preparing agreements and writing opinions. He was part of a professional and interdisciplinary team that had a holistic approach toward all the Fund's projects. They had the responsibility to translate these very often new features in the relationship with borrowers to acceptable and innovative documentation. That kind of relationship was totally new to the Arab World and it required a great deal of imagination and understanding of the underlying legal framework as well as immense diplomatic

---

2 Since that time, the Abu Dhabi Fund for Development and the Saudi Fund for Development have been created. Other development finance institutions of a multilateral character were also established by the Arab countries, or with strong Arab participation. These institutions include the Arab Fund for Economic and Social Development, the Islamic Development Bank, the Arab Bank for Economic Development in Africa and the OPEC Fund for International Development. For a review of the role and orientation of Arab aid agencies *see* ABDLATIF Y. AL-HAMAD, PERSPECTIVE ON ARAB AID INSTITUTIONS AND INTERNATIONAL DEVELOPMENT ASSISTANCE, THE ROLE OF ARAB PETROFUNDS, addresses delivered at two international *fora* — (Kuwait Fund Publications, 1979).

skills to convince the borrowers of the unusual legal requirements. Ibrahim Shihata was most valuable in that stage of the Kuwait Fund development where he showed a flair for innovation to tackle new legal requirements within the limitations in these situations. In fact, this approach of "preventive lawyering," so to speak, served the Fund and its borrowers well in forestalling problems or dealing with them constructively at an early stage.

With his excellent legal background and natural team spirit, Ibrahim Shihata was eminently qualified to serve in that particular milieu and made exceptional contributions to the Fund's work. The foundations of the legal system in the Fund were laid down by his predecessor, Saad S. Al-Fishawy, who was seconded from the World Bank. But, as was expected, a lawyer of the caliber of Ibrahim Shihata was not merely content to follow in the footsteps of his predecessor. He took keen interest, beyond his own specialization, in the wider issues of development and participated actively in the shaping of a totally new discipline in the region. He indeed succeeded in giving law a central role in the work of the Fund. He contributed, in no small measure, in the shaping of such policies and was the author of the reorganization of the Kuwait Fund that led to the expansion of its operations to all developing countries and to the five-fold increase of the Fund resources.

Being very much at home in the area where law and development meet, Ibrahim Shihata enriched the intellectual climate in the Fund as well as in other circles. He represented the Fund at many conferences and published numerous papers, that elucidated various legal issues relating to investment and development, especially as those relate to international joint ventures and inter-Arab joint enterprises. Closer to home, his paper on the legal aspects of the Fund and its operations[3] continues to be an invaluable source for lawyers and researchers.

As Legal Adviser to the Fund, he was naturally called upon from time to time to give opinions on the interpretation of the Law and Charter of the Fund and resolutions of its Board of Directors. His interpretations were never only literal, and he invariably adopted a practical approach, which accorded primary importance to the purposes of the Fund and the promotion of its

---

[3] *See* IBRAHIM F.I. SHIHATA, THE KUWAIT FUND FOR ARAB ECONOMIC DEVELOPMENT: A LEGAL ANALYSIS (Kuwait Fund Publication 1974).

objectives. For instance, when the Fund first considered making technical assistance grants, the question arose as to the basis of charging such grants to the accounts of the Fund, particularly as there was no easily identifiable account to which they could be debited. The Charter of the Fund made specific reference to lending but not to providing grants, while the budget of the Fund was a purely administrative one that made no provision for grants. Ibrahim Shihata took the view that as the law establishing the Fund spoke generally of assisting Arab countries in developing their economies, the absence of a particular reference to grants or of a designated account for accommodating grants was no barrier to making them. A proposal to allocate a specific percentage of the Fund's income was proposed by him. This was accepted by the Board of Directors and has become a policy precedent in other regional development Funds. Another example is that, before the Fund commenced its co-operation with national development finance corporations and well before the Charter of the Fund was amended in 1981 to expressly allow for financing private sector projects, the question arose whether it would be compatible with the established policies of the Fund to make loans to the private sector through national financial institutions. Ibrahim Shihata saw no difficulty in squaring this with the Charter of the Fund on the basis of the developmental nature of the projects.

The fact that the Fund was an agency of a developing country had implications for the work and approach of the Fund. In a world divided by many political schisms, the Fund had to observe a high degree of neutrality with respect to political and economic systems.[4] Moreover, some of the recipients of the Fund were not used to the Fund's approach as they considered it intrusive. All that required considerable tact and diplomacy on the part of the Fund staff in dealing with beneficiaries, especially during the negotiation of loan agreements which usually took place in the field. Ibrahim Shihata's colleagues all testify that he had an inborn aptitude for diplomacy and was always aware of any particular sensitivities of the borrower, without compromising the principles of the Fund. He was always successful in gaining the agreement and

---

[4] *See* ABDLATIF Y. AL-HAMAD, FINANCING ARAB ECONOMIC DEVELOPMENT: THE EXPERIENCE OF KUWAIT FUND, *supra* note 1, at 2.

confidence of the borrowers by his personal attributes and diplomatic skills.

Ibrahim Shihata was often called on to give advice to borrowers in revising laws and regulations that impacted projects financed by the Fund. As procurement contracts for the execution of funded projects are routinely vetted by the Legal Department of the Fund, he applied himself unsparingly to this task and assisted borrowers in negotiating agreements with international contractors. Not infrequently, the effect of such assistance could be measured in monetary terms and, in one instance, due to a bold intervention on his part, savings of several million dollars were realized by a borrower.

As the Fund is a para-statal agency, it is subject, in addition to its Charter, to a number of laws of a public-law nature. Ibrahim Shihata exhibited considerable versatility in dealing with problems of administrative law. His experience with the *Conseil d'Etat* of his home country, Egypt, was handy to ensure that the Fund kept within the relevant legal bounds. On occasion, problems affecting the autonomy of the Fund were encountered and he staunchly defended such autonomy against any possible encroachment.

During his time at the Fund, Ibrahim Shihata played an important part in the endeavors of the Fund aimed at the creation and building of a number of national and regional institutions to advance the cause of development.

Prominent among these institutions are the Arab Fund for Economic and Social Development (AFESD) and the "*Banque Arabe de Développement en Afrique*" (BADEA). Both institutions came as an expression of solidarity among developing countries.

When the idea of the creation of the AFESD was put forward by Kuwait and approved by the Arab League, Ibrahim Shihata cooperated with other colleagues in putting together the necessary documentation and in drafting the agreement establishing the Arab Fund. The Arab Fund was the first regional institution contributed to solely by developing countries. What should be kept in mind is that it is a form of self-help and solidarity at the regional level.

Ibrahim Shihata was also responsible for the drafting and the negotiation of the Agreement establishing BADEA. The importance of BADEA stems from the fact that a group of developing countries, the Arab countries for that purpose, establish a Bank as a collective financial facility for providing concerted support to a region where most of the least developed countries exist, namely the African continent.

The Inter-Arab Investment Guarantee Corporation is another important case in point.[5] The conference on Arab Industrial Development, held in Kuwait in November 1966, approved a proposal by the Fund to establish an inter-Arab agency for the guarantee of investments against political risks in the Arab countries. This was prompted by acute awareness of the important role of private investment in the development of the Arab region and the need to create favorable conditions for the flow of such investment. The Kuwait Fund was entrusted with the responsibility of preparing the required studies. Ibrahim Shihata collaborated with Zakaria Nasr, head of research at the Kuwait Fund, in the preparation and negotiation of the agreement and the relevant documentation that led to the successful creation of the InterArab Investment Guarantee Corporation in 1974, as well as associated drafts on the principles relating to the treatment of Inter Arab investment and the settlement of disputes related to them. It was launched well ahead of any other multi-national institution with a similar agenda.

Following the entry into force of the Agreement in mid-1974, Ibrahim Shihata produced a legal analysis of the Inter-Arab Investment Guarantee Corporation, which continues to be an indispensable reference on the Corporation to this day. As it turned out, his contribution during the launching of the Corporation was a forerunner to the role he came to play on a larger scale much later, when he succeeded, almost single-handedly, in the creation of the Multilateral Investment Guarantee Agency (MIGA) of the World Bank. The irony of this situation was that the World Bank originally came forward with the idea, but failed to achieve it until it was created in a developing region by developing countries with the help of Ibrahim Shihata.

But, let me turn now to another institution, albeit of a different nature, on which Ibrahim Shihata left his unmistakable imprint. That institution, with which we were closely associated, was

5 *See* Robert Stephens, The Arabs' New Frontier, at 80 *et seq.* (2nd ed. 1976).

the OPEC Fund for International Development, originally established as the OPEC Special Fund by an agreement among the Member States of OPEC signed on January 28, 1976. Following the rise of oil prices in 1973, members of OPEC, out of solidarity with fellow developing countries, entered into consultations among themselves to consider the creation of a special vehicle to assist other developing countries.

It was considered desirable by these OPEC members, especially the Arab Gulf countries, that a collective effort be made in the field of international development.

The OPEC Member Countries are a diverse group of developing countries with huge needs for capital for their own development. That precluded the creation of a permanent international financial institution. However, OPEC members opted for the establishment of the OPEC Special Fund purely as an account jointly owned by them and dedicated to assisting other developing countries. Ibrahim Shihata was on loan from the Kuwait Fund to the delegation of the State of Kuwait to the Ministerial Meetings of OPEC Member States that created the OPEC Fund.[6] He participated actively and effectively in the deliberations of these meetings that passed the resolutions establishing the proposed Fund. In recognition of his advice and legal expertise, he was entrusted with the task of preparing the draft agreement of the OPEC Special Fund. He crafted a document with a great measure of ingenuity and creativity and in a manner which accommodated the views and concerns of the members. He was able, with his exceptional ingenuity, to find a compromise that gives every country political credit without, in this situation, putting additional financial burden on any of them. The agreement establishing the OPEC Fund was signed on January 26, 1976. It was, therefore, a fitting tribute to Ibrahim Shihata that the inaugural meeting of the Ministerial Council of the OPEC Special Fund unanimously decided to appoint him the first Director-General of the Fund.

The competent and imaginative management of the Fund by Ibrahim Shihata and his ability to design a well-thought-out program for providing support to the least developed countries and for forging relations with other financial institutions, earned him

---

6 For detailed information on the OPEC Fund, *see* the OPEC Fund's website <http://www.opec.org/opecfund.htm>.

world-wide acclaim. He led the OPEC Fund continuously in achieving the highest degree of operational efficiency. Though the original agreement envisaged a situation where the Fund would be dissolved once its initial resources were committed, members of OPEC came to realize the importance of the Fund as an instrument of co-operation with other developing countries. The success of Ibrahim Shihata in managing it gave the institution permanent status. That was not his only success, as the exceptional track record of the Fund under Ibrahim Shihata led to three replenishments within a period of less than six years. Ibrahim's remarkable adeptness in building consensus among OPEC countries was instrumental in this success.

With its increased resources, the Fund, under the leadership of Ibrahim Shihata, made wide strides within a short period of time in responding to the needs of developing countries. This, coupled with the innovative approach adopted by him in devising new approaches of channeling assistance to developing countries,[7] imparted to the Fund considerable weight and stature on the international development scene well in excess of its resource base. It is scarcely surprising, therefore, that the Fund came to be more than just a transient phenomenon and established itself as an important agency of international development cooperation. This was crowned in 1980, when the Agreement establishing the OPEC Special Fund was amended, thanks to the initiative of Ibrahim Shihata to transform the Fund from a joint account of the member countries to a full-fledged multilateral organization, endowed with an independent legal personality, and redesignated as the OPEC Fund for International Development.

As Director-General of the Fund, he played an instrumental role in the success of the international negotiations leading to the establishment of the International Fund for Agricultural Development (IFAD).[8] The OPEC countries, identifying fully with the interests of developing countries, strongly supported the creation of the proposed institution, while the idea received, to put it mildly, a lukewarm response from most of the industrial countries.

---

[7] *See* IBRAHIM F.I. SHIHATA, THE OPEC SPECIAL FUND — A NEW APPROACH TO DEVELOPMENT, (OPEC Fund Publication 1976).

[8] For a detailed description of IFAD's work and vision *see* the IFAD's website <http://www.ifad.org>.

Ibrahim Shihata was charged with the task of representing Kuwait and the OPEC countries in the negotiations for the creation of IFAD. On many occasions, he spoke on behalf of all developing countries. There is little doubt that, had it not been for the OPEC Special Fund (OSF) and the ingenuity of Ibrahim Shihata, the resolution to establish IFAD would have succumbed to the same fate that has begotten a number of other international schemes. He forcefully argued the case for the institution to be established with sufficient financial support from the donor community, especially the industrial countries, in a manner commensurate with their economic strength. The negotiations were arduous and protracted, with the question of burden sharing between the industrial countries and OPEC countries proving to be a stumbling block. Thanks to the determined commitment and imagination of Ibrahim Shihata, this was overcome when OPEC countries accepted more than their fair share of the initial burden. Through a sizeable commitment of US$435.5 billion OSF helped turn the idea into reality; its contribution served as an effective catalyst in the mobilization of other capital. But, that was not the end of the matter. The unique manner in which contributions to the financial resources of the proposed institution were assembled, with the industrial countries constituting one category of contributors and OPEC countries another, while other developing countries were a third category, called for further negotiations between the three groups concerning the organizational structure of the institution. Ibrahim Shihata brought to bear on this matter his tremendous legal expertise, and the final design of the structure of IFAD that emerged from the negotiations gave a strong voice to OPEC and other developing countries. This was a new direction for financial cooperation giving, for the first time in an international financial institution, two-thirds of the votes to developing countries while still leaving two-thirds of the votes in the hands of donors. Developing countries in this manner were certain to exercise a major influence on investment decisions for the resolution of their problems. The key element in this design was obviously the fact that the OPEC members were at the same time developing countries and major donors. This solution was due to Ibrahim Shihata and his negotiating skills.

The OPEC Fund played an important part in the subsequent evolution of IFAD through further financial contributions and through the service of Ibrahim Shihata on IFAD's Board of Executive Directors, as a representative of the State of Kuwait. Many of those intimately associated with IFAD would testify to his effective contribution in shaping its policies and development.

IFAD was by no means the only institution in whose creation and development the OPEC Fund, under Shihata's stewardship, played an important role. The Common Fund for Commodities stands out as an another example. The OPEC countries, as an expression of their solidarity with other developing nations, declared the full support for the Common Fund concept and requested, early in 1977, Ibrahim Shihata as Director General of the OPEC Fund to act as coordinator among their delegation to the negotiating conference. When protracted negotiation showed no sign of real progress, Ibrahim Shihata found the way to accelerate the pace of negotiation by declaring the OPEC countries' intention to contribute to the resources of the Fund, and the readiness of the OPEC Fund to consider providing financial support to the least developed countries (LDC), in order to enable them to meet part of their contribution to the Common Fund.

The importance of the Common Fund stems from the fact that it provided an overall approach to commodity problems and helped developing countries cope with the vagaries of supply and demand, as opposed to the earlier partial efforts of commodity by commodity approach which has failed to produce acceptable results.

It is not possible within the compass of a short paper to fully do justice to Ibrahim Shihata's contribution to international development. More importantly, this paper does not deal with his contribution to the work of the World Bank and its affiliates during his service in that institution. This omission was deliberate, as those of his colleagues, who were intimately associated with him at the World Bank Group, would be better qualified to bring out his highly laudable achievements. But the account given in this paper of only part of Shihata's immense services to international development, would not be complete without mentioning his instrumental role in the creation of the International Development Law Institute (IDLI).[9] Since his days at the Kuwait Fund, Ibrahim Shihata, with considerable prescience, was preoccupied with the

---

9 For general information on IDLI, *see* the IDLI' s website <http://www.idli.org>.

significant part played by law and lawyers in the development process and the need to equip lawyers from developing countries for the task of shaping legal institutions so as to be more conducive to meeting the needs of developing economies. At his suggestion, the Kuwait Fund cooperated in 1969 with the International Legal Center, which is based in New York, in carrying out a study concerning the establishment of a "Law and Development Center" to train lawyers from the Arab region. In 1983, Ibrahim Shihata who was then Director-General of the OPEC Fund, spearheaded the International Development Law Institute (IDLI) project with the assistance of three Western lawyers, who dedicated themselves to the Institute. With his full weight behind the Institute, he solicited support from various quarters, including the Kuwait Fund and the Arab Fund for Economic and Social Development, both of which needed little convincing of the importance of this unique Institute. Now, thanks to his inspired leadership as Chairman of its Board of Directors, the Center is a well-established edifice of training in the legal aspects of development.

It would not be an overstatement to say that Ibrahim Shihata is the development lawyer *par excellence*. But he also proved to be a resourceful policy-maker and an accomplished administrator in the field of development finance. With his remarkable record of achievement in serving the cause of development, he, no doubt, has already secured his place in the history of the human endeavors toward the goals of economic and social developments whose objective is the service of the poor throughout the world. Ibrahim Shihata has committed himself and his endless energies the task of creating a more equitable and secure world for billions of people in the Third World.

IBRAHIM SHIHATA AND THE ESTABLISHMENT OF THE INTERNATIONAL FUND FOR AGRICULTURAL DEVELOPMENT

*Fawzi H. Al-Sultan**

I. INTRODUCTION

I have known Dr. Shihata over many years during our association with the Kuwait Fund, the Organization of the Petroleum Exporting Countries (OPEC) and the World Bank. Dr. Shihata was closely associated with the establishment of the International Fund for Agricultural Development (IFAD) and was one of the key players in developing its early architecture. My own direct involvement with IFAD commenced of course, much later, at the beginning of 1993 when I was elected its third President. At that point, he gave me some valuable insight about IFAD based on his close involvement with the process of its establishment and participation in its governing bodies during IFAD's initial formative years after the Fund became operational as a UN specialized agency in December 1977.

I have always admired Dr. Shihata for his professional integrity and quiet competence, for his clarity of logic and articulation, and for an informed, reasoned and rational approach to any issue or task at hand, shorn of empty rhetoric, or populist drumbeat. As a negotiator, with long experience in the international arena, he is known to be strict and unyielding on fundamental principles. However, he is flexible and ready for working out compromise solutions based on ground realities. Because of these

---

* The views expressed in this paper are the personal views of the author and should not be attributed to the institution with which he is affiliated.

qualities, he acquired the trust and respect even of those who held opposing views, during the variety of conferences and debates on the restructuring of the international organizational framework through "the New International Economic Order" (NIEO).

In the above context, Dr. Shihata emerged in the 1970s as a key interlocutor for Kuwait and the OPEC Fund in many North-South deliberations. With his characteristic forthrightness, he has termed much of these discussions as "collective monologue," with both the North and the South adopting unduly rigid posturing on a wide-ranging and unwieldy agenda. In this connection, he has in some of his writings underscored a distinctive feature of the business-like negotiating process leading to the establishment of IFAD and illustrated why IFAD was effectively one of the few positive outcomes of the North-South dialogue against the backdrop of a somewhat disappointing record of the debates on the NIEO. According to him, IFAD became a working reality because all the parties to its negotiations followed the precept of "maximum of action and minimum of rhetoric" — a tradition which has continued to guide its subsequent evolution over the past two decades of its operations.

Through his writings during this period he also sought to bring to the North a clearer understanding of OPEC's approach to the development challenges faced by oil-importing developing countries and highlighted OPEC's significant record in terms of concessional development assistance as a responsible and responsive non-traditional donor. He has been one of the most authentic chroniclers of this "other face of OPEC" to counteract much of the uninformed criticism of OPEC after it raised oil prices in 1973. He was closely involved with the drafting of the agreement establishing the OPEC Fund and was its first Director General from 1976 to 1983, before he moved to the World Bank.

While I was Kuwait's Executive Director on the Executive Board of the World Bank for over eight years, prior to my moving to Rome in 1993, I had many occasions to interact with Dr. Shihata on a number of important policy initiatives, such as the Multilateral Investment Guarantee Agency (MIGA). Dr. Shihata took charge of the initiative of establishing MIGA in 1983 and substantially redesigned the proposal. This was a significant initiative designed to promote direct investment in developing countries through greater depoliticization of non-commercial investment risks. MIGA was intended to provide a comprehensive international institutional framework where an investor could refer claims as arbitrable disputes between it and the host country, besides carrying out a number of complementary research and training, advisory and promotional activities. In 1985, the World Bank's executive directors decided to discuss MIGA' s draft convention in a committee of the whole. Both of us had experience from the Inter-Arab Investment Guarantee Corporation, a regional agency established in 1974 to promote investments flowing among its Arab member countries. I recall the discussions I had with Dr. Shihata on issues such as how to balance MIGA' s effectiveness and viability with the host governments' desire to avoid any encroachment upon their sovereignty. Dr. Shihata was most impressive in his grasp of the issues and concepts, his ability to reduce complex questions to simple and clear statements, and his drafting and negotiating skills. As General Counsel, he added a new depth to his role in a changing world environment. As Bob Conable aptly mentions in his preface to Dr. Shihata's book of selected essays, *"The World Bank in a Changing World,"* Dr. Shihata "has been an innovator in agency formation, leaving valuable records of institutional philosophy for those who will be working in development long after we are all gone."

At a personal level, Dr. Shihata is a modest, private person. His excellent yet gentle sense of humor contributes greatly to his effectiveness in helping to achieve agreement on difficult matters. He always prepares himself extremely well for any discussion and is thus able to present his point of view on the basis of a firm grasp of the underlying issues and with clear, logical articulation. His vigorous presence is both persuasive and reassuring. In committee discussions he has been known to sway opinions and to reopen and turn around previously settled positions through the sheer force of his reasoning and the intrinsic soundness of the alternative formulations or solutions offered by him. This ability he amply demonstrated in the Bank, and I understand not infrequently in IFAD when he was on its Executive Board. He played an important role in refining many of the ground rules which have governed the conduct of business by IFAD' s governing bodies, such as a clear demarcation between the executive authority and responsibility of the President as the Chief Executive Officer of the Fund and the decision making role of the Executive Board and the Governing Council as the guardians of IFAD's charter, mandate, and its lending policies and criteria.

Dr. Shihata's professional record is an open book since wherever he has worked he has concisely documented his positions and views on the questions of law and policy that he encountered in the course of his official functions. The long list of his writings spanning over his entire career is a testimony to his versatility and the diversity and sweep of a broad spectrum of issues in development, international law and institutional reforms with which he has been concerned. A unifying theme which defines his work is to establish a bridge between law and economic development in all its complexity and dynamics. His example is unique and virtually unmatched, since many development practitioners and executives often get overwhelmed by the weight of the daily routine and are unable to find time to document and share with a wider audience the positions they take and solutions they offer in the discharge of their business. Much of their creative work and innovations get masked in the anonymity of internal policy papers or notes. Dr. Shihata has set an example which needs to be encouraged, within the framework of a flexible and forward looking disclosure policy, for the sake of greater transparency and openness in deliberating on major policy initiatives and strategic issues and options. This will bring the international financing institutions (IFIs) closer to their stakeholders and clients and keep the public at large better informed of the working and corporate strategic thrusts of these institutions.

II. IBRAHIM SHIHATA, AN IMPORTANT PLAYER IN THE EARLY ARCHITECTURE OF IFAD

Dr. Shihata's association with IFAD spans over almost a decade (1974–1983), starting with the World Food Conference in Rome in 1974, which first gave birth to the idea of an international institution concerned primarily with agricultural development in the developing world. His involvement with IFAD can be considered in three distinct phases:

- The initial years (1975–1976) when the idea got a concrete shape through policy level consultations which eventually led to the convening of the United Nations Conference on the Establishment of the International Fund for Agricultural Development. Dr. Shihata steered the meetings of interested governments and of the contact group which finalized the Agreement Establishing IFAD. The Final Act of the Conference was signed at its 4th meeting in June 1976, and the Conference adopted a Resolution establishing a Preparatory Commission.
- The Preparatory Commission (1976–1977) which prepared a number of draft legal documents, such as the Relationship Agreement between the UN and IFAD, the Agreement for the Provisional Headquarters of IFAD, the agreements with Cooperating Institutions, Operational Guidelines and Financial Regulations and a host of other drafts needed to make the organization operational. The Commission also approved, with some modifications, the Report of the Working Committee on IFAD' s Lending Policies and Criteria. Its work laid the ground work for the convening of the first Session of IFAD' s Governing Council on 13–15 December 1977 in Rome, when IFAD formally commenced its operations. The Prepcom was chaired by Mr. Abdelmuhsin M. Al-Sudeary of Saudi Arabia who later was elected IFAD's first President. The Conference was composed of eighteen Member States and seventeen Alternates. Its Interim Secretariat was ably headed by Dr. Sartaj Aziz, currently Pakistan's External Affairs Minister. It concluded its work at its fourth Session in July 1977. Dr. Shihata, representing Kuwait, played an active role in the Commission. Its deliberations greatly benefited from the advice and interventions of Dr. Shihata and drew extensively on his legal and drafting skills.
- The Executive Board of the Fund on which Dr. Shihata was an Executive Director of Kuwait (1977–1983). He also was Kuwait's Governor on a number of annual sessions of the Governing Council. He left a distinct imprint on the way the Board should transact its sessions in a business-like manner, avoiding long interventions which often characterize discussions in some other fora.

Dr. Shihata's participation in the entire negotiating process leading to its establishment, and later in the formative years of its operations, was in dual capacity. He was a full participant throughout his association with IFAD, representing the State of Kuwait. At an informal level, he also brought to his participation the full weight of his official position as the Director General of the newly established OPEC Special Fund. Thus, he functioned as the coordinator of the OPEC category of membership throughout the negotiations, and later in the context of consultative processes related to the deliberations in IFAD's governing bodies. This greatly contributed to reaching consensus on a number of controversial and sensitive issues. He was invariably able to crystallize the views and positions of the OPEC group, and often enough of the developing countries as a whole, and to articulate them clearly, forcefully and persuasively. This greatly facilitated arriving at compromise solutions and helped move forward the negotiations, notwithstanding protracted and heated discussions in the contact group and plenary meetings and diversity of view points. The high quality of representation from a number of member countries in all three categories of membership greatly helped in creating an environment of constructive dialogue and cooperation based on businesslike discussions.

Dr. Shihata always adopted a realistic and flexible approach to negotiations and was able to carry the OPEC countries behind him. The following summary record of his intervention on the agenda item relating to "membership and initial contributions" at the second Session of the Governing Council in December 1978 is illustrative of this approach. He "pointed out that the document under consideration was of necessity full of compromises but should be acceptable to all if the criteria were applied with sufficient flexibility. He appealed to the Members to adopt it as it stood, subject to later review by the Governing Council if necessary."

He also helped through his interventions to promote healthy precedents for business-like and orderly discussions. For instance he argued against substantive reopening of technical documents that had been fully deliberated in the Executive Board. In the discussion on the Lending Policies and Criteria of IFAD he argued at the second session of the Governing Council that it should not normally introduce substantive amendments into technical documents. He suggested that the Council should either adopt the document before it or refer it back to the Executive Board, bearing in mind, however, that the document was the fruit of two years' discussion.

He invariably emphasized the paramount need that the Fund would continue to operate within the framework outlined in the Agreement establishing IFAD. He had personally made a significant contribution to the crafting of the Agreement, bringing to bear on this task the considerable experience he had gained as the main architect of the Agreement establishing the OPEC Special Fund. IFAD was a product of the renewed vigor which was provided to the North-South dialogue by what Dr. Shihata has termed as the "oil revolution" of the early 1970s. Thus, the Agreement establishing IFAD had many unique features:

- Its membership comprised three categories, namely the developed countries; the oil exporting developing countries; and the other developing countries. Each of the three categories had 600 votes, which effectively gave to the developing countries a two-thirds voting power. (However, a healthy practice has evolved in IFAD which has encouraged decisions being taken on the basis of consensus.)
- The resources of IFAD were to be contributed primarily by the developed and OPEC developing countries, and the other developing countries were not obligated to contribute to IFAD resources, even though they had an equal share in the voting strength.
- IFAD's mandate was narrowly defined to assist developing countries with food production and agricultural development with focus on the economic well-being, nutritional standards, and improved quality of life of the rural poor. Thus, it is a unique institution established specifically with the objective of rural poverty eradication.
- IFAD is intended to stay small. Therefore, the appraisal of projects and programs, as a general rule, should be entrusted to other competent international institutions of a world-wide or regional character.

The above features of IFAD were agreed upon by the conference of interested governments as a result of intensive discussions during which agreement was hammered out on a number of underlying thorny issues about the structure and scope of the new institution. These agreements became possible because of parleys at formal and informal levels, particularly among a small group of facilitators from the three categories of potential members — a process of consensus-building in which Dr. Shihata participated as one of the most influential and proactive players. Some of these issues are briefly mentioned below to under-score the challenge faced by the framers of the IFAD charter.

(i) The first controversial issue, discussed early on, related to the status of IFAD in the UN system — as an organ of the UN, like the UNDP, or as an independent Specialized Agency of the UN, like the FAO, but operating as an international financial institution, and not as a technical assistance agency. A number of developing countries, with strong support from delegates like Dr. Shihata won the day and got a decision that IFAD will function as an autonomous Specialized Agency within the family of the UN system.

(ii) Another crucial issue related to the financial basis of IFAD. Dr. Shihata was among those who strongly advocated against IFAD being vested with authority to raise funds through external borrowing. In this he was perhaps guided by the similar discussions with which he was involved in connection with the establishment of the OPEC Fund. Most donors, both from OECD and OPEC, were of the view that IFAD should derive its resources from voluntary contributions and preserve its character as a Fund rather than copy the model of the World Bank or the Regional Development Banks. The majority of interested governments also did not favor the system adopted by the United Nations and FAO for example, which legally obligates members to pay an assessed level of contributions. IDA was perceived as a more appropriate model for IFAD, except that the bulk of the financing was to be pledged by the OECD and OPEC group members. For the initial resources of the Fund, Dr. Shihata was able to facilitate an indication of a combined pledge (US$435.5 million) from individual OPEC member countries to be paid collectively out of the resources of the OPEC Fund. Commenting on this, Shihata has written in his book "The Other Face of OPEC":[1]

> "The conclusion to the negotiations over the establishment of IFAD was reached after OPEC countries pledged, through the OPEC Fund, to contribute more than 40 percent of the initial resources, provided that the developing countries, as a group, acquired two thirds of the voting power while the non-OPEC developing countries remained under no obligation to contribute to IFAD' s resources. Through the large financial contribution of the OPEC Fund and the active role played by representatives of the OPEC countries in the negotiations of the Agreement Establishing IFAD, a new chapter in the history of international financial institutions was launched."

(iii) Another important debate, which perhaps raged more in the background than in the open, was whether IFAD should be merely a 'cheque-signing' institution, and largely provide funding support to the operations of the other IFIs which conformed to its lending policies and criteria, or whether it should shape its own distinct 'market niche' in the field of development assistance. Dr. Shihata, representing the OPEC group, took the view that IFAD should not build up a large bureaucracy, but did not want to see it acting simply as a paying agent for pre-existing institutions. IFAD' s name and standing in the international community today as an institution of excellence in rural poverty eradication owes much to the wisdom of the framers of its charter and its lending policies and criteria who opted for a small but dynamic and innovative institution which will search, experiment and evolve new and actionable approaches to target resources to the rural poor. This has helped IFAD evolve and promote a people-centered and participatory process of poverty-focused development for the benefit of the disadvantaged and marginalized sections of rural communities. Dr. Shihata contributed greatly to the debate, particularly in ensuring transparency, accountabil-

---

[1] IBRAHIM F.I. SHIHATA, THE OTHER FACE OF OPEC: FINANCIAL ASSISTANCE TO THE THIRD WORLD 38 (1982).

ity and a clear legal framework for IFAD' s operations to ensure stringent adherence to standards of financial rectitude and cost-effectiveness.

In some of his writings, Dr. Shihata has written about his experience with the creation of IFAD in the context of the North-South dialogue. In a paper published in 1983,[2] he attributed the success of the IFAD negotiations to three main factors: (i) a clear indication of the proposed OPEC pledge to contribute resources to IFAD, which underlined its commitment to the proposal, combined with a structured negotiating mechanism based on a business-like approach; (ii) the position of OPEC being orchestrated in a coordinated manner through a single spokesman, which enabled the group to speak with a single voice; and (iii) a consensus in the contact group on a framework setting out the basic parameters relating to the structure, scope and governance of the institution, with detailed guidelines and regulations being worked out by the Preparatory Commission concurrently with action on the ratification of the Fund's constituting agreement. This process contrasted sharply to the 'maximalist' and rhetorical approach of the developing countries in the Paris dialogue on the NIEO, which turned out in Dr. Shihata's words to be a 'collective monologue.'

While the objectives, lending policies and criteria, and basic structure of IFAD's institutional and operational framework has stood the test of time, the institution and its strategic thrusts and approaches to poverty alleviation have evolved over the years in response to the changing world environment. Much of the changes could be easily accommodated within the framework of its original charter. However, in some areas of governance it became necessary to revisit some of the earlier parameters, and the Agreement Establishing IFAD was amended in February 1997 after a carefully negotiated restructuring exercise. The allocation of votes and distribution of seats was realigned to the changing pattern and level of contributions to IFAD's resources by the members of the two main categories. The other developing countries are also expected to pitch in by making contributions in freely convertible resources. The Fund, denied the right to supervise the

---

2 Ibrahim F.I. Shihata, *The North-South Dialogue Revisited: Some Personal Reflections*, 5 THIRD WORLD QUARTERLY 569 (1983).

implementation of projects by the original terms of its establishment, has now secured the necessary continuity by being allowed to supervise a limited number of innovative or exceptional projects on an experimental basis. While targeting has been essential in enabling the Fund to direct its resources in accordance with its mandate, important lessons have been learnt about the modalities of doing so against the framework of a clear set of corporate strategic thrusts and quantifiable action plans. As recommended by a Rapid External Assessment Team that evaluated IFAD in 1994, the Fund is moving towards developing as a 'knowledge institution' in rural poverty, with a major emphasis on knowledge generation and dissemination.

III. LAW AND DEVELOPMENT: AN IFAD PERSPECTIVE

The ultimate goal of economic development is to achieve the well-being of people while ensuring inter-generational and intra-generational equity in resource use. A sustainable process of poverty-focused development however, is contingent on an enabling policy environment and an orderly legal and institutional framework. As Dr. Shihata has written, "'law' in its widest sense as encompassing the whole legislative, regulatory and institutional framework, can act as a supportive structure and mechanism for developmental activities."[3] Dr. Shihata, from his days with the OPEC Fund has emphasized the need to look at development assistance, irrespective of its source, as an essential instrument for economic transformation and growth, and not simply as a matter of "resource transfer". For the IFIs, the connection between 'law' and 'development' has become an acute operational reality.

An IFI in directing its financial assistance to its developing member countries can not be oblivious to the broader concerns on the issues of corruption, human rights, democracy, and ethnic or racial discrimination. These concerns touch public sensibilities in a world where information flows instantly to the homes and hearths of people across the globe. These concerns for international normative standards of "good behavior" pose a dilemma for

---

3 Ibrahim F.I. Shihata, *Law and the Development Process,* ON THE RECORD, THE BANK'S WORLD, March 1990.

the IFIs who are generally prohibited by their charters from being influenced by the political character of its members in its decision-making. They can take "only 'economic' considerations" into account in its decisions. As observed by Dr. Shihata, while "good governance" challenges are critical for sustainable development, this means "walking a tightrope" between applying policy pressures that could be justified on economic grounds and crossing over the line into unacceptable political interference.

From IFAD's perspective, the major concern is with legal and institutional frameworks that touch the lives of the rural communities. These frameworks include both formal laws and regulations and informal or customary practices and traditions which govern the use of common property resources or the working of community-based associations. Much of the discussion on complementary legal and institutional reforms in the developing countries has focused on issues of macro-economic growth, industry, commerce and foreign direct investment. These issues are no doubt of great importance for developing countries to meet the challenges of market reforms and global integration. Dr. Shihata's writings on complementary reforms constitute part of seminal literature on this subject. However, there is a down-stream policy arena which is located closer to the challenge of rural poverty eradication. This calls for reforms at the level of 'local governance.' As the main focus of IFAD operations is on target-group specific interventions embedded in local socio-economic contexts, it has attempted to capture the changing boundaries and perceptions of poverty. The cornerstone of IFAD's operations is to sharpen IFAD's focus on the poor in a situation of changing dynamics of poverty. In the process it encounters a whole range of policy, legal and institutional impediments which condition the effectiveness and impact of micro-level poverty-focused investments. They can broadly be categorized as those that affect: (i) access of the poor to productive assets, facilities and resources, such as laws and regulations that have an impact on their land and water rights, and enhance their food security; (ii) active participation of the poor, especially of women, in local and community level processes of economic and social development, and a more active role of civil society organizations operating at the grass-roots; (iii) the representation of the underprivileged and marginalized sections of rural society, particularly that of women, and tribal or indigenous populations in local governance institutions; and (iv) the decentralization and devolution of authority to local governance organs. It is equally crucial that the reforms of relevant laws, rules and procedures to address these issues are transparent and enforceable, and have the back-up support of dispute-resolution institutions.

Dr. Shihata's enduring contribution throughout his professional work is to use his deep knowledge of the law and apply it in the service of improving the conditions of humankind. In this process, he has brought the law into the global development agenda, giving development initiatives and institutions a sound legal foundation. He has recognized that the law is not simply a matter of protecting property or personal rights. Beyond that, it should serve as the embodiment of society's conception of justice. To his credit and to the benefit of all of us, Dr. Shihata has applied a conception of justice and an approach to the law, that foster conditions in which men and women are able to lead fruitful, secure and fulfilling lives.

SETTLEMENT OF DISPUTES BETWEEN PARTIES FROM DEVELOPING AND INDUSTRIAL COUNTRIES

Karl-Heinz Böckstiegel

I. INTRODUCTION

Ibrahim F.I. Shihata is one of the great figures of this century for the legal relations between developing and industrial countries. This is shown in more detail in another section of this *Liber Amicorum* and is illustrated particularly by his long functions as Vice-President and General Counsel of the World Bank and as Secretary-General of the International Centre for Settlement of Investment Disputes (ICSID). His professional efficiency goes along with a personal sincerity that I have found to appreciate not only in a great number of professional meetings but also in private meetings such as lunches in Washington and The Hague. It was therefore with great pleasure that I accepted the invitation to contribute to this *Liber Amicorum*.

The topic of my contribution is obviously closely related to the long-year interest of Ibrahim Shihata as well as to my own academic interest and arbitration practice of almost thirty years. Therefore, this contribution does not claim to present all aspects of the topic, but rather will try to deal with some specific selected aspects of the topic within the limitations of space for contributions in this book. In particular, I have agreed with the Editorial Committee for this book not to deal in any extensive way with the ICSID practice and my own experience in this regard, because other authors in this book will present more detailed contributions on ICSID.

A further preliminary note seems necessary: If we look at the global picture of states and their economic development, it is even more obvious than it was in earlier times that the distinction between developing and industrial countries was a great simplification and that many countries might nowadays well be characterized as falling under both categories or as having moved partly or fully from a developing country to an industrial country. Many so-called developing countries have built up important industries and many so-called industrial countries are still developing such as from a dominance of industrial production to a dominance of a service industry. Furthermore, though the former socialist countries of Eastern Europe are normally considered as industrial countries, their transition from a socialist to a free market economy has brought for some of them challenges regarding necessary changes in their national laws and court systems which are similar to those traditionally known by developing countries. Nevertheless, this traditional distinction, if one remains aware of its simplification, is still relevant in many ways, not only but also regarding the settlement of international disputes.

II. TYPES OF PARTIES INVOLVED

If we look at the parties involved in disputes between developing and industrial countries, on the side of the industrial countries we find mostly private enterprises. The state itself and its government may, however, appear as a party in disputes concerning relationships in public international law, be it multilaterally within the World Trade Organization or bilaterally, such as in the implementation of investment or aviation treaties.

From the side of the developing countries, less private enterprises will be involved in these kinds of disputes, because in many developing countries there will be less private enterprises of the size involved in international business relations that would lead them to be parties in the international contracts and disputes considered here. On the other hand, the state and its state enterprises will appear more often from the side of the developing country as a party in such a dispute such as the host state for a foreign investment or as the owner or builder of large infrastructure projects.

III. TYPES OF OBJECTS OF THE DISPUTE

Objects of the dispute could first of all come from the range of international relations, particularly economic relations ruled by public international law. If one looks at the survey of Stuyt[1] on arbitration between 1794 and 1970, it becomes evident that economic disputes were often the subject of proceedings before the Second World War but more seldom in the first decades afterwards. Insofar, there is a parallel to cases before the Permanent Court of International Justice which was more often seized with economic disputes than later the International Court of Justice. Economic questions were either directly or at least indirectly in dispute in the intergovernmental arbitration proceedings in the Palena case of 1966 between Argentina[2] and Chile, the Rann of Kutch case of 1968 between India and Pakistan,[3] the Beagle Channel case of 1977 between Argentina and Chile,[4] the Guinea-Guinea Bissau case of 1986,[5] and the Taba case of 1987 between Egypt and Israel.[6] At least indirectly, economic matters were the object of the several proceedings before *Ad Hoc* Chambers of the International Court of Justice in the Frontier Dispute of 1985 between Burkina Faso and Mali[7] and the Maritime Frontier Dispute of 1987 between El Salvador and Honduras.[8]

Also at the level of public international law, issues of international trade in goods and services are at stake in disputes under the very extensive dispute settlement machinery of the World Trade Organization. Matters of civil aviation are objects of dispute settlement under the Chicago Convention of 1944 and before the International Civil Aviation Organization (ICAO) as well as of dispute settlement clauses in bilateral air transport agreements as thousands exist between developing and industrial states. Finally,

---

1 ALEXANDER MARIE STUYT, SURVEY OF INTERNATIONAL ARBITRATIONS 1794–1970 (1972).

2 Argentine-Chile Frontier Case (Arg. v. Chile), 38 INT'L. L REP. 10 (1969).

3 Indo-Pakistan Western Boundary (Rann of Kutch) Case (India v. Pak.), 50 INT'L. L REP. 2 (1976).

4 Beagle Channel Arbitration (Arg. v. Chile), 52 INT'L. L REP. 93 (1979).

5 *See* 25 I.L.M. 251 (1986).

6 *See* 27 I.L.M. 1421 (1988).

7 *See* 1986 ICJ REPORTS, 554.

8 *See* Procedural briefs and decisions *in* 1987 ICJ REPORTS, at 10, 12.

of course, the protection of foreign investment is at stake under dispute settlement methods adopted in hundreds of bilateral investment treaties between industrial and developing states insofar as disputes arise between the High Contracting States.

In connection with investments as the objects of dispute, in addition to disputes between the host state and the home state of the investor, there are disputes directly between the private investor, normally from an industrial country, and the host state itself. As we all know, in this context often ICSID is the chosen institution for the settlement of disputes either already in the bilateral investment treaty, or in a contract between the host state and the foreign investor or, more recently, also in national investment laws of developing countries in which the host state unilaterally submits to ICSID and the foreign investor can, without the need of further agreement, start ICSID proceedings. But already before ICSID became a more popular choice for the settlement of investment disputes, over many decades we already find contracts, particularly concession contracts regarding natural resources, providing for some kind of international arbitration directly between the host state and the private foreign investor. There is a number of well-known cases in this field which do not have to be reiterated here.

Also beyond the scope of foreign investment, international business practice has had and still has a great number of commercial contracts between on one side a state, state institution, or state enterprise, and on the other side a foreign private enterprise. Typical objects of such contracts — and of resulting disputes — are the delivery of military goods, the delivery of oil, gas, and other products of natural resources, the construction and maintenance of infrastructure projects for the supply of energy, water, communication services, airports, dams, and finally also often the construction and maintenance of large plants in the various branches of industry.

In view of the special importance of the transfer of technology between industrial and developing countries, all contracts in that context must also be considered as of prime relevance. As far as patent rights and other industrial property rights are concerned, obviously the monopoly of state institutions to decide on the validity of such rights cannot be changed by arbitration clauses. On the other hand, many contracts in this field do contain arbitration clauses which cover all other aspects of industrial property rights. Arbitration and technology, arbitration and international economic co-operation towards industrial, scientific and technical development, and arbitration concerning transfers of patents, know-how, trademarks and similar rights for promoting international industrial co-operation have been dealt with quite some years ago already by the International Arbitration Congresses in Moscow 1972 and in Mexico City 1978 as well as at the Interim Meeting of the International Council for Commercial Arbitration (ICCA) in Vienna 1976.[9] And regarding the specific field of intellectual property rights, the World Intellectual Property Organization (WIPO) has developed highly sophisticated dispute settlement machineries which may be used in the future.

Very often in commercial relations and in arbitration between parties from industrial and developing countries one finds varying types of long-term contracts. Already the contracts on the erection of large industrial plants and turn-key factories, which one often finds in these relationships, lead to a contractual period of several years due to the volume of the deliveries and services involved. Contracts on investments and on co-operation, be it in the developing country or be it by a joint venture in a third country, as well as license and know-how contracts will usually involve even much longer contractual periods. Arbitration regarding such long-term contracts will often be more complicated than other arbitration procedures due to the new, not foreseeable or at least not foreseen developments which at least from the stand-point of one of the parties disturbs the balance of the contract or certain contractual obligations. The arbitral tribunal in such cases will often be asked to adapt the contract, a function which is not permitted to arbitration in all national systems.[10]

In commercial relations and arbitration cases between parties from industrial and developing countries, one will also often find

---

9 USSR Chamber of Commerce and Industry, COLLECTION OF THE IVTH INTERNATIONAL CONGRESS ON ARBITRATION MATERIALS, 54 *et seq.*, 409 *et seq.*; International Council of Commercial Arbitration, VITH INTERNATIONAL CONGRESS, 317 *et seq.*; Schiedsgerichtsbarkeit und gewerblicher Rechtsschutz, INTERIMSTAGUNG DER ICCA, Wien 1976 (Bd. 30 der Schriftenreihe der Bundeskammer für Gewerbliche Wirtschaft, 1976).

10 For a most recent research on all related questions, *see* S. Kröll, *Ergänzung und Anpassung von Verträgen durch Schiedsgerichte, in* INTERNATIONALES WIRTSCHAFTSRECHT, VOL. 16 (Cologne 1998).

a situation where not one contract, but several contracts forming a certain interdependent system of relationships will have to be taken into account. An example are those frequent relationships where, parallel to contracts on delivery and services or to investments, financing agreements have to be concluded since sufficient financing is not available in the developing country. In such cases often third parties especially national and international banking or insurance institutions are involved. Another system of several interrelated contracts appears, if for the erection of a large industrial plant in a developing country contracts have to be concluded on the delivery of equipment, on the civil engineering, on the delivery of equipment, on the erection of equipment, and on consultation regarding the erection and running of the plant, contracts which involve different partners, different contents and structures, but which nevertheless are in many ways interrelated. In all such cases of contractual systems, disputes lead to specific problems in arbitration especially regarding the question, among which parties a valid arbitration agreement has been concluded, regarding the status of interested third parties in an arbitration proceeding and the question which effect an award may have on related contracts with other parties. Problems of this kind have been extensively discussed under the heading of "multi-party arbitration" in recent years and, indeed, have led to amendments of modern arbitration rules.[11]

IV. CHOSEN METHODS OF DISPUTE SETTLEMENT

There exists a great variety of options of methods for dispute settlement available to parties from developing and industrial countries. Even if one discounts the "paper tigers" of arbitration, i.e. the many options which only exist on paper but are never or very seldom used in practice, the survey of actual cases presents a great diversity.

Regarding disputes in the range of public international law between states from the industrial and the developing world, reference has already been made to the cases before the Permanent

---

11 Such as: ICC Arbitration Rules, Art. 10 (1998); LCIA Arbitration Rules, Art. 8 (1998); Arbitration Rules of the German Arbitration Institution (DIS), § 13.

Court of International Justice and the more recent cases before the International Court of Justice at The Hague. The dispute settlement machinery of the World Trade Organization, though still relatively young, has already been used widely though opinions differ as to the effectiveness of this rather complicated system, including an appeal level. Another frequent choice for interstate disputes found in bilateral aviation and investment treaties is arbitration, in the latter case often ICSID arbitration. But if one goes through the great volume and great variety of multilateral and bilateral treaties in international law it will still be found that, with the exception of those mentioned above, states have been hesitant to choose a binding third-party settlement method for disputes between themselves and have rather relied only on non-binding methods such as diplomatic negotiations, conciliation and mediation.

In view of this traditional and general hesitation of states it is surprising — and on the other hand encouraging for the peaceful settlement of disputes — that in one of the most delicate political relationships between two states, namely between Iran and the United States after the Iranian Revolution in 1979, binding dispute settlement by arbitration was accepted by both states. This by far largest international arbitration procedure in history both with regard to the number of cases and the financial amounts involved was conducted, as is well known, by the Iran-United States Claims Tribunal in The Hague created by the Declaration of Algiers to decide on all claims which one of the two states or their citizens have against the other state. In the limited framework of this contribution it is not possible — and in view of the extensive literature[12] on the Tribunal also not necessary — to go into any detail

---

[12] Most recent comprehensive books are: CHARLES N. BROWER & JASON D. BRUESCHKE, THE IRAN-UNITED STATES CLAIMS TRIBUNAL (1998); GEORGE H. ALDRICH, THE JURISPRUDENCE OF THE IRAN-UNITED STATES CLAIMS TRIBUNAL (1996); JOHN A. WESTBERG, INTERNATIONAL TRANSACTIONS AND CLAIMS INVOLVING GOVERNMENT PARTIES — CASE LAW OF THE IRAN–UNITED STATES CLAIMS TRIBUNAL (1991).

Examples of further publications are: Jones, *The Iran-United States Claims Tribunal: Private Rights and State Responsibility*, 24 VIRGINIA JOURNAL OF INTERNATIONAL LAW 259 *et seq.* (1984); Clagett, *The Expropriation Issue Before the Iran-United States Claims Tribunal: Is "Just Compensation" required by International Law or Not?*, 16 LAW AND POLICY IN INTERNATIONAL BUSINESS 813 *et seq.* (1984); Carbonneau, *The Iran-United States Claims Tribunal 1981–1983, in* THE ELABORATION OF SUBSTANTIVE LEGAL NORMS AND ARBITRAL ADJUDICATION: THE CASE OF THE IRAN-UNITED STATES CLAIMS TRIBUNAL

of its more than 3,800 cases virtually all of which concern economic disputes. The jurisdiction of this Tribunal covers both intergovernmental disputes as dealt with above and disputes involving private enterprises which I will deal with below. Though the great majority of these cases are claims by private enterprises or private individuals against the other state, 94 truly intergovernmental disputes have been placed before the Tribunal of which some 25 are so-called A-Cases (interpretative disputes referred to in Article II (3) and VI (4) of the Claims Settlement Declaration) and 69 so-called B-Cases (official claims of one government against the other based on Article II (2) of the Claims Settlement Declaration). For its procedure, the Tribunal used the UNCITRAL (United Nations Commission for International Trade Law) Arbitration Rules in an adapted version. By agreement between the two Governments, a special Security Account amounting to one billion US-Dollars was created for the enforcement of any decisions against Iran, and Iran undertook to fill this account up as soon as it ran under US$500 million, an obligation which it has fulfilled in practice. The work of the Tribunal since its creation in 1981 has been overshadowed by the hostile relationship between the two Governments, but nevertheless has found its way — under these difficult circumstances — to a surprisingly professional working atmosphere and to a great number of decisions all of which are published.[13] Even in the fall of 1987, when

104 *et seq.* (Lillich ed., 1984); Gold, *The Iran-United States Claims Tribunal and the Articles of Agreement of the International Monetary Fund,* 18 GEORGE WASHINGTON JOURNAL OF INTERNATIONAL LAW AND ECONOMICS 537 *et seq.* (1985); Leurent, *Problèmes soulevées par les demandes des double nationaux devant le Tribunal des différents irano-américains,* 74 REVUE CRITIQUE DE DROIT INTERNATIONAL PRIVÉ 273 *et seq.* (1985); McCabe, *Arbitral Discovery and the Iran-United States Claims Tribunal Experience,* 20 THE INTERNATIONAL LAWYER 499 seq. (1986); Caron, *Interim Measures of Protection: Theory and Practice in Light of the Iran-United States Claims Tribunal,* 46 ZEITSCHRIFT FÜR AUSLÄNDISCHES ÖFFENTLICHES RECHT UND VÖLKERRECHT 466 *et seq.* (1986); MAIWALD, DAS IRAN-UNITED STATES CLAIMS TRIBUNAL (Cologne 1987); Brower, *Current Development in the Law of Expropriation and Compensation: A Preliminary Survey of Awards of the Iran-United States Claims Tribunal,* 21 THE INTERNATIONAL LAWYER 639 *et seq.* (1987), and *The Iran-United States Claims Tribunal after Seven Years: A Retrospective from the Inside,* 43 THE ARBITRATION JOURNAL 16 *et seq.* (December 1988).

13 Shortly after being filed the awards are published — and commented — in the Iranian Assets Litigation Reporter and in Mealey's Litigation Reports (Iranian Claims). All awards are reprinted in IRAN-UNITED STATES CLAIMS TRIBUNAL REPORTS, Grotius Publications, Cambridge, 29 volumes since 1983. Selection reprinted regularly in YEARBOOK: COMMERCIAL ARBITRATION, Deventer.

Iran and the United States performed military actions against each other at the Gulf, a large oral hearing of the Tribunal took place in the Peace Palace in The Hague on a dispute which could not have been more delicate under the circumstances, namely a claim by Iran against the United States to return great quantities of certain military equipment, and the hearing could be performed in a professionally adequate manner. In the practice of the Tribunal, a number of typical procedural problems of international arbitration have occurred to which the jurisprudence of the Tribunal is of relevance for other and future international dispute settlement and especially arbitration such as regarding the questions of jurisdiction in case of double nationality, presentation and evaluation of evidence, and interim measures of protection. The jurisprudence is even wider on matters of substantive law as an obvious consequence of the wide ranging competence of the Tribunal and the variety of the cases before it ranging from questions of public international law such as interpretation of treaties, treatment and expulsion of foreigners, expropriation and nationalization, and the law of military co-operation up to practically all questions occurring in international business relations of private enterprises regarding international contracts, payments, and investments. This variety is the result of the intensive co-operation which existed in all these fields between the United States and Iran, at state and private levels. In these fields, the jurisprudence of the Tribunal deals with questions such as the applicable law, lifting the corporate veil, interpretation of contracts, *force majeure,* letters of credit and bank guarantees, exchange restrictions for payments, expulsion of foreigners and liability for interest. But the author — as a former President of the Tribunal — should for obvious reasons refrain from evaluating this jurisprudence[14] and leave that to outside observers.

Contrary to the often found hesitation of states in interstate disputes to rely on binding dispute settlement, commercial rela-

---

[14] Not an evaluation, but a selective *resumé* of issues in the decisions of the Tribunal can be seen in Böckstiegel, *Zur Bedeutung des Iran-United States Claims Tribunal für die Entwicklung des internationalen Rechts, in* FESTSCHRIFT DER RECHTSWISSENSCHAFTLICHEN FAKULTÄT ZUR 600–JAHR-FEIER DER UNIVERSITÄT ZU KÖLN (Cologne 1988); *id., Practice of International Dispute Settlement — Thoughts after Resigning as President of the Iran-United States Claims Tribunal, in* LIBER AMICORUM FOR NICOLAS MATTE (Montreal 1989).

tions between on one side states, state institutions or state enterprises and on the other side foreign private enterprises are in modern practice almost always subjected to binding dispute settlement methods. This is most probably due to similar reasons as those that have made arbitration popular for international commercial relations in other areas: Often both contractual partners try to avoid the national jurisdiction of the home state of the other partner so that agreeing on international arbitration is an obvious compromise; often both parties also expect a better knowledge of the facts and usages of international commerce from arbitrators which — contrary to the judges of state courts — they can choose themselves; the procedure of arbitration is most often more flexible than national codes of procedure and obviously does not grant one of the parties the advantage of a legal procedure which is well-known to it but unfamiliar to the other party; advantages regarding the language of procedure may also be avoided more easily in international arbitration; often — though not always — arbitration will also be faster than litigation before a national state court, especially since one single arbitration procedure, but normally only proceedings in three levels of state courts will lead to a final decision; at least in comparison with three instances of court litigation, arbitration will also normally be cheaper; and finally, especially due to the New York Convention of 1958 and the other arbitration conventions, enforcement of arbitration awards is assured in a much higher number of states throughout the world than is the enforcement of court judgements. These reasons, in varying combinations and relevance, may have led to the situation that, generally in international commerce, arbitration is the preferred instrument for the settlement of disputes at least for larger contracts.

In addition, there may be some further specific reasons why this trend can also be found in contracts involving parties from developing countries: The social and legal differences between many industrial and developing countries may make it even more difficult for parties from this background to agree to the national law and national jurisdiction of the other party; sometimes, not only the party from the industrial but also from the developing country may come to the opinion that neither are the judges from industrial countries well enough acquainted with the situation in developing countries nor are judges in developing countries well enough acquainted with the specific legal problems connected with industrial equipment and high technology services which very often are the object of contracts of this kind. On the other hand, it should not be neglected that experiences with older concession contracts and arbitration cases dealing with such contracts may make a party from a developing country hesitate to agree to traditional arbitration which it may consider as a "western" arbitration. It is in this context that one may find the reasons why still some Latin-American and Arab states take a reluctant attitude toward international commercial arbitration. Another reason for this attitude may be that, due to their different traditions, one may be less familiar in certain of these states with the instruments and alternatives available in international commercial arbitration. Closer examination shows, however, that not seldom more reservations are phrased in abstract terms at the international level than actually play a role in commercial practice and negotiations on concrete contracts. This is illustrated by the fact that a considerable number of the parties agreeing to and involved in the arbitration of the International Chamber of Commerce comes from the developing world, the UNCITRAL Arbitration Rules have been elaborated and are chosen by parties from developing countries, and finally also by the high record of ratification which can be noted from developing countries for the ICSID Convention. Furthermore, an indication that also developing countries, in spite of the hesitations mentioned, consider arbitration as the relatively better method for the settlement of international commercial disputes, seems to be confirmed by the Law of the Sea Convention which includes an accepted highly sophisticated mechanism for the settlement of disputes, giving the parties a choice between certain options, but providing for arbitration in case the parties do not agree on any other method.

If thus, there is a general trend to submit to arbitration for the settlement of disputes between parties from developing and industrial countries, the obvious next question is, which methods are primarily chosen in practice. In this context, one has to be aware that, as is true for international arbitration in general — also here the hundreds of institutions and arbitration rules created both at the national and international levels over the years do by no means imply that all these are actually used in practice. Quite to the contrary, it is in fact a relatively small number of institutions and rules to which parties seem to be ready to submit when they conclude an international commercial contract. Only a short reference to these practically relevant institutions and rules can be given hereafter within the limited space available for this paper.

If one first turns to *ad hoc* arbitration, one finds that this "tailor-made" method of dispute settlement is not chosen too frequently for the settlement of disputes between parties from developing and industrial countries. The reason for this may be twofold: On the one hand, as in international arbitration in general, agreements for *ad hoc* arbitration, in order to be effective, have to be negotiated and developed in great detail as they have to deal with all major issues and possible problems that may occur in an international dispute settlement procedure. And even if drafted with the greatest care, it cannot be excluded that, particularly in a long-term contract, situations arise which were not foreseen in the contract and its arbitration agreement and which, therefore, are either not covered by the arbitration agreement or at least highly difficult for the arbitral tribunal to deal with efficiently. Secondly, *ad hoc* arbitration have a relatively better chance of functioning in the practice of an actual dispute, if the place of arbitration is in a state which has a modern arbitration law subsidiarily dealing with all major issues in case they are not dealt with in the arbitration agreement itself. Though, in the last twenty years, we have had quite a number of new legislation in various countries introducing modern arbitration laws, this can by no means be said for all industrial and even less for developing countries though the adoption of the UNCITRAL Model Arbitration Law in almost thirty countries throughout the world by now has improved the situation. But in all other countries, *ad hoc* arbitration is still exposed to the risks mentioned above.

A compromise solution is available and by now quite often found in contracts between parties from developing and industrial countries, namely the choice of the UNCITRAL Arbitration Rules. As is well known, the UNCITRAL Arbitration Rules have been elaborated with the specific intention to serve as a subsidiary framework for *ad hoc* arbitration in order to deal with the difficulties mentioned above. From the point of view of parties in developing countries, it may be also a special attraction of the UNCITRAL Arbitration Rules, that these have been negotiated in the United Nations Commission for International Trade Law (UNCI-

TRAL) between experts both from industrial and developing countries and that they are considered by both the industrial and the developing world as an efficient framework for international dispute settlement. This basic acceptability is confirmed on one hand by the fact that — as mentioned above — the Iran-United States Claims Tribunal used the UNCITRAL Arbitration Rules in an adapted version for its many cases and also by the fact that the United Nations use the UNCITRAL Arbitration Rules for dispute settlement when they conclude commercial contracts with private enterprises at the international level.

Nevertheless, the still most popular choice found in international practice for the settlement of disputes between parties from developing and industrial countries are the arbitration rules of certain arbitral institutions at the international and sometimes also at the national level. This reflects the picture in general international arbitration where institutional arbitration is the preferred choice because at least the rules of the most frequently chosen institutions present the parties the advantage of an experience of many years, of foreseeability, and also of the relatively best efficiency, because these rules are regularly adapted to changes in the international environment. Thus, the present rules of the International Chamber of Commerce (ICC) and of the London Court of International Arbitration (LCIA) are regularly examined by experts both from the industrial and the developing worlds and have both most recently been adopted in modern versions from the beginning of 1998. It is therefore not surprising that a major part of the cases before the ICC and the LCIA are disputes between parties from developing and industrial countries.

Though the ICSID Convention is of 1965, and the ICSID Arbitration Rules have been unchanged for many years, recent years show a growing popularity of ICSID arbitration. This is an impressive contrast to the early years of ICSID when an average of one case per year could only be found in practice. This growing trend to choose ICSID arbitration may partly be due to the fact that submission to ICSID arbitration is not only found by the traditional method of a specific contract between the host state and the foreign investor, but also by modern bilateral investment treaties and — as mentioned above — sometimes by specific investment laws of states unilaterally submitting to ICSID. A further explanation may also be that the nullification procedure, which was relatively too often used in the early years of ICSID and made ICSID lose one of the major advantages of arbitration, namely an undelayed final and binding decision on the case, has been used and has been successful much less in recent years so that the parties can normally expect a final and binding decision by an ICSID arbitral tribunal within a foreseeable time.

Finally, some national institutions of arbitration are also chosen sometimes for the settlement of disputes between parties from developing and industrial countries. An example in an industrial country is the arbitration of the Stockholm Chamber of Commerce, and an example in what some may still consider as a developing country is the arbitration of CIETAC in China which gets the bulk of cases arising between Chinese parties on one hand and foreign enterprises on the other hand.

V. PERSPECTIVE

If one looks for a short perspective at the end of this limited presentation in this *Liber Amicorum,* the practice up to the present time seems to indicate a trend to a growing acceptance of binding methods of settlement of disputes between parties from developing and industrial countries and, in particular, of arbitration as the preferred method of dispute settlement. For the future, the growing adoption of the UNCITRAL Model Law for commercial arbitration in many industrial and developing countries throughout the world will create a more and more harmonized legal framework for such arbitration supported by the growing harmonization of the major institutional arbitration rules used in the practice of this field.

IBRAHIM SHIHATA AND THE RESOLUTION OF INTERNATIONAL INVESTMENT DISPUTES: THE MASTERFUL MISSIONARY*

Charles N. Brower

I. INTRODUCTION

In his position as the Secretary-General of the International Centre for Settlement of Investment Disputes ("ICSID" or "the Centre"),[1] Dr. Ibrahim F.I. Shihata has played a significant and decisive role in the cause of peaceful and successful resolution of international investment disputes. His efforts have been concentrated quite naturally at ICSID, where he has served since October 1, 1983,[2] but he also has worked unselfishly and energetically to foster a general acceptance of, and confidence in, all manner of international alternative dispute resolution mechanisms. Moreover, Dr. Shihata has followed a grand vision, concentrating his efforts not simply on improving the procedural workings of international

* This Article is an updated and expanded version of a speech originally given at a March 22, 1999 Symposium held in honor of Ibrahim F.I. Shihata at Georgetown University Law Center. I would like to thank Lee A. Steven of the Virginia and Washington, D.C. Bars for his very able assistance in the preparation of this Article.

1 Established by the Convention on the Settlement of Investment Disputes between States and Nationals of Other States, Mar. 18, 1965, 575 U.N.T.S. 159, 17 U.S.T. 1270 [hereinafter ICSID Convention].

2 Dr. Shihata was elected Secretary-General of ICSID on September 29, 1983 at the Seventeenth Annual Meeting of the ICSID Administrative Council and began his first term on October 1, 1983. *See* ICSID, 1984 ANNUAL REPORT 17, 20 (1984). The Administrative Council, consisting of one representative of each Contracting State to the ICSID Convention, meets annually and is the chief governing body of ICSID. *See* ICSID Convention, *supra* note 1, arts. 4–8.

dispute resolution, but also on using such mechanisms to promote the general welfare by improving the investment climate worldwide. Such efforts should not go unsung and this Article seeks to outline some of Dr. Shihata's more significant contributions both within ICSID itself and in the broader context of international dispute resolution.

II. IBRAHIM SHIHATA'S CONTRIBUTIONS TO ICSID

If Dr. Aron Broches brought ICSID to life — and truly he did[3] — Dr. Ibrahim Shihata raised it almost from infancy, through adolescence, to its present young, but rapidly maturing, adulthood. Statistics alone bear this out. At the time of his arrival on duty at ICSID, the Centre had registered a mere sixteen cases, or about one a year.[4] In the intervening years (not yet quite sixteen) its docket has quadrupled and its "rate of climb" is steepening.[5] Before 1997 the Centre had never registered more than four cases in a single year; in 1997, however, ICSID registered ten cases, in 1998 it registered eleven cases, and in 1999 it registered nine cases.[6]

In part, of course, this increased case load must be due to the fact that under Dr. Shihata's leadership the Centre has come both to merit and, consequently, to be accorded a large measure of trust and confidence on the part of sovereign States and private

---

3 As General Counsel of the World Bank in the 1960s, Dr. Broches led the team that formulated the first draft of the ICSID Convention and was instrumental in shepherding the long negotiation process that preceded the adoption of the final draft. *See, e.g.*, 1 ICSID, History of the Convention on the Settlement of Investment Disputes between States and Nationals of Other States: Analysis of Documents 2–10 (1970). Dr. Broches also served as ICSID's first Secretary-General, serving from the inauguration of ICSID on February 2, 1967 to October 2, 1980. *See* ICSID, Fifteenth Annual Report 1980/1981 3 (1981).

4 *See* ICSID Cases, Doc. ICSID/16/Rev. 6 (Sept. 30, 1998). The Centre provides a continuously updated version of this publication on its new Internet website. In the on-line version, ICSID Cases is divided into two documents. *See* ICSID, *List of Concluded Cases*, <http://www.worldbank.org/icsid/cases/conclude.htm>, and ICSID, *List of Pending Cases*, <http://www.worldbank.org/icsid/cases/pending.htm> [hereinafter *List of Concluded and Pending Cases*].

5 From January 1984 to August 1999, ICSID registered forty-nine cases compared to the sixteen cases of the preceding years, for a total of sixty-five cases. *See List of Concluded and Pending Cases, supra* note 4.

6 *See ibid.*

investors in a world of ever increasing foreign direct investment. The causes nevertheless lie, however, in more than just good stewardship on the part of a diligent and conscientious Secretary-General. Other factors are at play.

Dr. Shihata has been a tireless, creative, politically adept, and thoroughly committed exponent of the cause he espouses and indeed personifies — in short, a masterful missionary. Thus early in his tenure he was determined to go beyond simply promoting the ICSID arbitration machinery and to use it as an "instrument of international public policy," seeking to enhance the legal framework of foreign direct investment and to forge new ties of confidence and goodwill between foreign investors and host States.[7] He then undertook to achieve this goal through a number of initiatives, including:

- Renovating the ICSID machinery itself;
- Disseminating information regarding ICSID;
- Sponsoring educational programs about ICSID, and indeed about international arbitration more broadly; and
- Targeting efforts to recruit new States Parties to the ICSID Convention, particularly from those theretofore indifferent to it, if not downright hostile.

A. Renovation of the ICSID Machinery

Renovation of ICSID's arbitral operations consisted partly of revising the ICSID Arbitration Rules in 1984[8] so as, on the one hand, to

---

[7] As Dr. Shihata wrote in his first Annual Report as ICSID's Secretary-General:

> I take it that it is my duty to find ways for ICSID to assume a more important role in improving the investment climate at large, and in developing countries in particular. ICSID can play that role only to the extent that its potential clients, the investors and the host countries, agree to resort to the ICSID machinery either at the time of drafting or when disputes arise out of such an agreement.
>
> . . . .
>
> . . . [Yet] ICSID should not be viewed merely as a mechanism of conflict resolution. It should be regarded as an effective instrument of international public policy which is meant in the final analysis to secure a stable and increasing flow of resources to developing countries under reasonable conditions.

1984 ANNUAL REPORT, *supra* note 2, at 4–5.

[8] *See ibid.* at 10 ("Given the experience acquired in conciliation and arbitration proceedings, the Secretary-General deemed it timely to revise the Rules. The pur-

simplify and streamline ICSID procedure,[9] and, on the other hand, to insulate ICSID arbitration more fully from any pre-award resort to municipal courts by a party without the other's consent.[10] Further, Dr. Shihata prevailed upon ICSID's Administrative Council the same year to continue indefinitely ICSID's Additional Facility,[11] thereby insuring the Centre's availability in many circumstances to States not yet party to the ICSID Convention and to their nationals.[12] In recommending the continuation of the Additional Facility in 1984, Dr. Shihata showed remarkable prescience: the Centre did not register the first Additional Facility case until 1997, but since then has registered a total of seven cases invoking that facility.[13] Further, these seven cases, all of which are still pending, constitute more than twenty percent of ICSID's currently active docket.[14]

---

pose of this revision is not to make major modifications to the Rules, but rather to simplify or clarify certain provisions and to allow for more flexibility in the handling of proceedings.").

9 *See* Antonio R. Parra, *Revised Regulations and Rules,* 2 NEWS FROM ICSID, Winter 1985, at 4–6 (detailing the changes implemented by the 1984 revisions); ICSID, 1985 ANNUAL REPORT, 14–15 (1985).

10 *See* Parra, *supra* note 9, at 6 (discussing the changes to Arbitration Rule 39, which clarified that, unless expressly provided otherwise in their arbitration agreement, parties to an ICSID arbitration may not seek provisional measures from a municipal court but must instead seek such relief exclusively from the ICSID tribunal itself); 1985 ANNUAL REPORT, *supra* note 9, at 14.

11 *See* 1984 ANNUAL REPORT, *supra* note 2, at 17 (announcing the Secretary-General's report to the Administrative Council recommending that the Additional Facility be maintained); 1985 ANNUAL REPORT, *supra* note 9, at 14 (reporting the Administrative Council's approval of the Secretary-General's proposal to continue indefinitely the Additional Facility).

12 The Additional Facility administers certain proceedings that fall outside the scope of the ICSID Convention, namely: "(i) conciliation or arbitration proceedings for the settlement of Investment Disputes arising between parties one of which is not a Contracting State or a national of a Contracting State; (ii) conciliation or arbitration proceedings between parties at least one of which is a Contracting State or a national of a Contracting State for the settlement of investment disputes that do not directly arise out of an investment; and (iii) fact-finding proceedings." ICSID, ADDITIONAL FACILITY FOR THE ADMINISTRATION OF CONCILIATION, ARBITRATION AND FACT-FINDING PROCEEDINGS, at v (June 1979) (also available at <http:// www.worldbank.org/icsid/facility/facility.htm>).

13 *See List of Concluded and Pending Cases, supra* note 4. All but one of these cases have been brought under Chapter 11 of the North American Free Trade Agreement (NAFTA).

14 As of April 12, 2000 there were 30 pending cases on the ICSID docket. *See ibid.* (visited April 12, 2000).

Renovation took place in less formal structural ways as well. When the ICSID-user public became alarmed over the success of the first two proceedings brought to annul an ICSID award,[15] which was compounded by concern over the test for annulment applied in the first annulment case,[16] Dr. Shihata acted swiftly. To better ensure a correct and uniform jurisprudence in future annulment proceedings, he saw to it that the Chairman of the Ad-

---

[15] The first two annulment proceedings were *Klöckner Industrie-Anlagen GmbH v. United Republic of Cameroon,* ICSID Case No. ARB/81/2, First Annulment Decision of May 3, 1985, *reprinted in* 2 ICSID REP. 95 (1994), and *Amco Asia Corp. v. Republic of Indonesia,* ICSID Case No. ARB/81/1, First Annulment Decision of May 16, 1986, *reprinted in* 1 ICSID REP. 509 (1993).

Shortly after these early annulment decisions commentators expressed concern over the future viability of ICSID, several of them openly predicting the ultimate demise of ICSID. *See, e.g.*, STEPHEN J. TOOPE, MIXED INTERNATIONAL ARBITRATION 256–59 (1990); Mark B. Feldman, *The Annulment Proceedings and the Finality of ICSID Arbitral Awards,* 2 ICSID REV.–FOREIGN INV. L.J. 85 (1987); D.A. Redfern, *ICSID — Losing its Appeal?,* 3 ARB. INT'L 98 (1987); W. Michael Reisman, *The Breakdown of the Control Mechanism in ICSID Arbitration,* 1989 Duke L.J. 739.

[16] A request for annulment of an award under the ICSID Convention may be granted only where the *ad hoc* Committee constituted to hear the annulment petition finds that at least one of the following five grounds for annulment is present:

(a) that the Tribunal was not properly constituted;
(b) that the Tribunal has manifestly exceeded its power;
(c) that there was corruption on the part of a member of the Tribunal;
(d) that there has been a serious departure from a fundamental rule of procedure; or
(e) that the award has failed to state the reasons on which it is based.

ICSID Convention, *supra* note 1, art. 52(1). The *ad hoc* Committee in *Klöckner* took the view that a "finding that there is one of the grounds for annulment in Article 52(1) must in principle lead to total or partial annulment of the award, without the Committee having any discretion." *Klöckner,* 2 ICSID REP., at 162.

Professor Reisman of Yale Law School has criticized this "technical discrepancy" approach, advocating instead a "material violation" standard that would require annulment only if a technical discrepancy in procedure actually materially affects the interests of the losing party. *See* W. Michael Reisman, *Repairing ICSID's Control System: Some Comments on Aron Broches' "Observations on the Finality of ICSID Awards,"* 7 ICSID REV.–FOREIGN INV. L.J. 196, 204–05 (1992). Reisman notes that the *ad hoc* Committee in the *Amco Asia* case did not follow *Klöckner's* "technical discrepancy" approach but instead applied the "material violation" standard:

> This [material violation] approach is, in fact, what the *Amco I ad hoc* Committee took when it noted that the *Amco* Tribunal had made an incorrect choice of law but then confirmed that the Tribunal's choice of law produced the same result as would have been achieved by the proper choice of law. Hence, the *Amco I ad hoc* Committee did not annul on this ground.

Ibid. at 204.

ministrative Council judiciously exercised his authority to appoint the members of the *ad hoc* Committees constituted to hear applications for annulment[17] so as to appoint to each such Committee at least one member (if not two) who already had sat on a previous Committee.[18] The result has been that following a total of six annulment proceedings in just four cases within a period of eight years,[19] not a single annulment petition has been registered in the almost eight years since May 27, 1992 (the date of registration of the last annulment petition),[20] and confidence in ICSID is at an all-time high.

B. Dissemination of Information Regarding ICSID

Dr. Shihata has expanded the dissemination not just of information about ICSID itself, but also of knowledge likely to facilitate its use, in a number of ways. The "information technology" revolution began almost immediately with the reformatting of the *ICSID Annual Report* in 1984. In this regard, Dr. Shihata paid particular attention to reaching out to States Parties to the ICSID Convention by including suggestions for, and reports on, the expansion of the Centre's participation in the peaceful settlement of investment disputes and the promotion of mutual confidence between investors and States.[21] That same year Dr. Shihata also initiated publication of the biannual *News from ICSID* so as to spread his message to

---

17 *See* ICSID Convention, *supra* note 1, art. 52(3) ("On receipt of the [annulment] request the Chairman shall forthwith appoint from the Panel of Arbitrators an *ad hoc* Committee of three persons.").

18 *See List of Concluded and Pending Cases, supra* note 4 (listing the composition of the arbitral tribunals and *ad hoc* Committees constituted in each ICSID case).

19 In addition to the first annulment proceedings in the *Klöckner* and *Amco Asia* cases cited *supra* note 15, both of these cases involved a second annulment proceeding. The decisions from these second annulment proceedings remain unpublished, but in each case the *ad hoc* Committee denied the annulment petition. *See List of Concluded and Pending Cases, supra* note 4.

The two other annulment proceedings were *Maritime International Nominees Establishment v. Republic of Guinea,* ICSID Case No. ARB/84/4, Annulment Decision of Dec. 22, 1989, *reprinted in* 4 ICSID Rep. 79 (1997) (partial annulment granted), and *Southern Pacific Properties (Middle East) Ltd. v. Arab Republic of Egypt,* ICSID Case No. ARB/84/3 (case settled and annulment proceedings discontinued at the parties' request). *See List of Concluded and Pending Cases, supra* note 4.

20 *See List of Concluded and Pending Cases, supra* note 4.

21 *See, e.g.*, 1984 ANNUAL REPORT, *supra* note 2, at 4–5.

an even larger audience,[22] and this publication has become an invaluable source for, *inter alia,* articles on the procedural workings of ICSID, reports of significant developments, updates on pending proceedings, and a continuously updated bibliography of publications by and about ICSID.

Dr. Shihata has extended his outreach to the academic community as well. In 1986 Dr. Shihata launched *ICSID Review–Foreign Investment Law Journal,* a well-respected law review containing scholarly, in-depth articles, comments on recent developments, notes on both ICSID and non-ICSID arbitrations, pertinent book reviews, and documents on national investment laws and investment treaties. This Journal is published twice a year and has become an important outlet for the work of academics and practitioners alike. Of particular importance, and as an example of the kind of material published, *ICSID Review–Foreign Investment Law Journal* recently has presented installments of a ground-breaking commentary on the ICSID Convention by Christoph Schreuer.[23] This commentary promises to be a definitive analysis not only of the ICSID Convention itself but also of existing ICSID case law.

Concurrent with the publication of *ICSID Review–Foreign Investment Law Journal,* Dr. Shihata has commissioned and published studies of ICSID jurisprudence for the purpose of verifying its consistency with the rulings on similar issues by other international tribunals as yet another "confidence-building measure"[24] and has expanded the scope and coverage of the two ICSID publications *Investment Laws of the World*[25] and *Investment Treaties.*[26]

---

22 In the first issue of *News from ICSID* Dr. Shihata wrote that a "lack of information has kept resort to ICSID at a modest level in spite of its wide membership [. . .]. *News from ICSID* will attempt to fill this gap by systematically providing basic data on the role which ICSID is playing and is able to play in the fulfillment of its ultimate objective of improving the investment climate, globally, and in developing countries, in particular." Ibrahim F.I. Shihata, *Editorial,* 1 News from ICSID, Winter 1984, at 1.

23 *See* Christoph Schreuer, *Commentary on the ICSID Convention,* 11 ICSID Rev.–Foreign Inv. L.J. 318 (1996); 12 ICSID Rev.–Foreign Inv. L.J. 59 and 365 (1997); 13 ICSID Rev.–Foreign Inv. L.J. 150 and 478 (1998). Further installments of this commentary are planned for future volumes of the Journal.

24 *See, e.g.,* John A. Westberg, *Applicable Law, Expropriatory Takings and Compensation in Cases of Expropriation: ICSID and Iran-United States Claims Tribunal Case Law Compared,* 8 ICSID Rev.–Foreign Inv. L.J. 1 (1993).

25 ICSID, Investment Laws of the World (10 vols.) (1972–).

26 ICSID, Investment Promotion and Protection Treaties (7 vols.) (1983–).

In addition, by encouraging the systematic analysis of the contents of *Investment Laws of the World* and *Investment Treaties,* Dr. Shihata has helped give birth to further important publications, prominently including the seminal *Bilateral Investment Treaties* by Rudolf Dolzer and ICSID's Margrete Stevens.[27]

It was Dr. Shihata's idea also to compile and publish *ICSID Cases,* which, for every case registered for ICSID arbitration and conciliation, presents information on the nature of the dispute, identifies the members of the tribunal, notes the outcome of the case, and lists publications in which the case is reported or discussed.[28] This booklet has been an invaluable aid to the practitioner. Dr. Shihata's regard for gathering information on ICSID and making it available to the ICSID-user public continues to evolve and keep pace with emerging technology. Thus, the Centre recently developed a comprehensive Internet website,[29] which is not limited to the usual generic information regarding the institution but includes full text versions of the ICSID Convention (including a continuously updated list of States Parties and Signatories), the Arbitration Rules for both ICSID and the Additional Facility, an on-line version of *ICSID Cases,* an on-line version of *News from ICSID,* and on-line versions of numerous other ICSID publications. The website is also beginning to publish electronic versions of available ICSID decisions and awards.[30]

C. Educational Programs on ICSID and International Commercial Arbitration

Dr. Shihata has been particularly active in causing ICSID to organize or sponsor educational programs throughout the world on ICSID and international commercial arbitration generally. Since

---

27 RUDOLF DOLZER & MARGRETE STEVENS, BILATERAL INVESTMENT TREATIES (1995).

28 *See* ICSID CASES, *supra* note 4. The increasing importance of ICSID case law and the need for wider dissemination of publicly available decisions has led the Lauterpacht Research Centre for International Law at the University of Cambridge to publish *ICSID Reports,* a collection of ICSID arbitral decisions and related municipal court opinions. This publication, which began in 1993, has reached four volumes.

29 *See ICSID Home Page,* <http://www.worldbank.org/icsid/>.

30 *See* ICSID, *Online Decisions and Awards,* <http://www.worldbank.org/icsid/cases/ awards.htm>.

November 1983, ICSID annually has joined the International Chamber of Commerce International Court of Arbitration and the American Arbitration Association in a symposium, rotated among New York City, Paris and Washington, D.C. (and occasionally other cities), designed to facilitate greater and more knowledgeable use of international arbitration in the resolution of investment disputes.[31] Dr. Shihata and his ICSID colleagues also have co-sponsored and participated in numerous other conferences and seminars all over the world, including in "non-ICSID States."[32] They have reached still broader audiences through the many papers and articles resulting from these conference and seminar presentations that persuasively explain the role of international arbitration in general, and ICSID in particular, in depoliticizing investment disputes and in thereby promoting an investment climate conducive to greater foreign direct investment in developing countries.[33]

---

[31] *See, e.g., The World Bank Hosts a Second ICSID, AAA, ICC Symposium,* 2 NEWS FROM ICSID, Winter 1985, at 7–8 (reporting on the second such symposium and noting that "the three sponsoring institutions have reached the conclusion that this type of international gathering should become a permanent feature of their promotional activities."). Papers presented at these symposia have been published in several ICC and ICSID publications. *See, e.g.,* ICC INTERNATIONAL COURT OF ARBITRATION, THE ARBITRAL PROCESS AND THE INDEPENDENCE OF ARBITRATORS (1991); ICC INTERNATIONAL COURT OF ARBITRATION, CONSERVATORY AND PROVISIONAL MEASURES IN INTERNATIONAL ARBITRATION (1993); ICC INTERNATIONAL COURT OF ARBITRATION, THE STATUS OF THE ARBITRATOR (1995); *Arbitration and the Courts,* 2 ICSID REV.–FOREIGN INV. L.J. 402 (1987) (collecting three papers from the Fifth Joint Symposium); *Arbitration and the Courts,* 3 ICSID REV.–FOREIGN INV. L.J. 107 (1988) (collecting three further papers from the Fifth Joint Symposium); *How to Draft Arbitration Clauses,* 7 ICSID REV.–FOREIGN INV. L.J. 141 (1992) (collecting three papers from the Eighth Joint Symposium); *Institutional Arbitration: Uniformity and Diversity,* 13 ICSID REV.–FOREIGN INV. L.J. 1 (1998) (collecting papers from the Fourteenth Joint Symposium); Ahmed S. El-Kosheri, *ICSID Arbitration and Developing Countries,* 8 ICSID REV.–FOREIGN INV. L.J. 104 (1993); Horacio A. Grigera Naón, *ICC Arbitration and Developing Countries,* 8 ICSID REV.–FOREIGN INV. L.J. 116 (1993); Eric A. Schwartz, *The Domain of Arbitration and Issues of Arbitrability: The View form the ICC,* 9 ICSID REV.–FOREIGN INV. L.J. 17 (1994).

[32] Reports on these many conferences may be found in almost every issue of ICSID's *Annual Report* and *News from ICSID.*

[33] *See especially* Ibrahim F.I. Shihata, *Towards a Greater Depoliticization of Investment Disputes: The Roles of ICSID and MIGA* (Jan. 1992) (unpublished updated version of an article originally published in 1 ICSID REV.–FOREIGN INV. L.J. 1 (1986), available from the Centre).

D. Recruiting New States Parties to the ICSID Convention

Dr. Shihata's spectacularly successful work in proselytizing the non-believers among States is especially impressive. Specifically, his assiduous wooing of Latin American countries, where the Calvo Doctrine[34] for so long was king, has been instrumental in the fact that now thirteen countries from that region are party to the ICSID Convention,[35] and four more have signed it.[36] This is a long way from zero, which was the count, as it were, for many years.[37] The first arbitration at ICSID involving a Latin American State came in 1996,[38] and now fully twelve of ICSID's thirty currently pending cases arise in that region.[39] Forty percent truly is a long way from zero.

---

[34] In its strongest form, the Calvo Doctrine, named after the Argentinean statesman who first propounded it, holds that an alien may not to seek the diplomatic protection of its own State but instead must rely on the law and procedure of the local jurisdiction for the resolution of disputes arising from its commercial activities in the local jurisdiction. *See, e.g.*, IAN BROWNLIE, PRINCIPLES OF PUBLIC INTERNATIONAL LAW 546 (4th ed. 1990).

[35] Argentina, Bolivia, Chile, Colombia, Costa Rica, Ecuador, El Salvador, Honduras, Nicaragua, Panama, Paraguay, Peru, and Venezuela. *See* ICSID, *List of Contracting States and other Signatories of the Convention (as of March 21, 2000)*, <http:// www.worldbank.org/icsid/constate/c-states-en.htm>.

[36] Belize, Dominican Republic, Guatemala, and Uruguay. *See ibid.*

[37] The first Latin American country to sign and ratify the ICSID Convention was Paraguay, which signed on July 27, 1981 and deposited its notice of ratification on January 7, 1983. *See ibid.* Costa Rica signed on September 29, 1981 (but did not ratify until April 27, 1993), while El Salvador signed on June 9, 1982 and ratified on March 6, 1984. *See ibid.* All other Latin American signatories to the ICSID Convention have signed (and, where applicable, ratified) the ICSID Convention during Dr. Shihata's tenure as Secretary-General of ICSID. *See ibid.*

[38] *Compañía del Desarrollo de Santa Elena S.A. v. Government of Costa Rica*, ICSID Case No. ARB/96/1 (case currently pending). *See List of Concluded and Pending Cases, supra* note 4.

[39] *See ibid.* The cases and their subject matter are as follows: *Compañía del Desarrollo de Santa Elena S.A. v. Government of Costa Rica*, ICSID Case No. ARB/96/1 (valuation of land holding); *Metalclad Corp. v. United Mexican States*, ICSID Case No. ARB(AF)/97/1 (waste disposal enterprise); *Compañía de Aguas del Aconquija S.A. v. Argentine Republic*, ICSID Case ARB/97/3 (water and sewer services concession agreement); *Azinian v. United Mexican States*, ICSID Case No. ARB(AF)/97/2 (waste disposal enterprise); *Lanco Int'l, Inc. v. Argentine Republic*, ICSID Case No. ARB/97/6 (port terminal concession agreement); *Houston Indus. Energy, Inc. v. Argentine Republic*, ICSID Case No. ARB/98/1 (electricity distribution and sale concession); *Casado v. Republic of Chile*, ICSID Case No. ARB/98/2 (publishing enterprise);

III. IBRAHIM SHIHATA'S CONTRIBUTIONS OUTSIDE ICSID

Ibrahim Shihata has pursued the Siamese-twin goals of peaceful settlement of investment disputes and improvement of foreign investor-host State relations just as relentlessly outside the strict framework of his ICSID responsibilities as within it. His prolific writings — seemingly innumerable books, a wealth of articles, Hague Academy lectures, etc.[40] — his leadership and reformation of the International Development Law Institute;[41] his cooperation in the founding and establishment of the Institute for Transnational Arbitration;[42] his parental role as regards the Multilateral Investment Guarantee Agency (MIGA);[43] his chairing of the World Bank-IMF task force that produced the World Bank Group's *Guidelines on the Treatment of Foreign Direct Investment*;[44] his

---

Olguín v. Republic of Paraguay, ICSID Case No. ARB/98/5 (food products enterprise); *Compagnie Minière Internationale Or S.A. v. Republic of Peru,* ICSID Case No. ARB/98/6 (gold mining project); *USA Waste Servs., Inc. v. United Mexican States,* ICSID Case No. ARB(AF)/98/2 (waste disposal enterprise); *Karpa v. United Mexican States,* ICSID Case No. ARB(AF)/99/1 (foreign trade enterprise); *Empresa Nacional de Electricidad S.A. v. Argentine Republic,* ICSID Case No. ARB/99/4 (hydroelectric power concession).

40 Dr. Shihata's list of publications, reproduced in part at the end of this book, encompasses twenty-seven books and more than two hundred and fifty published articles and essays in both Arabic and English, and numerous translations of his writings into French, Spanish, Chinese, and Russian.

41 *See, e.g.,* 1984 ANNUAL REPORT, *supra* note 2, at 16; 1985 ANNUAL REPORT, *supra* note 9, at 13; ICSID, 1986 ANNUAL REPORT 14 (1986).

42 *See* ICSID, 1987 ANNUAL REPORT 12 (1987).

43 MIGA was established by the Convention Establishing the Multilateral Investment Guarantee Agency, *opened for signature* Oct. 11, 1985, 1 ICSID REV.-FOREIGN INV. L.J. 147 (1986) (entered into force April 12, 1988). For background on the Convention's development and purpose, and Dr. Shihata's role therein, *see* IBRAHIM F.I. SHIHATA, MIGA AND FOREIGN INVESTMENT: ORIGINS, OPERATIONS, POLICIES AND BASIC DOCUMENTS OF THE MULTILATERAL INVESTMENT GUARANTEE AGENCY (1988); *Convention Establishing the Multilateral Investment Guarantee Agency, Introductory Note,* 1 ICSID REV.-FOREIGN INV. L.J. 145 (1986); Shihata, *Towards a Greater Depoliticization of Investment Disputes, supra* note 33, at 16–30; *Commentary on the Convention Establishing the Multilateral Investment Guarantee Agency,* 1 ICSID REV.-FOREIGN INV. L.J. 193 (1986).

44 *See Legal Framework for the Treatment of Foreign Investment,* 7 ICSID REV.–FOREIGN INVESTMENT L.J. 295 (1992) (containing *Guidelines on the Treatment of Foreign Direct Investment* as well as other documentation produced in connection with

work as Vice President and General Counsel of the World Bank — all of these have been of a piece with his ICSID work. All form the medium through which his prodigious drive and determination have been brought to bear on the achievement of the goals he set himself.

IV. CONCLUSION

Much has been written on the remarkable surge in the number of bilateral investment treaties that have been concluded in the last decade, as well as the increasing importance of such treaties in the international regulation and protection of foreign investment.[45] Indeed, it can hardly be disputed that as the millennium comes to an end, bilateral investment treaties have become the principal means by which States are regulating investment on the international plane.

---

the work of the task force). The *Guidelines* are also reprinted in 31 I.L.M. 1363 (1992). *See also* ICSID, 1992 ANNUAL REPORT, at 9 (1992) and ICSID, 1993 ANNUAL REPORT 9 (1993) (describing the purpose and results of the task force's work).

45 *See, e.g.*, DOLZER & STEVENS, *supra* note 27; M. SORNARAJAH, INTERNATIONAL LAW ON FOREIGN INVESTMENT 225–75 (1994); U.N. CENTRE ON TRANSNAT'L CORPS., BILATERAL INVESTMENT TREATIES (1988); Andrew T. Guzman, *Why LDCs Sign Treaties that Hurt Them: Explaining the Popularity of Bilateral Investment Treaties*, 38 VA. J. INT'L L. 639 (1998); Michael A. Geist, *Toward a General Agreement on the Regulation of Foreign Direct Investment*, 26 LAW & POL'Y INT'L BUS. 673 (1995); Ibrahim F.I. Shihata, *Recent Trends Relating to Entry of Foreign Investment*, 9 ICSID REV.–FOREIGN INV. L.J. 47 (1994); Todd S. Shenkin, *Trade-Related Investment Measures in Bilateral Investment Treaties and the GATT: Moving Toward a Multilateral Investment Treaty*, 55 U. PITT. L. REV. 541 (1994); Jose L. Siqueiros, *Bilateral Treaties on the Reciprocal Protection of Foreign Investment*, 24 CAL. W. INT'L L.J. 255 (1994); Kenneth J. Vandevelde, *Of Politics and Markets: The Shifting Ideology of BITs*, 11 INT'L TAX & BUS. LAW 159 (1993); Mohamed I. Khalil, *Treatment of Foreign Investment in Bilateral Investment Treaties*, 7 ICSID REV.–FOREIGN INV. L.J. 339 (1992); Asoka de Z. Gunawardana, *The Inception and Growth of Bilateral Investment Promotion and Protection Treaties*, 86 AM. SOC'Y INT'L L. PROC. 544 (1992); Jeswald W. Salacuse, *BIT by BIT: The Growth of Bilateral Investment Treaties and Their Impact on Foreign Investment in Developing Countries*, 24 INT'L LAW. 655 (1990); Adeoye Akinsanya, *International Protection of Direct Foreign Investments in the Third World*, 36 INT'L & COMP. L.Q. 58 (1987); Aron Broches, *Bilateral Investment Protection Treaties and Arbitration of Investment Disputes*, *in* THE ART OF ARBITRATION, LIBER AMICORUM FOR PIETER SANDERS 63 (J. Schultsz & J. Van den Berg eds., 1982).

Perhaps less well noticed, but equally important, however, is the fact that of the approximately 1125 bilateral investment treaties that have been concluded around the world since Dr. Shihata began his tenure at ICSID[46] (not to mention some rather significant multilateral investment treaties such as NAFTA[47] and the Energy Charter Treaty[48] that also were concluded during this time), about eighty percent include ICSID arbitration as an option for settling investment disputes between foreign investors and the host State.[49] Moreover, a full twenty-five percent of such treaties look to ICSID as the *exclusive* means of dispute resolution.[50] The predominance and importance of these treaties and their dispute resolution provisions is reflected in the fact that they form the basis of jurisdiction in approximately sixty percent of the currently pending ICSID cases.[51]

With characteristic modesty, Dr. Shihata may disclaim responsibility, but it cannot be doubted that Dr. Shihata's determined contributions to the cause for which he so long has labored have played a significant and decisive role in elevating international arbitration in general, and ICSID in particular, to its present high esteem amongst both sovereign States and private investors. The nearly universal reliance on ICSID arbitration in the ever growing and important regime of bilateral and multilateral investment

---

46 According to the Centre's records, the total number of bilateral investment treaties concluded between 1959–1983 was 206, while the total number concluded between 1984–1998 was 1125. Direct communication from the Centre. This latter figure is likely to rise, however, because ICSID's data on the number of treaties concluded in the years 1996–1998 is still incomplete.

47 North American Free Trade Agreement, Dec. 17, 1992, U.S.-Can.-Mex., 32 I.L.M. 296 & 612 (1993) (entered into force Jan. 1, 1994).

48 Energy Charter Treaty, *opened for signature* Dec. 17, 1994, 33 I.L.M. 360 (1994) (entered into force April 16, 1998). *See* Jan Linehan, *Investment, Trade and Transit: Dispute Settlement under the Energy Charter Treaty,* 15 NEWS FROM ICSID, Summer 1998, at 4.

49 Direct communication from the Centre. For an analysis of such dispute resolution provisions in relation to the jurisdictional requirements of the ICSID Convention, *see* DOLZER & STEVENS, *supra* note 27; Antonio R. Parra, *Provisions on the Settlement of Investment Disputes in Modern Investment Laws, Bilateral Investment Treaties and Multilateral Instruments on Investment,* 12 ICSID REV.–FOREIGN INV. L.J. 287 (1997).

50 Direct communication from the Centre.

51 *Ibid.*

treaties is testament to Dr. Shihata's unflagging zeal and commitment. It is therefore fully appropriate and timely to recognize his long labor and to extend appreciation for all that he so impressively has achieved in his many years as a dedicated international public servant.

ARBITRATING ENTITLEMENT TO DORMANT BANK ACCOUNTS*

*Thomas Buergenthal***

I. INTRODUCTION

The Second World War ended in 1945. In 1996, fifty one years later, the Swiss Bankers Association and two leading Jewish organizations — the World Jewish Restitution Organization and the World Jewish Congress — concluded a Memorandum of Understanding[1] designed to enable the heirs of Holocaust victims who deposited money or other securities in Swiss banks to claim these accounts. A variety of obstacles — Swiss bank secrecy laws, unreasonable demands made by the banks on those seeking to claim these accounts, motivated in part no doubt by a desire to retain the free use of these funds,[2] as well as the loss and destruction of documents belonging to Holocaust victims — had prevented the rightful owners of these accounts or their heirs from reclaiming them.

---

* This article is written as a tribute to Dr. Ibrahim F.I. Shihata in recognition of his important contribution to international law in general, and international arbitration in particular.

** The opinions expressed in this paper are the author's and should not be attributed to the institutions he is affiliated with.

1 The text of the Memorandum of Understanding is reproduced in *Independent Committee of Eminent Persons Report on Dormant Accounts of Victims of Nazi Persecution in Swiss Banks* (hereinafter cited as *Volcker Report*), appendix A, 1 (1999).

2 Swiss law does not require banks to relinquish long dormant accounts to the State or to publish the names of their account holders. It is consequently in their interest not to find the heirs to dormant accounts. The Volcker Commission recommended the adoption of laws that would reverse that situation. *Volcker Report, supra* note 1, at 22–23.

One can only speculate why it took more than half a century for this agreement to be concluded. The end of the Cold War was certainly a factor. One argument in the past for not publishing dormant accounts was fear that the funds belonging to people living behind the Iron Curtain would be confiscated by various Communist regimes. The desire to maintain good relations with neutral Switzerland and its banking establishment, deemed useful by the allies, particularly in the early days of the Cold War, probably explains why some of the countries, and particularly the US, showed little interest in pressuring Switzerland to address Holocaust-related issues.

The aforementioned Memorandum of Understanding established the Independent Committee of Eminent Persons (ICEP). Chaired by Paul Volcker, ICEP assumed responsibility for the implementation of the decision to search for dormant accounts belonging to Holocaust victims and to design a mechanism for the resolution of claims to these accounts. ICEP exercised this mandate by establishing the Independent Claims Resolution Foundation, a Swiss legal entity. The Foundation, in turn, created the Claims Resolution Tribunal for Dormant Accounts in Switzerland (the CRT or Tribunal) and charged it with the adjudication of entitlement to these accounts. The Tribunal began its work early in 1998.

While the negotiations leading to the Memorandum of Understanding were in progress, the Swiss banks undertook their own search of bank accounts dormant since 1945 that appeared to belong to non-Swiss nationals. With the permission of the Swiss Federal Banking Commission, the Swiss Bankers Association eventually published two lists, one in July and the other in October 1997, containing approximately 6,500 names. Potential claimants to these accounts were at the same time invited to submit their claims to the CRT. The two lists did not distinguish between Holocaust and non-Holocaust-related accounts. As a matter of fact, it now appears that no more than twenty to twenty-five percent of these accounts belonged to victims of the Holocaust.

The distribution and initial processing of the claims forms for these two lists were entrusted to the international accounting firm ATAG Ernst & Young. It established contact offices in various parts of the world to assist those wishing to file claims. The roughly

10,000 claims[3] received in this fashion were eventually referred to the CRT for adjudication. This article discusses the structure, procedure and practice of the CRT in dealing with the claims to these dormant accounts.[4]

Here it should also be noted that in December 1999, ICEP identified more than 25,000 dormant accounts after a massive search of Swiss bank files carried out under its auspices by a group of foreign bank auditors.[5] While the two earlier lists, as noted above, included foreign dormant accounts, whether Holocaust-related or not, the new list is presumed to consist of only such accounts. ICEP has recommended to the Swiss Federal Banking Commission that this list be published and that the CRT also be charged with the adjudication of entitlement to these accounts.[6] No action has as yet been taken by the Swiss authorities on this recommendation.

II. INSTITUTIONAL FRAMEWORK

The CRT is an arbitral tribunal operating under the Rules of Procedure of the Claims Resolution Process (Rules of Procedure), adopted on October 15, 1997 by the Board of Trustees of the Independent Claims Resolution Foundation.[7] The CRT is also subject to the relevant provisions of the Swiss Private International Law Act. This law applies to the CRT because it has its seat in Switzerland and exercises arbitral jurisdiction over disputes between non-Swiss claimants and Swiss banks.[8]

---

3 It is noteworthy that these claims were filed only against less than 60 percent of the published accounts. More than 40 percent went unclaimed.

4 On the same subject, *see generally* Amance Dourthe-Perrot, *Le Tribunal Arbitral pour les Comptes en Déshérence en Suisse,* REVUE DE L'ARBITRAGE, vol. 1 (1999), at 21; Lucy Reed, *Arbitration Principles Prove Effective in Resolving Holocaust Bank Claims,* TRANSLEX — TRANSNATIONAL LAW EXCHANGE, vol. 2, no. 3 (1999), at 1; Shai Wade, *Mass Claims Arbitration: The Experience of the Claims Resolution Tribunal for Dormant Accounts in Switzerland,* MEALEY'S INTERNATIONAL ARBITRATION REPORT, vol. 14, no. 11, 1 (1999).

5 *Volcker Report, supra* note 1, at 20.

6 *Ibid.* at 19–21.

7 For the text of the Rules of Procedure, *see Volcker Report, supra* note 1, at A–31.

8 *See* Swiss Private International Law Act, art. 176; Nathalie Voser, *Arbitrability*

The Tribunal consists of seventeen arbitrators designated by the Trustees of the Independent Claims Resolution Foundation. Five of the arbitrators are Swiss, including the Chairman of the Tribunal, four are Israelis, four US nationals, including the Vice-Chairman, and one each from the United Kingdom, Canada, Cyprus and Belgium. Most members of the Tribunal are well-known international commercial arbitrators, judges and law professors. The three arbitrators who are not lawyers have extensive business, accounting or banking experience. All arbitrators were selected with a view to ensuring that the Tribunal would consist of a majority of non-Swiss arbitrators and that all arbitrators would be persons known for their professional standing, integrity and independence. The Tribunal is assisted by some thirty Swiss and foreign lawyers and a smaller number of paralegals.

Under its Rules of Procedure, the arbitrators act as Sole Arbitrators and in Claims Panels consisting of three arbitrators.[9] When claims are referred to a Claims Panel, the panel must consist of one Swiss and two non-Swiss arbitrators.[10] Claims Panels deal with appeals or so-called resubmissions from adverse Initial Screening Procedure decisions and in Ordinary Procedure cases involving disputes of 3000 Swiss Francs or more. These procedures are described below.

III. THE ARBITRAL PROCESS

The Rules of Procedure provide for three distinct proceedings: Initial Screening (IS), Fast Track (FT) and Ordinary Procedure (OP). Of these, as will be seen, only OP most closely resembles arbitration in its traditional sense.

A. Initial Screening

The IS Procedure is a mechanism for the preliminary determination of a claimant's entitlement to a dormant account under the relaxed standard of proof established in Article 22 of the Rules

---

and the Applicable Law in the Claims Resolution Process for Dormant Accounts in Switzerland, 15 ARBITRATION INTERNATIONAL 237 (1999).

9 Rules of Procedure, arts. 3–5.

10 *Ibid.* art. 6.

of Procedure. Whereas Article 22 of the Rules requires the successful claimant to show that "it is plausible in light of all the circumstances that he or she is entitled, in whole or in part, to the dormant account," the IS Procedure requires substantially less in terms of proof. Here, only if "(i) the claimant has not submitted any information on his or her entitlement to the dormant account, or (ii) if it is apparent that the claimant is not entitled to the dormant account," the claim will be dismissed at the IS stage.[11] In short, the IS Procedure is an admissibility proceeding with a very low threshold. To survive it and move to the merits, claimants merely have to provide some information indicating that they *might* plausibly be entitled. To be successful on the merits, however, claimants will have to show that it *is* plausible, applying Article 22 of the Rules, that they are entitled to the account or a part thereof. The relaxed standard of proof under which the Tribunal operates is designed to take account of the obvious difficulties claimants are likely to have, due to the destruction of entire families and of documents during the Second World War and the Holocaust, in establishing their entitlement to a long dormant account.

The IS Procedure was designed to balance the needs of the claims resolution process against the requirements of Swiss bank secrecy. It provides a method for not disclosing bank information protected under Swiss law to individuals who are obviously not entitled to it. To achieve this objective, the two lists of dormant accounts published by the Swiss Bankers Association in 1997 did not identify the banks holding the account. They merely provided the names of the account holders and, where known, their place and country of residence. More specific information concerning the particular dormant account, including the name of the bank and the amount in it, may be disclosed only after a claimant has survived IS.

The IS Procedure works as follows: when ATAG Ernst & Young receives a completed claims form in which claimants are asked to provide information about their relation to the account holder, it transmits the form to the bank holding the account. The bank has twenty days to indicate whether it agrees to the disclosure of its name. During that period the bank reviews the docu-

---

11 *Ibid.* art. 10.

ments it has on file concerning the account holder and the information provided by the claimant in the claims form. If the bank concludes that, on the evidence, the claimant might plausibly be entitled to the account, it will agree to disclosure. The file is then transferred to the CRT for the formal determination of entitlement, either under the FT or OP Procedure.

If the bank refuses to disclose, the claim is automatically referred to the CRT for an IS decision. That is, every negative decision by the bank comes to the CRT, which makes its own independent disclosure determination. That decision is made in the first place by a Sole Arbitrator. If the arbitrator decides against ordering disclosure, the claimant has thirty days within which to appeal to a Claims Panel and to submit whatever additional evidence he or she deems relevant.[12] The Claims Panel's review is a *de novo* review of all the evidence before the CRT. If the Sole Arbitrator or Panel order disclosure, the claimant will receive the documents in the bank file, including the name of the bank and the amount in the account. At that point, the claimant will also be invited to sign a claims resolution (arbitration) agreement, consenting to the adjudication of the claim by the CRT under the FT and OP Procedures. Claimants to whom the bank disclosed will also have to sign that agreement before they may proceed to the next stage. The banks are parties to a master claims resolution agreement, accepting in advance the jurisdiction of the CRT to arbitrate these claims.

The evidence before the CRT in the IS Procedure consists of all available documents on file in the bank relating to the account holder, such as signature cards, information about the account holder's profession and nationality, complete addresses, etc. The Sole Arbitrator or Claims Panel will also have access to information provided by other claimants to the account, if any. At the IS stage, none of this information, other than the information published by the banks, is provided to the claimant. This policy can be justified on the ground that the IS Procedure is not an arbitral proceeding and that it is designed merely to screen out claimants who cannot demonstrate even a remote connection to the account holder.

---

[12] *Ibid.* art. 10.

As a rule, claimants who can provide some minimal information about the account holder beyond what appears on the published lists and an indication of a family connection to the account holder will receive a favorable IS decision. At this stage, moreover, all doubts are resolved in favor of the claimant. Disclosure will usually be denied where the claimant provides no information other than that he or she has the same family name as the account holder. But where the name is rare and the claimant's family comes from the same town as the account holder, disclosure may well be ordered, particularly if the bank files contain no information that would clearly demonstrate that the claimant is not related to the account holder.[13] Disclosure will be denied if the information provided by the claimant demonstrates that he or she is not entitled. That will be the case, for example, where the claimant identifies the account holder as a relative who died before the account was opened, or where the profession and place of residence of the alleged relative differ significantly from the information in the bank's files.

IS decisions, whether rendered by a Sole Arbitrator or Claims Panel are reasoned decisions in which the grounds for denial or disclosure are set out and related to the information supplied by the claimant and the bank. About ten percent of the claimants who were denied disclosure by a Sole Arbitrator have taken advantage of their right to resubmit their claim to a Claims Panel. This number is surprisingly small considering that claimants do not have to be represented by counsel and that all proceedings are free. Of these appeals, roughly ten percent have been successful, usually because the claimant, after reading the reasons advanced by the Sole Arbitrator for denying disclosure, is able to produce additional information that tips the scale.

Following disclosure, either by the bank or by the CRT, the case will be decided under the FT or OP Procedure, provided the claimant has signed the claims resolution agreement. A claimant who does not sign the agreement is free to sue the bank in the courts, or attempt to negotiate a settlement directly with the bank.

---

13 This article will not provide specific citations to the claims adjudicated by the CRT because the CRT has not yet published its decisions. They are to be published soon on its website <http://www.crt.ch>.

A vast majority of claimants has availed itself of the Tribunal's claims resolution process, and some have negotiated direct settlements with the banks. I am unaware of any law suits filed against the banks by claimants who received disclosure in the IS Procedure.

B. Fast Track

The FT Procedure was designed to avoid lengthy arbitral proceedings in cases where the banks recognize that the claimant is entitled to the account and are willing to offer to pay the amount the CRT determines to be due. The applicable provisions in the Rules of Procedure dealing with FT — particularly Articles 11 and 12 — are not models of clarity, however. That is why some banks have assumed that FT may be used by them not only to offer payment of the funds in the account and whatever additional amounts may be due, but also to obtain a speedy determination from the CRT that the claimant is not entitled to the account.

The reason for the confusion regarding the scope of the FT Procedure has to do with the language of Articles 11 and 12 of the Rules of Procedure. Article 11 reads as follows:

> "Claims may be submitted to a Sole Arbitrator for Fast Track review at the request of the Swiss bank or upon agreement of all parties involved.
>
> Claims submitted to a Sole Arbitrator shall be resolved within thirty days (30) after submission to the Fast Track approval.

Article 12 of the Rules of Procedure provides that:

> To make an award to a claimant using the Fast Track Procedure, a Sole Arbitrator shall decide:
>
> (i) that the claimant has a valid claim applying the standards of proof provided for in Article 22, provided that such a conclusion is possible by simple legal and factual inquiries, taking into account any sworn written or oral statement from the claimant in accordance with Article 24; and

(ii) that the payment offered by the Swiss bank to the claimant complies with the guidelines on interest and fees . . . ; and

(iii) that the claim does not have to be referred to a Claims Panel under the provisions of Article 13."[14]

These provisions do not stipulate that FT may be used only when the bank believes that the claimant is entitled and is willing to pay out the required amount. Those reading them as authorizing FT also for a speedy denial of a claim on the merits, interpret Articles 11 and 12(i) to mean that if the Sole Arbitrator can make a finding "by simple legal and factual inquiries" that the claimant does not have a "valid" claim, he or she may so find and dismiss the claim. The CRT, on the other hand, has consistently read these provisions to mean that FT may be resorted to only in cases where the bank believes that claimant is entitled and is willing to make the payment which is due. Pursuant to this interpretation, the Tribunal will refer a claim to OP when the bank requests FT but is not prepared to offer payment. The claim must be referred to OP, moreover, if the Sole Arbitrator determines that it cannot be treated in FT for one of the reasons spelled out in Article 13.

The CRT has also interpreted Article 12(i) to require the Sole Arbitrator to make an independent finding of entitlement, even when the bank acknowledges that the claimant has a valid claim

[14] Article 13 reads as follows:
"A claim submitted to the Fast Track Procedure shall be referred to a Claims Panel for decision in the ordinary procedure if the Sole Arbitrator

(i) has reason to believe that
    (a) the named account holder may have acted as an intermediary for a victim of Nazi persecution;
    (b) the claimant may have submitted a fraudulent claim; or
    (c) the assets deposited in the account may have been looted from victims of Nazi persecution.

In making these determinations, the Sole Arbitrator may request factual information related to the matters referred to in (i)(a)–(c) above from ICEP; or

(ii) determines that
    (a) the entitlement of the claimant cannot be verified by simple inquiries in accordance with Article 12(i);
    (b) the determination of the amount due to the claimant requires detailed and complicated calculations or inquiries; or
    (c) a full review by a Claims Panel is appropriate for other reasons."

and is willing to pay out. That conclusion is clearly compelled by the language of the provision. However, in order not to delay proceedings in cases where a bank is willing to pay out to a claimant whose entitlement is doubtful, and to avoid the formal determination of entitlement required by Article 12(i), the CRT,will, as a rule, invite the banks to conclude so-called small- and large-amount settlements with claimants on terms previously agreed upon between the Swiss Bankers Association and the CRT. Once concluded, the agreement is incorporated by reference into the Tribunal's award.

The small-amount settlements are used for accounts up to 100 Swiss Francs. They are resorted to where the bank documents contain little more than the name of the account holder and the amount in the account. These accounts were, as a rule, consolidated by the banks with many others of the same type and carried on their books as collective accounts.[15] Here it is often impossible to determine who among various often unrelated claimants is entitled. Because of the sparsity of bank information about the account holder, many claimants appear to be equally entitled. In these cases, it is also impossible to know what the original amount in the account was and whether it was depleted by bank charges. To take all these factors into consideration, the small-amount settlements provide for a payment of the amount in the account, multiplied by a factor of ten. These payments are usually offered to all claimants to a given account who survived IS. Claimants do not have to accept this settlement and may decide to arbitrate their claims instead, but the vast majority accepts the settlement offer.

The large-amount settlement was designed to permit a rapid payout of the amount due in cases where the bank is willing to make such payment and waives the determination of entitlement provided for in Article 12(i). To anticipate the risk that other heirs with equal or better entitlement might file a later claim, the large-amount settlement stipulates that the agreement does not protect the bank against subsequent meritorious claims by third parties. The claimant, in turn, undertakes to share the amount of the set-

---

15 Swiss law allows banks to destroy most bank documents ten years after an account has become dormant and requires them only to maintain a record containing personal information provided by the account holder on opening the account (frequently little more than a name and nationality) and the amount in the account.

tlement with other equally entitled family members. The large-amount settlement also requires the banks to agree to pay claimants whatever additional compensation may be due under the Interest and Fee Guidelines to be adopted by the Independent Claims Resolution Foundation.[16] A large number of claims have been resolved by means of these agreements.

C. Ordinary Procedure

Article 14 of the Rules of Procedure reads as follows:

> "All claims that are not approved in the fast track procedure shall be resolved in ordinary procedure before a Sole Arbitrator or Claims Panel. The ordinary procedure involves a full review of the claim and all available evidence in an expedited procedure."

Pursuant to Article 15 of the Rules of Procedure, the determination of entitlement is to be made by applying the relaxed standard of proof spelled out in Article 22 of the Rules. It requires the claimant to show that "it is plausible in light of all the circumstances that he or she is entitled, in whole or in part, to the account."[17] While all FT proceedings are resolved by a Sole Arbitrator, this is true for OP proceedings only where the funds in the dormant account amount to 3,000 Swiss Francs or less; a Claims Panel must decide claims to accounts above that amount.[18]

Claims are referred to OP in a number of different circumstances. At the IS stage, as has been seen, doubts are resolved in favor of the claimant. Many claims of questionable entitlement are frequently approved for IS disclosure if there appears to be even so much as a likelihood that the claimant will be able to come up with a stronger case at the next stage. But once disclosure is or-

---

16 These Guidelines, which have not as yet been adopted, will seek to compensate claimants to Holocaust-related accounts for interest that was not paid and for bank charges that were deducted. *See* Rules of Procedure, arts. 12 & 16. The Guidelines, once adopted, will in all likelihood provide for the multiplication by a factor of ten of the amount in a Holocaust-related account after the fees previously deducted and interest due have been added to the account.

17 For the text of art. 22 and discussion relating to its application, *see infra* sec. IV.

18 Rules of Procedure, art. 4.

dered and the case moves into FT or OP, the claimant will have a significantly greater burden of proof. If the claimant's case appears on its face to be strong and there are no other unrelated claimants, the case will more often than not be referred by the bank to FT for speedy disposition. When there are doubts on that score or where there are multiple claimants with divergent interests, or claimants who are not related, the case will go to OP. Even if a bank asks for FT, the request may be denied by the Tribunal and the claim referred to OP. This is usually done when the Tribunal concludes that the case raises difficult inheritance or conflict of laws issues or because other claimants appear to have equally strong or better claims to the same account. Put in another way, FT is resorted to in cases that can be resolved easily because they present no complicated legal or factual issues. All other cases, particularly those which raise the issues referred to in Article 13(i),[19] go to OP.

Article 20 of the Rules of Procedure provides for the joinder of "all relevant claims" where "a specific dormant account is claimed by several persons."[20] Experience has shown that of the many claims to an account which have survived IS and were referred to OP, only some appear to be meritorious. If all of these claims, regardless of their probable entitlement, were to be joined, the proceedings would become unmanageable, unnecessarily expensive and result in a significant slowdown of the entitlement process. Here it should be noted that there are on the average four claimants to an account. The maximum number of claimants to one account is substantially greater. The record is held by one account which received more than 100 claims. Moreover, the exchange of documents between claimants living in different countries, the translation of documents sent to and received from claimants,

19 That provision is reproduced in *supra* note 14.

20 Article 20 reads as follows:

"The Claims Resolution Tribunal shall join all relevant claims in one procedure before the same Claims Panel or Sole Arbitrator, if

(i) a specific dormant account is claimed by several persons;

(ii) one person claims dormant accounts with several banks; or

(iii) a combination of (i) and (ii) occurs.

If a claim with respect to a dormant account is pending and a third party submits a claim with respect to the same account to the Claims Resolution Tribunal, the Chairman of the Claims Resolution Tribunal shall assign the new case to the already competent Sole Arbitrator or Claims Panel."

and the staff resources necessary to service large multiple-party claims, not to mention the costs connected with such proceedings, suggest the need for avoiding automatic joinders of claims to the same account unless justice cannot be served otherwise. Consequently, the Tribunal has consistently held that, since only "relevant" claims need be joined, the Sole Arbitrator and the Claims Panel have considerable leeway in deciding which claims to join. In making this decision, the Sole Arbitrator or Claims Panel must be guided, of course, by considerations of procedural fairness and the need for determining entitlement in an "expedited procedure" as that concept is understood in Article 14.[21]

The Tribunal will usually only join claims if a preliminary review of the information provided by the claimants and the bank documents suggest that entitlement to the account could not be fairly and properly decided without joinder. This will be the case, for example, if the claimants represent different branches of a family or if two or more unrelated claimants point to different ancestors as the purported account holder and each appears to make out a *prima facie* case of entitlement. Illustrative of the latter situation are claims to an account with regard to which the bank documents contain merely the name of the account holder and the city where he or she resided. Here two unrelated families might submit claims pointing to one of their relatives as the account holder who had the same name and lived in the same city. Such claims may have to be joined before a final determination of entitlement can be made. The ultimate outcome in these cases will depend upon a showing by one or the other party that it is more plausible that their ancestor, rather than the ancestor of the other claimant, was the account holder. The answer to this question may turn on the particular ancestor's profession, his or her business relations, evidence of travel to Switzerland or neighboring countries, age, etc. Joinder may also be necessary to permit the parties to test conflicting allegations by other claimants.

Article 22(ii) provides that "a finding of plausibility requires, *inter alia,* . . . that no reasonable basis exists to conclude that

---

21 Article 14 reads as follows:
"All claims that are not approved in the fast track procedure shall be resolved in the ordinary procedure before a Sole Arbitrator or Claims Panel. The ordinary procedure involves a full review of the claim and all available evidence in an *expedited* procedure." (Emphasis added.)

fraud or forgery affect the claim or evidence submitted; *or that other persons may have an identical or better claim to the dormant account.*" (Emphasis added.) This language, which is hardly a model of clarity, appears to provide that if two unrelated claimants produce equally convincing evidence of their entitlement, neither of them should be deemed to be entitled. This is clearly not an equitable solution particularly when, as a rule, it is the sparsity of bank documents which prevents the Tribunal from finding who, as between the two claimants, has a better entitlement. In these situations, the Tribunal has tended to adopt one of two solutions: where the account is relatively small, the Tribunal will ask the bank whether it would be prepared to conclude a settlement, paying each of the claimants the full amount. The bank usually accepts this suggestion, if only because its cost of arbitrating the claim fully would be greater than the multiple payment. Where the amount in the account is quite large, and the bank is not prepared to make a multiple payment, the Tribunal will frequently suggest that the claimants conclude a settlement agreeing to share the amount in the account. Most of the time claimants will accept this solution. It is clear, of course, that the language of Article 22(ii) appears to prevent the fairest solution of all, namely, where two or more unrelated claimants appear to be equally entitled, they each should get the full amount in the account, especially since it is the absence of bank documents which prevents a clear finding of entitlement.

The absurd result that the English text of Article 22(ii) of the Rules appears to produce is not duplicated by the German text of that same provision. It reads as follows in the here relevant part: "Beim Entscheid, ob ein Anspruch plausibel ist, soll unter anderem berücksichtigt werden, ob . . . andere Personen einen identischen oder besseren Anspruch auf den nachrichtenlosen Vermögenswert besitzen." Unlike the English text, which provides that a "finding of plausibility requires, *inter alia* . . . ," the German text merely stipulates that "in determining plausibility, *account* shall be taken, *inter alia,* of. . . ." The German text thus does not preclude a finding of plausibility if "other persons have an identical . . . claim," it merely provides that this factor should be taken into account. It would follow that in determining plausibility, the existence or non-existence of other equally entitled claimants, that is, claimants related in the same degree to the account holder and those with a better claim, should be taken into account. This type of a provision makes good sense, whereas the English text would prevent two unrelated claimants with "identical" claims from recovering anything.

Although under Article 35 of the Rules, the English text of the Rules is to prevail in case of a conflict between it and translations thereof, it is known that the drafters of the Rules worked with English and German draft texts in drawing up these provisions before preparing the final English version. It is therefore quite likely that the English text is a poor translation from the German. Besides, the English text, if applied literally, would produce the absurd result of rejecting the claims of claimants who, because of poor record keeping by the banks, are prevented from demonstrating their clear entitlement. A much more reasonable interpretation, consistent with the German text, is to read the provision as requiring the Tribunal, in determining plausibility, to take the existence of other claimants with identical or better claims into account.

IV. ENTITLEMENT

We have already noted that entitlement to an account is to be determined by the application of the relaxed standard of proof formulated in Article 22 of the Rules of Procedure. That provision reads as follows:

> "The claimant must show that it is plausible in light of all the circumstances that he or she is entitled, in whole or in part, to the dormant account. The Sole Arbitrators or the Claims Panels shall assess all information submitted by the parties or otherwise available to them. They shall at all times bear in mind the difficulties of proving a claim after the destruction of the Second World War and the Holocaust and the long time that has elapsed since the opening of these dormant accounts.
>
> A finding of plausibility requires, *inter alia,*
>
> (i) that all documents and other information have been submitted by the claimant regarding the relationship between the claimant and the published account holder that

can reasonably be expected to be produced in view of the particular circumstances, including, without limitation, the history of the claimant's family and whether or not the published account holder was a victim of Nazi persecution; and

(ii) that no reasonable basis exists to conclude that fraud or forgery affect the claim or evidence submitted; or that other persons may have an identical or better claim to the dormant account."

In theory, the plausibility test is not difficult to sustain. But even this relaxed standard of proof can present problems for claimants three or four generations removed from the account holder. This is particularly true for Holocaust survivors or their descendants. Their families were frequently not able to preserve documents or other evidence that might help establish family ties to the account holder. The matter of proof is further complicated by the fact that in many cases the bank files contain very little information about the account holder. This is so not only because, as we have seen, the banks were free to discard most documents after more than ten years, but also because at the time when most of these accounts were opened — usually in the late 1920's and early 1930's — Swiss banks were not required to and frequently did not demand detailed personal information from their customers.

Where the document relating to the opening of the account is still available, it may contain a specimen of the account holder's signature and place of residence. Some bank files contain additional information about the account holder, including notations of his or her nationality, profession, academic or other titles, marital status, as well as the name of a power of attorney or spouse. The availability of this additional information makes it much easier for the Sole Arbitrator or Claims Panel to test the claimant's allegations about the account holder. But even where the banks have kept this type of information, and many have, it is not always reliable. At the time when most of these accounts were opened, Swiss banks were not required to have their customers present identification when opening accounts. They could therefore use pseudonyms or provide false information about their domicile, nationality or profession. Unless a claimant knows the pseudonym that was used by the account holder, or has other relevant information, it will be impossible to establish entitlement, even with the benefit of the relaxed standard of proof. Considering that many foreign customers had good reason in the 1930's to use pseudonyms or otherwise to try to disguise their identities, it can be assumed that these accounts will never be recovered by their heirs.

The language of Article 22 and the reality confronting the Tribunal in applying the relaxed standard of proof, particularly in Holocaust-related accounts, explain why claimants need not present formal documentary evidence to win their cases. Depending on the circumstances, the Tribunal will accept other information claimants might have about their family and its relationship to the account holder, including personal recollections, letters, pictures, obituaries, entries on grave stones, etc. This information is evaluated and compared with the information in the bank files, as well as with information provided by other claimants. Thus, although the process of establishing entitlement to long dormant accounts under the relaxed standard of proof is much more informal than in traditional judicial or arbitral fact-finding, it is well suited to the task confronting the Tribunal. Interestingly enough, while the Rules of Procedure envisage written and oral proceedings,[22] the Tribunal has thus far not had occasion to resort to oral proceedings.

V. APPLICABLE LAW

The question whether a specific claimant has a right to an account depends on his or her relationship to the account holder. The law to be applied by the Tribunal in determining whether the claimant is entitled to an account is laid down in Article 16 of the Rules of Procedure, which reads as follows:

> "The Sole Arbitrator and the Claims Panels shall apply the law with which the matter in dispute has the closest connection in deciding matters concerning the relationship between the

---

22 Rules of Procedure, art. 24.

> published account holder or holder of power of attorney and the claimant (e.g., to inheritance matters or fiduciary agreements). At the request of all involved parties other than the Swiss bank, inheritance matters may be resolved according to Talmudic law.
>
> The relationship between the claimant and the Swiss bank shall be governed by Swiss law, except as provided by these Rules of Procedure. In deciding matters relating to interest, fees and charges, the Sole Arbitrators and Claims Panels shall apply the Interest Guidelines."

The formulation of the "closest connection" test copies the relevant Swiss conflicts of law rule.[23] Under this test, if the account holder was a German national and resident, for example, German law would apply in determining the validity of his or her will. German law would also apply in deciding whether the claimant's relationship entitles him or her to inherit from an account holder who died intestate.

One important initial question that arises in using this test to determine entitlement to a dormant account is whether the law to be applied is the law that was in effect at the time of the account holder's death, which is the normal rule, or whether the Tribunal is free to apply the law in force today. In answering this question, it must be kept in mind that in many cases before the Tribunal, the determination of entitlement to the dormant account is made more than fifty years after the death of the account holder, assuming the date and place of death are known, which is frequently not the case. In other words, the Tribunal is not dealing with an estate that is being settled shortly after the death of the decedent, who may be presumed to be aware of the likely line of succession at the time of death or when making the will. In these normal type of cases, it makes good sense to apply the law in force at the time of the making of the will or the testator's death. That is not necessarily so with regard to the claims the Tribunal has to deal with. Here the applicable law may have changed a number of times during the years the account remained dormant.

---

23 Swiss Private International Law Act, art. 187. *See generally,* Voser, *supra* note 8, at 243.

Public policy considerations or laws which may in the past have discriminated against women or persons born out of wedlock, for example, or which did not recognize common law marriages or had special rules applicable to adoptions, may also have been substantially modified and modernized. And even if that did not happen, some of these laws may today conflict with otherwise applicable international obligations under human rights treaties. This will most likely be the case as far as the rights of women and children born out of wedlock are concerned. It is thus readily apparent that the formalistic application of the law in force at the time of the account holder's death could produce results difficult to square with the demands of a claims resolution process that is designed to do justice in a world far removed from that of the account holder, and which he had no way of anticipating.

Depending upon the circumstances, the Tribunal has in these types of cases approached the issue of applicable law in a flexible manner, consistent with the unique factual context within which it has to operate. At times it has been forced to fall back on what it has characterized, for lack of a better expression, as "general principles of inheritance law," looking to what would be fair under the circumstances and seeking to divine what the decedent would most likely have wanted to happen in the light of the evolution of his or her family. Here it should be remembered that the Tribunal is often dealing with families or potential heirs four or even more times removed from the deceased account holder, many of them not even in a direct line of descent from him or her.

The determination of entitlement of individual members of various branches of a family living in different countries, presents complicated problems of applicable foreign law. Here the Tribunal will apply the law of the place where the respective claimants are domiciled. In many cases, this will require it to look to the law of a number of countries with different legal systems. Issues of fairness arise even here. For example, what should the Tribunal do when then the applicable law requires it to deny the descendants of one of the account holder's sons the right to share in his father's long dormant Swiss account because more than three decades earlier, while living behind the Iron Curtain and totally unaware of his father's dormant account, the son waived the right to share in his father's estate which was then being probated by his siblings in the West? Here the Tribunal concluded that it was bound by a thirty years statute of limitations applicable to such waivers that had expired a few years earlier. Increasingly though the Tribunal seeks to avoid the problems that arise in this context by leaving the distribution within a branch of a family to the claimants themselves. That is usually done by means of settlement agreements. This approach has the added advantage of preventing undue delay in completing the claims resolution process.

The application of Talmudic law, also envisaged in Article 16 to determine entitlement under certain circumstances, has to date not been applied. In the only case known to me in which a claimant sought to invoke Talmudic law, it was not applied because the other "relevant" claimant declined to give the consent required by Article 16. Moreover, the Interest and Fee Guidelines to which the second paragraph of Article 16 makes reference have as yet not been issued by the Independent Claims Resolution Foundation. The lack of these Guidelines has made it necessary for the Tribunal to render only partial awards. Final awards will be rendered when the Guidelines are issued.[24]

VI. CONCLUSION

A. The Past

By the fall of 2000, the CRT should be able to conclude the adjudication of all claims to the accounts identified on the two lists which the Swiss banks published in 1997. This process has lasted much longer — more than two and a half years — than those who established the CRT expected it would take. Their assumption was that the work would be completed in about six months.

The miscalculation is in large part attributable to the fact that the CRT was entrusted with the administration of a process that had no precedent. It is a novel experiment for the resolution of a set of problems whose complexity and massive scale was not, and probably could not, be anticipated. This is not to say that as an abstract proposition it would have been impossible to design a more

24 For the likely contents of the Guidelines, *see supra* note 16.

rational and speedy claims resolution process. But the political climate which led to the search for dormant accounts in Switzerland and eventually produced the CRT prevented such solutions. That climate was characterized by mutual recrimination and mistrust among the major players — the Jewish organizations on the one hand, and the Swiss Government and Swiss banks, on the other. Moreover, the work of the CRT was also slowed down by a number of other factors that had not been anticipated: that there would be so many related and unrelated claimants to individual accounts, that the applicable bank documents were as incomplete as they turned out to be, and that compliance with the due process requirements expressly provided for in the Rules of Procedure or implicit in the arbitral process required additional time to complete.

With 20x20 hindsight it is clear that, given the way the CRT claims resolution process was set up and the more than fifty years that had elapsed since the accounts had become dormant, it was totally unrealistic to assume that the Tribunal would be able to complete its task in the short time envisaged for it. That is why the often heard criticism by Swiss banks that the CRT process is too slow and costly is largely unjustified, if only because their lawyers helped to create this complex process. The mistrust between the Jewish and Swiss sides led these two parties to establish a claims resolution system with many cumbersome safeguards. Illustrative is the provision permitting all IS denials to be automatically appealed and treated *de novo* by a Claims Panel consisting of three arbitrators, one of whom has to be Swiss, and this regardless of the amount in the account or the possible merit of the appeal. Another example is the requirement for a three-member Claims Panel, constituted in the same manner, for dealing with claims in OP involving all accounts valued at 3,000 Swiss Francs and above. The fear that a single arbitrator, whether Swiss or non-Swiss, would let his or her prejudice sway a decision in favor of the bank or a claimant, no doubt explains these unusually low threshold requirements. The fact that each of the parties wanted to show their constituencies that the Tribunal was comprised of a highly respected and distinguished group of arbitrators has had the consequence that the arbitrators' predictably busy schedules make it difficult to convene Panel meetings as soon as a case is ready for adjudication.

Because claimants are permitted to submit their applications and all relevant documentation in their own language, much of this material must be translated; that again takes time. Further delays result, particularly in OP proceedings, from the exchange of documents between the banks and various joined related and unrelated claimants to the same account, which is required as a matter of due process by law. Since these claimants often live in different countries and speak different languages, a long time may lapse before the Tribunal may be able to compile the relevant material in one of the working languages of the arbitrators to enable them to address the merits of the claim. The dispersal of families caused by the Holocaust and World War II, and the fact that three or more generations of descendants frequently separate the account holder from the claimants, also explain why there are usually many more related and unrelated claimants to an account with plausible entitlement than would be the case under ordinary circumstances. The relaxed standard of proof (plausibility), provided for in Article 22 of the Rules of Procedure, while clearly necessary for the type of the claims the CRT has to arbitrate, compounds this problem. It tends to make adjudication cumbersome because claimants who would otherwise fail to meet the stricter traditional burden of proof might more easily satisfy the plausibility test. In determining entitlement, the Tribunal will thus have to work with a much larger pool of claimants who appear *prima facie* to be entitled.

The work of the CRT has also taken longer than expected because the Tribunal has no direct or independent access to bank documents. It depends on the banks to provide it with all the relevant documentation relating to an account. But that documentation is not always forthcoming. On various occasions, the Tribunal has found that even though a bank previously certified that it had transmitted all relevant documentation to the CRT, internal evidence from the documents submitted indicates that it has in fact not done so. Sometimes a bank will on its own advise the CRT that it has found some additional document of relevance to the case. Most of the time the failure to provide missing documents is innocent and appears to not have been designed to mislead. It is usually due to carelessness by a lowly bank employee charged with copying documents or an erroneous assumption that the missing documents would not be needed by the Tribunal. Be that as it may, it is quite clear that a great deal of time and money has been wasted by the Tribunal searching and waiting for missing bank documents. It is hard to say how many more such documents never came to the attention of the Tribunal and thus affected its decision-making process to the detriment of individual claimants. Clearly, the less documentation is available in a bank file transmitted to the Tribunal the more difficult it is to apply the plausibility test, which depends on finding links between the account holder and the claimant's family.

B. The Future

In January 1999, the two Swiss banks which, because of numerous bank mergers, accounted for more than eighty percent of all dormant accounts in Switzerland, concluded a class action settlement agreement — the so-called Global Settlement — with various class action plaintiffs who had sued these banks in the United States.[25] In the Global Settlement, the banks agree to pay the sum of US$1.25 billion to settle all claims against Swiss banks in return for the withdrawal of these law suits. The Global Settlement was also subscribed to by the two Jewish organizations responsible for the creation of the claims resolution process that established the CRT.

Once approved by the federal district court judge with jurisdiction over it, the Global Settlement will, to a very significant extent, transform the claims resolution process currently administered by the CRT. While the present system envisages adversarial proceedings between the banks and claimants, the Global Settlement will for all practical purposes remove the banks from the arbitral proceedings. It converts these proceedings into a dispute resolution mechanism for the determination of entitlement between the claimants *inter se*. The banks will no longer have an interest in the outcome of these proceedings because the Global Settlement provides that all monies already paid or to be paid by them to successful claimants to dormant accounts of victims of

[25] While the agreement still has to be approved by the Federal District Court in charge of the consolidated class action suits, its terms are unlikely to change in any major respect. *See generally*, Sean Murphy, *Contemporary Practice of the United States Relating to International Law*, 93 AMERICAN JOURNAL OF INTERNATIONAL LAW 879, 888–892 (1999).

Nazi persecution will be credited against the US$1.25 billion Settlement Fund.

As noted earlier, in 1999 ICEP auditors compiled a new list of more than 25,000 additional dormant accounts, which had not been found by the Swiss banks in their 1997 search. This new list remains to be published. The Volcker Commission recommended that the accounts on this list also be adjudicated by the CRT under an arrangement to be worked out between ICEP, its Independent Claims Resolution Foundation and the US federal judge responsible for the implementation of the Global Settlement. Because of the large number of accounts on the list, the CRT and the above entities decided that the claims resolution process applicable to the new list should be substantially simplified to permit a speedier determination of claims. The new procedures are likely to do away with the Claims Panels, to restrict appeals from adverse decisions, to simplify the initial screening process, and to limit the number of languages in which the parties will be able to communicate with the Tribunal.

These changes build on the CRT's experience with the first two lists. They are justified not only by the large number of claims that will have to be adjudicated, but also because the Global Settlement removes the banks from the claims resolution process. The tensions and mutual suspicions between the Jewish side and the Swiss banks that explain many of the cumbersome procedures under which the CRT had to work in dealing with the first two lists, have lost their relevance given the new arrangements. Of course, the cooperation of the banks will still be needed in providing the CRT with full access to the bank documents it will need to discharge its responsibilities. The fact that the banks will then no longer have a strong incentive to cooperate with the CRT in providing this documentation suggests that all bank records relating to the newly discovered accounts be transferred to a central location with direct access to it by the CRT.

TAIWAN AND INTERNATIONAL FINANCIAL ORGANIZATIONS

Hungdah Chiu

I. INTRODUCTION

The proposals of John Maynard Keynes in the United Kingdom and Harry Dexter White in the United States were the main influences in the creation of the International Monetary Fund (IMF). The chief objective of those proposals was to avoid the monetary disorders of earlier decades before World War II. In July 1944, before the defeat of Germany in May 1945, a Conference convened by the United States was held at Bretton Woods, New Hampshire. The Conference led to the creation of the IMF[1] and the International Bank for Reconstruction and Development (IBRD or Bank).[2] China's quota for the Fund was set at US$550 million, while the United States' was set at US$2.75 billion, the United Kingdom's at US$1.3 billion and the Soviet Union's (Russia) at US$1.2 billion. The Soviet Union changed its policy at the end of World War II and did not ratify the Agreement. The Fund began operations in the spring of 1946. The Bank was inaugurated in the latter part of 1946.[3]

At the time of concluding both Agreements, China, under the leadership of Chiang Kai-shek, was at its wartime capital, Chungk-

1 Articles of Agreement of the International Monetary Fund, formulated at the Bretton Woods Conference, July 1-22, 1944. Opened for signature at Washington, DC on December 27, 1945; entered into force on December 27, 1945. 60 Stat. 1401; TIAS 1501; 3 Bevans 1351; 2 UNTS 39.

2 Articles of Agreement of the International Bank for Reconstruction and Development, formulated at the Bretton Woods Conference, July 1-22, 1944. Opened for signature at Washington, DC on December 27, 1945; entered into force on December 27, 1945. 60 Stat. 1440; TIAS 1502; 3 Bevans 1390; 2 UNTS 134.

3 *See* ARTHUR N. YOUNG, CHINA AND THE HELPING HAND 1937-1945 (1965), at 360-361.

ing, and became an ally of the United States by signing the Declaration by the United Nations on January 1, 1942.[4] The Republic of China (ROC) was a member of the Fund until it was notified by the Fund, that the government of the People's Republic of China (PRC) would represent China in the Fund, on April 18, 1980.[5] Similarly, the ROC also was notified that PRC would represent China in the Bank on May 16, 1980.[6]

Since late 1949, the Chinese mainland has been under the control of the Chinese Communist Party, which, on October 1, 1949, inaugurated the Central People's Government and renamed China as the People's Republic of China (PRC), with its capital in Beijing (Peking).[7] The Republic of China first moved its capital from Nanking to Kuang Chou (Canton), and on December 8, 1949, from Kuang Chou to Taipei, Taiwan Province.[8] The PRC foreign minister, Zhou En-lai, on November 15, 1949 immediately requested the Secretary-General of the United Nations (UN) to expel the delegation of the Republic of China. Similar requests were sent to the International Labour Organisation (ILO) on June 5, 1950; the International Telecommunications Union (ITU) on August 26, 1950; the IMF on August 26, 1950; and the IBRD on August 26, 1950. By August 26, 1950 the PRC had appointed a delegation to attend the 5th Session of the General Assembly of the United Nations, and a delegation to attend the ITU. On December 5, 1950 it notified the Universal Postal Union (UPU) that the PRC had accepted the Universal Postal Convention.[9] However, all these requests were rejected by the United Nations and other UN affiliated international organizations, which continued to rec-

---

4 55 Stat. 1600; EAS 236, 3 Bevans 697.

5 *ROC Statement*, 1 Chinese Yearbook of International Law and Affairs, (1981), at 142.

6 *Ibid.*, at 142-143.

7 Proclamation on the establishment of the Central People's Government of the People's Republic of China announced by Chairman Mao Zedong, October 1, 1949. Chinese text is available *in* 1 Zhonghuo Renmin Gonghequo Duiwai Guanxi Wenjianji (1949-1950) [Collection of Foreign Relations Documents of the People's Republic of China]; Beijing: Shijie Zhishi Chupanshe 3-4 (1958) [hereinafter Collection of Foreign Relations Documents].

8 *Taipei: Government Information Office*, The Republic of China Yearbook 734 (1995).

9 Collection of Foreign Relations Documents, *supra* note 7, at 85-87, 128, 136-140 & 188-189.

ognize only the delegation of the ROC located on Taiwan until October 25, 1971.

II. THE PRC, THE IMF AND THE WORLD BANK

On October 25, 1971, the General Assembly of the United Nations adopted Resolution 2758 (XXVI) to transfer the seat occupied by the ROC delegation to the PRC. The Resolution stated:

> "*Decides* to restore all its rights to the People's Republic of China and to recognize the representatives of its Government as the only legitimate representatives of China to the United Nations, and to expel forthwith the representatives of Chiang Kai-shek [i.e., the delegation of the ROC] from the place which they unlawfully occupy at the United Nations and in all the organizations related to it."[10]

All other UN affiliated international organizations followed the General Assembly's resolution,[11] except the IMF and the Bank.[12] The United States eventually recognized the PRC on January 1, 1979[13] and supported the PRC's joining the IMF and the Bank, despite the fact that the US-Taiwan Relations Act of 1979[14] specifically provides in Section 4(a) that "[n]othing in this Act may be construed as a basis for supporting the exclusion or expulsion of Taiwan from continued membership in any international financial institution or any other international organization." In this context, it must, however, be noted that in the United States, it is the Pres-

---

[10] VIII UN MONTHLY CHRONICLE 61, No. 10, Nov. (1971).

[11] *See Representation of China Within the United Nations System–Developments within the Organizations of the UN System Concerning Chinese Representation*, XI INTERNATIONAL LEGAL MATERIALS 561-570., No. 3, May (1972).

[12] The United States did not recognize the PRC until Jan. 1, 1979. Both the IMF and the Bank have a weighted voting system, by Oct. 10, 1963, the United States itself constituted 22.93% of the total voting power of the Fund. *See* HANS AUFRICHT, THE INTERNATIONAL MONETARY FUND, LEGAL BASES, STRUCTURE, FUNCTIONS 42 (1964). For a list of other countries' voting powers, *see ibid.*, at 99-104. The ROC has 3.54% of the total voting power, *see ibid.*, at 100.

[13] Joint Communique on the Establishment of Diplomatic Relations between the United States of America and the People's Republic of China, January 1, 1979, 79 DEPARTMENT OF STATE BULLETIN 25, No. 2022, Jan. (1979).

[14] Public Law 96-8, Apr. 8 (1979), 93 STAT. 14.

ident who can recognize foreign governments and decide foreign policy issues, not Congress.

The PRC, from its founding on October 1, 1949, has consistently adhered to the "one China" policy and insisted on being treated as "the only legal government in China"; it has also decided to represent Taiwan, though the latter is *not* under its effective control. In April 1980, the ROC was no longer recognized to exercise China's representation in the IMF,[15] and in May 1980, in the Bank.[16]

III. THE ASIAN DEVELOPMENT BANK AND ITS IMPLICATIONS FOR TAIWAN TO PARTICIPATE IN THE IMF AND IN IBRD

The Asian Development Bank (ADB) was established on August 22, 1966;[17] the ROC was a founding member.[18] A Chinese Communist scholar, Chen Tiqiang, argued later after the 1971 UN General Assembly resolution pertaining to China that, since Taiwan (ROC) was no longer recognized by the United Nations and many countries in the world, it should automatically lose its membership status at ADB.[19] However, subsequent events belied his position. On June 26, 1983, Chinese leader Deng Xiaoping told a Chinese-American Professor, Winston Yang of Seton Hall University, that Taiwan could retain its membership at the ADB by

---

15 *See ROC Ministry of Foreign Affairs Statement issued on Apr. 18. 1980,* 1 CHINESE YEARBOOK OF INTERNATIONAL LAW AND AFFAIRS 142 (1981).

16 *ROC Ministry of Foreign Affairs Statement Issued on May 16, 1980; ibid.*, at 142-143.

17 Articles of Agreement Establishing the Asian Development Bank, done at Manila on Dec. 4, 1965, entered into force on Aug. 22, 1966, 576 UNITED NATIONS TREATY SERIES, at 123.

18 At that time, the ROC government made it clear that its representation was limited to the Taiwan area only.

19 *See* Chen Tiqiang, *Taiwan Shouldn't Hang On in Asian Development Bank*, PEOPLE'S DAILY, May 3, 1983, at 7 [English translation *is available in* CHINA DAILY, May 4, 1983, at 4].

changing its name to "China, Taipei."[20] On March 10, 1986, the PRC was admitted to the Bank without demanding the expulsion of Taiwan,[21] though ADB, under PRC pressure, would use "Taipei, China" to refer to the ROC in its official documents or correspondence.[22] The ROC on Taiwan refused to accept this change and did thus not send a delegation to the ADB's 1986 meeting. It, however, still maintains its membership.[23] Later on, after President Lee Tenghui succeeded as President of the ROC in 1988, the ROC became more flexible and attended the 1998 meeting of the ADB, though it filed a protest on the name change. The ROC has since attended the meetings of the ADB, including the 22nd Annual Meeting of the ADB held in Beijing, in the PRC.

Whether the ADB model can be applied to the ROC's participation in the IMF and the World Bank depends on the negotiations between the ROC's "unofficial" Strait Exchange Foundation (SEF) and the PRC's "unofficial" Association for Relations Across the Taiwan Strait (ARATS). Despite reaching certain agreements at Singapore on April 29, 1993,[24] those negotiations have been indefinitely "postponed" since June 16, 1995. At the time of this writing, in September 2000, the negotiations have not been resumed.[25]

---

20 *See* Li-yu Yang (Winston Yang), *Deng Xiaoping's New Idea on Peaceful Unification–A Two Hours Talk with Deng Xiaoping*, 8 QISAI NIANDAI [THE SEVENTIES] 17-19 (1983).

21 *See People's Republic of China Joins ADB as its 47th Member Country*, ADB NEWS RELEASE NO. 33/86 (MAR. 10, 1986).

22 Multilateral Treaties Deposited with the Secretary-General, Status as of Dec. 31, (UN Doc. 97/LEG/SER.E/16) No.5, 391(1997).

23 Official Protest Lodged with ADB Over Name Change, *FREE CHINA JOURNAL, Mar. 17, 1986, at 1.*

24 *See* Hungdah Chiu, *The Koo-Wang Talks and Prospect of Building Constructive and Stable Relations Across the Taiwan Straits,* 29 ISSUES & STUDIES, JOURNAL OF CHINESE STUDIES AND INTERNATIONAL AFFAIRS, No. 8 Aug. (1993), at 1-33.

25 *See* Xinhua Says Wang-[Koo] Meeting "Postponed," FBIS-CHI-95-117 June 19, 1995, at 86. The quoted part of the letter from ARATS is from Commentary Blames Taiwan for Delaying Talks, FBIS-CHI-95-128 July 5, 1995, at 78. For analysis of the reasons for postponing the negotiations, *see* Hungdah Chiu, *Recent Cross-Strait Relations and the United States*, 32 ISSUES & STUDIES, No. 12 Dec. (1996), at 1-13.

THE VISION OF IBRAHIM F.I. SHIHATA: A MULTILATERAL INVESTMENT INSURER TO ENCOURAGE PRIVATE FOREIGN INVESTMENT

*Luis Dodero**

I. INTRODUCTION

In October of 1989, I joined the Multilateral Investment Guarantee Agency (MIGA or the Agency) as the first General Counsel. At that time MIGA was still a new experiment that had been created after more than 35 years of World Bank reports and studies on variations of the concept and two unsuccessful initiatives. Dr. Ibrahim F. I. Shihata, who joined the World Bank as Vice President and General Counsel in 1983, was the catalyst for the creation of MIGA. He directed a small cadre of dedicated World Bank staff and turned a series of well-intentioned proposals into reality.

MIGA was created under the Convention Establishing the Multilateral Investment Guarantee Agency (the Convention) dated October 11, 1985. The Convention entered into force on April 12, 1988, and MIGA concluded its first contract of guarantee in January of 1990. The Agency is a member of the World Bank Group, consisting of the International Bank for Reconstruction and Development (IBRD) and the International Development Agency (IDA) (collectively the World Bank), the International Finance Corporation (IFC), and the International Centre for the Settlement of Investments Disputes (ICSID).

---

* The views expressed in this paper are those of the author and should not be attributed to the organization with which he is affiliated.

MIGA's mandate is to encourage the flow of private investment into its developing member countries through two types of activities: (i) issuance of guarantees (or insurance) against political risks to private investors; and (ii) provision of advisory services to developing member countries on how to improve their foreign investment climates.

Dr. Shihata explained in great detail his efforts to create the Agency and his vision for its future in his book entitled *MIGA and Foreign Investment.*[1] This book has been the 'bible' for anyone interested in foreign investment and is still the most trustworthy source of legal interpretation for all matters concerning the Agency. Dr. Shihata personally dedicated my copy of his book as follows: "This is only the background. The evolution of MIGA's legal work is in your hands."

I was very surprised when I joined MIGA to find that many World Bank staff were still very skeptical about the future of this new agency. Even more startling was the prevailing attitude among the World Bank member countries towards MIGA. Some of them, mostly the developed nations, believed that providing investment guarantees (or insurance) to private investors did not make much sense, given that most of the industrialized countries had their own investment insurance schemes. They felt that MIGA should focus on its advisory activities so that developing member countries could improve their foreign investment climates. They believed that once this aim was achieved, private investors would be willing to invest in the developing countries without the need for coverage against political risks. On the other hand, a number of the developing countries (or 'Category Two countries,' as termed by the Convention) voiced their concern about being lectured by MIGA on how to organize their laws and infrastructure in order to attract foreign investment. As a result of these reservations, less than fifty countries, out of a then potential 160 members of the World Bank, had joined the Agency by the time I came to MIGA in October 1989.

This chapter sets out the significant developments in MIGA that have taken place during the first eleven years of operations of

---

1 *See* IBRAHIM F.I. SHIHATA, MIGA AND FOREIGN INVESTMENTS — ORIGINS, OPERATIONS, POLICIES, AND BASIC DOCUMENTS OF THE MULTILATERAL INVESTMENT GUARANTEE AGENCY (MIGA AND FOREIGN INVESTMENT) (1988).

the Agency, comparing them with Dr. Shihata's forecasts for the future and giving my reflections on the experiences as its General Counsel during those years.

II. MEMBERSHIP

Membership in MIGA was originally open to any member of the World Bank and to Switzerland.[2] MIGA can only conduct its guarantee and advisory activities in its member countries; thus, persuading countries to join the Agency was a priority from the very beginning. This membership drive required extensive efforts by MIGA's counsel to explain to the governments of prospective member countries the rights and obligations that the ratification of the Convention implied, and to counter specific legal issues that some countries deemed insurmountable obstacles to their accession to membership. Not unexpectedly, one of the most debated provisions of the Convention relates to the settlement of disputes between the Agency and its members when MIGA is acting as subrogee to the rights of its guarantee holder once a claim is paid by the Agency.[3] According to Article 4(j) of Annex II to the Convention, entitled 'Settlement of Disputes Between a Member and the Agency Under Article 57": "Each member shall recognize an award rendered pursuant to this Article as binding and enforceable within its territories as if it were a final judgment of a court in that member."

The Calvo Doctrine, which was adhered to by most Latin American and some Asian countries, was in direct conflict with Article 57 of the Convention and Article 4(j) of Annex II and, therefore, constituted the primary legal impediment to membership. This doctrine led to the adoption by many state legal systems of the principle that any dispute between a foreigner and the state must be settled in local courts. This principle also proved to be one of the main impediments to globalization and attraction of foreign investment, but has slowly been abandoned by most countries either totally (Argentina, Bolivia, Peru) or partially

---

2 Switzerland was not a member of the World Bank at the time the Convention was opened for signature.

3 *See* Convention Establishing the Multilateral Investment Guarantee Agency, Oct. 11, 1985, art. 57 [hereinafter, MIGA Convention].

(India, Mexico). When the Convention was being drafted, Dr. Shihata was well aware of the difficulties that MIGA would encounter in its efforts to persuade these countries to ratify a multilateral treaty containing an arbitration provision. He elaborated on this issue in Chapter Seven of his book.[4] In order to facilitate the accession to MIGA of those countries that had difficulty accepting the settlement of disputes mechanism in Annex II, the Convention in Article 57 contemplates an alternative method of dispute resolution to be agreed between MIGA and the country concerned; however, such an agreement requires approval by the Board of Directors by a special majority.

To date, the experience in MIGA has been that Dr. Shihata was right in his assumption. The arbitration provision has been one of the most controversial topics of discussion with potential member countries, and some of them requested utilization of the alternative method of dispute settlement referred to above. But my position has always been to advise those countries to forego this alternative, because I do not think that it would be easy to persuade the Directors to accept the granting of special treatment to one country when most of the countries represented by them have accepted the settlement of disputes procedures set forth in Annex II. This approach has proven to be the correct one. A number of countries who wanted to negotiate the alternative method eventually accepted the standard mechanism, and therefore the Board of Directors has not had to consider this alternative.

There is, however, one remaining holdout — Mexico. Mexico is the only Latin American country that has not joined MIGA because of the provision on the settlement of disputes. The argument set forth in Dr. Shihata's book that "[a] dispute between MIGA and the host country of a guaranteed investment is a conflict between two international persons, both subjects of international law, unlike the typical case of a dispute between a foreign investor and the host government"[5] has not been accepted as yet by the Mexican authorities. In our discussions with Mexican lawyers, their position has been that, as subrogation implies that MIGA acquires the rights of the investor against Mexico, MIGA is acting as an agent of the investor, and therefore the latter has, in-

4 *See* SHIHATA, *supra* note 1, at 257.

5 *See ibid.* at 264.

directly, access to arbitration against the Mexican state, which is unacceptable under Mexican law.

Another crucial development related to membership, which naturally had not been contemplated by Dr. Shihata, nor anyone else for that matter, was the dissolution of the Soviet Union and the collapse of the other Communist regimes in Eastern Europe — 18 of which became members of MIGA. These countries were not included in the list in Schedule A to the Convention because they were not members of the World Bank, and therefore had been ineligible for membership in MIGA. Soon after these countries gained their independence, they signaled to MIGA a keen interest in attracting foreign investment and joining the Agency, but there was a prevalent hesitation among prospective investors to venture their capital in such countries due to a high perception of political risks. These countries also sorely needed advice on how to attract foreign investors, and MIGA's advisory services were the right instrument to assist them. It was therefore an easy task to convince most of these countries to join MIGA. However, their membership had serious ramifications in the Agency, particularly on the number of available shares of capital stock for new members and on parity of voting power, as shall be discussed later.

For an overall view of the steady rise in the membership of MIGA for the Fiscal Years 1989–1999, see *Figure 1* below.

FIGURE 1. COUNTRY MEMBERSHIP, FISCAL 1989–1999 (as of 6/30/1999)

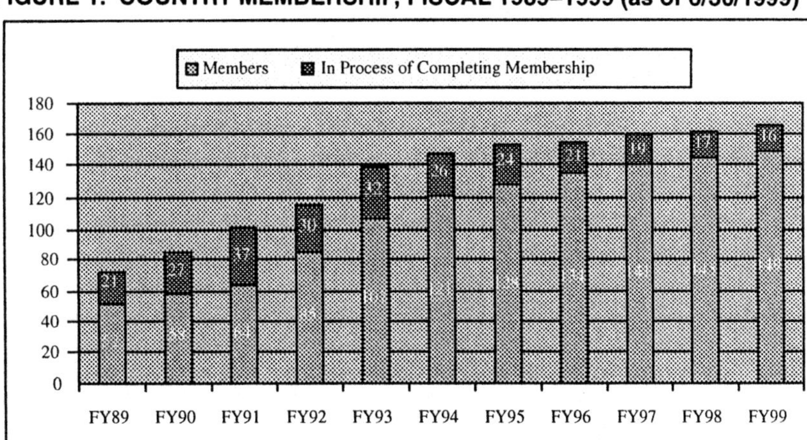

Source: MIGA Annual Report 1999

At present, there are twenty-two Category One or industrialized member countries and 129 Category Two or developing member countries. See *Table 1* below for the present list of MIGA member countries.

In Category One, New Zealand is the one country remaining that has not yet joined MIGA. In Category Two, the two main holdouts are the Islamic Republic of Iran and the aforementioned Mexico.

III. CAPITAL OF THE AGENCY

The capital stock of MIGA was set in the Convention (Article 5) at one billion Special Drawing Rights (SDR) at a fixed rate of exchange of US$1.082 per each SDR. The capitalization of an agency like MIGA, whose main activity is to provide long-term insurance against unpredictable risks, is of paramount importance, especially during its formative years, because it serves as the basis for the calculation of the limit on contingent liability that can be assumed by the Agency. Obviously, diversification is one key factor in the avoidance of financial failure, but an optimal level of diversification can only be achieved by insuring a large number of investments in as many countries as possible. This could not be achieved very quickly, especially by a new, little-known agency with relatively few members whose guarantee activities are subject to a somewhat lengthy administrative process. Article 22 of the Convention allows the Board of Directors to prescribe limits by host country, number of projects, type of investment, and type of risk, so that the Agency would not be exposed to a dangerous concentration of risks.

During the early years, MIGA's growth in membership proceeded much slower than anticipated by Dr. Shihata, and most of the applications received were ineligible since the host countries or the investor's home countries were not yet members of MIGA. Despite these drawbacks, in 1989 the Agency issued its first contract of guarantee for an investment in Indonesia. Henceforward, more countries joined MIGA, and its guarantee business and risk diversification grew in tandem. However, as MIGA became more successful, the constraints on MIGA's capital increased and the limits on its guarantee operations became more restrictive.

TABLE 1. 151 MIGA MEMBER COUNTRIES

22 INDUSTRIALIZED MEMBER COUNTRIES

Australia	France	Japan	Spain
Austria	Germany	Luxembourg	Sweden
Belgium	Greece	Netherlands	Switzerland
Canada	Iceland	Norway	United Kingdom
Denmark	Ireland	Portugal	United States
Finland	Italy		

129 DEVELOPING MEMBER COUNTRIES

AFRICA	ASIA/PACIFIC	MIDDLE EAST/ NORTH AFRICA	EUROPE/ CENTRAL ASIA	LATIN AMERICA/ CARIBBEAN
Angola	Bangladesh	Algeria	Albania	Argentina
Benin	Cambodia	Bahrain	Armenia	Bahamas, The
Botswana	China	Egypt, Arab Rep. of	Azerbaijan	Barbados
Burundi	Fiji	Israel	Belarus	Belize
Burkina Faso	India	Jordan	Bosnia-Herzegovina	Bolivia
Cameroon	Indonesia	Kuwait	Bulgaria	Brazil
Cape Verde	Korea, Rep. of	Lebanon	Croatia	Chile
Congo, Dem. Rep. of	Malaysia	Libya	Cyprus	Colombia
Congo, Rep. of	Micronesia, Fed.States of	Malta	Czech Republic	Costa Rica
Cote d'Ivoire	Mongolia	Morocco	Estonia	Dominica
Equatorial Guinea	Nepal	Oman	Georgia	Dominican Republic
Eritrea	Pakistan	Qatar	Hungary	Ecuador
Ethiopia	Palau	Saudi Arabia	Kazakhstan	El Salvador
Gambia, The	Papua New Guinea	Tunisia	Kyrgyz Republic	Grenada
Ghana	Philippines	United Arab Emirates	Latvia	Guatemala
Guinea	Samoa	Yemen, Rep. of	Lithuania	Guyana
Kenya	Singapore		Macedonia, FYR of	Haiti
Lesotho	Sri Lanka		Moldova	Honduras
Madagascar	Vanuatu		Poland	Jamaica
Malawi	Viet Nam		Romania	Nicaragua
Mali			Russian Federation	Panama
Mauritania			Slovak Republic	Paraguay
Mauritius			Slovenia	Peru
Mozambique			Turkey	St. Kitts and Nevis
Namibia			Ukraine	St. Lucia
Nigeria			Uzbekistan	St. Vincent & the Grenadines
Senegal				Trinidad & Tobago
Seychelles				Uruguay
Sierra Leone				Venezuela
South Africa				
Sudan				
Swaziland				
Tanzania				
Togo				
Uganda				
Zambia				
Zimbabwe				

15 DEVELOPING COUNTRIES IN PROCESS OF FULFILLING MEMBERSHIP REQUIREMENTS

Chad	Lao People's Dem. Rep.	Syrian Arab Republic	Tajikistan	Antigua and Barbuda
Central African Rep.	Solomon Islands		Yugoslavia, Fed. Rep. of	Suriname
Gabon	Thailand			
Guinea-Bissau				
Liberia				
Niger				
Rwanda				

Source: MIGA Finance & Administration

IV. LIMITS ON GUARANTEES — PRACTICAL AND CREATIVE SOLUTIONS

A. Increases in Limits on Guarantees

At the end of 1993, it became apparent that the very conservative, initial maximum aggregate amount of contingent liabilities (overall limit on guarantee capacity) that could be assumed by MIGA — i.e., 150 percent of the subscribed capital plus reserves less a percentage of reinsurance obtained by the Agency, as set forth in Article 22 of the Convention — was a major barrier to the growth of its guarantee operations. As contemplated in the Convention, the Council of Governors, by special majority, approved Resolution No. 47 on February 8, 1994, increasing the limit in two stages. The first one, to 250 percent, became effective immediately; the second increase to 350 percent became effective in 1996. Concurrently, limits per project rose from an initial US$50 million to US$110 million, and per country from US$220 million to US$350 million. In 1997, it was obvious that, despite the above measures, MIGA was rapidly outgrowing even these increases in the guarantee limits in view of the number of applications for guarantee in the pipeline. Therefore, a general capital increase (GCI) would be necessary much sooner than anyone had anticipated.

B. Collaboration with Other Investment Insurers

Until a GCI could be approved by the Council of Governors, MIGA had increased its collaboration with many private and national insurers. MIGA is able to complement the national insurers by offering coverage to investors who do not meet their eligibility requirements. MIGA is particularly important in the private market because the Agency is often the only source of long-term insurance. The Agency has turned to both treaty reinsurance as well as facultative reinsurance and coinsurance in order to cushion the impact on the Agency's capacity. At the same time, MIGA has initiated some more creative instruments, such as the Cooperative Underwriting Program (CUP) and the Investment Guarantee Trust Funds (IGTFs).

Treaty Reinsurance

In 1997, MIGA concluded its first 'quota share' reinsurance agreement with ACE Insurance Company Limited (ACE), a private insurance company domiciled in Bermuda. In fiscal year 1999, MIGA revised its agreement with ACE and signed a treaty reinsurance agreement with XL Insurance Ltd. (XL), also based in Bermuda. According to these reinsurance treaties, a percentage of all projects insured by MIGA over a certain threshold is automatically reinsured by the treaty partner. ACE and XL will each reinsure up to US$50 million per project and US$150 million per country. Treaty reinsurance allows MIGA to increase its capacity to issue additional amounts of coverage per project from US$110 million to US$200 million and per host country from US$350 million up to US$620 million. The Agency's experience with these types of arrangements so far has been excellent, and they have contributed to a significant increase in the flow of foreign investments to developing countries, despite MIGA's still insufficient guarantee capacity.

Facultative Reinsurance and Coinsurance

Facultative reinsurance and coinsurance (i.e., that which is applicable to a specific project) was utilized soon after MIGA commenced operations and obtained from both national insurance agencies and private insurance companies. MIGA has signed facultative reinsurance agreements with EDC of Canada, COFACE of France, OPIC of the United States, SACE of Italy, EID/MITI of Japan, CESCE of Spain, ECGD of the United Kingdom, as well as Lloyds of London.

Cooperative Underwriting Program

Another interesting and unusual method of supplementing MIGA's capacity was the establishment of the Cooperative Underwriting Program (CUP). This instrument is a form of coinsurance set forth in an agreement between MIGA and a private insurer under which, in case of a claim, each insurer is only liable for their respective portion. However, under the agreement, MIGA is the insurer of record and, as such, exercises its recovery actions against the host country as subrogee to the rights of the investor for both the amount insured by the private insurer and that insured by the Agency. As mentioned above, the Convention recognizes MIGA's rights of subrogation and its recourse to *ad hoc* arbitration and other types of instruments to facilitate its prospects of recovery. Needless to say, the private insurer shares in MIGA's advantages and benefits from other aspects of the arrangement. Thus, private insurers, that would not otherwise be willing to cover a certain project in a particular developing country, are willing to do so under the CUP. MIGA leverages more foreign investment without expending its capacity, and the host country is the ultimate beneficiary. The Agency has signed CUP arrangements with ACE Global Markets, Lloyds of London, Sovereign Risk Insurance Ltd. of Bermuda, and Zurich-American Political Risk of the United States.

C. Investment Guarantee Trust Funds

Annex I of the Convention encourages the establishment of Sponsorship Trust Funds (STFs). These funds were conceived as instruments for MIGA to bring more investments to its member countries without utilizing its scarce guarantee capacity. Under the STF, one or more sponsor countries contributes funds that are deposited in an account and are used as capital to back guarantees issued by MIGA on behalf of the STF for investments in one or more host countries. In brief, a STF is a parallel MIGA, focussing on specific host countries and voluntarily capitalized by sponsor countries.

During MIGA's first years, several attempts to create STFs were made by the Agency. However, they were unsuccessful because, among other things, candidate sponsor countries preferred to use their own investment insurance facilities to promote investments by their national companies rather than to capitalize a STF to be administered by MIGA.

Despite these obstacles, MIGA was able to create two instruments which are very similar to the STF concept and serve the same purpose. These instruments are the Investment Guarantee Trust Funds (IGTFs), and the first two were established for the benefit of the West Bank and Gaza as well as Bosnia and Herzegovina.

West Bank and Gaza: Private sector investors were extremely interested in the new investment opportunities in this region but their perception of the political risk was extremely high. However, it did not seem possible at first that the Agency could provide its services there. Setting up a STF as contemplated in Annex I to the Convention was considered but had to be abandoned because the purpose of these funds is to encourage the flow of investments into the territories of a member country of MIGA, and the West Bank and Gaza was neither a member nor a territory of a member. Furthermore, sponsors can only be MIGA member countries (Convention, Arts. 1, 6). Since certain multilateral organizations (i.e., non-members) were interested in contributing to the fund, I gave this issue a lot of thought, and finally decided that MIGA would not be deviating from its objectives if a different type of fund, not subject to the conditions of the STF, was created instead.

Article 2 of the Convention allows MIGA "to exercise such other incidental powers as shall be necessary in the furtherance of its objective," and contributing to the peace process in the West Bank and Gaza clearly met the requirements of this provision since political stability in these territories would contribute to the attraction of foreign investment to Jordan, Egypt and Israel, all member countries of MIGA, and in turn encourage investors from those countries to invest in the territories. On January 21, 1997, the Board of Directors accepted my reasoning by approving the fund. Japan, the European Investment Bank, and the Palestinian Authority (the latter through a credit from the International Development Agency (IDA)) have made contributions to the fund. The first MIGA guarantee was issued in June 1999 to Phoenix International for a cultural center for tourists and business visitors. Located just south of Bethlehem, the center will include several restaurants, a professional crafts center, a museum, an amphitheater, and a park; and it encompasses several significant archeological sites. There are presently five active applications in the guarantee pipeline as of September 30, 1999.

Bosnia and Herzegovina: In 1997, another IGTF, the Investment Guarantee Trust Fund for Bosnia and Herzegovina, was created with a credit line provided by the European Union (EU) totaling 10.5 ECU (or approximately US$12 million). Because the EU is not a member of MIGA (although all of the members of the EU are members of the Agency), this fund did not meet the requirements of the STF covered in Annex I of the Convention. Thus, Article 2 of the Convention was also applied to enable MIGA to create this guarantee trust fund. To date, no projects have been insured as yet under this fund. However, there are 15 active applications in the guarantee pipeline as of September 30, 1999.

IGTFs and STFs — Capital-to-Risk Ratio

A problem inherent in both IGTFs and STFs is how to set a capital-to-risk ratio. Most of these types of funds are created to encourage investments in a single country or in specific areas, and thus the concentration of risk is very high. It would be very risky to set a ratio higher than one-to-one (i.e., the maximum amount to be insured is one dollar for each dollar of the fund's capital), and therefore the funds require a considerable amount of capital. One mitigating factor of this large capital requirement is that some investors would be willing to make their investments even if MIGA — through the fund — is providing coverage for only a portion of the investment, because they feel the Agency's involvement is sufficient protection.

V. 1998 GENERAL CAPITAL INCREASE

According to MIGA's earlier forecasts, the Agency would have run out of insurance capacity around the year 2002. While reinsurance, CUPs, and trust funds are useful instruments in relieving constraints on guarantee capacity up to a certain point, the only definitive and totally effective remedy was a general capital increase (GCI).

In 1997, MIGA began the necessary steps towards the approval of the 1998 GCI by the Council of Governors. Since a vote by special majority (i.e. "an affirmative vote of not less than two-thirds of the total voting power representing not less than fifty-five percent of the subscribed shares of the capital stock of the Agency" [6] was required, it was imperative to secure the support of the maximum number of member countries.

During the Annual Meetings of the World Bank Group on September 22, 1997, the Development Committee[7] recognized the constraints MIGA was facing due to lack of capital and endorsed a 'funding package' comprising an IBRD grant of US$150 million

6 MIGA Convention, *supra* note 3, art. 3(d).

7 The Development Committee of the Boards of Governors of the International Monetary Fund and the World Bank.

and a GCI of US$850 million, of which, US$150 million would be paid-in and US$700 million would be callable capital. At the same time, the Committee urged the MIGA Board 'to also reach clear understandings on core policy issues as soon as possible.'

The reason for the US$150 million grant from IBRD was due to the need for the Agency to increase its guarantee capacity as an interim measure while all the steps required to obtain the formal GCI were completed. These steps are cumbersome and very lengthy in a multilateral organization; it may take more than five years from the preparation of the necessary documentation to obtain the Board's recommendation to, and the approval of, the Council of Governors until the end of the subscription period. The US$150 million grant was approved by the Board of Executive Directors of the World Bank in December 1997 and was used by the Agency as operating capital and *not* as a part of the GCI, because only member countries — and thus not the World Bank — can subscribe to MIGA's capital stock. This capital injection helped MIGA to continue providing guarantees in a number of new host countries and to further diversify its risk exposure.

The directive by the Development Committee to MIGA's Board of Directors to "reach clear understandings on core policy issues" was included in the Committee's communiqué at the initiative of a number of industrialized countries who wanted to emphasize the developmental role of MIGA as a multilateral agency. The 'core policy issues' referred to in the communiqué were: labor standards, environmental guidelines, developmental effectiveness, and an inspection mechanism. Each of these issues were discussed with the Board and understandings were reached as follows:

Labor Standards: The purpose of this issue was to encourage investors guaranteed by MIGA to adopt certain labor standards that would constitute a minimum common denominator for all investments to be guaranteed by the Agency. These investments must have a positive developmental impact in the host country, and therefore the Agency should not use its limited capacity to provide guarantees to transactions that do not meet these standards. It was decided that the Agency should incorporate in its standard contract of guarantee, provisions under which the contract could be canceled if the project enterprise in the host country hired harmful child labor and/or forced labor. The task to define what constituted 'harmful child labor' proved to be much more difficult than anticipated. On the one hand, a number of developing countries did not agree with what they considered interference with their local legislation, while others alleged that their own labor laws were sufficiently protective to avoid such unwanted practices. On the other hand, not all industrialized countries applied the same standards; some of them had not ratified the international conventions on these issues and some others thought that MIGA should go well beyond these conventions. Finally, the definitions of 'forced labor' and 'harmful child labor' taken from the International Labour Organization (ILO) Convention No. 29 and the United Nations Convention on the Rights of the Child (ratified by 140 countries and 190 countries, respectively) were adopted. The definitions read as follows:

> "Forced Labor' means all work or service, not voluntarily performed, that is exacted from an individual under threat of force or penalty.
>
> 'Harmful Child Labor' means the employment of children that is economically exploitative, or is likely to be hazardous to, or to interfere with, the child's education, or to be harmful to the child's health, or physical, mental, spiritual, moral, or social development."

Environmental Guidelines: The Convention does not refer to any type of environmental standards to be met by MIGA's guaranteed projects. MIGA's Operational Regulations[8] refer to "the effects of the investment project on the social infrastructure and environment of the host country" (para. 3.06), among other factors that the Agency must consider to determine whether or not the investment project to be guaranteed contributes to the development of the host country. However there is no elaboration on the scope of these factors. A set of environmental guidelines were submitted to the Board and approved by it in 1998. It took more than one year for the Directors to reach a consensus on these guidelines. MIGA' s Environmental Guidelines classify the projects into three categories: 'A' — environmentally sensitive, diverse, or unprecedented; 'B' — site-specific, adverse environmental impacts on human populations or environmentally important areas; and 'C' —

8 The Operational Regulations were adopted by the MIGA Board of Directors on June 22, 1998.

minimal or no adverse environmental impacts. The environmental assessment of those projects classified as category 'A' must be disclosed to the public (MIGA releases the sponsor's environmental impact assessment report to the Bank's InfoShop in Washington, D.C. and posts a notice of the release on its home page on the Internet) 60 days before the project is discussed with the Board, so that affected parties can provide their comments.

Developmental Effectiveness: MIGA conveyed its proposal for the evaluation of the developmental impact of guaranteed investments to the Board of Directors in July 1998. The directors endorsed the report's approach and the new project selection and evaluation process. As of June 1999, a total of 32 projects had been evaluated, and the results verified that all 32 projects have positively impacted the development of the host countries. MIGA will continue its program of site visits and project evaluations.

Inspection Mechanism — First MIGA-IFC Compliance Advisor/ Ombudsman: The position of Compliance Advisor/Ombudsman, a vice presidential level post reporting directly to the President, is the first of its kind in a multilateral development institution. Ms. Meg Taylor was appointed to this position in July 1999, and she will advise senior management on issues arising from the new policies on environmental assessment and disclosure of information as well as analyze claims by parties affected by projects to be insured by MIGA.

All the above issues could be considered unwieldy factors that impede the processing time for the Agency's underwriting decisions. They are, however, extremely relevant to any member of the World Bank Group, the objective of which must be to contribute to the development of its member countries. Because of the adoption of these measures, MIGA is now being recognized as one of the standard setters in the investment insurance field and other insurers are following the Agency's lead.

VI. ISSUE OF PARITY OF VOTING POWER

More than eighteen pages of Dr. Shihata's book, *MIGA and Foreign Investment,*[9] deals with the voting structure in MIGA's Board

9 *See* SHIHATA, *supra* note 1, at 293–327.

of Directors and Council of Governors, an issue that, in principle, should not require very lengthy elaboration. There is even a critique of Article 39 of the Convention (Voting, Adjustments of Subscriptions and Representation) in which Dr. Shihata foresees that certain future problems would arise from the final drafting of this Article.[10] Dr. Shihata's predictions have certainly proven to be correct. These problems (and others) have arisen, and it has been necessary for the office of the General Counsel, the Board and Council to arrive at some creative solutions in order to avoid these problems becoming a major obstacle to the functioning of the Agency.

MIGA is the only member of the World Bank Group that has a voting structure which was created in such a way that the aggregate voting power of its developing member countries should be equal to that of the industrialized members. Achievement of parity of voting power was one of the issues that took the most discussion time during the setting up of the Agency. The ultimate result was a compromise, described in detail by Dr. Shihata, that in theory seemed logical, but in practice could never work for two reasons: (i) it overestimated the willingness of the members of the World Bank to become members of the Agency; and (ii) it did not take into account the possibility that a large number of countries, which were not members of the World Bank when MIGA was created, would join the Agency later.

The voting structure that was the result of that compromise, was the following: as in the Bretton Woods institutions, member countries would get a number of 'membership votes' (a fixed equal number of votes that every country obtains when joining the institution, which in MIGA was set at 177) in addition to one vote per share.[11] The membership votes in MIGA would be calculated in such a way that, when all members of the World Bank, at the time the Agency was created (which were listed in Schedule A of the Convention), joined the Agency, the aggregate voting power of Category One (industrialized) countries would be the same as that of Category Two (developing) countries. A period of three years was set up in Article 39(c) of the Convention to review the allocation of shares and to redistribute or reallocate them be-

---

10 *See ibid.* at 319.

11 *See* MIGA Convention, *supra* note 3, art.39(a).

tween the two categories of member states in order to obtain parity of voting power.

First Review of the Allocation of Shares

On April 12, 1991, the third year after the Convention came into force, Resolution No. 20 on Review of Allocation of Shares was approved by the Council of Governors postponing the reallocation of shares until the fifth year after entry into force of the Convention or 1993. The 1991 Review contained the following findings as of December 31, 1990:

- Seventeen Category One and eighty Category Two countries were members of the Agency.
- Category One countries had 67.89 percent voting power and Category Two 32.11 percent; therefore, to achieve real parity, the voting power of Category Two countries had to be increased by 17.89 percent. This increase should have been achieved, as set forth by Article 39, by allocating to Category Two countries 19,498 shares. However, only 17,199 shares remained at that time to be reallocated to countries that were not signatories of the Convention, of which 4,034 shares would have to be set aside for Category One countries and 13,165 shares for Category Two countries.
- If all signatory countries had became full members, the voting power would have been 59.75 percent for Category One versus 40.25 percent for Category Two.

Had MIGA proceeded at the time with the reallocation of shares, the following consequences would have occurred:

- Once parity was achieved, the admission of new members would upset the parity because any new member would bring additional voting power to the category to which it belonged, to the detriment to the other category.
- Should a member be allowed to move from one category to the other — some members had announced that they wished to do so — the hard to realize parity would have disappeared once again.

- The only answer would have been to close the Agency to new members and to prohibit any change from one Category to another (the Council of Governors must approve any such change). This solution would have, among other things, jeopardized the future growth of the Agency because MIGA may only do business, both issuance of guarantees and provision of advisory services, in its member countries.

The Board of Directors clearly realized that the reallocation would have an extremely negative impact on the Agency and recommended to the Council of Governors to postpone the reallocation for two years, until June 1993.

However, after the postponement was approved, a new and unforeseen issue arose: 18 of the former Soviet Republics and other former communist countries in Eastern Europe joined the World Bank and thus were eligible to join MIGA. Since they were not listed in Schedule A to the Convention, the Council of Governors had to approve their memberships and did so without casting a single negative vote. All of these countries when they joined the Agency became Category Two members. The result was that the aggregate voting power of the Category Two countries, once all or most of the countries listed in Schedule A joined the Agency, would be much higher than that of Category One. Furthermore, Greece, Portugal and Spain, who are classified in the Schedule A as Category Two, opted to move to Category One. South Africa took the opposite position and opted to move to Category Two. All these events, of course, caused a major disruption in the carefully conceived calculations for achieving parity of voting power instituted by the founders of MIGA.

Second Review of the Allocation of Shares

On June 8, 1993, the Council of Governors approved Resolution No. 43 on Review of Allocation of Shares, resolving that the decision referred to in Article 39(c) of the Convention, be postponed for five years, or taken during the tenth year after entry into force of the Convention. It further resolved that: (i) the shares of the capital stock of the Agency should continue to be allocated to the countries and in the number set forth in Schedule A annexed to the Convention; and (ii) should the number of shares of capital stock of the Agency that is available for new signatories be exhausted, the capital of the Agency shall be increased to provide sufficient shares to be subscribed by each new member in accordance with Article 5(b) of the Convention.

At the time of the 1993 Review, there were seventeen Category One member countries and eighty-four Category Two member countries. Two Category One countries and thirty Category Two countries were in the process of completing their membership. Category One members had 59,734 votes or fifty-seven percent of the voting power, and Category Two had 45,067 votes or forty-three percent of the voting power (as of February 28, 1993). Thus, MIGA was inching towards parity.

Another issue the drafters' compromise agreement on parity of voting power overlooked was: 'What would happen in the case of a capital increase?' Under a GCI, members cannot be compelled to subscribe to all the new shares created by the increase. Had parity of voting power been achieved prior to a GCI, that parity would be upset if only one country decided not to subscribe the new shares. As mentioned before, MIGA is now undergoing the subscription period for its first GCI. In view of all the difficulties mentioned above, it was decided that the best course of action would be to postpone once again trying to achieve voting parity until the end of the GCI subscription period in the year 2003. At that time, the shares that are as yet unallocated to any member, in theory, would be used to achieve the desired parity.

It is, of course, obvious that once the reallocation exercise has been completed, any new country will find it difficult to join MIGA because its membership would automatically disrupt the parity. One way to facilitate the accession of new members would be to reserve a certain number of unallocated shares — if any are left — and offer them to the Category that must increase its voting power (most likely Category One) because the other Category (most likely Category Two) would increase its voting power with the addition of a new member or members. Dr. Shihata, in his critique on Article 39, did not think that offering shares to just one group of countries would be without its own set of problems. I fully agree with him, and the reason being that every member of the Agency has a preemptive right to subscribe to any unsubscribed shares; and if the reserved shares are offered just to one Category of countries, countries in the other Category may exercise their preemptive rights, and then it would be impossible to ever achieve parity. This is a major dilemma we will have to tackle in the future.

VII. GUARANTEES

The number of guarantees, investment amounts facilitated and number of countries benefiting from investments guaranteed by MIGA, have increased steadily during the last ten years. As I explained before, during the first years of operations, the number of projects guaranteed by MIGA was disappointing and below all expectations. Yet, today MIGA is one of the five largest investment insurers in the world. For an overview of the growth in MIGA's number and amounts of guarantees issued, as well as the foreign direct investment (FDI) generated by those guarantees, see *Table 2* below:

TABLE 2. MIGA's GUARANTEE PORTFOLIO AND FDI FACILITATED, FISCAL 1990-99
(as of 6/30/99)

Category	1990	1991	1992	1993	1994	1995	1996	1997	1998	1999	Total
Number of Guarantees Issued	4	11	21	27	38	54	68	70	55	72	420
Amount of Guarantees Issued (millions of US dollars)	132	59	313	374	372	672	862	614	830	1,310	5,538
Estimated FDI Facilitated (billions of US dollars)	1.0	0.9	0.6	1.8	1.3	2.3	6.5	4.7	6.1	5.2	30.4

Source: MIGA Annual Report 1999

In Fiscal Year 1999 alone, MIGA's outstanding guarantees were issued for projects in fifty-seven developing member countries, of which twenty-eight were IDA-eligible[12] countries.

A. Risks

Although the Convention authorizes MIGA to cover four risks (expropriation, transfer restrictions, war and civil disturbance, and breach of contract), until December 1999 only coverage of the first

12 The International Development Association (IDA) is the World Bank's concessional lending facility, which concentrates its activities on the very poor countries.

three were offered by the Agency, with the sole exception of the very first project which included a guarantee for breach of contract. The continuous growth in the number of infrastructure projects being operated by private investors in recent years has motivated MIGA to review its policy of not offering breach of contract coverage. Investors, mainly in the infrastructure sector, want to be covered against breaches of contractual obligations by the host government. In many cases, the contracting party to these contracts is not the government of the host country but a sub-sovereign or a territorial subdivision, such as a province or municipality or even a state-owned company.

The way in which the Convention directs MIGA to cover breach of contract implies that the breach of a contractual obligation is not the event that generates the claim. Once the breach has occurred, one of the three following situations must take place before MIGA can accept the claim: (i) the investor cannot have recourse to a forum (either judicial or arbitral) to establish the breach; (ii) an arbitration award or a judicial decision is not rendered within the time period stipulated in the guarantee contract; or (iii) the award or decision cannot be enforced. Out of these situations which constitute denial of justice, MIGA, for the time being, is only willing to cover the last one. MIGA has recently begun to offer this coverage to investors in response to a number of applications (that have been filed) requesting it. In any case, the involvement of sub-sovereigns, the different types of dispute resolution provisions included in the investment contracts, the complexity of the contracts, as well as other factors have resulted in a greatly increased workload for its Legal Department.

B. Claims

At the time of writing this article in December 1999, no claim had been paid by the Agency.[13] However, this does not mean that all projects guaranteed by MIGA have been free of trouble. It is quite natural that during the first years after the setting up of an

---

[13] However, MIGA has registered a claim and it is at present negotiating a solution with the host government. The claim has not been paid yet because the date for payment in accordance with the contract of guarantee has not yet elapsed.

insurance entity such as MIGA, there are few or no claims, simply because there are few guaranteed projects and the likelihood of one of them experiencing a claim is, to a point, directly proportional to the overall number of guaranteed projects. On the other hand, although there are no actuarial calculations to ascertain the probability of a political risk materializing, the risk assessment made by MIGA for each project is very reliable — at least in the short term. No one can predict ten years into the future whether there will be a new government in a host country that would decide to expropriate foreign interests; nor can one predict the likelihood that in a future election an opposition party, which espouses nationalistic policies, would be voted into power. If the risk analysis indicates that there exists a bias in the present government, or a real possibility of one in a future government, against foreign investment, then the insurer should not provide a guarantee against a specific and highly probable risk.

But the main reason for a lack of claims was foreseen by Dr. Shihata on page 183 of his book, where he says that: "It will also be seen that MIGA is expected in most cases either to facilitate negotiated settlements between the host country and the investor or reach such settlements with the host country itself."[14] During its relatively short span of operations, MIGA has successfully negotiated five 'near-claim' situations in which guaranteed investors informed the Agency that the host government was taking measures that were tantamount to expropriation ('creeping expropriation'). In these cases, MIGA succeeded in finding mutually acceptable solutions by engaging in negotiations with the respective host governments, all of them, of course, shareholders of the Agency. MIGA's standing as a multilateral organization whose members are represented on the Board of Directors greatly facilitates the access by the staff of the Agency to the decision-making authorities of the government. The Agency is uniquely positioned as a claims prevention instrument, and investors appreciate this role when they are seeking coverage for their investment risks.

Due to the above, the Arbitration procedure set forth in Annex II to the Convention has not been tested yet, and there is a high likelihood that it may not be utilized in the future.

---

14 SHIHATA, *supra* note 1.

VIII. NON-GUARANTEE ACTIVITIES

As mentioned above in my Introduction, MIGA's mandate to encourage the flow of investments into its developing member countries is carried out by the Agency through two different methods. The first one is the issuance of guarantees; this activity generates an income and, once the necessary reserves for claims are set aside, a profit. The following *Figure 2* summarizes the dramatic growth in MIGA's income:

FIGURE 2. MIGA INCOME, FISCAL 1990–99 (as of 6/30/99)

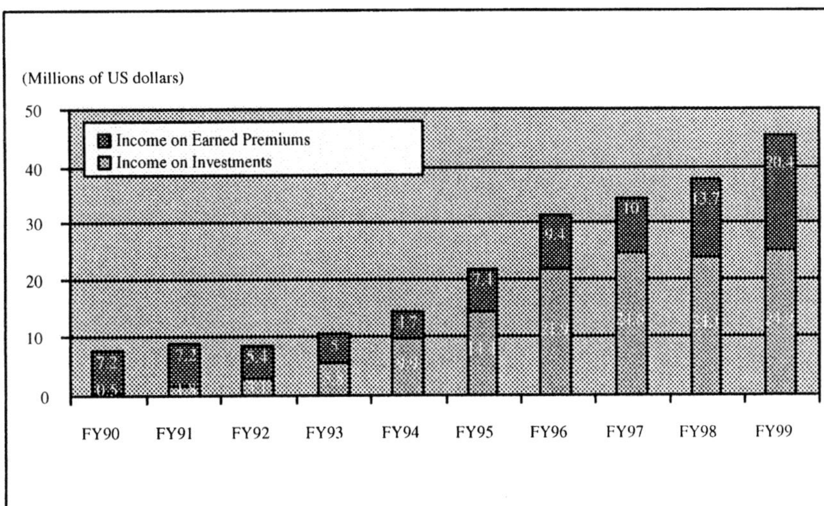

Source: MIGA Annual Report 1999

The Agency cannot distribute this profit among its shareholder countries until the reserves reach five times the subscribed capital (Art. 27 of the Convention). Since MIGA is a developmental, non-profit multilateral agency, it makes sense that at least part of these profits be used to carry out the second activity mandated by the Convention, i.e., to provide advice to developing member countries on how to improve their foreign investment climate. This is a costly activity that requires highly specialized staff, a significant amount of travel, and frequent hiring of short-term, outside consultants.

Dr. Shihata dedicates Chapter Five, entitled *MIGA's Non-Guarantee Operations,* of *MIGA and Foreign Investment*[15] to this program and describes there an extremely ambitious set of activities which were also incorporated into Chapter Seven of the Agency's Operational Regulations. These activities include: research, dissemination of information, technical advice and assistance, consultation on investment policies and programs, and negotiation of agreements with host governments. He also points out the need for MIGA to cooperate with other multilateral agencies that carry out similar types of activities in order to avoid duplication and specifies that there must be a level of complementarity between its guarantee program and the other activities of the Agency.

From the beginning, the main obstacle to MIGA providing the very ambitious program described by Dr. Shihata has been funding. During the Agency's initial years, MIGA's reserves consumed most of the premiums received due to the amount of risk caused by the relatively few guaranteed projects and a lack of diversification in its portfolio. Although some of the advisory activities were provided on a charge-back basis, covering one hundred percent of the fixed costs simply was not possible. These obstacles were accurately predicted by Dr. Shihata, and as a consequence Chapter Seven of the Operational Regulations (para. 7.02) takes into account that these activities "shall be initiated as rapidly and comprehensively as may be feasible in the light of the Agency's initial financial and administrative limitations."

During the first four years of operations, as set forth in the Operational Regulations, many of MIGA's external advisory activities were provided through the participation of the Agency in a joint venture with the World Bank and the IFC, called the Foreign Investment Advisory Service (FIAS). It was later realized that MIGA simply could not afford to pay its share in the expenses of FIAS, and therefore, in June 1994 it decided to abandon its involvement in FIAS but to continue its cooperative efforts when feasible. At the same time, MIGA's Policy and Advisory Services (PAS) was renamed the Investment Marketing Services (IMS) to reflect the unit's changed role.

---

15 *See* SHIHATA, *supra* note 1, at 191–213.

A. Investment Marketing Services

IMS and its activities were designed in such a way that they would not duplicate nor compete with those carried out by FIAS. IMS technical assistance activities can be summarized as follows:

- *Dissemination of Information*: MIGA provides two distinct and internationally recognized information services to its member countries and the public, its IPA*net*™ and its PrivitizationLink;
- *Capacity Building*: MIGA provides assistance to its member countries on how to organize and operate investment promotion agencies; and
- *Investment Facilitation*: MIGA provides support to its members in the attraction of potential investors in sectors which have been identified as having strong potential for growth and development.

Dissemination of Information

The two main vehicles for the dissemination of information by IMS are the *IPA*net and the PrivatizationLink.

IPAnet: MIGA directed its energies towards the creation of cutting-edge management and marketing techniques, particularly in the area of information technology. The primary beneficiaries that were targeted were the investment promotion agencies (IPAs) in its developing member countries. These agencies encompassed boards of investment and investment promotion centers, sectoral ministries, business associations, chambers of commerce, and financial intermediaries. The ultimate goal was to utilize the Internet as a cost-effective and efficient vehicle for information exchange and communications to assist developing countries and transition economies in promoting their investment opportunities. IPA*net* is an on-line information clearinghouse of investment databases, business news, market intelligence, and other features designed to make global investment activity more efficient and productive. IPA*net* has become a one-stop center for investment promotion, providing easy desktop access to information on investment opportunities, sources of finance, investment-related laws and regulations, market intelligence, and lists of key players in international investment. All registrants in IPA*net* with e-mail addresses automatically receive a newsletter six times a year. The newsletter highlights news and events related to international investment. IPA*net* was selected as Website of the Week by the *Financial Times* in April 1998.

PrivatizationLink: Perceiving a dearth of available information on investment opportunities arising from privatization of state-owned enterprises, IMS launched a new internet-based initiative to provide on-line information on privatization to potential investors. This site contains profiles of state-owned enterprises being privatized, background information on privatization agencies and their programs, and directories of privatization personnel, consulting firms, and other advisors. It also disseminates information on relevant laws and regulations, country-specific information on the market environment, business operating conditions, tax incentives, and related data. Most importantly, the PrivatizationLink provides concerned agencies with a free means to advertise globally the enterprises in their individual privatization programs.

Capacity Building

A core objective of IMS is to strengthen the institutional capacity of its developing members countries so that they can attract and retain foreign direct investment. This type of assistance is conducted at present on three levels through: (i) training programs and workshops on how to enhance investment promotion skills and utilize best practices in investment promotion; (ii) sector and region-specific strategy workshops and executive training programs; and (iii) the AFRI-IPA Support Program (ASP). The first two are self-explanatory; however the third initiative, the AFRI-IPA Support Program, represented a significant change in the way MIGA operates. This field-based technical assistance program was launched in February 1998 to provide hands-on technical assistance to investment promotion agencies and sectoral ministries in Sub-Saharan Africa — a region that the World Bank deemed to be particularly in need of all types of assistance. ASP operates on a multi-country basis from field offices in Southern, West/Central, and East Africa, which are supported by headquarters staff. Its goal is to facilitate the sharing of investment-related experiences among African countries and to keep external institutions and potential investors up to date on the opportunities in the region.

Investment Facilitation

IMS supports the efforts of its developing member countries to attract potential investors in rapidly growing sectors. Recently, IMS has concentrated its efforts on the mining and tourism sectors by capitalizing on established networks. Besides organizing its own symposiums and conferences in these two sectors, IMS works very closely with such disparate institutions as, among others, the World Bank, IFC, the Organization of American States (OAS), the U.S. Department of Commerce, the Organization for Economic Cooperation and Development (OECD), and the Turkish International Cooperation Agency.

B. Legal Technical Assistance

The MIGA Convention cites other types of non-guarantee activities in which the Agency has been very active besides the direct promotion of investment. These activities are of a legal nature and serve to facilitate the issuance of guarantees, and are contemplated in Article 23(b) of the Convention as follows:

> "(i) encourage the amicable settlement of disputes between investors and host countries;
>
> (ii) endeavor to conclude agreements with developing member countries, and in particular with prospective host countries, which will assure that the Agency, with respect to investment guaranteed by it, has treatment at least as favorable as that agreed by the member concerned for the most favored investment guarantee agency or State in an agreement relating to investment [. . .]; and
>
> (iii) promote and facilitate the conclusion of agreements, among its members, on the promotion and protection of investments."

Mediation of Investment Disputes: The Legal Department offers the services of its experienced counsel to act as mediators in the resolution of disputes between member countries and investors that are not recipients of MIGA's guarantees. The Agency has been extremely successful in its efforts to date, and eight disputes have been resolved through MIGA's offices, some of which commenced before MIGA was created. Several more disputes are advancing toward resolution. Mediation is voluntary, informal and inexpensive, and is increasingly attractive as a viable alternative to formal diplomatic solutions or costly arbitration. In addition, as mentioned above, counsel act as mediators in disputes between the Agency's guaranteed investors and its member countries, which is one reason no claims have been paid to this date.

Conclusion of Agreements on Legal Protection: These agreements endow the Agency with most favored treatment in case a dispute arises between a guaranteed investor and a developing member country, thus serving to aide in the resolution of a dispute or expedite the recovery of monies paid for eventual claims. Ninety-one Agreements on Legal Protection have entered into force between MIGA and the 91 developing member countries listed in *Table 3* below:

Promotion of Bilateral Investment Treaties (BITs) among Member Countries: The Legal Department provides advice to member countries on the main characteristics involved in the negotiation of BITs. When this service was initiated, many developing countries had never signed such treaties and were at a loss on how to proceed with negotiations and what terms they should ensure were included in the treaties. Counsel have reviewed draft BITs and conducted a number of seminars and workshops on this topic, using as its handbook, the *Legal Framework for the Treatment of Foreign Investment—Volume II: Guidelines* (Guidelines)[16] prepared by a team of expert Counsel of the World Bank Group, under the direction of Dr. Shihata, José Camacho who at the time was General Counsel of IFC, and myself.

In addition, when feasible, the Legal Department conducts legal technical training workshops and assists in the creation of national investment insurance programs in its member countries.

---

16 The Development Committee of the Boards of Governors of the International Monetary Fund and the World Bank.

TABLE 3. AGREEMENTS ON LEGAL PROTECTION

Albania	Czech Republic	Latvia	Russian Federation
Algeria	Dominica	Lebanon	Saudi Arabia
Angola	Dominican Republic	Lithuania	Senegal
Armenia	Ecuador	Madagascar	Slovak Republic
Azerbaijan	El Salvador	Malaysia	South Africa
Bahamas, The	Equatorial Guinea	Mali	Sri Lanka
Bahrain	Eritrea	Mauritania	St. Lucia
Bangladesh	Estonia	Mauritius	St. Vincent and Grenadines
Barbados	Gambia	Moldova	Tanzania
Bolivia	Georgia	Morocco	Togo
Bosnia and Herzegovina	Ghana	Nepal	Trinidad and Tobago
Brazil	Guatemala	Nicaragua	Tunisia
Bulgaria	Guinea	Nigeria	Turkmenistan
Burkina Faso	Guyana	Oman	Uganda
Cameroon	Honduras	Pakistan	Ukraine
Cape Verde	Hungary	Panama	United Arab Emirates
China	India	Papua New Guinea	Uruguay
Colombia	Indonesia	Paraguay	Uzbekistan
Congo, Rep. of	Israel	Peru	Venezuela
Congo, Dem. Rep. of	Jamaica	Philippines	Vietnam
Costa Rica	Jordan	Poland	Yemen, Rep. of
Cote d'Ivoire	Kazakhstan	Qatar	Zambia
Croatia	Kenya	Romania	

Source: MIGA Legal Department

IX. EVOLUTION OF THE OPERATIONAL REGULATIONS

One of Dr. Shihata's most perceptive bequests has been the inherent flexibility of MIGA's Operational Regulations. As he says in his book *MIGA and Foreign Investment*:

> "The Convention was carefully drafted so that the Agency should not deviate from a number of fundamental principles; however, it is flexible enough to allow MIGA to adapt to the changing needs of the marketplace by including most its policies and procedures in the Operational Regulations, which can be amended by simple majority of the Board of Directors at anytime."[17]

This flexibility has allowed MIGA to respond quickly to the demands of investors, changes in the policies of national and private insurers, and transformations in its developing member countries. To date, the Board of Directors has approved every one of the seventeen recommended amendments to the Operational Regulations. The first was in October 1988 and the most recent in December of this year. Even though the composition of the Board has evolved and the names of the Directors have changed over time, when MIGA's rationale for an amendment is convincing, Directors have readily assented because they have been reassured by Dr. Shihata's directive.

X. THE FUTURE

MIGA has grown from a staff of seventeen (including the first Executive Vice-President who was appointed in June 1988) as of December 31, 1988 to a staff of 124 as of December 30, 1999; and from a small suite of offices in the old 'A' Building of the World Bank to its present headquarters on the 12th floor and part of the 11th floor of the 'U' Building. In addition MIGA now has field offices in Sarajevo, Bosnia; Tokyo, Japan; Windhoek, Namibia; Moscow, Russian Federation; Berne, Switzerland; Lomé; Togo; and Harare, Zimbabwe. MIGA had zero income in the beginning of its operations and relied heavily on the World Bank for all financial and administrative support. In Fiscal Year 1990, MIGA issued four guarantees and realized a gross income of US$7.7 million, and in Fiscal Year 1999, MIGA issued seventy-two guarantees and had a gross income of over US$45 million.

"Where will MIGA be in another ten years?" No one can state for certain but, if history is prologue, MIGA will continue to grow

---

17 SHIHATA, *supra* note 1 at 109.

steadily as long as investors and developing countries require its guarantee and advisory services. It will also continue to adapt itself to the demands of the market and to the individual needs of its member countries as well as to set benchmarks for the political risk insurance industry as a whole. Dr. Shihata left us an important legacy — a very dynamic institution — comprising, among others, MIGA's broad Convention, including its very useful Commentary; flexible Operational Regulations; and his *MIGA and Foreign Investment,* with its detailed history and analysis of MIGA. I personally would like to thank Dr. Shihata for giving us the tools to make our progress a bit smoother, our challenging work a little simpler, and our future more secure.

THE WORLD BANK AND THE GLOBAL ENVIRONMENT: NOVEL FRONTIERS?

Rudolf Dolzer

Dr. Ibrahim Shihata deserves to be designated a lawyer's lawyer. His legal skills and the clarity of his opinions, written or oral, have found international recognition on the highest levels. The quality of his work has also been ensured by his ability and his willingness to work unusually long hours so as to guarantee thoroughness and breadth of analysis, also allowing him time for academic writing beyond the duties and hours dedicated to the World Bank. Respect for the law has been his central concern, not just in his writing and speaking, but in his thinking and his decisions in his daily professional conduct. In the world of international organizations in which so many currents and cross-currents are bound to pressure those responsible for decision-making, such steadfastness and loyalty to legal principle are never to be taken for granted, as has been evident on many fronts.

Beyond the realm of law, personal courage to defend the law will occasionally be required, and Dr. Ibrahim Shihata's combined characteristics of personal warmth and detachment have allowed him to speak and to act effectively for the rule of law in periods of stability and in difficult situations.

Fortunately, the management of the World Bank has known and has appreciated his role as the guardian of law, which gradually has encompassed a nearly unique institutional memory. Personal preferences, national distinctions, ideological inclinations or political priorities found their barriers in Dr. Ibrahim Shihata's willingness to protect the law. For those not familiar with his style and orientation of his work, he may at times have appeared to be inflexible or even insensitive to their demands or expectations; in reality, such perceptions failed to understand that the existing law, for the sake of the rule of law, will have to stand higher than preferences or choices.

At the same time, his mind at the World Bank has excelled not only in the application of existing law: when it came to recognize existing gaps or deficiencies, the constructive, forward-looking side of his creative personality allowed him to present innovative approaches and solutions which gained support, which were translated into law and practice and which have rightly been hailed as promoting the stature of the Bank and its mission to promote development. In particular, he has left his stamp on the creation of the Multilateral Investment Guarantee Agency (MIGA), on the establishment of the Global Environment Facility (GEF) and on the construction of the World Bank's Inspection Panel (IP). As is true for national governments, international organizations and international civil service, their failures and their achievements are largely influenced by the role of individual leaders. The World Bank was fortunate to benefit from the talents of Ibrahim Shihata during a long period which was crucial for its institutional formation and its adaptation in its role as a leading organization to promote development and justice.

Environmental issues have long occupied Dr. Ibrahim Shihata's work at the Bank, as is evident from his writings.[1] In this area in particular, his dedication to the rule of law was occasionally mistaken and resented as being insensitive to new and complex challenges in the work of the Bank. My personal impression was that in reality, Dr. Ibrahim Shihata's mind was very open for environmental concerns within the boundaries of the law which was laid down to govern the World Bank. In this spirit, the following short remarks on novel issues arising out of global environmental politics for the World Bank are offered in honor of Dr. Ibrahim Shihata.

Within the last decade, the rapid evolution of environmental politics acquired a new dimension with the sudden emergence of

---

1 *See, e.g.*, IBRAHIM F. I. SHIHATA, THE WORLD BANK IN A CHANGING WORLD, VOL. 1, at 135 *et seq.* (1991); *id.*, THE WORLD BANK IN A CHANGING WORLD, VOL. II, at 183 *et seq.* (1995); *id.*, *The World Bank's Contribution to the Development of International Environmental Law*, *in* LIBER AMICORUM PROFESSOR IGNAZ SEIDL-HOHENVELDERN IN HONOUR OF HIS 80TH BIRTHDAY 631 *et seq.* (Gerhard Hafner et al. eds., 1998).

global environmental concerns, which now exist side by side with the traditional local areas of concern, such as air pollution or river pollution.[2]

I. THE WORLD BANK AS KEY ACTOR IN THE ENVIRONMENTAL AREA

While the Stockholm Conference of 1972 has been widely hailed as the beginning of international environmental cooperation,[3] the international environmental agenda has since undergone a rapid transformation in order to respond to the globalization of environmental issues which have since been recognized. Whereas such matters as the transnational air pollution stemming from Germany and the United Kingdom and harming Scandinavian forests or the environmental consequences of individual riparian States of the Rhine or of the Danube for other riparian States prompted the Stockholm Conference and dominated its agenda,[4] the truly global dimensions of environmental politics which dominate, or should dominate, the debate and actions in the foreseeable future had not yet moved to center stage.[5] The protection of biodiversity on the global scale, the effort to mitigate climate change, the need to preserve the ozone layer in the stratosphere, the halting of the degradation of the oceans and the combat against increasing desertification all have causes which predate the Stockholm Conference, but the scientific understanding and the awareness of the urgent need for international cooperation to address these issues have only evolved thereafter. It is true that the main international forum which exists today specifically to deal with international environmental issues, the United Nations Environment Program (UNEP), has indeed been created on the basis of the Stockholm

---

2 For an overview of the development of international environmental law *see, e.g.*, PHILIPPE SANDS, PRINCIPLES OF INTERNATIONAL ENVIRONMENTAL LAW 25 *et seq.* (1995).

3 *See, e.g.*, LYNTON KEITH CALDWELL, INTERNATIONAL ENVIRONMENTAL POLICY 55, 60 (1990); *see also* PHILIPPE SANDS, *supra* note 2, at 38.

4 For the Conference *see* Louis B. Sohn, *The Stockholm Declaration on the Human Environment*, 14 HARVARD INTERNATIONAL LAW JOURNAL 423 *et seq.* (1973).

5 Rudolf Dolzer, *Global Environmental Issues: The Genuine Area of Globalization*, 7 JOURNAL OF TRANSNATIONAL LAW AND POLICY 174 (1998).

deliberations.[6] However, this organization as well reflects the more narrow view of the need for global environmental cooperation which informed the leaders present in Stockholm; meanwhile, more and more observers have called in the past decade for a new or a renewed organization whose powers, competencies, structure and infrastructure are commensurate with the evolution of the nature and the magnitude of global environmental problems.[7]

The World Bank has, by necessity, gradually been drawn into these new challenges inasmuch as its decisions and projects have an immediate direct bearing upon all of these issues and also because its attitude and actions stand out as representing the willingness on the ground to effectively address these problems, beyond high level speeches and conferences on the diplomatic and political front of global environmental politics. The adoption of universal treaties to protect the ozone layer (1985 and 1987),[8] the adoption of treaties to protect biodiversity[9] and to mitigate climate change[10] in Rio in 1992[11] and the negotiation of a convention against desertification[12] in 1994 have been milestones, erected in a relatively short period, in this new era of environmental chal-

---

6 UN General Assembly Resolution 2997 (XXVII) of Dec. 15, 1972, *reprinted in* 1972 YEARBOOK OF THE UNITED NATIONS 331 *et seq.* For UNEP *see, e.g.*, T.C. Bacon, *The Role of the United Nations Environment Program (UNEP) in the Development of International Environmental Law,* 1974 CANADIAN YEARBOOK OF INTERNATIONAL LAW 255 *et seq.;* Pierre-Marie Dupuy, *UNEP, in* 5 ENCYCLOPEDIA OF PUBLIC INTERNATIONAL LAW 319 *et seq.* (Rudolf Bernhardt ed., 1983); K. Ramakrishna, *UNEP: An Assessment of its Impact,* 24 INDIAN JOURNAL OF INTERNATIONAL LAW 346 *et seq.* (1984); Peter H. Sand, *Environmental Law in the United Nations Environment Program, in* ACADÉMIE DE DROIT INTERNATIONAL DE LA HAYE, *Colloque 1984: L'avenir du droit international de l'environnement, préparé par René-Jean Dupuy* 51 *et seq.* (1985).

7 *See, e.g.*, FRANK BIERMANN & UDO E. SIMONIS, NEEDED NOW: A WORLD ORGANIZATION FOR ENVIRONMENT AND DEVELOPMENT (1998); Rudolf Dolzer, *Time For Change,* 9 OUR PLANET No. 1, at *19 et seq.* (1997).

8 Vienna Convention for the Protection of the Ozone Layer, March 22, 1985, *reprinted in* 26 I.L.M. 1529 *et seq.* (1987); Montreal Protocol on Substances that Deplete the Ozone Layer of June 29, 1987, *reprinted in* 26 I.L.M. 1550 *et seq.* (1987).

9 Convention on Biological Diversity of June 5, 1992, *reprinted in* 31 I.L.M. 822 *et seq.* (1992).

10 United Nations Framework Convention on Climate Change, May 9, 1992, *reprinted in* 31 I.L.M. 849 *et seq.* (1992).

11 United Nations Conference on Environment and Development (UNCED) of June 3-14, 1992.

12 Convention to Combat Desertification in those Countries Experiencing Serious Drought and/or Desertification, particularly in Africa, Oct. 14, 1994, *reprinted in* 33 I.L.M. 1328 *et seq.* (1994).

lenges and politics. The precise meaning and significance of these treaties for the operations of the Bank have been the subject of a growing and ongoing political and legal debate which shall be addressed briefly at the end of these remarks. The challenge of the World Bank to respond to these issues has been twofold. Firstly, the need to "mainstream" these concerns into all of its operations has arisen, an ongoing enormous task of tremendous magnitude in which the operational complexity of defining "sustainable development" as balancing of economic, ecological and social priorities, has become evident. On a second level, the Bank has been faced with the need for, and the legitimacy of, specific Bank initiative to address some of the most pressing issues of global environmental concern for which funds have been lacking on the national and international level. In its search for its own appropriate role in the evolving global environmental agenda, the Bank has in recent years gone beyond research and seminars and has adopted projects which have, without fanfare, made the Bank to be in practice the most important actor on the global environmental level,[13] a novel situation and a far cry from the period in which the Bank's reputation was far from benign from an environmental perspective. A short summary of recent initiatives of the Bank to respond to the global environmental concerns may serve to illustrate its role of leadership, but also the attendant political and legal complexity.

II. SOME RECENT WORLD BANK ENVIRONMENTAL INITIATIVES

As a result of the Bank's Global Carbon Initiative, set up in February 1997, President Wolfensohn, in June 1997, announced at the United Nations General Assembly Special Session that the World Bank will launch a Carbon Fund. The objectives of this Fund which has started its operations in the year 2000 are to demon-

---

13 *See also* IBRAHIM F.I. SHIHATA, THE WORLD BANK IN A CHANGING WORLD VOL. II, *supra* note 1, at 184: "[The] World Bank has been a pioneer in addressing the environmental consequences of development activities and a world leader in the establishment of new environmental policies and procedures." For an overview of the Bank's role in global environmental politics *see* recently Ibrahim F.I. Shihata, *The World Bank's Contribution to the Development of International Environmental Law*, *supra* note 1.

strate that project-based emission reduction transactions can promote and contribute to the sustainable development of the Bank's clients countries, and to provide the parties to the Framework Convention on Climate Change[14] with an opportunity to "learn by doing" as they deliberate on the rules and procedures which will govern project-based emission reduction transactions under the Kyoto Protocol.[15] Furthermore, the Fund is to provide an example of how the World Bank can work in partnership with both the public and private sectors to mobilize new resources for its client countries while addressing global environmental concerns. The target size of the Fund is US$ 100–120 million. The Fund is to be administered by the Bank without a separate legal entity. The Bank intends to fund project activities in host countries that reduce or sequester greenhouse gas emissions. These activities will be additional to the Bank's regular lending activities and are supposed to last until the end of 2012.

As far as the protection of global waters is concerned, the World Bank is involved in the activities of the Global Water Partnership (GWP), an international network open to governments, UN agencies, multilateral banks, research organizations, NGOs etc., which was established at a founding meeting in Stockholm in August 1996. The Consultative Group, which is the highest policy-making body of the network, is chaired by Mr. Serageldin, the Vice President of the Bank. The sub-sectors of the GWP include programmes which are intended to have a catalytic effect on investment in their specific fields (water and sanitation, irrigation and drainage) operating according to the Partnership's shared principles. The Technical Advisory Committee, consisting of twelve internationally known professionals and scientists in disciplines related to water resources management, held an initial meeting in Copenhagen in June 1996.[16]

As to the conservation of biological diversity, the World Bank considers, in cooperation with the International Union for Conservation of Nature and Natural Resources (IUCN), implementing

---

14 United Nations Framework Convention on Climate Change, *supra* note 10.

15 Kyoto Protocol to the United Nations Framework Convention on Climate Change, Dec. 10, 1997, UN Doc. FCCC/CP/1997/L.7/Add. 1, *reprinted in* 37 I.L.M. 32 *et seq.* (1998).

16 For further information on the Global Water Partnership *see* <http://www.gwp.sida.se/gwp/gwp/welc.html>.

a programme on the protection on biological diversity in fifteen regions in the Third World. The first potential projects concern the atlantic forests in Brazil, the ecosystem in the border zone between Ecuador and Peru, and the Delta of the Okavango River in Botswana. In these three regions, an extremely high number of endangered species can be found.

Also, the World Bank and the World Wildlife Fund (WWF) have announced, in July 1997, a global alliance for forest conservation and sustainable use which provides for a network of protected areas across both developing and developed countries including at least 10 percent of each of the world's major forest types by the year 2000.[17] Furthermore, the two partners agree that large areas of natural forest in developing countries and transitional economies should be brought under real sustainable management starting from a negligible amount today. The Bank announced that it will help client countries establish an additional 50 million hectares of new forest protected areas in its client countries, and bring an additional 200 million hectares of the world's forests under independant certification by the year 2005.[18]

The areas and the projects mentioned raise a number of legal and political issues which are distinct yet interrelated. Some of the more important ones shall be briefly outlined.

III. WORLD BANK ENVIRONMENTAL ACTIVITIES IN THE CONTEXT OF INTERNATIONAL TREATIES

A first legal issue concerns the World Bank's mission of "development" as laid down in Art. 1 of its Articles:

The purposes of the bank are:

> (i) To assist in the reconstruction and development of territories of members by facilitating the investment of capital for productive purposes, including the restoration of economies destroyed or disrupted by war, the reconversion of productive facilities to peace-

[17] For the World Bank — WWF alliance *see* Ken Newcombe, Juergen Blaser & Kerstin Canby, *The World Bank and Forests,* Environment Matters at the World Bank, Annual Review 56 *et seq.* (Fall 1998).

[18] For further information on the agreement between the World Bank and the WWF *see also* <http://www.panda.org/news/press/news_130.htm>.

time needs and the encouragement of the development of productive facilities and resources in less developed countries [...]."[19]

The Articles having been formulated in Bretton Woods in 1945, the notion of development is not qualified as "sustainable", as, for instance, in the preamble of the World Trade Organization[20] or the European Bank for Reconstruction and Development.[21] In fact, it is obvious that the drafters of Art. 1 of the Bank's Articles thought of economic aspects when they formulated the agreement. Thus, the question arises whether and to what extent the evolution of the concept of development in the past fifty years and, in particular, the incorporation of non-economic factors into that concept may find their way into the Bank's operation.[22] Dr. Ibrahim Shihata has rightly explained that it is inevitable that the Bank has adapted its work to the changing understanding of the process of development.[23] This view of the necessity to understand broad legal notions in a dynamic and evolutionary way has been sanctioned by the International Court of Justice,[24] and, in

---

19 International Bank for Reconstruction and Development (IBRD), Articles of Agreement (as amended effective Feb. 16, 1989), *reprinted in* 2 UNTS 134 *et seq.*; 606 UNTS 294 *et seq.*

20 *See* Preamble of the Agreement Establishing the Multilateral Trade Organization (World Trade Organization, WTO) of Dec. 15, 1993, *reprinted in* 33 I.L.M. 13 *et seq.* (1994): "The Parties to this Agreement, recognizing that their relations in the field of trade and economic endeavour should be conducted with a view to rising standards of living [...], while allowing for the optimal use of the world's resources in accordance with the objective of sustainable development, seeking both to protect and preserve the environment and enhance the means for doing so in a manner consistent with their respective needs and concerns at different levels of economic development [...]."

21 *See* Art. 2 (vii) of the Agreement Establishing the European Bank for Reconstruction and Development (EBRD) of May 29, 1990, *reprinted in* 29 I.L.M. 1077 *et seq.* (1990): "[T]he Bank shall assist the recipient member countries [...] to help their economies become fully integrated into the international economy by measures [...]; (vii) to promote in the full range of its activities environmentally sound and sustainable development [...]."

22 *See generally* ROBERT L. AYRES, BANKING ON THE POOR: THE WORLD BANK AND WORLD POVERTY (1983).

23 *See* IBRAHIM F.I. SHIHATA, THE WORLD BANK IN A CHANGING WORLD, VOL. I, *supra* note 1, at 177.

24 *See* International Court of Justice, Legal Consequences for States of the Continued Presence of South Africa in Namibia (South West Africa) notwithstanding Security Council Resolution 276 (1970), 1971 ICJ REPORTS, 16, at 31, para. 53 (Advisory

principle, no disagreement seems to have been voiced with Dr. Shihata's positive approach.

Nevertheless, questions remain specifically with regard to the effect of existing treaties for the protection of the global environment upon the Bank's operation. In this regard, the various facets of the general issue of the binding nature of such international agreements upon an international organization accepted by its member states would have to be examined. In the current context, a lack of identity of Bank membership and of countries adhering to the relevant conventions would have to be taken into account. Also, the specificity of the mandate of the Bank as laid down in the Articles of Agreement as distinct from the specific language and purpose of the conventions will not be without a bearing on the matter. A general reference to the conventions on sustainable development as contemporary expressions of the interest of the international community may have legal significance, and finds growing recognition in legal doctrine,[25] but cannot as such replace thorough legal examination of the legal issues mentioned earlier. Generally speaking, States have retained the right to fashion international organizations and their missions as narrowly or as broadly as they wish, and to express their intention in the constituent document. Interpretation of the constituent document will take into account subsequent practice and the generally accepted rules, including that of the evolutionary nature of broad legal notions,[26] but the principle of the power of the member states to independently determine the purpose of their organization must not thereby be contradicted or undermined.

A separate but related issue arises in respect of the nature of the modern conventions on sustainable development and the

---

Opinion of June 21, 1971). *See also* International Court of Justice, Gabcíkovo-Nagymaros Project (Hung. v. Slovk.), 1997 ICJ REPORTS, 7, at 64 *et seq.* paras. 111-113 (Judgement of Sept. 25, 1997).

25 *See, e.g.*, Günther Handl, *The Legal Mandate of Multilateral Development Banks as Agents for Change Toward Sustainable Development*, 92 AMERICAN JOURNAL OF INTERNATIONAL LAW 642 *et seq.* (1998).

26 *See generally* HENRY G. SCHERMERS & NIELS M. BLOKKER, INTERNATIONAL INSTITUTIONAL LAW 719 *et seq,*. paras. 1155f (1995), who speak of a " 'living constitution,' the interpretation of which changes with the development of society." *But see* also, for a different point of view, International Court of Justice, Certain Expenses of the United Nations, 1962 ICJ REPORTS 151 (Advisory Opinion of July 20, 1962), Separate Opinion of Judge Sir Percy Spender, at 195 *et seq.*

legal powers of the organs of these conventions on the one hand, and the freedom of the World Bank to act in concert, to act more aggressively or more slowly than these organs, on the other hand. The treaties on sustainable development have been phrased in broad terms regarding their objectives and purposes.[27] In the area of climate change, specific time tables and targets for industrial countries and countries in transition have been agreed upon in Kyoto[28] without, however, denying the principle of freedom of means to reach timetables and targets. So far, no comparable obligations have been included in the legal framework for developing states. In the areas of biodiversity and desertification, the existing agreements spell out objectives, but retain a framework character due to the generality of the envisaged means of implementation.[29] This is even more so with regard to the protection of oceans and the applicable rules of the 1982 Law of the Sea Convention, giving rise to considerations of a specific protocol or some other form of expressing of the need for sustainable development which has been contained in the Law of the Sea Convention only in a rather rudimentary manner,[30] also due to an

---

27 *See, e.g.*, Vienna Convention for the Protection of the Ozone Layer, *supra* note 8, Art. 2: "1. The Parties shall take appropriate measures [...] to protect human health and the environment against adverse effects resulting or likely to result from human activities which modify or are likely to modify the ozone layer [...]"; Framework Convention on Climate Change, *supra* note 10 , Art. 2: "The ultimate objective of this Convention and any related legal instruments that the Conference of the Parties may adopt is to achieve [...], stabilization of greenhouse gas concentrations in the atmosphere at a level that would prevent dangerous anthropogenic interference with the climate system. Such a level should be achieved within a time-frame sufficient to allow ecosystems to adapt naturally to climate change, to ensure that food production is not threatened and to enable economic development to proceed in a sustainable manner"; Convention on Biological Diversity, supra note 9, Art. 1: "The objectives of this Convention [...], are the conservation of biological diversity, the sustainable use of its components and the fair and equitable sharing of the benefits arising out of the utilization of genetic resources, including by appropriate access to genetic resources and by appropriate transfer of relevant technologies, taking into account all rights over those resources and to technologies, and by appropriate funding."

28 *See* Kyoto Protocol, *supra* note 15.

29 *See* Convention on Biological Diversity *supra* note 9, and Convention to Combat Desertification, *supra* note 12.

30 Rudolf Dolzer, *Implications of Agenda 21 and UNCLOS for International Waters as a GEF Focal Area,* GEF Working Paper Number 15, at 7 *et seq.*

assumption that coastal states are able and willing to legislate the necessary arrangements.

In addition to these broad objectives and the limited specific obligations which are more or less common to the treaties concerned, the obligations on the part of recipients of the Bank's credits are in some areas further qualified by certain clauses which recognize the limited financial and technological capabilities of developing states. Thus, as is also encapsulated in the phrase "common but differentiated responsibilities",[31] the double nature of the legal effect of ratification of these treaties shows: while the goals and objectives are accepted as legitimate and even as necessary in view of the problem as defined by science or by best available assumptions, the developing states condition their required contributions in view of their limited financial and technological obligations. Against this background, a simple reference to the international goals of the international community pursued by the convention will not answer all questions when it comes to setting forth the obligations incumbent upon the World Bank in its legal relations to the recipient states. It is true that the World Bank has formally adopted the policy not to contribute to a violation of an international obligation on the part of a member state in granting and implementing a loan.[32] Given the legal nature of the treaties described, this operational directive is of limited assistance in determining the legal consequences for the conduct of the Bank when it comes to delineating specific consequences of this directive.

In this context, it will also have to be considered that the GEF, being the provisional or definitive financial mechanism of the biodiversity and the climate convention,[33] has been based upon

---

31 *See, e.g.*, United Nations Framework Convention on Climate Change, *supra* note 10, Art. 3 (1). For the principle of common but differentiated responsibility *see generally* PHILIPPE SANDS, *supra note* 2, at 217 *et seq.*

32 Thus, the World Bank has pledged not to finance "projects that contravene any international environmental agreement to which the member country concerned is a party", World Bank, Operational Manual Statement (OMS) 2.36, Environmental Aspects of Bank Work (1984), para. 9 (e).

33 For the GEF, *see generally*, Rudolf Dolzer, *The Global Environment Facility — Towards a New Concept of the Common Hertitage of Mankind, in* THE LIVING LAW OF NATIONS, ESSAYS IN MEMORY OF ATLE GRAHL-MADSEN 331 *et seq.* (Gudmundur Alfredsson & Peter Macalister-Smith eds., 1996); Sand, *The Potential Impact of the Global Envi-*

the recognition that those incremental costs which developing states incur to protect global (as distinct from national) environmental interests will ultimately be borne by the developed countries.[34] These costs are not in any way quantified in the conventions, and the resources available for these purposes are ultimately decided by the developed states during the process of replenishment of the GEF. The openness of the financial limitations of the developed states corresponds to the described openness of the substantive obligations of the developing states.

The practicalities of the matter from the point of view of the World Bank will also be influenced by the Bank's institutional need to protect competitiveness on the international financial markets. In case the standards set by the Bank for the granting of a loan will appear to be too burdensome from the viewpoint of its potential recipients, these may turn to the private markets which do not in any way place environmental restrictions upon their loans. Practice has illustrated the potential ensuing dilemma: the result would be negative both from the Bank's institutional perspective and from the vantage point of environmental protection. This situation would change as soon as the private sector would be held to the same or similar standards as the World Bank, and possibly, guidelines in this direction would indeed be useful to avoid this dilemma. As long as this is not the case, it would not be appropriate to require that the Bank set standards which in fact put its competitive situation in question and do not promote environmental objectives either.

A broader general consideration also places limitations upon the requirements set by the Bank. Put squarely, the ceiling for standards for developing states cannot be higher than is observed in practice by developed states. The principle of common but differentiated responsibility as recognized in binding treaties[35] would otherwise be ignored and contradicted. The issue may appear to be academic. However, the point bears emphasis, for instance in view of demands to immediately withdraw Bank sup-

---

ronment Facility of the World Bank, UNDP and UNEP, in ENFORCING ENVIRONMENTAL STANDARDS: ECONOMIC MECHANISMS AS VIABLE MEANS? 479 *et seq.* (Rüdiger Wolfrum ed. 1996).

34 *See* Instrument for the Establishment of the Restructured Global Environment Facility, March 13, 1994, Part IV, para. 25, *reprinted in* 33 I.L.M. 1273 *et seq.* (1994).

35 *See* United Nations Framework Convention on Climate Change, *supra* note 31.

port for coal mining in China and India in view of the practice of enormous subsidies for coal and of the low degree of energy efficiency in industrialized countries.

In their sum, all of these considerations indicate that a differentiating approach will be required in answer to the question of the binding effect of global treaties for sustainable development upon the conduct of the Bank. More precise analysis will be required to set forth a comprehensive review than is possible in these short remarks which are only intended to describe the contours of the issues. An obvious differentiation so far not expressly mentioned will also be made between standards requested by member States and such imposed by the Bank in its policies and guidelines. In view of the broad concept of development as it is widely accepted today, it would appear inappropriate to argue that the Bank would be legally prohibited from promoting higher standards of sustainable development than those universally embodied in its Articles of Agreement or its secondary rules.

IV. CONCLUSION

In the *Gabcíkovo Case* (Hungary vs. Slovakia), decided by the International Court of Justice in 1997,[36] the notion of sustainable development has made its way into the realm of legal construction and into the forefront of international legal thinking. The Court's majority preferred a cautious approach and spoke of the concept of sustainable development,[37] drawing from a critical individual opinion of Judge Weeramantry, who goes further and speaks of a legal principle.[38] Both attitudes appear to be plausible and both will call for a synthesis in applications to specific areas and configurations of law.[39] The time for a new legal paradigm to address

---

[36] *See supra* note 24.

[37] International Court of Justice, Gabcíkovo-Nagymaros Project (Hung.v. Slovk), *supra* note 24, at 78, para. 140.

[38] *Ibid.*, Separate Opinion of Judge Weeramantry, at 95.

[39] For a survey of the development and the legal implications of the concept of sustainable development in international law *see, e.g.*, Ulrich Beyerlin, *The Concept of Sustainable Development, in* ENFORCING ENVIRONMENTAL STANDARDS: ECONOMIC MECHANISMS AS VIABLE MEANS?, *supra* note 33, at 94 ff.; Günther Handl, *Sustainable Development: General Rules Versus Specific Obligations, in* SUSTAINABLE DEVELOPMENT AND INTERNATIONAL LAW 35 *et seq.* (Winfried Lang ed., 1995); David Luff, *An Overview of In-*

the emerging pressing issues of sustainability has come, and, as with other novel broad legal propositions, gradual evolution and refinement in particular fields and cases will shape the development of the law along the lines of such complementary notions as the necessity of prevention, the concepts of the common concerns and heritage of mankind, the principle of common but differentiated responsibility or a version of the principle of strict liability for actions which endanger the global environment. In order to be orderly, timely and successful, this unfolding process of developing the new paradigm will require all those talents and skills which have characterized Dr. Ibrahim Shihata's attitude and work: analytical skill, balance of judgment, the ability to look beyond immediate concerns and, perhaps most important, a sense of international community which is both realistic and transcends the interests of individual nations.

---

ternational Law of Sustainable Development and a Confrontation Between WTO Rules and Sustainable Development, REVUE BELGE DE DROIT INTERNATIONAL 90 *et seq.* (1996).

MORGAN V. WORLD BANK (TEN YEARS LATER)

Christian Dominicé

I. INTRODUCTION

As a prominent international civil servant, Dr. Ibrahim F.I. Shihata contributed significantly to the development of the institutions of the World Bank Group and to its orientation towards greater justice, attention to the environment, and respect for the human being. This concern can be seen, among many other examples, in the procedure which gives to groups of individuals the opportunity to file complaints with the World Bank Inspection Panel,[1] to which Dr. Shihata devoted much of his talent and efforts.[2]

The development of the protection of human rights is one of the main features of the evolution of international law over the last decades of the twentieth century. Quite recently, on a very specific topic, new thoughts have been put forward concerning immunity from jurisdiction and its relationship to the respect of the fundamental rights of the individual. The question is being raised in connection with the various entities and persons enjoying jurisdictional immunities, particularly States (sovereign immunity).[3]

---

1 *See* Ibrahim F.I. Shihata, *The World Bank's Contribution to the Development of International Environmental law, in* LIBER AMICORUM PROFESSOR IGNAZ SEIDL-HOHENVELDERN 631–649 (G. Hafner et al. eds., 1998).

2 *See id., The World Bank Inspection Panel* (1994), and *id.*, THE WORLD BANK INSPECTION PANEL IN PRACTICE (2nd ed. 2000).

3 *See* G. Ress, *The Changing Relationship Between State Immunity and Human Rights, in* LIBER AMICORUM CARL AAGE NORGAARD 175 (M. De Salvia & M.E. Villger eds., 1998); J. BRÖHMER, STATE IMMUNITY AND THE VIOLATION OF HUMAN RIGHTS (1997).

International organizations are also the focus of attention.[4] Ten years ago, the World Bank was sued in the United States District Court of the District of Columbia by a former employee, whose complaints concerned acts and behavior of some officials of the Bank.[5] The complaint was dismissed on the ground that the Organization benefits from immunity and thus the Court lacked jurisdiction. The question which arises ten years later, is whether today the decision would be the same, or should the Court in a similar case recognize the plaintiff's right of access to court and set aside the plea of immunity if no legal remedy is available to him?

II. THE DECISION OF THE COURT

The plaintiff, Charles Morgan, was an employee of *Going Places,* a temporary employment agency. He received an assignment at the World Bank, in a secretarial position, and worked in other respects as a directly hired employee. His complaint was that in late 1989 bank officials and security guards forcibly detained him and denied him access to an attorney, accused him of stealing money without presenting any evidence, and subsequently made unwarranted threats in the course of continuing harassment. Morgan sought compensatory and punitive damages for intentional infliction of emotional distress, false imprisonment, libel and slander.[6] The World Bank asserted that it was immune from suit and filed a motion to dismiss.

Granting the motion, the Court first stated that pursuant to applicable statutory provisions[7] and principles of international law, international organizations such as the World Bank are, in the ab-

---

4 *See* M. Singer, *Jurisdictional Immunity of International Organizations: Human Rights and Functional Necessity Concern,* 36 VIRGINIA JOURNAL OF INTERNATIONAL LAW 53 (1995).

5 *See* Charles Morgan v. The International Bank for Reconstruction and Development, 752 F. Supp. 492, (D.C., Sept. 13, 1990).

6 *Ibid.* at 493.

7 *See* International Organizations Immunities Act, 22 U.S.C. §288 *et seq.* [hereinafter IOIA]; Foreign Sovereign Immunities Act, 28 U.S.C. §1602 *et seq.* [hereinafter FSIA].

sence of a waiver, absolutely immune from suits arising out of their internal operations. The Court then rejected the argument that the Bank had waived its immunity through the waiver provision of Article VII, Section 3, of its Articles of Agreement.[8] Referring to the case of *Mendaro v. World Bank*,[9] it rightly stated that that provision was limited in its scope to the external operations of the Bank.[10]

Another argument against immunity was based upon the Foreign Sovereign Immunity Act (FSIA).[11] It was contended that since the International Organizations Immunities Act (IOIA) said that qualified international organizations . . . "shall enjoy the same immunity from suit and every form of judicial process as is enjoyed by foreign governments . . ." the FSIA was to be applied, particularly the "commercial activity" exception to immunity. The Court did not decide whether or not the FSIA was to be applied, an issue which is controversial.[12] Assuming *arguendo* that the restrictive standard of that Act, rather than the absolute immunity of international organizations, applied to the World Bank, the judgment was that Morgan's claim did not fall within the "commercial activity" exception.

For the Court, the suit concerned an employment relationship, because Morgan "has been assigned for a substantial period as a regular World Bank staff member."[13] The alleged course of

---

8 Article VII, sec. 3 of the International Bank of Reconstruction and Development's [hereinafter IBRD] Articles of Agreement, 2 UNTS 180 ("Actions may be brought against the Bank only in a court of competent jurisdiction . . . no actions shall, however, be brought by members or persons acting for or deriving claims from members. The property and assets of the Bank shall, wheresoever located and by whosoever held, be immune from all forms of seizure, attachment or execution before the delivery of final judgment against the Bank").

9 *See* Mendaro v. World Bank, 230 U.S. App. D.C. 333, 717 F. 2d 610 (D.C. Cir. 1983), 78 American Journal of International Law 221 (1984).

10 For similar provisions in the articles of agreement of other banks, *see* Ch. Dominicé, *L'immunité de juridiction et d'exécution des organisations internationales*, Vol. 187, No. 4 Recueil Des Cours de L'Academie De droit International 145, 196 (1984).

11 *Supra*, note 7.

12 The IOIA was adopted in 1945, the FSIA in 1976. Does the reference to State immunity in IOIA mean the rule of 1945 (absolute immunity) or that of 1976 (restrictive immunity)?

13 Morgan, 751 F.Supp., at 494.

conduct of Bank officials arose directly from Morgan's work at his job. The employment practices of the World Bank did not constitute "commercial activity" within the Statute's meaning.

It is interesting to quote here the following sentence of the decision: ". . . the fact that Morgan is not in all respects formally an employee of the Bank but serves on detail from his agency is of no legal consequence."[14] The legal nature of the employment relationship, in my opinion, may have legal consequences. These will be discussed later.

The Court added a last argument, saying that, even if the FSIA was held to apply, the Act's tort exception[15] provided no basis for proceeding.[16]

III. OBSERVATIONS

The purpose of the present paper is to ask whether, today, the decision on immunity would be different, due to human rights concerns. There is no need to discuss here all issues considered in the judgment. However, two important questions must be dealt with in order to make clear in which legal context, in our opinion, the issue "immunity versus human rights" could be raised. The first relates to the immunity of international organizations and the second concerns employment relationships.

There is already substantial literature on the immunity from jurisdiction of international organizations, as well as a growing practice.[17] The focus here is merely on a specific feature of the case of *Morgan*. The law which was to be applied by the District Court was primarily US law (IOIA and FSIA). International law

---

14 *Ibid.*

15 28 U.S.C. §1605(a)(5).

16 Two of the four counts of the complaint (those alleging libel and slander) did not fall within the exception to immunity, and the two others (false imprisonment and intentional infliction of emotional distress) were foreclosed in this instance by the "discretionary function" exemption of the FSIA.

17 *See supra*, notes 4 and 10; S. Muller, International Organizations and Their Host States (1995); J. Duffar, Contribution à l'étude des privilèges et immunités des organisations internationales (1982); M. Wenckstern, *Die Immunität internationaler Organisationen, in* Handbuch des internationalen Zivilverfahrensrechts (Max-Planck Institut ed., 1994); P. Bekker, The Legal Position of Intergovernmental Organizations 122 (1964).

was considered mainly in relation to the question of waiver of immunity, since the Articles of Agreement of the Bank were invoked. In other countries, the legal status of an international organization is generally governed by international law. Very frequently there is a bilateral headquarters agreement, sometimes a multilateral treaty on privileges and immunities.

It is true that even when there is a treaty, the judge must in some countries apply national law, for the reason that he or she is not entitled to apply provisions of international conventions. The most conspicuous example is the United Kingdom.[18] However, in these situations, the municipal law must be in accordance with the relevant treaty, or there is a breach of international law. In the United States, the situation is different. That country has concluded a Headquarters Agreement with the United Nations,[19] and more recently another, even if partial, with the Organization of American States.[20] For the other organizations, municipal law is relevant, (i.e., the IOIA), whenever the President has designated an organization to fall under that Act.

As a consequence, it is clear, that in the absence of a waiver, immunity from jurisdiction is absolute and complete for the United Nations.[21] For the other organizations, it has never been clearly decided whether the IOIA, when prescribing that the organizations "shall enjoy the same immunity from suit and every form of judicial process as is enjoyed by foreign governments, . . . ," refers to the situation as it was when the Act was adopted in 1945 (absolute immunity) or means that since the FSIA was enacted, it has to be applied to international organizations, in-

---

18 *See* H. Fox et al., *United Kingdom,* in THE INTEGRATION OF INTERNATIONAL AND EUROPEAN COMMUNITY LAW INTO THE NATIONAL LEGAL ORDER 494 (P.M. Eisemann ed., 1996). *See also* Arab Banking Corporation v. International Tin Council (ITC) et al., 77 INTERNATIONAL LEGAL MATERIALS (I.L.M.) 1 (despite a Headquarters Agreement between ITC and the United Kingdom, the courts held that the *International Tin Council [Immunities and Privileges] Order 1972,* promulgated as Statutory Instrument 120 of 1972, was relevant).

19 Headquarters Agreement of 26 June 1947 (St/LEG/SER.B/10.204). *See also* Applicability of the Obligation to Arbitrate under Section 21 of the United Nations Headquarters Agreement of 26 June 1947, 1988 ICJ REP. 12 (Apr. 26).

20 Agreement between the United States of America and Organization of American States relating to Privileges and Immunities of Representatives to the Council of the Organization and other Members of Delegations, March 20, 1975, 26 UST 1025.

21 *See* M. Singer, *supra* note 4, at 96.

cluding the restrictive doctrine of immunity.[22] In the *Morgan* case, the Court took no decision on that controversy, granting immunity to the World Bank even under FSIA, *arguendo* considering that it was to be applied.

Whereas the matter is normally governed by treaty, given there is one, it is difficult to assert that, today, there are rules of customary international law according to which international organizations enjoy absolute immunity from jurisdiction,[23] although it might be the case for certain important international organizations.[24]

It can be concluded that generally the scope of the immunity from jurisdiction, is still fairly broad or far-reaching,[25] perhaps with more flexibility in the United States, where, but for the UN, as restrictive interpretation of the law is possible, provided it is not contrary to a rule of customary international law.

Employment-related relationships are certainly of particular importance. The *Morgan* case concerned employment, as was stressed by the District Court, which referred to previous decisions, in particular to the leading cases *Broadbent v. Organization of American States* and *Mendaro*. In *Broadbent*,[26] the claimants were seven former staff members of the General Secretariat of the OAS.

---

22 For that reason, there seems to be more flexibility in the United States than in other countries, because, when there is a Headquarters Agreement, the immunity of the organization is absolute and complete, but for exceptions expressly enunciated. The discussion by Singer (*supra* note 4) of a functional approach to immunity may be well adapted to U.S. law (but for the UN), but not to Headquarters Agreements. It is to be added that a recent decision of the United States Court of Appeals seems to indicate that the IOIA is preferably to be interpreted as referring to the law as it existed in 1945, Atkinson v. Inter-American Development Bank, et.al., 9 Oct. 1998, 322 U.S. App. D.C. 307, 156 F. 3d 1335 (D.C. Cir.1998).

23 The existence of a customary rule has been affirmed, for example, in the Netherlands (Spaans v. The Netherlands, 107 INTERNATIONAL LAW REPORTS 1), and in Switzerland (Malek c. Ligue des Etats Arabes, Judgement of 25 January 1999, IPRAx 1999, 257, published in French), but it is not general practice of the national courts.

24 *See* Ch. Dominicé, *supra* note 10, at 174, 219; M. Singer, *supra* note 4, at 72, 87, 98.

25 One recent Headquarters Agreement concerning an important international organization, the Agreement between the World Trade Organization and Switzerland, concluded in 1995, grants to the Organization absolute and complete immunity from jurisdiction. *See* art. 8 of that Agreement.

26 Broadbent et al. v. Organization of American States, 202 U.S. App. D.C. 27, 628 F.2d 27 (D.C. Cir. 1980).

After their dismissal from the Secretariat on August 31, 1976, they filed complaints with the Administrative Tribunal of the Organization, which held that they should be reinstated or awarded indemnities. The Secretary General chose the latter solution. Then the seven claimants brought action in the District Court, which held that OAS was immune from suit. The Court of Appeals dismissed the appellants action. It based its decision on the law governing the immunity of international organizations, avoided a decision as to whether according to IOIA (and FSIA) international organizations enjoy absolute or restrictive immunity and held that even under the restrictive doctrine employment by an international organization could not be characterized as a commercial activity.

In *Mendaro,*[27] the claimant was a former employee of the World Bank, who alleged various employment-related grievances. The Court of Appeals followed the reasoning adopted in *Broadbent*[28] and concluded that it did not have jurisdiction to entertain Mendaro's action. It can be observed here that the plaintiff had not filed a complaint with the Administrative Tribunal of the World Bank, as pointed out by the Court.[29] This is a right belonging to any staff member.[30]

The decision in *Morgan* does not mention the Administrative Tribunal. This is no doubt due to the status of the claimant, because the appeal procedure to the Administrative Tribunal, in the World Bank as in other organizations, is open only to staff members, namely to officials whose employment is governed by the Organization's staff rules. The Court says in *Morgan* that he "had been assigned for a substantial period as a regular World Bank Staff member." But a few sentences later it reads: ". . . the fact that Morgan is not in all respects formally an employee of the Bank

---

27 Mendaro v. World Bank, 230 U.S. App. D.C. 333, 717 F. 2d 610 (D.C. Cir. 1983).

28 ". . . the same issues and principles are involved here and under the rationale of Broadbent." *Ibid.* at III.

29 "This plaintiff had another recourse, that was to file a complaint with the Administrative Tribunal. She was specifically informed of that right by the Bank." *Ibid.* at II.

30 *See* Statute of the Administrative Tribunal of the IBRD, International Development Association, and International Finance Corporation, art. II. *See also* C.F. AMERASINGHE, THE LAW OF THE INTERNATIONAL CIVIL SERVICE, VOL. II (2nd ed. 1994), Chapter Nine (*Principles of Staff Employment of the World Bank*), at 511.

but serves on detail from his agency is of no legal consequence." The conclusion is that Morgan was not a staff member. He had another type of status and was not entitled to the appeal procedure leading to the Administrative Tribunal.[31]

That difference with the *Broadbent* and *Mendaro* cases is of importance in respect of immunity. It is a common practice of practically all organizations to have locally recruited employees, assigned generally to minor tasks. These employees are not international civil servants; their contractual relationship with the organization is, in most cases, governed by domestic law.

In this regard, some analogy may be drawn with State accredited diplomatic missions. The members of the missions are civil servants of the sending State, whose status is defined by the laws of that State. But there may be locally recruited personnel, with contracts governed by local law. This can be seen in the case law of some of the countries which have adopted the restrictive doctrine of immunity from jurisdiction, where labor relations of the locally recruited employees of foreign embassies are considered to be *acta iure gestionis* and fall under the exception to immunity, but the practice is particularly heterogeneous.[32]

Concerning the immunity of international organizations, there are strong arguments for affirming that employment-related law suits of international civil servants (staff members) against their organization belong entirely to the internal sphere of the organization. Consequently, there is incompetence of the forum *ratione materiae*.[33] This is not the same as immunity from jurisdiction *stricto sensu*. In *Broadbent*, the question had been raised,[34] but the Court preferred to decide on the basis of immunity from jurisdiction. It was easier. However, the difference is important be-

---

31 For staff members, administrative tribunals may hear complaints such as those of Morgan, *see* Eben-Moussi v. WHO, International Labour Organisation's Administrative Tribunal (ILOAT) Judgment No. 1619 (1997); Fahmy No. 3 v. UNIDO, ILOAT Judgment No. 1637 (1997).

32 *See* H. Fox, *Employment Contracts as an Exception to State Immunity: Is all Public Service Immune?*, LXVI British Yearbook of International Law 97 (1995); W. Gloor, Employer States and Sovereign Immunity (1999).

33 In the same way, if a diplomat would attempt to bring a complaint concerning his employment against his sending State before a court of the receiving State, that court ought to declare that there is lack of jurisdiction.

34 Broadbent, 628 F.2d, at 29 (Part II A).

cause in the case of immunity, there can be a waiver,[35] whereas in the case of lack of jurisdiction the question of waiver is not relevant. In *Morgan,* the Court was facing a case where immunity proper was at stake, because the employment relationship was not such as to imply lack of jurisdiction. It is precisely when there is immunity that the issue of the right of access to a Court may arise.

IV. THE ISSUE OF HUMAN RIGHTS

Recently, the question of the conflict between immunity from jurisdiction and human rights has arisen. More precisely, it is argued that to oppose immunity to a claimant is a breach of the latter's "right to his/her day in court" (access to a tribunal). The breach is committed by a court and leads to the international responsibility of the State of which it is an organ. The argument is that every State bound to give effect to that fundamental right should not tolerate that a claimant be deprived of his right to a judge. Consequently, immunity should not be granted when the claimant is not offered a fair procedure for presenting his claim.

In relation to international organizations, the question has been raised both before some national courts, and before the European Court of Human Rights.[36] For example, in an employment-related case between a locally recruited employee and the permanent Delegation of the Arab League in Geneva, the Swiss Federal Tribunal confirmed the decisions of the lower labor Courts which recognized the immunity of the Arab League, but expressly stated that immunity should not be granted in a particular case if no procedure is available to the claimant.[37] In that case

---

35 *See* Lutcher S.A. Celulose e Papel v. Inter-American Development Bank, 127 U.S. App. D.C. 238, 382 F.2d 454 (D.C. Cir. 1967).

36 The only human right which is considered here is the right of access to a court. Immunity as a procedural right may conflict with it. The approach is thus different from that of Singer (*supra* note 4), who, commenting on *Morgan,* says that the officials of the World Bank had acted in a way contrary to human rights and that this was a reason for denying immunity. This, however, concerns the merits of the dispute between *Morgan* and the Bank.

37 *See* Malek, *supra* note 23.

the claimant had the possibility of bringing his claim before the Administrative Tribunal of the League in Cairo.[38]

In a case against UNESCO, the plaintiff indicated that he had an arbitration clause in a contract with that Organization, which however refused to cooperate with the arbitral procedure. The Cour d'Appel de Paris decided that UNESCO could not rely on the immunity from jurisdiction, as provided for by the Headquarters Agreement, to oppose the designation of an arbitrator by the French judge.[39] The main argument has been that to recognize immunity in such a case would constitute a breach of Article 6 of the European Convention on Human Rights and Fundamental Freedoms (European Convention).[40]

On the international level, the European Court of Human Rights in Strasbourg had to deal with cases brought by former employees of the European Space Agency (ESA) in Darmstadt, Germany.[41] The German courts had dismissed their claims on the basis of the immunity from jurisdiction granted to the ESA by its Headquarters Agreement. The complaint before the European Court was against Germany for breach — by its courts — of Article 6 of the European Convention. The complaint was dismissed by the Court on the ground that, according to the judgment, the employees could have resorted to a specific procedure within the ESA. Such decisions imply that, failing an alternative procedure, immunity must be set aside in order to avoid a denial of justice (breach of Article 6 of the European Convention).

---

[38] Several similar cases have been brought before the "tribunal des prud'hommes" of Geneva against the League of Arab States. The decisions were the same as in Malek.

[39] *See* Boulois v. UNESCO, Cour d'appel de Paris, 19 juin 1998, REVUE DE L'ARBITRAGE 343 (1999).

[40] European Convention for the Protection of Human Rights and Fundamental Freedoms [hereinafter European Convention], Nov. 4, 1950, art. 6, 213 U.N.T.S. 221 ("(1) In the determination of his civil rights and obligations or of any criminal charge against him, everyone is entitled to a fair and public hearing within a reasonable time by an independent and impartial tribunal established by law. . . .").

[41] *See* Richard Waite and Terry Kennedy v. Germany; Beer and Regan v. Germany. Both cases were brought before the former European Commission of Human Rights and then before the European Court, which issued two similar Judgements on February 18, 1999 (No. 26083/94 and 28934/95), 93 AMERICAN JOURNAL OF INTERNATIONAL LAW 933 (1999).

In *Morgan,* immunity was granted on the basis of municipal law (IOIA and FSIA). When in such a case, there is a conflict with a rule of international law, the latter must prevail. However, in most countries immunity from jurisdiction is granted to an international organization by a rule of international law, in general a provision of the Headquarters Agreement. The conflict which may arise is between two rules of international law. The assumption is, of course, that there exists a rule of international law which recognizes the right of a person to have access to court, and that that specific rule must be given primacy over other rules of international law, here the rule of immunity from jurisdiction of the international organization.

Today, there are good arguments for affirming that the most important human rights obligations apply as customary international law and that they may be among those which can be described as *erga omnes.*[42] The right of access to court is one of those fundamental rights which has become part of customary international law. It is provided for in Article 10 of the Universal Declaration of Human Rights,[43] and also in the various conventions for the protection of human rights, which have been broadly ratified.[44] The process by which rules such as those which protect human rights become customary rules is slightly different from the usual process of creation of custom, the reason being that they incorporate a strong ethical value.[45]

---

[42] *See* 1 OPPENHEIM'S INTERNATIONAL LAW 1000 (Sir Robert Jennings & Sir Arthur Watts eds., 9th ed. 1992); T. MERON, HUMAN RIGHTS AND HUMANITARIAN NORMS AS CUSTOMARY LAW 79 (1989).

[43] Universal Declaration of Human Rights, art. 10, G.A. Res. 217A(III), U.N. Doc. A/810 (1948) ("Everyone is entitled in full equality to a fair and public hearing by an independent and impartial tribunal, in the determination of his rights and obligations and of any criminal charge against him").

[44] *See* UN Covenant on Civil and Political Rights, art. 14, *adopted* Dec. 16, 1966, *entered into force* Mar. 23, 1976, G.A. Res. 2200, 21 U.N. GAOR Supp. (No. 16) at 52, U.N. Doc. A/6316 (1966); European Convention, *see supra,* note 40, art. 6; Inter-American Convention on Human Rights, art. 8, Nov. 22, 1969, O.A.S. Treaty Series No. 36, at 1, Doc. OEA/Ser. L./V/II. 23 doc. Rev.2; African [Banjul] Charter on Human and Peoples' Rights, art. 7, adopted June 27, 1981, OAU Doc. CAB/LEG/67/3 rev. 5, 21 INTERNATIONAL LEGAL MATERIALS (I.L.M.) 58 (1982) (entered into force Oct. 21, 1986).

[45] *See* Ch. Dominicé, *Le grand retour du droit naturel en droit des gens,* in MÉLANGES EN L'HONNEUR DE JACQUES-MICHEL GROSSEN 399 (Faculté de droit de Neuchâtel ed., 1992).

In a conflict between the rule of immunity, even if it is a rule of international law, and the right of access to court, the latter must prevail, according to principles which deserve some attention. In my opinion, rules *erga omnes* and rules of *jus cogens* are the same rules.[46] The first notion puts emphasis upon the effect of the rule in relations between States, whereas the second expression relates primarily to the nature of the rule. According to article 53 of the Vienna Convention on the Law of Treaties of 1969, a treaty is void if, at the time of its conclusion, it conflicts with a peremptory norm of general international law. However, *jus cogens* is a notion which does not belong merely to the international law of treaties. A rule of *jus cogens* may have various types of effects. For example, in cases of extradition, the Swiss Federal Tribunal, in a situation where it should have applied a bilateral treaty of extradition, refused in several decisions to grant extradition to the requesting State, the reason being that the individual concerned would be exposed to torture or inhuman treatment.[47] This would be contrary to *jus cogens*. In none of those cases, of course, was the extradition treaty held to be void, but it was considered that to apply it in a particular case would be contrary to *jus cogens*.

Mutatis mutandis, this type of reasoning could be followed in a conflict between immunity and the right of access to a court. If the international organization concerned enjoys immunity, the judge has to examine if the claimant is offered a fair procedure as an alternative to the normal lawsuit before the national judge. If not, the court must set aside the rule granting immunity, in order to give effect to the fundamental right of access to a judge. The trend is in that direction.[48]

It must be added here that the time has come for the main international organizations to institute fair procedures for private claimants. It is an obligation which is stipulated in almost every

---

[46] *See* B. Simma, *From Bilateralism to Community Interest in International Law,* No. 4 RECUEIL DES COURS DE L'ACADEMIE DE DROIT INTERNATIONAL 250, 300 (1994) ("... *ius cogens* and obligations *erga omnes* are but two sides of one and the same coin").

[47] *See* Ch. Dominicé & F. Voeffray, *Suisse,* in THE INTEGRATION OF INTERNATIONAL AND EUROPEAN COMMUNITY LAW INTO THE NATIONAL LEGAL ORDER 494, 562, *supra* note 18; *see also, Judgement of the Swiss Federal Tribunal, Case F., 10 July 1991,* REVUE SUISSE DE DROIT INTERNATIONAL ET DE DROIT EUROPÉEN 552 (1992).

[48] *See* Malek, *supra* note 23; Boulois, *supra* note 39; Waite, *supra* note 41.

headquarters agreement, and of course in the most important conventions on privileges and immunities.[49] With some exceptions what has been done so far is not satisfactory.[50] The example of the Administrative Tribunals could be followed.

V. CONCLUSIONS

A most important question is: if a *Morgan*-type case was to be decided in year 2000, ten years later, what would be the decision? One important change has occurred in the last few years: The right of access to court, as a fundamental right that may be contrary to immunity from jurisdiction has attracted growing concern. Some indications are already to be found in the case law of both national and international courts. It is with regard to this human rights concern that the *Morgan* case has to be reconsidered. Other points that have been discussed here may also be briefly summarized.

Since Morgan was not a member of the staff, with the status of an international civil servant, the reference to *Broadbent* and *Mendaro* was not quite appropriate. However, the point at issue was the question of immunity of the World Bank. It was decided on the basis of the US law (IOIA and FSIA) and immunity from jurisdiction was recognized. The same conclusion could have been reached under international law: this means that to deny immunity would have been a breach of international law, but for the human rights exception.

The basis for immunity is the waiver provision of Article VII, Section 3, of the World Bank's Articles of Agreement. As the District Court rightly observed, the waiver is restricted to the financial/capital investment operations of the Bank. Therefore, if there is a waiver of limited scope, the conclusion is that, except for that waiver, there is immunity. Although controversial,[51] it can furthermore be said that for the important international organizations,

---

49 *See* Convention on the Privileges and Immunities of the United Nations, Feb. 13, 1946, 21 UST 1418, 1 UNTS 17, Sec. 29; Convention on the Privileges and Immunities of the Specialized Agencies, approved by the General Assembly Nov. 21, 1947, 33 UNTS 263, Sec. 31.

50 *See* P. KLEIN, LA RESPONSABILITÉ DES ORGANISATIONS INTERNATIONALES 247 (1998).

51 *See supra*, notes 23 and 24.

particularly those of the UN system, immunity from jurisdiction is now granted under customary international law.

Considering that, in *Morgan,* it was right to recognize the immunity of the Bank, the question is now whether it should be set aside for human rights reasons. There is a clear conflict, in a "*Morgan*-type" case, between immunity and the right of access to Court. In *Broadbent* and *Mendaro* — apart from the fact that there was lack of jurisdiction (incompetence of the forum *ratione materiae)* — the claimants could avail themselves of the procedure and appeal leading to the Administrative Tribunal. There was no case of denial of justice.

In a new *Morgan* case, the Court should note that the claimant is not offered any fair procedure for presenting his claims and decide that, although the Bank enjoys immunity from jurisdiction, it ought to be set aside in that particular case. This is clearly one consequence of that extraordinary evolution, over the last fifty years or so, which aims at giving more respect to the human being.

THE CONTRIBUTION OF IBRAHIM SHIHATA AS SCHOLAR TO THE DEBATES OF *L'INSTITUT DE DROIT INTERNATIONAL* DURING THE LAST DECADE

Ahmed S. El-Kosheri

Since his election during the Helsinki Session of 1985, Dr. Ibrahim Shihata participated actively in the academic activities of *L'Institut de Droit International,* manifesting his scholarly qualities as a distinguished international law specialist.

This was the case when he expressed — *inter alia* — his opinion about the difficulty of classifying the UN General Assembly resolutions into "Law-declaring" and "Law-making" resolutions,[1] about the danger of making reference to "vague concepts which give unlimited discretion to arbitrators"[2] in arbitration between States and foreign enterprises, as well as with regard to the issue of the autonomy of private parties in the choice of the applicable law when he emphasized that the national courts have only to respect the choice by the parties to the extent that it "was based on *bona fides* and the law was not in breach of the public policy provisions of the law of the forum."[3]

A detailed analysis of all contributions by Dr. Shihata enriching the debates of *L'Institut* would require a lengthy study. Hence, it is more appropriate, within the limits of the present paper, to

1 Ibrahim F. I. Shihata, 62 ANNUAIRE DE L'INSTITUT DE DROIT INTERNATIONAL (SESSION DE CAIRO), Part II (1987), at 91 *et seq*.

2 Ibrahim F. I. Shihata, 63 ANNUAIRE DE L'INSTITUT DE DROIT INTERNATIONAL (SESSION DE SANTIAGO DE COMPOSTELLA), Part II (1990), at 171 *et seq*.

3 Ibrahim F. I. Shihata, 64 ANNUAIRE DE L'INSTITUT DE DROIT INTERNATIONAL (SESSION DE BASEL), Part II (1991), at 145–146.

focus on three specific subjects which illustrate the magnitude of his ability as a scholar and the diversity of the domains he masters.

The first subject relates to the "[o]bligations of a company belonging to an international group and their effect on other companies of that group." In response to the questions raised by the Rapporteur, Dr. Shihata provided an extensive study accompanied with eight annexes which cover forty pages.[4]

The learned scholar started by indicating that the concept of corporate group revolves around the "centralization of decision-making authority" factor, rather than around the element of common ownership. According to him, this concept is close to the concept of "control" adopted in national legal systems, and if the majority ownership may be a *prima facie* evidence of control, there are situations in which control will still exist despite the absence of majority ownership."[5] "This is particularly the case in many of the so-called 'new forms of investments'; i.e. investment projects where the foreign investor holds no or little equity but nevertheless exercises demonstrable powers over the projects through contractual arrangements (e.g., through licensing agreements, management contracts, franchising, production sharing, risk-service contracts, product-in-hand contracts, etc.). In such instances, while majority equity is absent, control can still flow from other factors, such as appointment of managers and retention of power over major policies, operational decisions, competitive technology or marketing."[6]

The relevance of the said control with regard to the liability of the group as a whole is illustrated by the two groups of cases reported by Dr. Shihata in Annex 8, which are the *Swift v. Esperenza* Argentinean court decisions and the *Bhopal v. Union Carbide* cases in both New York and India where an amicable settlement took place.

Dr. Shihata's analysis of the reasons behind the recourse by a parent enterprise to the creation of a large chain of subsidiaries

---

4 Ibrahim F.I. Shihata, 65 ANNUAIRE DE L'INSTITUT DE DROIT INTERNATIONAL (SESSION DE MILAN), Part I (1993), at 195–235.

5 *Ibid.* at 196.

6 *Ibid.* at 197.

worldwide led him to formulate the following three important observations:

(i) "Subsidiaries are often created with a view to carrying out activities that are forbidden for the parent or that would be *ultra vires* if done directly by it. National legal systems do not seem to yield a general rule to the effect that the parent must transpose to the subsidiary the legal restrictions which affect its operations;"

(ii) "[A]ffiliates are not to be used in bad faith to circumvent the application of otherwise binding requirements of applicable laws;"

(iii) "[T]he parent's desire for insulation from liabilities that might be incurred while entering into various business transactions in foreign countries — thereby limiting its losses to the assets in the subsidiary — has been found a sufficient business purpose for forming the subsidiary abroad and legitimizing the tax avoidance advantages derived therefrom."[7]

With regard to the scope of the jurisdiction of national courts over members of the group located outside that territory, Dr. Shihata attracted the attention to the example provided under Article 25 of the ICSID (International Centre for the Settlement of Investment Disputes) Convention as "a criterion which can be used to extend jurisdictions over an investor who may seem otherwise to fall outside the scope of this jurisdiction."[8]

In commenting on an ICSID arbitration case, Dr. Shihata noted, within a different context, that "the legal significance that can be given by an international arbitral tribunal to the 'developing' stage of the law of a country in partnership with a multinational group." He interpreted the first award rendered in the said case as implicitly adopting a "principle of international law of development according to which an industrialized country enterprise has a more stringent duty of good faith and disclosure towards its less sophisticated developing country partner than

---

7 *Ibid.* at 200.

8 *Ibid.* at 203.

would be the case if its contracting partner were a developed country." He added: "The language of the award recognized implicitly the differential legal connotations that can be attached to operations taking place in a developing country."[9] Dr. Shihata continued by indicating that the said award "was annulled *in toto,* on the grounds that in reaching the above-mentioned conclusion the tribunal was found to have applied equity rather than the proper law."[10] In Dr. Shihata's opinion, the second tribunal constituted in the case "did not pronounce on the existence of the principle of international law of development . . . , since it considered that the national law applies to the dispute provided a sufficient basis of decision."[11]

The second subject to which Dr. Shihata devoted considerable attention concerns "the legal consequences for member States of the non-fulfillment by international organizations of their obligations toward third parties." In responding to the Rapporteur's questions, Dr. Shihata was keen to emphasize in four successive communications the following crucial rules:

(i) "In case member States confer international legal personality on the organization, the latter will have such a personality *vis-à-vis* its members (and other parties who recognize it as such) even if the activities of the organization are *jure gentionis.* This has been the case for many economic joint ventures."[12] However, in Dr. Shihata's opinion, the legal personality conferred by member States on an international organization should not be considered of *erga omnes* application, since he believes "that it would be more realistic to limit this to the member States which recognize such personality, expressly or through dealings with the international organization as a separate entity."[13]

(ii) "There is no established rule of customary international law which states *in the abstract* whether and to what ex-

---

9 *Ibid.* at 205.

10 *Ibid.*

11 *Ibid.* at 206.

12 Ibrahim F. I. Shihata, 66 ANNUAIRE DE L'INSTITUT DE DROIT INTERNATIONAL (SESSION DE LISBONNE), Part I (1995), at 291.

13 *Ibid.* at 425.

tent member States are directly liable for the acts or missions of an international organization."[14]

(iii) "Generally speaking, a member State may be held separately liable for its behavior related to an international organization to the extent that such behavior is in violation of an established international law obligation."[15]

In application of the above-stated rules, Dr. Shihata envisaged a number of concrete situations that could emerge in practice, such as the non-responsibility of the State for acts of an official of the organization, even when the person in question is appointed by such a State and participates in decision-making organs of the organization. Equally, the liability of member States has to be based on the provisions of the organization's constitutive and other relevant instruments.[16]

Based on his long experience as General Counsel of the World Bank, Dr. Shihata formulated a number of useful guidelines as demonstrated by the following propositions:

(a) "Where members of the governing bodies of the organization are considered" officials of the organization (as in the case of the IBRD and most other international financial institutions), "the actions of such officials (in the decision-making process) will be attributed to the organization, not to their states;"

(b) "[T]he State cannot normally be liable for the acts of the organization merely as a result of voting in favor of such acts in the appropriate forum as long as such voting is a legally valid act under the organization's charter;"

(c) "A State may be liable, however, if it causes or supports an action which is in violation of general international law or the organization's charter. The basis of such liability would be the State's fault, rather than the organization's own action;"

(d) "The unlimited liability of member States for the acts of the organization cannot be assumed as a general principle

14 *Ibid.* at 291.

15 *Ibid.*

16 *Ibid.* at 291–292.

of international law: it has to be established on the basis of the charter and the practice of the organization involved;"

(e) "There is a preliminary presumption that international organizations, being separate legal persons, are solely liable for their acts. In the absence of a clear evidence to the contrary, a member State is not liable for the act of the organization regardless of whether the alleged liability is based on contract or tort;" and

(f) As supported by Annexes prepared by World Bank lawyers and submitted by Dr. Shihata with regard to the experiences of the League of Nations and of the East African Community's joint enterprises, the general rule is that in cases of dissolution and liquidations the "claims of the organization's creditors will be satisfied through the assets of the organization, with no residual responsibility on the part of the members."[17]

The third subject to which the eminent scholar devoted particular attention relates to the Law of Environment. Even before receiving the questions of the Rapporteur, Dr. Shihata stressed the importance of reinforcing the preventive function of state responsibility, the need to control the environmental activities of multinational corporations, the issue of criminal responsibility of the operators, as well as the protection of the areas beyond the limits of national jurisdiction which remain to a great extent unregulated when it comes to preventing and restoring environmental degradation.[18]

Within the context of liability for environmental degradation resulting from private activities, Dr. Shihata emphasized, *inter alia,* the relevance of the distinction between:

(i) "the responsibility or liability of the operator (whether or not it is based on fault or negligence);" and

---

[17] *Ibid.* at 311–313.

[18] Ibrahim F. I. Shihata, 67 ANNUAIRE DE L'INSTITUT DE DROIT INTERNATIONAL (SESSION DE STRASBOURG), Part I (1997), at 235–236.

(ii) "the responsibility or liability of the State of the operator (mainly for not taking adequate measures to prevent the operator from harming the environment)."[19]

He stressed later that "the operators' civil liability and state liability should not be seen as mutually exclusive, but rather as complementary."[20]

Dr. Shihata also indicated that due to "the irreversible nature of environmental damages," compensation "while possibly adequate for the present victims, cannot be an adequate remedy for the environment itself. Punitive damages may therefore help as a greater deterrent. They should also assist in financing remedial actions."[21]

At the same time, Dr. Shihata demonstrated how to reconcile the apparent "conflicts of interest" between sovereignty, culture and economic developments in environmental issues, by stating:

> "Complementarity between cultural, economic and environmental concerns should be achieved to assure culturally and environmentally sustainable development. Law has an important role in reconciling these concerns and allowing them to interact in a mutually re-enforcing manner, taking account also of the political realities in the society addressed by it, whether this society is domestic or international."[22]

In concrete terms, Dr. Shihata proposed certain measures, among which it seems important to mention the following:

(a) "The State which has control over the environmentally damaging activities of the multinational corporation should have jurisdiction over such corporation. International conventions addressing operators' liability can identify the responsible parties, the applicable rules and the methods of Settlement of disputes."[23]

---

19 *Ibid.* at 272.

20 *Ibid.* at 275.

21 *Ibid.* at 273.

22 *Ibid.* at 274.

23 *Ibid.* at 275.

(b) "The need for introducing adequate safeguards to reduce as much as possible environmental degradation is a matter of international public policy which must be addressed both in international environmental law and international aid efforts."[24]

(c) "Ideally, only an international organization with an agreed upon mandate should take up claims at the international level on behalf of the environment, in which case an international fund would receive the compensation and use it for rehabilitation and conservation purposes;" and

(d) "A standing World Environmental Court may not be needed at this stage. If the chamber for environmental disputes of the ICJ is not deemed adequate or sufficiently specialized for environmental disputes among States, a facility for the international arbitration or adjudication of these disputes as well as of disputes between States and operators could be established following the systems of the International Court of Arbitration or ICSID, i.e., by having a list of potential arbitrators or judges to be drawn upon when needed and a small secretariat to serve it."[25]

Finally, it may be appropriate to conclude with an observation about Dr. Shihata's deeply rooted attachment to his home legal traditions, as witnessed by his reference within the context of environmental protection to "the principles of Islamic law established since the seventh century." This law assumes that man, being the "steward of God" on earth, is under an obligation "not to corrupt the earth." From this general obligation, many subsidiary obligations ensue, including obligations with respect to the protection of water sources, land reserves, reclamation of land, treatment of animals and plants, etc. The liability resulting from non-compliance with these obligations is not always based on private damage suffered by a specific party.[26]

---

24 *Ibid.* at 276.

25 *Ibid.* at 279.

26 *Ibid.* at 276–277.

SWALLOWING INJUSTICE TO BUILD COMMUNITY: LATIN AMERICA AFTER THE ERA OF STATE TERROR*

Tom J. Farer

I. INTRODUCTION

From the mid-1960's to the late 1980's (even later in certain countries), militarized governments in most of Latin America enforced their view of a desirable public order by terrorizing great numbers of citizens who happened to have different views, and also their friends and relations and persons who, whatever their views or lack thereof, and objected them to terror as a means of governing. One Argentine general put the matter with admirable brevity. "First we will kill all the subversives," he said. "Then we will kill their collaborators, then their sympathizers, then those who remain indifferent and finally the indecisive."[1] To be sure, even many of his fellow senior officers and some of the civilians who supported them thought the General's views a bit excessive, requiring as they would a rather sharp contraction in the Argentine population. But Argentina is a sophisticated sort of place where people pride themselves on their urbanity. Had he spoken at a plantation-owner's dinner or in the officer's club in a country like

---

* This contribution to the Liber Amicorum for Ibrahim F.I. Shihata is based on a lecture delivered at the Institute of International Studies of the University of California, Berkeley, on April 20, 2000 as part of the Rockefeller Foundation series. The author wishes to thank Harry Kreisler, Director of the Institute, and his colleagues for their gracious hospitality on the occasion of his lecturing at Berkeley.

1 Various persons interviewed by the Inter-American Commission on Human Rights during its on-site visit to Argentina in September 1979 cited the statement attributed to General Saint Jean.

Guatemala, where those who rule live closer to the bone, his remarks would have been unremarkable, hardly more than a gratuitous restatement of conventional wisdom.

As is always the case, local circumstances color the ideas and methods of like-minded people. As the former's heirs are quick to remind us, Mussolini's Italian fascism was not identical with Hitler's German Naziism. Variations on a theme doubtless matter. Mussolini and friends killed far fewer people and not only, one supposes, because they were less competent. As a percentage of the population, far fewer Chileans died at the hands of Augusto Pinochet and his merry men than Salvadorans at the hands of the armed forces and their paramilitary allies.[2] The Uruguayans had a bias in favor of detention and torture followed by psychological annihilation.[3] The Argentines preferred the physical sort.[4]

For all their possibly interesting variations, terror states had a number of things in common, and prominent among them was the withdrawal of immunity from the middle and upper classes. In less affluent times, it used to be said (perhaps first by Abraham Lincoln) that God must love the poor because he had made so many of them. There are many of them in Latin America, but other signs of God's love have long been missing. Independence from Spain in the early nineteenth century did not make life conspicu-

---

[2] Chile's Truth Commission concluded that 4,000 people were killed or disappeared during Pinochet's rule (*Report of the Chilean National Truth and Reconciliation Commission, May 1991*), while in contrast, more than 70,000 in political violence in El Salvador during the 1980s when the US sponsored military and paramilitary death squads wantonly killed their fellow citizens. Marjorie Miller, *A Rush to Judgment on Duarte of El Salvador*, LA TIMES, June 19, 1988, at E2.

[3] Beginning in the 1960s, the government of Uruguay engaged in a reign of terror as part of its efforts to repress the Movement for National Liberation, otherwise known as Tupamaros. The military used torture as a method of breaking wider society by engendering fear in the general population. As a result, between 300,000 and 400,000 of Uruguay's 3 million people went into exile and one in every 50 of those remaining was detained for interrogation or imprisoned. LAWRENCE WESCHLER, A MIRACLE, A UNIVERSE 88-89 (1990).

[4] The Argentinean truth commission revealed that the military government — which ruled from 1976 to 1983 — systematically tortured, murdered, and disappeared almost 9,000 Argentine citizens. Finally, the military executed many of the disappeared by dropping them from airplanes over the ocean, so that their bodies would never be found. *Commission Nacional Sobre la Desaparicion de Personas, Nunca Mas* [National Commission on the Disappearance of Persons, Never Again] (Universitaria de Buenos Aires, 4th ed. 1984), at 235-36 & 479.

ously less nasty for the Latin poor any more than the Universal Declaration of Human Rights did in the middle of the twentieth. Towers of affluence continued to grow on their backs. They populated the prisons and hungered in the plains, strangers as much to due process as to the welfare state. Whether under the regime of tweedle-de-and-dum political parties or old-fashioned autocrats, they lived at the mercy of a state able at will to license the powerful or itself to beat, steal, starve, incarcerate and kill. The picture of the lives of ordinary citizens implied by the long lists of human rights embedded in national constitutions connected with reality, however loosely, only for members of the comfortable classes. Velasquez was the appropriate portraitist for the upper classes and perhaps Renoir for the middle. For the rest — Goya. But in the time of state terror, Goya would have found rich material in all classes, for ideological wars are great levelers.

In the name of Western civilization, governments in most of Latin America made the world unsafe for everyone, regardless of class, everyone, that is, who found fault with the goals and practices of governments or with the private interests they served or, as may happen when the dogs of terror are unleashed, who managed to offend some member of the apparatus of repression. Such was the fate of one suave Argentine diplomat, briefly home on leave, plucked one day out of his car on a Buenos Aires boulevard, by anonymous men in unlicensed vehicles, and never seen again. His widow, as by then she must have been, finally managed a meeting with President Videla, the retired General chosen by his colleagues to serve as head of state, a social acquaintance of the woman. "Please help me find my husband," she pleaded. Imperially slim, his long body twisting in apparent discomfort, Videla replies, by implication denying nothing: "In this matter, I am absolutely impotent."[5]

In the early 1980's, as the slaughter intensified in Central America, with the avid support of the Reagan Administration,[6] re-

---

5 Confidential communication from a trustworthy informant made to the author during his participation in the on-site observation of the Inter-American Commission on Human Rights in Argentina during September 1979.

6 *See, e.g.*, The Massacre at El Mozote 110-140 (1993) (Mark Danner's account of its reaction to the now confirmed massacre at El Mizote in Danner); or UN Ambassador Jean Kirkpatrick's efforts to mitigate or exculpate the rape-murder of four churchwomen by members of the Salvadoran armed forces, claiming "They were not

pression began to ease in much of South America, most notably in Brazil and, above all, in Argentina where, following its abortive effort to wrest the Malvinas or Falkland Islands from Great Britain, the military withdrew in disarray from the heights of political power.[7] In Chile, however, once the Latin American exemplar of stable democratic government, the military regime directed by Augusto Pinochet and supported by the upper classes maintained a harsh grip on civil society virtually to the end of the decade.[8] So the restoration in Chile of a political order compatible with at least minimalist conceptions of human rights roughly coincided with the initiation of peace processes in Central America made possible by the end of the Cold War and the subsequent collapse of the Soviet Union.

Before the era of state terror, one feature of the Latin left — and not only of the Marxist revolutionaries within it — was a tendency to devalue the importance of civil and political rights or at least of the power diffusing and often lumbering constitutional restraints and administrative procedures that liberals deem essential means for protecting those rights.[9] Arresting inequalities and a long experience of state structures effectively colonized by the wealthy classes encouraged the view that the institutions and methods of liberal democracy were primarily instruments to inhibit the exercise of popular power on behalf of justice. At best they were luxuries not affordable until deep inequalities of opportunity and result had been addressed.

---

just nuns, they were political activists;" *See also* Charles Austin, *Maryknollers Pursue Risky Paths in the Third World*, N.Y. TIMES, June 21, 1981, Section 4, Page 9, Column 1.

7 *See* Geoffrey P. Miller, *Constitutional Moments, Precommitment, and Fundamental Reform: The Case of Argentina*, 71 WASHINGTON UNIVERSITY LAW QUARTERLY 1061, 1070-72 (1993); MARTIN E. ANDERSEN, DOSSIER SECRETO: THE MYTH OF ARGENTINA'S "DIRTY WAR" 299-301 (1993). One thousand Argentine compared with 250 British lives were lost during Argentina's failed attempt to wrest the islands from British control.

8 Pinochet ruled Chile for 17 years from the 1973 coup that overthrew the Allende government until Patricio Alywin was voted into power in the December 1989 presidential elections, following a plebiscite in which 54.7percent of the people voting said "no" to continued military rule. Edward C. Snyder, *The Dirty Legal War: War Human Rights and the Rule of Law in Chile 1973-1995*, 2 TULSA JOURNAL OF COMPARATIVE & INTERNATINAL LAW, Spring 1995, at 253

9 *See* TOM FARER, THE GRAND STRATEGY OF THE UNITED STATES IN LATIN AMERICA, Ch. 4 (1988).

If the terror regimes accomplished nothing else, they contributed to an adjustment of this attitude. Leftist intellectuals and political leaders who experienced unrestrained state power, albeit employed to maintain rather than reform the social order, discovered in hiding, exile or prison the real value of institutionalized restraints. One result was a pronounced tendency toward convergence in the value priorities of centrist and leftist political parties, helped along, of course, by the public autopsy performed on dead Marxist governments in the Soviet block which exposed the long accumulation of their internal rot. And although they did not attend the school of electrical shock, while terror served their ends, by the end of the period some part of the traditional political right — no longer united by the petrifying fear of revolution — also began moving to embrace liberal constitutionalist government with all its implicit compromises — agreeably constrained, to be sure, on questions involving the allocation of income, wealth and power. Changes in the calculus of value and interest internal to Latin countries coincided, of course, with Washington's calculation that US interests in the post Cold-War era were best served by moving from a rhetorical to a substantive policy of democracy promotion, a policy that had among its several virtues the reduction of cognitive dissonance in the practice and discourse of American foreign policy.[10]

The condition precedent to promoting democracy in polarized and war-ravaged Central America was peace building, a complex project initially of cease fire, security guarantees, demobilization, integration of combatants, resettlement of displaced persons and development of understandings about at least the outline of post-war institutions and policies and the terms on which peaceful political competition would be waged.[11] In the southern cone of Latin America, where military governments had quickly shattered the spine of armed opposition, peace of a kind existed, but democracy (much less its consolidation) awaited a measure of reconciliation and a degree of consensus on the means and limits of electoral politics.

---

[10] *See, e.g.*, G. John Ikenberry, *Why Export Democracy?: The 'Hidden Grand Strategy' of American Foreign Policy*, 23 THE WILSON QUARTERLY, No. 2 (Spring 1999).

[11] For an examination of the relationship between democracy and the peace building process, *see* LUC REYCHLER, DEMOCRATIC PEACE BUILDING AND CONFLICT PREVENTION, THE DEVIL IS IN THE TRANSITION (1999).

Whether in Central or South America, one widely but not universally accepted condition for advancing the democratic project was to face openly and in some way to redress the crimes and sins of the dictatorships. Peace and democracy, in other words, demanded some accounting, some measure of justice. But if justice was a necessity, so also, many people felt, it was a threat. For in no case was it clear just how much justice each fragile process of democratization could bear. Few imagined that anything approaching full justice could be done. The villains, after all, were not in chains and, quite apart from their commitment to self-defense, did not in most cases seem disposed to regard themselves as villains. That irrepressible enthusiast for tea with Mrs. Thatcher, General Pinochet, put the military view most publicly and succinctly when, on the eve of Chile's first free elections since his 1973 coup, he declared: "The day they touch one of my men, the rule of law ends. This I say once and will not say again."[12]

In Central America, doing justice could mean more than punishing those who had murdered and tortured in the name of the state and Western civilization, that all-purpose moral solvent. People had originally opposed the established order and thereby exposed themselves to the terror in a desperate effort to mitigate the structural injustice of mortal poverty and quotidian humiliation, either their own or of people with whom they sympathized. So at least for some who demanded justice as part of peace building in Central America, justice meant not only the punishment of criminals but also some positive action to alleviate the conditions that had led in the first place to war; that is, in the words of the Nobel Laureate Amartya Sen,[13] to increase the life chances of the general population.

I intend to look at two countries — Argentina and Guatemala — and in relation to them attempt two things. One is to recall, as vividly as I can, the crimes crying out for exposure, condemnation and restitution. For memory fades, one crime begins to blend into another until it becomes lost in a tranquilized undifferentiated sense, not even a memory any more, that bad things have happened in the course of the human adventure. The

---

[12] *See* Tina Rosenberg, *Overcoming the Legacies of Dictatorship,* 74 Foreign Affairs, Iss. 3 at 134 (1995).

[13] AMARTYA KUMAR SEN, DEVELOPMENT AS FREEDOM (1999).

other is to sketch the outcome of the efforts in these countries to address past injustices in the course of processes aiming to construct or consolidate a liberal capitalist order.

II. ARGENTINA

Systematic state terror arrived in Argentina in 1976 when the armed forces displaced the disintegrating government of Isabel Peron and launched a carefully planned campaign of extermination against the two clandestine armed movements of the left, the Monteneros and the ERP.[14] Three operational guidelines structured the campaign. It would be decisive and quick; the High Command would share strategic direction and responsibility, but tactical direction and responsibility would be decentralized; and it would not generate large numbers of detainees who could become subjects of international petition by liberal governments and human rights organizations.

By the time I arrived in Buenos Aires in September of 1979 as a member of the team dispatched by the Inter-American Commission on Human Rights, "The Dirty War" ("*La Guerra Sucia*"), as its executors often called it, was effectively over. Estimates of the number of persons, mostly young, who disappeared into the secret detention centers of the armed forces vary across a wide spectrum. The respected Sabato Commission, set up by the first post-junta elected government, concluded that the minimum figure was nine thousand,[15] but that it could be considerably higher. Some unofficial counts put the figure closer to 30,000.[16]

For seventeen days and through the larger parts of many nights, the six Commission members, together with Commission legal staff, roamed the country, collecting evidence including eye witness testimony from the relatively few people who had come out of the detention centers alive. Among the witnesses were Mr.

---

14 Report on the Situation of Human Rights in Argentina, Organization of American States, OEA/Ser.L/V/11.49 doc. 19 corr.1 April 11, 1980.

15 *See* Nunca Mas, *supra* note 5.

16 Encarta's on line encyclopedia (entry on the history of Argentina), Online Encyclopedia 2000, available at *http://encarta.msn.com* © 1997-2000 Microsoft Corporation; Americas Watch and Amnesty International have cited figures between 12,000 and 15,000.

and Mrs. Samuel Falikoff. They had contacted us through an American Rabbi, Marshall Meyer, then serving as a Director of South America's only Jewish seminary. A heroic figure, as large in courage as in size, he took me and two staff members one morning on a circuitous journey designed to expose any tailing vehicle, a journey that culminated at a school in an undistinguished Buenos Aires neighborhood. There awaiting us in a small room were a middle aged couple who struck one immediately as members of the professional classes. Quiet, conservatively dressed, soft-bodied, in appearance the epitome of people who lead a dignified, useful, mildly intellectual, undramatic life of impeccable propriety. Mrs. Falikoff's testimony, I don't recall her husband uttering a word, lasted several hours. Her husband had been a doctor practicing in Cordoba, a city that had been a stronghold of left-wing agitation. Since the military takeover, it had been under the control of General Menendez, by reputation one of the hardest line figures and harshest regional commanders in the Argentine Army. Shortly after the repression began, they moved to Buenos Aires. On November 25, 1976 she and her husband were abducted from their apartment and held thereafter for more than a month in a clandestine center. Here are a few excerpts from her account of their detention.

> "They took me down a spiral staircase to a basement. There they told me to close my eyes and they put a very tight blindfold, with elastic in the back, on me, which immediately gave me an intense headache. They handcuffed me and shackled my feet together by a chain with padlocks on both shackles. They were very tight and had sharp edges . . . After a while, I began to hear, coming through one of the walls of pressed board, the sound of a lot of running water, and then the cries of my husband insulting them and repeatedly calling them 'murderers'. This is repeated approximately every hour, or perhaps less. Obviously the torture room is next door. . . . On the following day — I guess — they took me out and led me to a corridor on the same floor. My legs are so swollen that the shackles begin to cut into my skin . . . One of the ones who had been to my house approached me and put a hood of thick white cloth over my head. He explained that with that hood they would not bother me. That was because they were taking people to the torture room according to the order of their chairs [unless they had the white hood] . . . The door was nearby and every time they took

someone out, the noise of running water and the desperate screams of pain could be heard, despite the fact that a record player was constantly playing very loud music. There were certain songs that they played more frequently, and despite the fact that the tapes were worn, I could hear the lyrics which went roughly: 'And now what are they? Where are they? What are their ideals?, etc.' . . . Afterwards I noticed that they brought my husband to the chair alongside me, because I recognized his pants and shoes. . . .

During the entire time I was there, I heard the same sound; the loud record player, screams of pain, running water. The guards wore rubber boots . . . asked [the young guard] why I was there, and he said it was a mistake. His only job was to see that the prisoners did not speak, did not take off their hoods, and those who did so, he could beat at will until he knocked them out. He and the others were taught karate and self defense.

They were made to . . . hate the prisoners, about whom the only thing they knew was that they 'are enemies of the country, who want to destroy it, by destroying the army.' . . . This guard told me that some of them were taken on raids, and sometimes they were given special commendation or merit awards. They were very proud of that. For example, he told me that the previous day he has been assigned to go to a house that someone had denounced. It answered the description, and when the owners tried to escape, they had to shoot them: a young woman with a two or three years old child. Later they learned that the people were not involved. He had felt bad about that, but the persons who denounced innocent people were to blame . . .

I managed to see my husband, shirtless, with marks everywhere from the cattle prod. I realized that he had no more than two centimeters in a row of unmarked skin. He breathes heavily and asks for 'water, water,' but his voice is very weak and it is hard for him to move his tongue so the words do not come out. A guard came, and told him not to bother them, that they could not give him water because if they did he would die . . .

They called one of the prisoners 'peg-leg.' He was very near me, and by his voice seemed to be an older person and very weak. One night the guards got drunk and began to bet that they could make him stand on his peg-leg. They brought him into the middle of the room and ordered him to do it. He begged them, said it was impossible, that he was going to fall. They began to kick him, punch him, and they stood him up. Of course, he fell. They stood him up again, he fell again, and so on, throughout the night. It was a most macabre spectacle. The guards went crazy, they beat him

> without interruption and the poor man was begging them to stop. There was the sound of blows to the lungs, the abdomen, the noise of broken bones. They stopped when he fell unconscious. Afterwards he was delirious for two or three days until they called the doctor. The doctor said he had many broken bones and ordered him to be taken away. I didn't hear him again. . . .
>
> In early December, a transfer occurred. Apparently they were taking away those who had been there the longest; however, they included among them the lawyer who was next to me; in all, some forty persons. They adjusted the handcuffs, the shackles and the hoods. They assembled them together, were taking them out when the noise of an airplane was heard that seemed to be landing nearby. After a time, the sound of an airplane was heard again, then nothing more. A guard asked another where they were being taken, and he answered: 'Fishfood.'"[17]

By the end of 1982, the military was splintering from the multiple blows of its military defeat,[18] its disastrous stewardship of the Argentine economy,[19] the ostentatious corruption permeating its administration of the state[20] and the authoritative exposure of its crimes by the Inter-American Commission Report.[21] Its power lying more in its unity than in its guns, the military establishment decided to carry out an un-negotiated withdrawal to its barracks. To that end it terminated its ban on party politics and prepared

---

17 Excerpts from case No. 2662 — Alberto Samual Falicoff, *Report on the Situation of Human Rights in Argentina*, Organization of American States, OEA/Ser.L/V/11.49 doc. 19 corr.1 April 11,1980.

18 *See* Anderson, *supra* note 7. The Argentine Military put out press releases claiming that it was winning the war until near the end.

19 During the Military's rule, Argentina's foreign debt ballooned from 8 billion in 1976 to 40 billion in 1983. *See* DONALD B. HODGES, ARGENTINA'S "DIRTY WAR": AN INTELLECTUAL BIOGRAPHY 7 (1991). By the time the military relinquished power, inflation was at an annual rate of 600 percent. William C. Smith, *Hyperinflation, Macroeconomic Instability, and Neoliberal Restructuring in Democratic Argentina, in* THE NEW ARGENTINE DEMOCRACY, at 20 & 26. *See also* THE SEARCH FOR A SUCCESSFUL FORMULA (Edward C. Epstein ed., 1992).

20 The National Commission of the Disappeared reported that during the military's rule "the judiciary became a sham jurisdictional structure, a cover to protect its image," instead of being a "brake on the prevailing absolutism," Nunca Mas, *supra* note 5, at 387.

21 *Report on the Situation of Human Rights in Argentina*, Organization of American States, OEA/Ser.L/V/11.49 doc. 19 corr.1 April 11, 1980.

the country for elections in the fall of 1983 that propelled Raul Alfonsin into the Presidency.[22] Assuming power in December 1983, he almost immediately began to implement his campaign promise to investigate human rights violations and to indict both military chiefs who ordered the secret extermination of persons deemed subversive and the officers who committed the worst excesses in implementing that order and also guerrilla leaders found to have violated human rights, primarily through attacks on civilians. He secured Congressional ratification of the most important international human rights conventions and approval of legislation punishing the commission of torture with the same penalty that applied in the case of murder. More significantly, he secured approval of legislation abrogating military jurisdiction over crimes against civilians committed by serving members of the military establishment.[23]

At about the same time, President Alfonsin established a Commission composed of respected citizens armed with full powers to investigate the disappearance of persons during the dirty war. Within a year, it produced the report "*Nunca Mas*" that laid out in even greater detail than the Commission's 1980 exposé the facts the military had struggled so hard to conceal. It did so without the cooperation of the armed forces from which no word of contrition was heard.[24] Meanwhile, the President, in the face of united opposition from the military establishment, prepared for criminal prosecution of the military high command during the dirty war. His strategy was one of *exemplary* trial and punishment, in other words he proposed to set sharp limits on the scope of accountability.[25]

In order to effect any prosecution at all — at least to do so consistent with Argentina's constitutional system and legal tradi-

---

22 Radical party candidate Raul Alfonsin was elected President and assumed office on December 10, 1983. Carlos Nino, *The Duty to Punish Past Abuses of Human Rights put into Context: The Case of Argentina*, 100 YALE LAW JOURNAL 618, 620 (1991) (hereinafter the "Case of Argentina").

23 *See* Nino, *supra* note 23, at 620.

24 Nunca Mas, *supra* note 5. The report is sometimes referred to as the "Sabato Report," after the commission's chairperson, writer Ernesto Sabato.

25 The following account of Alfonsin's strategy and tactics draws heavily on the lucidly incisive work of Carlos Nino. *See, e.g.*, Nino, *supra* note 23; Carlos Nino, Comment, *The Human Rights Policy of the Argentina Constitutional Government: A Reply*, 11 YALE JOURNAL OF INTERNATIONAL LAW (1985).

tions — he and his legal advisors had to find their way around a plethora of procedural and practical obstacles including the amnesty the *de facto* military government had awarded to itself before leaving office[26] and the existing procedural norm granting military tribunals jurisdiction over acts of military service in military places. On his initiative, Congress declared the amnesty null and void. It did so with the help of a novel theory in Argentina, namely that norms declared by an unelected authoritarian government did not enjoy the presumption of validity enjoyed by norms emanating from a democratic one. Hence, legislative acts of the military junta were to be deemed valid only if their content was found to be consistent with the demands of justice. The auto-amnesty was held not to pass that test.[27]

Getting around the military jurisdiction law without being found to have violated prohibitions against *ex post facto* modification of procedural norms required greater creativity. Noting that the Constitution prohibited the President from exercising judicial functions and arguing that military courts (like the rest of the military) form part of the executive branch, he secured Congressional and ultimately judicial support for a compromise that gave initial jurisdiction to military tribunals but allowed the Federal Courts of Appeals to supersede them if they did not complete trials within six months. In the event, the initial trials, those involving the members of the successive military juntas that had governed during the dirty war and of the commanders of the region of Buenos Aires — had to be taken over by the Federal Courts where the prosecutions were successfully completed. Whereupon the previous masters of the Argentine Universe found themselves to be guests of the state although under conditions ineffably more benign than those their victims had experienced.[28] For the moment a fair measure of justice had been done and done without great risk of a military riposte perhaps because their failures in the realm of economic policy and of the Falklands war made the defendants re-

26 Law of National Pacification, Law No. 22924, Sept. 22, 1983. The law granted immunity from prosecution to suspected terrorists and members of the armed forces for human rights violations committed between May 25, 1973 and June 17, 1982.

27 *See* Nino, *supra* note 23, at 621.

28 *Ibid.* at 622.

sponsible for the precipitate termination of military government and the huge loss of the armed forces' prestige.

But then things began to get complicated. To limit the potential number of middle rank officers, Alfonsin's legislation established a revocable presumption that those who committed crimes under orders, and without decision-making capacity, had believed that the orders were legitimate. But the legislation that emerged from Congress eliminated the presumption in the case of "abhorrent or atrocious" acts. Since practically everything that went on in the dirty war could be so classified (for example, participating in the original detention of persons and bringing them to the officers in charge of the interrogation centers), the risk of indictment now loomed for a large part of the officer corps of all ranks. If a number of cases had been tried expeditiously in the military tribunals, the latter might have given a relatively narrow definition to the statute and thus made clear that prosecution would be limited to the most gross and brutal participants. But instead the tribunals dallied whereupon the Federal Court of Appeals in Buenos Aires stepped in and asserted jurisdiction.[29] With military unrest growing, Alfonsin pushed a new law through Congress, the so-called "Full-Stop" Bill that established a sixty-day statute of limitations for new indictments related to the war.[30]

The result was disastrous on every count. Previous supporters of the government at home and abroad condemned what they saw as a pusillanimous and immoral sell-out to military pressure. The Appeals Courts of the interior, which had hitherto moved at a snails pace, suddenly sprang into action and seized jurisdiction in cases that had languished in military tribunals in their respective regions. Within weeks, more than 450 officers had been brought within civil jurisdiction.[31] The military response was mutiny in Easter Week, 1987. A group of indicted officers holed up in a military garrison where comrades announced they would repel with violence any effort to enforce detention orders.

Alfonsin learned that, while only a small part of the armed forces was directly involved, the military as a whole would not

---

29 *Ibid.* at 622 & 623.

30 Ley de Punto Final, Law No. 23492, Dec. 24, 1986.

31 Nino, *supra* note 23, at 623.

obey a command to suppress the mutiny. Literally millions of people poured into the streets of Buenos Aires and other major cities to defend the civilian government with their bodies. The President flew to the garrison by helicopter to obtain by himself the surrender of the rebels. After hours of high tension, he went on television to announce that the rebels had yielded to constitutional authority, that they were under arrest and that people should return to their homes. He wished everyone a happy Easter.[32]

But the worst challenge was yet to come. For almost immediately, the President learned that other indicted officers were preparing to resist court orders. At his request, the Supreme Court asked the appeals courts for the files in the cases before them, in effect suspending the process. But at the same time, it became clear that the Court would not itself take responsibility for articulating limits to the due obedience law. Threatened with a rolling series of mutinies, believing that they would at a minimum abort the whole effort to end the military's historic freedom from civilian control, rejecting a general amnesty that would have covered even the junta leaders, barred by the constitution from pardoning lesser officers who had not yet been convicted, Alfonsin pushed new legislation through Congress making irrefutable in all cases other than those involving very senior officers the presumption that officers had acted in the belief that orders were legitimate. This was the much excoriated "due obedience" law.[33]

For this act a torrent of abuse poured over the President. He was condemned by the very human rights organization he had co-founded.[34] His party suffered at the polls. But as far as the military was concerned, the move worked. When incorrigible military elements rebelled again, Alfonsin called on the commander-in-chief to act and the rebels were quickly repressed.[35]

Alfonsin had sought to overcome the dense tradition of military impunity without aborting the process of democratic consolidation. He had to find his way without the compass of precedent. His successor, Carlos Menem, had other priorities. Shortly after as-

32 *Ibid.* at 623 & 624.

33 Ley de Obediencia Debida., Law No. 23521, June 4, 1987.

34 *See* AMERICA'S WATCH, TRUTH AND PARTIAL JUSTICE IN ARGENTINA 83 (1987).

35 *See* Nino, *supra* note 23, at 624.

suming office, he granted presidential pardons to all those convicted or under trial for state and subversive acts of terrorism, for misconduct in the war, or for rebelling against democratic institutions. Even the members of the military juntas were covered.[36] Then he set about rejuvenating the super-inflated and yet moribund Argentine economy.[37]

Two years ago, I returned to Argentina for the first time since I had testified in the trial of the high command back in 1985. In the course of two weeks I interviewed prominent representatives of all sectors of society, including the President of the Association of Bankers and other important figures in the vibrant financial community, two leaders of the political party that has emerged to the left of Alfonsin's Radical Party (which is as radical as the Holy Roman Empire was Holy) and also the commander-in-chief of the Armed Forces. The one thing everyone agreed on was that for the first time in the modern history of Argentina, the military had disappeared from the political equation. No social group could envision calling on the military to veto electoral outcomes and the military could no longer imagine itself assuming power. And so it appeared that, at long last, Argentine society had tranquilized its Leviathan.

In this way as in others, Argentina is a different country although it still lives very far East of Eden. And the past is still a presence. The wall of silence that so long shielded the perpetrators of the dirty war has been leaking. Every few months there is another public confession.[38] And even the trials are not over. The disappeared children, born in the captivity of their mothers and placed years ago with families deemed to have the right sort of values, retain the character of disappeared persons inherited from their dead mothers. Hence the crime (in effect of kidnaping and

---

36 *Ibid.* at 625.

37 In 1995, inflation in Argentina was 2 percent per year. Per annum growth of gross national product reached as high as seven percent under President Menem. *Latin Realities*, ECONOMIST, Mar. 30, 1996, at 19. Between 1991 and 1993, Argentina's economy grew by 25.5percent. Stephen Fidler & John Barham, *Argentine Miracle Needs More Foreign Capital*, FINANCIAL TIMES, June 22, 1994, at 8.

38 *See Argentina Purges "Dirty War" Guilt*, GUARDIAN, Apr. 28, 1995, at 10 (recounting the public confessions of senior military officers).

illegal detention) is ongoing, not covered by Menem's pardon.[39] So life is not so good for Videla and the others who led the armed forces in those days, ordinary men much like Eichman,[40] who made a desolation and called it victory.

III. GUATEMALA

If Guatemala were the whole world, then one would have to agree with Washington Irving's *dictum* that "[h]istory is a register of the crimes and miseries that man has inflicted on his fellow man,"[41] revised to reflect the fact that in Guatemala humiliation, mutilation and murder have been inflicted on men and women indiscriminately. Guatemala is the Rwanda of the Western Hemisphere. I noted earlier that the Sabato Commission in Argentina concluded that just under 10,000 people had been liquidated. That was out of a population of some thirty million. The Truth Commission established by the Guatemala Peace Accord of 1996, surveying the entire period of state terror — which extends back to the 1960s but which did not reach a shrieking pitch until about 1980 — put the death toll at 200,000 out of a population of about nine million, over ninety percent of which are attributable to the armed forces and paramilitary death squads collaborating with them.[42] In proportion to the national population, the Argentine military government would have had to kill about 600,000 people in order to compare with its Guatemalan peer.

Kurtz's tortured epiphany in Joseph Conrad's Heart of Darkness — "The horror! The horror!" — would be a fitting epitaph for this country where even today sixty percent of the population is unassimilated Mayan Indian. As late as 1940, the Mayans were subjected to forced labor in the plantations of the country's land

---

39 The "full stop" or "punto final" law which established a sixty-day period beyond which no new charges could be brought for state-sponsored crimes committed during the "dirty war" contained an exception for crimes involving the theft and irregular adoption of the children of the disappeared. Law No. 23.492, Art. 5, (1986).

40 *See* HANNAH ARENDT, EICHMANN IN JERUSALEM: A REPORT ON THE BANALITY OF EVIL (1994).

41 WEBSTER'S NEW WORLD DICTIONARY OF QUOTABLE DEFINITIONS (Eugene E. Brussell ed. 1996).

42 *See Report of the Guatemalan Historical Clarification Commission*, Feb. 25, 1999.

holding oligarchy and the United Fruit Company.[43] That is almost a century after the liberation of the serfs in Russia.

Comprehensive Terror in Guatemala stems in a literal sense from the failed effort by nationalist modernizers in the period between 1944 and 1954 to moderate the bestial conditions of rural life and generally to drag Guatemala into the 20th century. The 1954 coup against the country's elected government, organized, financed and orchestrated by the United States ended, as intended, the prospect of reform by political means. Purged modernizers within the military establishment, including a number of young officers trained by the United States, initiated the first insurrection against the primitives confirmed in power by the Eisenhower Administration's intervention. The response was state terror that ebbed and flowed, depending on how long it took for a new generation of wildly courageous dissidents to replace their liquidated predecessors. Even in ebb, it never ceased to take its toll of victims: first because the military establishment and its oligarchic allies believed in the prophylactic virtues of exemplary horrors that could perpetuate the memory of unspeakable suffering; secondly, because prophylaxis was seen to require atomization of the potentially disaffected classes, hence all organizational efforts — however meliorative their objectives — were latently subversive; and thirdly, because capital preferred that labor be servile.[44]

The experience of the employees of the Coca-Cola bottling plant in Guatemala City, owned by a gentleman from Houston, was atypical, if at all, only in its dramatic intensity. The OAS Commission on Human Rights' 1981 Report on Guatemala records a chronology of events at the plant between October 1978 and April 1979. On October 16, 1978, following a discussion between union representatives and plant managers at which the former were warned of what could happen to them, Israel Marquez, Secretary General of the Union at the plant was attacked with machine guns while driving home. He survived. In November, three former lieu-

---

[43] For a discussion of the relationship between United Fruit and its Guatemalan workers, *see* Texas Papers on Latin America, Paper No. 95-01; Alejandra Batres, *The Experience of the Guatemalan United Fruit Company Workers 1944-1954: Why Did They Fail* — ILAS Distinguished Paper Award University of Texas at Austin (1995).

[44] For a discussion of the genesis of the Guatemalan conflict, *see Report on the Situation of Human Rights in the Republic of Guatemala,* OEA/Ser.L.II.53doc.21 rev.21 Oct. 13, 1991, at 19-22 (hereinafter Commission Report).

tenants in the army assumed personnel positions in the plant. Early on the morning of December 12, eight members of the military police arrived on the premises for no apparent reason. Shortly after noon, Pedro Quevado, the union's financial secretary, while seated in a company truck on his distribution route, had twelve bullets pumped into his face and throat by persons unknown. He did not survive. All members of the union's executive committee began receiving threatening notes at their homes, notes encouraging them to cease union activities. Some stepped down. But others took their place. On January 16, two bus loads of men from the so-called Police Model Squad attempted to arrest Israel Marquez when he entered the premises. He escaped and ultimately found sanctuary with his wife and son in the Venezuelan Embassy. Manuel Lopez Balan replaced him as Secretary-General. On April 5, 1979, while on his distribution route for the company, Balan was beaten with an iron tube and his throat was slit. He did not survive. On May 1, four union members were abducted. Of the four, two disappeared altogether, the bodies of the other two, one showing unmistakable signs of torture, were found respectively on the 2nd and 3rd of May.[45]

During the murderous reign of General Romero Lucas, terror was more prominent in the cities. Leaders of centrist and democratic socialist political parties, including the former mayor of Guatemala City and the distinguished former foreign minister, Fuentes More, were machine-gunned to death on main streets in the city. The faculty of the leading university, San Carlos, and educators generally were decimated. In 1980, 226 elementary school teachers and eighty nine university professors were murdered. When General Rios Montt and his oligarchic faction seized power in 1982, the main burden of repression moved to the countryside where guerrillas had for some years been quietly working among the Mayans of the highlands, and once there it assumed almost holocaustal proportions as entire villages, literally hundreds, were wiped out.[46]

Part of the world view that allowed this to happen was encapsulated for me early one morning in the officer's mess of a fort

---

45 *Ibid.* at 94-111 (discussing the chronology of violence at the Coca-Cola Bottling company between Oct. 1978 and Apr. 1979, and attacks against union members).

46 *Ibid.* at 24-27 & 84-89.

in the Guatemalan highlands not far from the scene of reported massacres my Mexican colleague and I had come to investigate. It was a large room with long tables, most of them filled at that hour, not long after dawn, with men just back from night patrols. Their faces still striped with black camouflage paint, their confident rough chatter reminiscent of a football team at ease after a tough practice, they worked their way through bowls of thick, hot cereal, large plates with high stacks of sweet rolls and toast on which they swabbed thick lumps of butter topped with honey or jam from a great assemblage of clay pots. Stunted Mayan women hardly taller than the children of the middle classes moved ceaselessly among the tables refilling plates and pouring steaming coffee and mate. If testosterone had a smell, the room would have reeked of it. In the front of the room on two giant television screens a big band clothed in white, satin-lapeled jackets played the jazz of another era, the sax and trumpet sections rising alternatively to twist to the rhythm of their obsolete songs.

Our host is the Deputy Commander of the region, a physical parody of a Guatemalan officer with his bull neck, almost wider than his head, and his thick wrists and heavy-knuckled hands. He raises one of those hands and points at the Mayan women moving silently, with closed faces, among the tables. "*Estos Inditos*, [These little Indians]," he begins in an expansive, didactic tone. "*Un pueblo muy humilde*, [A very humble people]," he says as if tendering us a lapidary insight. "*Pero*" [But] and now his tone changes histrionically: "But they have been penetrated by the virus of Marxism. And we must cut it out as you would cut out a cancer." He looks at us expectantly, perhaps waiting for a remark that will justify tossing us out of the helicopter on the ride back to Guatemala City.

So when, in 1987, the recently elected Christian Democratic Government of Vinicio Cerezo opened negotiations with the leadership of the ravaged guerilla movement, meeting his obligations under the Esquipulas Agreement of Central American Heads of State requiring every conflicted country to initiate dialogue leading to peace, the prospects for positive results seemed bleak. When the guerrillas tabled a proposal calling for a "Truth Commission" to investigate human rights violations and the demilitarization of the countryside, along with full freedom of speech and association, application of the Geneva Conventions to the conflict and a formal dialogue between the major economic and social forces in the country, the military successfully demanded suspension of official contacts.[47] But under the sponsorship of friendly governments in Europe and Latin American, and with the aid of elements of the Guatemalan Catholic Church, the guerrillas began contacts with political parties and social and economic groups, even, finally, with the organizational expression of the industrial and landed elite, the Coordinating Committee of Agricultural, Commercial, Industrial and Financial Associations (CACIF). It, however, flatly rejected negotiation of socio-economic reform.[48]

These discussions occurred within the context of a rapidly changing international environment. The Cold War ended and the Soviet Union disintegrated. In Nicaragua, the Sandinistas relinquished office after losing an open election and, with US support, the Contras were demobilized. In a radical change of stance, the US also threw its support behind a negotiated settlement in El Salvador managed by the United Nations which during the Cold War had been forced by the US to treat Latin America as a no-go zone. Concluded finally in 1992, the Salvadoran Accords provided for a UN-funded Truth Commission constituted by three distinguished foreign experts to be selected by the Secretary General, a commission authorized to make recommendations the Salvadoran Government would be obligated to implement. While requiring the demobilization of the FMLN, it envisioned a parallel process whereby the military would be downsized, stripped of internal security functions and purged of officers found by an *ad hoc* committee of respected Salvadorans to have engaged in major violations of human rights. Meanwhile, a new national police force, independent of the military, would assume internal security functions. The accords also contained specific government commitments to provide land for ex-combatants.[49]

When the accords were signed, they were dismissed by persons known to speak for the Guatemalan military and agro-industrial elite as irrelevant to Guatemalan reality since in Guatemala the guerrillas had been defeated and Guatemala was

---

[47] JAMES DUNKERLEY, THE PACIFICATION OF CENTRAL AMERICA 79-80 (1994).

[48] *Ibid. see* Table 6, the Guatemalan Peace Process 81 (1987-92).

[49] *Ibid.* at 65 et seq, the Chapultepec Accords (named after the Mexico City castle in which they were signed) Jan. 16, 1992.

not dependent on US support.[50] Writing a year later, James Dunkerley concluded that the failure of the guerrillas on the battlefield "makes it unlikely that any eventual Guatemalan Peace Settlement will go much further than the rebels' demobilization, re-reincorporation into the legal sphere, and, if conditions were propitious, some judicial consideration of the violation of human rights since the late 1970's."[51]

At the time, it seemed less a prediction than a statement of fact. Yet, beneath the surface there was already movement in the tectonic plates of this volcanic society. Within the elite-dominated economy, the long dominant plantation-export sector with its commitment to feudal labor practices was losing ground proportionately to a modern export-oriented manufacturing and assembly sector in which somewhat more educated workers and less repressive labor practices could arguably contribute to productivity. It was, moreover, a sector more subject to boycott threats directed at its partners in the US and other developed countries. In addition, it was a sector whose future would depend largely on Guatemala's inclusion in any extension of the North American Free Trade Agreement.[52]

A second source of movement was the elite's previous decision in the mid 1980's that its interests would be served better by a more orderly constitutional and nominally civilian political system. Consistent with that move, limits began to appear in the scope of urban repression. As limits became manifest, popular organization began anew. Among the groups that began to organize were Mayans, hundreds of thousands of whom had been driven into Guatemala City by the poverty and terror in the countryside. Relaxation of terror in the City also allowed middle-class leaders to return from self-exile and help provide leadership.[53]

---

50 Dunkerley, *supra* note 47, at 76-77.

51 *Ibid.* at 78.

52 The large non-agricultural sectors such as the textile industry favored free trade agreements.

53 *See* Dinorah Azpuru, *Peace and Democratization in Guatemala* (noting that "the increasing participation, organization and consciousness among the Mayan population [. . .] is one of the greatest contributions of the peace process to democratization in Guatemala"), at 111; and Robert Plant, *Indigenous Identity and Rights in the Guatemalan Peace Process* (discussing the role of indigenous organizations in the peace process), both in COMPARATIVE PEACE PROCESSES IN LATIN AMERICA (Cynthia Arnson ed. 1999).

Even what at first glance appeared to be an ugly side to civilianization, metastasizing corruption in politics and public administration constituted a force for peace in that it seemed to encourage some of the civilian and military elite to seek a more normal, more modern and efficient political order, one with elements of popular accountability. Corruption produced deterioration in services like light and power necessary to the elite as well as the rest of society. Deterioration together with the gradual meliorization of the climate of fear led to large scale protests and even riots uniting workers, students, the floating proletariat and even the lower middle class. The broadening support for modernization of Guatemala suddenly cohered when, in 1993, President Serrano attempted to consolidate autocratic power by suspending the Congress and declaring a state of emergency.[54] Popular organizations and trade unions found themselves in alliance with the CACIF[55] in determined opposition. Influencing the agro-industrial hierarchy was a threat from the US to cut Guatemalan access to the US market for its manufactured goods. The Organization of American States (OAS), speaking for the democratic regimes now proliferated in the Hemisphere, threatened to request bi-lateral sanctions. European states suspended economic aid. Under this pressure, the military withdrew support first from Serrano and then from his ally who tried to succeed him.[56]

Though awful in many respects, Serrano did restart peace negotiations but without observable progress. Negotiations continued fitfully under his successor, the former human rights ombudsman, Ramiro de Leon Carpio who proved profoundly disappointing once in office.[57] Until 1994, perhaps the most useful efforts were those outside the official process, so-called Second Track Diplomacy in which Norway, but also the US, Spain and Mexico played useful roles. It allowed confidence building contact between guerrilla leaders and some officers of the armed forces, an institution which gradually began to appear a bit less

54 *See* Dunkerley, *supra* note 47, at 84.

55 The CICAF disfavored negotiations with the guerillas. SUSANNE JONAS, OF CENTAURS AND DOVES, GUATEMALA'S PEACE PROCESS 41-42 (2000).

56 Jonas, at 42 *et seq.*

57 *Ibid.* at 124 (noting that the de Leon government was presiding over a worsening human rights situation).

monolithic.[58] Then, in 1994 at the request of both the guerrillas and the government, the United Nations assumed the role of moderator and the parties agreed to an agenda-setting accord which included establishment of a civil society institution, the Assembly of Civil Society ("*Assemblea de Sociedad Civil*") in which popular, indigenous, labor, and business groups would be urged to participate.[59] The Assembly was charged with making consensus recommendations to the negotiators and to evaluate the accords with which the negotiations would hopefully conclude. Beginning with a comprehensive agreement on human rights, calling for UN verification of compliance, one by one the accords emerged, always painfully, until December 29, 1996, when the final accord was signed and in a scene bordering on mass ecstasy, the end of thirty five years of civil war was declared.[60] The accords would have been remarkable in many Latin countries; in Guatemala they seemed almost to imply some behind-the-scenes Divine Intervention. These were their main elements:

1. The Accords

The first and what many regarded as the breakthrough accord was the one on human rights. Its substance would have been unremarkable in many countries. It consisted largely of the government's commitment to do all of the things it was theoretically obligated to do under international human rights and humanitarian law which included decent treatment of captured combatants and effective guarantees of freedom of movement and association. A bit more striking, perhaps, were the explicit commitments in effect to eliminate secret security units and to professionalize and purge existing security forces. What was remarkable was the agreement to invite the United Nations to deploy a human rights verification mission inside the country empowered to look into accusations of human rights violations, to issue periodic reports assessing the general situation as well as commenting on specific cases, to disseminate those reports through the mass media, to

58 *Ibid.* at 43 *et seq.*

59 *Ibid.* at 140.

60 *Ibid.* at 92.

move freely about the country and to make visits without notice to state institutions and guerrilla camps in order to collect information for its reports, to make recommendations to the parties concerning measures to promote human rights and guarantee compliance with the accord and to assure that national organizations charged with the defense of human rights were autonomous and effective. All this from a military/oligarchic regime that had furiously rejected US military aid with human rights strings attached as an unacceptable interference in the country's internal affairs. This from the most articulately xenophobic government in Central America was indeed a breakthrough.[61]

Next in time came the agreement on the resettlement of population groups uprooted by the conflict. The government committed itself either to return land to refugees (whose abandonment of it had hitherto been taken as evidence of guilty involvement with the insurgency) or to compensate them. The guerrillas demanded and the government agreed that representatives of the uprooted peoples would be able to participate in decision making, both general and specific, about their resettlement. And, evidencing epochal change in Latin American culture, the government agreed to eliminate all forms of discrimination in the allocation of benefits under the accord.[62]

Equally if not more surprising in the Guatemalan context and the military's triumphalist claims was the third accord establishing what amounted to a truth commission. Having less than two years previously said in effect — "never here in Guatemala" — in June 1994 the Government signed an accord that called for the establishment of an Historical Clarification Commission. To be constituted in part by two Guatemalan citizens, by implication acceptable to both sides, the chair would be a distinguished foreign expert whom the Secretary General of the United Nations would select. Again the Guatemalan elite was accepting the kind of international involvement in its affairs to which it had hitherto been reflexively hostile. Acceptance, however, came only after great pressure from the most interested European and Latin gov-

---

61 Comprehensive Accord on Human Rights (March 1994). For a discussion of the main provisions of this accord, *see* Jonas, *supra* note 55, at 71 *et seq.*

62 Resettlement of Population Groups uprooted by the Armed Conflict (June 1994). *See* Jonas, *supra* note 55, at 73 *et seq.*

ernments and on the basis of a compromise condemned by human rights groups, namely that, unlike the Salvador Report, this one would name no names and have no judicial consequences.[63]

If the third was striking, the fourth accord on the identity and rights of indigenous peoples probably has to be called miraculous. Guatemala is, after all, a country in which the indigenous majority had been virtually enslaved for four hundred years, a period extending into practically the middle of the 20th century, and thereafter had been excluded from the political process and incorporated into the national economy largely as beasts of burden might. The accord's taproot, from which all of its detailed provisions stemmed, was a government commitment to seek a constitutional amendment redefining the Guatemalan Nation as "multi-ethnic, multi-cultural and multi-lingual." The accord itself explicitly recognized and identified the various Maya peoples and also the two non-Maya indigenous groups.

The Government's branching commitments included securing legislation making ethnic discrimination a crime, decentralizing the educational system in accordance with the needs of indigenous peoples, including protection of their linguistic heritage, officially recognizing and respecting indigenous languages in the provision of public services, incorporating customary law into the legal code, and amending the Municipal Code so that local organization in predominantly indigenous areas could conform with indigenous norms and traditions for group action. In addition, the government committed to adopt or seek Congressional adoption of measures that would institutionalize indigenous representation in decision-making at every level of government. Furthermore, the accord provided for the immediate creation of several joint commissions, composed of an equal number of governmental representatives and representatives of indigenous organizations, to guide implementation of educational reforms and land tenure arrangements. This accord was ratified in 1996 by the Guatemalan Congress albeit with an amendment specifying that it was subordinate to the still unamended constitution which defined the nation in unitary terms.[64]

---

63 Historical Clarification Commission (June 1994). *See* Jonas, *supra* note 55, at 74.

64 Identity and Rights of Indigenous Peoples (Mar.1995). *See* Jonas, *supra* note 55, at 75.

Equally remarkable if not also miraculous was the 1996 socioeconomic accord. Here was a regime, in recent decades probably the most socially retrograde in Latin America, committing itself, among other things, to:

- encourage the formation and legal recognition of grassroots organizations to facilitate broader citizen participation in a decentralized development-planning process;
- adopt certain detailed mechanisms to assure the participation of women in the process and to eliminate all forms of gender discrimination embedded in existing laws;
- increase state spending on health, education, housing and social security and specifically to increase the proportion of spending on education and health in relation to GDP by at least 50 percent of 1995 levels;
- insure that the literacy rate would be increased to 70 percent (up from 55 percent, the second lowest in Latin America) within four years;
- provide vocational training for at least 200,000 people by the year 2000;
- create a land trust fund that would acquire land and make it available to peasants at affordable prices;
- and in a country where elite views about progressive taxation and the welfare state generally would make Malcolm Forbes a centrist and Prince Otto von Bismark, founder of the German welfare state, a communist, a commitment to raise the ratio of taxes to GDP by 50 percent, from under 8 percent to at least 12 percent also by the year 2000 and to do so in a way consistent with the principal that the tax system should be "fair, equitable, and on the whole progressive, in keeping with the constitutional principle of ability to pay."[65]

Chronologically, the last substantive accord was the one on what had till then been the ultimate "no-go" issue area, namely the strengthening of Civilian Power and the Role of the Armed

---

65 Socio and Economic Aspects and Agrarian Situation (May 1996). *See* Jonas, *supra* note 55, at 78.

Forces in a Democratic Society.[66] This remarkable document's main elements were the following:

- A commitment to redefine the army's role by means of a constitutional amendment limiting that role to external defense;
- Concomitant transfer of internal security responsibilities to a new national civilian police force. Existing police forces would be disbanded or integrated into the new force which would also acquire supervisory authority over all private security forces. The new force would fall under the administrative responsibilities of the Minister of the Interior rather than the Army or its traditional cabinet proxy, the Minister of Defense;
- Recruitment of members of the new force so as to reflect the multi-cultural and multi-ethnic composition of the national population and training of its members in a new police academy designed to enhance the professional capacities and self-image of force members;
- Reduction by a third of the army's size and budget;
- Amendment of the constitution to confirm the President of the Republic as the commander-in-chief of the army;
- Dissolution of the Special military units that had evolved during the decades of civil conflict, in particular the unit based in the Presidential Palace ostensibly to protect the President but in fact to plan and implement secret operations against persons and groups deemed subversive;
- Subjecting crimes committed by military personnel to the jurisdiction of the civilian courts.[67]

An accord with such revolutionary dimensions, particularly one negotiated between parties of markedly unequal strength, was bound to be marked by ominous omissions and conditions. At least three are notable. First, many of its key elements could not

---

66 A fifth set of agreements (The Operational Accords, Dec.1996), were strictly operational in nature and established the specific conditions of the cease-fire and the separation of forces. *See* Jonas, *supra* note 55, at 88 *et seq.*

67 Strengthening of Civilian Power and Role of the Armed Forces in a Democratic Society, (Sept.1996). *See* Jonas, *supra* note 55, at 81 *et seq.*

be implemented without amendment of the national constitution. Under the existing constitution, which the Accords did not purport to displace, every amendment requires a two-thirds affirmative vote in the Congress followed by a majority vote in a national referendum.[68] The accords, indeed even the decision to negotiate with the armed opposition, did not enjoy the unanimous support of the traditional parties and the elite-military establishment whose several elements the parties reflected. On the contrary, some establishment factions and figures condemned the accords from the moment they were announced and insisted that they constituted commitments only of the then President and his coalition rather than of the state.

That was one very serious problem, hugely compounded by a political culture that had discouraged mass electoral participation and by the murderous repression that had decimated the ranks of potential leaders for the effectively disenfranchised majority of Guatemalans. Repression had also inhibited efforts to build ties among the multiple indigenous groups or even to provide them with the lingua franca of Spanish. In short, it was hard to feel confidence that the requisite amendments would be passed in the near future. Threatening ultimate defeat of the military accord and, indeed, of all the others was a circle of irony. The accords were intended to create conditions for the effective incorporation of the Guatemalan masses into the national political system, to give them real citizenship. Yet, until incorporation occurred, it would be difficult to get the accords implemented and thus to established the conditions seemingly required for incorporation.[69]

With respect to the military accord itself, there were two additional problems. One was the absence of any commitment to or specific mechanism for purging the military of persons guilty of the most heinous human rights violations.[70] In this respect, as in certain others, the Guatemalan accords differed profoundly from the Salvadoran which had established an investigative body with a mandate to identify the worst delinquents for the very purpose

---

68 Jonas, *supra* note 55, at 85-86.

69 *See* Jonas, *supra* note 55, Chapter 6 for a discussion of the roadblocks to implementation of the Accords.

70 *See* Jonas, *supra* note 55, at 85.

of triggering their forced retirement.[71] This difference was intended by the Guatemalan military who, it is reported, viewed the Salvadoran accords with a bitter conviction that it could and would not happen to them. If the army was not to be cleansed but simply removed from internal security duties, the composition of the new force that would assume those duties had to be a matter of the highest consequence. One evident danger was that the army would retain *de facto* control of internal security operations by insinuating its most intractable unreconstructed delinquents into the new national police force and reinforcing them with killers from paramilitary groups often staffed with former army members. For the unreconstructed members of the army and its civilian allies, the ideal would be a force packed with their friends and off limits to persons who had served in or been sympathetic to the armed opposition. Despite this danger's salience, the accord did not specify whether ex-army and security force members or ex-guerrillas could serve. [72]

Post-Conflict Guatemala

Perhaps societies do experience redefining moments when some unique conjuncture alters their historical path. Perhaps the accords evidence such a shift in Guatemala. Perhaps. But at any moment in time, societies are clusters of patterned and deeply rooted behaviors, behaviors corresponding to powerful individual and group interests and mentalities. Hence a moderately cautious observer will assume that, except where the *ancient regime* is either destroyed or at least challenged by forces it cannot repress, the new path will not immediately and sharply diverge from its predecessor. Until they change in the face of the altered circumstances encountered on new terrain, interests and identities erect quotidian barriers pressing social forces back toward the familiar way.

---

71 For an overview of El Salvador's peace accords, *see* Antonio Canas & Hector Dada, *Political Transition in El Salvador*, *in* COMPARATIVE PEACE PROCESSES IN LATIN AMERICA (Cynthia Arnson, ed., 1999).

72 Jonas, *supra* note 55, at 85.

Certainly any deviation, unless it is illusory, increases over time. Meanwhile, societies inch forward in the face of entrenched resistance. Such has been the experience of Guatemala. Let's begin with the very specific commitment on tax reform. It had to be a central feature of any sustained program for poverty alleviation. For decades prior to the accords, Guatemala had trailed the rest of Latin America in the percentage of gross domestic product available for the production of public goods. Its system of taxation, markedly regressive, generated relatively exiguous revenues. In other words it was both unjust and feeble. Despite the letter of the accord and pressure from the international donor community, the government failed to get the requisite legislation through Guatemala's Congress in the face of quiet but unambiguous hostility from the economic elite acting through CACIF, its main organ for collective action. A level of progressive taxation that would simply make Guatemala an average Latin country in this respect remains unacceptable to the agro-business interests that still rule Guatemala in cooperation with the military establishment. [73]

As action to enhance government revenues was a condition precedent for sustainable poverty reduction, so constitutional reform was essential for extending true citizenship to the indigenous majority. First the Arzú administration delayed pushing the substance of the accord on multi-culturalism and indigenous rights through the Congress. In this and other ways it implied a low priority for executing the relevant agreements. Finally, in May 1999, Congressional approval having been achieved, the requisite constitutional amendments were submitted to a national referendum. Opponents dominated the media, particularly television.[74] The traditional parties of the center and left were either lukewarm or hostile. The government failed to disseminate any clear account of the amendments much less to campaign on their behalf or markedly to ease the economic and logistical as well as educational obstacles to voting by the amendments' beneficiaries, the indigenous majority. True, they were no longer liable to be murdered for the delinquency of organizing and attempting to vote.

---

73 *See ibid.* at 169 *et seq.* for an analysis of Guatemala's failed tax reforms.

74 *For example,* two days before the vote on the reforms, the CACIF published a newspaper ad pronouncing its strong opposition to the reforms. *Ibid.* at 196.

But after decades of pitiless decimation, a new infrastructure of emancipatory political organizations was not yet in place. In the event, only eighteen and one-half percent of the eligible voters participated in the referendum. The amendments were defeated by a vote constituting six percent of all theoretically eligible voters.[75]

A third important statement of the obstacles to social, economic and political transformation was the murder of Bishop Juan Gerardi. The Catholic Church's leading advocate of reform and a central figure in promoting the peace process, Bishop Gerardi, was found on April 27, 1998, with his skull smashed by a cement block and its contents spread over the floor of his garage. Two days previously, on behalf of the Archbishop's human rights office which he directed, he had presented to the nation a monumental report on violations of human rights during the decades of state terror. The report laid the overwhelming majority of those violations at the door of the military institution.[76]

He died struggling for justice in a society where less than one-third of the work force held formal jobs paying at least the exiguous minimum wage, where only twenty-seven percent of the population lived above the poverty level and where 2.4 million people, about a quarter of all Guatemalans living in Guatemala (perhaps as many as a fifth live in the United States), survived (to the extent they did) in conditions defined by intergovernmental organizations as "extreme poverty."[77]

As we look back to the ecstatic moment in 1996 when hundreds of thousands of people poured into the center of the capital to celebrate the appearance of peace, what can we say about this tortured, pitiable country? Because life without hope is unbearable, we at this safe distance can eulogize the space that has been opened for political mobilization and the incipient struggle to construct a national society that might, someday, be pocked by no more than the normal quotient of poverty and inequality and injustice in the application of the law. But between hope and reality falls the shadow of contemporary Guatemala. In the realm

---

75 *Ibid.* at 199.

76 *Ibid.* at 146 & 147.

77 *Ibid.* at 182.

of economic misery and public action to alleviate it, I note the Year 1999 Human Development Report of the United Nations Development Programme. It reveals that Guatemala, with a per capita gross domestic product nearly three times greater than Bolivia and Honduras, ranks below them on the human development index, ranks lower, indeed, than any country in the Hemisphere with the single exception of Haiti.[78] In the realm of justice, I cite the Year 1999 World Report of Human Rights Watch, in particular the following two items in its report on Guatemala. One deals with the investigation into the Assassination of Father Gerardi. Every material witness has found it prudent to leave the country. So has the investigating magistrate and also the second prosecutor in the case who, unlike his predecessor, was willing to consider the hypothesis that Gerardi's murder was politically motivated. Previously, despite the uncanny coincidence of Girardi's report and his death (carried out with the sort of horrific dramaturgy frequently used in the past by the Guatemalan armed forces and its paramilitary allies), the official investigators operated exclusively on the assumption that the death was no more than a common crime.[79]

A second suggestive criminal process was the prosecution of members of a military patrol accused of murdering eleven persons in a rural community. All of the victims had recently been repatriated from refugee camps outside the country, camps to which they had fled during the terror campaign waged by the armed forces. After a process characterized by the presiding judge's dilatory tactics, intractable resistance from the military and anonymous threats to prosecutors, the second lieutenant who had led the patrol and ten soldiers were found guilty of manslaughter. Another fourteen soldiers were found guilty of complicity. The presiding judge sentenced the two groups respectively to five and four years imprisonment, then declared each sentence commutable to a fine of five quetzals for each day of the sentence. At

---

78 1999 Human Development Report prepared by the United Nations Development Programme, at 260. Out of 174 countries, Guatemala ranked 117 while Haiti ranked 152. The Human Development Report measures development on components of education, longevity and income per head.

79 Human Rights Watch, 2000 World Report 130 *et seq.*

the time of the sentence, five quetzals equaled sixty-seven US cents. In other words, each soldier found guilty of multiple manslaughter was required to pay a total of 1,218 dollars, slightly over US$100 per dead peasant.[80]

Summing up post-peace-accords Guatemala in the apt idiom of New Orleans blues, one would have to say: "Justice? He not be comin' to Guatemala anytime soon."

---

80 *Ibid.*

REFLECTIONS ON GOOD GOVERNANCE, DEVELOPMENT AND JUDICIAL REFORM: SOME PERSPECTIVES ON THE PROBLEM OF JUDICIAL CORRUPTION*

*Florentino P. Feliciano***

I. PRELIMINARY — GENERAL CONSIDERATIONS

This brief essay proposes to focus on the problem of corruption in the judicial department of government and its relationship with broader, contemporary concerns about good governance, development and judicial reform. Its more specific objective is to address some of the aspects of this problem relating to judges themselves, as distinguished from officials and staff of auxiliary or support offices in the judicial department such as clerks of court or court registrars; court administrators; and sheriffs or enforcement-related officers. These latter types of subordinate officials present different kinds of regulatory or control problems than do judges, problems which do not seem to differ qualitatively from those which relate to officials in the executive department of government.

---

* This essay is based on an address delivered on Jan. 11, 1999 at a Symposium at the East Asian Legal Studies Program, Harvard Law School. The address in turn constituted a revision and enlargement of a paper delivered at a Conference held in Rome, Italy, under the aegis of the International Development Law Institute (IDLI) and the *Avvocatura Generale dello State,* Government of Italy, in Apr. 1998. An earlier version of this essay was published *in* 73 PHILIPPINE LAW JOURNAL 429 (1999). The consent of the Philippine Law Journal to the inclusion of the present, somewhat enlarged essay in this *Liber Amicorum* is recorded with appreciation.

** The views expressed in this paper are those of the author and should not be attributed to the institution he is affiliated with.

Two aspects of the problem of judicial corruption will be explored in this essay: the first relates to the context in which corruption among judges takes place; the second is concerned with the strategies or modes of control which are being employed to reduce or mitigate the incidence of judicial corruption. Necessarily, this paper draws from experience in my own country, since this is the only part of the world with which I have sufficient detailed familiarity.

These aspects are sought to be presented in terms sufficiently concrete and operational so as to generate a feel of the "real world," as it were, in which the judiciary operates in the Philippines. Preliminarily, however, it seems useful to explore some considerations of a fairly general nature which bear upon the subject of judicial corruption and reform and good governance.

The first general submission which may be made is that — whatever else it may be — and it is often referred to as a social and economic and institutional problem — judicial corruption is at bottom a personal and moral problem. From this perspective, a judge's response to a corrupt promise of some sum of money or of higher office or of any of the multitude of things that commonly are objects of human desire, will be affected by, *inter alia,* the judge's personal conception of his relationship with the rest of the universe. Given the ultimate nature of the problem of judicial corruption, judicial reform must realistically draw upon the wellsprings and methods of moral reform and these of course include religious and spiritual and social resources and methods. One lesson that history teaches us is that movements aimed at basic moral and social reform are often accompanied by religious fundamentalism. This was true in the Reformation of the late medieval Christian Church in the 15th century by Martin Luther and the Counter-Reformation of St. Ignatius of Loyola. Recall, in more recent times, the role of fundamentalist Islam in the revolution against and eventual overthrow of the Shah of Iran; of the so-called "liberation theology" of many Catholic priests in Central and South America during the decades of the 1960s, 1970s and 1980s; and the strategic role of the Catholic Church in the Philippines in the 1986 revolution against the Marcos regime.

A second general point that may be worth making is that corruption in the judiciary is a reflection of corruption in the civil service of a country. And the latter may be a symptom of corruption in the private sector and in society itself. Significant corruption among judges does not, and cannot, exist autonomously where the rest of the civil service and the civil society are substantially unaffected and in a healthy condition.

My third general consideration is in part a trite one: it is that corruption, public and private, has existed, and does exist, in all forms of human society as we know it from history.[1] Nevertheless, certain cultural factors in a particular society may bear significantly upon the incidence, growth and amenability to legal and social controls of corruption in general, and judicial corruption in particular. This is clearly a task for social anthropologists, but certain fairly common features in Philippine culture need examination in this regard. For instance, (a) deference to authority is clearly a desirable thing insofar as generating habits of law-observance is concerned; but it also makes difficult open complaints against and reporting or denouncing dishonest or incompetent public officials;

---

1 J. T. NOONAN, JR., BRIBES: THE INTELLECTUAL HISTORY OF A MORAL IDEA (1984) traces the 4000 years history of the concept of a bribe in the context of the culture or society in which the bribe-giver and the bribe-taker carry out their non-legitimate reciprocity. Noonan (a judge of the Ninth Circuit US Court of Appeals and Robbins Professor of Law Emeritus, University of California, Berkeley) describes the central concept of a bribe as "an inducement improperly influencing the performance of a public function meant to be gratuitously exercised. The concrete constituent elements . . . change with culture. The concept of a bribe contracts or expands with conventions, laws, practices." *See ibid.* at XI.

Noonan's work remains the standard scholarly examination of the moral philosophy, law and cultural anthropology of various societies' responses to, and efforts to control corruption, including, in particular, judicial corruption.

W. M. REISMAN, FOLDED LIES: BRIBERY, CRUSADES AND REFORM (1979), at 2 and Chapter 2, refers to bribery as "tendering and accepting a private reward for defection from a manifest duty." He distinguishes between a "myth system" and an "operational code": "an observer may distinguish in any social process a *myth system* that clearly expresses all the rules and prohibitions (the 'rights' and 'wrongs' of behaviour expressed without nuances and shadings), and an *operational code* that tells 'operators' when, by whom, and how certain 'wrong' things may be done. An operator is someone who knows the code in his own social setting — certain lawyers, some police officers, some business men, an agent, a kid at school." *See ibid.* at 1.

The myth systems of all human societies stigmatize varying forms of bribery; the operational codes of differing segments of a society frequently recognize that bribery continues to be practiced, under differing names and in varying circumstances, notwithstanding the prohibitory norms of the myth system. He describes his book as "an attempt at exploration into the inter-relations of the myth system and operational code as they pertain to bribery. It is a study of the processes and techniques of social stabilization rather than of social change." *Ibid.* at 6.

(b) *"Pakikisama"*— one aspect of which relates to submission to demands for group harmony and reluctance to "upset the official applecart," — is important in a society like ours which prizes consensus-building; however, such reluctance frequently renders problematical the discovery and investigation of official wrong doing; and (c) the concept of gratitude as constitutive of a personal social debt or obligation seems of central relevance. Gratitude for what? Among other things, for securing a judicial appointment or promotion. Most generally put, the relevant point appears to be that the agenda of judicial reform must include, among other things, the gradual modification of the systems of identifications and loyalties prevailing in our society. Effective identification with national ideals and institutions will need to be cultivated; loyalties to family clan or linguistic tribe or other sub-grouping will need to be restructured and modernized.

Another general submission which may be essayed is that judicial corruption is particularly deleterious in its consequences for the institutions of government and the body politic in general. Corruption of any public officer or employee is bad enough; corruption of a judicial officer is infinitely worse. The judicial process is often described as a system for delivery of justice; it is also sometimes described as a system and process for resolution of disputes. In responsible and representative governments, both the delivery of justice and the resolution of disputes are to be carried out on the basis of and in accordance with law. From this perspective, one effect of judicial corruption may be seen to be the substitution of the private exclusive interest of one of the parties to the dispute, and of the judge, instead of the public inclusive interest of the general community, as expressed in law, as the effective determinant of decision. In this very basic sense, judicial corruption subverts the role of law as the authoritative instrument of peaceful and legitimate change in society.

Insofar as impact upon the legal system is concerned, it may be observed that corrupt judgments may be rendered with or without distortion of the written norm. There is no necessary distortion of the relevant norm if that norm itself contemplates the exercise of judicial discretion within certain limits and the corrupt decision is rendered arguably within the limits of that discretion. The result, in other words, may be reached without a clear and palpable violation of the applicable norm. The ensuing result may even be plausibly regarded as the correct or a reasonable outcome normatively speaking; in such situation, the detection and proof of accompanying judicial corruption becomes more difficult.[2] The judge, however, who acts from a corrupt motive and receives extra-judicial consideration, nevertheless commits a separate violation of the criminal law.[3] Where the terms of the ap-

---

2 Prof. G. Gunther in his authoritative biography of Judge Learned Hand (LEARNED HAND, THE MAN AND THE JUDGE (1995), chapter XII) provides detailed, fascinating illustration in respect of Chief Judge Martin Manton who was forced to resign from the Second Circuit Court of Appeals in Feb. 7, 1939. The resignation came after then New York County District Attorney Thomas E. Dewey forwarded to the Chairman of the House of Representatives Judiciary Committee, whose tasks include consideration of possible impeachment, detailed charges concerning receipt by Chief Judge Manton, in six incidents, of more than US$400,000 from parties involved in litigation before the Second Circuit.

Judge Learned Hand himself had sat in two cases in which Manton had accepted bribes. In the first case, *General Motors Corp. v. Preferred Electric & Wire Corp.* 79 F.2d 621 (2d. Cir. 1935), the Second Circuit (Manton, Learned Hand and Swan, JJ.) unanimously invalidated the General Motors patent on which suit was brought. The pre-conference memoranda showed that all three judges agreed on the result from the outset and that nothing in Manton's memorandum "could clearly provoke suspicions of corruption" and that Manton's analysis of the legal issues closely resembled those of Hand and Swan. *See* GUNTHER, referred to at the beginning of this note, at 506–507. The Second Circuit, on rehearing granted after Manton had resigned, been charged and convicted, upon a fresh review of the old record and with full knowledge of Manton's bribery, once again found the patents invalid; 109 F.2d 615 (2d Cir. 1940).

The second case was much more complex: *Art Metal Works v. Abraham & Straus*, 70 F.2d 641 (2d Cir. 1934). Hand had dissented from Manton's majority opinion. In 1939, the Second Circuit, several months after Manton's conviction, unanimously reversed the earlier decision and adopted Hand's dissenting opinion. Prof. Gunther commented that "[b]y thus limiting his corrupt votes to reasonably close cases and arguably plausible positions, Manton made much of his dishonesty difficult to detect." *See* GUNTHER, referred to at the beginning of this note, at 507.

The Second Circuit continued to enjoy its reputation as the most highly respected US Circuit Court of Appeals with the great triumvirate of Learned Hand, as Chief Judge, Thomas Swan and Augustus Hand.

3 After his resignation from the Second Circuit, and on appeal from his conviction under a federal statute penalizing conspiracy "to defraud the United States," "in any manner or for any purpose," Manton argued that there had been no defrauding of the US and no obstruction of justice because the cases in which he had received payments from, or on behalf of, litigants, had been correctly decided. Moreover, he had been merely one of the members of the Division sitting on the cases involved and could not by himself have delivered success to the litigants who had paid him. *See* NOONAN, *supra* note 1, at 569.

Retired US Supreme Court Justice Sutherland, who had been designated to sit

plicable legal norm do not allow the exercise of discretion by the judge, or where the result is otherwise evidently inconsistent with the requirements of the norm, the corrupt decision necessarily distorts and undermines that norm. Such is the ordinary, garden-variety concept of judicial corruption.

The next general submission that might be made is that if corruption in the judiciary is sufficiently widespread, or (what may be functionally equivalent) if the public perception is that such corruption is sufficiently widespread,[4] the other institutions of government — legislative, executive and administrative — may be substantially weakened and the government's claim to legitimacy or official rectitude may be substantially eroded. In a community like that we have in my country, erosion and eventual loss of legitimacy must be carefully and self-consciously guarded against. Legitimacy is a vital but finite and exhaustible resource of governments that may be squandered by, among other things, widespread corruption, especially corruption in the judiciary which in the perception of the public, is uncontrolled and unchecked for a prolonged period of time. This is a principal lesson that may be derived from the contemporary still unfolding events in Venezuela and Pakistan.[5]

---

with the Second Circuit to hear Manton's appeal, was willing to assume that all the cases concerned had been correctly decided. Nevertheless, Sutherland rejected Manton's argument, holding that correctness of those decisions was not the issue. Sutherland wrote: "Judicial action, whether just or unjust, right or wrong, is not for sale." United States v. Manton, 107 F.2d 834 at 846.

4 Public awareness of corruption is essential if the community's efforts and resources are to be mobilized for the task of combating and controlling corruption. At the same time, the cautionary note sounded *in* IBRAHIM F.I. SHIHATA, THE WORLD BANK IN A CHANGING WORLD (2000), Chapter Nine (*Role of the Judiciary in the Prevention and Control of Corruption)* is noteworthy: "If corruption grows faster in an environment of under-regulation or over-regulation, *corrupt and corrupting individuals have a vested interest in spreading the perception that it is dominant and prevalent in all cases. Through them it becomes self-perpetuating. Public perception of widespread corruption often produces an actual increase in corruption.*" (Emphasis supplied.)

5 The current turmoil and constitutional crisis in Venezuela have been attributed by commentators to the loss of political legitimacy by the traditional political and juridical institutions of Venezuela. It is reported that 94 percent of the Venezuelan people distrust the judiciary as corrupt and inept and frequently take the law into their own hands by lynching persons accused of crimes while disputes involving business enterprises remain mired in court for years. The Venezuela legislature is reportedly viewed with the same widespread distrust. In the Feb. 1999 presidential

Our community relies heavily, almost instinctively, on legal (i.e., statutory) prohibition and criminalization as modes of control of socially undesirable types of behavior. The resulting prescriptions naturally require judicial interpretation and application. Our judiciary is also empowered to intervene decisively in the processes of government by striking down legislative measures as unconstitutional, and executive and administrative acts as unconstitutional or illegal. We have not seriously developed (outside the field of labor relations) alternative, private, non-judicial, methods of dispute resolution — such as mediation and conciliation — and we have barely begun with commercial arbitration. In other words, the judiciary, in our system of government, has a very large and important role to play. By intervening or failing to intervene under certain circumstances, or by the quality of their intervention, the judiciary can in measure affect the course and direction and the pace of social, economic and political development of the country. The nature of the functions entrusted to the judiciary in our governmental system, underscores the fundamental importance of preserving the integrity and independence of the judiciary from the ravages of corruption. At the same time, those very same functions constitute the judiciary as principal and indispensable bulwark

---

elections, a former unsuccessful coup leader, Mr. Hugo Chavez, was elected President by a landslide vote and a "constituent assembly" consisting almost completely of Mr. Chavez' party mates was elected. This " constituent assembly" has effectively claimed power and authority to "transform the state" and to dismiss the Venezuelan Supreme Court and to strip the Venezuelan Congress of its legislative functions. The judges of the Supreme Court preferred to resign *en masse* rather than be physically thrown out of office. *See* the report entitled *Debunking Democracy* by R. Colitt & R. Lapper, FINANCIAL TIMES, Aug. 31, 1999, at 12.

Note may also be taken of a recent decision of the Supreme Court of Pakistan *reported in* THE WASHINGTON POST, May 13, 2000, at A22. The Pakistan Supreme Court is said to have ruled on May 13, 2000 that widespread corruption justified the ouster of former prime Minister Nawaz Sharif in a military coup. The Court gave General Pervez Musharraf, the country's military leader who had seized power on Oct. 12, 1999, charging runaway corruption and economic mismanagement on the part of the previous Sharif government, three years "to clean up Pakistan and return to democracy." The Court is quoted by THE WASHINGTON POST as having said that "the military takeover was justified under the doctrine of necessity. Sufficient evidence was presented by the state of corruption of the former government."

The Venezuelan and Pakistan developments provide illustration of the possible consequences of total loss of legitimacy in the eyes of substantial portions of the population of a country.

against the corruption and degradation of the other institutions of government and of society itself.[6]

Thus we arrive at the nexus between the basic principles and constitutive practices of good governance — of which legal and judicial reform and control of corruption are integral — and national development processes. In the last several decades, there has been increasing recognition that a sound legal framework or system is a basic prerequisite for the success of the social and economic development efforts of a state.[7] A sound legal system is not simply a black box which, at one end, takes in problems and which, at the other end, mechanically grinds out solutions in the form of legally binding decisions. It is most appropriately conceived of as comprising a series of processes by which laws and regulations are formulated and prescribed, applied and enforced, and evaluated and amended or terminated. Good governance relates to the participatory nature, the quality and efficiency and transparency of these processes of law-prescribing, law-applying and law-enforcing, and law-revising or law-repealing. Indispensable for the efficacy of these inter-related processes is the existence of "well functioning public institutions" staffed by trained

---

6 SHIHATA, *supra* note 4, expresses the relevant point succinctly:

"The more checks and balances exist within a society, and the more strong institutions are in place to protect such checks and balances, in an overall environment of free expression and free press, the fewer opportunities there may be for corrupt practices which remain unchecked or unpunished. The judiciary is the ultimate institution to protect these checks and balances. It can, and in fact is expected to, act as a model for other institutions and as a necessary mechanism to enforce law efficiently and fairly against corrupt behavior, thus serving as a deterrent to any further behavior of this kind." (Footnote omitted.)

7 *See*, in particular, the extensive work done by Dr. Ibrahim F. I. Shihata on this subject, *e.g.*, *Good Governance and the Role of Law in Economic Development, Preface in* MAKING DEVELOPMENT WORK: LEGISLATIVE REFORM FOR INSTITUTIONAL TRANSFORMATION AND GOOD GOVERNANCE (A. Seidman, R. B. Seidman & T. Wälde EDS., 1999); *id.*, The World Bank in a Changing World, Vol. II (1995), Chapter Three (*Legal Framework for Development and the Role of the World Bank in Legal Technical Assistance*); *id.*, COMPLEMENTARY REFORM — ESSAYS ON LEGAL, JUDICIAL AND OTHER INSTITUTIONAL REFORMS (1997), Chapter One (*Law, Development and the Role of the World Bank*); *id.*, *The Role of Law in Business Development*, 20 FORDHAM INTERNATIONAL LAW JOURNAL 1577 (1997); and *id.*, *Corruption — A General Review with an Emphasis on the Role of the World Bank*, 15 DICKINSON JOURNAL OF INTERNATIONAL LAW 451 (1997).

individuals who are accountable to the general community and who are bound by and do comply with laws and regulations applying them in an efficient and observable manner, without arbitrariness or corruption.

Arguably the most important of those "well functioning public institutions" is an independent, fair and impartial, honest and well-trained judiciary. In all well-ordered modern societies, the judiciary is not merely the arbiter of disputes between private individuals. It must also — and more importantly — resolve citizens' problems with their own government, their charges of unconstitutional, illegal, arbitrary, corrupt or disgraceful behavior on the part of public officials as well as conflicting claims of jurisdiction and competence by public agencies *inter se.*

It should also be noted that the requirements of good governance — which include, again, an independent, impartial, honest and competent judiciary — and the extent to which they are effectively realized within the internal processes of a state, are widely regarded as giving rise to legitimate concerns on the part of other states. Legislation by home countries of multinational corporations have, for instance, defined the giving of bribes to officials of foreign governments as criminal behavior punishable in the home country and the bribes themselves as non-tax deductible.

In 1977, the Foreign Corrupt Practices Act[8] was enacted by the US Congress. It defines as a criminal offense the bribery of foreign officials by US corporations seeking to obtain and do business abroad. The Act did not render criminal all acts of bribery of foreign officials. It explicitly excludes gratuities frequently paid to low-level foreign government officials to secure or expedite the performance of routine, non-discretionary, duties. These are commonly referred to as "facilitating" or "grease" payments and typically are not made "for the purpose of obtaining business."[9] Payments unlawful under the Foreign Corrupt Practices Act are also denied deductibility under Section 162(a) of the US Internal Revenue

[8] 15 U.S.C. Secs. 78m, 79dd-1, 78dd-2, 78ff. Text *in* 17 INTERNATIONAL LEGAL MATERIALS (I.L.M.) 214 (1978); the Foreign Corrupt Practices Amendments of Aug. 23, 1988 appear *in* 28 INTERNATIONAL LEGAL MATERIALS (I.L.M.) 455 (1989).

[9] *See* L.A. Low, A.K. Bjorklund & K.C. Atkinson, *The Inter-American Convention Against Corruption: A Comparison with the United States Foreign Corrupt Practices Act,* 38 VIRGINIA JOURNAL OF INTERNATIONAL LAW 243, 257 & 269 (1998).

Code which authorizes US taxpayers to deduct "ordinary and necessary" expenses incurred in carrying on trade or business.[10]

On March 29, 1996, twenty one out of the thirty four member states of the Organization of American States (OAS) signed the Inter-American Convention Against Corruption.[11] In the same year, the United States and Canada, the principal capital- and technology-exporting countries in the hemisphere, signed this Convention and on March 6, 1997, the OAS Convention went into effect after the deposit of the second instrument of ratification. The Preamble of the OAS Convention eloquently underlines the relationship between democratic legitimacy, development and efforts to combat and control corruption:

> "The Member States of the Organization of American States
>
> *Convinced* that corruption undermines the legitimacy of public institutions and strikes at society, moral order and justice, as well as at the comprehensive development of peoples;
>
> *Considering* that representative democracy, as an essential condition for stability, peace and development of the region, requires, by its nature, the combating of every form of corruption in the performance of public functions, as well as acts of corruption specifically related to such performance;
>
> *Persuaded* that fighting corruption strengthens democratic institutions and prevents distortions in the economy, improprieties in public administration and damage to a society's moral fiber;
>
> *Recognizing* that corruption is often a tool used by organized crime for the accomplishment of its purposes;
>
> . . .
>
> *Deeply concerned* by steadily increasing links between corruption and the proceeds generated by illicit narcotics trafficking which undermine and threaten legitimate commercial and financial activities, and society, at all levels; [and]

---

10 On the deductibility of bribes or "questionable foreign payments" for tax purposes, *see*, e.g., M. Chu & D. Magraw, *The Deductibility of Questionable Foreign Payments*, 87 YALE LAW JOURNAL 1091 (1978); and L. Denys et al., *Bribes as Deductible Business Expenses*, 16 EUROPEAN TAXATION 370 (1976).

11 *See* text *in* 35 INTERNATIONAL LEGAL MATERIALS (I.L.M.) 724 (1996). It may be noted that under Art. XXIII of the Convention, states which are not members of the OAS may accede to the Convention.

> *Bearing in mind* the responsibility of States to hold corrupt persons accountable in order to combat corruption and to cooperate with one another for their efforts in this area to be effective, and
>
> . . ."

Probably the most important provision of the OAS Convention for present purposes, is Article VIII which sets forth the undertaking of states parties to the Convention to criminalize what is often called "active bribery" or the giving or offering of bribes, as distinguished from "passive bribery" understood as the soliciting or accepting of bribes in transnational commerce by foreign government officials. This article (Article VIII on Transnational Bribery) reads in part as follows:

> "Subject to its Constitution and the fundamental principles of its legal system, each State Party shall prohibit and punish the offering or granting, directly or indirectly, by its nationals, persons having their habitual residence in its territory, and business domiciled there, to a government official of another State, of any article of monetary value, or other benefit, such as a gift, favour, promise or advantage, in connection with any economic or commercial transaction in exchange for any act or omission in the performance of that official's public functions.
>
> . . ."

Two observations might usefully be made in this connection. Firstly, the definition of "transnational bribery" now includes the "facilitation payments" typically made to minor foreign public officials.[12] Secondly, the applicability of the Convention's provisions is not dependent upon a showing that the acts of corruption imputed to the accused resulted in harm to state property, that is, that the country of the official bribed has suffered some economic injury by reason of the acts of corruption involved.[13]

---

12 Art. I, OAS Convention defines "public official," "government official" or "public servant," as meaning "any official or employee of the State or its agencies, including those who have been selected, appointed or elected to perform activities or functions in the name of the state or in the service of the state, *at any level of its hierarchy*." (Emphasis supplied.)

13 *See* Art. XII, OAS Convention.

Soon after the OAS Convention went into effect, the member states of the Organization for Economic Cooperation and Development (OECD) followed suit and signed a Convention on Combating Bribery of Foreign Public Officials in International Business Transactions on December 17, 1997. The OECD Convention, like the OAS Convention, recognizes in its preambular paragraphs that the use of bribery by multinational corporations as an instrument in securing and expanding business opportunities, had become common place in some developing countries and that efforts to control and suppress corruption must be supported by international cooperation:

> "[B]ribery is a widespread phenomenon in international business transactions, including trade and investment, which raises serious moral and political concerns, undermines good governance and economic development, and distorts international competitive conditions; [and]
>
> [A]ll countries share a responsibility to combat bribery in international business transactions."[14]

---

[14] *See* text *in* 37 International Legal Materials (I.L.M.) 1 (1998). It is noteworthy that the bribery of a public official is required, under the Convention, to be penalized as a criminal offence "irrespective of, *inter alia,* the value of the advantage [secured through bribery], its results, perceptions of local custom, the toleration of such payments by local authorities, or the alleged necessity of the payment in order to obtain or retain business or other improper advantage." *See* Commentaries on the OECD Convention Adopted by the Negotiating Conference on Nov. 21, 1997, par. 7 *in* 37 International Legal Materials (I.L.M.) 8, 9 (1998). Moreover, bribery of a foreign public official to obtain or retain business or other improper advantage is required to be criminalized "whether or not the company concerned was the best qualified bidder or was otherwise a company which could properly have been awarded the business." Commentaries etc., par. 4, 37 International Legal Materials (I.L.M.) 8 (1998).

See, further, *Convention on the Fight Against Corruption Involving Officials of the European Communities or Officials of Members of the European Union,* recommended by the Council of the European Union on May 26, 1997 for adoption by the Member States in accordance with their respective constitutional requirements, 37 International Legal Materials 12 (I.L.M.) (1998). The EU Convention requires each Member State to render both "passive corruption" and "active corruption" criminal offenses.

Reisman, *supra* note 1, at 157, referring to earlier proposals relating to an international agreement to criminalize bribery by multinational corporations, expresses doubt as to the prospects of success of such an agreement. He notes that the

The OECD Convention establishes, again much like the OAS Convention, treaty undertakings by states parties to it to enact domestic legislation criminalizing the employment of "active bribery" by their nationals, individual or corporate, in promoting their business interests abroad. That parties to the OAS Convention or to the OECD Convention may carry out such undertakings not necessarily or exclusively for moral or ethical reasons, but as well for more pragmatic objectives of reducing the comparative cost of doing business abroad and achieving equality of competitive conditions — need not detract from the importance and desirability of implementing those treaty undertakings.[15]

From a national criminal law perspective, the noteworthy effect of statutes like the US Foreign Corrupt Practices Act and of legislation implementing the OAS and the OECD Conventions, is that, although some or all of the constituent elements of the act of bribery may occur outside the territorial domain of the state party enacting the legislation, the courts of that state nevertheless acquire jurisdiction to try and punish the corporate officials or representatives offering or dispensing the bribes. Sometimes the realistic prospects of detecting and punishing bribery in transnational business may be greater in the national state or domicile of the multinational enterprise than in the home country of the bribe-taker. Practical immunity in that home country may well form part of the corrupt bargain. There is, too, clear recognition that the bribery of foreign officials affects the interests of the national state or domicile of the bribe-giver.

Finally, it may be observed that the same requirements of good governance are also taken into account, with varying degrees of explicitness, by multilateral financial institutions in the

formal code of virtually every country in the world already prohibits bribery. An international agreement might win quick acceptance but result in no more enforcement than is currently obtained under the different domestic laws it replicates.

15 The OECD has had no monopoly of concerns over the use of, or acquiescence in, bribery of foreign public officials by multinational enterprises. The UN Commission on Transnational Corporations produced lengthy studies on a code of conduct for transnational corporations prohibiting, *inter alia,* bribery of foreign public officials; so did the UN Social and Economic Council. A useful list of these studies may be found in the extensive bibliography on bribery appended to REISMAN, *supra* note 1, at 266–267. The 1984 Draft UN Code of Conduct on Transnational Corporations appears *in* 23 INTERNATIONAL LEGAL MATERIALS (I.L.M.) 602 (1984).

granting (or withholding) and structuring of development loans to developing and transition-economy countries.[16]

II. THE CONTEXT OF CAUSES AND CONDITIONS

We turn to the context of more specific causes and conditions within which the problem of corruption among judges may be examined.

By context, one commonly refers to the aggregate of causative and conditioning (that is, environmental) factors within which judicial corruption occurs. It is commonly difficult to distinguish, in the real world, between causes and conditioning factors but, one might believe, it is not really necessary to make such a distinction for preventive and regulatory purposes.

The first of these factors relates to the protracted and complex nature of the judicial process as we know it, which in itself is the result of many factors including the great number of statutes and administrative regulations which have to be judicially applied and controlled. The ultimate outcome is multiplicity of litigations which are processed through the judicial system. The sheer volume of incoming cases is such as to lead to significant congestion of judicial dockets and the slow but inexorable accumulation of backlogs of judges, at least those who are stationed at urban and commercial-industrial centers.[17]

In our country, the congestion of dockets is observable at just about all levels of the judiciary. A sense of the realities of the sit-

---

16 Sometimes the message is conveyed with considerable explicitness indeed. Consider the following: Recently, THE FINANCIAL TIMES, Aug. 25, 1999, at 12, carried a report entitled *World Bank Threatens To Stop Lending To Indonesia*. It had been previously reported that senior officials took bribes to transfer government funds to a private bank, Bank Bali, which then transferred more than half the payment (i.e., US$80 million) to an agency run by a senior member of the then ruling Golkar party. Opposition leaders accused senior advisers and a younger brother of former President B.J. Habibie of involvement in the scandal. Mark Baird, the World Bank's Indonesia Director, was quoted as stating that "[I]f this case is not resolved early, and satisfactorily, it is difficult for us to provide budget support to the Government of Indonesia." Mr. Baird was described by THE FINANCIAL TIMES as "now exerting the heaviest foreign pressure on Mr. Habibie's government since it took office in May [of 1998]."

17 *See* generally, F. P. Feliciano & E. L. Caparas, *The Problem of Delay in the Philippine Court System*, 62 PHILIPPINE LAW JOURNAL 201 (1987).

uation may perhaps be conveyed by citing that in the Supreme Court of the Philippines, in the last ten years (1989–1998), the average number of newly filed cases per year has been 5,555.3 cases. The average number of cases disposed of per year during the same period has been 5,282.8 cases.[18] While the jurisdiction of the Supreme Court is, in theory, optional in character, the Constitution requires the Court to explain why it rejects a petition for review or petition for *certiorari*, which means that each case must be processed and decided one way or the other.[19] This is true for all courts below the Supreme Court.

It should also be noted that our Judiciary Act, as it stands at present, permits successive appeals — from the Municipal Court to the Regional Trial Court, and then to the Court of Appeals and finally to the Supreme Court. Decisions of administrative agencies may also be tested in the courts, from the Regional Trial Court and onwards.

The net result of the system is that the losing party may try, in successive appeals up the hierarchy of courts, to reverse the original judgment or at least delay the finality of the judgment and the execution thereof. This situation creates incentives for at-

---

18 "Newly filed cases" with the Supreme Court include both judicial cases and administrative (disciplinary) cases involving judges and other officials of the judicial department. The above figures may be grossed up and broken down as follows:

I(1) Total judicial cases filed Jan. 1, 1989 to Dec. 31, 1998	51,638
average over 10 years	5,163.8
(2) Total administrative cases filed Jan. 1, 1989 to Dec. 31, 1998	3,915
average over 10 years	391.5
II(1) Total judicial cases disposed of Jan. 1,1989 to Dec. 31, 1998	49,950
average over 10 years	4,995
(2) Total administrative cases disposed of Jan. 1, 1989 to Dec. 31,1998	2,878
average over 10 years	287.8

The yearly figures relating to judicial cases were provided by the Judicial Records Office, Supreme Court of the Philippines, courtesy of Atty. Natalie Mendoza of the Office of the Clerk of Court *(en banc),* Supreme Court. The year by year figures pertaining to administrative (disciplinary) cases were supplied by the Office of the Court Administrator, Supreme Court; the assistance of Deputy Court Administrator Zenaida Elepaño is acknowledged. The figures relating to the dockets of trial courts throughout the country, are much more difficult to assemble. It is believed that the differential between cases disposed of and cases filed, in respect of trial courts, is probably significantly higher than that pertaining to the Supreme Court.

19 1987 PHILIPPINE CONSTITUTION, art. VIII, sec. 14.

tempts by litigants and their lawyers to short-circuit the ordinarily lengthy procedure by extra judicial means.

The second element of the context which should be noted is that the levels of compensation in the judiciary are very low, indeed, unreasonably low. A certain disparity in the compensation structures of civil servants and the private sector is, of course, commonplace, especially in developing countries. In the case of the judiciary, however, the disparity is so severe as to be appalling. Not more than one and a half percent of the national budget is allocated to the judicial department. The figure used to be one percent until a former Chief Justice lobbied with the Department of the Budget and Management and the legislative department of the government. He quickly found out, however, that there was a limit beyond which the independence of the judiciary would be endangered by further lobbying and he decided against further efforts to obtain a higher allocation of budgetary resources.

It is therefore not easy to attract bright young lawyers to the judiciary, except where they have independent means. Of course there are able lawyers who enter the judiciary at a relatively late stage in their professional careers, where substantial savings permit them to treat low judicial compensation levels as secondary in importance. For all, however, acceptance of judicial office requires a strong moral commitment to reject blandishments from, for instance, litigants who go to court to protect an economic interest from either the internal revenue officers or business competitors.

Some perspective is necessary in looking at this factor. Prosperity (in the form of high compensation levels) is not a guarantee of judicial integrity, competence and independence,[20] any more than poverty (understood as modest pay scales) necessarily

---

20 A former senior law officer who comes from Asia made the interesting comment (to the author) that the pay of judges could also be raised to such generous levels as to create marked, if unspoken, inclinations on the part of judges to uphold the position of the government in crucial litigations. It was stated that the pay scale of judges of the highest court in one Asian country very significantly exceeds that of justices of the Supreme Court of the United States. The suggestion, apparently, is that judges, when so generously treated, may be less likely to take an aggressively independent stance *vis-à-vis* the Legislative and Executive Departments which control the public purse.

means easy judicial virtue or loss of judicial innocence. There is no more inevitability about either judicial corruption or judicial reform than about other important aspects of personal and social life and development.[21]

Another factor to be considered is the public perception of the judiciary in general, to the extent that this perception is reflected in the mass media and opinion polls. There are, of course, in my country as elsewhere, dishonest judges who accept different kinds of bribes, as well as ignorant judges and those whose personal behavior render them unfit for judicial office. It is not possible to tell whether we have more than our "fair share" of corrupt judges.[22] It seems to me, however, that in the last few years, public perception has been generally severe with respect to judges. My personal belief is that there are many, many judges out there who are honest and committed and reasonably competent, but who are voiceless and largely unnoticed in the hurly-burly of episodic media crusades. Two considerations are worth mentioning. One is wide-

---

21 Striking illustration is provided in Professor Andrew Kaufman's superb biography of Mr. Justice Benjamin N. Cardozo. Justice Cardozo is widely regarded as second only to Mr. Justice Oliver W. Holmes of the US Supreme Court in the enduring importance and quality of their contributions to the caselaw of that Court. *See* ANDREW KAUFMAN, CARDOZO (1998). Justice Cardozo's father, Judge Albert Cardozo who had been elected to and had sat in the New York Supreme Court during the period of Tammany Hall dominance of New York City politics, was forced to resign on charges of corruption, fee-splitting with receivers and Masters of the Rolls appointed by him, etc. Justice Cardozo almost never spoke of his father, except to say that the affair had taken place a long time ago when he was a young boy and he remembered Albert as a loving father. By the end of Mr. Justice Cardozo's life, he had redeemed his family honor by the sheer force of the exemplary moral and intellectual qualities of the life he led as a man and as a judge; Kaufman, *ibid., passim*, notes that this extraordinary redemption was accomplished within a single generation. Justice Cardozo prevented a "like father, like son" syndrome from arising. In the end, the name "Judge Cardozo" ceased totally to refer to the disgraced father and recalled instead only the great and universally respected judge the son had become.

22 REISMAN, *supra* note 1, at 9, acknowledges the methodological problems arising from the fact that although bribery in a particular society might be extant in a greater or lesser degree, "it is conducted in an atmosphere of understandable secrecy." Part of the reason for secrecy, he suggests, arises from fear of sanctions "not for violation of the laws against bribery but rather for violation of the operational code that some types of bribery are acceptable but are not to be talked about," and from the readiness of members of a group to impose effective sanctions on those who deviate from that code.

spread lack of familiarity among the general public about the structure and requirements of our system for delivering justice. When, for instance, a person accused of a crime is acquitted in court, there is an unfortunate tendency on the part of the victim or his family readily to assume either that the judge was ignorant or had been bribed by the accused person.

What is often forgotten is that the courts constitute only the last phase of the justice delivery system and that earlier phases — such as police investigative work, finding and protecting witnesses and other evidence, and preparation and handling of the public prosecutor's case — effectively limit what courts can do by way of reducing criminality. If insufficient admissible evidence is adduced in court — because the police did not do their work or because the public prosecutor was inept — the courts must acquit.

Another consideration is that litigants or their lawyers and even the bar associations have often been reluctant to come out openly against judges they might suspect or who are rumored to be dishonest so that investigation may be commenced. We noted earlier that cultural influences may be at work here. Still another consideration is that there are unfortunately some lawyers who are quick to explain an unfavorable court decision, or a large billing for legal fees, by telling the client that the judge had been "bought" by the opposing litigant or that a portion of his legal "fees" had to go to the judge. The client will never know whether or not his lawyer is telling the truth; and the judge, who could be completely innocent, is totally defenseless.

The general point that should be made is that corrupt judges do not exist in a vacuum. There are corrupt judges because, *inter alia,* there are corrupt lawyers and litigants willing to offer a bribe or who, for diverse reasons, are unwilling to resist a demand for a bribe from an aggressively corrupt judge and who refuse to go to the appropriate judicial authority which can discipline and remove such judges. Judicial reform must begin and go hand in hand with reform of the bar. Clearly, members of the bar and the general public must learn to cooperate with judicial authority, and the latter must, in turn, convincingly demonstrate its own ability to identify and remove unworthy and unfaithful judges so as to generate and reinforce the habits of trust and cooperation.

III. MODES OF REGULATING AND CONTROLLING JUDICIAL CORRUPTION

The modes which have been employed in my country to regulate and control corruption among judges, are multiple. There is, firstly, a general effort to upgrade the levels of judicial compensation, on the part of the Executive and Legislative Departments of government. However, there are structural limitations to this strategy, since such upgrading has to take into account the compensation levels of the entire civil service. It simply has not been politically possible to upgrade judicial compensation levels without at the same time upgrading the pay scales of the rest of the government sector. There is constant competition for finite budgetary allocations and the judicial department is at a severe disadvantage in such competition.

More specific strategies relate to the recruitment of judges. In the end, the problem of judicial corruption is the problem of the quality — moral and professional — of members of the bar; for judges are recruited exclusively from the bar.[23] There are no elective judges in our jurisdiction; there have never been any. Under our earlier (i.e., the 1935 and 1973) Constitutions, the appointment of all judges was vested in the President of the Republic, but such appointment was subject to confirmation by the Commission on Appointments — consisting of Members of the Senate and the House of Representatives. To minimize the perceived influence of political factors on the selection of judges, our present (1987) Constitution has done away with the need for confirmation by the Commission on Appointments. Instead, nominations to judicial posts are made by a Judicial and Bar Council composed of seven members: the Chief Justice of the Philippines, the Secretary of Justice and a Member of Congress as *ex-officio* Members; and a representative of the Integrated Bar, a law professor, a retired Member of the Supreme Court and a representative of the private sector.[24] The Chief Justice is *ex-officio* Chairman of the Council. Three or more nominations are made for each judicial vacancy; the final choice and the appointment is made by the President of

---

23 1987 PHILIPPINE CONSTITUTION, art. VIII, sec. 7, par. (2).

24 *Ibid.* at art. VIII, sec. 8, par. (1).

the Republic.[25] This procedure makes possible a more focused effort to scrutinize carefully the record and credentials (personal and professional) of would-be judges. The list of names under consideration for nomination is published in national newspapers and bar associations and the public are invited to comment on those names. The Judicial and Bar Council may also interview the candidates for nomination. The process is generally analogous to the process of recruitment for positions in private corporations and enterprises.

The next effort to upgrade the quality of judges comes promptly upon the appointment of new judges. They are required to undergo training courses at the Philippine Judicial Academy, an entity originally created by an administrative order of the Supreme Court and later reconstituted and chartered by statute and maintained by Government.[26] In addition, special courses and seminars are offered at the Academy; those hopeful of promotion to higher courts must confront the task of taking and passing these courses.

A third mode of control of judicial corruption relates to the administrative supervision exercised by the Supreme Court, by constitutional mandate,[27] over all courts and court personnel. An important aspect of this supervision is the monitoring of the administrative performance of judges, i.e., the state of their judicial dockets and the disposition of cases within the prescribed period of time. This monitoring makes possible the rationalization of the distribution of case loads; additional judges are moved to districts generating high numbers of cases.

The supervisory jurisdiction of the Supreme Court over lower courts is not, however, limited to administrative matters.[28] The Supreme Court has disciplinary jurisdiction over all judges of lower courts.[29] It receives and investigates complaints against judges.

---

25 *Ibid.* at art. VIII, sec. 9.

26 *See*, in this connection, A. A. Melencio-Herrera, *Legal and Judicial Education Reforms and the Narvasa Court, in* ODYSSEY AND LEGACY: THE CHIEF JUSTICE ANDRES R. NARVASA CENTENNIAL LECTURES SERIES 40 *et seq.* (1998).

27 *See* 1987 PHILIPPINE CONSTITUTION, art. VIII, sec. 6.

28 In *Maceda v. Vazquez,* G.R. No. 102781, Apr. 22, 1993, 221 SCRA 464, the Supreme Court declared that this administrative supervisory and disciplinary authority over all lower courts is vested *exclusively* in the Supreme Court, and not shared by, *e.g.*, the Office of the Ombudsman.

29 1987 PHILIPPINE CONSTITUTION, art. VIII, sec. 11.

When probable cause is shown, formal charges are filed against a judge by the Court Administrator and hearings where the respondent judge is given the opportunity to defend himself, are held by a Regional Trial Court judge or by a Member of the Court of Appeals designated by the Supreme Court. The designated judge renders a report which is reviewed in a formal proceeding by the Supreme Court. In this proceeding, the respondent is accorded the opportunity to rebut the findings and recommendations of the investigating judge or justice. Thereafter, the Supreme Court renders judgment either dismissing the charges or penalizing the respondent judge. The penalties range from reprimand to dismissal.[30]

---

30 The following figures were provided by the Office of the Court Administrator, an agency directly under the supervision of the Supreme Court of the Philippines; the assistance of Deputy Court Administrator Zenaida Elepaño is once again acknowledged with appreciation:

- As of Mar. 31, 1999, the total number of lower court (i.e., trial) judges in the Philippine judiciary was 1,524. On the same date, the number of vacant positions of trial judges was 694.
- During the period from 1989 to 1999, a total of 43 lower court judges were *dismissed from office* by the Supreme Court: 14 were Regional Trial judges; 28 were Metropolitan or Municipal Trial or Circuit Trial judges and one Shariá Circuit Court Judge. Of these, eight were dismissed on charges of violation of the Anti-Graft and Corrupt Practices Act; 12 on charges of gross misconduct; seven on charges of grave abuse of authority; five on charges of immorality and disgraceful conduct; five on charges of inefficiency and failure to decide a case within the reglementary period; two on charges of ignorance of the law; one for violation of the Code of Judicial Conduct; one for knowingly rendering an unjust decision; and two for habitual absenteeism and falsification of certificates of service (i.e., disposition of pending cases).
- From 1995 to 1999, a total of 12 lower court judges were penalized with *suspension from office,* without pay for varying periods of time, for offenses ranging from violation of the Anti-Graft and Corrupt Practices Act, through gross ignorance of the law, sexual harassment and delay in rendering decisions.
- From 1987 to 1999, 137 lower court judges were penalized with *monetary fines* in amounts equivalent to from 10 days salary to two months salary, for offenses ranging from gross ignorance of the law (the most common offense) through serious misconduct in office and grave abuse of authority to immorality and knowingly rendering an unjust judgment.
- Finally, from 1990 to 1999, 57 lower court judges were "reprimanded" for a variety of minor offenses while from 1987 to 1999, 75 lower court judges were "admonished" for much the same kinds of offenses.

Where appropriate, the Court may also order the initiation of criminal proceedings against the offending judge. Formal proceedings against respondent judges of course take time. But once they are ripe for decision, the Court assigns high priority to the resolution of such disciplinary proceedings.

A fourth mode of control — a fairly obvious one — is legislation that would limit the availability of successive appeals and provide for finality of judgments of the Court of Appeals in many types of cases, except those which, by constitutional provision, pertain to the exclusive jurisdiction of the Supreme Court. During the decade of the '90s, at least two bills were filed in our Congress seeking to do just that with respect to decisions of certain administrative, quasi-judicial agencies, such as the National Labor Relations Commission, whose decisions may be reviewed by the Court of Appeals on *certiorari*. The bills failed of enactment.

Another measure adopted by the Supreme Court, in the exercise of its administrative supervision, relates to the introduction of new electronic methods of court reporting. The objective here has been the reduction of the period of delay in the conduct of trials occasioned by the need for manual transcription of court stenographers' notes. The new methods make possible the completion of the transcript of oral hearings almost immediately after the end of each hearing. The acquisition of this new technology requires very significant capital investment, as does the re-training of present stenographers. It remains to be seen what degree of success in shortening litigation can be achieved with these new methods.

The degree of success of any particular strategy of prevention and control is commonly difficult to determine. What is perhaps most important, in the end, is that all available strategies must be employed with sustained commitment, fairness and large quantities of common sense. A sense of the human condition and an understanding of both the dynamics and the constraints of social processes would also be valuable in this enterprise.

A final reflection. Judicial reforms must be institutionalized if they are to survive the term of office of the reformer. The role of personal leadership in the task of judicial reform must not, however, be overlooked. Necessarily, in our system, the main burden of this leadership falls on the Chief Justice of the Supreme Court of the Philippines. Certain qualities of heart, mind and will are indispensable for the successful assumption and discharge of the burdens and responsibilities entailed by that leadership.[31] This burden, however, must realistically be shared by the Presiding Justice of the Court of Appeals and the Executive Judges of the Regional Trial Courts and of the Municipal Trial Courts. With such leadership, and with an informed and supportive citizenry, and a strong and vigilant bar itself deeply committed to professional reform, much may be expected by way of progress in judicial reform.

POST SCRIPTUM: CURRENT DEVELOPMENTS

Noteworthy efforts aimed at judicial development and judicial reform have gone on stream, as it were, in the last couple of years in the Philippines. The principal effort has been directed at the formulation of a comprehensive but detailed and operable plan for addressing identified priority problems and concerns of the judiciary. A "Medium Term Public Investment Program for the Supreme Court [really the Judicial Department]" (MTPIP) was formally approved by the Supreme Court in May, 2000.[32] The MTPIP is the result of a series of intensive studies on and investigations of particular problems of the judiciary determined to constitute priority concerns, followed by extensive consultations with judges, the Philippine Judicial Academy, the Institute of Judicial Administration of the University of the Philippines, the Department of Justice, the Integrated Bar of the Philippines and voluntary bar associations and other professional organizations. These problems include those relating to: fiscal autonomy; court per-

---

31 *See*, in this connection, A.V. PANGANIBAN, LEADERSHIP BY EXAMPLE (1999) where a Member of the Supreme Court of the Philippines outlines some of the judicial management policies and practices recently adopted by that Court under Chief Justice Hilario G. Davide, Jr. These efforts include, notably, the acceleration of the rate of investigation and disposition of disciplinary charges brought against judges and other officers of the judiciary.

Special note should be taken of the comprehensive and systematic agenda of judicial reform and the enhancement of judicial capabilities as instruments of good governance and national development, and the available menus of fairly concrete steps, outlined and explored in SHIHATA, *supra* note 4.

32 *See, generally,* C. B. Espeleta, *The Judicial Reform Program: A Work in Progress,* BENCHMARK, VOL I, no. 2 (July–Aug. 2000), Public Information Office, Supreme Court of the Philippines.

formance; judicial education including capacity-building, and development and upgrading of skills in decision-making; modernization of court facilities and acquisition of new technologies in, e.g., documents filing, processing, storage and retrieval; and adaptation and use of alternative dispute resolution methods. The MTPIP is designed as a framework within which particular judicial reform projects addressing and focusing on particular problems may be undertaken and courses of corrective and ameliorative action formulated, developed and implemented. Cost estimates of reform projects and implementation thereof are provided. The Supreme Court has forwarded the MTPIP to the National Economic Development Authority for review and integration into the Medium-Term Philippine Development Plan. The Court may also be expected to forward the MTPIP to the Department of Budget and to Congress to support requests for an enhanced budgetary allocation for the judiciary.

The MTPIP thus formulated by the Philippine Supreme Court seems noteworthy for a number of reasons. It reflects recognition of the need for systematic planning and organization if judicial reform and corruption-control are earnestly to be sought and achieved. The MTPIP has been designed and developed with technical assistance secured from a mix of multilateral institutions (such as the United Nations Development Program, the World Bank, the Asian Development Bank and the International Development Law Institute) and development agencies of donor countries (the United States, Japan, Australia and Canada). This is the first time in its history that the Supreme Court has gone outside the Philippine Government to obtain assistance for the enhancement of the judicial system of the country. The Court has done so with a certain tentativeness, very probably due, *inter alia,* to its awareness that it must maintain, and be seen to maintain, its independence as the administrator and ultimate dispenser of justice. The Court also recognizes that valuable as is the start-up assistance given by the international donor community of the Court's agenda for reform, the sustainability of its reform program ultimately depends on its obtaining access to domestic resources and effectively mobilizing the essential supporting commitments from the Executive and Legislative branches of government, from the judges themselves and members of the bar, and finally, from the general community.

THE CRIMINAL LAW CONVENTION ON CORRUPTION OF THE COUNCIL OF EUROPE

*Louis Forget**

I. INTRODUCTION

Over the last five years or so, combating corruption has become a world-wide movement. Most international organizations involved in economic or political development have applied their own skills and resources to this cause. For example, while the World Bank was developing its own strategy to help its borrowing member countries in their efforts to combat corruption,[1] a number of other international organizations were undertaking work of their own. This article describes a particularly important initiative taken by the Council of Europe: its Criminal Law Convention on Corruption.

On January 27,1999, the Council of Europe opened its Criminal Law Convention on Corruption (the Convention) for signature. As of October 10, 2000, thirty-five of the forty-one members of the Council of Europe had signed it, and five countries had ratified it.[2]

---

* The author is grateful to Mr. Bertrand de Speville, scientific expert of the Council of Europe's Multidisciplinary Group on Corruption (GMC), and Mr. Manuel Lezertua, Secretary of the GMC, for their valuable comments. Responsibility for the contents of this article rests solely with its author. The views expressed are the author's, and do not necessarily represent the views of the World Bank.

1 For a detailed discussion of corruption and the World Bank's strategy to combat it, *see* IBRAHIM F.I. SHIHATA, THE WORLD BANK IN A CHANGING WORLD, Vol. III, 603 (2000), Chapter Eighteen (*Corruption — A General Review with an Emphasis on the Role of the World Bank*).

2 As of October 10, 2000, the member states of the Council of Europe that have signed the Convention are: Albania, Belgium, Bulgaria, Croatia, Cyprus, the Czech

By the nature of its contents and the number of countries that have already signed it, the Convention can be expected to take its place among the important international instruments concluded over the past few years to coordinate the international fight against corruption, alongside the Inter-American Convention Against Corruption[3] concluded under the auspices of the Organization of American States (the OAS Convention), the Convention on Combating Bribery of Foreign Public Officials in International Business Transactions[4] concluded within the OECD (the OECD Convention), and the various instruments adopted within the European Union.[5]

The Convention shares a number of characteristics with the other instruments mentioned above.[6] First, all these instruments are recent: the Inter-American Convention was opened for signature in April 1996, and the OECD Convention in December 1998. The first protocol of the European Communities dates from July 1995. Second, all these conventions were prepared and negotiated

---

Republic, Denmark, Estonia, Finland, France, Georgia, Germany, Greece, Hungary, Iceland, Ireland, Italy, Latvia, Lithuania, Luxembourg, Moldova, Netherlands, Norway, Poland, Portugal, Romania, Russia, Slovakia, Slovenia, Sweden, "The former Yugoslav Republic of Macedonia," Ukraine and the United Kingdom. Two non-members, Bosnia and Herzegovina, and the United States have also signed it. The Czech Republic, Denmark, Slovakia, Slovenia and "The former Yugoslav Republic of Macedonia" have ratified the Convention.

3 *Inter-American Convention Against Corruption,* 35 INTERNATIONAL LEGAL MATERIALS 724 (1996) (adopted at Caracas, Venezuela, Mar. 3, 1996, and entered into force Mar. 6, 1997).

4 *Convention on Combating Bribery of Foreign Public Officials in International Business Transactions, opened for signature* Dec. 17, 1997, 37 INTERNATIONAL LEGAL MATERIALS 1 (1998) (entered into force Feb. 15, 1999).

5 *See* Protocol to the Convention on the Protection on of the European Communities' Financial Interest, drawn up on the basis of Article K.3 of the Treaty on European Union, 1996 O.J. (C 313) 1, (signed in Dublin Sept. 27, 1996); Second Protocol to the Convention on the Protection of the European Communities' Financial Interests, drawn up on the basis of Article K.3 of the Treaty on European Union, O.J. (C 221) 0012-0022 (signed in Brussels June 6, 1997); and the Convention drawn up on the basis of Article K.3(2)(c) of the Treaty on the European Union on the Fight Against Corruption involving Officials of the European Communities or Officials of the Member States of the European Union, 1997 O.J. (C 195) 1 (signed in Brussels May 26, 1997).

6 For a detailed comparison of the three conventions mentioned in the text and the US Foreign Corrupt Practices Act, *see* Lucinda Low & Michael L. Burton, *Emerging Global Anti-corruption Standards: New Prosecutorial Tools for Transnational Investigations and Enforcement,* paper prepared for the 13th Annual National Institute on White Collar Crime, San Francisco, California, Mar. 4-5, 1999.

within the framework of international organizations, all of which, with the exception of the OECD,[7] are regional in character. The regional focus of these organizations may have contributed to the success of these initiatives. The relatively small membership, together with the strong traditions of cooperation among their members, may have made cooperation on this politically sensitive topic easier. This, together with the advent of a more favorable climate for such initiatives, may explain why these regional efforts were successful. Also, the use of international organizations, with their pre-existing staff and infrastructure, may have simplified the process of preparing the groundwork for the conventions and, where it was desired, have provided the organizational basis for the follow-up mechanisms attached to the conventions.

Third, the conventions share a common objective: establishing formal arrangements for cooperation among the parties in combating corruption, by agreeing among themselves on common substantive definitions of the offences that the parties agree to criminalize, and on methods of cooperation among them in the investigation and prosecution of the offences defined in the conventions. The conventions differ as to their scope: the OAS Convention and the Council of Europe Convention share a broad scope, and aim at internal as well as international corruption. By contrast, the OECD Convention is designed to deal with one important but limited objective: to establish among the parties to it a common definition of the offence of corruption of foreign public officials in international business transactions and to lay the basis for cooperation among themselves in their fight against this type of corruption. Among the broad-based conventions, the Council of Europe Convention has two outstanding characteristics: it goes further than the OAS Convention in defining the corruption offences that are to be criminalized, and it contains a follow-up mechanism, which the OAS Convention lacks.

In the following sections, a brief description of the Council of Europe's work on corruption will be given (Section II), following which the structure of the Convention will be examined (Section

---

7 While the OECD is not a regional organization, its membership shares certain characteristics with regional organizations that have contributed to its success in negotiating the OECD Convention, including a relatively even level of economic development, and a long tradition of cooperation in economic matters.

III). In Section IV, certain specific issues related to the offences established in the Convention will be discussed. Thereafter, Section V will deal with jurisdiction, Section VI will deal with international cooperation, Section VII will discuss the follow-up mechanism, Section VIII will deal with signature and entry into force, and Section IX will offer some conclusions.

II. BACKGROUND: THE COUNCIL OF EUROPE AND THE GMC

The Council of Europe is a regional organization of which forty-one European countries are members. Its objective is "to achieve a greater unity between its members for the purpose of safeguarding and realizing the ideals and principles which are their common heritage and facilitating their economic and social progress."[8] It sees its main role as "to strengthen democracy, human rights and the rule of law throughout its member states."[9]

The Council of Europe's work on corruption dates from 1994. In response to a request made by the 19th Conference of European Ministers of Justice in Valetta, Malta, in 1994, the Committee of Ministers of the Council of Europe established the Multidisciplinary Group on Corruption (GMC).[10] This is a committee of experts whose members are nominated by the member countries of the Council of Europe. All members of the Council of Europe are invited to appoint experts in the GMC.[11] In addition, non-member countries that have observer status in the Council of Europe are

---

8 Statute of the Council of Europe, art. 1(a), 1 EUROPEAN TREATY SERIES OF AGREEMENTS AND CONVENTIONS OF THE COUNCIL OF EUROPE, *available* at <http://www.coe.fr/eng/legaltxt/1e.htm>.

9 *About the Council of Europe* (Oct. 12, 1999) <http://www.coe.fr/eng/present/about.htm>.

10 In the tradition of the Council of Europe, the French acronym is used in English as well as in French. 'GMC' stands for *Groupe Multidisciplinaire sur la Corruption*. The term 'multidisciplinary' denotes the fact that the GMC deals with criminal, civil and administrative law aspects of corruption, and reports to two standing committees of the Council of Europe: the European Committee on Crime Problems (CDPC) and the European Committee on Legal Cooperation (CDCJ).

11 The budget of the Council of Europe bears the costs of attendance at meetings of the GMC of one expert per country. All members have appointed one expert. Some have appointed two.

invited to appoint observers (this was the case of Georgia until it became member, and is the case of Belarus, Bosnia and Herzegovina and the Holy See). In view of the close links between the work of the GMC and that of the OECD on combating bribery of foreign public officials, members of the OECD which are not members of the Council of Europe were invited to appoint observers to the GMC, namely Australia, Canada, Japan, Mexico, New Zealand and the United States, and many of these countries appointed observers who participated actively in the work of the GMC. Also invited were international organizations such as the Commission of the European Communities, the OECD, the United Nations, the International Criminal Police Organization (ICPO-Interpol), the European Bank for Reconstruction and Development, the World Bank, and the International Commission on Civil Status.

The GMC first elaborated a draft Programme of Action against Corruption, to which were attached draft terms of reference,[12] and submitted it to the Council of Ministers through the two standing committees through which it reports to the Council of Ministers. As approved in November 1996, the terms of reference call for the GMC to "elaborate as a matter of priority one or more international conventions to combat corruption, and a follow-up mechanism to implement undertakings contained in such instruments, or any other legal instrument in this area; to elaborate as a matter of priority a draft European Code of Conduct for Public Officials." The terms of reference also call for the GMC to organize or promote research projects and to implement the other parts of the Programme of Action against Corruption, and to take into account the work of other organizations and bodies with a view to ensuring a coherent and coordinated approach.

Originally, the GMC had envisaged drafting a framework convention that would have contained principles to be applied in the fight against corruption, and specific instruments dealing with the criminal, civil and administrative aspects of the topic. After considerable work had been done on the framework convention, it became evident that the principles to be incorporated in it were so general in nature that they could be adopted by the political organs of the member states without the need to enshrine them in a

12 *Programme of Action Against Corruption*, adopted by the Council of Ministers in Nov. 1996.

formal treaty. Consequently, they were adopted by the Council of Ministers of the Council of Europe in November 1997 as the Twenty Guiding Principles for the Fight Against Corruption.[13] This led the way for the GMC to work on the criminal law convention. After consulting the European Committee on Crime Problems (CDPC) and the Parliamentary Assembly of the Council of Europe, the GMC finalized the draft Convention in September 1998, and submitted it to the Committee of Ministers, which adopted it and decided to open it for signature on January 27, 1999.[14]

III. THE STRUCTURE OF THE CONVENTION — BALANCING FAR-REACHING SUBSTANTIVE PROVISIONS AND THE OBJECTIVE OF WIDE RATIFICATION

The Convention contains a set of corruption offences the parties agree to incorporate in their national legislation, as well as provisions regarding cooperation among them in the repression of these substantive offences, including provisions on the grounds on which the parties agree to take jurisdiction over them. With respect to the list of corruption offences the parties agree to criminalize and the grounds on which they agree to take jurisdiction over these offences, the Convention goes beyond the current law of many countries. But it was also the aim of the drafters of the Convention that it be ratified by the widest number of parties possible, both within the membership of the Council of Europe and

---

13 Resolution (97) 24 adopted by the Committee of Ministers on Nov. 6, 1997.

14 In addition to its work on the Criminal Law Convention, the GMC has prepared the text of the Civil Law Convention on Corruption (174 EUROPEAN TREATY SERIES OF AGREEMENTS AND CONVENTIONS OF THE COUNCIL OF EUROPE), *opened for signature* by the Committee of Ministers on Nov. 4, 1999, as well as the text of a Model Code of Conduct for Public Officials, which was considered by the Committee of Ministers on May 11, 2000. The Committee of Ministers recommended that the governments of member states promote, subject to national law and the principles of public administration, the adoption of codes of conduct for public officials based on the Model Code. The GMC is currently considering a protocol to the Criminal Law Convention dealing with bribery in the field of arbitration, as well as possible international rules intended to combat corruption in the funding of political parties and electoral campaigns. The GMC is also sponsoring annual conferences of specialized services responsible for the fight against corruption. Such conferences have been held in Strasbourg (1996), Tallinn (1997), Madrid (1998) and Limassol (1999).

outside of it. The Convention is structured in a way that balances these two objectives.

The list of corruption offences is wide-ranging: it contains not only the traditional corruption offence of active and passive domestic bribery of public officials (Articles 2 and 3) and of members of domestic public assemblies (Article 4), bribery of foreign public officials (Article 5) and of members of foreign public assemblies (Article 6), but also bribery in the private sector (Articles 7 and 8), bribery of officials of international organizations (Article 9), of members of international parliamentary assemblies (Article 10) and of judges and officials of international courts (Article 11). It also includes the related offenses of trading in influence (Article 12), money laundering of proceeds of corruption offences (Article 13) and "account" (i.e., accounting) offences (Article 14). The list of offences is broader than that contained in the OAS Convention, which does not deal with corruption of international officials, nor with private sector corruption.[15] The Convention also expands on the grounds on which the Parties must take jurisdiction on offences established under it. This aspect of the Convention is discussed below, under the heading "Jurisdiction."

The wide scope of the corruption offences set out in the Convention, as well as the novel grounds for jurisdiction could act as a deterrent to the participation of a large number of States, another necessary objective if cooperation is to be established among a large enough number of States to deal successfully with an issue that by definition knows no borders. This was a particularly important consideration in the drafting of the Convention, given the differing degrees of development of the anti-corruption mechanisms among the States participating in the GMC. For this reason, a complex system of reservations is put in place which allows, to a degree defined in the Convention, States to bring their legislation into conformity with the Convention in a gradual way.

Article 37 defines the power of the parties to enter reservations to the Convention. Certain provisions are not subject to reservations, namely those requiring the criminalization of the offence of bribery of local public officials (active and passive), bribery of members of domestic public assemblies, active bribery

---

15 By contrast to the OAS Convention, the Council of Europe Convention does not deal with the topic of "unjust enrichment."

of foreign public officials, bribery of officials of international organizations, and bribery of judges and officials of international courts. Also not subject to reservations are money laundering and "account" offences.[16] In the matter of jurisdiction, the provision requiring parties to take jurisdiction over offences committed in whole or in part in their territory is also not subject to reservations. These offences, when committed in the territory of a State party to the Convention, may be considered the 'core' offences under the Convention, which all State parties agree to criminalize and over which they agree to take jurisdiction.

Reservations are possible to the provisions requiring the criminalization of the following offences: passive bribery of foreign public officials, bribery of members of domestic and foreign public assemblies,[17] active and passive bribery in the private sector, bribery of members of international parliamentary assemblies, and trading in influence.[18] The power to make reservations to these provisions is limited in three ways. First, reservations can be made only at the time of signature or when depositing an instrument of

---

16 While art. 37 does not refer to art. 13 on Money Laundering, and therefore reservations to that provision would not be acceptable, the text of art. 13 itself defines money laundering by reference to art. 6, paras. 1 & 2 of Council of Europe Convention No. 141 on Laundering, Search, Seizure and Confiscation of the Proceeds From Crime of Nov. 1990, and states that the parties are obligated to establish money laundering as a criminal offence under the conditions set out in that Convention when the predicate offence is one of the offences the party is required to criminalize under arts. 2-12 of this Convention, but only to the extent that (i) the party has not made a reservation to the criminalization of the offence in question pursuant to art. 37, or (ii) it "does not consider such offences as serious ones for the purposes of [its] money laundering legislation."

17 While one can see, generally, that the offences in this second list constitute a 'second tier' set of bribery offences, one would have expected bribery of members of domestic public assemblies to be included in the list of 'core' offences not subject to reservations. However, at present, certain States restrict the amenability of members of public assemblies to criminal liability.

18 States may also by declare that they reserve the right not to apply, or to apply only in specific cases or conditions, the jurisdiction rules in art. 17, para. 1(b) (based on the nationality of the accused) and art. 17, para. 1(c) (based on the fact that the accused is a public official or a member of a domestic public assembly of the reserving State, or is an official of an international organization, a member of an international parliamentary assembly or a judge or official of an international court and a national of the reserving country). Making use of this reservation to the fullest extent would limit the jurisdiction of the reserving State with respect to offences defined in the Convention to cases where the offence is committed on its territory in whole or in part. Art. 37, para. 3 also allows parties to make a reservation by which

ratification, acceptance, approval or accession. Second, under Article 37, paragraph 4, each State is limited to making five such reservations (but "reservations of the same nature with respect to Articles 4, 6 and 10 shall be considered as one reservation" — Article 37, paragraph 4).

Third, while a State may maintain its reservations to certain provisions permanently, the Convention requires that such a State make a periodic declaration to this effect. Article 38 provides that reservations are valid for a period of three years after the entry into force of the Convention in respect of the State concerned and that they may be renewed for periods of the same duration (paragraph 1). However, if a State does not make a statement regarding its reservation within three months of the expiry of the reservation (after being notified by the Council of Europe one year before that date), the reservation lapses six months after the end of the current three-year period of validity (paragraph 2). Furthermore, the party that makes a reservation must provide, before its renewal or upon request, an explanation to the Group of States Again Corruption (GRECO) on the grounds justifying its continuance (paragraph 3).

The issue of reservations was controversial throughout the drafting of the Convention.[19] The GMC's Explanatory Report admits that Article 37 "contains, in its paragraphs 1 and 2, for *(sic)* a large number of reservation possibilities."[20] It explains that this stems from the fact that "the Convention is an ambitious document, which provides for the criminalization of a broad range of corruption offences, including some which are relatively new to many States," and that, in addition, "it provides for far reaching rules on grounds of jurisdiction."[21] The Convention thus attempts to balance the objectives of allowing as many States as possible to become parties to it, with that of gradually achieving the broadening of the measures to be taken by each State Party to combat corruption.

---

they would not be under an obligation to provide legal assistance to another party under art. 26, para. 1 "if the request concerns an offence which the requested Party considers a political offence."

[19] In addition to the list of offences to which reservations could be made, another controversial issue was that of jurisdiction. *See infra*, sec. 5.

[20] Explanatory Report, para. 143.

[21] *Ibid.*

It may be noted that the drafters of the other conventions against corruption have faced the same dilemma. The case of the OAS Convention is particularly interesting in this regard. The convention contains a limited set of offences the parties agree to criminalize, and two other sets of provisions: in Article III ('Preventive Measures') the parties agree "to consider the applicability" of certain measures to prevent corruption, which bear some resemblance to the Council of Europe's Guiding Principles, and in Article XI ('Progressive Development'), the parties state that they "view as desirable, and undertake to consider, establishing as offences under their laws," a further set of corruption acts.[22] For their part, the drafters of the OECD Convention have agreed to a provision in the Preamble which is intended to signify that reservations affecting its substantive provisions would not be acceptable.[23]

IV. SPECIFIC ISSUES

Some of the provisions of the Convention regarding the definition of the offences covered and related matters will be commented on in this section.

A. Bribery

Apart from the definition of "public official," the definition of bribery in the Convention is very similar to that found in the OAS

[22] In spite of the limited number of 'hard' commitments it contains, the OAS Convention allows members to make an unlimited number of reservations to the Convention, "provided that each reservation concerns one or more specific provision and is not incompatible with the object and purpose of the Convention" (art. XXIV).

[23] Convention on Combating Bribery of Foreign Public Officials in International Business Transactions, Dec. 17, 1997, 337 INTERNATIONAL LEGAL MATERIALS 8, preamble, consideration 8 (OECD Convention). For details, *see* Philippe Cavalerie, *La Convention OCDE du 17 décembre 1997 sur la lutte contre la corruption d'agents publics étrangers dans les transactions commerciales internationales*, XLIII ANNUAIRE FRANÇAIS DE DROIT INTERNATIONAL 109 (1997), at 614-616.

and the OECD conventions. The similarities between the three definitions stand out in Table 1 below:

TABLE 1. "BRIBERY" IN THREE INTERNATIONAL CONVENTIONS ON CORRUPTION

	OAS	Council of Europe	OECD
Solicitation, giving	"solicitation or acceptance;" "offering or granting"	"promising, offering or giving;" "request or receipt"	"offer, promise or give"
Advantage — Nature and Recipient	"an article of monetary value, or other benefit or advantage for himself or for another person or entity"	"any undue advantage to any of its public officials, for himself or herself or for anyone else"	"any pecuniary or other advantage to a foreign public official for that official or for a third party"
Link Between Advantage and Purpose of Advantage	"in exchange for any act or omission in the performance of his public functions"	"for [the public official] to act or refrain from acting in the exercise of his or her functions"	"in order that the official act or refrain from acting in relation to the performance of official duties"
Intention	(no mention)	"when committed intentionally"	"intentionally"

B. Public Officials

The definition of "public officials" in the Council of Europe Convention differs from that found in the other two conventions in that it is not 'self-contained,' but refers to the law of the country where the duties of the official are performed. (Table 2 sets out the definitions of "public officials" in the three major conventions.) Article 1, paragraph (a) states that "'public official' shall be understood by reference to the definition of 'official,' 'public officer,' 'mayor,' 'minister' or 'judge' in the national law of the State in which the person in question performs that function and as applied in its criminal law." Paragraph (c) adds that in the case of proceedings involving a public official of another State, the prosecuting State may apply the definition of public official only insofar as it is compatible with its national law. Such a reference to the national law may lead to some uncertainty, to the extent that not all legal systems provide a clear definition of 'public officials'. However, this technique appeared as a reasonable way of dealing

TABLE 2. "PUBLIC OFFICIAL" IN THREE INTERNATIONAL CONVENTIONS ON CORRUPTION

OAS	Council of Europe	OECD
"a government official or a person who performs public functions;" "'public official,' 'government official,' or 'public servant' means any official or employee of the State or its agencies, including those who have been selected, appointed, or elected to perform activities or functions in the name of the State or in the service of the State, at any level of its hierarchy"	"interpreted by reference to the definition of 'official,' 'public officer,' 'mayor,' 'minister' or 'judge' in the national law of the State in which the person performs the function and as applied in its criminal law"	"any person holding a legislative, administrative or judicial office of a foreign country, whether appointed or elected: any person exercising a public function for a foreign country, including for a public agency or public enterprise; and any official or agent of an public international organization"

with the fact that the scope of the notion of 'public official' varies among countries, and that it would not have been possible to agree, in the context of the Convention, on a uniform definition. The use of a 'self-contained' definition would have had the disadvantage of resulting in some accused persons being found to be 'public officials' under the Convention, when they were not considered as such in the legislation of their own country. In any event, an accused person who is not a 'public official' is likely to be an officer of a private sector entity, and subject to the rules applicable to corruption in the private sector.

The States that become parties to the Convention may find it expedient to include in their domestic law a definition of 'public official'. This would considerably reduce the uncertainty resulting from the indirect definition contained in the Convention. States that also become parties to the OECD Convention could use the same definition of 'public official' as they have agreed to in the latter convention. Under Article 1, paragraph 4(a) of the OECD Convention, "'foreign public official' means any person holding a legislative, administrative or judicial office of a foreign country, whether appointed or elected; any person exercising a public function for a foreign country, including for a public agency or public enterprise; and any official or agent of a public international organization." Furthermore, the Commentaries to the OECD

Convention contains a detailed elaboration of the terms 'public function,' 'public agency' and 'public enterprise.'[24]

C. Private Sector Corruption

One of the most novel features of the Convention is its treatment of private sector corruption. No other international convention has dealt with it before. The GMC's Explanatory Report provides three reasons for the inclusion of this form of bribery in the Convention. First, it states that corruption in the private sector undermines the climate of trust, confidence and loyalty, which are necessary to maintain and develop social and economic relations, and that private corruption causes damage to society as a whole. Second, the GMC sees criminalization of private sector corruption as necessary to ensure the respect of fair competition. Third, the GMC refers to the privatization process. It notes that over the years, important public functions have been privatized (in education, health, transport, telecommunications, etc.), and that the privatization process has entailed transfers of substantial budgetary allocations and regulatory powers. It adds that "it is therefore logical to protect the public from the damaging effects of corruption in business as well, particularly since the financial or other powers concentrated in the private sector, necessary for their new functions, are of great social importance."[25]

Nevertheless, the Convention does not treat private sector bribery exactly in the same way as it treats that occurring in the public sector. The most important difference is that in the former, but not the latter, the Convention requires as an element of the offence of bribery, that the bribed persons acted or refrained from acting "in breach of their duties." As a result, prosecution of private sector bribery may be somewhat more difficult, as conviction would be conditioned on proof of such a breach of duties. The

---

[24] *Commentaries on the Convention on Combating Bribery of Foreign Public Officials, in* INTERNATIONAL BUSINESS TRANSACTIONS, paras. 12-15, adopted by the Negotiating Conference on Nov. 21, 1997.

[25] Explanatory Report, para. 52.

Explanatory Report states that in the case of public officials, it is immaterial whether there had been a breach of duties, given the general expectation of transparency, impartiality and loyalty in the public sector. In the case of the private sector, what is being protected according to the Report is "the trust, the confidence and the loyalty that are indispensable for private relationships to exist." The Report adds: "The employee, partner, managing director who accepts a bribe to act or refrain from acting in a manner contrary to his principal's interest, will be betraying the trust placed upon him, the loyalty owed to his principal."[26]

Two other aspects of the provisions on private sector corruption are worth noting. First, with respect to the definition of 'private sector', only the 'business' sector is included in the scope of Articles 7 and 8. This is the meaning of the words 'when committed [. . .] in the course of business activity' in these two articles. The Explanatory Report states that these words exclude the non-profit sector, but also that the Convention would not prevent a State party from implementing the provision without this restriction, so as to make it applicable to all non-governmental entities.[27] Second, by contrast to the definition of 'public officials' in the Convention, with respect to which the Convention refers to the law of the State in which the person in question performs a function, in the case of private sector bribery, the Convention provides its own definition of a person working in the private sector. Articles 7 and 8 require criminalization of bribery of and on the part of 'any persons who direct or work for, in any capacity, private sector entities.' The Explanatory Report states that "this is a sweeping notion to be interpreted broadly as it covers the employer-employee relationship but also other types of relationships such as partners, lawyer and client and others in which there is no contract of employment."[28]

---

26 *Ibid.* para. 55.

27 *Ibid.* para. 53.

28 *Ibid.* para. 54. The report adds: "Within private enterprises it should cover not only employees but also the management from the top to the bottom, including members of the board, but not the shareholders. It would also include persons who do not have the status of employee or do not work permanently for the company — for example consultants, commercial agents etc. — but engage the responsibility of the company. [. . .] For the purposes of this provision, the word 'entity' should be understood as meaning also, in this context, an individual."

D. Trading in Influence

Article 12 requires the parties to criminalize the offence known as 'trading in influence.' By contrast to bribery, which involves only two parties, trading in influence involves three persons. One person represents that he or she can exert an improper influence over the decision-making of another person who is a public official, and the first person is given, offered or promised by a briber an undue advantage in order to exert this improper influence over the public official, or the person requests, receives or accepts an undue advantage for this purpose.

Under Article 12 of the Convention, the parties agree to criminalize "the promising, giving or offering, directly or indirectly, of any undue advantage to anyone who asserts or confirms that he or she is able to exert an improper influence over the decision-making of any person referred to in Articles 2, 4 to 6 and 9 to 11 in consideration thereof, whether the undue advantage is for himself or herself or for anyone else, as well as the request, receipt or the acceptance of the offer or the promise of such an advantage, in consideration of that influence, whether or not the influence is exerted or whether or not the supposed influence leads to the intended result." The persons referred to are public officials (Article 2), members of domestic public assemblies (Article 4), foreign public officials (Articles 5), members of foreign public assemblies (Article 6), officials of international organizations (Article 9), members of international parliamentary assemblies (Article 10) and judges and officials of international courts (Article 11). As can be seen from this list, the offence of trading in influence deals only with improper influence exerted towards public officials in the broad sense of the term. It does not deal with improper influence exerted over persons working in the private sector. Also, the offence is committed whether or not the influence is exerted or, if exerted, whether or not it leads to the result intended by the briber.

The Explanatory Report states that criminalizing this conduct seeks to reach the close circle of the official or the political party to which he belongs and to tackle the corrupt behavior of those persons who are in the neighborhood of power and try to obtain advantages from their situation.[29]

[29] *Ibid.* para. 64.

E. Money Laundering

The Convention requires parties to, in effect, make corruption a 'predicate offence' under their money laundering legislation. In this respect, the Convention goes further than the two other conventions on corruption. The OAS Convention is silent on this topic, and the OECD Convention merely requires the parties to it which have made bribery of its own officials a predicate offence to do so on the same terms for the bribery of a foreign public official without regard to the place where the bribery occurred.[30]

Article 13 of the Convention defines money laundering by reference to Article 6, paragraphs 1 and 2 of Council of Europe Convention No. 141 on Laundering, Search, Seizure and Confiscation of the Proceeds from Crime of November 1990. The Article states that the parties are obligated to establish money laundering as a criminal offence under the conditions set out in that Convention when the predicate offence is one of the offences the party is required to criminalize under Articles 2 to 12 of this Convention, but only to the extent (i) the party has not made a reservation to the criminalization of the offence in question pursuant to Article 37, or (ii) it "does not consider such offences as serious ones for the purposes of their (*sic*) money laundering legislation."[31]

---

30 Article 7 of the OECD Convention.

31 Article 6, paras. 1 and 2 of Convention No. 141 reads as follows:
"1. Each Party shall adopt such legislative and other measures as may be necessary to establish as offences under its domestic law, when committed intentionally:
a. the conversion or transfer of property, knowing that such property is proceeds, for the purpose of concealing or disguising the illicit origin of the property or of assisting any person who is involved in the commission of the predicate offence to evade the legal consequences of his actions;
b. the concealment or disguise of the true nature, source, location, disposition, movement, rights with respect to, or ownership of, property, knowing that such property is proceeds;
and, subject to its constitutional principles and the basic concepts of its legal system:
c. the acquisition, possession or use of property, knowing, at the time of receipt, that such property was proceeds;
d. participation in, association or conspiracy to commit, attempts to commit and aiding, abetting, facilitating and counselling the commission of any of the offences established in accordance with this article.
2. For the purposes of implementing or applying paragraph 1 of this article:
a. it shall not matter whether the predicate offence was subject to the crim-

F. Account Offences

The Convention also includes an obligation on the part of the parties to establish as offences two types of offences related not to the offences of bribery set out in the Convention, but rather related to the use of books of accounts in the commission of such offences or in the process of hiding them. Two kinds of acts are to be made offences when committed intentionally, in order to commit, conceal or disguise the offences set out in Articles 2 to 12 of the Convention (to the extent the party has not made a declaration or reservation limiting its commitment to any of these offences): (i) creating or using an invoice or any other accounting document or record containing false or incomplete information; and (ii) unlawfully omitting to make a record of a payment (Article 14).

The treatment of this offence in the Convention differs from the bribery offences in that, by contrast to bribery offences, which are to be criminalized, the parties have a choice as to the method of repression of account offences: they can be made subject to either criminal or administrative sanctions. Article 14 states that the parties are required to establish these offences as 'liable to criminal or other sanctions' under their domestic laws. The Explanatory Report also notes that "the obligations arising out of this Article to establish certain acts as offences is to be implemented in the framework of the Party's laws and regulations regarding the maintenance of books and records, financial statement disclosures, and accounting and auditing standards."[32]

The OECD Convention contains a provision on "accounting" which covers some of the same ground as the one in Article 14. In its Article 8, the OECD Convention requires the parties to it to "prohibit the establishment of off-the-books accounts, the making of off-the-books or inadequately identified transactions, the recording of non-existent expenditures, the entry of liabilities with incorrect identification of their object, as well as the use of false documents, by companies subject to [their] laws and regulations."

---

inal jurisdiction of the Party;

b. it may be provided that the offences set forth in that paragraph do not apply to the persons who committed the predicate offence;

c. knowledge, intent or purpose required as an element of an offence set forth in that paragraph may be inferred from objective, factual circumstances."

32 *See supra* note 25, at para. 74.

As in the case of the Council of Europe Convention, the OECD Convention allows the parties to select the appropriate means of punishing such offences. The parties are required to provide "effective, proportionate and dissuasive civil, administrative or criminal penalties." (Article 8, paragraph 2.) The Commentaries on the OECD Convention note that "one immediate consequence of the implementation of this Convention by the Parties will be that companies which are required to issue financial statements disclosing their material contingent liabilities will need to take into account the full potential liabilities under this Convention, in particular its Articles 3 and 8, as well as other losses which might flow from conviction of the company or its agents for bribery."[33]

G. Corporate Liability

One of the difficulties of reaching international agreement on criminal offences involving corporations is that not all systems recognize that corporations, as distinct from the individuals that manage them or work for them, may be found criminally liable. In some legal systems, only individuals may be found criminally liable. Neither the Convention, nor the OECD Convention requires parties whose system does not recognize the criminal liability of corporations to change their system in this respect. These conventions do require that the parties establish the liability of corporations for certain defined corruption offences, but leave it to the parties to decide what type of liability — criminal, civil or administrative — will be applied.[34] The standard for the sanction, however, is the same as for natural persons: the sanction must be "effective, proportionate and dissuasive."[35]

In Article 18, paragraph 1, the Convention establishes the principle that parties are required to establish the liability of 'legal persons' for the following criminal offences: active bribery, trading

---

33 Commentaries, para. 29.

34 Article 2 of the OECD Convention requires the Parties to "take such measures as shall be necessary, in accordance with its legal principles, to establish the liability of legal persons for the bribery of foreign public officials." The Commentaries (para. 20) state: "In the event that, under the legal system of a Party, criminal responsibility is not applicable to legal persons, that Party shall not be required to establish such criminal responsibility."

35 Article 19, para. 1.

in influence and money laundering, when two conditions are met: first, the offence has been committed for the benefit or on behalf of the corporation, and second, the offence is committed by a person "who has a leading position within the legal person." That "leading position" may be based on the natural person having (i) a power of representation of the legal person, (ii) an authority to take decisions on behalf of the legal person, or (iii) authority to exercise control within the natural person.

Paragraph 2 of Article 18 broadens the scope of paragraph 1 to cases where "the lack of supervision or control by a natural person referred to in paragraph 12 has made possible the commission of the criminal offences referred in paragraph 1 for the benefit of that legal person by a natural person under its authority." The Explanatory Report states that the aim of the provision is "holding legal persons liable for the omission by persons in a leading position to exercise supervision over the acts committed by subordinate persons acting on behalf of the legal person."[36]

H. Sanctions

Article 19, paragraph 1 requires that the Parties, "having regard to the serious nature of the criminal offences established in accordance with this Convention," provide "effective, proportionate and dissuasive sanctions and measures, including, when committed by natural persons, penalties involving deprivation of liberty which can give rise to extradition." With respect to legal persons, paragraph 2 requires that they also be subject to "effective, proportionate and dissuasive" sanctions, which can be criminal or non-criminal, but must include monetary sanctions. The OECD Convention establishes the same standard of "effective, proportionate and dissuasive" penalties for the offence of bribery of foreign public officials.[37]

Article 19, paragraph 3 requires the Parties to enable themselves to confiscate the 'instrumentalities' and 'proceeds' of the

---

36 Explanatory Report, para. 87.

37 OECD Convention, art. 3, para. 1. The OECD Convention goes on to specify that: "The range of penalties shall be comparable to that applicable to the bribery of the Party's own public officials and shall, in the case of natural persons, include deprivation of liberty sufficient to enable effective mutual legal assistance and extradition."

criminal offences established in accordance with the Convention. The Explanatory Report states that the paragraph must be read in light of the Council of Europe Convention No. 141 on Laundering, Search, Seizure and Confiscation of the Proceeds form Crime.[38] The terms 'confiscate,' 'instrumentalities,' 'proceeds' and 'property' used in the Convention may be better understood when read in light of the Money Laundering Convention. The GMC explains that "by the word 'confiscate,' reference is made to any criminal sanction or measure ordered by a court following proceedings in relation to a criminal offence resulting in the final deprivation of property."[39] "'Instrumentalities' cover the broad range of objects that are used or intended to be used, in any way, wholly or in part, to commit the relevant criminal offences established in accordance with Articles 2-24 of the Convention."[40] "The term 'proceeds' means any economic advantage as well as any savings by means of reduced expenditure derived from such an offence. It may consist of any 'property' in the interpretation that the term is given below."[41] The Convention takes into account that different systems define differently the property that may be confiscated, which can be the assets that form the proceeds of the offence, or other property belonging to the defendant, equal in value to the illegal proceeds illegally gained (so-called 'substitute assets'). "'Property' is defined broadly to cover these different cases. The Explanatory Report states that: "'Property' therefore has to be interpreted . . . as including property of any description, whether corporeal or incorporeal, movable or immovable, and legal documents or instruments evidencing title to or interest in such property."[42]

---

38 Explanatory Report, para. 93.

39 *Ibid.* para. 94. Convention No. 141 defines 'confiscation' as a penalty or a measure, ordered by a court following proceedings in relations to a criminal offence or criminal offences resulting in the final deprivation of property." (art. 1(d)).

40 Explanatory Report, par. 94. Convention No. 141. defines 'instrumentalities' as "any property used or intended to be used, in any manner, in whole or in part, to commit a criminal offence or criminal offences." (art. 1(c)).

41 Explanatory Report, para. 94. Convention No. 141 defines 'proceeds' as "any economic advantage from criminal offences. It may consist of any property as defined in sub-paragraph (b) of this article." (art. 1(a)).

42 Explanatory Report, para. 94. Convention No. 141 defines 'property' as including "property or any description, whether corporeal or incorporeal, movable or im-

I. Gathering of Evidence

Article 23, paragraph 1 requires the Parties to adopt such legislative and other measures as necessary "including those permitting the use of special investigative techniques, in accordance with national law" to facilitate the gathering of evidence and the confiscation of proceeds with regard to the offences covered by the Convention. Paragraph 2 adds the requirement that courts or other competent authorities be empowered to "order that bank, financial or commercial records be made available or be seized for this purpose." Finally, paragraph 3 states that bank secrecy shall not be an obstacle to such measures. The Explanatory Report notes the difficulty of gathering evidence in a field where secrecy is a key element of the offence. It notes that, while they did not provide a list of the special investigation techniques they were referring to in the Convention, the drafters of the Convention were referring "in particular to the use of under-cover agents, wire-tapping, bugging, interception of telecommunications, access to computer systems and so on."[43] The Explanatory Report also notes that such techniques are "highly intrusive" and "may give rise to constitutional difficulties as regards their compatibility with fundamental rights and freedoms."[44] The Report notes that reference to similar techniques may be found in the 1988 United Nations Convention Against Illicit Traffic in Narcotic Drugs and Psychotropic Substances[45] and in the Council of Europe Convention No. 141, as well as in the Forty Recommendation of the Financial Action Task Force.[46] The Convention leaves the Parties free to de-

---

movable, and legal documents or instruments evidencing title to, or interest in such property." (art. 1(b)).

43 *Ibid.* para. 114.

44 *Ibid.*

45 United Nations Convention Against Illicit Traffic in Narcotic Drugs and Psychotropic Substances of Dec. 19, 1988, U.N. Doc. E/CONF.82/15 (1988), *reprinted in* 28 INTERNATIONAL LEGAL MATERIALS 493 (1989). Article 5, para. 3 states: "In order to carry out the [confiscation] measures referred to in this Article, each Party shall empower its courts or other competent authorities to order that bank, financial or commercial records be made available or be seized. A Party shall not decline to act under the provisions of this paragraph on the ground of bank secrecy."

46 Financial Action Task Force on Money Laundering (FATF), *The Forty Recommendations*. Recommendation No. 7 states in part:

cide which of these special investigative techniques they will use, and, by the use of the expression "in accordance with national law" leave it to the Parties to provide such safeguards in the applications of these techniques as may be required in order to meet the applicable standards of human rights and fundamental freedoms.

J. Jurisdiction

The Convention contains provisions that extend the grounds for taking jurisdiction beyond those found in the laws of most States. The Convention requires all States parties to assert jurisdiction over offences contained in the Convention committed in whole or in part in their territories (Article 17, paragraph (a)). This is the normal ground for jurisdiction on criminal matters found in most systems. But the Convention further requires a State Party to take jurisdiction in two other cases on the basis of an extensive view of the principle of nationality. In the first case, the State party must take jurisdiction not only when the offender is a national of that State, but also if the offender, not being a national of that State, is a public official of that State or a member of one of its public assemblies (Article 17, paragraph (b)). In this case, a non-national offender who is exercising public functions in a State is assimilated to a national of that State. In the second case, the State Party must take jurisdiction when the offence involves one of its public officials or a member of its domestic public assemblies, or an official of an international organization, an official of an international parliamentary assembly or an official of an international court who is also a national of that State (Article 17, paragraph

"Countries should adopt measures similar to those set forth in the Vienna Convention [Against Illicit Traffic in Narcotic Drugs and Psychotropic Substances], as may be necessary, including legislative ones, to enable their competent authorities to confiscate property laundered, proceeds from, instrumentalities used in or intended for use in the commission of any money laundering offence, or property of corresponding value, without prejudicing the rights of bona fide third parties.

Such measures should include the authority to: 1) identify, trace and evaluate property which is subject to confiscation; 2) carry out provisional measures, such as freezing and seizing, to prevent any dealing, transfer or disposal of such property; and 3) take any appropriate investigative measures."

(c)).[47] However, a Party may by declaration decide not to apply the provisions of paragraphs (b) and (c), or apply them only in specific cases.[48]

The intention to maximize the grounds for taking jurisdiction over corruption offences is further highlighted by the fourth paragraph of Article 17, which states that: "This Convention does not exclude any criminal jurisdiction exercised by a Party in accordance with its own law." The GMC explains that there may be cases where a Party may wish to exercise jurisdiction over offences which affect its interests but are not committed on its territory or by its nationals. It adds that "the universality principle would permit States to establish jurisdiction over serious offences, regardless where and by whom they are committed, because they may be seen as threatening universal values and the interests of mankind." According to the Explanatory Report, so far, this principle has not yet gained a general international recognition, although some international documents make reference to it.[49]

K. International Cooperation

Corruption is an international phenomenon and countries that wish to combat it effectively need to take into account its international dimension. For this reason, in addition to the agreement on the definition of corruption offences and the sanctions applicable to them, the Convention contains detailed provisions regarding the assistance the Parties will give one another in the investigation and prosecution of the defined offences. While there are already a number of treaties dealing with mutual judicial assistance and extradition in criminal matters, the Convention nevertheless contains a chapter on the topic. The need for such a relatively detailed treatment of the subject is explained by the fact that the Convention is an open treaty, while many of the existing treaties on legal assistance and extradition are closed treaties to which non-members of the Council of Europe could not become

47 The Explanatory Report makes it clear that para. (c) refers to the bribed person, something that does not come out clearly in the text.

48 Art. 17, para. 2.

49 Explanatory Report, para. 83. The Report does not provide examples of the international documents to which it alludes.

parties. The GMC also refers to the difficulties in obtaining the required cooperation in this field, "a problem widely recognized and eloquently stated, *inter alia,* by the *Appel de Genève*" — a notable incursion of public opinion in the work of the GMC.[50]

In effect, the Convention provides a set of subsidiary rules, to be applied by the parties in the absence of a treaty providing more favorable provision between them. In this context, 'more favorable' means that the provisions of the Convention must be applied "if thanks to their application it will be possible to afford a form of co-operation that it would not have been possible to afford otherwise."[51] Chapter IV on International Cooperation starts by requiring of the Parties that they cooperate with each other in accordance with relevant instruments, to the widest extent possible for the purpose of investigations and proceedings concerning the offences defined in the Convention, and states that Articles 26 to 31 of the Convention will apply (i) in the absence of such instruments, and (ii) where they are more favorable than such instruments.[52]

L. Mutual Legal Assistance

Article 26, paragraph 1 requires the Parties to afford each other "the widest measure of mutual assistance by promptly processing requests from authorities that, in conformity with their domestic laws, have the power to investigate and prosecute criminal offences established in accordance with this Convention." Paragraph 2 limits the cases in which mutual legal assistance may be refused to those where compliance with a request for assistance "would undermine its fundamental interests, national sovereignty, national security or *ordre public.*" The Explanatory Report states that the expression 'fundamental interests of the country' "may be interpreted as allowing the requested State to refuse mutual legal assistance in cases where the fundamental principles of its legal system are at stake, where human rights' consideration should prevail and, more generally, in cases where the requested State

50 *L'Appel de Genève* is a manifesto signed initially by seven magistrates from five European countries demanding greater cooperation among the governments involved in fighting corruption. *See* Denis Robert, La Justice ou le Chaos (1996).

51 Explanatory Report, para. 123.

52 Art. 25.

has reasonable grounds to believe that the criminal proceedings instituted in the requesting State have been distorted or misused for purposes other than combating corruption."[53]

M. Extradition

Article 27 provides a set of rules that are intended to maximize the cases where extradition will be granted. Paragraph 1 provides that the offences established in accordance with the Convention will constitute extraditable offences in any existing extradition treaty among the Parties, and that the Parties undertake to make these offences extraditable under any future treaty they conclude among themselves. Paragraph 2 provides that when a Party which makes extradition conditional on the existence of a treaty receives an extradition request from a Party with which it does not have such a treaty, it may consider the Convention as the legal basis for extradition with respect to any criminal offence established in accordance with the Convention. Conversely, paragraph 3 requires that Parties that do not make extradition conditional on the existence of a treaty recognize criminal offences established in accordance with the Convention as extraditable offences between themselves. Paragraph 4 states that extradition shall be subject to the conditions provided in the law of the requested Party or by applicable extradition treaties, including the grounds on which the requested Party may refuse extradition. Finally, paragraph 5 establishes the principle of *"aut dedere aut judicare"* — extradite or punish. As the Explanatory Report states, "[t]he Party that refuses extradition and institutes proceedings against the offender is under the specific obligation to institute criminal proceedings against him and to inform the requesting party of the result of such proceedings."[54]

N. The Follow-up Mechanism

It was the intention, when the Action Plan was finalized, that the parties would monitor their respective performance under the Convention by a follow-up mechanism. The terms of reference of

---

53 Explanatory Report, para. 125.

54 *Ibid.* para. 130.

the GMC, as finally adopted, require it to "elaborate as a matter of priority a framework convention against corruption as well as other international conventions to combat corruption and a follow-up mechanism to implement undertakings contained in such instruments."[55] It became clear during the preparation of the Convention in the GMC that what was envisaged was a mechanism similar to the OECD Working Group on Bribery in International Business Transactions which provides the follow-up to the OECD Convention,[56] and the Financial Action Task Force (FATF), which follows-up on its own Forty Recommendations of 1989 on money laundering. While the principle was not in question, the difficulty for the GMC resided in finding a structure that would be anchored in the Council of Europe, while allowing the participation of parties to the Convention that were not members of the Council of Europe on an equal footing with those that were.

The solution was the establishment of GRECO, by resolution of the Committee of Ministers of the Council of Europe.[57] The objective of GRECO is set out in Article 1 of its statute, and it is "to improve the capacity of its members to fight corruption by following-up, through a dynamic process of mutual evaluations and peer pressure, compliance with their undertakings in this field."[58] GRECO will monitor not only compliance by the parties to the Convention of their obligations under the Convention, but also the observance by its members of the Guiding Principles for the Fight Against Corruption adopted by the Committee of Ministers on November 6, 1997.[59] Membership in GRECO is open to all members of the Council of Europe, and to non-member States which have participated in the elaboration of the Enlarged Partial

55 Program of Action, para. 33.

56 *See* OECD Convention, art. 12, and Explanatory Report, paras. 34-36.

57 Resolution (98)7 of the Committee of Ministers, which authorizes the establishment of the Group of States Against Corruption (GRECO) by means of an Enlarged Partial Agreement to which the statute of the GRECO is appended (the agreement is said to be enlarged because it is open to States not members of the Council of Europe, and partial, because not all members of the Council of Europe are automatically parties to it).

58 Resolution 98(7) of the Committee of Ministers, app., art. 1.

59 It will also monitor the compliance of parties to other conventions which provide for such follow-up by GRECO, when such convention come into force. This will be the case of the Civil Law Convention.

Agreement. Since non-members are not affected directly by the adoption by the Committee of Ministers of the 20 Guiding Principles, these States must declare, at the time they notify the Secretary General of the Council of Europe of their joining GRECO, that they undertake to apply the Guiding Principles. In addition, membership in GRECO is compulsory for States Parties to international legal instruments adopted pursuant to the Program of Action against Corruption, which provide for such compulsory membership. This is the case as regards the Criminal Law Convention and the Civil Law Convention.[60] GRECO's Statutory Committee is comprised of representatives to the Committee of Ministers of member States having joined GRECO and of representatives specifically appointed for that purpose by GRECO member countries not members of the Council of Europe. It adopts GRECO's budget.

The procedures of GRECO, as they were envisaged in September 1999, have been described as follows:

> "In order to carry out its tasks, GRECO will proceed to evaluation procedures in respect of each of its members. For each evaluation round, it will start by selecting specific provisions on which the evaluation procedure will be based. GRECO will also adopt a questionnaire for each evaluation round, which will be addressed to all members concerned by the evaluation. Moreover, GRECO will appoint a team of experts for the evaluation of each member. Indeed, this team will examine the replies given to the questionnaire, and will request, where appropriate, additional information from the member undergoing the evaluation. The team of experts may also visit the member concerned, for the purpose of seeking additional information concerning its law or practice.
>
> The team of experts will prepare a draft evaluation report on the state of the law and practice in relation to the provisions selected for the evaluation round. After having received any comments by the member undergoing the evaluation, this draft report will be discussed and adopted by GRECO.
>
> These reports will be confidential. They may contain specific recommendations addressed to the member concerned, with a view to improving its domestic laws and practices to combat corruption. However, the Statutory Committee may issue a public statement when it believes that a member remains passive or takes

60 *See* Resolution 98(7) of the Committee of Ministers, art. 32, paras. 3-4.

insufficient action in respect of the recommendations addressed to it by GRECO."[61]

GRECO began functioning in May 1999.[62] It has adopted its rules of procedure, and undertaken its first round of evaluations (2000-2001).

O. Signature and Entry Into Force

The Convention is open for signature by the member States of the Council of Europe and the other States that have participated in its elaboration. These latter States are Belarus, Bosnia and Herzegovina, Canada, the Holy See, Japan, Mexico and the United States. The Convention will come into force when fourteen States have expressed their consent to be bound by the Convention.[63] Any State that is not a member of GRECO at the time it ratifies the Convention automatically becomes a member when the Convention enters into force in its respect.[64]

While the Convention was elaborated within the Council of Europe, and is initially open to signature only by Member States of the Council of Europe and the small number of non-members that were invited to participate in its elaboration, it nevertheless could become a convention of wider application. Article 33 provides that after the Convention has entered into force, other States may be invited to accede to the Convention. A decision to issue such an invitation would be made by the Committee of Ministers of the Council of Europe, after consulting the Contracting States to the Convention, by the majority required under Article 20(d) of the Statute of the Council of Europe (a two-thirds majority of the representatives casting a vote and a majority of the representatives entitled to sit on the Committee), and the unanimous vote of

---

61 *See* Anti-corruption Activities 6-7.

62 As of October 2000, it was composed of the following members: Belgium, Bosnia-Herzegovina, Bulgaria, Cyprus, Denmark, Estonia, Finland, France, Georgia, Germany, Greece, Hungary, Iceland, Ireland, Latvia, Lithuania, Luxembourg, Poland, Romania, Slovakia, Slovenia, Spain, Sweden, the United Kingdom and the United States. *See Council of Europe, An Overview of Anti-Corruption Activities from 1994 to 1999* (document P:/gmcc/act1994-1999.eng rev2.) (hereinafter called 'Anti-corruption Activities') and subsequent information from the Council of Europe.

63 See Convention, art. 32, paras. 1 & 3.

64 *See ibid.* art. 32, para. 4.

the representatives of the Contracting States entitled to sit on the Committee of Ministers.[65]

V. CONCLUSION

The Council of Europe Criminal Law Convention on Corruption constitutes an important contribution to the international combat against corruption. Its wide scope, its far-reaching provisions and its follow-up mechanism are among the features that are likely to contribute to its success as an effective instrument in the fight against corruption. The Criminal Law Convention also represents a remarkable example of cooperation between the Western European States and the transition economies of Eastern Europe. In meetings supported by the Council of Europe Secretariat, experts from the Member States of the Council of Europe and the invited observers worked together towards the objectives set out in the Programme of Action against Corruption. The follow-up mechanism will continue this form of cooperation.

From the point of view of the World Bank, the Convention is also important. As the Bank continues to emphasize good governance and transparency in economic management, and continues to put the fight against corruption at the forefront of its programs and its dialogue with its borrowing member countries, it is fully conscious of the importance of the actions of other organizations sharing the same goals. In this respect, the actions of the Council of Europe in Eastern Europe and its own are highly complementary. The Council of Europe, through its Plan of Action and, more specifically, the Criminal Law Convention, brings together the countries of Eastern Europe, with their neighbors to the West as well as other countries in a concerted effort to agree on the actions to be taken to combat corruption and on a mechanism to follow-up on their undertakings. This is an undertaking that the Bank fully supports.

---

65 *See ibid.* art. 33, para. 1.

THE WORLD BANK'S PROTOTYPE CARBON FUND: MOBILIZING NEW RESOURCES FOR SUSTAINABLE DEVELOPMENT

*David Freestone**

On July 20, 1999 the Executive Directors of the World Bank approved IBRD Resolution 99-1 on the establishment of a Prototype Carbon Fund (the "Fund" or PCF). This Fund, which the Board recommended should not be launched until after the Fifth meeting of the Conference of the Parties (CoP-5) to the United Nations Framework Convention on Climate Change (UNFCCC),[1] represents a first attempt to demonstrate systematically the way that the innovative market mechanisms introduced in the 1997 Kyoto Protocol to the UNFCCC[2] might operate to the advantage of the

* The views expressed in this article are the views of the author and do not necessarily represent the views of the World Bank. The author co-ordinated the legal work on the development of the Fund. He is pleased to have the opportunity to acknowledge the contribution of his colleagues in the Legal Department, including Charles Di Leva, Jean-Phillipe Brisson, Hanneke van Tilburg, Tom Duvall, Scott White, Sophie Smith, Peter Barcroft, and Peter Epp. The Fund is the brainchild of Ken Newcombe in the Environment Department and it has been a challenge and a pleasure to work with him and his team. I am also grateful to Melanne Civic for her invaluable editorial assistance.

1 The United Nations Framework Convention on Climate Change (UNFCCC) was concluded in New York on May 9, 1992 (UN Doc. Distr. General A/AC.237/18 (Part II)/Add.1.15 May 1992). It was opened for signature at the United Nations Conference on Environment and Development in Rio de Janeiro, Brazil, on June 4, 1992. It came into force on March 21, 1994 and on May 17, 2000 had 184 Parties. The Fifth Conference of the Parties took place in Bonn, Germany, from Oct. 25 to Nov. 5, 1999. "COP/MOP" means the Conference of the Parties to the UNFCCC serving as the meeting of the Parties to the Kyoto Protocol.

2 The text of the Protocol to the UNFCCC was adopted at the third session of the Conference of the Parties to the UNFCCC (COP-6) in Kyoto, Japan on December

World Bank's borrowing countries. It was recognized by the Bank's Board that although the Parties to the UNFCCC still had to reach decisions on a number of issues which could be crucial to the ultimate success of such a Fund, nevertheless there were important ways in which a demonstration fund such as the PCF could actually assist the Parties in the process of identifying key practical issues for their deliberation. As a prototype, the Fund has three principal objectives: first, to demonstrate how projects which are designed to reduce emissions of Greenhouse Gases (GHG) can promote and contribute to the sustainable development of the Bank's borrowing member countries, and the ways in which these projects can channel additional public and private capital for development, as well as provide both financiers and project host countries with an equitable share of the resulting benefits;[3] second, to provide the Parties to the UNFCCC an opportunity to "learn by doing" as they themselves deliberate on the rules, regulations and procedures that will govern such GHG emission reduction projects under the framework of the UNFCCC/Kyoto Protocol; and third, to provide an important example of how the Bank can work in partnership with both the public and private sector to mobilize new resources for its borrowing member countries while addressing global environmental concerns.

This article will briefly set out the background to the establishment of the Fund, namely the evolving regime of the 1992 UN Framework Convention and its Kyoto Protocol. It will explain the process of development of the Fund; highlight the key legal challenges faced in its design and; finally, draw a few wider conclusions.

11, 1997. (UN Doc FCCC/CP/1997/7/Add.1. It should be read together with decisions 1/CP.3, 2/CP.3 and 3/CP.3). It was opened for signature from March 16, 1998 to March 15, 1999 at UN Headquarters, New York. By that date the Protocol had received 84 signatures. It will enter into force on the ninetieth day after the date on which no less than 55 Parties to the Convention, incorporating Annex I Parties which accounted for at lest 55% of the total carbon dioxide emissions for 1990 from that group, have deposited instruments of ratification, acceptance, approval or accession. On Sept. 12, 2000, 84 countries had signed the Protocol and 29 had ratified, of which only one (Estonia) is an Annex I country.

3 As well as promoting the transfer of environmentally sound and socially acceptable technology, and reducing local pollution.

I. THE UN FRAMEWORK CONVENTION ON CLIMATE CHANGE

The UNFCCC was opened for signature in June 1992 as a part of the 1992 UN Conference on Environment and Development in Rio de Janeiro (UNCED).[4] It now has 186 parties. The basic objective of the Convention is to achieve "stabilization of greenhouse gas concentrations in the atmosphere at a level that would prevent dangerous anthropogenic interference with the climate system. Such a level should be achieved within a time frame sufficient to allow eco-systems to adapt naturally to climate change, to ensure that food production is not threatened and to enable economic development to proceed in a sustainable manner."[5] The Convention is based on a number of the innovative principles set out in the 1992 Rio Declaration, notably the precautionary principle,[6] inter-generational equity,[7] and the principle of "common but

---

4 See *UNFCCC, supra* note 1.

5 *Ibid.*, art. 2.

6 *See* Article 3(3) UNFCCC, *supra* note 2. *See also* Principle 15 of the Rio Declaration (UN Doc Distr. General A/Conf.151/5/Rev.1 (June 13, 1992). There is an extensive literature on the Precautionary Principle, *see e.g.*, Lothar Gündling, *The Status in International Law of the Principle of Precautionary Action, in* THE NORTH SEA: PERSPECTIVES ON REGIONAL ENVIRONMENTAL CO-OPERATION 23 (David Freestone & Ton IJlstra eds., 1990); James Cameron & Julie Abouchar, *The Precautionary Principle: A Fundamental Principle of Law and Policy for the Protection of the Global Environment*, 14 BOSTON COLLEGE INTERNATIONAL LAW REVIEW 1–27 (1991); David Freestone, *The Precautionary Principle, in* INTERNATIONAL LAW AND GLOBAL CLIMATE CHANGE 21 (Robin Churchill & David Freestone eds., 1991); Ellen Hey, *The Precautionary Approach: Implications of The Revision of the Oslo and Paris Conventions*, 15 MARINE POLICY (1991). *See also* INTERPRETING THE PRECAUTIONARY PRINCIPLE (Tim O'Riordon & James Cameron eds., 1994), and THE PRECAUTIONARY PRINCIPLE AND INTERNATIONAL LAW: THE CHALLENGE OF IMPLEMENTATION (David Freestone & Ellen Hey eds., 1996).

7 *See* Article 3(1) UNFCCC, *supra* note 1, which provides that: "The Parties shall protect the climate system for the benefit of present and future generations of humankind, on the basis of equity and in accordance with their common but differentiated responsibilities and respective capabilities." *See also* Principle 3 of the Rio Declaration, *supra* note 5. On the principle of intergenerational equity *see* EDITH BROWN WEISS, IN FAIRNESS TO FUTURE GENERATIONS: INTERNATIONAL LAW, COMMON PATRIMONY AND INTERGENERATIONAL EQUITY (1989); Catherine Redgwell, *Intergenerational Equity and Global Warming, in* INTERNATIONAL LAW AND GLOBAL CLIMATE CHANGE, *supra* note 6, at 41–56.

differentiated responsibility."[8] The generally hortatory obligations of all Parties are set out in Article 4(1), but the full significance of the common but differentiated obligations emerges in Article 4(2)[9] where the developed countries and countries with economies in transition (which are listed in Annex I) undertake to adopt policies and measures that will "demonstrate that developed countries are taking the lead in modifying longer term trends in anthropogenic emissions consistent with the objective of the Convention." While a number of particular factors are listed, the Article does recognize that "a return by the end of the present decade to earlier levels of anthropogenic emissions [. . .] would contribute to such modification." The Convention does not, however, provide any modality by which this return to "earlier" levels can be made — nor indeed does it prescribe which particular earlier levels should be used as the benchmark. Nevertheless, Article 4(3) does provide an unequivocal obligation that the developed countries listed in Annex II[10] shall provide "new and additional financial resources" to meet the agreed costs incurred by developing countries in meeting their communication obligations under Article 12 and to meet the "agreed full incremental costs" in implementing the measures envisaged in Article 4(1) and which are agreed between the developing country Party and the "entity or entities referred to in Article 11" (i.e., the Financial Mechanism).[11] The Annex II countries also undertake to assist countries particularly vulnerable to the impacts of climate change in meeting the costs of adaptation to those adverse effects[12] and to take all practicable steps to promote, facilitate and finance, as appropriate, the transfer of, or access to, environmentally sound technologies and know-how to other Parties, particularly developing countries, to enable them to implement the provisions of the Convention.[13]

---

8 Article 3(1) UNFCCC, *supra* note 1. The text of the Article continues: "Accordingly the developed country Parties should take the lead in combating climate change and the adverse impacts thereof." *See also* Principle 7 of the Rio Declaration, *supra* note 5.

9 As well as other articles of the Convention, *see, e.g.*, art. 12.

10 Annex II does not contain Economies in Transition (EIT) countries.

11 Under art. 21(3), the Global Environment Facility, *infra* note 43, shall be "the international entity entrusted with the operation of the financial mechanism referred to in Article 11 on an interim basis."

12 *See* Article 4(4).

13 *See* Article 4(5).

A. The Berlin Mandate

The Convention came into force on March 21, 1994. The First Conference of the Parties (CoP-1) was held in Berlin, Germany, in April 1995. The major issue was the need for the Convention to develop more concrete obligations and a more precise time frame for the reduction of emissions of GHGs by the industrialized countries in Annex I. To the extent that the Conference produced a negotiated paper setting both a process and a time line for the development of another instrument to achieve this objective, CoP-1 may be regarded as a success. Indeed at the final Plenary session of the Conference, the President, Angela Merkel, introduced the review of the adequacy of commitments in Article 4.2(a) and (b).[14] She said that the industrialized countries' agreement to specific measures and the developing countries' agreement to reaffirm and advance existing commitments meant that the process would advance.[15] This was the "Berlin Mandate."

The Conference also endorsed the concept of a pilot phase for joint implementation activities. This pilot phase was to be called "activities implemented jointly under the pilot phase."[16] The objective was to allow investments by Annex I countries in a range of GHG mitigation projects outside their own borders to allow them to begin to understand more clearly the implications of developing such off-shore projects. The decision does not envisage Annex I countries being able to claim credit against future reduction targets for investments made under the Activities Implemented Jointly (AIJ) pilot phase. This issue still has to be decided by the CoP.

The so called AGBM (Ad Hoc Group on the Berlin Mandate) met regularly at CoP-2 and the intervening Subsidiary Bodies[17]

---

14 *See* FCCC/CP/1995/L.14, review of the adequacy of commitments in art. 4.2(a) and (b).

15 India for the G77 and China said the decision to launch a process to strengthen the commitments made CoP-1 a success, noting that consultations were not easy. The European Union (EU) stated its understanding that the wording "developed countries/other Parties" in section II(2)(a) must be interpreted as "developed countries and/or other Parties" and means that this sub-paragraph applies to Annex I Parties within the European Community, individually or jointly among themselves, in accordance with art. 4.2(a) and (b) of the Convention.

16 FCCC/CP/1995/L.13.

17 The Subsidiary Body for Scientific and Technological Advice (SBSTA), estab-

meetings to advance the concepts of the adequacy of the commitments under Article 4. The culmination of the process, which involved a series of submissions by the Parties of observations and of draft language, was the CoP-3 meeting in Kyoto.

B. The Kyoto Protocol

In December 1997, at the eleventh hour, indeed, early in the morning of the day after that scheduled for the completion of CoP-3, after twelve hours of continuous negotiation,[18] the Parties to the 1992 UNFCCC concluded the long awaited protocol. The 1997 Kyoto Protocol is designed to strengthen the commitments of the 1992 Convention — particularly Article 4(2) (a) and (b) — by setting out a firm schedule for reductions of GHG emissions by Annex I countries and firm targets to be met within an agreed commitment period. In adopting the Protocol the CoP recalled that it had decided in Berlin in 1995, at its first Conference, to start a process by which it could take "appropriate action" for the period beyond 2000 by the adoption of a protocol or another legal instrument at its third session; and recalled that one aim of that process was to strengthen the commitments in Article 4(2) (a) and (b) for developed country parties and other parties included in Annex I of the 1992 Convention both to require them to elaborate policies and measures and to set quantified limitation and reduction objectives (QELROs) within specified time frames for the reduction of anthropogenic emission by sources, and removal by sinks of greenhouse gases.[19]

---

lished by art. 9 of the Convention and the Subsidiary Body for Implementation (SBI), established by art. 10, meet in conjunction with the Conference of the Parties and also inter-sessionally.

18 *See Report of the Third Conference of the Parties to the United Nations Framework Convention on Climate Change*, 12 EARTH NEGOTIATIONS BULLETIN 4 (Dec. 1–11, 1997).

19 Typical anthropogenic sources of GHGs are set out in Annex A to the Kyoto Protocol and include combustion of fossil fuels for energy, industrial processes, solvent manufacture and agricultural practices. The measurement of the effects of natural "sinks" like trees which sequester carbon and other GHGs is more controversial.

The UNFCCC and its Kyoto Protocol both purport to regulate greenhouse gases "not controlled by the Montreal Protocol." This form of words is used as some gases which contribute to global climate change also deplete the ozone layer and

The CoP decision also recalled that according to the Berlin Mandate, the process would not introduce any new commitments for Parties not included in Annex I, but would reaffirm existing commitments in Article 4(1) and continue to advance the implementation of these commitments in order to achieve sustainable development, taking into account Article 4 (3), (5) and (7).

The specific commitments of Annex I Parties are set out in Annex B to the Protocol (reproduced as Appendix I to this article). These envisage that during the five years of the "commitment period" from 2008 to 2012, those parties will have reduced their emissions by an average of 5.2 percent from 1990 levels. The individual country commitments (or assigned amounts), however, range from Iceland and Australia which were able to increase their emissions from the 1990 base levels (by ten and eight percent respectively) to the countries of the European Union, which accepted an eight percent reduction from 1990 levels.

Since 1990, many of the Annex I countries have substantially further increased their GHG emissions through growth in their economies. The commitments to reduce emissions below 1990 levels are therefore commensurably even more rigorous, and the potential economic impacts of these obligations are unparalleled in international environmental law.[20] However, the most innovative aspects of the Protocol may in fact not be these strict commitments but the introduction of so called market mechanisms, initially called flexibility mechanisms (or "Flex-mechs") but now known as the Kyoto Mechanisms, into the process by which Annex I countries can meet their obligations. Some degree of cooperation had been envisaged by the 1992 Convention itself,

---

are already subject to the legal regulatory regime of the Montreal Protocol, *see infra* note 20. To avoid undue repetition, this important qualification is not used in the text of this paper but should be borne in mind.

[20] The potential impacts of the economic changes necessary to meet the commitments are different in kind from the very significant commitments made by developed countries under the 1987 Montreal Protocol (as amended and adjusted) to the 1985 Vienna Convention for the Protection of the Ozone Layer, 26 International Legal Materials 1527 (1987). *See* the text of the *Montreal Protocol on Substances that Deplete the Ozone Layer,* 26 International Legal Materials 1550 (1987). The text of the Montreal Protocol as changed by the London adjustments and amendments of 1990, 1992, 1995 and 1997 can be found at <http://www.unep.org/ozone/mont_t.htm>.

which in Article 4(2) (b) talks of the aims of "returning [GHG emissions] individually, *or jointly*, to their 1990 levels [. . .]."[21] The wording of the 1992 Convention is echoed in Article 3(1) of the Protocol, which re-affirms that these commitments may be made individually or jointly, and has also been developed further in Article 4 in response to requests by the EU to allow it to be done within the EU group of nations as a whole. This mechanism, the so called EU "Bubble," requires that Parties in Annex I, which reach an agreement to fulfil their commitments under Article 3, jointly shall be deemed to have met those commitments if their total combined aggregate emissions do not exceed their assigned amounts calculated in accordance with Annex B. Such an interstate agreement must be formally concluded and notified to the Parties through the UNFCCC Secretariat and in the event of failure of the group of states to meet the required reductions, each party becomes again individually liable for its own levels of emissions.[22]

C. The Kyoto Mechanisms

More radical than the joint responsibility agreements envisaged under UNFCCC Article 4, however, are the provisions of Articles 6 and 12 of the Kyoto Protocol — each of which envisages that in various ways emission reductions financed in other countries might be set off against the financiers' GHG reduction targets. The theory behind this approach is that the "marginal abatement cost," i.e., the cost of financing an emission reduction in a relatively fuel efficient industrialized country, will usually be far higher than in a country such as an EIT or a developing country, which may have less efficient fuel-use technology. As the global climate system benefits from these reductions wherever they are made, making reductions in an EIT or a developing country *as part of* a national strategy which also, of course, includes the introduction of domestic "policies and measures" to reduce emis-

---

21 Emphasis added. The idea that the Parties might seek to do this jointly was the basis for the AIJ pilot phase, *supra* note 16, in which the modalities of international co-operation would be explored.

22 *See also* Article 4(6) which applies the same principles to co-operation within a "regional economic integration organisation" (the standard treaty language for bodies such as the EU) that is itself a Party to the Protocol.

sions at home, will make the cost of reaching these reduction targets cheaper and increase the chances that they will actually be reached. The consequential advantages will be new resource and technology transfers, including access to cleaner technology and contributions to sustainable development. In addition, Article 17 even contemplates a system of emission rights trading, whereby one Annex I country might directly purchase from another Annex I country some of its rights to emit GHG, known as Assigned Amounts. At the time of writing, the modalities for implementing all these innovative mechanisms are still being discussed by the UNFCCC Parties. However, the underlying principles of the project based mechanisms are described in the Kyoto Protocol itself.

Article 6

This article builds directly on the wording of Article 4(2)(b) of the 1992 Convention (above) which envisages that countries listed in Annex I may act individually or jointly to meet their emission reduction objectives. Article 6 of the Kyoto Protocol allows any Annex I country to transfer to, or acquire from, another Annex I country, reductions of GHG emissions, described as Emission Reduction Units (ERUs), achieved by project activities.[23] These ERUs may be generated by any projects that reduce anthropogenic emissions of designated greenhouse gases or that enhance the anthropogenic removal by sinks[24] of such gases. The key feature of this mechanism is that all the emission reductions need to be brought about, and verified, within specific projects. It is also subject to a number of further requirements. First, these projects require the express approval of both State Parties acting as transferor and transferee. The Protocol uses the term "Parties," hence both States must be parties to the Protocol. Second, the reduction of GHGs that takes place as a result of the project must also be "additional" to any that would otherwise have occurred.[25]

---

23 Once verified and reported in accordance with guidelines to be elaborated by the UNFCCC CoP/MoP, art. 6(2).

24 Such removal could include the sequestering of carbon by trees. *See* Woods Hole Research Center website at <http://www.whrc.org/science/carbon/carbon.htm>.

25 Sometimes called the "but for" test: "But for the project" . . . would not have happened.

Third, no State Party can acquire ERUs if it is not itself in compliance with a number of other obligations under the protocol;[26] and finally, the acquisition of such ERUs is not a substitute for domestic action to reduce GHG emissions, for all such acquisitions must be "supplemental to domestic actions."[27]

In order to make it clear that the full risk of any non-compliance with other provisions of the Protocol rests entirely with the acquirer of the ERUs, the Protocol goes on to provide that where an issue of non-compliance is raised, transfer and acquisition transactions may continue but entirely at the risk of the acquirer. As the usual modality for these transfers will be by investment or purchase, this is known as "buyer risk."[28]

The final issue of importance is that although the Protocol talks clearly about Party-to-Party transactions, it does envisage others, such as the private sector (or even international organizations, e.g., the IBRD) participating in the financing and organizing of such projects. Article 6(3) permits any party to authorize a legal entity to participate in "action leading to the generation, transfer or acquisition" of ERUs, provided, however, that that authorization is under the responsibility of the authorizing State Party.

Article 12

This article was the great surprise of the Kyoto Meeting. The Brazilian delegation had proposed some form of Green Development Fund at an earlier meeting but the forms and modalities of the Clean Development Mechanism (CDM) defined in Article 12 were truly the results of the negotiations at Kyoto.[29] Perhaps as a result of the fact that the negotiation of Article 12 took place in a different drafting group from that of Article 6, or perhaps deliber-

---

26 *See* Articles 5 and 7, Kyoto Protocol, *supra* note 2.

27 Discussions continue of the meaning of "supplemental" in this context.

28 Article 6(4) reads:

> "If a question of implementation by a Party included in Annex I of the requirements referred to in this Article is identified in accordance with the relevant provisions of Article 8, transfers and acquisitions of emission reduction units may continue to be made after the question has been identified, *provided that any such units may not be used by a Party to meet its commitments under Article 3 until any issue of compliance is resolved.*" (Emphasis added).

29 *See* Jacob Werksman, *Unwrapping the Kyoto Surprise*, 7 REVIEW OF EUROPEAN COMMUNITY AND INTERNATIONAL ENVIRONMENTAL LAW 147, 151 (1998).

ately,[30] each article uses rather different language to describe concepts that are essentially very similar. The most important aspect of Article 12 is the fact it would be used by Annex I countries to finance emission reductions in countries that have not made commitments under the Protocol to meet GHG emission reduction targets, i.e., developing countries that are not listed in Annex I. Article 12(2) sets out clearly the objective which is "to assist Parties not included in Annex I to achieve sustainable development and in contributing to the ultimate objective of the Convention, and to assist Parties included in Annex I in achieving compliance with their [. . .] commitments under Article 3."

The particular appeal as well as the tension of the CDM, however, lies in the fact that States with commitments would be financing projects in countries without commitments. This should mean, of course, that developing countries can share the benefits of project-financed clean technology within their economies, but also that a far wider pool of possible reductions are possible than would be available through reductions in Annex I countries. Despite some initial concerns that this might be seen as the "thin end of the wedge" in the introduction of commitments to developing countries, in fact, the basic assumptions on which the CDM is based are sound. Even if the majority of the responsibility for the historical emissions leading to climate change can be laid at the doors of the developed world, a reduction of emissions anywhere in the world has an equally beneficial impact on the global climate system, and it is in the developing world — notably in India and China — where much of the increase in future emissions of GHG seems likely to take place in this new century. A mechanism, therefore, that encourages investments in climate friendly projects in developing countries should also have a beneficial impact on the global climate system as well as a net beneficial impact on sustainable development. There is, however, also a global community interest in ensuring that Annex I countries or entities only be permitted to claim credit for those projects in developing countries that demonstrably reduce GHG emissions. Hence, the

30 *See* UNFCCC Secretariat paper from early 1998 which views different terminology in arts. 6 and 12 as drafting errors and suggests unifying language. This approach was firmly rejected by the G77.

Protocol envisages a supervisory structure including an emission certification system. The CDM will have an Executive Board acting under the guidance of the CoP/MoP.[31] Emission reductions, and possibly even projects themselves,[32] will need to be certified by "operational entities" designated by the CoP/MoP. An emission reduction so certified is therefore termed a Certified Emission Reduction (CER) — to distinguish it from the product of Article 6 projects, which is termed an Emission Reduction Unit (ERU).

The administrative expenses of the Convention servicing these bodies will be covered, *inter alia*, by a levy of "a share of the proceeds" from certified project activities. This share will also be used to "assist developing countries that are particularly vulnerable to the adverse effects of climate change to meet the cost of adaptation."[33] In a number of other respects CDM projects will resemble Article 6 projects. Participation in CDM projects must be voluntary; projects must manifest real measurable and long-term benefits relating to mitigation of climate change; and a project activity generating CERs must be "additional" to that which would have occurred in its absence.[34] Participation in the CDM is also open to the involvement of private and/or public entities,[35] subject to guidance of the Executive Board. More significant, however, is the absence of a distinction again made in Article 6 between emission reduction activities and those designed to enhance anthropogenic removal by sinks of GHGs. Given the overarching responsibility of the CoP/MoP to provide "authority and

31 *See* Article 12(4).

32 Compare Article 12 (5) which provides that "emission reductions resulting from each project activity shall be certified . . ." with Article 12(5)(c), 12 (6) and 12(8) which use the term "certified project" activity and activities. No modality for certifying projects, as opposed to emission reductions, is provided in Article 12.

33 The modalities for this have yet to be determined. Even the issue of whether it will be a fund is open to debate at time of writing. The Chief Executive Officer of the GEF (Mohammed El-Ashry) has indicated that the GEF stands ready to act as the financial mechanism for such a fund if that is the preferred option.

34 *See* Article 12(5)(c).

35 *Cf.* Article 6(3) which says legal entities may participate in "actions *leading to* the generation, transfer or acquisition [. . .] of emission reduction units. This could be interpreted as saying that they may not be transferred or acquired (and therefore perhaps not owned?) by such entities. By contrast, art. 12 envisages "participation [. . .] in the acquisition of certified emission reductions," suggesting that private/public entities might own these CERs.

guidance" and its responsibility to "elaborate modalities and procedures"[36] for the operation of the CDM, a decision on whether the CDM will include sink projects will have to emanate from the CoP/MoP.

Article 17

The third mechanism envisaged by the Kyoto Protocol allows the trading of parts of Assigned Amounts among Annex I Countries (Article 17 of the Protocol). "Assigned Amounts" refers to the quantity of GHGs a Party to the Kyoto Protocol is allowed to release into the global atmosphere during the 2008–2012 commitment period. These amounts, calculated as a percentage of emissions during the base year (usually 1990), are set out in Annex B of the Protocol. This mechanism is also referred to as "emission trading."

D. The Buenos Aires Plan of Action

The Kyoto Protocol has not yet entered into force, but, in the meantime, the Parties to the UNFCCC have been negotiating the ways in which its mechanisms would operate if and when it does enter into force. An understanding between the Parties to the UNFCCC on how to proceed was advanced at the Fourth Conference of the Parties to the UNFCCC (CoP-4), held in Buenos Aires in November 1998. CoP-4 resulted in a number of decisions including the "Buenos Aires Plan of Action" (Decision I/CP.4). The Plan of Action declares the determination of the Parties to the UNFCCC to strengthen the implementation of the UNFCCC and to prepare for the future entry into force of the Kyoto Protocol. It includes a resolution to demonstrate, *inter alia*, substantial progress on the Kyoto mechanisms. More significantly, Decision 7/CP establishes that the deadline for reaching decisions on all three of the market mechanisms will be CoP-6 — the Sixth Conference of the Parties which is planned to be held in November 2000 in The

36 Article 12(7) empowers the CoP/MoP at its first meeting, to "elaborate modalities and procedures with the objective of ensuring transparency, efficiency, and accountability through independent auditing and verification of project activities."

Hague. It also outlines the detailed work program for developing the mechanisms.

II. THE WORLD BANK AND CLIMATE CHANGE

As Peter Sand has said, "the World Bank has come a long way since the days it was the preferred villain of the environmental movement."[37] In addition to the development of policies governing the environmental and social impacts of the project activities that it finances,[38] the Bank is also the Trustee for the world's largest environmental fund — the Global Environment Facility (GEF). In response to a French and German proposal at the 1989 World Bank Annual Meeting,[39] a meeting was held in Paris in November 1990 to finalize a proposal for a Global Environment Facility with a commitment of some US$1 billion over a three year pilot phase.[40] A proposal for the establishment of a Global Environment Trust Fund was approved by the Bank's Board of Exec-

---

37 Peter H. Sand, *Trusts for the Earth: New International Financial Mechanisms for Sustainable Development, in* SUSTAINABLE DEVELOPMENT AND INTERNATIONAL LAW (W. Laing ed. 1995), *reprinted in id.*, TRANSNATIONAL ENVIRONMENTAL LAW: LESSONS IN GLOBAL CHANGE 291, 299 (1999).

38 Since the 1980s the World Bank has developed internal policies and procedures designed to prevent its projects from causing environmental harm. Since 1993 these policies have been subject to review by an independent Inspection Panel. For the text of the World Bank "Safeguard Policies" *see* <http://www.worldbank.org>. For a discussion of the evolution of these policies and the role of the Inspection Panel *see* IBRAHIM F.I. SHIHATA, THE WORLD BANK INSPECTION PANEL: IN PRACTICE 41–46 (2nd ed. 2000).

39 Sand reports that this proposal can be traced back to a suggestion by the Brundtland Commission for the "development of a special international banking programme or facility linked to the World Bank" *in* PETER SAND, OUR COMMON FUTURE 338 (1987). This idea was developed by the Washington, D.C. based World Resources Institute (WRI), as a proposal for an global International Environmental Facility (IEF), *see* WRI, NATURAL ENDOWMENTS: FINANCING RESOURCE CONSERVATION FOR DEVELOPMENT 14 (F. van Bolhuis ed., 1989).

40 At the same time the World Bank was also involved in the finalization of an Interim Multilateral Fund of about US$240 million as part of the amendment and adjustment procedures agreed to the Montreal Protocol, *see supra* note 19, at the London Meeting in June 1990 and in a joint funding proposal of some US$255 million for a Pilot Programme to Conserve the Brazilian Rain Forest, which emanated from the Houston G7 Summit in July 1990. *See further*, SAND, *supra* note 37.

utive Directors by Resolution No. 91-5 on March 14, 1991.[41] By a tripartite procedural resolution on October 28, 1991 the United Nations Development Programme (UNDP), the UN Environment Programme (UNEP) and the World Bank agreed to cooperate in the implementation of the Facility.[42] The Bank acts as Trustee of the Fund as well as one of the three Implementing Agencies.

At the Rio Conference, a great deal of heat was generated about the governance of the GEF and Agenda 21 Chapter 33.16 (a)(iii) recommended that the GEF should be "restructured" so as to, *inter alia*, "ensure a governance that is transparent and democratic in nature, including in terms of decision-making and operations, by guaranteeing a balanced and equitable representation of the interests of developing countries, as well as giving due weight to the funding efforts of donor countries." A similar provision is expressly included in the text of Article 21 of the UNFCCC.[43] The restructuring process, involving negotiations among seventy-three states, was completed in Geneva in March of 1994; a replenishment of $US2 billion was agreed for an initial three year period to 1998, and the Instrument setting out the new governance structure and operational modalities was adopted by the governing bodies of the three Implementing Agencies.[44] In March 1998, at a meeting in Paris, the negotiations for a second replenishment — GEF-2 — were completed with commitments totaling US$2.75 billion for the three year period to 2001.[45]

---

41 *See Documents Covering the Establishment of the Global Environment Facility*, 30 INTERNATIONAL LEGAL MATERIALS 1735. *See also* I.F.I. Shihata, *The World Bank and the Environment: a Legal Perspective*, 16 MARYLAND JOURNAL OF INTERNATIONAL LAW AND TRADE 1–42 (1992).

42 Replacing earlier arrangements based on a joint statement of the heads of the three agencies dated Sept. 17, 1990.

43 The final sentence of Article 21(3) reads: "[. . .] The Global Environment Facility should be appropriately restructured and its membership made universal to enable it to fulfill the requirements of Article 11." On Article 11, *see supra* note 11.

44 For the text of the *Instrument for the Establishment of the Restructured Global Environment Facility, Report of the GEF Participants Meeting, Geneva 14–16 March 1994, see* 33 INTERNATIONAL LEGAL MATERIALS 1273 (1994). *See further* I.F.I. Shihata, *The World Bank's Contribution to the Development of International Environmental Law*, LIBER AMICORUM PROFESSOR SEIDL-HOHENVELDERN — IN HONOUR OF HIS 80TH BIRTHDAY 631–657 (G. Haffner, et al. eds., 1998).

45 *See The World Bank Group (1999)*, 10 YEARBOOK OF INTERNATIONAL ENVIRONMENTAL LAW 2000. (David Freestone, et al. 790-796).

Largely as a result of its role as one of the three Implementing Agencies of the GEF, the World Bank has the largest investment portfolio of climate friendly energy projects in the world. In the last three fiscal years (1998-2000) the GEF council approved the inclusion in its Work Programme of some 21 projects proposed by the World Bank with total financing of over US$2 billion, of which US$122 million was to be provided by the GEF. In addition, since 1995, the Bank has — in collaboration with the Government of Norway — invested some US$10 million of "additional" funding in four "Activities Implemented Jointly" projects under the AIJ Pilot phase established by the Berlin CoP-1 of the UNFCCC.[46]

Climate change should be a matter of serious concern to the World Bank. Analysis by the Intergovernmental Panel on Climate Change (IPCC) estimates that, should the level of CO_2 concentration in the world be doubled, developing countries would suffer economic costs of five to nine percent of GDP, several times higher than industrialized countries, and that the poor in the Bank's borrowing countries would be at the greatest disadvantage.[47]

III. THE PROTOTYPE CARBON FUND

The Prototype Carbon Fund (the "Fund") builds on the World Bank's significant experience in investing in climate friendly technology projects in many parts of the world. It is called a prototype, because its primary intent is that it will be able to act as a "trail blazer" for other similar funds that may be launched by the other IFIs or the private sector. Because of its existing portfolio and its pipeline of projects, including renewable energy and en-

---

46 *See* Rolf Selrod and Patrick Karani, *Evaluation Report of the Norway-World Bank AIJ Programme: Lessons learned from the Pilot phase under the UNFCCC*, World Bank Environment Department, July 2000. *See also* David Freestone, *World Bank Initiatives on AIJ: The Potential Role of the World Bank Group in the Carbon Offset Investment Business, in* GREENHOUSE GAS MITIGATION: TECHNOLOGIES FOR ACTIVITIES IMPLEMENTED JOINTLY 34 (P. W. F. Riemer, et al. eds., 1998).

47 *Climate Change 1995: The Economic and Social Dimensions of Climate Change* (INTERGOVERNMENTAL PANEL ON CLIMATE CHANGE [IPCC], 1996).

ergy efficiency projects in both developing countries and EITs, the Bank is able to provide baseline projects, or underlying projects, onto which the additional resources and environmental benefits required by the Kyoto protocol can be relatively easily grafted.[48] Similarly, after nearly 10 years of experience in working at a project level with the "incremental costs" requirements of GEF funding, many of the basic concepts of baseline projects from which additionality (as required by Kyoto) must be shown, are relatively well understood by its operational staff. In order to mobilize the sorts of investments necessary to bring about the global changes in energy consumption patterns necessary to meet the Kyoto commitments within the commitment period, it has been estimated that resource flows in the order of US$30 billion a year may need to be available.[49] Although the negotiation of the details of the Kyoto regulatory framework are proceeding apace, there is still some evidence of mistrust between the Annex I countries and those countries without emission reduction commitments, the majority of which are members of the G77. A fund that was able to make investments in a participative and open way could, it is argued, assist both host and financing countries to appreciate the benefits which may be derived from the Kyoto mechanisms. The development of a new commodity — an emission reduction — which is an asset with a saleable value, will make many renewable energy and other sustainable development projects that are currently financially non-viable, more profitable and hence, fundable. But at the early stages in the development of these transactions there are many lessons to be learned and practices to be developed. The objective of the Prototype Fund is to show how these transactions can be concluded in a manner which assists both the industrialized world and also those host countries which are interested in developing the capacity to take full advantage of the opportunities offered by the Kyoto mechanisms.

The Fund evolved out of the Bank's Global Carbon Initiative, set up in February 1997 to attempt to respond to a broader development agenda. The costs of developing the Fund were met by the "New Products Committee" within the Bank, which was es-

---

[48] For additionality *see supra* note 25.

[49] A. Denny Ellerman et al., *The Effect of Developing Countries of the Kyoto Protocol and* CO_2 Emissions Trading *(IBRD Paper, Sept. 1998).*

tablished by the Strategic Compact — approved by the Bank's Executive Board in March 1997. The overarching objective of the Fund was to explore how market based mechanisms — contemplated even in 1997 by the Parties to the UNFCCC — could help reduce the global concentrations of GHGs and contribute to the sustainable development of the Bank's borrowing member countries. In June 1997, it was announced at the United Nations General Assembly Special Session that the Bank would launch a carbon fund should the UNFCCC Parties be favorably disposed towards such an initiative. The basic concept of the Fund is remarkably simple. It will collect money from both public and private sector entities, use the pooled funds to convert normal energy projects into a portfolio of climate-friendly projects in return for the emission reductions which they generate. The emission reductions so generated would then be distributed *pro rata* to those entities which had contributed to the Fund. The portfolio approach would spread the risks that result from total project failure (which some AIJ projects had faced) and also allow economies of scale and replication of basic transactions. By entering into the field at an early stage of the development of the market for emission reductions the Bank also felt that it could provide comfort to the private sector and provide important experiences for those who follow.[50]

In developing this initiative, there has been an extensive consultative process. In addition to extensive "one-on-one" meetings with potential contributors to the Fund and potential host countries, there have been four consultative meetings with Potential Participants: two in Washington, D.C., one in Interlaken, Switzerland supported by the Swiss government, and one in Porvoo, Finland with the support of the Finnish Government. Three consultative meetings were held with potential host countries, one for EITs in Bratislava, Slovakia, in April 1998; the second in Goa, India, in June 1998, in collaboration with a UNEP Capacity Building Project; and the third in Cape Town, South Africa, in Septem-

---

50 There is evidence that this prototype argument is justified. A Swiss Bank is about to launch a similar fund which is explicitly modelled on the PCF and intends to "slipstream" the PCF on issues such as baselines, certification etc. *See* Swiss AIK Pilot Program (SWAPP), <http://www.admin.ch/swissaij/>.

ber 1998. The team has also had regular contacts with the UNFCCC Secretariat and other relevant bodies, such as the Organisation for Economic Co-operation and Development International Energy Agency (OECD-IEA). Presentations on the Fund and other Bank Climate Change activities have been made as side events at UNFCCC Conferences and meetings of the UNFCCC Subsidiary Bodies. Ad hoc meetings with potential participants and potential host countries have also been held on the sidelines of UNFCCC events. Within the Bank, extensive briefings and consultations were held with Country Directors, and the relevant sector Boards. The possible design of the Fund was also discussed with the Executive Directors at two informal Board meetings: the first on May 18, 1998, the second on February 22, 1999.

A. Basic Features of the Fund

The Fund is established as an IBRD Trust Fund, with the IBRD acting as Trustee of the Fund. The detailed design features of the Fund are set out in the "Instrument establishing the Prototype Carbon Fund" which was approved as an Annex to the Board Resolution of July 20, 1999. The Fund requires a minimum of US$60 million to be viable and was originally capped at US$150 million. It is open to both public and private sector entities that fulfill standard participation requirements. The public sector entity contribution is US$10 million and the private sector entity contributes US$5 million, although for both, the payment schedule under which the contribution must be made is spread over the life of the Fund. The Instrument envisages that the Fund will have two Closings. The first in the spring of 2000 and the second a year later.[51] The Fund will run until the end of the first commitment period in 2012, with such "winding-up" period as may be necessary thereafter. To operate any longer than this would require the explicit agreement of the Bank's Board as well as prior agreement of all the Participants. No investment in a single project may be less than two percent or more than ten percent of the Fund's assets so

[51] To reward the "early-movers" who join at first closing, there is a 10 percent surcharge for participation in the second closing for the same *pro-rata* benefits.

it is envisaged that it will fund approximately twenty projects. In the process of developing the Fund, the potential participants provided guidance on the proposed Project Portfolio Criteria, which may, however, be amended by the Participants during the course of the operation of the Fund.[52] Project selection criteria have also been developed on the same basis.[53]

---

52 "Project Portfolio Criteria. The Trustee will develop a Project portfolio with the intention that during the term of the Fund:

a broad balance will be achieved in the number of Projects undertaken in Economies in Transition and in Developing Countries and that, notwithstanding potential Projects identified prior to the establishment of the Fund, emphasis should be directed initially to the development of Projects in Developing Countries;

a major emphasis should be directed at development of Projects in the area of renewable energy technology such as, but not limited to, geothermal, wind, solar and small hydro energy;

no less than approximately 2% nor more than approximately 10% of the Fund's assets should be invested in any one Project;

no more than approximately 20% of the Fund's assets should be invested in Projects in the same Host Country;

no more than approximately 10% of the Fund's assets should be invested in land-use sector Projects, and, in addition, any such Project should be located in an EIT unless the Parties to the UNFCCC deem it appropriate that land-use sector projects may also be located in Developing Countries; and

no more than approximately 25% of the Fund's assets should be invested in Projects using the same technology."

53 "Project Selection Criteria. The Trustee shall select Projects in accordance with the following Project Selection Criteria:

Consistency with UNFCCC and/or the Kyoto Protocol. The Trustee shall seek to ensure that Projects comply with all current and future guidelines, modalities and procedures adopted by the Parties to the UNFCCC and/or the Kyoto Protocol, in particular those pertaining to sustainable development and additionality.

Consistency with Relevant National Criteria. The Trustee shall seek to ensure that the Projects' designs are compatible with and supportive of the national environment and development priorities of the Host Countries. In addition, the Projects and the transfer of Emission Reductions should be consistent with the rules and criteria adopted by Host Countries regarding Article 6 and Article 12 Projects.

Consistency with the IBRD's Country Assistance Strategy. The Trustee will seek to ensure that Projects are designed to be consistent with, and supportive of, the then current Country Assistance Strategy of the IBRD for the Host Country and the Host Country's own development objectives.

Complementarity with GEF. The Trustee shall seek to ensure that Projects are complementary to the GEF and do not compete with the GEF's long-term operational program nor with its short-term response measures. In furtherance of this criterion, potential Projects will be reviewed by the Secretariat of the GEF to determine their GEF eligibility. Only if it is determined that a potential Project will not receive

B. Institutional Arrangements

Design as a World Bank Trust Fund

The overarching objective of the Fund is to model the way in which the private sector might set up a similar fund. However, given the nature of the IBRD as a public international organization, a number of the design options open to the private sector were not available for practical or policy reasons.[54] The international trust fund was quickly identified as the favored vehicle for the Fund. Sand has traced the evolution of the use of the trust fund mechanism for environmental purposes and has pointed out that the World Bank alone administers more than 1600 trust funds.[55] In 1978, Sir Joseph Gold, former General Counsel of the International Monetary Fund (IMF), identified the proliferation of arrangements bearing the name "trust" within the practice of in-

---

GEF financing will the Fund Manager consider including it as a Fund Project.

Achievement of National and Local Environmental Benefits. The Trustee shall seek to ensure that Projects provide at least the same level of national and local environmental benefits as the Underlying Projects.

Consistency with the Fund's Strategic Objectives and Operating Principles. The Trustee shall seek to select Projects with a view to achieving the strategic objectives and operational principles of the Fund as set forth in the Instrument.

Consistency with the General Guidance Provided by Participants. The Trustee shall seek to ensure that Projects comply with the general guidance provided by Participants at their meetings.

Additional Characteristics of Projects. The Trustee shall seek to ensure that Projects are selected to mitigate various types of risk. Projects should generally entail manageable technological risk. The technology to be used in a Project should be commercially available, have been demonstrated in a commercial context, and be subject to customary commercial performance guarantees. The technical competence in the Host Country to manage this technology should be established in the course of Project appraisal. Projected Emission Reductions over the life of the Project should be predictable and should involve an acceptable level of uncertainty. GHG Reductions should also be amenable to standardised Validation and Verification processes with existing methodologies."

54 Such as incorporation of the Fund as a special purpose company under a national legal system, possibly in an off-shore tax friendly location.

55 *See Trusts for the Earth, in* P. H. SAND, TRANSNATIONAL ENVIRONMENTAL LAW: LESSONS IN GLOBAL CHANGE 291–31 (1999). This is a revised version of the 10th Onoh Memorial Lecture given at the University of Hull, England, in Feb. 1994. Note that the GEF, the Ozone Trust Fund, and the Brazilian Rain Forest Trust Fund are all Trusts Funds for which the Bank acts as Trustee.

ternational organizations and analyzed their key characteristics.[56] According to Gold, "[. . .] the establishment of trust funds for administration by existing international organizations [based on] implied or express powers avoids the need to create new organizations with limited purposes and makes use of the experience and demonstrated skills of organizations already in the field."[57]

Approval of Projects and Authorization of Legal Entities

Another key issue was the way in which the Fund would be able to facilitate private sector involvement in the Fund. Article 6(1) reflects the traditional State-to-State arrangement which had been the model for AIJ under the pilot phase.[58] The operative part reads as follows: "For the purpose of meeting its commitments, [. . .] any Party included in Annex I may transfer to, or acquire from any other such Party emission reduction units."[59] The restrictions that this approach would impose on arrangements such as the Carbon Fund were discussed at the First Consultative Meeting with potential participants in Washington, D.C. on September 29, 1997, prior to the Kyoto Conference. Many of the participants at the Consultative Meeting were, and remain, negotiators within

---

56 *See* J. Gold, *Trust Funds in International Law: The Contribution of the International Monetary Fund to a Code of Principles*, 72 AMERICAN JOURNAL OF INTERNATIONAL LAW 856–866 (1978).

57 *Ibid.* at 860, *cited in* SAND, *supra* note 36, at 293. Note that by the use of implied powers there is a general requirement that the objectives of the Fund be consistent with the aims of the organisation administering the Fund. Within the IBRD, Operational Policy 14.40(4) addresses this requirement.

58 *See supra* note 16. The World Bank has acted as broker for a number of such arrangements between, for example, Norway and Poland and Norway and Mexico. *See* Freestone, *World Bank Initiatives on AIJ: The Potential Role of the World Bank Group in the Carbon Offset Investment Business, supra* note 46. *See also* Rolf Selrod & Patrick Karani, *Evaluation Report of the Norway-World Bank AIJ Programme: Lessons Learned from the Pilot Phase under the UNFCCC* (World Bank Environment Department, July 2000). For further details, *see* <http://www.unfccc.com>, <http://www.esd.worldbank.org/aij>, and <http://www.usaij.com>.

59 There is similar wording in Article 12, which says that under the CDM (a) Parties not included in Annex I may benefit from project activities resulting in certified emission reductions and (b) Parties in Annex I may use [CERS] accruing from such projects to contribute to compliance with part of their [. . .] commitments under art. 3."

the UNFCCC process. At that point, the draft Convention contained no reference to the private sector or the role of possible brokers. To address this issue, the Swiss Government introduced new wording into the draft protocol at the Bonn Negotiating Session in October 1997.[60] This wording eventually became Article 6(3). The Swiss original wording used the term "intermediaries" — envisaging bodies which need not be established in either the receiving or transferring states, and obviously including international organizations, such as the World Bank. At Kyoto, this term was changed to "legal entities" with the understanding that this also included private sector entities acting under the responsibility of the State Party.

Article 6(3) now reads: "A Party included in Annex I may authorize legal entities to participate, under its responsibility, in actions leading to the generation, transfer or acquisition under this Article of emission reduction units." Under this final text, Parties may authorize any "legal entity" they choose. This therefore extends to bodies established under either national and international law. It includes private sector entities in carbon offset importing and exporting countries as well as "third party" entities such as international organizations. Because the State Party ultimately retains international legal responsibility for meeting the obligations of the Protocol, any action it authorizes would still be "under its responsibility." This is reinforced by the use of the phrase "leading to the generation, transfer or acquisition [. . .]." This suggests that each transfer accepted for registration by the UNFCCC Secretariat (or whatever is the body ultimately given such a task) against Kyoto targets would have to identify the State Party from which the offset has come and the State Party to which it is going, so as to enable proper accounting to take place for the purposes of meeting commitment obligations. The purpose of Article 6(3) seems to be, therefore, to introduce expressly the concept of flexibility in the modalities parties may authorize for organizing such transfers, including the use of the private sector, on the understanding that for registration purposes, the transfers will still be Party-to-Party. It is in this light that Article 6(1) should therefore be read.

---

60 Switzerland ultimately decided not to join the Fund.

C. Approval of the Parties

Article 6(1)(a) requires that every project have the "approval of the Parties involved." The most obvious way in which this approval could be given is by a specific treaty between the two State Parties (as was the case with the AIJ activities discussed above). However, "approval" is a rather wider international law concept which covers more than just a specific treaty agreement. A State Party may, in the exercise of its sovereignty, give this approval in a number of different ways. These could include passing national legislation establishing the modalities by which such approval would be given nationally, or signing an agreement with a third party (including an international organization such as the World Bank) approving a project or a portfolio of projects (as is envisaged by the Fund). This approval does not mean that the State Party will, or indeed will be able to, claim credit for the project, merely that it has met one of the pre-conditions for this. The key concept is the fact that the Party is ultimately responsible for meeting its carbon emission targets and for regulating the way in which this is done (i.e., by approval of projects).

D. The Significance of the Fund

For the purposes of the Fund, the "approval" process envisaged by Article 6(1)(a) has been split into two distinct processes. Until such time as the CoP/MoP decides otherwise, it appears that each project will require the approval of both the acquiring State and the transferring State (the hosts). The Trustee of the Fund will be the "authorized legal entity" for each side. Given the portfolio approach of the Fund, for the public sector participants the signing of a Participation agreement with the Trustee explicitly constitutes the grant of "authorization" as well as the "approval" of the projects undertaken by the Trustee in accordance with the modalities of the Fund Instrument. The private sector participants are in a different position. If they wish to obtain emission reductions for the purposes of Articles 6 and 12 from the projects undertaken by the Fund,[61] which can be used for the purposes of meeting Kyoto

---

61 Of course, the primary focus of many private sector participants is not the Kyoto system but the national legislation/ requirement which they may wish or need

commitments, they must also be "authorized" for the purposes of Article 6(3) by their State Party and meet whatever other requirements that may be developed by the CDM.[62] This authorization can be given by a variety of means — individual communication, development of a voluntary "national trading scheme" or legalization. This was always a *caveat emptor* risk for the private sector, of which they were well aware.

The second step will be to secure the approval of the transferring Party (the host state). Before beginning project preparation the Trustee will obtain from the Host Country a letter of endorsement that explicitly approves the project and authorizes the Trustee for the purposes of Articles 6 or 12, as applicable. Once the project is prepared the Host Country and the Trustee will sign a formal agreement (a "Host Country agreement") which will, *inter alia*, contain formal provisions relating to approval and authorization.

These two sets of agreements constitute "approval" of the Parties for the purposes of Article 6(1)(a). The Fund structure is flexible enough to adapt to whatever rules may emerge from the UNFCCC process, but is currently premised on the understanding (derived from Article 3) that any emission reduction units or certified emission reductions which are generated by the Fund, will be registered under the UNFCCC system as having been generated by the host State Party and transferred to all of the State Parties of all the contributors (i.e., State to State). These registered units will then be distributed by the Fund between the contributors in proportion to the level of their contributions to the Fund. Whether private sector investors can receive these, or whether they go to their national Governments, will depend on the "authorizations" they have received from their own Governments and the details of the UNFCCC registration scheme, which has yet to be elaborated.

Given all these uncertainties, the Fund does not guarantee that the offsets generated by the Fund will qualify for registration for the purposes of the Kyoto Protocol. Even the modalities for this process are still unknown. The participants are fully aware of this risk which they will have to take themselves. The investments under the Fund are planned to be scheduled over a three to four

---

to meet. The development of a national scheme — even a voluntary one — as in Japan — must meet the requirements of authorization.

[62] Subject to "the guidance which will be provided by the executive board" of the CDM Article 12(9).

year period during which time the guidelines on the technical aspects of the verification and reporting envisaged by Article 6(2) and Article 12(5) should become clearer. There is a further risk, of which participants are also aware: it is possible no grandfathering of existing projects may be permitted for credit once these guidelines are elaborated.

E. Adaptability to the Emerging Regime of the UNFCCC/Kyoto Protocol

As discussed above, the PCF is an attempt to lead from behind, i.e., to start the process of implementing the Protocol before the rules are finalized under the Buenos Aires Plan of Action. Much of the hostility that the Fund encountered in its early days stemmed from fears that the Bank was attempting to usurp the negotiating process, to assume a dominant role in the emission reductions market, and to impose its own practices on projects under the Kyoto Mechanisms. The size of the Fund and its limited time span are specifically designed to show that the Fund is intended as a prototype for others to follow — not as a prototype for the Bank to further elaborate such funds. The dual objectives of the Fund are not only to provide participants with independently certified emission reductions in return for their contributions, but also to develop understanding about the way projects can be implemented that meets the basic criteria adumbrated in the Kyoto Protocol. Public sector Participants hope to feed some of this information into the negotiations, but many of the private sector Participants hope to achieve a better understanding for themselves of the opportunities that the emerging emission reduction market is likely to offer. In this sense, the Fund aims to build capacity in both industrialized and Host Countries.

However, the plethora of key issues that have still to be decided by the CoP under the Buenos Aires Plan of Action both provide a reason for launching the Fund (in the sense of assisting with identifying key practical issues that need to be decided) but also pose problems for the venture. The Protocol was concluded at the eleventh hour at CoP-3, and it shows. Many crucial issues relating to the way in which the innovative mechanisms will work are still to be settled by the CoP or CoP/MoP. Indeed, in this sense Kyoto is a framework Protocol to a framework Convention. Having said that, some parts of the Protocol structure are clearer than others. It is, for example, instructive to contrast the wording of Articles 6, 12 and 17 with one another. Whereas, under Article 6, the Conference of the Parties is given the role of "further developing *guidelines* for the implementation of the article," under Article 12 not only does the CoP have the ongoing mandate of exercising "authority and guidance" over the CDM, but the CoP/MoP still has to "elaborate *modalities and procedures*." Guidelines are usually non-binding, hence the role of the CoP in relation to Article 6 is much lighter than the more regulatory role which seems to be envisaged under Article 12. At the extreme end of the scale, under Article 17, the CoP has still to develop the whole system of emissions trading, namely, it has to define "the relevant principles, modalities, rules and guidelines."

Faced with this incomplete regulatory system, the design of the Fund reflects the need to respond to all the emerging requirements. It has developed its own modalities for the validation of baselines (to ensure additionality) and for the certification and verification of emission reductions generated by projects by independent third party certification agencies. These modalities have already been of assistance to the UNFCCC process, but baselines may need to be revalidated and reductions re-certified if the UNFCCC requirements differ. Similarly, while the procurement of the certification agencies themselves will initially be in accordance with the IBRD procurement guidelines, the PCF Instrument specifically envisages that once the CDM designates the operational entities for the certification of emission reductions as required by Article 12(5) of the Protocol, those procedures will govern in the case of any inconsistency.[63]

Elsewhere in reference to selection of projects, the validation, certification, registration, ownership and distribution of emission reductions,[64] the collection of a share of the proceeds of CDM[65] or even Article 6 projects, the modalities of the Fund will be able to respond to the UNFCC requirements as they are developed. The Fund even provides for the involuntary removal of Participants in the unlikely event that the regulatory framework developed means

63 *See* PCF Instrument art. 3.4.

64 *See notably* PCF Instrument sec. 13.1 entitled: "Adaptability to the requirements of the UNFCCC."

65 *See* Kyoto Protocol, *supra* note 2, art. 12(8).

that the continued participation of one entity prevents the rest of the Participants from receiving registerable emission reductions.[66]

F. The Closing of the Fund

The First Closing of the Fund took place on the April 10, 2000. Fifteen companies and six governments contributed US$135 million.[67] The Instrument had envisaged the First Closing in early 2000 with a Second Closing approximately a year later. To reward early movers, the Instrument also envisaged a ten percent premium payable by those entities that joined the Fund at the Second Closing.

At the Organizational Meeting held immediately after the closing, the Participants decided to recommend that the Instrument be amended to allow the Second Closing to be brought forward to the summer of 2000 but only in relation to those potential participants who had registered their interest in advance by May 17, 2000. The instrument was amended by the IBRD Board by the streamlined "no-objections" procedure in May, 2000, and the cap on the Fund war raised to US$180 million.[68] The Board also agreed that the premium payable be reduced to 2.5 percent. The Second Closing took place on October 31, 2000. Two further private sector entities joined the Fund. The size of the Fund closed at US$145 million.

IV. CONCLUSIONS

The amount of money that needs to be spent in industrialized countries to meet the cost of the Kyoto commitments is enor-

---

66 *See* PFC Instrument, sec. 9.2.

67 Public Sector Entities: Canada, Finland, Japan Bank for International Cooperation, the Netherlands, Norway, and Sweden. Private Sector entities: British Petroleum-Amoco, Chubu Electric Power Co, Chugoku Electric Power Co., Deutsche Bank, Electrabel/Suez-Lyonnaise des Eaux, Gaz de France, Kyushu Electric Power Co., Mitsubishi Corp., Mitsui, Norsk Hydro, R.W.E., Shikoku Power.Co., Statoil, Tohoku Electric Power Co., and Tokyo Electric Power Co. At the second closing, Fortum and Rabobank joined the Fund.

68 *See Resolution 2000-1, Bank Minutes and IFC* [International Finance Corporation] *Minutes, Meeting of the Executive Directors of the Bank and IDA* [International Development Association] *and the Directors of IFC*, May 23, 2000.

mous[69] and is unlikely to be generated by the public sector alone. The Kyoto Protocol therefore presents unparalleled opportunities for developing countries and economies in transition to capture some of the benefits from the trade in emission reductions which Kyoto has designed to help the industrialized countries meet their GHG reduction obligations. These benefits include not only access to cleaner technology and investments that would not otherwise have taken place, but they also give the opportunity to capture resources as projects financed under the Kyoto Mechanisms will generate a new valuable commodity — GHG emission reductions.

The PCF is designed to pilot a few projects, to identify contentious issues as well as possible solutions. It has mobilized resources from both the public sector and the private sector. Commentators agree that it is the private sector which will have to be the major driving force if the changes in technology which the UNFCCC envisages are to take place and industrialized countries are to meet their Kyoto commitments.[70] The know-how that the PCF seeks to generate and share is intended to assist the parties to the UNFCCC at a practical level as they continue to negotiate the guidelines, modalities and rules, as well as to assist individual countries at a strategic level in appreciating the opportunities which Kyoto presents. In the implementation of the PCF projects (not all of which will come from the World Bank Group portfolio), the World Bank does have some comparative advantage from more than fifty years of project-based investment experience, as well as nearly a decade of work with the GEF in isolating the global incremental benefits of environmental projects that it implements. On the World Bank Board of Executive Directors sit representatives of industrialized countries, countries with economies in transition, and developing countries. The Fund is designed to provide benefits to all three groups.

---

69 *See* Ellerman, et. al, *supra* note 49, which estimates the annual cost at US$30 billion per annum.

70 *See Press Briefing by the US Delegation to the Fifth Session of the Conference of the Parties to the UN Framework Convention on Climate Change (CoP-5),* Bonn, Germany, Nov. 4, 1999.

APPENDIX I

KYOTO PROTOCOL ANNEX B[+]

PARTY	QUANTIFIED EMISSION LIMITATION OR REDUCTION COMMITMENT (Percentage of Base Year or Period)		
Australia	108	Liechtenstein	92
Austria	92	Lithuania*	92
Belgium	92	Luxembourg	92
Bulgaria*	92	Monaco	92
Canada	94	Netherlands	92
Croatia*	95	New Zealand	100
Czech Republic*	92	Norway	101
Denmark	92	Poland*	94
Estonia*	92	Portugal	92
European Community	92	Romania*	92
Finland	92	Russian Federation*	100
France	92	Slovakia*	92
Germany	92	Slovenia*	92
Greece	92	Spain	92
Hungary*	94	Sweden	92
Iceland	110	Switzerland	92
Ireland	92	Ukraine*	100
Italy	92	United Kingdom of Great Britain and Northern Ireland	92
Japan	94		
Latvia*	92	United States of America	93

* Countries that are undergoing the process of transition to a market economy.

+ *Editorial Note:* This table sets out the extent of the GHG reductions which the countries list in this Annex must make during the 2008–2012 commitment period. Expressed as a percentage of their base year — which for most is GHG emission levels in 1990.

APPENDIX II

INTERNATIONAL BANK FOR RECONSTRUCTION AND DEVELOPMENT

RESOLUTION NO. 99-1

AUTHORIZING ESTABLISHMENT OF THE PROTOTYPE CARBON FUND

AS AMENDED BY RESOLUTION NO. 2000-1[71]

WHEREAS the International Bank for Reconstruction and Development (the "Bank") desires to promote project-based mechanisms that will help countries to reduce global concentrations of greenhouse gases and therefore minimize the adverse impacts of climate change on developing countries and countries with economies in transition;

WHEREAS in order to further that objective, the Bank desires to establish the Prototype Carbon Fund to be administered by the Bank to provide participants in the Prototype Carbon Fund with the opportunity to finance projects in developing countries and countries with economies in transition to generate greenhouse gas emission reductions which could be transferred to the participants, thereby assisting them in satisfying their obligations under the United Nations Framework Convention on Climate Change, related international agreements and domestic legislation;

---

71 Resolution No. 2000-1, "On Changing the Terms of a Second Closing and on Certain Other Amendments to the Instrument establishing the Prototype Carbon Fund," approved by the Executive Directors of the International Bank for Reconstruction and Development (IBRD) on May, 2000.

NOW THEREFORE IT IS HEREBY RESOLVED AS FOLLOWS:

The Executive Directors hereby establish the Prototype Carbon Fund on the terms and conditions set forth in, and substantially in the form of, Annex I attached to this Resolution.

INTERNATIONAL BANK FOR RECONSTRUCTION AND DEVELOPMENT

Instrument Establishing the Prototype Carbon Fund

WHEREAS:

(A) The International Bank for Reconstruction and Development [IBRD] desires to promote project-based mechanisms that will help countries to reduce global concentrations of greenhouse gases and therefore minimize the adverse impacts of climate change on developing countries through the establishment of a Prototype Carbon Fund to be administered by the IBRD to provide Participants in the Fund with the opportunity to provide resources to projects in developing countries and countries with economies in transition to generate greenhouse gas Emission Reductions which could be transferred to the Participants, thereby assisting them in satisfying their obligations under the United Nations Framework Convention on Climate Change and related international agreements and domestic legislation;[72]

(B) The IBRD has three strategic objectives in establishing the Fund: first, to demonstrate how project-based Emission Reductions transactions can promote and contribute to the sustainable development of developing countries and countries with economies in transition that are members of the IBRD; second, to share with the Parties to the United Nations Framework Convention on Climate Change and other interested parties knowledge gained by the Trustee and Participants in the course of the Fund's operations during the period when the guidelines, modalities and procedures

72 Text as amended by Resolution 2000-1.

that will govern project-based Emission Reduction transactions are being negotiated; and third, to demonstrate how the IBRD can work in partnership with the public and private sectors to mobilize new resources for its borrowing member countries while addressing global environmental concerns; and

(C) The IBRD is prepared to establish and administer the Prototype Carbon Fund on the terms and conditions set forth below.

NOW THEREFORE it is hereby resolved that:

ARTICLE I
DEFINITIONS

Section 1.1. *Definitions.* Unless the context otherwise requires, the following terms shall have the meanings set forth below:

1) "Activities Implemented Jointly" means project activities undertaken under the Activities Implemented Jointly Pilot Phase of the UNFCCC;
2) "Additional Participants" means those Participants that enter into Participation Agreements with the Trustee after the First Closing;
3) "Annex I" means Annex I of the UNFCCC;
4) "Annex I Countries" means the countries listed in Annex I of the UNFCCC and, when appropriate, in Annex B of the Kyoto Protocol;
5) "Annex B" means Annex B of the Kyoto Protocol;
6) "Article 6" means the mechanism defined in Article 6 of the Kyoto Protocol that provides for the transfer and acquisition of Emission Reduction Units between Annex I Countries;
7) "Article 12" means the mechanism (known as the Clean Development Mechanism) defined in Article 12 of the Kyoto Protocol that provides for the transfer of Certified Emission Reductions from non-Annex I Countries to Annex I Countries;
8) "Assigned Amounts" means the quantity of GHG an Annex I Country can release during the first commitment period of the Kyoto Protocol and is equal to the percentage, spec-

ified in Annex B, of an Annex I Country's aggregate anthropogenic carbon dioxide equivalent emissions of GHG in 1990, or in another base year as provided by the Kyoto Protocol, multiplied by five;

9) "Association" means the International Development Association, a member of the World Bank Group;

10) "Baseline" means the situation that would have occurred without the implementation of a Project, in particular with respect to Greenhouse Gas emissions or sequestration;

11) "Certification" means the process by which either (i) operational entities designated by the COP/MOP for the purposes of Article 12 and/or, if the UNFCCC Parties deem it appropriate, Article 6 of the Kyoto Protocol or (ii) properly qualified Independent Third Parties certify that the GHG Reductions achieved by a Project comply with a relevant set of standards or conditions;

12) "Certified Emission Reductions" means the GHG Reductions that are achieved by an Article 12 Project and are certified by operational entities designated by the COP/MOP for the purposes of Article 12 of the Kyoto Protocol;

13) "COP/MOP" means the Conference of the Parties to the UNFCCC serving as the meeting of the Parties to the Kyoto Protocol;

14) "Developing Countries" means those countries not listed in Annex I;

15) "Economies in Transition" or "EIT" means the countries listed in Annex I or Annex B that are undergoing the process of transition to a market economy;

16) "Eligible Private Sector Participant" means any person, other than an Eligible Public Sector Participant, organized in a country Party to the UNFCCC and whose participation in the Fund has been approved by the Trustee;

17) "Eligible Public Sector Participant" means any government, agency, ministry or other official entity of a country Party to the UNFCCC and whose participation in the Fund has been approved by the Trustee;

18) "Emission Reductions" means Emission Reduction Units, Certified Emission Reductions, and, pending the adoption of the relevant guidelines, modalities and procedures un-

der the regulatory framework of the UNFCCC and/or the Kyoto Protocol, GHG Reductions certified by Independent Third Parties as complying with a relevant set of standards or conditions;

19) "Emission Reduction Units" means the GHG Reductions achieved by an Article 6 Project that meet the conditions specified in Article 6 of the Kyoto Protocol including, if the Parties to the UNFCCC deem it appropriate, certification by operational entities designated by the COP/MOP;

20) "First Closing" means the initial closing of the Fund that is expected to occur on or about February 1, 2000, or such later date as may be determined by the Trustee in consultation with the Participants;

21) "Fund Management Committee" means the Committee comprised of the individuals selected by the President of the IBRD and which is responsible for overseeing the operations of the Fund;

22) "Fund Management Unit" means the Fund Manager and other staff selected by the Fund Manager who will perform services for the Fund on a full-time basis;

23) "Fund Manager" means the IBRD staff member selected by the President of the IBRD to head the Fund Management Unit and to act as chairperson of the Fund Management Committee;

24) "Fund Property" or "Property" means all property contributed to the Fund and all other assets, receipts and interests of the Fund;

25) "GHG Reductions" means, with respect to an Article 6 Project, the reduction of GHG emissions and the enhancement of GHG sequestration achieved by such Project and, with respect to an Article 12 Project, the reduction of GHG emissions and, if the Parties to the UNFCCC deem it appropriate, the enhancement of GHG sequestration achieved by such Project;

26) "Global Environment Facility" or "GEF" means the mechanism established by the 1994 Instrument for the Establishment of the Restructured Global Environment Facility;

27) "Greenhouse Gases" or "GHG" means the six gases listed in Annex A of the Kyoto Protocol, which are carbon diox-

ide, methane, nitrous oxide, hydrofluorocarbons, perfluorocarbons, and sulphur hexafluoride;

28) "High Quality Emission Reductions" means Emission Reductions of a sufficient quality so that, in the opinion of the Trustee at the time a Project is selected and designed, there will be a strong likelihood, to the extent it can be assessed, that Participants may be able to apply their share of Emission Reductions for the purpose of satisfying the requirements of the UNFCCC, related international agreements, or applicable national legislation;

29) "Host Country" means a country that is a member of the IBRD and in which a Project is located;

30) "Host Country Agreement" means an agreement entered into between the Trustee and the Host Country in respect of a Project;

31) "Host Country Committee" means the committee described in Article VII of this Instrument;

32) "Host Country Observer" means a member of the Host Country Committee who is elected to serve as a non-voting observer at a Participants' meeting or a Participants' Committee meeting;

33) "IFC" means the International Finance Corporation, a member of the World Bank Group;

34) "Independent Third Party" means an entity, such as an environmental auditing company, which is independent from the IBRD, the relevant Host Country and the relevant Project Entity;

35) "Initial Participants" means those Participants that entered into Participation Agreements with the Trustee on or before the First Closing;

36) "Instrument" means this Instrument establishing the Prototype Carbon Fund;

37) "Kyoto Protocol" or "Protocol" means the Protocol to the United Nations Framework Convention on Climate Change adopted at the Third Conference of the Parties to the United Nations Framework Convention on Climate Change in Kyoto, Japan on December 11, 1997;

38) "Letter of Endorsement" means the letter from the Host Country to the Trustee confirming that the Host Country is prepared to endorse further development of a Project;

39) "Monitoring" means activities pursuant to which the Project Entity or another person collects and records data which assess the GHG Reductions resulting from a Project pursuant to the terms of the Monitoring and Verification protocol for that Project;
40) "Operational Policies and Procedures" means those policies and procedures included within the IBRD's Operational Manual from time to time;
41) "Participant" means any Eligible Private Sector Participant or Eligible Public Sector Participant that has signed a Participation Agreement, or any assignee thereof pursuant to the terms of this Instrument;
42) "Participants' Committee" means the committee described in Article VI of this Instrument;
43) "Participation Agreement" means an agreement between a Participant and the Trustee with respect to the Participant's contribution to, and participation in, the Fund;
44) "Person" means and includes individuals, corporations, partnerships, trusts, unincorporated associations, unincorporated organizations, joint ventures and other entities, and governments and agencies and political subdivisions thereof;
45) "Private Sector Participant" means a Participant that is a person, other than a Public Sector Participant, organized in a country Party to the UNFCCC;
46) "Project" means an activity for which the Trustee has agreed to provide financing under Project Agreements, or project resources, in the form of the purchase of Emission Reductions, to Recipients under Project Agreements;[73]
47) "Project Agreement(s)" means a Host Country Agreement, or a Host Country Agreement and a Project Entity Agreement;
48) "Project Concept Note" means a brief description of a Project prepared by the Fund Management Unit that is to be presented for consideration by the Fund Management Committee and the Participants' Committee;
49) "Project Entity" means one or more persons with which the Trustee has entered into a Project Entity Agreement;

[73] Text as amended by Resolution 2000-1.

50) "Project Entity Agreement" means an agreement between the Trustee and a person defined as a Project Entity that provides, *inter alia,* for the implementation, operation and Monitoring of a Project;
51) "Project Portfolio Criteria" means the criteria specified as such in Schedule 1 to the Instrument;
52) "Project Selection Criteria" means the criteria specified as such in Schedule 1 to the Instrument;
53) "Public Sector Participant" means a Participant that is a government, agency, ministry or other official entity of a country Party to the UNFCCC;
54) "Quantified Emission Limitation or Reduction Commitment" or "QELRO" means the commitment by countries listed in Annex B to reduce Greenhouse Gas emissions by the percentage provided for in such Annex from a base year established pursuant to the Kyoto Protocol;
55) "Recipient(s)" means a Host Country, or a Host Country and a Project Entity;
56) "Second Closing" means the additional closing of the Fund that may occur on or about July 14, 2000, or such later date as may be determined by the Trustee in consultation with the Participants;[74]
57) "Third Party Project" means a Project that originates from outside the World Bank Group's project pipeline;
58) "Trustee" means the IBRD acting not in its individual or personal capacity but solely in its capacity as trustee of the Fund;
59) "Underlying Project" means a project financed by the IBRD, the IFC or a third party for which the Fund agrees to provide supplementary financing or resources through a Project;[75]
60) "UNCITRAL" means the United Nations Commission on International Trade Law;
61) "United Nations Framework Convention on Climate Change" or "UNFCCC" means the United Nations Framework Convention on Climate Change adopted in New York on May 9, 1992;

---

74 *Ibid.*

75 *Ibid.*

62) "Validation" means the assessment by a third party of a Project design, including its Baseline, before the Project's implementation;
63) "Verification" means the periodic auditing of the data recorded by the person responsible for Monitoring to verify the amount of Emission Reductions achieved by the Project in relation to its Baseline and the Project's compliance with other relevant requirements; and
64) "World Bank Group" means the International Bank for Reconstruction and Development, the International Finance Corporation, the International Development Association and the Multilateral Investment Guarantee Agency.

ARTICLE II
ESTABLISHMENT

Section 2.1. *Establishment.* The Prototype Carbon Fund is hereby established as a trust fund of the IBRD, constituted of the funds that shall from time to time be contributed in accordance with the provisions of this Instrument, and any other Fund Property. The IBRD shall be the Trustee of the Fund and in this capacity shall, as legal owner, hold in trust the Fund Property which constitutes the Fund, and manage and use the Fund Property only for the purposes of and in accordance with the provisions of this Instrument, keeping the Fund Property separate and apart from all other accounts and assets of, or administered by, the IBRD.

Section 2.2. *Trust Only.* It is the intention of the parties to this Instrument to create only the relationship of trustee and beneficiary between the Trustee and each Participant and not to create a general partnership, limited partnership, joint stock association, corporation, bailment or any form of legal relationship other than a trust. Nothing in this Instrument shall be construed so as to make the Participants, either by themselves or with the Trustee, partners or members of a joint stock association.

Section 2.3. *Authority to Enter into Participation Agreements; Maximum Size of Fund.* The Trustee may enter into Participation Agreements with Initial Participants during the period commencing on a date to be determined by the Trustee but not earlier than

November 15, 1999, and ending on and including the date of the First Closing. The Trustee may, thereafter, at its discretion, enter into Participation Agreements with Additional Participants during the period commencing after the First Closing and ending on and including the date of the Second Closing; provided that the aggregate amount of contributions to be provided under all of the Participation Agreements shall not exceed US$180 million.[76] Except as otherwise provided in this Instrument, the Trustee shall not enter into any Participation Agreements or accept any new contributions from any Participant after the Second Closing.

ARTICLE III
OPERATIONAL PRINCIPLES AND OPERATIONS OF THE FUND

Section 3.1. *Operational Principles.* The operational principles of the Fund are: (i) to provide resources for Projects which are intended to generate High Quality Emission Reductions; (ii) to endeavor to effect an equitable sharing between the Participants and the Host Countries of any Emission Reductions and other benefits arising from Projects; and (iii) to disseminate broadly the knowledge gained by the Trustee in the development of the Fund and the implementation of Projects.[77]

Section 3.2. *Operations of the Fund.* The Fund shall finance Projects designed to achieve GHG Reductions in return for (i) the exclusive right as against any third party, other than a person authorized under the regulatory framework of the UNFCCC and/or the Kyoto Protocol, to have an Independent Third Party certify the quality and quantity of any GHG Reductions generated by the Projects; and (ii) the right to have transferred to Participants an agreed amount of any Emission Reductions generated. The operations of the Fund may include the provision of project resources in the form of the purchase of Emission Reductions, either directly or through intermediaries.[78] The Trustee shall facilitate the pro-

---

76 *Ibid.*

77 *Ibid.*

78 Text introduced by Resolution 2000-1.

cesses of Validation, Verification and Certification whereby an Independent Third Party certifies the quality and quantity of any GHG Reductions achieved by the Projects in accordance with relevant standards and/or criteria to be developed under the regulatory framework of the UNFCCC and/or national laws. The Trustee shall also facilitate the transfer of an agreed amount of any Emission Reductions achieved by each Project from the Recipient to the Participants, on a pro rata basis.

Section 3.3. *Selection of Projects.* The Trustee shall select Projects in accordance with the Project Selection Criteria and with the intent, over the term of the Fund, of meeting the Project Portfolio Criteria. No material changes may be made to the Project Selection Criteria without the prior consent at a Participants' meeting of Participants holding not less than two-thirds of the votes of the Fund.

Section 3.4. *Compliance with IBRD's Operational Policies and Procedures.* The operations of the Fund shall comply with the Operational Policies and Procedures of the IBRD, except to the extent that such Operational Policies and Procedures may be inconsistent with the guidelines, modalities and procedures adopted by the Parties to the UNFCCC regarding the procurement of services by Independent Third Parties, in which case the latter shall govern.

ARTICLE IV
CONTRIBUTIONS FROM PARTICIPANTS

Section 4.1. *Payment of Contributions.*[79] Each Public Sector Participant will be required to contribute U.S.$10 million to the Fund and each Private Sector Participant will be required to contribute U.S.$5 million to the Fund. Each Initial Participant's and Additional Participant's required contribution to the Fund will be paid at the First Closing and the Second Closing, respectively, through the issuance and delivery of a promissory note made payable to the Trustee on demand. At the First Closing and Second Closing, the Trustee will provide Participants with an anticipated schedule of demands for payment of their respective promissory notes.

79 Text as amended by Resolution 2000-1.

However, such schedule of payments will remain at the sole discretion of the Trustee, having regard to the financial requirements of the Fund, including the anticipated requirements for payments to Recipients under Project Agreements. The Trustee will make demands for payment by Participants under the promissory notes on a pro rata basis; provided, that the failure of any Participant to make any such payment when due shall not relieve any other Participant of its obligation to make its respective payment. Participants will be entitled to prepay up to the entire amount of their required contribution. No interest will be payable by Participants on any portion of the required contribution not yet demanded by the Trustee or by the Fund on any prepaid portion of the required contribution. The first payment from Initial Participants will be due within 30 days following the First Closing, and the first payment from Additional Participants and a further payment from Initial Participants, if any, will be due within 30 days following the Second Closing. The Trustee will provide Participants with at least 30 days' notice of all subsequent payment demands.

Section 4.2. *Payment of Premium.* All Participation Agreements entered into after the First Closing shall provide that the Additional Participants shall, in addition to their required contribution, pay a premium in an amount equal to 2.5% of the amount of such contribution.[80] The premium shall be payable on the same terms as the contribution. The premium shall not be taken into account in determining the Participant's interests in the Fund or in the calculation of the size of the Fund.

ARTICLE V
PARTICIPANTS' MEETINGS

Section 5.1. *Participants' Meetings.* A meeting of the Participants shall be held annually, at such date and time and in such place as shall be determined by the Trustee. At each such annual meeting, the Participants may review the operations of the Fund and existing Projects to provide the Trustee with general policy and strate-

80 *Ibid.*

gic guidance on the operations of the Fund and shall have the following powers and duties:

a) reviewing and approving the business plan and annual budget for the Fund for the next fiscal year;
b) reviewing and approving by a two-thirds majority of the votes of the Fund any amendments to the Project Selection Criteria or the Project Portfolio Criteria, other than amendments that in the Trustee's opinion are merely technical in nature; provided, that any such amendment shall be consistent with the Operational Policies and Procedures of the IBRD in the opinion of the Trustee and otherwise be acceptable to the Trustee;
c) providing general guidance to the Trustee on the selection of Projects;
d) commencing with the second annual Participants' meeting, electing the members of the Participants' Committee to serve until the next annual Participants' meeting;
e) for each of the first ten annual Participants' meetings, reviewing and, if acceptable, approving the recommendation, if any, of the Participants' Committee regarding a performance-linked payment to be paid to the Trustee for the preceding fiscal year pursuant to Section 11.3 hereof;
f) at the first annual Participants' meeting, reviewing and authorizing the payment to the IBRD of any development costs related to the Fund's establishment not presented at the organizational Participants' meeting; and
g) taking any other action that may be taken by the Participants under this Instrument.

Special meetings of the Participants may be called at any time by the Trustee for any purpose consistent with this Instrument, including without limitation voting on the removal of Ineligible Participants pursuant to Section 9.2 hereof. At any such special meeting, one or more Participants may, if all of the other Participants participating in the meeting consent, participate by means of such telephone or other communications facilities as permit all Participants participating in the meeting to hear each other or participate by other electronic means, and a Participant participating in such a meeting by such means is deemed for the purposes of this Instrument to be present at that meeting.

Section 5.2. *Organizational Meeting.* The Trustee shall convene an organizational Participants' meeting within 14 days of the First Closing, at such date and time and in such place as shall be determined by the Trustee. At such organizational Participants' meeting, the Participants shall have the following powers and duties:

a) reviewing and approving the business plan and budget for the Fund for the period from the First Closing to the last day of the fiscal year of the Fund in which the organizational Participants' meeting is held;
b) electing the members of the Participants' Committee to serve for a term running from the date of the organizational Participants' meeting until the second annual Participants' meeting; and
c) reviewing and authorizing the payment to the IBRD of the development costs related to the Fund's establishment.

Section 5.3. *Notice.* The Trustee shall provide each Participant and each Host Country Observer with written notice of a Participants' meeting not less than 30 days before the date of the meeting unless such notice has been waived by the intended recipient. Such notice shall state the place, date and time of the meeting and, in the case of a special meeting, the purpose or purposes for which the meeting is called. Notwithstanding this Section, written notice of the organizational Participants' meeting shall be given to the Participants and each Host Country Observer on the First Closing.

Section 5.4. *Voting.* Each Participant shall be entitled to one vote for each U.S. dollar of its contribution to the Fund (exclusive of any premium paid) on each matter submitted for a vote at a meeting of the Participants. Except as otherwise provided, every matter submitted to a Participants' meeting shall be decided by the majority of the votes cast by Participants represented at such Participants' meeting.

Section 5.5. *Quorum.* Participants represented at a meeting of the Participants holding a majority of all the votes of the Fund shall constitute a quorum for the transaction of business at a Participants' meeting.

Section 5.6. *Action Without Meeting.* Action required or permitted to be taken at a Participants' meeting may be taken without a meeting if a consent in writing, setting forth the action to be so taken, has been circulated to all of the Participants and Host Country Observers and signed in one or more counterparts by Participants holding not less than two-thirds of the votes of the Fund or, in the case of an action requiring unanimous approval, by all Participants.

Section 5.7. *Proxies.* Any Participant entitled to vote at a Participants' meeting may vote by proxy if a duly executed proxy has been received by the Trustee for verification prior to the meeting.

ARTICLE VI
PARTICIPANTS' COMMITTEE

Section 6.1. *Participants' Committee.*

(a) At the organizational Participants' meeting, the Participants will establish a Participants' Committee, which shall be comprised of seven members during its first term and five members at all times thereafter. The members of the Participants' Committee shall be officers, directors, employees or officials of Participants; provided, that not more than one member shall be a representative of the same Participant. The members of the Participants' Committee shall be elected by majority vote of the votes cast at a Participants' meeting. At the organizational Participants' meeting, the Participants shall elect members of the Participants' Committee for a term running from such meeting to the date of the second annual Participants' meeting. At the second annual Participants' meeting and at each annual Participants' meeting thereafter, the Participants shall elect members of the Participants' Committee to be members until the next succeeding annual Participants' meeting. The Participants' Committee shall elect one of its members to serve as chairperson until such time as such member has ceased to be a member of the Participants' Committee or until such member's successor as chairperson has been elected.

(b) Each member of the Participants' Committee shall serve until the member's successor shall have been elected; provided, that at the time a member of the Participants' Committee ceases to be an officer, director, employee or official of a Participant, such member's term as a member of the Participants' Committee shall cease. That Participant may appoint another officer, director, employee or official of such Participant to fill any vacancy in the Participants' Committee resulting from the resignation, death or incapacity of a member that is or was an officer, director, employee or official of such Participant, failing which, after 30 days, any vacancy in the Participants' Committee shall be filled by the affirmative vote of a majority of the remaining members of the Participants' Committee. A member elected to fill such a vacancy shall be elected for the unexpired term of the member's predecessor in office. At any time, any member of the Participants' Committee may be removed by the Participant for which such member is a representative and replaced with another representative of that Participant.

(c) The Participants' Committee elected at the organizational Participants' meeting shall be comprised of four members who are officials of Public Sector Participants and three members who are officers, directors or employees of Private Sector Participants. The Participants' Committee elected at the second annual Participants' meeting shall be comprised of two members who are officials of Public Sector Participants and three members who are officers, directors or employees of Private Sector Participants. Thereafter, the representation of Public Sector Participants and Private Sector Participants on subsequent Participants' Committees will alternate annually between two and three members, respectively.

Section 6.2. *Actions of the Participants' Committee.* Each member of the Participants' Committee shall be entitled to cast one vote, and a majority of the members of the Participants' Committee present at a meeting shall constitute a quorum for the transaction of business. Every matter submitted to the Participants' Committee shall be decided by the majority vote of the votes cast at the meeting; provided, that the actions referred to in Section 6.4(c) hereof shall be approved unless at least two members of the Participants' Committee object within 30 days of the presentation, by the Trustee, of the relevant Project Concept Note to the Participants.

Section 6.3. *Meetings of the Participants' Committee.* Meetings of the Participants' Committee shall be called by the chairperson or the Trustee. Each member of the Participants' Committee, each Host Country Observer and the Trustee shall be given at least 14 days' written notice of any Participants' Committee meeting unless such notice has been waived by the intended recipient. Such notice shall specify the matters to be considered and shall designate the place, date and time of the meeting. One or more members of the Participants' Committee may, if all of the other members of the Participants' Committee participating in the meeting consent, participate in a meeting of the Participants' Committee by means of such telephone or other communications facilities as permit all members participating in the meeting to hear each other or participate by other electronic means, and a member of the Participants' Committee participating in such a meeting by such means is deemed for the purposes of this Instrument to be present at that meeting. No member of the Participants' Committee shall receive any compensation from the Fund for its services as such, nor shall any member of the Participants' Committee be entitled to payment or reimbursement from the Fund or Trustee for travel or other costs incurred in attending meetings of the Participants' Committee.

Section 6.4. *Powers and Duties of Participants' Committee.* The Participants' Committee shall have the following powers and duties:

a) providing general advice to the Trustee on issues regarding the operation of the Fund;
b) reviewing the operations of the Fund and advising the Trustee on the extent to which the Project Agreements negotiated and to be entered into by the Trustee accord with the Project Selection Criteria;

c) reviewing Project Concept Notes for each proposed Project in order to determine whether to object to the inclusion of such Project in the Fund's portfolio;
d) for each of the first ten years of the Fund, providing recommendations to the annual Participants' meeting regarding the making of a performance-linked payment to the Trustee pursuant to Section 11.3 of this Instrument for the preceding fiscal year of the Fund; and
e) for any fiscal year, authorizing expenditures, other than those incurred pursuant to Section 8.1(i) and Article XII of this Instrument, which exceed the total annual budget previously approved by the Participants for that fiscal year by more than 10%.

ARTICLE VII
HOST COUNTRY COMMITTEE

Section 7.1. *Host Country Committee.* The Trustee shall invite each Host Country and each potential Host Country that has signed a Letter of Endorsement or a memorandum of understanding with the Trustee with respect to the Fund to appoint a representative to serve on the Host Country Committee. Such Host Country or potential Host Country may also invite one Project Entity or potential Project Entity which is expected to implement a Project in its territory to appoint a representative to attend meetings of the Host Country Committee as a non-voting observer.

Section 7.2. *Powers of the Host Country Committee.* The Host Country Committee shall have the following powers:
a) providing advice to the Trustee, copied to the Participants, on proposed amendments to the Project Selection Criteria and Project Portfolio Criteria;
b) providing advice to the Trustee, copied to the Participants, on the composition of the Project portfolio and providing views on the consistency of the Project portfolio with the regulatory framework of the UNFCCC;
c) providing advice to the Trustee, copied to the Participants, on how to effect an equitable sharing between the Participants and the Host Countries of any Emission Reductions and other benefits arising from Projects;

d) providing advice to the Trustee, copied to the Participants, on Project implementation, including the processes of Validation, Verification and Certification; and

e) providing advice to the Trustee on the development and improvement of vehicles for the dissemination of the knowledge gained by it in the development of the Fund and the implementation of Projects.

Section 7.3. *Election of Chairperson and Host Country Observers.*

(a) At its first meeting, the Host Country Committee shall elect one of its members as chairperson of the Host Country Committee to serve as such until the chairperson's successor has been elected. The Host Country Committee shall also elect three of its members to serve as Host Country Observers at Participants' meetings and one of its members to serve as a Host Country Observer at Participants' Committee meetings, until each such member's successor has been elected. Such Host Country Observers shall be entitled to be present at all Participants' meetings or Participants' Committee meetings, as the case may be. The Host Country Observers shall receive no compensation from the Fund or Trustee for their services as such nor shall they be entitled to payment or reimbursement from the Fund or Trustee for travel or other costs incurred in attending the relevant meetings.

(b) Until such time as the initial Host Country Observers have been elected, the Trustee shall designate and invite specific members of the Host Country Committee to attend meetings of the Participants and meetings of the Participants' Committee.

Section 7.4. *Meetings of the Host Country Committee.* Meetings of the Host Country Committee shall be held at least annually, at such dates and times and in such places as shall be determined by the Trustee to permit the Host Country Committee to interact with the Participants.

Section 7.5. *Notice.* The Trustee shall provide each member of the Host Country Committee with written notice of a Host Country Committee meeting not less than 30 days before the date of the meeting unless such notice has been waived by the intended recipient. Such notice shall state the place, date and time of the meeting.

ARTICLE VIII
ADMINISTRATION

Section 8.1. *Authorization and Administration*. The administration of the Fund shall be governed by the following provisions:

a) The Trustee shall hold all Fund Property in trust for the benefit of the Participants. The Trustee shall manage and use Fund Property only for the purposes of, and in accordance with, the provisions of this Instrument, keeping it separate and apart from the assets of the IBRD, the IFC and the Association but may commingle it for investment purposes with other trust fund assets maintained by the IBRD, the IFC or the Association. At its discretion, the Trustee may at any time exchange any funds received from a Participant or any other Fund Property for one or more other currencies in order to facilitate the administration of the Fund.

b) The Trustee shall exercise the same care in the discharge of its functions under this Instrument as the IBRD exercises with respect to its own affairs and shall not have any additional obligation in respect hereof. The privileges and immunities accorded to the IBRD shall apply to the Property, archives, operations and transactions of the Fund. The obligations of the Trustee pursuant to this Instrument are not obligations of any government.

c) The Trustee is authorized to enter into Participation Agreements and accept contributions in the required amount from Participants at any time after a date to be determined by the Trustee, but not earlier than November 15, 1999, through the Second Closing, as provided in this Instrument. The Trustee shall not be authorized to recognize more than one person joining together as a joint Participant. Participation Agreements shall be in form and substance satisfactory to the Trustee. The Trustee shall use the contributions to the Fund and the income earned from the investment of such contributions pending disbursement solely for the purposes set out in this Instrument.

d) The Trustee may, at any time and with the approval of Participants holding not less than two-thirds of the votes cast at any meeting of Participants, solicit an amount of voluntary supplementary contributions from Participants. No Participant will have any obligation to contribute such additional amount. Any such voluntary supplementary contribution made by a Participant will be taken into account in determining the Participants' pro rata interests in the Fund, and the pro rata interest of a Participant may be reduced or increased depending upon the amount, if any, of such voluntary supplementary contributions. No premium (as described above) will be payable by Participants in respect of any supplementary contributions. The aggregate amount of contributions to be made to the Fund, including any voluntary supplementary contributions under this Section, will under no circumstances exceed U.S.$180 million (exclusive of any premium paid by Participants).[81]

e) The Trustee is authorized to perform all acts and enter into all contracts as it shall deem necessary or desirable to accomplish the purposes of the Fund, including, without limitation, Project Agreements. Subject to the terms of this Instrument, the selection of Recipients and Projects, the preparation and negotiation of Project Agreements and the monitoring and supervision of Projects shall be the responsibility solely of the Trustee.

f) The Trustee is authorized to invest funds held by the Fund pending disbursement in such manner as it may decide. All the income from such investments shall be credited to, and used exclusively for the purposes of, the Fund. Without limiting the foregoing, the Trustee shall have the power to invest Fund Property in such securities, instruments and other obligations as are authorized investments for other trust fund assets maintained by the IBRD, the IFC or the Association or retain Fund assets in cash; from time to time to change the investments of the assets of the Fund; and to exercise any and all rights, powers and privileges of own-

81 *Ibid.*

ership or interest in respect of any and all such investments of any kind and description, including, without limitation, the right to consent and otherwise act with respect thereto, with power to designate one or more individuals, firms, associations or corporations to exercise any of said rights, powers and privileges in respect of any of said instruments. The Trustee shall not be limited to investing in obligations maturing before the possible termination of the Fund, nor shall the Trustee be limited by any law limiting the investments which may be made by fiduciaries.

g) To ensure the efficient operation of the Fund's cash management and investment transactions, the Trustee shall have the power to borrow from commercial banks and other financial institutions, for periods of up to thirty days, in any currency or currency unit.

h) The Trustee shall have the power to incur and pay any costs or expenses which in its opinion are necessary or desirable to carry out any of the purposes of the Fund, and to make payments from Fund Property to itself as Trustee to the extent provided in this Instrument; provided, that without the approval of the Participants' Committee, such costs or expenses, other than those incurred pursuant to Section 8.1(i) and Article XII of this Instrument, shall not exceed the total annual budget for the Fund previously approved by the Participants by more than 10%.

i) The Trustee shall have the power to collect all property due to the Fund and to pay all claims against Fund Property. The Trustee shall have the power to engage in and to prosecute, defend, compromise, abandon, or adjust, by arbitration, or otherwise, any actions, suits, proceedings, disputes, claims, and demands relating to the Fund, including without limitation those relating to Project Agreements, and out of the Property of the Fund to pay or to satisfy any debts, claims or expenses incurred in connection therewith, including those of litigation, and such power shall include without limitation the power of the Trustee to dismiss any action, suit, proceeding, dispute, claim, or demand, derivative or otherwise, brought by any person, including a Participant in its own name or the name of the Fund, whether or not the Fund or the Trustee may be named individually therein or the subject matter arises by reason of business for or on behalf of the Fund.

j) The Trustee shall have the power to: (i) employ or contract with such individuals or persons as it may deem desirable to conduct the business of the Fund; (ii) enter into joint ventures, partnerships and any other combinations or associations; (iii) subject to the terms of this Instrument, elect and remove such officers and appoint and terminate such agents or employees of the Fund as it considers appropriate; (iv) purchase and pay for out of Fund Property, to the extent available on commercially reasonable terms, such insurance as the Trustee deems desirable to protect it, the IBRD, the Participants and any other individual or person entitled to indemnification by the Fund; and (v) make amendments to the Project Selection Criteria or Project Portfolio Criteria that in its opinion are merely technical in nature.

k) The Trustee may from time to time appoint or otherwise engage one or more banks or trust companies or other financial institutions to serve as escrow agent(s) on behalf of the Fund in respect of Fund Property that may be deposited into an escrow account pending disbursement.

l) Except as otherwise provided in this Instrument, the Trustee shall have the exclusive power to conduct the business of the Fund and carry on its operations wheresoever the Trustee deems necessary, proper or desirable in order to promote the interests of the Fund. Any determination made by the Trustee in good faith as to what is in the interests of the Fund shall be conclusive. In construing the provisions of this Instrument, the presumption shall be in favor of a grant of power to the Trustee. The enumeration of any specific power herein shall not be construed as limiting the aforesaid power. Such powers of the Trustee may be exercised without order of or resort to any court or other authority.

m) Nothing in this Instrument shall preclude the IBRD from acting for its own account and from entering into or being interested in any contract or transaction with any person, including, but not limited to, any Participant, Host Country or Project Entity, with the same rights as it would have had if it were not acting as the Trustee, and the IBRD need not account for any profit therefrom.

n) Any power, duty or discretion to be exercised by the Trustee pursuant to the terms of this Instrument shall, unless otherwise provided, be exercised by the Trustee in its sole discretion.

Section 8.2. *Project Validation, Verification and Certification of Greenhouse Gas Reductions.* The Trustee may from time to time enter into one or more contracts with persons for such services, and on such terms and conditions, as the Trustee shall consider appropriate with respect to Project Validation, as well as for Verification and Certification of GHG Reductions. Without limiting the foregoing, such services may include:

a) Validation of the Project's design, primarily on the basis of the Project Appraisal Document and other relevant documentation prepared during Project development;
b) Verification of GHG Reductions and of Project compliance with relevant requirements specified in the Project Entity Agreements;
c) Certification of GHG Reductions by operational entities designated by the Parties to the UNFCCC or, pending the adoption of the relevant guidelines, modalities and procedures, by an Independent Third Party; and
d) Submission of periodic reports to the Trustee concerning (i) actions recommended to be taken by the Trustee or the Recipient to address problems relating to Project specifications, criteria or objectives; (ii) risks that may materialize in future Verification periods; and (iii) any suggested means of improving Project performance.

Section 8.3. *Administrative Services.* The Trustee may from time to time contract with one or more persons (including with related persons such as the IBRD) for goods, services, and personnel whereby such persons will provide to the Trustee or to the Fund, goods, services or administrative personnel on such terms and conditions as the Trustee may determine.

Section 8.4. *Registrar, Transfer Agent and/or Custodian Services.* The Trustee may from time to time engage one or more persons to act as registrar, transfer agent and/or custodian on behalf of the Fund in respect of Fund Property, instruments evidencing entitlement to Emission Reductions, or other interests of the Participants, on such terms and conditions as the Trustee may determine.

Section 8.5. *Parties to Contract.* Any payment, transaction or contract which is authorized under this Instrument may be made or entered into, as the case may be, with any person, and the validity of any such payment, transaction or contract shall not be affected by reason of the existence of any relationship between the Trustee and any such person; nor shall any person holding such relationship be liable merely by reason of such relationship for any loss or expense to the Fund under or by reason of said payment, transaction or contract or accountable for any profit realized directly or indirectly therefrom.

Section 8.6. *Limits on Trustee's Powers.* Notwithstanding any other provision of this Instrument, the Trustee shall not:

a) incur any costs or expenses, other than those incurred pursuant to Section 8.1(i) and Article XII of this Instrument, for the account of the Fund in any fiscal year or thereafter which exceed the total annual budget previously approved by the Participants by more than 10%, excluding development costs reimbursable under Section 11.2, without the approval of the Participants' Committee; or
b) commit Fund Property to the preparation of a Project unless the Trustee has presented a Project Concept Note to the Participants' Committee and less than two members of the Participants' Committee have objected to the preparation of the Project within 30 days thereafter.

Section 8.7. *Fund Management Committee.* The Trustee shall establish a Fund Management Committee comprised of five members, consisting of the Fund Manager and four other members of the IBRD's management, who shall be selected by the President of the IBRD. The Fund Manager will chair and coordinate the business of the Fund Management Committee, including its meetings and decision-making schedules. The Fund Management Committee shall be responsible for overseeing the operations of the Fund, and it shall also (i) approve each Project proposal prior to the Participants' Committee review of such Project; (ii) review and decide whether to proceed with a Project after due consideration of comments received by any Participants after the Participants' Committee review; (iii) review and, if acceptable, approve each Project Agreement following its negotiation by the Trustee with the Host Country and Project Entity, but prior to its execution; (iv) approve each business plan and annual budget for the Fund prior to their submission to the Participants at their annual meeting; (v) approve expenses for the account of the Fund which exceed the total annual budget previously approved by the Participants by more than 10% of that budget, if deemed necessary for the continuation of the Fund's operations; and (vi) supervise the knowledge-sharing activities of the Fund in furtherance of the Fund's knowledge dissemination principle set forth in Section 3.1(iii) of this Instrument.

Section 8.8. *Fund Management Unit.* A Fund Management Unit shall be established by the Trustee. The Fund Manager shall head the Fund Management Unit as the chief executive officer and shall have overall responsibility for the day-to-day operations of the Fund, including, without limitation: (i) overseeing the operations of the Fund Management Unit, including the selection of its staff; (ii) representing the Fund's interests at international fora and maintaining contact with Participants and Recipients; (iii) overseeing the selection of Projects, reviewing Projects during their appraisal, implementation and operation, and negotiating Project Agreements; (iv) ensuring compliance with Project Selection Criteria and Project Portfolio Criteria; (v) seeking to ensure consistency, to the extent possible, of the Fund's operations with the regulatory framework of the UNFCCC and the Operational Policies and Procedures; and (vi) collecting, organizing, managing and disseminating the knowledge and information obtained by the Trustee in the course of its operation of the Fund.

ARTICLE IX
DEFAULT AND REMOVAL OF PARTICIPANTS

Section 9.1. *Default in Paying Installment.*

(a) If, after demand by the Trustee, a Participant (the "Defaulting Participant") fails to pay any installment of a contribution (or any part thereof) when due and such failure continues for 15 days, the Trustee shall notify the Defaulting Participant and the other Participants of such default. If, after 30 days from such notification, the Defaulting Participant fails to pay such amount in full, the Trustee will so notify the other Participants. Any of the other Participants may, between 15 and 30 days following such notice from the Trustee, notify the Trustee that it intends to purchase the Defaulting Participant's interest in the Fund. If only one Participant so notifies the trustee, the Trustee shall notify such Participant that it may purchase the Defaulting Participant's interest in the Fund by making payment (i) to the Defaulting Participant of an amount equal to 50% of the fair market value (as determined by an independent third party selected by the Trustee) of the Defaulting Participant's pro rata interest in the Fund (the "Purchase Price"), less any expenses incurred by the Trustee or the Fund in connection with the sale, and (ii) to the Trustee of the amount of the unpaid installment due to the Fund from the Defaulting Participant.

(b) If more than one Participant notifies the Trustee of an intention to purchase the Defaulting Participant's interest in the Fund, then the Trustee shall so notify each such Participant that elects to purchase a portion of the Defaulting Participant's interest in the Fund, and each such Participant may purchase that portion of the Defaulting Participant's interest that corresponds to the electing Participant's proportion of the interest of all the electing Participants' interests in the Fund.

(c) If no Participant notifies the Trustee of an intention to purchase the Defaulting Participant's interest in the Fund, the Trustee may arrange for a private sale of such interest to a person acceptable to the Trustee.

(d) The Defaulting Participant shall receive from the proceeds of the sale an amount equal to the lesser of the sale proceeds or the Purchase Price, less any expenses incurred by the Trustee or the Fund in connection with the sale. Upon disposition of the Defaulting Participant's interest as described above, the Defaulting Participant shall be deemed to have transferred to the purchaser(s) all of its rights and interest in the Fund, including without limitation, any further distributions of Fund Property which it is entitled to receive, and the Trustee shall consent to such transfer.

(e) If there is no sale of a Defaulting Participant's interest in the Fund within 90 days following the default of such Defaulting Participant, such Defaulting Participant shall thereupon, without any further notice or action by the Trustee, be deemed to have forfeited all of its rights and interest in the Fund, including, without limitation, the right to further distributions of Fund Property which it is entitled to receive, and such rights and interest shall thereupon, without any further notice or action by the Trustee, be cancelled.

Section 9.2. *Removal of Ineligible Participants.*

(a) If, following the development by the Parties to the UNFCCC and/or the Kyoto Protocol of criteria for the financing of Article 6 or Article 12 Projects or for the transfer of Emission Reductions, in the opinion of the Trustee the continued participation of any Participant (the "Ineligible Participant") will prevent the transfer to the Participants of Emission Reductions which are capable of being credited towards Annex I Countries' QELROs and/or prevents the Fund from financing Article 6 or Article 12 Projects, the Trustee, having obtained approval of a two-thirds majority of the votes of the Fund, exclusive of the Ineligible Participant, may require the removal of the Ineligible Participant from the Fund and shall notify the Participants of such decision. Any of the other Participants may, between 15 and 30 days following such notice from the Trustee, notify the Trustee that it intends to purchase the Ineligible Participant's interest in the Fund. If only one Participant so notifies the Trustee, the Trustee shall notify such Participant that it may purchase the Ineligible Participant's interest in the Fund by making payment to the Ineligible Participant of an amount equal to the fair market value (as determined by an independent third party selected by the Trustee) of the Ineligible Participant's pro rata share of the Fund (the "Purchase Price").

(b) If more than one Participant notifies the Trustee of its intention to purchase the Ineligible Participant's interest in the Fund, then the Trustee will so notify each such Participant that does elect to purchase a portion of the Ineligible Participant's interest and each such Participant may purchase that portion of the Ineligible Participant's interest that corresponds to the electing Participants' proportion of the interest of all the electing Participants' interest in the Fund.

(c) If no Participant notifies the Trustee of an intention to purchase the Ineligible Participant's interest in the Fund, the Trustee may arrange for a private sale of such interest to a purchaser acceptable to the Trustee.

(d) The Ineligible Participant shall receive from the proceeds of a sale referred to in Section 9.2(b) or (c) above an amount equal to the lesser of the Purchase Price or the amount realized from such sale less the costs of such sale, as determined by the Trustee. The Ineligible Participant shall be deemed to have transferred to the purchaser(s) all of its rights and interest in the Fund, including any further distributions of Fund Property which it is entitled to receive, and the Trustee shall consent to such transfer.

(e) If there is no sale of an Ineligible Participant's interest in the Fund within 90 days following notice from the Trustee of the removal of the Ineligible Participant, the Trustee shall redeem the Ineligible Participant's interest in the Fund upon payment, out of then available Fund resources, of an amount equal to the Purchase Price (or a part thereof) as provided below. In the event that there are then insufficient available Fund resources to make such payment in full, the Purchase Price (or any part thereof remaining unpaid) shall be paid out of the proceeds of the next succeeding drawdown of the remaining Participants' funding obligations, in which case the Ineligible Participant shall be entitled to receive interest (at the prevailing rate as determined by the Trustee) on the Purchase Price remaining unpaid from the date of redemption of the Ineligible Participant's interest to the date payment is made. If there is no sale of a Ineligible Participant's interest as described above or if, within 120 days following notice from the Trustee of the removal of the Ineligible Participant, the Trustee determines that there are then insufficient available Fund resources and insufficient further funding obligations of the remaining Participants to pay the Purchase Price, such Ineligible Participant shall, without any further notice or action by the Trustee, be deemed to have forfeited all of its rights and interest in the Fund, including, without limitation, the right to Emission Reductions and any further distribution of Fund assets which it is entitled to receive, and such rights and interest shall be cancelled.

ARTICLE X
FISCAL YEAR; RECORDS AND REPORTS

Section 10.1. *Fiscal Year.* The fiscal year of the Fund shall be the same as the fiscal year of the IBRD, which runs from July 1 to June 30 of the following year.

Section 10.2. *Business Plan; Annual Budget.* The Trustee shall prepare a business plan which shall include a proposed budget for the operation of the Fund for each fiscal year and submit such proposed business plan and budget to the Participants for their consideration at the annual Participants' meeting no later than 30 days prior to the commencement of such fiscal year, except that the business plan and budget to be submitted to the Participants at the organizational Participants' meeting shall be provided to the Participants at the First Closing.

Section 10.3. *Financial Statements.* The Trustee shall maintain separate record and ledger accounts in respect of the Fund. Within 90 days of each March 31, June 30, September 30 and December 31, the Trustee shall prepare financial statements with respect to the Fund and forward a copy to each of the Participants. The annual financial statements shall be audited financial statements. The Trustee shall cause such annual financial statement to be audited by the same auditors as are engaged by the IBRD from time to time and shall send a copy of the auditors' report to each of the Participants.

Section 10.4. *Reports to Participants.* The Trustee shall within 90 days of each June 30 and December 31 prepare a report on the operation of the Fund for the preceding six-month period and send a copy to each of the Participants. Each such report shall contain a Project status report, including a cash flow, cost analysis and disbursement schedule for the Projects, and information on any changes to the structure or operations of the Fund resulting from decisions of the Participants at the preceding annual Participants' Meeting. Each such Participants' report shall be accompanied by a statement of account for each Participant evidencing such Participant's share of Fund Property.

Section 10.5. *Other Documentation.* To the extent consistent with the IBRD's, the IFC's or a Third Party Project sponsor's policies, as applicable, with respect to disclosure of information, the Trustee shall provide the Participants with copies of all final documents prepared or received by the Trustee with respect to each Project (including, without limitation, Project Concept Notes, project concept documents, project appraisal documents, Validation reports and Verification reports) and, from time to time as warranted, in the Trustee's discretion, with information on good practices and lessons of experience learned by the Trustee from the development and operation of the Fund, including, without limitation, methodological research and procedures for Validation and Verification. The Trustee shall prepare and keep updated a specific "Project Information Document" for each Project which shall be made publicly available through IBRD's Public Information Center. The Trustee will report to the UNFCCC Secretariat on Projects in accordance with reporting requirements established by the Parties to UNFCCC as and when such requirements are established.

ARTICLE XI
EXPENSES AND FEES

Section 11.1. *Expenses.* Fund Property shall be used by the Trustee to pay or reimburse it or any other person, including the IBRD and the IFC, for all costs and expenses incurred in the administration of the Fund, including without limitation: (i) all costs incurred in connection with the appraisal, selection and supervision of Projects; (ii) costs of office space and facilities, equipment and supplies and services, including, without limitation, the cost of utility services; (iii) communication expenses, including, without limitation, mailing, telephone and facsimile expenses; (iv) salaries, benefits, travel, accommodation and subsistence expenses of all personnel performing services in respect of the Fund, including, without limitation, those incidental to the appraisal, selection and supervision of Projects; (v) expenses for documentary and other relevant requirements, including fees relating to the UNFCCC and/or the Kyoto Protocol, Project approval and Validation, Verification and Certification processes; (vi) any payments required in connection with Article 12 Projects and, if the Parties to the UNFCCC deem it appropriate, in connection with Article 6 Projects; (vii) any compensation and expenses of any consultant, agent, adviser, contractor or subcontractor engaged by the Trustee for the Fund; (viii) costs of any insurance policies obtained in connection with, or on behalf of, the Fund, Participants or other persons; (ix) costs of legal, accounting and auditing services provided in respect of the Fund; and (x) public relations and representation costs.

Section 11.2. *Fund Development Costs.* Upon presentation to the Participants at the organizational meeting or a subsequent annual meeting of the Participants of an itemized statement thereof, Fund Property shall also be used by the Trustee to reimburse the IBRD for 80% of all costs and expenses incurred by the IBRD prior to the First Closing of the Fund in relation to the development of the Fund, including, without limitation: (i) the salaries and benefits of personnel of the IBRD; (ii) the travel, accommodation and subsistence expenses of personnel of the IBRD; (iii) compensation and expenses of any consultant, adviser, contractor, subcontractor, or auditor retained by the IBRD, including, without limitation, legal advisers, and (iv) costs and expenses associated with the preparation of all legal documentation in respect to the formation and operation of the Fund; provided however, that the aggregate amount of Fund Property so used for such purposes shall not exceed U.S.$2 million, and the amount of Fund Property to be so used shall be paid to the IBRD in five equal annual installments. In addition to the foregoing, Fund Property may also be used by the Trustee to reimburse the IBRD for all costs and expenses incurred by the IBRD prior to the First Closing of the Fund in relation to the identification, preparation and appraisal of proposed Projects, provided the IBRD has obtained the express agreement of Participants therefor.

Section 11.3. *Performance-linked Payment.* During each of the first ten years of the Fund's operations, the IBRD may be entitled to receive a performance-linked payment of up to U.S.$100,000, payable annually as soon as practicable after June 30 of each fiscal year, based upon the performance of the Fund during the preceding fiscal year. The amount of this payment, if any, to be paid to the Trustee for any fiscal year shall be determined by the Participants at their discretion at the annual Participants' meeting taking into account performance indicators determined by the Participants, including, without limitation, the number and quality of the Projects developed, compliance with the Project Selection Criteria and Project Portfolio Criteria, and the cost effectiveness of the Trustee's management of the Fund.

ARTICLE XII
INDEMNIFICATION

Section 12.1. *Indemnification of Trustee and IBRD.* The Trustee, the IBRD, and any person who is, or has been, an officer, employee or agent of the Trustee, the IBRD or the Fund (each an "Indemnified Party") shall be indemnified out of Fund Property against any loss, liability, cost, claim, action, demand or expense (including, but not limited to, all reasonable costs, charges and expenses paid or incurred in disputing or defending any of the foregoing) which any Indemnified Party may incur or which may be made against any of them arising out of or in connection with the Fund's activities (including, without limitation, any such claims arising from Participants' actions or failure to act pursuant to this Instrument), except as may result from the Trustee's gross negligence or willful misconduct.

Section 12.2. *Indemnification of Participants.* The Trustee will indemnify, out of Fund Property only, each of the Participants against any loss, liability, cost, claim, action, demand or expense (including, but not limited to, all reasonable costs, charges and expenses paid or incurred in disputing or defending any of the foregoing) which a Participant may incur or which may be made against a Participant arising out of or in connection with the Fund's activities, except as may result from its gross negligence or willful misconduct.

Section 12.3. *No Waiver of Privileges and Immunities.* Nothing in this Instrument shall be considered to be a waiver of any privileges and immunities of the Trustee, the IBRD, or where applicable, the Participants or their respective officers, employees or agents, under the Articles of Agreement of the IBRD or any applicable law, all of which are expressly reserved.

Section 12.4. *No Personal Liability.* Neither the Trustee, the IBRD and the Participants nor any officer, employee or agent of any of the foregoing shall be subject to any personal liability whatsoever to any third party in connection with the activities of the Fund, and all such third parties shall look solely to Fund Property for satisfaction of claims of any nature arising in connection with Fund activities. Every written obligation, contract, instrument, certificate or undertaking made or issued by the Trustee shall recite that the same is executed or made by it not personally or in its individual capacity, but as Trustee of the Fund under this Instrument, and that the obligations of the Fund under any such instrument are not binding upon the Trustee or any of the Participants, personally or in their respective individual capacities, but bind only the Fund, and may contain any further recital which the Trustee may deem appropriate, but the omission of such recital shall not affect the validity of such obligation, contract, instrument, certificate or undertaking and shall not operate to bind or obligate the Trustee or the Participants personally or in their respective individual capacities.

Section 12.5. *No Duty of Investigation.* No individual or person dealing with the Trustee or any officer, employee or agent of the Trustee or the Fund shall be bound to make any inquiry concerning the validity of any transaction purported to be made by the Trustee or by said officer, employee or agent or be liable for the application of money or property paid, loaned to or delivered to or on the order of the Trustee or of said officer, employee or agent. Every obligation, contract, instrument, certificate or undertaking, and every other act or thing whatsoever executed in connection with the Fund, shall be conclusively presumed to have been executed or done by the executors thereof only in their capacity as officers, employees or agents of the Trustee or the Fund.

Section 12.6. *Reliance on Experts.* The Trustee and each officer and employee of the Trustee or the Fund shall, in the performance of its duties, be fully and completely justified and protected with regard to any act or any failure to act resulting from reliance in good faith upon the books of account or other records of the Fund, upon an opinion of counsel, or upon reports made to the Trustee or the Fund by any of its officers or employees or by any accountant, auditor, appraiser or other expert or consultant selected with reasonable care by the Trustee or by any officer, employee or agent of the Trustee or the Fund.

ARTICLE XIII
INTERESTS IN AND LEGAL OWNERSHIP OF EMISSION REDUCTIONS; DISTRIBUTIONS TO PARTICIPANTS

Section 13.1. *Adaptability to the Requirements of the UNFCCC.* In recognition that the regulatory framework of the UNFCCC and/or the Kyoto Protocol relating to the ownership, holding and transfer of Emission Reductions is still under development, and to maximize the likelihood that the Fund may achieve its stated objectives, the Trustee will endeavor to ensure that the contractual arrangements entered into among the Trustee, Participants, Host Countries, Project Entities and other parties will be structured flexibly so as to enable them to conform with the guidelines, modalities and procedures of the regulatory framework of the UNFCCC and/or the Kyoto Protocol if, when and as they are developed.

Section 13.2. *Statements of Accounts.* At the request of a Participant, the Trustee will produce a statement of account confirming the number of Emission Reductions to which a Participant is entitled. Such statement will reflect the Trustee's records indicating the total number of Emission Reductions to which the Participants are entitled and the Participant's pro rata share thereof. The Trustee may also send such statements of account to Participants from time to time in the absence of requests.

Section 13.3. *Distributions Subject to UNFCCC Requirements.* Subject to such guidelines, modalities and procedures as may be determined by the parties to the UNFCCC and/or the Kyoto Protocol, it is the intent of the parties to this Instrument that Project Agreements shall provide for Emission Reductions to be transferred from Recipients to or to the order of the Participants. Subject to such procedures as may be determined by the parties to the UNFCCC and/or the Kyoto Protocol, the Trustee shall, at the request of Participants, make all reasonable efforts to ensure that the Emission Reductions generated by the Projects will be capable of being credited towards Annex I Countries' QELROs. If, for any of the Participants, it is not possible to ensure that Emission Reductions generated by the Projects will be credited towards Annex I Countries' QELROs, the Trustee will seek to provide, or to cause others to provide, the necessary documentation to establish the Participants' entitlement to such Emission Reductions. Notwithstanding any other provision of this Instrument, none of the IBRD, the Trustee or the Fund assumes any responsibility for the right of Participants to receive Emission Reductions under the UNFCCC, any other applicable law or otherwise or for the right of Participants to use Emission Reductions to fulfill any obligation to which the Participant may be subject under the UNFCCC, any other applicable law or otherwise.

Section 13.4. *Withdrawal.* No Participant shall have the right to withdraw any part of its contribution to the Fund or to receive any distributions from the Fund except as provided in this Instrument.

ARTICLE XIV
ASSIGNMENT OF PARTICIPANTS' INTERESTS

Section 14.1. *Assignment of Participants' Interests.* A Participant may assign all, but not part, of its interest in the Fund or any of its rights under the Participation Agreement or this Instrument to an Eligible Private Sector Participant or an Eligible Public Sector Participant with the prior written consent of the Trustee, such consent not to be unreasonably withheld, provided that such assignee agrees, in form and substance acceptable to the Trustee, to be bound by the terms of this Instrument and the Participation Agreement entered into between the Trustee and the assignor Participant.

ARTICLE XV
DURATION; TERMINATION OF THE FUND; AMENDMENT

Section 15.1. *Duration.* Except as otherwise provided in this Article XV, the Fund shall terminate on December 31, 2012. The Participants may, by unanimous vote, decide to continue the business of the Fund after December 31, 2012 on such terms as they may determine, provided, that the Trustee will continue to serve as trustee only if the Executive Directors of the IBRD have expressly agreed to the extension and to the terms of such extension.

Section 15.2. *Termination of the Fund.*

(a) The Fund may be terminated before December 31, 2012 by (i) the resolution of Participants passed at a Participants' meeting by not less than a two-thirds majority of the votes cast at such meeting; or (ii) a unanimous consent in writing, setting forth the action to be taken, circulated to and signed by all of the Participants.

(b) The Fund shall terminate if, as of the First Closing, (i) the Trustee has not entered into Participation Agreements providing in the aggregate for contributions to the Fund from Participants of at least U.S.$60 million, or (ii) the Trustee determines that the group of Participants that have entered into Participation Agreements is not sufficiently diverse to achieve one of the IBRD's strategic objectives in establishing the Fund, namely working in partnership with the public and private sectors to mobilize new resources for the IBRD's borrowing member countries while addressing global environmental concerns.

(c) The Fund shall also terminate upon the resignation of the IBRD as Trustee of the Fund.

(d) Upon the termination of the Fund:

  i) the Trustee shall carry on no business for the Fund except for the purpose of winding up its affairs;

ii) the Trustee shall proceed to wind up the affairs of the Fund, and all of the powers of the Trustee under this Instrument shall continue until the affairs of the Fund shall have been wound up; and

iii) after paying or adequately providing for the payment of all liabilities, and upon receipt of such releases, indemnities and refunding agreements as it may deem necessary for its protection, the Trustee shall distribute the remaining Fund Property in cash or in kind, or partly each, among the Participants according to their respective rights; notwithstanding the foregoing, in the event the remaining Fund Property includes the right to purchase Emission Reductions to be generated after the termination date of the Fund, the Trustee shall, subject to any applicable restrictions under international law, national law or otherwise, including regulations under the UNFCCC and/or the Kyoto Protocol, endeavor to make such arrangements as are necessary to effect a transfer of such rights to or to the order of the Participants, but shall not have any liability to the Participants if it is unable to do so.

Section 15.3. *Amendment Procedures*. This Instrument may only be amended by the Executive Directors of the IBRD with the prior unanimous consent of Participants. Notwithstanding the foregoing, this Instrument may be amended by the Trustee without prior notice to or consent from any Participant if such amendment is (i) to supply any omission, or cure, correct or supplement any manifest error or ambiguous, defective or inconsistent provision hereof, or (ii) for any other purpose which does not adversely affect the rights of any Participant; provided, that all Participants are notified of any such amendment within 15 days after the effective date of such amendment.

Section 15.4. *Further Assurances*. Upon the request of the Trustee, each of the Participants shall do, execute, acknowledge and deliver or cause to be done, executed, acknowledged or delivered all such further acts, deeds, documents, instruments, assignments, transfers, conveyances, powers of attorney and assurances as may be necessary or desirable to effect the purpose of this Instrument and carry out its provisions.

ARTICLE XVI
APPROVAL AND AUTHORIZATION

Section 16.1. *Approval.* By entering into a Participation Agreement, a Participant shall be deemed to have approved the Projects for the purposes of Article 6 and 12 of the Kyoto Protocol.

Section 16.2. *Authorization.* By entering into a Participation Agreement, a Participant that is entitled to authorize legal entities to participate, under its responsibility, in actions leading to the generation, transfer or acquisition of Emission Reductions shall be deemed to have expressly authorized the Trustee to act on its behalf in this respect.

ARTICLE XVII
CONFLICTS OF INTEREST

Section 17.1. *Trustee Withdrawal from Dispute or Claim.* In order to avoid any potential conflict of interest between the IBRD and the Trustee, and notwithstanding any other provision of this Instrument, the Trustee shall not have any obligation to prosecute, defend, compromise, negotiate, abandon or adjust, by arbitration, or otherwise, any action, suit, proceeding, dispute, claim or demand or any default or potential default by a Host Country or Project Entity under a Project Agreement (collectively a "dispute") in any way relating to any Project Agreement. If the Trustee determines that it will refrain from taking any such action, the Trustee shall so notify the Participants and the Trustee and the Participants shall use their best efforts to endeavor to agree to satisfactory arrangements for dealing with such dispute including the assignment and transfer of all or part of the Trustee's rights and obligations under the relevant Project Agreement to the Participants or to a third party acting on their behalf. The Trustee shall have no liability to the Participants as a result of the Trustee's determination to refrain from taking any such action in respect of a dispute or as a result of the failure of the

Trustee and the Participants to reach such satisfactory arrangements in a timely manner or otherwise.

Section 17.2. *Participant Disclosure of Competing Interests.* Prior to the Participants' Committee's review of the relevant Project Concept Note, a Participant which participates, or which has affiliates or employees which participate individually and/or collectively, in funds or other investment vehicles having objectives and policies similar to those of the Fund which, as a result, may compete with the Fund for investment opportunities, supplies of raw materials, government franchises, customers or otherwise ("Other Ventures"), or a Participant or its affiliate or employee which has an interest in an Underlying Project, shall fully disclose such interest in Other Ventures or in an Underlying Project to the Trustee. If the Trustee determines that such participation or interest is such that the Participant should not participate in the Participants' Committee's deliberations on whether or not to object to the Project subject to this conflict or potential conflict of interest, it shall advise the Participant making the disclosure to recuse itself from the Participants' Committee's deliberations with respect to that Project. If the Participant disagrees with the Trustee's determination, it shall advise the Participants' Committee of the conflict or potential conflict, and the Participants' Committee (excluding the Participant making the disclosure) will decide whether such Participant should be permitted to participate in the Committee's deliberations on the Project concerned. The failure of a Participant to disclose such participation or interest in an Underlying Project or Other Venture in a timely manner will constitute a breach of this Instrument by such Participant, and the Trustee shall determine what remedies to exercise after consultation with the other Participants.

ARTICLE XVIII
ARBITRATION; EXERCISE OF REMEDIES

Section 18.1. *Validity.* The rights and obligations of the Trustee and the Participants with respect to the Fund shall be valid and enforceable in accordance with the terms of this Instrument and any agreement between the Trustee and the Participants. Neither the Trustee nor any Participant shall be entitled in any proceeding to assert any claim that any provision of this Instrument or such agreement is invalid or unenforceable because of any provision of the charter or constitutive documents of the Participant or the Articles of Agreement of the IBRD.

Section 18.2. *Arbitration.* Any dispute between the Trustee and a Participant arising out of or relating to this Instrument or such Participant's Participation Agreement shall be settled by arbitration in accordance with the UNCITRAL Arbitration Rules as at present in force. The number of arbitrators shall be three. The appointing authority shall be the Secretary-General of the Permanent Court of Arbitration at The Hague. In the event of a conflict between the UNCITRAL Arbitration Rules and the terms of this Instrument or of the Participation Agreement, the terms of the Instrument and Participation Agreement shall prevail.

Section 18.3. *Delays.* No delay in exercising, or failure to exercise, any right, power or remedy accruing to any party under this Instrument or any agreement between the Trustee and a Participant, whether or not upon any default, shall impair any such right, power or remedy or be construed to be a waiver thereof or an acquiescence in such default. No action of such party in respect of any default, or any acquiescence by it in any default, shall affect or impair any right, power or remedy of such party in respect of any other or subsequent default.

SCHEDULE 1 TO INSTRUMENT

PROJECT SELECTION CRITERIA
and
PROJECT PORTFOLIO CRITERIA

Project Selection Criteria. The Trustee shall select Projects in accordance with the following Project Selection Criteria:

a) *Consistency with UNFCCC and/or the Kyoto Protocol.* The Trustee shall ensure that Projects comply with all current guidelines, modalities and procedures adopted by the Parties to the UNFCCC and/or the Kyoto Protocol, as well as all future guidelines, modalities and procedures when adopted, in particular those pertaining to sustainable development and additionality.

b) *Consistency with Relevant National Criteria.* The Trustee shall seek to ensure that the Projects' designs are compatible with and supportive of the national environment and development priorities of the Host Countries. In addition, the Projects and the transfer of Emission Reductions should be consistent with the rules and criteria adopted by Host Countries regarding Article 6 and Article 12 Projects.

c) *Consistency with the IBRD's Country Assistance Strategy.* The Trustee will seek to ensure that Projects are designed to be consistent with, and supportive of, the then current Country Assistance Strategy of the IBRD for the Host Country and the Host Country's own development objectives.

d) *Complementarity with GEF.* The Trustee shall seek to ensure that Projects are complementary to the GEF and do not compete with the GEF's long-term operational program nor with its short-term response measures. In furtherance of this criterion, potential Projects will be reviewed by the Secretariat of the GEF to determine their GEF eligibility. Only if it is determined that a potential Project will not receive GEF financing will the Fund Manager consider including it as a Fund Project.

e) *Achievement of National and Local Environmental Benefits.* The Trustee shall seek to ensure that Projects provide at least the same level of national and local environmental benefits as the Underlying Projects.

f) *Consistency with the Fund's Strategic Objectives and Operating Principles.* The Trustee shall seek to select Projects with a view to achieving the strategic objectives and operational principles of the Fund as set forth in the Instrument.

g) *Consistency with the General Guidance Provided by Participants.* The Trustee shall seek to ensure that Projects comply with the general guidance provided by Participants at their meetings.

h) *Additional Characteristics of Projects.* The Trustee shall seek to ensure that Projects are selected to mitigate various types of risk. Projects should generally entail manageable technological risk. The technology to be used in a Project should be commercially available, have been demonstrated in a commercial context, and be subject to customary commercial performance guarantees. The technical competence in the Host Country to manage this technology should be established in the course of Project appraisal. Projected Emission Reductions over the life of the Project should be predictable and should involve an acceptable level of uncertainty. GHG Reductions should also be amenable to standardized Validation and Verification processes with existing methodologies.

Project Portfolio Criteria. The Trustee will develop a Project portfolio with the intention that during the term of the Fund:

a) a broad balance will be achieved in the number of Projects undertaken in Economies in Transition and in Developing

Countries and that, notwithstanding potential Projects identified prior to the establishment of the Fund, emphasis should be directed initially to the development of Projects in Developing Countries;

b) a major emphasis should be directed at development of Projects in the area of renewable energy technology such as, but not limited to, geothermal, wind, solar and small hydro energy;

c) no less than approximately 2% nor more than approximately 10% of the Fund's assets should be invested in any one Project;

d) no more than approximately 20% of the Fund's assets should be invested in Projects in the same Host Country;

e) no more than approximately 10% of the Fund's assets should be invested in land-use sector Projects. Further, unless the Parties to the UNFCCC deem it appropriate, no such Project shall be located in a Developing Country; and

f) no more than approximately 25% of the Fund's assets should be invested in Projects using the same technology.

PRIORITIES FOR RAPID AND SHARED ECONOMIC GROWTH IN EGYPT

*Ahmed Galal**

I. INTRODUCTION

There is a general agreement that no economic objective deserves more emphasis than rapid and shared economic growth. By growing rapidly and distributing the benefits widely, society can create jobs, provide social services, and maintain political stability. Less consensus exists, however, with respect to the appropriate set of reform priorities for a particular country at a given point in time. This paper attempts to identify these priorities for Egypt, given past reforms and future aspirations.

The paper shows that the pay-off is greatest if efforts are focused on reforming the education system, reducing the size of government, promoting saving and investment, and improving the rule of law, in that order. Additional gains can be expected from opening up the economy. Macroeconomic stability has been achieved, and only requires prudent management and adjustment where necessary. These conclusions are based on answering two questions: (1) What does it generally take to grow fast?; and (2) How does Egypt compare with the fast-growing economies?

II. WHAT DOES IT GENERALLY TAKE TO GROW FAST?

Economists believe that growth can only come from factor accumulation (physical and human), efficient allocation of resources, and

* Dr. Ibrahim F.I. Shihata and I share deep interest in Egypt's future development. This paper is a modest contribution to this end, but it by no means matches his dedicated effort and vast contributions.

productivity. What is less well-known, is that it is the combination of these sources of growth that makes a difference. The accumulation of investment in machines and human capital does not suffice, nor does the efficient allocation of resources or productivity.

Three examples illustrate this point. First, the former Soviet Union and other Eastern European countries were able to invest and grow rapidly for decades. Yet, the system eventually collapsed in the 1980s. Why? There was too much emphasis on the accumulation of physical and human capital, and too little emphasis on the efficient allocation of resources and productivity. The system provided distorted prices and failed to motivate managers and workers to improve productivity. The same point can be made with respect to Egypt in the period of 1975–1985. During this period, investment and Gross Domestic Product (GDP) grew fast (*see* Figure 1), aided by favorable oil prices, high remittances of workers and access to foreign loans. However, distortion of prices was pervasive and the domination of state-owned enterprises meant that economic agents had limited incentives to increase productivity.

In contrast, East Asian countries — despite their current short-term crisis — were able to grow fast for an extended period of time because they accumulated substantial physical and human capital, provided appropriate prices, and linked compensation to performance. In this context, it is noteworthy that more than fifty percent of the difference in per capita growth rate between East Asian countries (including Korea, Taiwan, Hong Kong, Singapore, Indonesia, Malaysia and Thailand) and a sample of Middle Eastern

FIGURE 1. REAL GDP GROWTH IN EGYPT, 1961–94

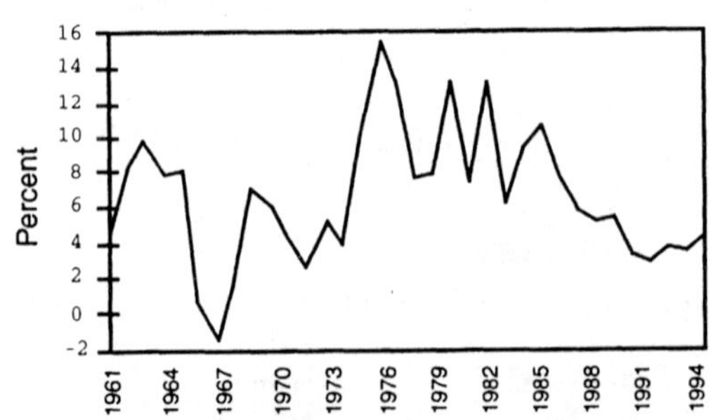

Source: Calculated from IMF, IFS, different issues.

FIGURE 2. SOURCES OF DIFFERENCE IN PER CAPITA GROWTH BETWEEN EAST ASIA AND MENA

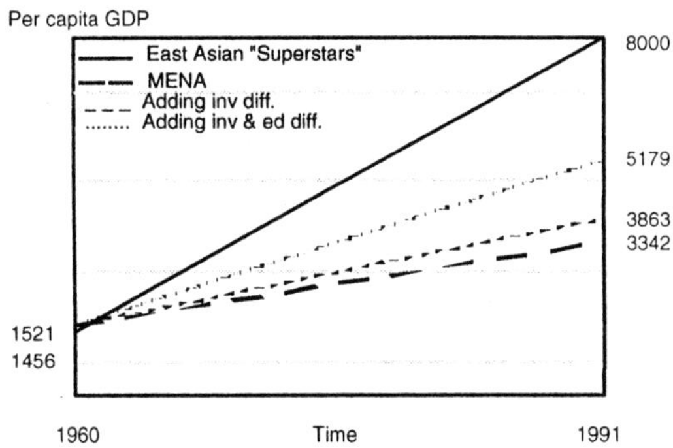

Source: John Page (1996).[1]

countries (including Morocco, Algeria, Tunisia, Egypt, Jordan, Syria, Iran and Iraq) is attributed to differences in productivity (*see* Figure 2).

What determines the fast accumulation of capital, efficient resource allocation and productivity? Economists have long tried to answer this question, and their thinking has evolved over time. According to the most recent literature concerned with accounting for growth, the factors leading to fast economic growth are of two types: basic conditions and choice variables (*see* columns 1 and 2 of Table 1 for a list of the most frequently used variables and their relationship to growth). Under basic conditions, the most critical variables are the initial level of per capita income and investment in human capital. Growth is higher in countries of lower initial per capita income because these countries tend to have less capital per worker and, therefore, offer higher rates of return on investment, which translates into higher growth rates. Growth is also higher the greater the investment in human capital because an educated labor force can use technology more efficiently. Related to the same variable, a more egalitarian education system helps growth because it produces good citizens, thus better governance and policies and less instability.

---

1 *See* John Page, *A Middle Eastern Miracle? Development Policy Lessons from East Asia*, Distinguished Lecture Series No. 4, Cairo: The Egyptian Center for Economic Studies (1996).

TABLE 1. FACTORS EXPLAINING GROWTH

Variables	Relation to growth	Deviation from the avg. of fast-growing economies	Regression coefficient	Predicted growth (%)
Initial conditions				
Per capita GDP	Negative	—	–0.026	—
Human capital *(mean years of schooling)*	Positive	–0.90	0.012	1.06
Choice variables				
Investment *(% of GDP)*	Positive	–17.95	0.043	0.77
Size of government *(Gov. expenditure % of GDP)*	Negative	6.80	–0.136	0.93
Openness *(average tariff rates)*	Positive	14.91	–0.018	0.26
Macroeconomic stability *(inflation rate)*	Negative	1.92	–0.043	0.08
Rule of law	Positive	1.5	0.004	0.63

Sources: Robert J. Barro (1997);[2] Robert J. Barro and Xavier Sala-I-Martin (1995);[3] and author's calculations.

Among the choice variables, the most important are saving/investment, size of government, openness, macroeconomic stability, and protection of property rights. Higher savings correlates positively with growth because it makes funds available for investment. Smaller government contributes to growth because this means lower non-productive spending and lower taxes, freeing more resources for the private sector to save and invest. More open economies grow faster because lower tariffs and other trade barriers reduce distortions in domestic markets and increase competition. Macroeconomic stability is associated with lower inflation, which reduces uncertainty and encourages investment. Finally, investors care about the effectiveness of law enforcement when choosing to invest.

2 *See* Roberto Barro, Jr., Determinants of Economic Growth: A Cross-Country Empirical Study, MIT (1997).

3 *See* Roberto Barro, Jr. & Xavier Sala-I-Martin, Economic Growth (1995).

III. HOW DOES EGYPT COMPARE WITH THE FAST-GROWING ECONOMIES?

Compared with a number of fast-growing economies, Egypt does well on some determinants of growth, but not as well on others. Per capita income in Egypt is relatively low, which means that there is room for catching up (*see* Figure 3). Egypt has also achieved macroeconomic stability and curbed inflation to levels comparable to those of fast-growing economies. Egypt, however, lags behind on several accounts, the most important of which is education (measured by the average years of school completed) and education equality (measured by the standard deviation of the average year of schooling, (*see* Figures 4 and 5). Although the government invests six percent of GDP on education, the return on this investment has been low due to a legacy of vast illiteracy, skewed expenditure on higher education, and high drop-out rates.[5]

Egypt also lags behind in domestic savings, the size of government, the degree of openness to the rest of the world, and investors' perception of property rights protection. Domestic savings relative to GDP is only eighteen percent, compared with over thirty percent in the fast-growing economies (*see* Figure 6). The share of government expenditure relative to GDP is still high (*see* Figure 7). Tariffs on imports are also high (*see* Figure 8) and the perception of investors (measured by an index of their willingness to accept established institutions to make and implement laws and adjudicate disputes) ranks low for Egypt. The extent to which

---

4 In a very insightful book on Egypt, MY WILL FOR MY COUNTRY (1995), IBRAHIM F.I. SHIHATA also emphasized the importance of education for Egypt's future. He also elaborated how the system can be improved in details.

5 *See* WORLD ECONOMIC FORUM, THE GLOBAL COMPETITIVENESS REPORT (1997).

6 *See* Nemat Shafik, *Big Spending, Small Returns: The Paradox of Human Resource Development in the Near East,* WORKING PAPER NO. 2, CAIRO: THE EGYPTIAN CENTER FOR ECONOMIC STUDIES (1995).

7 Nancy Birdsall, *Inequality and Human Capital Accumulation in Latin America*, DISTINGUISHED LECTURE SERIES NO. 7, CAIRO: THE EGYPTIAN CENTER FOR ECONOMIC STUDIES (1997).

8 *See* GLOBAL COMPETITIVENESS REPORT, *supra* note 3.

9 *Ibid.*

FIGURE 3. PER CAPITA GDP IN EGYPT AND SELECTED FAST-GROWING ECONOMIES, 1996

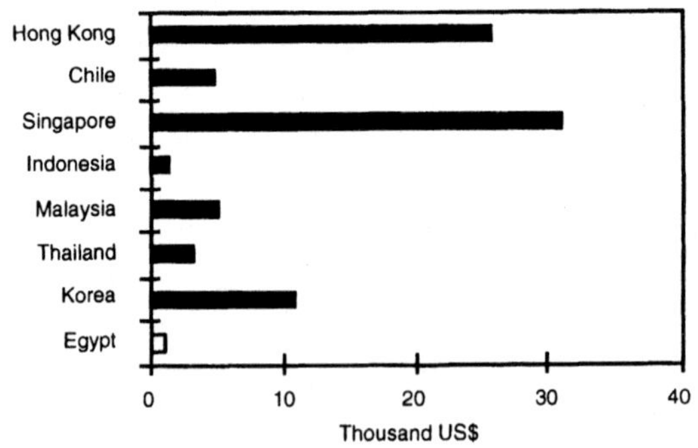

Source: The Global Competitiveness Report (1997).[4]

FIGURE 4. HUMAN CAPITAL ACCUMULATION

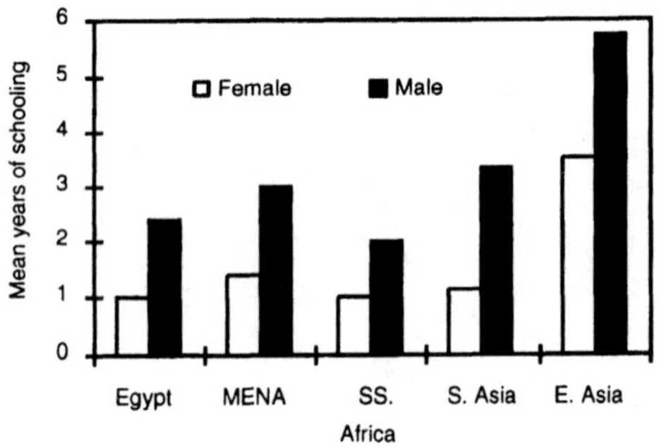

Source: Nemat Shafik (1996).[6]

FIGURE 5. HUMAN CAPITAL INEQUALITY

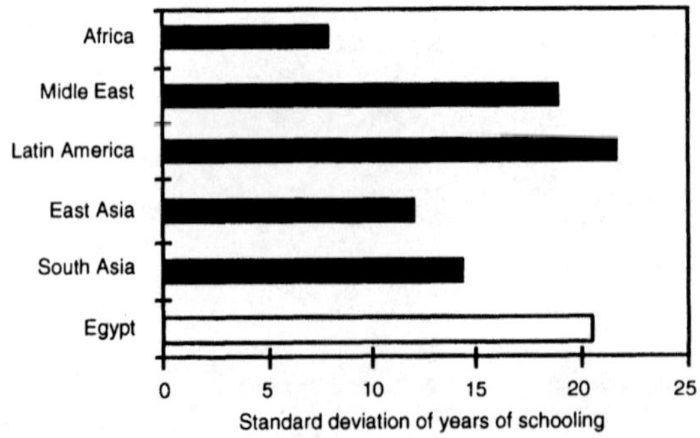

Source: Nancy Birdsall (1997).[7]

FIGURE 6. SAVINGS IN EGYPT AND SELECTED FAST-GROWING ECONOMIES, 1996

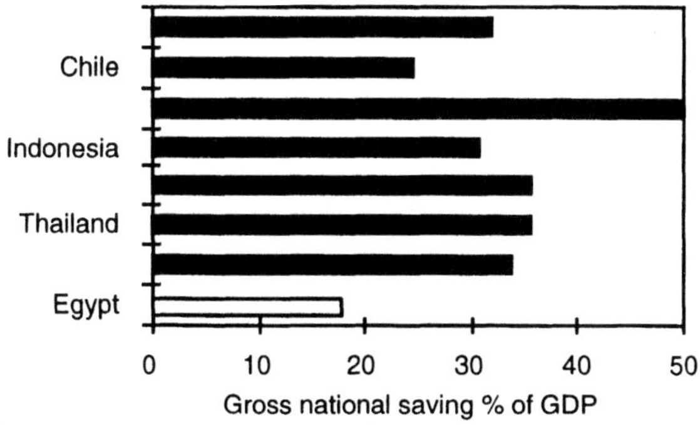

Source: The Global Competitiveness Report (1997).[8]

FIGURE 7. SIZE OF GOVERNMENT IN EGYPT AND SELECTED FAST-GROWING ECONOMIES, 1996

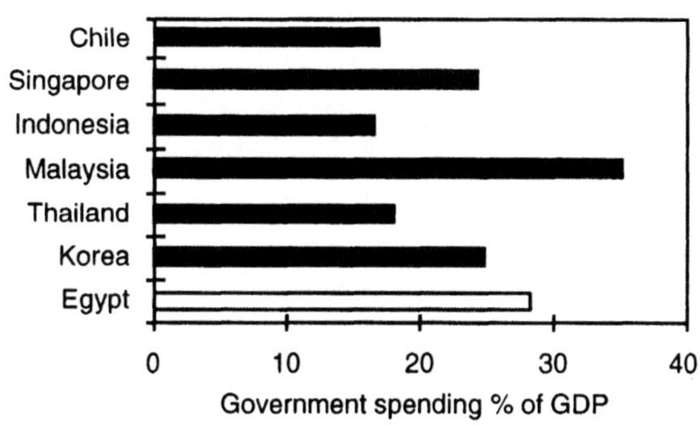

Source: The Global Competitiveness Report (1997).[9]

Egypt deviates from the average for fast-growing economies on each variable is given in column 3 of Table 1. The magnitude of deviations suggests that significant reforms are needed to put Egypt on a path of rapid economic growth. The question is where to start.

IV. PRIORITIES FOR FASTER ECONOMIC GROWTH

Policy makers cannot tackle all problems simultaneously. If they were to allocate their political capital to reforms with the highest

FIGURE 8. AVERAGE TARIFF RATES, 1996

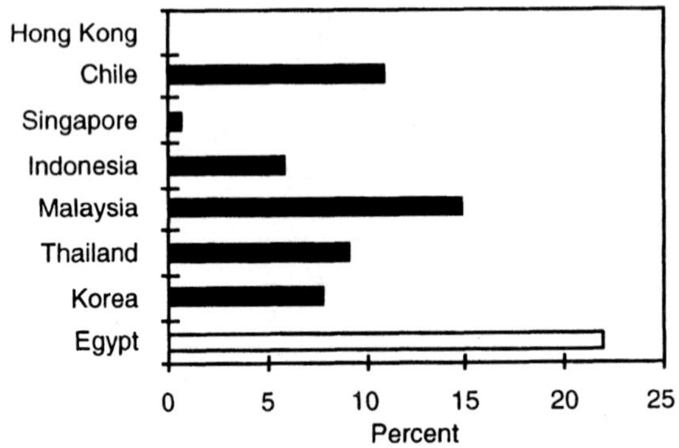

Source: The Global Competitiveness Report (1997).[10]

return in terms of potential growth, then their focus should be on education, reducing the size of government, promoting saving and investment, improving the perception of property rights protection and opening up the economy, in that order (column 5 of Table 1 gives an order of magnitude of the additional gains in growth units resulting from reforms in each of these areas). If successful, Egypt could increase per capita income by as much as 3.7 percent and exceed the desired target of 7 percent.

To bridge the policy and institutional gap between Egypt and the fast-growing economies, the following key reforms are necessary:

- **Education.** While government expenditure on education is not low, it is biased in favor of higher education. A shift in expenditure to basic education has been shown to generate more returns to society. Along the same lines, it has also been shown that the social return on educating girls is the best investment government can make. Accordingly, it may be socially desirable to subsidize the education of girls. Finally, even if the government were to continue financing education, the experience of other countries suggests that private sector participation in the delivery of education services, adopting performance-based incentives for teachers, and encouraging the participation of parents in monitoring schools, help improve the education system.

---

10 *Ibid.*

FIGURE 9. RULE OF LAW INDEX, 1995

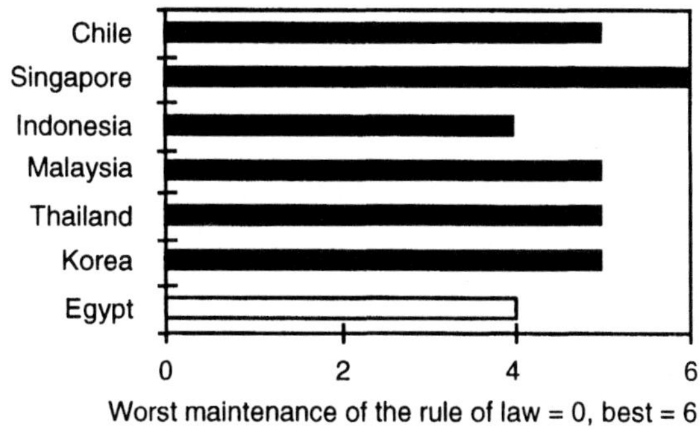

Source: International Country Risk Guide.[11]

- **Size of government.** Although the size of government expenditure relative to GDP has declined over time, it remains over thirty percent compared with about twenty percent in the fast-growing economies. Reducing the size of government requires lowering tax rates and curtailing investment, which the private sector could undertake more efficiently. Besides the level of government expenditure, a review of this pattern is necessary to ensure greater complementarity to private sector investment and better targeting to the most needy.
- **Saving/investment.** Greater domestic private saving is generally believed to follow growth. However, it may be possible to stimulate savings by reforming the pension system such that pensioners see a strong link between their contribution and benefits, as in Chile. Privatization is another channel, which has been shown to have the potential to increase savings by as much as two percentage points of GDP[12] from selling one-third of State Owned Enterprises (SOEs) in Egypt, because privatization is associated with improved productivity and the mobilization of foreign savings. Finally, deepening financial sector reform could promote savings and help channel these funds into efficient uses. Ensuring that the generated savings are translated into investment requires a stable macroeconomic environment, low transaction costs, high policy credibility and a supporting infrastructure. These preconditions are required for both domestic and foreign investment.

---

11 *See* POLITICAL RISK SERVICES, INTERNATIONAL COUNTRY RISK GUIDE (1982–1995).

12 *See* Ahmed Galal, *Savings and Privatization*, WORKING PAPER NO. 8, CAIRO: THE EGYPTIAN CANTER FOR ECONOMIC STUDIES (1996).

• **Protection of property rights.** Protecting the right to exchange, use and reap the benefits of assets is key to faster growth. This involves providing stable and transparent rules, enforcing them efficiently, and settling disputes fairly and expeditiously. But these reforms are too general and cover a wide range of issues. One place to start is by relying on what the private sector considers to be the most binding constraint. In this regard, a recent survey of 150 firms shows that the most binding institutional constraints relate to tax administration and conflict resolution mechanisms.[13]

• **Openness**. Opening up the economy to the rest of the world involves lowering tariff rates gradually and moving to a more flexible exchange rate system. Both measures reduce the bias against exports, expand labor intensive industries, and thereby improve income distribution. To further reduce the bias against exports, it is necessary to liberalize services (telecom, power, transport, ports and banking). It is estimated that the inefficiency of services is currently taxing exporters by as much as fifteen per cent. Finally, while pursuing liberalization through integration with the major trading partners, the objective should be to open up the economy multilaterally to avoid trade and investment diversion.

This list of priority actions may seem too long and difficult to implement, but Egypt of the 1990s appears to be up to the task. With a concerted effort on the part of government, private sector, donors and research institutes, the job is within reach.

---

13 *See* Samiha Fawzy, *The Business Environment in Egypt, in* PARTNERS FOR DEVELOPMENT: NEW ROLES FOR GOVERNMENT AND THE PRIVATE SECTOR IN NORTH AFRICA AND THE MIDDLE EAST (Fawzy & Galal eds., World Development Institute) (forthcoming).

IDLI: A NEW MODEL FOR NGO STRUCTURE, SUSTAINABILITY AND GROWTH

L. Michael Hager

I. INTRODUCTION

Not the least of the organizational achievements of Ibrahim Shihata is the International Development Law Institute (IDLI), based in Rome, Italy. IDLI offers training and technical assistance for legal professionals in developing and transition economy countries. The brainchild of three lawyers (Bill Loris, Gilles Blanchi and the author), the Institute was established in 1983 as a non-governmental organization. Dr. Shihata was an informal advisor to the organizers, helping them assemble a distinguished international Board of Directors, the first meeting of which was held at the OPEC Fund in 1983.

When the Institute began, it faced a wall of skepticism. People asked, "Why train lawyers? What do they have to do with economic development?" The rise of business globalization in the mid-eighties, however, brought about a sea change. The Institute's modest training activities quickly moved from the margin to the mainstream. Its potential markets expanded geographically with the opening of Central and Eastern Europe and the Former Soviet Union, peaceful transition in South Africa and a more outward-looking Latin America. At the same time, IDLI's substantive topics moved beyond capacity building (with an emphasis on win-win negotiation and dispute resolution) and international contracting to include economic law reform and good governance. The Organisation for Economic Co-operation and Development (OECD) Development Assistance Committee (DAC) consensus on "good governance," with its rule of law component, and the ending of the Cold War were additional factors which enlarged IDLI's role.

Now, sixteen years later, the Institute has more than 8,000 alumni from 161 countries, legally established alumni associations in more than 15 countries, a network of top quality visiting instructors of more than 1,000, and counterpart organizations with whom the Institute has worked in some 60 countries. Invariably, visitors to the Institute's headquarters in Rome or its Asia Regional Training Office in Manila, Philippines applaud both IDLI's accomplishments and the spirit of its staff. They sense that there is something "different" about this organization.

What is the difference with IDLI? Can it serve as a useful model for other international organizations? There are at least three elements worth citing: its structure (organization and governance), sustainability strategy, and vision for the future.

II. STRUCTURE

For almost a decade, IDLI operated as a non-governmental organization. Because the law of the Netherlands in the early-eighties was more hospitable to international NGO's, IDLI established itself as a Dutch "stichting" (foundation). However, with a legal headquarters in Rotterdam and a principal place of activity in Rome, operational constraints were frequent. For this reason, IDLI initially proposed that Italy as host government provide a headquarters agreement which would ameliorate the major problems: foreign exchange, contracting and local labor law restrictions. Understandably, the Government of Italy was reluctant to "open Pandora's Box" with respect to non-governmental organizations. However, the Ministry of Foreign Affairs, mindful of the increased attention the Institute was receiving from both funding organizations and user governments, proposed that IDLI become a full-fledged autonomous public international organization. This would then, they said, permit the negotiation of a proper headquarters agreement with a full range of privileges and immunities.

In 1986, IDLI achieved agreement in principle with three UN organizations to establish the Institute as an "internationally organized organization." Although there was limited legal precedent for such a creature of purely intergovernmental organizations, the then Legal Advisor of the United Nations refused to put his stamp of approval on the arrangement. As a result, with the somewhat hesitant approval of its Board of Directors, the Institute began the process of inviting potential state members to join together in an "Establishment Agreement."

Because IDLI's Board of Directors included a number of distinguished and highly placed representatives of various countries, the process of securing support turned out to be much faster than Management had expected. In February 1988, eight governments came together in Rome to sign the "Agreement for the Establishment of the International Development Law Institute." The full text of that Agreement is appended as "Appendix A."

In subsequent years, another six governments acceded to the Agreement, giving IDLI a current international membership of 14 countries. At this writing, Australia has signified its intention to become the 15th member state. A list of Member States is appended as "Annex B."

Elements of the "Establishment Agreement" are distinctive and worth citing here:

(1) Financial Support. Unlike most public international organizations, IDLI has no regular "assessments." As noted below, emphasis was placed on user charges for services. The only contributions and donations were to be "voluntary." (Article V(1)). Furthermore, the parties to the Agreement were not to be held responsible for "debts, liabilities, or obligations of the Institute." (Article V(2)).

(2) Frequency of Assembly Meetings. Under Article VI(1)(B) the Assembly of States is to "meet at the invitation of the Board of Directors or upon the initiative of one-third of the Assembly's member." In Rules of Procedure adopted by the Assembly (*see* "Annex C" below), the Assembly is required to hold a session "at least every three years." In fact, the triennial Assembly has become the norm.

Experience has shown that the relative infrequency of Assembly Meetings reduced the risk of political interference. At the same time, however, Management routinely invites Assembly representatives to attend Annual Board

Meetings as observers. Thus what may be lost in terms of formal meeting time is made up for in institutional transparency.

(3) Perhaps the most significant barrier to Member State control is Article VI.(1)(D), which provides that a decision of the Board of Directors requiring Assembly ratification "shall be deemed to be ratified on a date ninety days after dispatch of notification by the Institute of such decision to the Members of the Assembly unless, before that date, a majority of the Members of the Assembly notify the Institute of their opposition to the decision." Given the number and variety of Member States and the fact that none of them has a legal obligation to provide funding, the likelihood of the Assembly overruling the Board appears remote. Indeed, in the decade following internationalization there has not been a single instance of Member State objection to a Board decision or the filling of a Board Member vacancy.

Thus, IDLI has been able to operate for all intents and purposes as an international non-governmental organization while having all of the trappings (and benefits) of internationality. Most significantly, it has meant that the Institute has been able to negotiate advantageous Headquarters Agreements with both the Italian and Philippine Governments for its headquarters and Asia Regional Training Office, respectively.

III. SUSTAINABILITY

As noted above, IDLI relies solely on user charges and voluntary contributions for its financial support. Article V(1) provides that the Institute "shall obtain its financial resources through such means as voluntary contributions and donations: course and seminar tuition; training workshop and technical assistance fees; publication and other service revenues; and interest income from trusts, endowments and bank accounts." Primarily, this approach causes the Institute to operate much like the free market, whose principles it espouses in the training programs. IDLI prices its service products in effect at market rate. The market factor not only helps the Institute's Management meet the changing requirements of its clientèle more rapidly, but also drastically reduces the amount of subsidy required. Over the past few years the Institute has managed to obtain some eighty percent of its annual budget requirements from user charges, leaving only the remaining twenty percent to be covered by voluntary contributions.

Cost-effective management techniques have kept the Institute within budget for each year of its existence. At the same time, the Institute has managed to have surplus of revenue over expenses each year. Early on, IDLI developed a financial plan aimed at eliminating the need for voluntary contributions in the long run. Put another way, the plan is an exit strategy for donors. Each year the Board of Directors allocates the current surplus less capital requirements for the following year to a general or "sustainability" endowment. This endowment, like others created by donors for specific purposes, is managed by the United Bank of Kuwait in London. Under investment policies approved by the Board, the Managers have substantial discretion under a mandate to "maximize income and minimize risk." Currently, the Managers are authorized to invest up to thirty per cent of the fund in equities, with the larger remainder in more conservative instruments. The Board has fixed US$20 million as a sustainability target. When the endowment reaches that level, its annual income will accrue to program, hopefully covering the gap between user charges and total requirements. Meanwhile, annual income from the Fund is reinvested as part of the general surplus.

With this strategy, IDLI expects to be one of the first international organizations to become institutionally self-sufficient.

With respect to fundraising, IDLI's strategy from the beginning has been to diversify. Initially, the focus was on bilateral cooperation agencies. Currently some sixteen governments contribute both project and unrestricted course support through their development organizations. By the mid-eighties, the Institute was adding foundations (the Ford Foundation and the John D. and Catherine T. MacArthur Foundation) to its list of sponsors. More recently, IDLI has attracted intergovernmental organizations (although the Arab Fund for Economic and Social Development was a contributor almost from the outset). While the World Bank provided modest innovation grants to IDLI during its first four years, it limited its support to the in-kind provision of legal experts as visiting instructors until 1996. On the ground the Institute needed breathing space to further diversify its support (in order to offset declining contributions from major bilateral donors), the World Bank Development Grant Fund (DGF) provided major support over five years. The DGF grant covered both core costs and fellowships.

More recently, IDLI has launched its Corporate and Law Firm Partnership Program. Based on a combination of "mutual benefit" and social responsibility, the program has attracted an increasing number of major international companies and law firms which buy into selected elements of IDLI's programs, most typically fellowships. Participation gives each Partner a seat at the Annual Partner's Roundtable, where legal constraints to international business and training needs are discussed. The Partnership Program is a major hope for the future as government budgets for development continue to decline.

IV. GROWTH

History shows that organizations that fail to grow stagnate and soon expire. IDLI's sixteen-year history reflects continuous growth: part of it resulting from a widening of geographic market and part from an increase of substantive offerings. This growth can be attributed largely to the Institute's responses to targets of opportunity as they occurred over the years. In a dynamic era, there was little opportunity or even need to plan for the longer-term future.

As the Institute has matured, that situation has changed. In 1999, the Board of Directors approved Management's proposed "Vision 2000." A summary of the Vision Statement is attached as "Annex D." Two elements of Vision 2000 warrant emphasis. First, decentralization. IDLI's positive experience with the Asia Regional Training Office has shown that local markets for IDLI training and technical assistance are strong and cannot be met by a purely headquarters operation. They require continuous project development and implementation from a nearby regional center. Accordingly, IDLI plans to establish over the coming years additional offices in Latin America, Central and Eastern Europe and Africa and the Middle East.

Another important element of Vision 2000 is its emphasis on bringing IDLI field experience into various development planning fora. For example, last fall, IDLI organized and facilitated a tailor-made colloquium on civil society organizations in collaboration with the Norwegian Agency for International Development (NORAD). A "Frame Agreement" with the State Economic Cooperation Office of the Government of Switzerland (SECO) puts Institute Managers in regular contact with SECO project officers. These meetings result in "action plans" covering activities ranging from concept papers to field training activities and technical assistance. More recently, the Institute has begun working with World Bank Procurement Specialists in the joint design and delivery of a tailor-made course for World Bank Procurement officers on local procurement systems in client countries. For the future, IDLI envisions additional collaboration with multilateral development agencies, such as regular secondments of legal officers to IDLI and consultancy arrangements similar to the Swiss "Frame Agreement."

The IDLI experience has shown and continues to demonstrate that a combination of innovative organization and governance, creative strategies for sustainability and enlightened planning for the future can widen the horizon of a non-profit organization. Hopefully, IDLI can be perceived as a useful model.

Of course it must be acknowledged that IDLI's successes in these innovations owe much to the Chairman of its Board of Directors, Dr. Ibrahim F.I. Shihata.

ANNEX A:

Agreement for the Establishment of the International Development Law Institute

The PARTIES signatory hereto,

RECOGNISING the importance of law in the development process and the need for training lawyers for the development;

NOTING that the International Development Law Institute (IDLI) was established in 1983 as an international non-governmental organisation under the law of the Netherlands to assist developing country lawyers improve their ability to negotiate agreements and advise in the implementation of transactions in the fields of development assistance, foreign investment, international trade and other international business transactions;

NOTING that in its first three years of operation IDLI has offered courses, seminars and training workshops which have been attended by more than 480 participants from nearly 80 countries;

NOTING that IDLI has now secured substantial funding in support of its activities from a variety of governments, international organisations, foundations and the private sector;

NOTING the willingness of the Government of Italy to enter into the negotiation of a headquarters agreement once IDLI has acquired international status; and

BELIEVING THAT it is now desirable that the International Development Law Institute be established as an international organisation with suitable governance, juridical personality and status;

NOW THEREFORE THE PARTIES HAVE AGREED as follows:

Article I
Establishment and Status

1. There is hereby established the International Development Law Institute, hereinafter referred to as the "Institute" or "IDLI", as an international organisation.
2. IDLI shall possess full juridical personality and enjoy such capacities as may be necessary for the exercise of its functions and the fulfilment of its purposes.
3. The Institute shall operate in accordance with this Agreement.

Article II
Purposes and Activities

1. The purposes of the Institute are:
   A. To encourage and facilitate the improvement and use of legal resources in the development process;
   B. To encourage adherence to the rule of law in international transactions; and
   C. To improve the negotiating capability of developing countries in the fields of development co-operation, foreign investment, international trade and other international business transactions.
2. In order to accomplish the foregoing purposes, the Institute may engage in the following types of activities:
   A. Training, technical assistance, research, publication, establishment and operation of legal documentation center; and
   B. Other activities which advance the purposes of the Institute.
3. The Institute shall not be influenced by political considerations in its activities, management and staffing.

Article III
Powers

In furtherance of the foregoing purposes and activities, the Institute shall have the following powers:

1. To acquire and dispose of real and personal property;
2. To enter into contracts and other types of agreements;
3. To employ persons;
4. To institute and defend in legal proceedings;
5. To invest the moneys and properties of the Institute; and
6. To take other lawful action necessary to accomplish the purposes of the Institute.

Article IV
Headquarters

1. The headquarters of the Institute shall be in Rome, Italy, unless the Assembly decides to relocate the Institute elsewhere.
2. The Institute may establish offices in other locations as required to support its programs.

Article V
Finance

1. The institute shall obtain its financial resources through such means as voluntary contributions and donations; course and seminar tuition; training workshop and technical assistance fees; publication and other service revenue; and interest income from trusts, endowments and bank accounts.
2. The Parties to this agreement shall not be required to provide financial support to the institute beyond voluntary contributions. Nor shall they be responsible, individually or collectively, for any debts, liabilities or obligations of the Institute.
3. The Institute shall establish arrangements satisfactory to the government of the country in which its headquarters are located with a view to ensuring the Institute's ability to meet its obligations.

Article VI
Organization

The organisation of the Institute shall consist of an assembly of the Parties to this agreement ("Assembly"), a Board of Directors and a Director and staff.

1. The Assembly

A. Each Party to this Agreement shall appoint one representative to act as a member of the Assembly.

B. The Assembly shall meet at the invitation of the Board of Directors or upon the initiative of one third of the Assembly's member. The Assembly shall adopt its own rules of procedure.

C. The Assembly shall from time to time review the activities of the Institute. The Assembly shall also appoint the first Board of Directors, ratify subsequent Board appointments and ratify the Institute's work plan and budget.

D. A decision of the Board of Directors which requires Assembly ratification under Article VI.1.C Above shall be deemed to be ratified on a date ninety days after dispatch of notification by the Institute of such decision to the members of the Assembly unless, before that date, a majority of the members of the Assembly notify the Institute of their opposition to the decision. Notifications shall be made by the most rapid means of communication available or, in the case of member states, through diplomatic channels.

2. The Board of Directors

A. The Institute shall operate under the direction of a Board of Directors ("Board") consisting of not less than ten (10) and not more than sixteen members, including one member to be appointed from time to time by the country in which the Institute has its headquarters ("Permanent Representative") and the Director, who shall be an ex-officio member. Other Board members shall be selected on the basis of professional accomplishments in the fields of law or development and shall serve in their personal capacities and not representatives of governments or organisations.

B. Subsequent to the establishment of the first Board by the Assembly, the Board shall appoint its new members whenever vacancies occur.

C. Except for the Director and the Permanent Representative, each board member appointed subsequent to the establishment of the first Board shall serve on the Board until the completion of the Third Annual Board meeting following his or her written acceptance of an invitation to serve on the Board. The terms of the first members of the Board shall be staggered in order to establish gradual transition of membership.

D. The Board shall meet together at least once a year to carry out its functions. At its first meeting the Board will appoint a Chairman, one or more Vice-Chairmen and an Executive Committee.

E. The Board shall also:

1. Issue by-laws for the governance of the Institute in accordance with this Agreement;
2. Appoint the Director and external auditor of the Institute;
3. Approve the Institute's policies, annual work programs, budgets and audited financial statements; and
4. Do and perform all other acts necessary to carry out the powers delegated to the Board in this Agreement;

3. The Director and Staff

A. The Institute shall be administered by a Director who shall be appointed by the Board for a term of five (5) years, subject to renewal.

B. The Director shall appoint such Professional and General Services staff as may be required to carry out the purposes of the Institute in accordance with personnel policies approved by the Board.

C. The Director shall be responsible to the Board for operating and managing the Institute in accordance with this agreement and the decisions of the Board.

Article VII
Co-operative Relationship

The institute may establish co-operative relationships with other institutions and programs and may accept personnel on a loan or secondment basis.

Article VIII
Rights, Privileges and Immunities

The Institute and its staff shall enjoy in the country of its headquarters such rights, privileges and immunities as shall be stipulated in a headquarters agreement. Other countries may grant comparable rights, privileges and immunities in support of the Institute's activities in such countries.

Article IX
External Auditor

A full financial audit of the operations of the Institute shall be conducted on an annual basis by an independent international accounting firm selected by the Board. The results of such audits shall be made available to the Board and the Assembly.

Article X
Amendments

This Agreement may be amended by the Assembly by a three-fourth majority vote of all of its members, provided that notice of such amendment, together with its full text, shall have been sent to all members of the Assembly at least eight weeks in advance of the time established for a vote on the proposed amendment.

Article XI
Dissolution

1. The Institute may be dissolved if a four-fifths majority of all members of the Assembly determines that the Institute is no longer required or that it will no longer be able to function effectively.

2. In case of dissolution, any assets of the Institute which remain after payment of its legal obligations shall be distributed to institutions having purposes similar to those of the Institute as decided by the Assembly in consultation with the Board.

Article XII
Termination

Any party to this Agreement, upon written notice may terminate its accession to this Agreement and withdraw its membership from the Assembly. Such termination shall become effective three months after the date on which the notification of termination is received by the Depository.

Article XIII
Signature, Ratification, Acceptance, Approval and Accession

1. This Agreement shall be open for signature by states and intergovernmental organisations. It may also be signed, in lieu of any state, by a national public development organisation delegated to act on its behalf by such a state. It shall remain open for signature for a period of two years from June, 1987, unless such period is extended prior to its expiry by the Depository. Signature of the Agreement by any party eligible under this provision thereafter shall require approval of the Assembly by a simple majority.
2. The government of Italy shall be the Depository of this Agreement.
3. Ratification, acceptance or approval of this Agreement shall be undertaken by the signatories in accordance with their own laws, regulations and procedures.

Article XIV
Coming into Force

This Agreement shall come into force immediately upon receipt by the Depository of notifications by the three state parties to this

Agreement that the formalities required by the national legislation of such parties with respect to this Agreement have been accomplished.

Article XV
Transition

Upon the coming into force of this Agreement, the Institute shall take all steps necessary to acquire the rights, obligations, concessions, property and interests of its predecessor organisation, the International Development Law Institute, a non-governmental organisation legally established in Rotterdam, the Netherlands.

IN WITNESS WHEREOF, the undersigned being authorized thereto, have signed this Agreement in a single original in the English and French languages, both texts being equally authentic.

Done in Rome on February 5, 1988.

ANNEX B:

Status of Ratification of the Agreement for the Establishment of the International Development Law Institute*

State	Signature/ Accession	Ratification
Arab Republic of Egypt	March 20, 1989	May 21, 1990
Austria	January 20, 1993	March 17, 1994
Bulgaria	November 28, 1995	June 5, 1996
Colombia	June 18, 1998	June 18, 1998
Ecuador	February 5, 1998	February 5, 1998
France	February 5, 1988	April 12, 1989
Italy	February 5, 1988	May 28, 1993
Netherlands	February 5, 1988	March 5, 1990
People's Republic of China	May30, 1989	May 30, 1989
Philippines	February 5, 1988	April 28, 1989
Senegal	February 5, 1988	September 24, 1990
Sudan	February 5, 1988	May 13, 1989
Tunisia	February 5, 1988	May 15, 1991
United States of America	February 5, 1988	July 12, 1988

* As notified to IDLI by the Depository, the Government of Italy.

ANNEX C:

Rules of Procedure of the Assembly of the International Development Law Institute

Preamble

These Rules of Procedure are adopted under the authority of, and are subject to, the Agreement for the Establishment of the International Development Law Institute "Establishment Agreement". In the event of a conflict between any provision of these rules and any provisions of the Establishment Agreement, the Establishment Agreement shall prevail.

I. Definition

Rule 1

Definitions

(a) "Assembly" means the organ of the parties to the Establishment Agreement;

(b) "Board of Directors" means the Board of Directors of IDLI;

(c) "Chairman" means the Chairman of the Assembly;

(d) "Director" means the Director of IDLI or a Deputy Director when acting in the place of the Director;

(e) "Establishment Agreement" means the Agreement for the Establishment of the International Development Law Institute;

(f) "IDLI" means the International Development Law Institute;

(g) "Member" means a Member of the Assembly of IDLI;

(h) "Representative" means the person whom a Member has designated as its principal representative at a session of the Assembly, including the alternate appointed by that Member when such alternate is acting for the Representative.

II. Assembly Sessions

Rule 2

Holding of Sessions

The Assembly shall hold a session at least once every three years. It shall convene at the invitation of the Board of Directors or upon the initiative of one third of the members of the Assembly.

Rule 3

Procedures

1. Unless the time of an Assembly session is fixed by the Assembly, the Director is responsible, in accordance with such directions as may be given by the Board, for fixing the time of Assembly sessions.
2. Any Member may address a proposal for holding a session to the Director, who shall immediately communicate it to all Members. If at least one-third of the Members concur within 30 days, the session shall be held accordingly.

Rule 4

Place of Sessions

The sessions of the Assembly shall be held at the seat of IDLI. The Assembly may decide to hold a session elsewhere, if this does not involve additional costs to IDLI.

Rule 5

Notification of Sessions

The Director shall, in accordance with such directions as may be given by the Board, notify each Member of the time, date and place of the first meeting of a session of the Assembly and its expected duration.

Rule 6

Provisional Agenda

The Director shall , in accordance with such directions as may be given by the Board of Directors, prepare a provisional agenda for each session of the Assembly.

Rule 7

Communication of the Provisional Agenda

The Director shall transmit to the Members the provisional agenda for a session and the documentation relating to items thereon together with the notification referred to in Rule 5, no later than four weeks before the commencement of a session.

Rule 8

Supplementary Items

After the communication of the provisional agenda pursuant to Rule 7, any Member or the Director may propose supplementary agenda items, which the Director shall promptly communicate to each Member together with documentation relating thereto.

Rule 9

Adoption of the Agenda

1. The Assembly shall at the beginning of each session adopt the agenda for that session on the basis of the provisional agenda and the supplementary items.
2. During a session the Assembly may revise the agenda by adding, deleting, deferring or amending items.

III. Representation and Credentials

Rule 10

Representatives and Alternates

Each Member shall appoint a Representative to the Assembly, and may, at its discretion, also appoint an Alternate.

Rule 11

Credentials and Notifications

The credentials of Representatives and alternates shall be established by the competent state authorities. These credentials and the notification of the names of the Representatives and alternates shall be delivered to the Director at least one week before the opening of the first session in which the designated persons are to attend. Unless otherwise specified, such credentials and notifications shall be considered valid for subsequent sessions until withdrawn by notification to the Director.

IV. Chairman and Steering Committee

Rule 12

Election and Term of Office

1. The Assembly shall elect from among the Representatives a Chairman, Vice-Chairman and a Rapporteur who shall serve as a Steering Committee for three years and, upon expiration of this period, until their successors are elected. The Steering Committee shall verify credentials and discuss and make recommendations on procedural and other matters referred to it by the Assembly.
2. If a member of the Steering Committee resigns or ceases to be a representative, he shall cease to hold his office and a special election shall be held at the next session.
3. In the absence of the Chairman, the Vice-Chairman shall serve as Acting Chairman.
4. A Vice-Chairman acting as Chairman shall have the same powers and duties as the Chairman.
5. If a Chairman ceases to hold office, the Vice-Chairman shall serve as Acting Chairman until a new Chairman is elected.
6. The Chairman or Acting Chairman shall have the right to vote.
7. The Chairman of the Board of Directors and the Director shall be invited to attend meetings of the Steering Committee.

V. Secretariat

Rule 13

The Secretariat

The Director shall organize a Secretariat, which shall be responsible for all arrangements necessary for the Assembly's sessions.

Rule 14

Statements by the Board

The Chairman of the Board of Directors or the Director or their representatives may make oral as well as written statements concerning any question under consideration by the Assembly.

VI. Languages

Rule 15
Languages of the Assembly

English and French shall be the languages of the Assembly.

Rule 16
Interpretation

Speeches made in a language of the Assembly shall be interpreted into the other language.

Rule 17
Languages of Decisions

All decisions of the Assembly shall be made available in the languages of the Assembly.

VII. Conduct of Business

Rule 18
Public Meetings

The meetings of the Assembly shall be held in public unless the Assembly decides otherwise.

Rule 19
Quorum

A quorum for any meeting of the Assembly shall be constituted by a majority of the Members of the Assembly.

Rule 20
Records

The Secretariat shall prepare a record of the decisions taken by the Assembly.

Rule 21
General Powers of the Chairman

In addition to exercising the powers conferred on him elsewhere by these rules, the Chairman shall declare the opening and closing of each meeting of the Assembly, direct the discussions, ensure observance of these rules, accord the right to speak, put questions to the vote and announce decisions. The Chairman, subject to these rules, shall have complete control of the proceedings of the Assembly and over the maintenance of order at its meetings.

Rule 22
Points of Order

1. During the discussion of any matter, a Representative may at any time raise a point of order which the Chairman shall decide immediately in accordance with these rules. Any Representative may appeal against the ruling of the Chairman. The appeal shall be put to the vote immediately and the ruling of the Chairman shall stand unless overruled by the Assembly.
2. In raising a point of order, a Representative may not speak on the substance of the matter under discussion or make any proposal or motion.

Rule 23
Submission of Proposals

Proposals, including substantive amendments, shall normally be submitted by Representatives in both languages of the Assembly.

Rule 24
Motions

A Representative may present any of the following motions, which the Chairman may put to the vote without or with limited debate and which shall have precedence in the indicated order over all proposals and other motions before the meeting:

(a) to suspend the meeting;
(b) to adjourn the meeting;
(c) to adjourn the debate on the item under discussion;
(d) to close the debate on the item under discussion;
(e) to vote on a proposal under discussion.

Rule 25
Right of Reply

The Chairman shall accord the right of reply to any Representative who requests it, but may determine the time when such right may be exercised and the maximum length of any reply.

Rule 26

Expenses

The Members of the Assembly shall be responsible for all costs and allowances of their representatives in connection with travel to and from and attendance at meetings of the Assembly.

VIII. Decisions

Rule 27

Voting Rights

1. Each Member shall have a single vote.
2. Each Representative, or in his absence, his alternate, if any, shall be entitled to express views on a proposal before the Assembly or, if a formal vote on a proposal is taken, to cast the vote of the Member he represents.

Rule 28

Majorities Required

1. Except as provided otherwise in Articles VI.I.D, X and XI of the Establishment Agreement, all decisions of the Assembly, whether within or outside a session, shall be taken by a majority of the votes cast.
2. At any meeting of the Assembly, the Chairman should attempt to secure a consensus on a proposal in lieu of taking a vote thereon. However, the Assembly shall take decisions by vote at the request of any Representative.

Rule 29

Conduct Relating to Voting

1. The Chairman shall announce the commencement of voting, after which no one shall be permitted to intervene until the results of the vote have been announced, except on a point of order in connection with the process of voting.
2. Representatives may make brief statements consisting solely of explanation of their votes, before the announcement of the commencement of voting or after the results of the vote have been announced.

IX. Amendments

Rule 30
Method of Amendment

These rules may be amended by the Assembly to the extent that such amendment is consistent with the Establishment Agreement.

ANNEX D:

Vision 2000

BACKGROUND

Over the past fifteen years IDLI has generally achieved the ambitious goals it set for itself at its founding. It has matured from an idea to a strong and creative institution which has acquired a worldwide reputation for excellence in its legal training. It has:

- Established its credibility with developing and transition economy countries;
- Acquired a dedicated staff of legal professionals and middle managers able to provide quality training and training-related technical assistance in any part of the world;
- Attracted a worldwide pool of distinguished lawyers, legal advisors and judges from which it can draw visiting instructors and consultants;
- Developed a global network of legal and civil society organizations;
- Served as a disseminator of transactional and regulatory "best practices";
- Gained recognition as a valuable instrument of the international community in providing legal training and technical assistance for economic development and governance; and
- Assisted its alumni in creating local associations for training and civil society.

In 1983, IDLI was one of the few international institutions offering legal training for development. Now there is intense competition in this field. Consulting companies, law firms, universities, national and international non-governmental organizations, and training institutions all vie for legal technical assistance and training projects.

In 1983 IDLI communicated by telex. Today it strives to keep up with the opportunities and challenges of the information revolution. Globalization of the economy has transformed the environment in which we operate. What may have been visionary in 1983 is now regarded as just common sense: international trade and investment, participatory government, human rights and the free market all require a sound legal and regulatory framework. Adherence to the rule of law and a skilled legal profession are necessary elements of a wealth-creating economy and a free and well-ordered society.

This paper considers how the Institute, taking into account present and potential new resources, should focus its energies over the next five years, setting its initial course in the new century.

To formulate the strategic objectives in this statement, the starting point was our Establishment Agreement. Its framers sought both to define a mandate and to create an organization with an international legal status to fulfill it. This approach allowed IDLI to respond as the role of law has evolved in the development agenda. It also implied a duty for IDLI to renew itself as its environment and constituencies changed.

The Board is invited to contribute to the final formulation of the Vision statement and will be called upon in the future to approve related specific budgets and, as in the past, those actions which go beyond the normal scope of management.

THE CASE FOR RENEWAL

The geo-political, technological and economic upheavals of the 80's and 90's have drawn attention to the intimate and interdependent relationships between law, democratic institutions, civil society, human rights and economic development. Changes in one area require changes in another. Thus, IDLI's priorities must be renewed from time to time to keep pace with change.

In 1990 IDLI expressed its statement of mission as follows:

"To provide the highest quality legal training related to economic development in developing countries and countries with emerging market economies, and to gain increased recognition for excellence in this field."

IDLI has largely fulfilled these goals, having gained an international reputation for excellence in the field of legal training. A new mission statement should now be articulated for the very different world in which we will find ourselves in the 21st century.

As part of the renewal process, management has determined that IDLI must improve its capacities in order to:

- Increase the number of program beneficiaries each year;
- Attract a broader range of legal and related professionals;
- Benefit additional developing and transition economy countries;
- Expand its program offerings and other products;
- Utilize information technology;
- Promote gender balance in both program and organization;
- Contribute to the international community's understanding of the relevance of law to economic development and governance;
- Contribute to the diffusion of legal "best practices:"
- Promote legal institution-building and the development of civil society;
- Respond quickly and flexibly to changing situations and to requests for multi-faceted legal technical assistance; and
- Design and deliver training in legal skills and knowledge more cost-effectively.

NEW DIRECTIONS

We propose to implement the strategic objectives described below over the next five years, taking into account the availability of human and financial resources, appropriate budgeting and Board authorizations. The components are outlined below.

1. Strengthen Our Regional Presence

Subject to the availability of funding, IDLI should establish fully-fledged Regional Training Offices in Africa, Central and Eastern Europe and Latin America, structured along the lines of the Asia Regional Training Office (Asia RTO). Such offices would be established only after headquarters arrangements have been concluded with the concerned host member states. To minimize costs, they would rely on locally-hired staff, with initial supervision by an experienced Program Legal Counsel. The choice of location of future RTOs would depend on the needs of countries in the region, and on the package of support offered by the candidate government. Other strategic considerations would also be taken into account, such as eligibility for particular funding and the infrastructure and other competitive advantages offered by the candidate countries.

Like the Asia RTO, these offices would have a regional mandate and would be expected both to support themselves and to contribute financially to the overall IDLI operation. Each regional representative would be charged with securing funding for and implementation of country and regional programs. Management from headquarters would be undertaken in the same manner as that now in place for the Asia RTO.

As a first step in the process of decentralization, the Institute should develop for year 2000 two regular programs for regional delivery in the field. This would in effect transform the programs conducted by the Rome headquarters from exclusively "Rome-based" to "regular programs" offered both in Rome and in the regions. Such reconfiguration would respond to demands for increasing field training to serve regional needs and would free more headquarters time to organize international and national program events, as foreseen elsewhere in this statement.

It should be emphasized that the proposed regional programs and longer term decentralization would in no way diminish the importance of the Rome headquarters. On the contrary, the role of the center would be enhanced. IDLI Rome would take on additional responsibilities for project development, monitoring and evaluation. In line with other projections of Vision 2000, headquarters activities would embrace a more active NGO unit, coordinate and service multilateral and bilateral donor agencies and develop international conferences on legal and judicial reform and similar topics. With a broader outreach, the requirements for headquarters staff would increase over time (not decrease) as our

Rome headquarters exercised its function as nerve center for a steadily increasing range of global activities. Furthermore, as our Manila and Warsaw Offices have demonstrated, more active field work not only generates qualified candidates and visiting instructors for our Rome courses and seminars, but also creates more coordination and monitoring responsibilities at the center. In short, regionalization can only enlarge and enhance the role of our Rome headquarters and the profile of IDLI as an international organization and premier training institute.

2. Diversify Products

As our Board of Directors has reiterated over the years, training is and should remain our core product. The Institute should promote its role as disseminator of legal and judicial "best practices" and legal harmonization. However, if IDLI is to retain its competitive position, it must develop the capability to produce by itself, or through commissions, original and practical research on substantive and training-related topics. Moreover, it should regularly participate in international meetings which address legal aspects of economic development.

Wealth-creating business globalization has dictated most of IDLI's training agenda to date. For the future, "lower end globalization issues" — addressing wealth distribution and poverty alleviation — will become more important in our selection of training topics.

IDLI should seek to "partner" with donor agencies and other international organizations in the design and implementation of legal and judicial reform projects. For example, projects which include local training and reference materials along the lines of the recently completed Mongolia benchbook are a valuable resource for the formulation of policies. Training-of-trainers and training methodology publications in the country's language would reinforce local legal education and institution-building efforts, adding a multiplier effect to IDLI training. At the same time, as noted below, the Institute should expand its services to civil society organizations.

IDLI should also develop a powerful electronic information base of practical legal materials which could be accessed through the Internet by its alumni and other development lawyers around the world. As new software permits interactive training on the Internet, IDLI should experiment with distance education, especially as follow-up training for its alumni.

3. Take Full Advantage of IDLI's Status as an International Organization

The member states have conferred international legal status on IDLI in order to enhance its impact and sustainability. The Institute should therefore make greater use of that status by becoming a primary instrument of the international community in legal and judicial reform projects. As it is already beginning to do, the Institute can cooperate with donor countries and international organizations to design specialized programs under expandable and renewable "framework" arrangements.

IDLI should also use its international status to secure more funding from bilateral and multilateral donors, directly or through trust fund arrangements. It should expand its effort to conclude cooperative agreements with global centers of excellence (on the model of its current cooperation with the Centre for Legal Education in Sydney, Australia). Moreover, the Institute should regularly organize international meetings (such as conferences on legal and judicial reform) to develop legal project agendas for consideration by international development organizations, governments and civil society organizations. As state-of-the-art information technology becomes available to an increasing number of our client countries, the Institute can provide useful inputs to legislators and legislative draftspersons in those countries.

4. Expand Cooperation with Civil Society Organizations

Having begun its own existence as a non-governmental organization, IDLI is well placed to promote and foster civil society organizations. Building upon its rich base of information and contacts and on its growing recognition by the international NGO community, IDLI should be in a position to contribute at the international level towards the setting of legal standards and role models, especially now, when the third sector is evolving and new legislation is being created.

Through its NGO Unit, IDLI has already assisted in the creation of non-profit legal training centers in several countries. Moreover, it has helped create legally established associations of

IDLI alumni in more than a dozen countries, as far removed geographically as Ecuador and India. Yet the Institute can do more to share the experience of its managers in strengthening civil society around the world. The Institute should increase its emphasis on legal aspects of civil society organizations and the legal framework for non-profit entities, while continuing to share its first hand expertise on organizational sustainability.

5. Achieve Gender Balance in our Organization and Programs

Over the past three decades women around the world have been entering the legal profession in increased numbers. As they join the ranks of the profession, they require the same if not more training and capacity building opportunities as their male colleagues. IDLI should not only intensify its effort to achieve gender balance among its participants and experts but also utilize the participation of women lawyers to identify and suggest ways of reforming gender balance in its own staff and visiting instructors, and to achieve it in its governing bodies.

6. Outreach

One of the persistent concerns of any training activity is follow-up with former participants, both to ensure continuing support and to assess long term impact. To address this concern, IDLI should enhance its "outreach" to its various constituencies. The first priority is to former participants, alumni associations and counterpart organizations. Secondly, IDLI should strengthen ties with other members of the legal profession, professional associations, other NGOs and local research and academic institutions. Expanding such networks will help in programming, provide a forum from which IDLI can expand its influence for change and ensure the continuity of contact with former participants for any serious long term evaluation impact assessment.

RESOURCE NEEDS

Management recognizes that enhanced resources will be required to pursue these objectives. If we are to bring our vision into reality, we cannot continue to rely solely on annual contributions. To become more proactive in the setting of an international legal and judicial reform agenda, the Institute must be able to tap new budget categories of institutional support. To obtain the added resources, new and more creative fundraising approaches must be found to secure sustained multi-year giving by public and private sector organizations, foundations and individuals.

On the other hand, most of the new activities envisaged in this statement will be funded on a project basis. Furthermore, the additional costs incurred in delivering the two regional programs suggested for the year 2000 and beyond will be more than offset by the overall increased tuition revenue.

IDLI has an opportunity to re-cast itself in a new role for the 21st century, in order to respond to the increasing demands of an increasingly global market. But to seize that opportunity, it must begin the effort now — with the full support of our Assembly of State Members and Board of Directors.

DEVELOPMENT FINANCING IN CONFORMITY WITH THE *SHARI'AH*: INSTRUMENTS AND LIMITATIONS

*Mohamed El Fatih Hamid**

I. INTRODUCTION

The Islamic Development Bank (IsDB)[1] is an international financing institution with a dual mission: (i) to foster economic development and social progress of its member countries and the Islamic communities in non-member countries; and (ii) to pursue the former mission in conformity with the principles of the *Shari'ah*.[2] In pursuing its first mission, the IsDB has liberally drawn from the experience and expertise of the World Bank Group and other international and regional financing institutions. However, since no other institution is carrying on development fi-

---

*Any views expressed in this paper represent the opinion of the author and, unless otherwise indicated, should not be interpreted as official Islamic Development Bank's views.

1 The Islamic Development Bank is known in its member countries by the acronym, IDB. However, in deference to the Inter-American Development Bank whose acronym is also IDB, the acronym IsDB is used in this paper for the Islamic Development Bank.

2 *See* art. 1 of the IsDB's Articles of Agreement. In a statement to the Board of Governors of the IsDB, Dr. Ahmad Mohamed Ali, the incumbent President, described the two missions of the IsDB in slightly different words when he said that it

> "[h]as two basic missions: the first, is to achieve all forms and patterns of financial and economic cooperation among member countries through this Institution so that it could be a practical manifestation of the unity and solidarity of the Islamic Ummah, as enshrined in its Articles of Agreement. The second mission is commitment to Islamic principles and values in Islamic Banking."

SUMMARY RECORD OF PROCEEDINGS OF NINETEENTH ANNUAL MEETING OF THE BOARD OF GOVERNORS OF THE IsDB, at 204.

nancing in conformity with the principles of the *Shari'ah,* IsDB has to rely on its own innovative skills to pursue its second mission. The purpose of this paper is to give a brief survey of the instruments that the IsDB has devised to enable it to operate in conformity with the *Shari'ah* and to function as an effective development financing institution.

While it will be difficult to give a full exposition of what is *Shari'ah* within the limited campus of this paper, a brief outline is necessary for appreciating the extent and complexity of IsDB's mandate. *Shari'ah* is the law of Islam that regulates all aspects of a Muslim's life from the cradle to the grave. The principles of the *Shari'ah* are enshrined in the twin sources of divine revelation, the Holy Book of Islam (the *Qu'rân*), and the *Sunnah* (the sayings, deeds and confirmations of the Prophet of Islam). The principles derived from these two primary sources are, for Muslims, sacrosanct and immutable.[3] These principles are also few in number and, often, general in import. The legal void in areas of human activity left unregulated by the two primary sources was filled by detailed rules devised by Muslim jurists through application of individual intellectual effort (*ijtihâd*) in the light of the principles and strictures enshrined in the primary sources. The *ijtihâd* of the jurists of the eighth and ninth century, primarily through analogical deductions (*qiyas*),[4] produced a formidable body of doctrine known as *fiqh* (literally, "understanding"). This consists of both the interpretations of the jurists of what they conceive to be the true meaning of the texts of the primary sources, and new rules devised to govern areas left unregulated by the primary sources. Unlike the principles of the *Shari'ah, fiqh* is flexible, dynamic and amenable to change. That the rules of *fiqh* are the product of human effort is underscored by the diversity and multiplicity of opinion which has become one of its distinguishing features. This difference of opinion is due to the difference in the juridical premises from which each jurist proceeded, and the methodology which he adopted to reach his conclusions. The eighth century witnessed the rise of the schools of law in which jurists ultimately grouped. The most well-known of these schools are the four

---

3 For the distinction between the principles of the *Shari'ah* and *Fiqh, see* M.A. AL-ZARQA, AL-FIQH AL-ISLAMI WA MASADIRUHU 16 (1st ed. 1995).

4 Other legislative sources used by jurists in the process of *ijtihâd* include *ijma'* (the consensus of the scholars), *istihsan* (preference), and *'urf* (custom).

Sunni schools, each of which is named after the master that has established it. These are the *Hanafi, Maliki, Shafi'i* and *Hanbali* schools, and the two *Shi'ite* schools *Imamiyyah* and *Zayediyyah*.

Unfortunately, *ijtihâd,* which is an indispensable tool for ensuring that rules of *fiqh* continue to be responsive to the exigencies of an ever changing world, was brought to an abrupt end by the beginning of the tenth century by arbitrarily disqualifying jurists from any further *ijtihâd*. This was, among other reasons, prompted by a desire to preempt the misuse of the facility of *ijtihâd*.[5] Be the reasons as they may, the result was the stagnation of *fiqh*. With the exception of the valiant effort of two jurists[6] to bring *ijtihâd* to life, *fiqh* remained in its medieval state and continued to be so until replaced by Western systems of law with the advent of foreign domination of Muslim countries. It is not, therefore, surprising that when the IsDB commenced business, *Shari'ah* was the law of the land in not more than two of its member countries. In all the others, *Shari'ah* had been relegated to matters of personal status (*viz.*, marriage, divorce and succession), while western-inspired laws held sway in all other matters.

Banks that operate in conformity with the principles of the *Shari'ah* have often been referred to as "non-interest banks," presumably on the ground that they all proceed from the assumption that the charging or receipt of interest amounts to usury and, therefore, violates the prohibition of usury which is enshrined in the *Qu'rân*. This description is, however, misleading in so far as it abridges the dictates of an immensely rich jurisprudence in the single prohibition of interest. Rather than being a regime of prohibitive injunctions, *Shari'ah* is a comprehensive system of rules designed to regulate and guide human conduct to a just and equitable path. As has been rightly pointed out, although the elimination of interest is certainly a central tenet of the Islamic economic system, it is by no means an adequate description of the system as a whole, or for that matter, even of Islamic banking.[7] As will be seen, there are other rules of the *Shari'ah* that have an impact on the conduct of Islamic banking business.

---

5 *See* M. Abu Zahra, al-Milkiyya wa Nazariyyat al-Aqd 45 (1976); M.A. al-Zarqa, 1 al-Madkhal al-Fiqhi al-Am 176 (9th ed. 1967–1968).

6 Ibn Taymiyya (1263–1328G) and Ibn al-Qayyim (1292–1350G).

7 *See* M.S. Khan, *Islamic Interest Free Banking, in* Theoretical Studies in Islamic Banking and Finance 16 (M.S. Khan & A. Mirakhor eds., 1987).

As would be expected of a system of law which is rooted in religious values, the *Shari'ah* requires a degree of moral and ethical rectitude which is woefully absent in contemporary secular business practices. This does not mean that every morally desirable conduct is incorporated in a rule of *Shari'ah;* for *Shari'ah* makes a clear distinction between what is only morally binding and what is legally enforceable, though Muslims are enjoined to abide by both rules. It does, however, mean that no rule of *Shari'ah* would incorporate morally iniquitous conduct.[8] This underlines the difficulty of the application of the principles of the *Shari'ah* in an environment where the parties are not imbued with a like moral creed.

II. IsDB'S FINANCING OF DEVELOPMENT

Nowhere has the impact of the requirement to act in conformity with the *Shari'ah* been more felt than in the deployment of resources in financing development projects through *Shari'ah* compliant modalities. IsDB commenced business with two financing instruments and a wide mandate to "invest in economic and social infrastructure projects by way of participation or other financial arrangement."[9] The two financing instruments explicitly mentioned in the Articles of Agreement are loan and equity.[10]

From the perspective of the *Shari'ah,* loan is not an instrument of financing that is revenue-generating, given that the charging of interest is prohibited according to the view held by the majority of classical and contemporary jurists. The prominent place that has been given to loans in the Articles of Agreement of the IsDB[11] as an instrument of financing for both public and private sector projects and enterprises, may at first sight seem strange for a banking institution. The explanation of this apparent anomaly lies in the fact that the IsDB is an association of developing

---

8 It has been argued that there are no necessary conceptual connections between the content of law and morality, and that morally iniquitous provisions may be valid as legal rules or principles. *See* H.L.A. HART, THE CONCEPT OF LAW 268 (2nd ed. 1997).

9 Article 2(ii) of the IsDB's Articles of Agreement.

10 *See* arts. 2(i) & 2(iii) of the ISDB's Articles of Agreement.

11 Articles 2(iii), 18 & 19 of the IsDB's Articles of Agreement.

countries including a large number of the countries classified by the United Nations as least developed. For these countries, concessional financing is an essential requirement. However, given that the financing needs of these countries are huge, and the resources of the IsDB are limited,[12] the founders of the IsDB were mindful of the need to strike a balance between loan financing and equity financing. The expectations of the founders were that if the right balance is struck, then the revenues that will be generated from equity investments will enable the IsDB to sustain its concessional lending. For this purpose, Article 16(4) of the IsDB's Articles of Agreement enjoins it "to maintain a suitable ratio between equity investments in, and loans granted to, member countries." As things turned out, the expectations of the founders in this regard, have not been realized for reasons that will shortly be explained.

Participation in the equity capital of a project means accepting to share in the profit and loss of an enterprise. Those familiar with the literature on Islamic banking will appreciate the importance of equity financing for an institution operating in conformity with the principles of the *Shari'ah*. Financing on the basis of profit and loss sharing has come to be regarded as the paradigm of Islamic financing.[13] It is not, therefore, surprising that equity financing is the only other mode of financing specifically mentioned in the Articles of Agreement of the IsDB.

As against loan which is not revenue-generating, equity participation, and profit-sharing, were expected to be the revenue-earners par excellence. The first IsDB document on Policies and Procedures for Financing Operations betrayed that optimism. It provided that

> "[i]t is the policy of the Bank not to charge any interest or commitment charge on any of its financing operations. Dividend earnings from equity participation in project/enterprises and income from investment in projects/enterprises on the basis of profit-sharing will constitute the major source of income for the Bank. It is, there-

---

12 Recognizing this need, the IsDB established in 1992 a Special Account for the Least Developed Member Countries to provide more concessionary loans for its Least Developed Member Countries.

13 One of the first authors to articulate this idea is Dr. Nejatullah Siddiqui. *See* N.S. SIDDIQUI, BANKING WITHOUT INTEREST (4th ed. 1981).

> fore, necessary that in the first five years of its operation, the Bank should concentrate on equity participation and investment in projects/enterprises on the basis of profit-sharing."[14]

Unfortunately, the hard facts of life have dampened that early optimism. The returns from the equity investments were at best modest. Among the reasons given in explanation of this state of affairs are the lack of capital markets, ineffective macro-economic policies and the poor quality of economic management. In addition, projects often faced difficulties of one type or another relating to project implementation, production, marketing and other operational and financial aspects.[15]

Until 1992, equity financing was carried out on the understanding that, being in essence a profit and loss sharing modality, it is compatible with the *Shari'ah* as long as the activity which the enterprise intends to carry out is benign from the *Shari'ah* vantage point. Thus, it will not be possible to participate in the equity of a conventional bank or of a brewery. However, in that year the Fiqh Academy of the Organization of the Islamic Conference ruled[16] that it will not be permissible to participate in the capital of a company that is financed through interest-bearing loans or is otherwise receiving interest by placing its liquidity in interest-bearing instruments. Given that a company that does not borrow money on interest basis is a rare bird, that decision of the Fiqh Academy virtually brought equity participation, in all but the capital of Islamic financing institutions, to a grinding halt. The Annual Report of the IsDB for the year 1418H (1997–1998) tells us that the IsDB "participated in three equity operations during 1418H with a combined value of ID2.1 million (US$2.86 million). . . . Two of the equity ventures involved increasing the capital of two finance houses[17] in Turkey, while the remaining venture was with an Islamic Bank in Pakistan." However, the amount invested by the IsDB during 1419H (1998–1999) increased to ID 13.18 million

---

14 IsDB Policies and Procedures for Financing Operations, at 14.

15 *See* S.A. Meenai, The Islamic Development Bank: A Case Study of Islamic Co-operation 72–75 (1989); D.M. Qureshi, *Agenda for a New Strategy of Equity Financing by the Islamic Development Bank,* Vol. 1, No. 1 Islamic Economic Studies, at 71.

16 *See* Resolution No. 65/1/7, Islamic Fiqh Academy.

17 The Twenty-third Annual Report, IsDB, at 110.

(US$18.05 million), of which was invested in four Islamic institutions.

The impact of the decision of the Fiqh Academy on equity participation is a salient reminder of the pervasive effect of interest. The basis of that decision is that the income that may be realized by a company that borrows on the basis of interest, to the extent that the income or part thereof could be traced to that borrowing, is tainted with the illegality resulting from the violation of the prohibition of usury.

One may be tempted to argue that by ascribing culpability to the shareholders for the delinquent act of the company, the Fiqh Academy failed to take into account that, in law, the company is a person separate from its shareholders. Except in the few cases where the veil of incorporation is lifted, shareholders cannot be held responsible for the act of the company.[18] However, as against this, it may be argued that the relationship between a shareholder and a company is contractual. The terms of this contract are embodied in the Memorandum and Articles of Association of the company. If these documents give the company the power to borrow and pay interest or to receive interest for its deposits, the shareholders cannot escape the conclusion that they are privy to this wrongdoing and should, therefore, be deprived of their ill-gotten gains. The real issue, however, is whether it is at all practical to expect, in the context of the IsDB's member countries, that companies can do away with borrowing, given their huge need for foreign exchange. The crippling effect which the application of this ruling had on the ability of the IsDB to invest in equity, would point to a negative answer. That, in my view, is a state of affairs that can only be remedied by a more enlightened and pragmatic approach to the issue.

Against the backdrop of the foregoing, the IsDB felt the need to increase and diversify its array of instruments for two purposes. The first is to generate adequate returns to cover its administrative expenses, offset the effects of inflation and subsidize its concessional lending. The second is to equip itself to finance different

[18] For a novel argument in which an analogy is drawn between the interest of a shareholder in the property of a company and the interest of a master in the property of his slave, *see* M.A. Al-Gari, *al-Shakhsiya al-'Itibariyya that al-Masuliya al-Mahduda,* Vol. 5, No. 2 DIRASAT IQTISADIYYA 9 (1998).

project components. To satisfy these, it has indeed succeeded in developing three important instruments of financing, namely, Leasing, Installment Sale and *Istisna'a*. Leasing is a medium term mode of financing through which IsDB finances machinery and equipment and other capital assets that are capable of productive output either independently or in conjunction with other assets. During the lease period, IsDB maintains the ownership of the leased asset. On full payment of the rentals, the IsDB transfers the ownership of the asset to the lessee. In Installment Sales, IsDB finances machinery and equipment which will not be suitable for leasing or for which leasing for any other reasons is not appropriate. Unlike in Leasing, in Installment Sales the ownership of the assets is transferred to the beneficiary of the IsDB financing (buyer) on delivery. On the other hand, *Istisna'a* (a contract for the manufacturing or construction of assets) which is the most recent addition to IsDB's instrument of financing is suitable for financing the manufacturing or construction of assets. It is used by the IsDB as a mode for extending pre-shipment financing of capital goods and for construction of physical infrastructure assets with assured cash flows such as toll roads, seaports etc.

All of the above three instruments have been designed to give the IsDB a fixed predetermined return on its investment. This return, in the case of Leasing, is built in the rental to be paid by the lessee, and in the case of Installment Sales and *Istisna'a,* is built in the price to be paid by the purchaser. The fact that this return has been fixed[19] *ex ante* does not by itself raise a problem of *Shari'ah* compliance in so far as it is a return on the use of assets in the case of Leasing, and a return for the transfer of ownership of the assets in the other two modes. That these three modes are intended to yield a fixed return to the IsDB distinguishes them from

[19] Khan makes a distinction between the cost of capital and the rate of return, the former being the amount which the recipient of the financing ends up paying to the financier. According to him, while the rate of return on capital is always supposed to be variable and certain and cannot be predetermined, it is possible for the cost of capital to be fixed and predetermined, if leasing or *murabaha* (resale for a profit) modes are used. Because of the risks which the financier have to bear in the said modes of financing, the rate of return is kept uncertain until the lessee or purchaser takes delivery of and accepts the goods. *See* M.F. KHAN, COMPARATIVE ECONOMICS OF SOME ISLAMIC FINANCING TECHNIQUES 14–15 (Islamic Research & Training Institute, IsDB, 1st ed. 1991).

loan, where no return is generated, and from equity, where there is only an expectation of return.

In developing these instruments, IsDB's starting point was the contractual modalities developed by the earlier jurists with which the classical manuals are replete. The advantage of this approach is that it ensures the compatibility of the instrument with the *Shari'ah*. However, to avoid forcing modalities of classic origin into affinities with twentieth century business practices, these instruments needed to be suitably modified to ensure their responsiveness to current business needs without flouting the principles of the *Shari'ah*. Although the IsDB has undertaken that task with a fair measure of success, the exercise was rather delicate and was not free of difficulty for primarily two reasons: exposure to and management of risk.

The first attendant difficulty stems from the natural desire of a banking institution to avoid exposure to contractual risks. For Islamic banks not only are contractual risks inherent in the instruments through which they extend financing, but the assumption of those risks is viewed as a *conditio sine qua non* of their entitlement to earn a return on their investment. Any attempt to avoid exposure to contractual risks may render the contractual form a mere device for concealing an otherwise usurious transaction. The question is whether this consideration should preclude the parties from allocating contractual risks between them in a manner that will not give one an unfair advantage at the expense of the other.

The freedom of the parties to allocate contractual risks between them is limited under the rules of classical *fiqh*. Under these rules, some of the obligations of a contract are perceived to be so essential for maintaining a just and equitable equilibrium between the parties that any attempt to modify them by exonerating one party of his obligations or shifting the obligations of one to the other will be void and ineffective. This may, on the face of it, seem surprising in view of the fact that most contemporary *Shari'ah* scholars adopt the position articulated by the *Hanbali* jurist Ibn Taymiyya relative to freedom of contract. According to him, the general rule is that acts and dispositions (including the making of contracts and stipulations) are valid and permissible (*mubah*) unless expressly prohibited. The only condition stipulated in the *Qu'rân* for the validity of contracts, he argued, is mutual consent. Given such consent, the parties are free to make whatever contracts and stipulations they may choose as long as they do not violate the principles of the *Shari'ah*.[20] This view was not shared by the earlier jurists who based their position on the doctrine of the prescribed effects of a contract (*nazariyyat ju'aliyat al-athar*). Taken literally, this doctrine appears to deny the parties any freedom to regulate their contractual obligations. This is because, the doctrine stipulates that the effects of a contract are prescribed by God (*al-Shari'*). The role of the human will is confined to the conclusion of the contract through the exchange of offer and acceptance; it has no role in determining the effects of a contract.[21] Thus, the passing of property in a contract of sale from the seller to the buyer is an effect that is prescribed, and not a result brought about by the will of the parties. Indeed the parties cannot prevent that result. Thus a sale in which the seller reserves the title will not in the eyes of the *Shari'ah* be a proper sale. But to deny that the parties' will has a role in determining the effects of a contract, is to deny the freedom of the parties to regulate their contractual relationship by means of stipulations.

As a logical step in the application of the said doctrine, the prescribed effects of each contract need to be spelled out. The classical jurists spent a great deal of effort doing precisely this. The prescribed effects of each and every contract were spelled in great detail in their massive manuals. By so doing, they had delineated the area that fell outside the pale of the will of the parties. Any stipulation that purports to negate or contradict the prescribed effects of a contract will be void and ineffective. Only stipulations that reinforce these effects or are sanctioned by custom will be permissible and valid.[22]

Unless the doctrine of the prescribed effect of contracts is little more than a contrivance of juridical craftsmanship, it will not be easy to rehabilitate ancient contractual modalities in the contractual and business environment of the twentieth century. There is, for instance, a world of difference between the terms of a classical contract of hire (*ijara*) and the terms of a current financial lease though both are based on the separation between the own-

---

20 *See* T. IBN TAYMIYYA, 3 MAJMU'AT FATAWA IBN TAYMIYYA 323–349 (1980).

21 *See* M. ABU ZAHRA, *supra* note 5, at 250–264. *See also* M.W. SUWAR, AL-T'ABIR 'AN AL-IRADA FI AL-FIQH AL-ISLAMI 577–595 (1960).

22 *See* A. AL-SANHURI, 3 MASADIR AL-HAQ FI AL-FIQH AL-ISLAMI 101–176 (3rd ed. 1967).

ership of the corpus and its usufruct. The most cursory look at the provisions of the Unidroit Convention on International Financial Leasing will illustrate this point.[23] It is not suggested here that each stipulation in a current financial leasing contract must be followed since some of them are obviously contrary to the *Shari'ah*. What is suggested, however, is that the parties may be allowed a degree of freedom that will enable them to allocate certain obligations among themselves in the interest of the business efficacy of the transaction. For example, under a lease contract, the casualty risk (the risk of the accidental loss of, or damage to, the leased assets) remains with the lessor during the lease period.[24] This risk is normally covered by an insurance policy for which a premium is to be paid. If the lessor pays the premium, he will naturally regard it as a cost and will capitalize and recover it from the lessee as a part of the rentals. The result is that, at the end of the day, the cost of insurance will be borne by the lessee. Yet, some jurists find it objectionable if a lease agreement stipulates that the lessee will pay the insurance premium on behalf, and for the benefit, of the lessor, though the lessee may have a perfectly legitimate reason for the payment of the premium on behalf of the lessor. He may, for instance, prefer, in a cross border lease, to pay the premium in his local currency to a local insurance company, rather than to have the lessor pay it and recover it in foreign exchange. Furthermore, the payment by the lessee of the premium will not shift the risk from the lessor to the lessee. Thus, if the risk materializes and the insurance company declines, or is unable, to indemnify the lessor, the loss will be borne by the lessor. The same could be said about other ancillary obligations of a lease agreement, such as, the obligation to maintain the assets during the lease period. The question is whether such obligations could not be seen as a legitimate attempt of the parties to arrange the manner in which transaction costs are to be paid.

The second difficulty that faced the IsDB in devising efficient instruments of financing is the ability to manage the risks associated with the manner in which the contractual process for the acquisition of assets to be acquired for the purpose of leasing or

---

23 *See* UNIDROIT Convention on International Financial Leasing, May 28, 1988, 27 INTERNATIONAL LEGAL MATERIALS (I.L.M.) 931, in particular arts. 8, 9 & 10.

24 *See* Resolution No. 1, Third Session (1986) of the Islamic Fiqh Academy.

installment sale. Obviously, IsDB will not have those assets before it has decided to finance their acquisition for the purposes of the project. At the time the IsDB enters into the lease or installment sale financing agreement with the beneficiary under which it undertakes to acquire the assets and lease (or sell them on installment sale basis) to the beneficiary, the assets are, in legal terms, "future goods" i.e., goods that will be manufactured or that IsDB will otherwise acquire from their suppliers. IsDB realizes that, from the legal point of view, such agreement will be an "agreement to sell" and not a present sale. No property in the goods will, therefore, pass to the IsDB or to the beneficiary, until these goods are ascertained.

Until 1986, the IsDB's lease and installment sale agreements were based on the above assumptions. In that year, the Fiqh Academy of the Organization of the Islamic Conference ruled that this practice is not in conformity with the principles of the *Shari'ah*. To be acceptable from the point of view of the *Shari'ah,* the IsDB should sell or lease the assets after it has become the owner thereof.[25] This ruling is an application of a *Shari'ah* principle that prohibits contracts in which there is *gharar* (uncertainty). According to the widely accepted definition, *gharar* occurs wherever the consequences of an act are concealed or indiscernible.[26] Thus, a contract of insurance, in its conventional form, violates this principle in so far as the happening or otherwise of the risk insured against is concealed or unknown. Thus, *gharar* will vitiate a contract because of the uncertainty of the genus (*jins*), the species (*naw'a*), the attribute (*sifa*), the quantity (*miqdar*) of the subject matter of the contract. Uncertainty regarding the inability to deliver the subject matter or its existence will also vitiate the contract.[27] It is the uncertainty regarding the ability to deliver, which is the basis of the Fiqh Academy's ruling. This is further explained by a contemporary authority in the *Shari'ah* in the following terms:

---

25 *See ibid.*

26 *See* S.M.A. Al-Dhareer, *al-Gharar in Contracts and its Effects on Contemporary Transactions,* 16 EMINENT SCHOLARS LECTURES SERIES 10 (Islamic Reseach & Training Institute, IsDB, 1st ed. 1997).

27 *See ibid.* at 21–34.

> "In this kind of sale, Islamic jurisprudence departs widely from the practices familiar in the markets. Islamic law does not permit a person to sell that which he does not own at the time of the contract. Ibn Abidin says: 'Among the conditions of the sale is that the subject matter of the contract is owned by the seller acting for himself. A sale of what one does not own is invalid even if he comes to own it afterwards. This view is based upon authentic *hadiths* (of the Prophet) that forbid a person to sell what he does not have. Ibn Qudama said: We know of no disagreement over this'. . . . The reason for the ban here is *gharar* resulting from the inability to deliver."[28]

The uncertainty regarding the ability to deliver arises on the assumption that, if the contract with the supplier is discharged by reason of frustration because the goods perish before their delivery to the IsDB, it will not be in a position to make delivery to the beneficiary of its financing. It is this uncertainty in the ability to deliver what is not in one's possession at the time of the contract that violates the principles of the *Shari'ah* relative to *gharar.*

To comply with the *Shari'ah* requirement, as it is bound by its charter to do, IsDB now enters into two agreements with the beneficiary under a lease or installment sale. The first agreement is an agency agreement under which IsDB authorizes the beneficiary to acquire the assets on its behalf. The provisions of this agency agreement require that such procurement shall be in accordance with the procurement procedures of the IsDB, and the draft contract with the supplier will have to receive the prior approval of the IsDB before it is concluded on its behalf. IsDB also ensures that one of the terms of this contract is that the goods shall be delivered from the supplier directly to the beneficiary of the financing. The agency agreement further stipulates that after the agent takes delivery of the goods and satisfies himself as to their conformity with the contract, he will offer to buy them (or take them on lease) from the IsDB, as the case may be, on the terms and conditions set out in an appendix to the agency agreement. The second agreement (lease or installment sale) will be concluded by

[28] *See ibid.* at 61. Salam, which is a forward purchase of goods for a price to be made immediately, is a notable exception to the rule stated in the text.

the exchange of telexes after the agent has taken delivery and has offered to buy the goods (or take them on lease) on the terms and conditions set out in the said appendix to the agency agreement.

The conclusion of the lease or installment sale agreement in the manner just described exposes the IsDB to several risks, the most obvious of which is the failure of the beneficiary, for any reason, to conclude the lease or installment sale agreement after he has taken delivery of the assets on behalf of the IsDB, or his refusal to accept the assets because of their non-conformity with the specifications. In the former case, IsDB will have to find a buyer for the equipment and, if he incurs a loss in the sale to such buyer, it will be able to recover such loss.[29] However, this loss will not, under the rules of the *Shari'ah,* include the loss of profit which it would have gained, had the contract with the beneficiary been concluded. In the latter case, IsDB will have to reject the assets, and ask for the return of the price.

III. CONCLUSION

From the foregoing survey, it is hoped that the limitations of the instruments of financing used by the IsDB have become apparent. Some of these limitations arise from the *ijtihâd* of the jurists in interpreting certain textual authorities in the primary sources, while others are rules developed by them to fill whatever *lacunae* existed in the laws. With the momentous change in the economic and social setting in the last twelve centuries, some of these interpretations may have to be revisited to see whether they require reinterpretations in the light of the prevailing circumstances. In all cases, it will be remembered that the instruments devised by the IsDB and successfully used by it in its operations were virtually unknown at the inception of the IsDB. They are now well-known and widely used both in IsDB member countries and in many quarters in the international financial markets. To many, this alone is a worthwhile contribution.

---

29 *See* Resolutions Nos. 2 & 3 (1988) of the Islamic Fiqh Academy (adopted in the Fifth Session).

THE ESTABLISHMENT AND DEVELOPMENT OF THE NORDIC INVESTMENT BANK — AN INSTITUTION SUI GENERIS

*Siv Hellén**

> *"I know a bank where the wild thyme blows,*
> *Where oxlips and the nodding violet grows,*
> *Quite over-canopied with luscious woodbine,*
> *With sweet musk roses and with eglantine."*
>
> William Shakespeare
> A Midsummer Night's Dream Act II, Scene 1

I. BACKGROUND OF ESTABLISHMENT

The idea of a common financial institution for the Nordic countries was first launched in the late 1950's in connection with the discussions on a common Nordic customs union. But it was only with the failure of the NORDEK plan (a plan creating a Nordic Common Market) in 1970 that a Nordic investment bank became a serious topic of discussion. One can therefore say that the establishment of the Nordic Investment Bank (NIB, the Bank) was the concrete result of the NORDEK plan. The establishment was also spurred by the oil crisis in 1973, when the Nordic countries realized that a financial institution of high credit-worthiness would be needed to channel financial resources to the Nordic countries. Such an institution could help further Nordic economic integration by financing large investments, in particular in the en-

* The views expressed in this article are the personal views of the author and do not represent the official view of the Nordic Investment Bank.

ergy sector, to make the Nordic countries less dependent on imported energy. The actual process in establishing the Bank was then rather quick. The Nordic Council of Ministers, representing the Nordic governments, decided in February 1975 to set up a working group to put forward a proposal on the legal framework for the Bank. The proposal was presented to the Nordic Council, the parliamentary body of the Nordic countries. After getting the Nordic Council's opinion, the Nordic Council of Ministers moved on to sign the Agreement on Establishing the Bank (the Agreement) on December 4, 1975. The Agreement and the original Statutes appended thereto were subsequently subject to parliamentary approval and ratification in each of the Nordic countries. The Agreement came into force on June 1, 1976 and the Bank could officially start its operations.

II. THE LEGAL FRAMEWORK

A. The Agreement

From the preparatory work on the Bank's Agreement it is clear that the status of the Bank received relatively little attention. Rather, it was the need for a bank of this kind as well as where the headquarters should be located that was debated. In the race that took place on this issue Finland, which was in the lead because it did not at the time possess any significant Nordic institution, promised the Bank full diplomatic status. Some of the other Nordic countries however objected to this as it was thought that a bank which was supposed to primarily operate within the Nordic area would not need so far reaching privileges. Eventually it was decided that the headquarters of the Bank should be located in Helsinki and that the Bank was to be given tax exemptions on its assets and income mainly because the host country should not gain any direct benefits from the location of the Bank. The employees of the Bank were not granted any privileges or immunities and would pay taxes to the Finnish State on their salaries.

The Agreement itself was made very short according to the Nordic tradition, containing only eight articles. The preamble to the Agreement sets out the signatory governments' desire to establish the Bank to strengthen and further increase economic co-operation among the Nordic countries. The Bank should implement this general purpose by making loans and giving guarantees in accordance with regular banking practice taking into account socio-economic aspects to encourage investment projects and promote exports of Nordic interest. In Article 1 of the Agreement, which is reiterated in para. 1 of the Statutes, several important principles are embedded. First, the Bank should pursue its purpose by giving loans or guaranteeing loans only — no other forms of financing were envisaged. Second, it should grant its loans on commercial terms which implied, *inter alia,* market rates and sufficient security. Third, its lending should be of Nordic interest, a requirement that has posed many problems and intriguing situations for the Bank over the years.

Under the Agreement, it was further stated that the Bank shall possess full juridical personality (Article 1) and further in each of the contracting states be granted the same legal status as a domestic juridical person conducting operations similar to those of the Bank (Article 5). The Agreement also stipulated that operations of the Bank be exempt from payment restrictions and credit policy measures that in any way would prevent or impede the fulfillment of commitments made by the Bank. Furthermore, the assets of the Bank and its income were declared exempt from all direct taxation. Moreover, the Bank was to be exempt from any stamp duty or other official charges as regards loan agreements in which the Bank is a debtor.

The provisions mentioned above are all familiar exemptions that the multilateral financial institutions enjoy. However, under the Agreement, the Bank enjoyed no explicit immunity and very few privileges in comparison with such institutions. Nevertheless, the Nordic countries had those institutions in mind when creating the Nordic Investment Bank although they did not feel the necessity of providing a full scale of privileges and immunities for NIB.

B. The Statutes

The model for the Statutes of the Bank, in particular the capital structure, was taken from the European Investment Bank (EIB). The authorized capital stock of the Bank was initially 400 million SDR (Special Drawing Rights). The authorized capital stock is fully subscribed by the Member countries. Any increase in the authorized capital stock is to be distributed among the Member countries according to the allocation system for joint Nordic financing in effect at the time of the subscription, which is based on the Member countries' respective gross national income. No adjustments will be made with respect to capital already subscribed.

According to the Statutes, each Member country is obliged to make available to the Bank a portion of its share of the authorized capital stock as paid-in capital (originally one-fourth) while the remainder of the subscribed stock is subject to call to the extent the Board of the Bank deems it necessary for the fulfillment by the Bank of its debt obligations. The payments could be made in any convertible currency but were then converted to SDR. Since the capital was kept in SDR and the payment obligations expressed in SDR, no adjustment of the capital, or level payments by the Member countries were needed.[1]

The Bank's statutory lending limit is set at 250 percent of the authorized and subscribed capital. This is the same as with EIB. It was thought that this relatively high ceiling compared with other multilateral financial institutions would still be sufficient to attain a high credit rating due to the envisaged high quality of the loan portfolio.

Further guidelines for the Bank's lending operations were laid down in the Statutes:

A. A loan may not be made or a guarantee given if it is opposed by the country of the beneficiary.
B. Loans from and the investment of funds in the Nordic countries must be made in agreement with the authorities of the Member country concerned.
C. In its operations the Bank must aim for a profit allowing the formation of reserves and a reasonable return on the paid-in capital.
D. The Bank may under special circumstances acquire shares or other assets in order to avoid losses.

---

1 As of 1 April, 1993, NIB changed its currency of account and converted its authorized and paid-in capital from SDR to ECU. The ECU was subsequently changed to Euro from January 1, 1999.

E. The Bank shall to the extent that it is practically possible, protect itself against the risk of exchange losses.

The Bank is expected to earn a profit and should allocate its surplus to the reserve fund until it equals ten percent of the authorized capital stock. Thereafter, the Nordic Council of Ministers, after proposal of the Board of the Bank, is to decide upon the allocation of the surplus between the reserve fund and dividends on the subscribed capital.

As for the administration of the Bank, the Statutes stipulate that the Bank should have a non-resident Board consisting of ten members and an equal number of alternates, a President and necessary staff. All the powers are vested in the Board, which may delegate these powers to the President. Each Member country appoints two members of the Board and two alternates. Each member has one vote. The President is responsible for the conduct of the ordinary operations of the Bank and must follow the guidelines and instructions given by the Board.

To ensure that the operations of the Bank are conducted in accordance with its Statutes, a Control Committee is established by the Statutes which has the responsibility of delivering an annual audit report to the Nordic Council of Ministers. The Control Committee is composed of ten members, five being appointed by the Nordic Council of Ministers and five by the Nordic Council.

While there are no provisions for admitting additional members of the Bank, the Statutes deal with the withdrawal of a member country and with the liquidation of the Bank.

III. FIRST YEARS OF OPERATION; EXPERIENCES GAINED

A. Lending Activities

The lending activities started with few but rather big loans, the majority of them in the energy sector. The political debate concentrated on the Nordic interest of the Bank's loans and not very much attention was paid to the fact that one of the first loans went to finance a nuclear power plant in Finland. All the projects were safely within the boundaries of the Nordic countries so Norway's fear that the Bank would grant loans to the Soviet Union proved to be unfounded. Although no limitations were set in the Statutes, Norway in the beginning, in fact banned the Bank from the financing of projects outside the Nordic region. The ban was lifted a couple of years later. A statement in the Bank's annual report that it had financed projects of small- and medium-sized enterprises resulted in an elaborate discussion and the Bank was asked by the politicians to give a clear definition of the size of such enterprises. Occasional criticism was raised also about the necessity of a bank like NIB but these voices gradually became fewer and far between.

B. Funding Activities

At this time the international activities, i.e. activities outside the Member countries, were confined to the liability side of the Bank's balance sheet. The Statutes envisaged that the paid-in portion of the capital stock would be used for lending and accordingly, the first loans were granted in SDR. The borrowers were educated in how to borrow in a basket currency which in fact was no currency in itself only a unit of account. When the Bank was less than a year old in the spring of 1977, the time was right to introduce a new issuer in the Euromarket. The investment banks being active in London were fighting over the mandate to arrange NIB's first bond issue. A lot of surprises, mainly on the legal side, surfaced, which led the Bank to decide to make its first issue under Luxembourg law.

C. Identity Problems

The Bank encountered for the first but not the last time the fundamentals of the Anglo-American legal system. There were doubts raised whether the Bank in fact existed under New York law or under English law. Ten years earlier doubts of this kind had been raised in connection with the International Bank for Economic Co-operation — an international organization established in 1963 by a treaty between the Soviet Union and a number of East European States. Could such an organization be deemed to have sufficient legal capacity in English law to sue and be sued on loan contracts governed by English law and subject to the jurisdiction of the English courts?[2]

In early 1978 NIB investigated the question from the standpoint of New York law. The Bank's legal advisers (Messrs. Cleary, Gottlieb, Steen & Hamilton) arrived at the conclusion that NIB could in fact be sued and sue in the courts of the State of New York which was the likely jurisdiction for any contract NIB would enter into in the United States. Moreover, it was investigated whether NIB, when filing securities with the US Securities and Exchange Commission (SEC), in fact would be eligible as a Schedule B issuer rather than as a Schedule A borrower, the latter having to comply with much more detailed and complex requirements. The question put to the lawyers was:

> "Does the Nordic Investment Bank have juridical personality in the United States so that it may properly be named a defendant in a suit to recover on its notes or bonds upon its default in payment thereof?"

The advisers' main conclusion was that it would be highly unlikely that a U.S. Federal or State Court would refuse to exercise jurisdiction over the Bank in a suit to recover payment on its debts on the ground that it does not have legal personality. The opinion further confirmed that the Bank is a corporation of any one of or all its members, incorporated under municipal laws; it is an 'international organization,' a type of juridical entity which the United States recognizes; it is an unincorporated association within the meaning of the laws of the State of New York; it is an 'agency or instrumentality of a foreign state.' Also, according to the opinion, the question is mooted for the purposes of the U.S. securities laws, and arguably for many other purposes, if the Bank is permitted to register with the Securities and Exchange Commission (SEC), the securities it proposes to offer in the United States. If it is permitted to register the securities on a registration statement containing information called for in Schedule B to the Securities Act of 1933, this would presuppose agreement by the staff of the SEC that the Bank is 'a foreign government.'

---

2 *See* F.A. Mann, *International Corporations and National Law*, The British Yearbook of International Law 145 (1967).

In ascertaining their opinion, the lawyers pointed to Article 1 of the NIB Agreement, which stated that the Bank shall possess full juridical personality. This suggests in the opinion of the lawyers, the intention of creating legal existence without reference to the municipal laws of any of the contracting states, i.e., an entity with international or supra-national legal personality. The Agreement also stated that in each of the contracting states the Bank should be granted the same legal status as a domestic juridical personality conducting operations similar to those of the Bank. Certain of the contracting states have passed legislation or taken other steps to fulfill the obligation created by Article 5, thus also suggesting that one may view the Bank as a corporation duly formed under the municipal law of any one of these states. The conclusion of these articles being that there is both assertion of the international legal personality of the Bank as among the contracting states and *vis-à-vis* the world (Article 1), and a particular covenant by each contracting state to take the steps necessary within each of them to permit the entity to carry on its proposed functions as a long- term investment bank (Article 5). These Articles are not unique. Similar provisions may be found, e.g., in the Charter of the Asian Development Bank.

An international organization has juridical personality even in a non-member state. There is a lot of persuasive evidence that the U.S. Government recognizes that international organizations are individual legal entities. It can be likewise argued that the Bank is a corporation of one or more of its contracting states and that the courts should recognize its status on the basis of comity. In conclusion, on the part of offering securities in the U.S., the opinion recommends that NIB would seek no-action from the staff of SEC for registering as a Schedule B issuer with reference to previous cases by EIB and the European Economic Community and the European Atomic Energy Community as well as the European Coal and Steel Community.

To qualify as a foreign governmental entity within the meaning of the U.S. Securities Acts of 1933 and 1939, NIB had to stress its governmental nature as well as highlight the immunities and privileges in the no-action letter. In other words, the resemblance between NIB and the other multilateral financial institutions that had previously qualified should be emphasized. On the one hand, there was no doubt that NIB had been brought into existence for the purpose of implementing certain policies of its five member governments. On the other hand, the elements emphasized by the SEC up to that time had included several issues, which were only partially applicable to NIB, if at all, and therefore showed the Bank's different nature. If possible, the Bank should state that it was an instrument designed primarily to foster economic development and co-operation, not to make profit for its shareholders. The Bank should show proof of recognition by governments other than the Member countries in some ways, e.g., by appointment or accreditation to the Bank of an ambassador or other official of traditional diplomatic rank. Participation by the Bank in any intergovernmental agreements or treaties, such as an agreement with the International Monetary Fund, another international bank or organization or a government of a non-member state would be desirable. The Bank should show proof of the inviolability of the records and archives of the Bank in the territory of the member state; the immunity of suit of the officers and directors of the Bank with respect to the performance of their duties and *de facto* and *de jure* recognition of these privileges and immunities referred to above by any non-member state.

Despite the shortcomings of NIB in terms of SEC filing criteria, NIB was allowed to offer securities in the US in 1978 based on registration with the SEC as a Schedule B issuer.[3]

In May 1978, the lawyers in the United Kingdom that had previously been in doubt about the existence of certain international organizations under English law were inclined to revise their opinion based upon an exchange of letters between the Bank of England and the Foreign and Commonwealth Office. This correspondence would also prove to be of some significance later in the case of the Arab Monetary Fund.[4] The Bank of England letter dated April 21, 1978 by the Deputy Governor Sir Jasper Hollom seemed pretty straightforward asking essentially the following question:

> "What position does the Foreign and Commonwealth Office take concerning the legal personality and capacity in English law of financial entities, set up by a group of foreign sovereign states by a

[3] The Bank finally sought concurrence from the SEC on Dec. 4, 1981 and got the no-action from the SEC on December 30, 1981.

[4] *See* the discussion further below.

treaty (UK not being one of them) and empowering them to engage in financial activities in non-member states and conferring upon them legal personality in one or more states outside the UK?"

The answer by the Minister of State of the Foreign and Commonwealth Office, Frank Judd, Esq., seems to a layman at least as clear when he states in part as follows :

> "I am advised that a bank or other entity of the kind indicated in paragraph 2 of your letter would enjoy legal personality and capacity in this country, without any formal statement by or on behalf of Her Majesty's Government, in the same way and to the same extent as any other banking, commercial or other trading organisation established in a country other than the United Kingdom and enjoying legal personality and capacity in that country."

Regarding the capacity to enter into contract, the minister expressed that he was advised that:

> "[T]he capacity of such a bank or other legal entity to enter into loan or other contracts and to sue and be sued on them in this country does not depend upon the entity's being recognised by the United Kingdom Government."

Finally, the Foreign and Commonwealth Office stated that it favors entities of the type concerned being accepted as having sufficient legal personality and capacity to enter into transactions of this kind.

One opinion rendered by a lawyer from a well-known law firm in the United Kingdom in relation to the above correspondence uses more than twenty pages analyzing the grammar and sequence of words in the answer of the Foreign and Commonwealth Office. While it is presumably without merit to just take the letter at face value, it is hard to believe that all the aspects that the English lawyer brings out in the interpretation could have been considered in this fairly straightforward text. The conclusion, however, is that although there is no 100 percent certainty as to the standpoint of English law on the recognition of the entities in question in absence of authoritative judicial determination, a formal opinion on the subject would no longer need to be qualified.

This opinion and the changing legal position of legal entities such as NIB in the eyes of some learned scholars, inspired NIB's legal advisers, in their correspondence with reference to the opinion, to resort to 'Alice in Wonderland' by Lewis Carroll with the following quotes:

> "'Bye-the-bye, what became of the baby?' said the Cat. 'I'd nearly forgotten to ask.' 'It turned into a pig,' Alice quietly said, 'just as if it had come back in a natural way.'"
>
> . . .
>
> "'How puzzling all these changes are! I'm never sure what I'm going to be, from one minute to another! However, I've got back to my right size [. . .].'"

Yet, already in November the very same year doubts about the legal existence of certain international organizations appeared again. Dr. F. A. Mann states in an article in The Banker, *inter alia*, the following:[5]

> "These are organisations which are not formed under any system of national law. They are created by a treaty between states. They are governed by such treaty, supplemented by public international law in general. They have the status, capacity, powers, duties and functions defined by the treaty. They frequently do not have a territorial seat or office attributed to them but conclude so-called Headquarters Agreements with their host state. Even if the treaty itself provides for a seat in a certain country, such a provision does not remove the organisation from the realm of international law or subject it to the law of the country of the seat."

According to Dr. Mann, there are also certain organizations that create the appearance of being international ones but in truth they are created under the law of a given state. To which group do international organizations in the true sense of the word belong? Are they like private corporations or like states? The point had so far never been judicially considered in England and was

---

[5] *See* F.A. Mann, *Lending to International Organisations,* THE BANKER SUPPLEMENT 6 (November 1978).

thus far from clear. Dr. Mann seriously doubts that the Foreign and Commonwealth Office would really be willing to accept as an international subject any body corporate, which any group of states or other international organizations may choose to form. Dr. Mann further points out that some of these animals are, or may be, so odd that the views expressed by the Office in 1978 should not be given greater weight than the opinion of other reputable lawyers. Dr. Mann concludes that it must be doubted whether the last word on these problems has been spoken. The risk of the non-existence of the international organizations should, like the risk of immunity, be taken into account as one of the factors in assessing what is essentially a commercial and political, rather than a legal problem.

This again spurred our legal advisors into further literary excellence by quoting Alice in conversation with the Cheshire Cat:

> "'I wish you wouldn't keep appearing and vanishing so suddenly: you make one quite giddy!' 'All right,' said the Cat; and this time it vanished quite slowly, beginning with the end of the tail, and ending with the grin, which remained some time after the rest of it had gone. 'Well, I've often seen a cat without a grin,' thought Alice; 'but a grin without a cat! It's the most curious thing I ever saw in all my life!'"

IV. INTERNATIONAL LENDING ACTIVITIES START

As early as two years after the start-up, NIB was gradually getting ready to start to follow Nordic industry on its ventures into third countries. In the field of energy, forestry and telecommunications, among others, the bigger Nordic companies started exporting turnkey projects. Often these involved more than only one Nordic company and there seemed to be a clear niche for a long term financier which would not be tied to the rules of officially supported export credits. A study carried out by NIB led to a proposal to the Nordic Council of Ministers and to a decision by the Council of Ministers to establish the Project Investment Loan Facility (PIL) for NIB — initially on an interim basis. The formal framework of the Member country guarantees extended for this facility found its model once more from EIB and its financing under the Lomé convention. In July of 1982, the facility was made operational preceded by careful considerations about the modalities of financing as well as the possible impact the new activities would have on the Bank's credit standing.

The PIL-facility was originally established at the level of 350 million SDR out of which amount the Member countries guarantee ninety percent of each individual loan. The facility has been three times increased since and amounts as of January 1, 1999 to 3,300 million Euro.

The PIL-facility represented at the time thirty-five percent of the total ordinary lending capacity of the Bank. It was considered significant also because it represented a risk profile totally different from the one the Bank had been used to in the Nordic countries. NIB would be lending to middle-income developing countries as well as to state-controlled economies basically in Central and Eastern Europe and in the USSR.

NIB sought close co-operation with the World Bank, the Inter-American Development Bank as well as with other regional development banks. This was done not only for co-financing purposes but also to obtain the institutional support from these important agencies for the Bank's new activities. NIB set the maturities of its PIL-loans to match those of the World Bank loans. The guiding principle was that NIB would be granted the same treatment in terms of debt service as its powerful peers. This was not an unpretentious approach. Not only did NIB lack the mandate of a true development bank; it embarked on lending to governments of countries that were not members of the Bank. Hence the recipient countries had very little influence on the Bank's decisions concerning lending to them. With the relatively limited resources that the Bank had at its disposal under the facility, the recipient countries could not count on a continuous positive cash flow from the Bank. In addition, the Bank had to observe the requirement of Nordic interest in its projects, which very often was viewed by others as constituting tied financing.

NIB also regularly required the borrowing governments to accept privileges for it, which were not explicitly granted to it by its own Member countries. To get accepted as belonging to the group of multilateral lenders was therefore a big challenge for NIB. The acceptance was required not only from the borrowers but also from the other multilateral banks, official and commercial creditors, from rating agencies as well as from other international organizations such as the Organisation for Economic Co-operation and Development (OECD). This acceptance would usually not take the form of explicit agreements but rather come about in the form of implicit behavior or action in a particular situation. However, it was felt in NIB that some kind of visible support was needed at least from one of the most important players. Hence, concurrently with the establishment of the PIL-facility, NIB concluded the first Memorandum of Understanding with the World Bank. NIB also had discussions with the OECD-secretariat about its lending under the PIL-facility stressing the distinction between NIB's lending and officially supported export credits. This of course aimed at excluding NIB's lending from debt rescheduling in the Paris club.

In the first years of the PIL-facility, NIB sought approval of its policies and its status directly in, or in connection with, individual loan agreements with its borrowers. Later NIB started to negotiate separate framework agreements with its government counter-parties also in countries where NIB was the only multilateral lending source. The purpose of these agreements was to get general acceptance for NIB's lending policies and to set the priority areas for financing. Recently, when NIB has also been gradually moving into the private sector, the framework agreements have grown in importance establishing the legal ground for NIB to embark on lending activities in any target country.

To induce new countries to sign such an agreement giving the Bank in those countries an even better status than it enjoys at home, proved difficult. This fact was one of the major reasons for NIB to propose to its Member countries to revise the Bank's establishment agreement. But this was still some years away from the time when the Soviet Union collapsed and defaulted on its foreign debt. NIB, as the only multilateral lender to the USSR at the time, had in relation to its overall activities a fairly sizeable Russian exposure. NIB had not had any success in convincing its Soviet borrowers to explicitly accept its policy regarding debt service or rescheduling of debt. The concept of preferred creditor was established by the Bretton Woods institutions of which the Soviet Union was not a member at the time. NIB' s loans were nevertheless serviced without any interruption and the debt to NIB was excluded from rescheduling both in the London club and the Paris club. This represented the most tangible result of acceptance of

NIB's status although NIB had had a previous positive experience also in the former Socialist Federal Republic of Yugoslavia in the early 1980's.

V. THE CREDIT RATING IS QUESTIONED

In the autumn of 1990 a new problem for NIB surfaced suddenly when the rating agency Moody's, in issuing a warning for downgrading of the debt of the Kingdom of Sweden, also put NIB on its watch-list. This turned out to be Moody's interpretation of the ceiling concept, namely that no national entity in a country could have a higher rating than the state itself. At the time all other Member countries of NIB rated by Moody's had lost their triple A-rating and Sweden, NIB's biggest member country, was about to lose its top rating. It looked like NIB's fate was sealed. The market already discounted a downgrading into NIB's bond prices but the Bank was not inclined to give up. Consultants familiar with the rating agencies' way of thinking were hired and NIB's international lawyers started to work on arguments and stress tests including different scenarios on the impact of a lowered rating of its Member countries, on NIB's ability to service its debt. The exercise showed that NIB would be able to honor its obligations even if its Member countries and its Nordic borrowers would default on their obligations towards NIB. For once ironically, the loan portfolio that NIB had established in the developing countries served as the stronghold in various domino theories. Sweden was eventually downgraded, NIB fought a 100-day war with the rating agency and on the day the Gulf war ended, Moody's removed NIB from the watch-list and confirmed its Aaa-rating.

VI. THE CASE OF THE ARAB MONETARY FUND; THE EXISTENCE ISSUE REVISITED

Having successfully managed to gain acceptance of NIB as a serious and reliable borrower and lender in important markets of the world, it was time for NIB to look for new challenges. However, before that was to happen, an incident occurred that for a while meant that English law for the second time banished NIB to the embarrassing status of non-existence and proved the prophecy of Dr. Mann.

In 1989, the Arab Monetary Fund begun proceedings in the Chancery Division of the High Court in England against its former Director General (*The Arab Monetary Fund* v. *Jawad Mahmoud Hashim and Others*). The Fund was established by treaty by a number of sovereign states and its Articles of Agreement contained all the relevant provisions for creating a legal person. But the UK was not a member nor did the Fund maintain an establishment in the UK. The defendant tried to get an order striking out the proceedings upon the grounds that the Fund had no capacity to sue in English courts. The Judge upheld the capacity of the Fund to sue in English courts on the grounds that the Fund had been constituted under a system of domestic law and should therefore be recognized as an ordinary foreign juridical entity.[6] The second ground argued by the Fund was that English law recognizes the existence of a legal entity constituted under international law the same way as one that is constituted under a foreign system of law. However, in the *Tin* case [7] the House of Lords held that English law did no such thing in the absence of specific statutory provision.

The Supreme Court of Judicature Court of Appeal Civil Division did allow the appeal and struck out the action although with greatest possible reluctance and without any enthusiasm. The Master of the Rolls stated:

> "As I see it, absent an order in Council, an international organisation is something which, in the eyes of English law is as much a fact as a tree, a road or a hill. But it is not a person and the law can only deal in the rights and liabilities of persons. Once it is touched by the magic wand of the Order in Council it becomes a person. But equally it is not a United Kingdom juridical person. Nor is it a

6 *See* Hoffman J, November 14, 1989.

7 *See J.H. Rayner, (Mincing Lane) Limited* v. *Department of Trade and Industry* [1989] 1 W.L.R. 969.

foreign juridical person. It is a person *sui generis,* which has all the capacities of a United Kingdom person, but is not subject to the controls to which such a person is subject under United Kingdom law. It is not a native nor is it a visitor from abroad. It comes from the invisible depths of outer space."

The long awaited (and in light of the *Tin* case) somewhat surprising decision by the House of Lords came in February 1991. The House of Lords restored the order of Hoffman J. In the deliberations in the House, the before-mentioned correspondence from the Foreign and Commonwealth Office was cited and special emphasis was put on the following:

> "[O]n the assumption that the entity concerned enjoys, under its constitutive instrument [. . .] and under the law of one or more member states or the state wherein it has its seat or permanent location, legal personality and capacity to engage in transactions of the type concerned governed by the law of a non-member state, the [FCO] [. . .] would be willing officially to acknowledge that the entity concerned enjoyed such legal personality and capacity [. . .]."

The House of Lords further stated:

> "[A]lthough a treaty cannot become part of the law of the United Kingdom without intervention of Parliament, the recognition of foreign states is a matter for the Crown to decide and by comity the courts of the United Kingdom recognise a corporate body created by the law of a foreign state recognised by the Crown."

Although the House of Lords finally gave the authoritative judicial determination to the issue on whether certain international organizations existed under English law, one can wonder whether common law always can be regarded as common sense.

VII. BALTIC INVESTMENT PROGRAM

In early 1991, the Nordic Council of Ministers entrusted NIB with the task of exploring investment opportunities in the Baltic states.

Some moves towards increased independence from the Soviet Union were already quite visible in the Baltic states but the fully regained independence was still around the corner and not really foreseen by anyone. However, the study was expanded to include also a financial mechanism to be set up for this region as it was found that available financing would be a prerequisite for any investments in the region. When the study was finalized, a lot of important events had indeed taken place. Not only had the three Baltic states become independent countries once again but also the European Bank for Reconstruction and Development (EBRD) had been officially established. Based on the study, the Nordic Council of Ministers and the Governments of the Baltic countries in a joint resolution set up the Baltic Investment Programme (BIP) in March 1992. This started a venture that would take NIB more closely into non-member country operations than ever before. For the first time NIB would finance primarily private sector projects in countries with virtually no legal infrastructure for private enterprise activities and no experience in financing those enterprises on commercial terms. In addition, the legal system based on Western principles created in the 1920's had been lost for a generation and was unknown to the young people who immediately took over in business life.

Being an international financial institution, it was important for NIB to get the recognition of its status and policies in the Baltic countries. This did not prove an easy task. Since NIB asked for more privileges than its Member countries originally had accorded it, it was particularly tough to ask the small Baltic countries to concede to immunities and privileges for the Bank. In some way this reminded them of a form of sovereignty in relation to themselves that they just had been able to get rid of. In the end, the status agreements signed with all three countries and ratified during the spring of 1994 proved to be not only comprehensive but useful instruments in putting NIB both politically and commercially on the map in these countries. None of the three countries have so far had serious problems in servicing their official debt, but they have certainly already in their short history as reborn independent nations experienced the volatility of a market economy, where one cannot hide the problems and where one is very likely to be hit hard by crises in nearby areas. NIB has been fairly successful in its financing in the Baltic countries both in the private sector under the BIP but also in the public sector under PIL. This is largely due to the fact that NIB through both technical assistance and equity investments in the financial institutions it has assisted in establishing, has gained thorough experience of the conditions prevailing in those markets. As a small institution close to the Baltic countries, NIB has also been able to adapt and show greater flexibility in its operations in the region compared to the larger and more rigidly run international financial institutions.

VIII. ENVIRONMENTAL INVESTMENT LOANS IN 1997

A small financial institution such as NIB will have to prove its *raison d'être* from time to time. It is therefore important that NIB develops new ideas and is willing to take on tasks when so required by the Nordic countries. For many years in the Nordic countries it had been discussed on high political level what could be done to reduce the pollution in the adjacent areas. It was consequently natural that NIB was given a mandate to grant loans for investments directed to improving the environment in the Baltic Sea region. The target areas include Poland, the Baltic countries and the north-western part of Russia. The Nordic Council of Ministers decided upon the Environmental Loan Facility in August 1996 and in 1997 NIB was ready to grant the first loans under this facility. Environmental projects are characterized by long lead times being often also politically difficult to implement. It is therefore not so surprising that NIB had until the end of 1999 only disbursed one loan while the facility was almost fully committed. The facility has also enabled NIB to re-assume its lending to the Russian Federation, which virtually came to a halt with the fall of the Soviet Union. As mentioned before NIB has a good track record in getting its loans serviced by the Soviet Union and now by Russia, but NIB's risk classification of Russia today still hampers significantly the Bank's operations involving regular investment projects there. All other formalities are in place since NIB managed during 1996 to 1998 to negotiate a status agreement with Russia, which was subsequently approved by the Duma. There is, of course, a great potential for NIB to lend to and in Russia under the right circumstances not at least because of the geographical proximity of Russia with many of the Nordic countries. Russia shares a land border with both Finland and Norway but is also closely connected by the sea to Sweden and Denmark.

IX. NEW LEGAL FRAMEWORK — STRUGGLE FOR RECOGNITION

A. The Preparation Process

In the midst of increased activities internationally, specifically in the adjacent areas and Central and Eastern Europe, an increasingly obvious need occurred to adjust the legal framework for the Bank. As mentioned in the beginning, NIB started out as a common bank in the Nordic countries to cater to projects within the Nordic countries. However, in the early 1990's it turned out that NIB played a relatively more important role for Nordic industry outside the Nordic countries rather than within. Hence NIB's profile as a multilateral financial institution was reinforced. But the legal framework did not reflect this. In 1995, when Sweden and Finland had joined Denmark as members of the European Union, NIB felt that the time was right to present the idea of a new framework to the Nordic countries. Up till then NIB had been in general quite successful in convincing both its borrowers as well as its peers and the commercial banking community of its rooted policies and its wish to be treated as a preferred creditor. With time though, NIB realized that it might be difficult to maintain a special status that was not formally laid down and acknowledged in its constitutive documents by its own Member countries.

Once again NIB took model from EIB, which by now had three of NIB's Member countries among its members. The draft of an amended framework was handed over to Finland, which happened to be not only NIB's host country but also had the chair in the Nordic Council of Ministers in 1996. The Finnish Ministry of Finance put together a working group with members from some other ministries to explore the possibilities for the Finnish authorities to change the status of NIB. The working group concluded that there were very few possibilities and not much need to change the treatment of NIB in its host country. In any case, most of the action required would be such that also the Bank's other Member countries had to be involved. In January 1997, a new working group was formed among the Nordic countries consisting of civil servants mainly from tax departments. This working group handed over their report to the committee of civil servants from ministries of finance and economy of the Nordic countries. The committee is in charge of preparing issues for decision making by the Nordic Council of Ministers (the preparatory committee).

In June of 1997, the Nordic Council of Ministers in reality took its decision to go ahead in revising the legal framework. It stressed the necessity of enhancing the multilateral nature of the Bank and also underlined the importance of solving the pension issues concerning both the Bank and the staff which had been pending since 1993.

After an expert report on the subject of the legal status of the Bank and its staff in relation to its host government was delivered, the Bank was asked in October 1997 to prepare the first revised draft for a legal framework. The preparatory committee required quite a number of alterations before the matter was again discussed in the Nordic Council of Ministers on November 10, 1997. This time, the Council of Ministers was extremely firm in its decision. It expected a new legal framework to be ready by January 1, 1998, and that the Bank and its host country Finland would also agree upon the details concerning the tax treatment of the staff and the already mentioned pension issues in a headquarters agreement.

Real negotiations started in the preparatory committee to which meetings NIB was occasionally invited. It was indeed a bit frustrating to watch from the sideline how the discussions progressed. Simultaneously with the progress on the text of the new agreement, NIB wanted to proceed with the headquarters agreement. After having studied at least ten different agreements, NIB prepared a first draft which was very much based on precedence found in other international organizations located in Helsinki, but also involving a few elements of what was stipulated for example in EBRD's headquarters agreement with United Kingdom. NIB on its part felt the importance of trying as closely as possible to meet the unrealistic deadlines decided upon by the Nordic Council of

Ministers. In particular, there was a need to formalize the open issues on how to solve and implement the questions embedded in the Council's decision from November. The Government of Finland took a different approach. First, in their opinion there was no immediate need to elaborate on the tax and pension issues in the headquarters agreement since the Council's decision was clear enough and binding upon the Government and NIB. Second, the headquarters agreement should be drafted ideally only after the new agreement was ready. The headquarters agreement should cover only issues left out of the new treaty. It was therefore not until June 1998 that the Government of Finland delivered its first response in the form of their own draft for a headquarters agreement.

In the meantime the new agreement on NIB moved into its final shape. First of all, it was decided to work on a completely new agreement instead of trying to amend and supplement the old one. For the sake of clarity it was a good choice but for the sake of continuity it proved to be slightly complicated. The Bank had after all been established and in existence under one agreement which would now be completely substituted for a new agreement which essentially would not change the status of the Bank but would elaborate and clarify it. The preparatory committee felt that there was little need to stipulate on all issues. Particularly on issues where the representatives of the different Member countries could not agree it was felt better to leave the issues out altogether.

The final agreement consists of seventeen articles. In the end, the most difficult articles were the ones which related to the travel facilities and immunity from immigration restrictions for the staff and their families. Some Member countries were preoccupied with preferential treatment, which possibly would have consequences under the EU-regulations. Some Member countries did not like wording used in the EIB agreement because they had not approved it before and therefore wanted to use wordings from EBRD's agreement instead. The result was a mixture between wording used in agreements with a very Anglo-Saxon influence and the fairly short straightforward texts common for treaties among the Nordic countries. One of the peculiarities of the new agreement is found in Article 16, which regulates the entry into force of the new agreement. It says that once the agreement has entered into force, the provisions of Article 9 shall be applied from January 1, 1998. Article 9 deals with tax issues.

In the proposal to the Nordic Council of Ministers, the idea was to further elaborate and give more in-depth explanations to the wording used for the articles of the new agreement. The proposal suffered, however, from the same difficulties as the text itself. The proposal mainly reiterated the general reasons for a new legal framework and the text of the articles themselves. The Nordic Council of Ministers approved the text of the new agreement in June 1998. They also required that the headquarters agreement should be attached to the bill to parliament seeking approval of the new agreement. The headquarters agreement therefore had to be finalized in a hurry. This lead to a peculiar stipulation in the headquarters agreement on the settlement of disputes, which has to be viewed as a purely political compromise rather than a legal solution.[8]

The next step was then to find a common procedure and timetable for the signature of the new agreement and the subsequent parliamentary procedure and the ratification process. Again, timetables envisaged where moved. On October 23, 1998, the new agreement was finally signed.

In NIB there had been hopes for an entry into force one year after the first deadline, namely on January 1, 1999. On that day, the fourth capital increase was in place as well as some substantially expanded lending limits for the international lending. Both of those issues involved serious strategic deliberations; yet they were approved and executed in the Member countries in much shorter time-period than the new legal framework, which essentially only enhanced and in very few aspects expanded the privileges of the Bank itself. The economical effects to the Member countries being negligible except maybe for the host country.

After some lengthy national deliberations in the Nordic countries, on June 18, 1999, the Norwegian Ministry for Foreign Affairs

---

8 The headquarter agreement stipulates in Article 5 that a dispute between the Government and the Bank that cannot be settled amicably, shall be settled by decision of the Nordic Council of Ministers. The Council, where the Finnish government is represented, can however only make decisions by consensus.

as depository finally declared the agreement to become effective on July 18, 1999. In Finland the agreement became part of domestic law on July 21, 1999.

B. Main Principles of the New Agreement

What then is now different for NIB? In short, as mentioned above, the old agreement was drafted for a basically Nordic institution, hence there was little need for a more international dimension. The first article of the Bank's new agreement (the New Agreement) has been changed to reflect a common interest, a more global approach to NIB's financing. It is no longer sufficient that the Bank's lending is in line with Nordic priorities alone, in addition the financing should have better focus on the priorities and needs of the recipient country. There should, in other words, be more value added for all parties involved. This new approach which politically could be rather interesting and worth discussing was unanimously approved without a single word of discussion. Article 2, which describes the Bank as an international legal person received a lot of attention by the different civil servants, involved in the drafting. Some of them where reluctant to include a comparison with other legal persons both international and domestic because they felt that this could also create for NIB further privileges and immunities in as far as the others would have more extensive privileges than NIB. The reference to other legal persons is therefore embedded in the preamble to the New Agreement.

The next significant change from the old Agreement is found in Article 5 which is new and contains the waiver of implied and explicit immunity which is normally connected with international financial institutions. The text of Article 5 was the result of long discussions although in principle it bears a strong resemblance to the similar articles of IBRD and EBRD agreements. Previously, NIB lacked all treaty provisions on immunity from jurisdiction and enforcement and even those on property and assets, which are now provided for in Article 6. Articles 7 and 8, which are also new, deal with the premises, the archives and the official communication. Article 9 deals with taxes and other duties. While NIB's property and assets previously were exempt from all direct taxes, the Bank is now virtually exempt from all taxes and other dues. The same goes for trust funds managed by the Bank. To illustrate the difficulty in agreeing on the wording of this article it can be mentioned that it took several months to agree on one particular word in the article. Articles 10 and 11 concern the immunities and privileges of the members of the Board, the Bank's staff and experts used. While none of these articles existed in the old agreement, it is worth noting that the staff of the Bank still pay taxes to the host state. The seven articles in the New Agreement mentioned are the ones that contain the expanded privileges, while the other articles are essentially repetitions from the old legal framework.

In the legal framework the question of functional necessity is brought forward in Article 14 as an explanation for the privileges and immunities. There has been the idea behind the new legal framework to use a consistent terminology to address the specific functional needs of international financial organizations.

It was therefore quite surprising to find out in discussions with some of the representatives of the Member countries concerning the implications of the tax exemptions, that they did not think NIB qualified as an international organization. For them, an organization with only five member states could hardly be international, and secondly, the type of activities carried out did have little to do with the activities of the most commonly known international organizations. In some respects, NIB was to be treated the same way as foreign missions, in some respects again NIB was to fall under exceptional treatment and tax exemptions which originally were created for totally different circumstances and not seldom had socio-political connotations.

The thinking is also reflected in the headquarters agreement. It was for a long time assumed by the Bank that the headquarters agreement would have the status of domestic law in Finland. The host country, however, argued that there was little need for that since the agreement they preferred did not in any significant way repeat anything from the agreement on the Bank itself. Hence it was only implemented by a presidential decree. Yet this is the only agreement that covers the tax reimbursement on taxes paid by the staff on their salaries and mentions the pension for the staff.

It became clear very early that tax exemptions for the staff would be a very difficult issue in connection with the revision of the framework agreement. This in fact turned out to be impossible to implement. However, the Member countries still were firm in their position that the host country should not derive any particular benefits from the location of NIB. Therefore, Finland ultimately agreed to reimburse to the Bank the taxes collected from the Bank's staff. This could essentially have been achieved in the model of self-taxation as NIB had suggested and for which there even was precedence in the Nordic countries. This has, however, to be seen as one of those political compromises which do not always feel quite rational.

Recent exercises in retroactive employment of reimbursement of taxes paid from January 1, 1998 to date according to the New Agreement have proven the difficulties both legally and practically in such an unorthodox concept. These are, however, only examples of the changes that have to take place both internally and in the mind-set of the authorities in the Member countries.

X. SUMMARY

Within the limited scope of this article, there has been an attempt to show how the Nordic Investment Bank, a child of its time, has developed trying to adapt to a radically changing world. During its twenty–four years of history the Bank has met several legal and operational challenges. The Bank works both in the private and the public sector in the most developed areas of the world, in western democracies as well as in less developed areas and centrally planned economies. The Bank should co-operate both with commercial banks as well as with other international financial institutions among them the multilateral development banks. This requires great flexibility, but at the same time, consistent behavior not to distort and blur the profile of the Bank. During its existence, the Bank has reached and passed several important milestones. After NIB had been established with a capital of 400 million SDR, the capital was raised in 1984 to 800 million SDR and in 1987 again doubled to 1,600 million SDR. In 1993 the third capital increase took place first bringing the capital to 2,400 million SDR but then converting it to approximately 2,800 million ECU. The fourth capital increase took effect from beginning of 1999 and the capital is now 4,000 million Euro bringing the ordinary lending limit for loans mainly in the Nordic region up to 10,000 million Euro. Simultaneously, the international lending facilities of the Bank have grown since 1982, when the PIL-facility was first introduced, from 350 million SDR almost tenfold to over 3,400 million Euro. The Bank has financed projects in over forty countries world-wide. It has got itself a totally new legal framework and very few now doubt its existence from a legal point of view. But there is neither time nor room for complacency. The Bank is small and must stand ready to meet new challenges and demands. The Member countries have got an international financial organization, which is recognized as such also outside of the signatories of the new treaty. Will the Member countries look at the Bank as Shakespeare? Will they recognize its privileges and their privilege to have such a unique instrument to carry out the mandate given by them to their benefit as well as to that of the recipient countries? Only time will tell! Let us at least hope that the cat will stop disappearing!

NOTES ON THE FOUNDING OF THE INTER-AMERICAN INVESTMENT CORPORATION

*Raul R. Herrera**

I. INTRODUCTION

The Inter-American Investment Corporation (IIC) was organized when the Agreement on the Establishment of the Inter-American Investment Corporation was signed in Washington, D.C., in November 1984. The IIC was established as an affiliate of the Inter-American Development Bank (the IDB), and it became operational upon the approval by its Board of Executive of its first financing transaction in 1989. The signing event in 1984 was the formal commencement of an international financial institution that focuses on promoting the economic development of Latin America and the Caribbean. Its establishment took several years from when it was first discussed amongst its shareholders and the IDB. The original concept of establishing a multilateral mechanism to encourage the establishment, expansion, and modernization of local private enterprises in the region, preferably those that are small and medium size, appeared in the late 1960s. There were numerous studies, meetings and deliberations prior to the IIC's start-up.

This note is in two parts: the first part describes the early years giving rise to the concept of the IIC and the environment in which it was launched, and the second part reviews the first ten years of IIC's operations (1989–1999). The review undertaken in

* The opinions expressed in this article are the author's personal views and do not necessarily represent those of the institution he works for.

the first part is interesting from the perspective of how the establishment of the IIC was a response to the region's social and economic needs and aspirations during that period.

II. THE ECONOMIC BACKGROUND OF THE REGION

During the second half of the last century, there was an important change in the original industrialization model, which reflected the particular evolution of policies. Initially, Latin America was pursuing a strategy of import substitution through high protective tariff walls, quantitative limitations on imports, and subsidized financing of investments. An important shift in the original model followed when the conclusion was reached that Latin American and Caribbean industry had to be modernized and become efficient if it was to continue its dynamic growth. Toward this end it would be necessary to lower tariff barriers and widen market possibilities, permit the establishment of larger production units, and lower the cost of goods in order to promote exports. Some of the economic thinkers of this period foresaw that Latin America would need to increase the efficiency of its labor force, improve management and administrative techniques, and take advantage of economies of scale. In other words, obsolete industries would have to be upgraded and the process of industrial integration accelerated.

The production processes in manufacturing and agribusiness in Latin America required large sums of financing and investment that, within that continent, was insufficient for the needs at large. This financing scarcity affected small and medium scale private enterprises, which faced problems similar to those confronting the industry in general. However, such enterprises had even less access to financial and capital markets and technical assistance to ensure efficient production. Due to its terms, equity financing has in the long run been a better way to finance private small enterprises without subjecting them to the debt service pressures found in loan financing. Thus, equity financing appears to be more effective as a developmental technique. Even though the IDB has made significant efforts to directly promote the development of small and medium size enterprises, the lack of equity capital is a major impediment to this sector's growth, and the IDB's Articles of

Agreement do not permit it to make equity investments. In 1975, the Government of Venezuela, as an IDB shareholder, agreed with the IDB to the establishment of a trust fund, setting the stage leading to the establishment, years later, of the IIC. It was also an important signal of support for Latin America's private sector. With this trust fund, the IDB entered the field of developmental equity investment and laid the groundwork for a future investment mechanism.

III. THE INITIAL CONCEPT: THE REGIONAL FINANCE CORPORATION

The Tenth Annual Meeting of the Board of Governors of the IDB was held in Guatemala City in April 1969. The meetings were the first stages of the process that led to the establishment of the IIC. One of the underlying themes addressed in the round-table sessions was the furthering of the industrialization of Latin America, including the feasibility of establishing a regional agency to support the development of Latin American private sector enterprises. The proposed agency would include members from industrialized countries not part of the Inter-American system that would contribute financial resources, management experience and technical know-how. The proposed agency would supplement the efforts of the IDB in relation to small and medium size private enterprises, have equity investment authority, finance working capital, extend guarantees, and contribute to the mobilization of private and public capital with a modern entrepreneurial approach.

The Board of Governors of the IDB requested additional research that would include, *inter alia,* "an analysis of the possibility of establishing an organization, subsidiary to the bank, for the financing of industries through loans and investment." The Board of Executive Directors of the IDB also requested that the research discuss the: (a) financing needs of the industrial sector in Latin America, including the role of the public and private sector and types of financing instruments available; (b) obstacles to channeling domestic savings to industrial investments; (c) experiences of national, regional and international organizations in industrial financing and in financing non-traditional activities; and (d) the future organization's possible functions, financial structure and administrative organization. The research was led by the reputed economist Raul Prebish and a team of experts from Latin America, Europe and the United States. (The group of experts included, among others, Enrique V. Iglesias, current President of the IDB and Chairman of the Board of Executive Directors of the IIC and then Chairman of the Board of Directors of the Latin American Institute for Economic and Social Planning and former President of the Central Bank of Uruguay). The proposed name for the agency was the Regional Finance Corporation. At the following Annual Meeting of the Board of Governors in Punta del Este, Uruguay, in April 1970, discussions ensued regarding the proposed new agency.

The group of experts' meetings continued through the year, with recommendations focusing on the establishment of a regional finance agency to provide financial support to Latin American industrial firms, principally those in the private sector. The proposed agency would have the following purposes: (i) to promote enterprises and finance non-traditional exports; (ii) to finance equity investments, medium-term working capital loans for the purchase of capital goods of domestic origin and for local expenses and investments in industrial projects, and to guarantee the obligations of third parties; (iii) to furnish technical advisory services for the transfer of technology; (iv) to further the participation of other institutions in its financial activities; and (v) to create new instruments for tapping national savings that will make it possible to channel such savings toward the financing of industrial development.

The new financing mechanism would possess independent legal status and decision-making procedures, and would have the task of balancing dual goals of obtaining profitability by generating an adequate return on capital while making a significant contribution promoting the region's economic and social development. Since equity capital was limited, it was suggested that the agency take minority interests in companies (ten percent to thirty-five percent); and since its financing required certain transparency, it was also suggested that such companies use external auditors, be subject to annual audits, introduce sound accounting systems, and regularly distribute financial statements. A major concern regarding the new agency's relationship with the IDB was that it not affect the IDB's risk perception in the capital markets. Accordingly, several possibilities for the new financing mechanism were analyzed, such as it being an IDB division, subsidiary or branch; a joint venture with majority or minority participation of the IDB; or an independent institution in which the Bank would not own stock. In the end, the recommended alternatives were reduced to either establishing an affiliated agency, as the International Finance Corporation (IFC) is affiliated with the World Bank, or an independent organization without any participation of or affiliation with the IDB. The findings of the group of experts was submitted to the IDB at its Twelfth Annual Meeting of the Board of Governors in Lima, Peru, in May 1971. The Governors were receptive to the findings and instructed the Board of Executive Directors to initiate contacts with member countries while using the IDB as an information clearinghouse.

IV. DISCUSSIONS CONTINUE: THE VENEZUELAN TRUST AND MULTINATIONAL FUND

The decade of the 1970s brought financial volatility to the region. The decade was marked by oil price hikes and crises, banks' need to recycle dollar surpluses, and the United States' abandonment of fixed parity. These events exacerbated the structural weaknesses of Latin American economies so that the development pattern of the prior twenty-five years was modified by domestic policies driven by the flows of financial resources, fiscal reform and individual adjustments. Many of the non-oil-producing countries of the region were in economic difficulty. As a result, the findings for the Regional Finance Corporation were tabled for a later date.

Drawing on the human resources and technical experience of the IDB, a US$20 million trust fund administered by the IDB was proposed by the Government of Venezuela to invest equity in small and medium size regional enterprises. The principal features of eligible equity investments and operating parameters of the proposed fund were: (w) investments of US$150,000 to US$2,000,000; (x) for minority interests from fifteen percent to thirty-three percent of the capital of enterprises; (y) in enterprises whose share capital is at least eighty percent owned by Latin American shareholders; and (z) in enterprises of intermediate size located in the IDB member countries that are relatively less developed and/or with limited markets. By year-end 1981, the fund had approved investments in six projects for a total of US$4.6 million. During the second half of the 1970s, the region's economic growth slowed down compared with previous years, resulting in a decrease in demand for goods, a cutback in industrial investments, and an increase in imports, thus creating a balance of payments deficit. At the XXth Annual Meeting of the Board of Governors, held in Montego Bay, Jamaica, in 1979, discussions ensued about establishing a Multilateral Investment Fund that would expand operations started by the Venezuelan Trust Fund. At the meeting, the then IDB President stated in support of this initiative:

> "Another objective that has long been emphasized by the countries of the region is that of helping to strengthen Latin American businesses by investing in share capital. A first step in this direction was the allocation of up to US$20,000,000 for these purposes from the Trust Fund made available by the Government of Venezuela. . . . This has encouraged us to begin consultations with our member countries with a view to establishing the Latin American Multinational Fund for Industrial Development with enough capital to meet a long felt need in the region. Businessmen in most Latin American countries need risk capital in very large volumes and are often compelled to operate under a heavy burden of indebtedness, which in adverse circumstances can jeopardize the very existence of the enterprise. Moreover, this program could open the door to an international market for securities floated by Latin American firms and so make possible the issuance of obligations convertible into stock."

Interests persisted over the years among several member countries of the IDB to support a new multilateral trust fund. The subject was included for discussion in the agenda of the XXIInd Annual Meeting of the Board of Governors in Madrid, Spain, in 1981, and subsequent meetings were held among the IDB member countries. In general terms, a framework agreement was being molded as to the orientation and priorities of the fund. The focus of such a fund would be to finance small and medium size enterprises in countries that were relatively less developed and with limited markets, to mitigate the problems caused by insufficient capitalization of this sector in Latin America. The fund would be authorized to invest in equity, make direct loans, provide technical assistance, act as financial agent, and help to mobilize new financial resources for the region. The Governors of the IDB were apprised of these developments, and they requested that further studies be conducted.

In early 1982, an initial proposal for the creation of a multinational trust fund was submitted to the IDB Board of Governors with the following characteristics: (a) the principal direct investment activity would be in medium scale enterprises, in association with local, regional and international financial institutions; (b) assistance to small enterprises would be given through private financial institutions; and (c) the mechanism could be established either as a trust fund or a separate entity in the form of an investment company affiliated with the IDB. The proposal focused on the importance of small and medium size enterprises to the economies of Latin America, particularly because of their impact on employment generation, contribution to value-added production, production of a distributive impact, and enhancement of the practical training of the labor force. It was thought that small and medium size enterprises faced significant problems that called for the use of public funds through bilateral or international programs. After subsequent discussions, it was concluded that the tasks to be undertaken by the financing mechanism would best be entrusted to an independent organization with an independent decision-making process, even if it were affiliated with the IDB. This possible affiliation led to the consideration of an alternative institutional framework other than a trust fund, including the possibility of establishing an independent investment corporation affiliated with the IDB but with its own capital, management and activities.

The revised proposal submitted to the IDB Board of Governors in 1982 considered the establishment of an affiliated multilateral institution named the Inter-American Investment Corporation. Several meetings were held in different capital cities over the course of the following twelve months to discuss the constitutive document, until agreement was reached by twenty-four member countries of the IDB in a meeting in Rome in 1983. The following year, the Agreement Establishing the IIC and the accompanying resolution were submitted for consideration at the XXVth Annual Meeting of the Board of Governors held in Punta del Este, Uruguay. The Agreement Establishing the IIC was signed by thirty-four founding member countries in November 1984 in Washington,

D.C. In 1986, the inaugural meeting of the IIC Board of Governors was held in Caracas, Venezuela, at which the first Board of Executive Directors was elected.

V. LATIN AMERICA AND THE CARIBBEAN REGION

The IIC's mandate is to promote the economic development of its regional developing member countries by encouraging the establishment, expansion and modernization of private enterprises, especially those of small and medium size. It commenced operations in late 1989 and pursues its mandate through two main areas of activity: first, directly through project financing or merchant banking operations, and second, indirectly through financial sector or capital markets activities. The IIC's projects must be commercially viable, preferably majority-owned by nationals of Latin America or the Caribbean, and for which traditional financing would otherwise not be available under adequate terms. Before describing the IIC's diverse activities and ten-year performance in greater detail, the following describes the economic context in which the IIC was launched.

During the last decade, Latin American countries have undergone an economic renaissance after the economic slowdown experienced during the so-called "Lost Decade" of the 1980s, as a result of a new economic development strategy effectively put in place in Latin America. All countries in the region have undertaken major economic policy reforms establishing the foundations for open, export-led market economies. Due in large measure to the on-going efforts of the IDB in the region, state intervention has been substantially reduced; responsible fiscal policies have been adopted throughout; private investment is acknowledged as having a crucial role; foreign investment is now welcomed; domestic capital markets are being created; most debt problems have been resolved; and a renewed access to international capital markets continues. All of these changes have been undertaken under democratically-elected regimes, thus allowing for better prospects for stability, transparency, and fairness — all essential elements of a positive business environment. Within this framework, investors are finding that assets in many countries can still be bought at a reasonable percentage of their perceived international value, and the policy reforms underway are unleashing their full earnings potential. The international business community is aware of the immense potential offered by these developments, and their interest is further increased by the positive investment environment. Inflation has been generally reduced throughout the region, and it should be noted that where progress has been made in the battle against inflation, such progress was based on sound bases: first, fiscal discipline derived from structural fiscal reforms, such as expenditure reductions, increased privatizations, greater tax collections, and monetary autonomy; second, open, market-driven economies which allow import competition, thereby containing local prices and sedating expectations; and lastly, anchor prices and exchange rates which do not vary dramatically.

Similarly, capital inflows have grown tremendously over the last decade, during the course of which Latin America registered net capital inflows, reversing the capital flight tradition that has effectively created the largest pool of overseas funds available to any region in the world. Much of the capital inflows stem from the repatriation of funds, reflecting the confidence of Latin Americans in their own markets. Initially, these inflows dramatically affected the growth of domestic stock exchanges, and it is now old news that of the top performing stock markets worldwide, several are located in Latin America. In sharp contrast with the 1980s, these capital inflows are mostly absorbed by the region's private sector and not by its governments. Thus, to many the 1990s was the "decade of opportunity" in Latin America. Looking to the future, one must recognize that efforts by Latin American countries to establish open, market-led economies will, more than at any time in the recent past, subject them to the vulnerability and uncertainty of the global marketplace. This is especially due to declining prices of commodities, obstacles to trade, industrial countries' sluggish growth, instability and uncertainty in the global financial and exchange markets, as well as existing domestic social pressures. Alongside such hazards, the external environment holds out extraordinary opportunities. To take advantage of these opportunities, the countries in the region are undertaking internal as well as regional structural changes that will, in turn, enable them to create globally-competitive production systems. Perhaps the most significant result associated with this positive transfer of funds is that investment resources are being directed primarily to the private sector rather than to the public sector, the traditional recipient of funds.

Although the scenario for the region is optimistic, the economic renaissance of Latin America and the Caribbean is still in its incipient stages. Generally, only the larger, well-established companies of the region have been able to obtain financing from the traditional capital market sources. Given the early stages of development of regional capital markets and the long-term nature of the transformation process, small and medium size businesses are not yet experiencing the availability of increased domestic savings and the flows of foreign direct investment necessary to cement the economic recovery. In order to achieve balanced economic growth, the needs of these smaller businesses — the IIC's target market — should be addressed.

VI. THE IIC

It is within this regional context that the IIC began operations and has now completed its first ten years in business. The IIC is a legally autonomous treaty organization, and its resources and management are separate from the IDB, although its activities are coordinated with a view to also complement the activities of the IDB. The IIC was originally capitalized with US$200 million; however, in December 1999 its member countries approved a 250 percent general increase in resources, taking its paid-in equity capital to US$700 million. It is owned by thirty-seven member countries, of which twenty-six are Latin American and Caribbean (Argentina, the Bahamas, Barbados, Belize, Bolivia, Brazil, Colombia, Chile, Costa Rica, the Dominican Republic, Ecuador, El Salvador, Guatemala, Guyana, Haiti, Honduras, Jamaica, Mexico, Nicaragua, Panama, Paraguay, Peru, Suriname, Trinidad and Tobago, Uruguay and Venezuela) and the remaining eleven comprise United States, Japan, Israel and eight European countries (Austria, Denmark, France, Italy, Germany, the Netherlands, Spain and Switzerland). At the recent Annual Meeting of the Board of Governors held in March 2000, in New Orleans, Louisiana, United States, the Committee of the Board approved the admission of five member countries of the IDB that had not yet joined the IIC, comprising Belgium, Finland, Norway, Portugal and Sweden.

The IIC's role as a direct investor takes various forms, reflecting the particular needs of its clients. Typical forms of direct financial support include loans; equity investments; quasi-equity instruments; and resource mobilization activities, principally through co-financing transactions with international financial institutions. In many Latin American and Caribbean countries only large companies have been able to tap into securities markets. The IIC has worked to expand access to capital markets and to fill a critical void by financing transactions that develop local underwriting and leasing capabilities by local financial intermediaries, in order to provide much needed technical and financial resources. Furthermore, to enhance the availability of equity capital for promising small and medium size companies in the region, the IIC has invested seed capital in Latin venture capital and private equity funds from its inception in 1989.

The IIC's development criteria are important factors in considering whether or not to invest in a project. In evaluating a project's developmental impact, the following criteria are considered: (a) development of material and human resources; (b) creation of jobs; (c) foreign exchange generation; (d) technology transfer and the development of managerial skills; (e) impact on saving and investment rates; (f) democratization of ownership; and (g) the project's environmental, labor and worker safety impact.

By its very nature, the IIC has three characteristics which uniquely position it to undertake projects that private international financial institutions may not consider attractive: its Articles' immunities and privileges, its affiliation with the IDB, and its longer-term investment horizon. Moreover, a key factor in the future economic development of Latin America and the Caribbean will be the enhancement of the region's attractiveness to international investors. Given the IIC's limited capital in light of the broad scope of its mandate, it is clear that an important measure of success will be its ability to mobilize third-party resources for the region. In this regard, the IIC has been increasingly catalytic in raising extra-regional resources for its regional small and medium size clients since initiating its co-financing activities in 1991.

After the first ten years in operation, the IIC approved the financing of US$1.2 billion for over 200 projects throughout the region, representing total project costs in excess of US$5 billion, generating more than 200,000 new jobs for the region's economies and more than US$900 million in annual exports. It is particularly noteworthy that IIC has achieved these results while dedicating the vast majority of its resources to its target market; that is, IIC financing has reached over 2,000 small and medium size companies of the region. Since the IIC was created, the role and size of the private sector has expanded dramatically. The challenges and opportunities for small and medium size enterprises in the region are great, and the IIC continues to play a leading role in their growth. The establishment of the Inter-American Investment Corporation was a lengthy process. Many of the underlying themes discussed over the many years were, to a large extent, incorporated into the process of creating a multilateral investment corporation dedicated to meeting the financing needs of the small and medium size enterprises of the region.

THE RESPONSIBILITY OF STATES MEMBERS FOR THE DEFAULTS OF INTERNATIONAL ORGANIZATIONS: CONTINUING THE DIALOGUE

*Rosalyn Higgins**

I have admired the scholarly work of Ibrahim Shihata from the moment I came across it. As a university teacher of international law, I found it essential that my students studying the use of force should read what Dr. Shihata had to say on international conflict and embargoes. It was equally important that the LL.M. course students studying the international law of natural resources should familiarize themselves with Dr. Shihata's pioneering work on investment guarantees that carried benefits for capital importers and exporters alike.

But it was not until Ibrahim Shihata joined the Commission established by the *Institut de Droit International* to study the liability of member States for the defaults of international organizations that I had the opportunity to work with him. In the wake of the collapse of the International Tin Council, and against the background of the never-ending Westland Helicopter affair, a myriad of legal and ethical problems had been revealed. The *Institut* had thus established a Commission to work on the question of whether the States who were members of international organizations had any liability — joint or secondary — for the defaults or delicts of the organization concerned; or whether any liability was that of the organization alone. As the Rapporteur of this topic, I had good reason to value the knowledge there represented, which was remarkable.[1] The contributions of Ibrahim Shihata were invaluable.

---

* The views expressed in this paper are the author's and should not be attributed to the institutions she works for.

[1] The Commission members were Higgins (Rapporteur), Amerasinghe, Bowett, Crawford, Lauterpacht, Monaco, Salmon, Schachter, Schermers, Seidl-Hohenveldern, Seyersted, Shihata, Vignes, Vukas, Waelbroeck, Zemanek.

Not only did he seem to have a total overview of a very complex field of international law, but he also took it upon himself to ensure that I should better understand the very particular ways in which this general problem of law presented itself in the practice of international financial institutions. To that end, he tirelessly produced arcane but highly pertinent data from within that specialized world. His interest in the project never flagged, his analytic responses to questions and drafts were both timely and informative. Dr. Shihata gave not only of his specialized knowledge: he provided important and much appreciated moral support to a somewhat anxious Rapporteur at difficult moments in the passage of the Resolution in the form finally adopted by the *Institut*.

In this short tribute, I have thought to resume our dialogue on these matters. The thoughts that follow have no pretensions to being a further scholarly contribution to the literature in this area. They are merely the continuation of a conversation with an esteemed colleague.

*

Inevitably, matters move on. There is in 2000 some relevant practice that did not yet exist when we were both, with others, studying those matters in the early 90s. Were I writing my Reports today, I am sure I would wish to address these matters also.

The first concerns the entitlements of staff members to pensions and other benefits, and the liability therefor. The *Institut's* work did look "outwards" rather than "inwards," and it is suggested in certain quarters that, even if generally liability for defaults is that of the organization alone, the claims of employees represent a "special case," qualitatively different from that of the position of third parties *vis-à-vis* the organization.

The sentiment underlying this insistence is very understandable. The position of the employee within an organization is entirely visible,[2] these employees are known to the organization and often also to the member States; the links are therefore closer than are the links with outside persons seeking some recourse, somewhere, for broken contracts or for negligent acts.

2 The *Institut* resolution, adopted Sept. 1, 1995, in its section on "Desirable Developments," Art. 9, places considerable emphasis on transparency.

It is not hard to accept that the financial obligation of an employer towards its employees is indeed a generally recognized rule in international law and is part of the internal law of international organizations. But that merely posits the question of whether the organization itself or the States members of it are the "employer" who holds the duty. And one may readily agree that the benefit entitlement of employees in international organizations are unalterable *droit acquis,* and cite many dicta from diverse administrative tribunals to that effect. But that tells one nothing at all as to who is the bearer of that obligation. Neither the undisputed nature of the right held, nor the moral importance that the right be redeemed, provides a satisfactory legal answer as to whether States members are the bearers of the legal obligation if that obligation is not met by the entity primarily responsible, namely the international organization itself.

Neither the certainty of employees' rights, nor the moral importance that they should be met (both of which operate strongly in the field of employees' pensions) are legal tools for identifying the holders of obligation to the employees. That can only be done by going through the legal steps spelled out in the *Institut's* Resolution and the Rapporteur's Reports. These steps entail seeing, first, if the organization has both legal personality and a real decision-making independence from the members who comprise it. It also entails a case by case study to see if the claimants were led to believe that a joint or secondary liability would lie with the member States in the event of a default by the organization; or if the financing provisions of the organization are such that calls may indeed be made upon members to meet debts of the organization beyond those provided for in the budgets.

These are the sort of questions that have to be addressed to see if, in a particular organization, States members as well as the organization bear liability for defaults or for injury. The emerging practice of transferability of employees, between international organizations, and thus also their accrued benefits, attests to the reality of these rights as *droits acquis* — but does not help in addressing the questions that are relevant to the location of liability. Nor, it may be added, does referring to States members as "hiding behind the legal personality" of the defaulting organization. The phraseology invokes an understandable distaste for certain behavior but it does not carry the legal analysis forward. Of course, it is laudable that States sometimes do act responsibly with regard to employees' pensions. For example, States members decided together to ensure the pension regime established by EFTA in 1977. But not only was this an example of specific practice relating to dissolution, or transmutation, of international organizations, but it cannot be said to evidence the existence of a general obligation by States members — even as regards pension rights.

Nor does it much help to urge the question of employees' pensions as a 'special case,' either in a general sense or in the sense of a case to which might apply the exception envisaged in paragraph 5 (b) of the *Institut's* resolution.[3] It is true, certainly, that that resolution focused on debts owed to, or damage done to, persons external to the Organization. But the legal principles to be applied — the intellectual steps to be gone through — are the same if an analysis based on law rather than on sentiment (albeit powerful and understandable sentiment) is to be arrived at.

The answers are profoundly complex. Whether there is a joint or secondary liability on the part of States members certainly cannot be answered by a head count of the answers given by learned writers. The truth of the matter is that in most of the early writings answers were proffered to the question of the secondary liability of States members without the detailed legal implications of the matter being understood or addressed. It was only with the prolonged Tin litigation and Westland arbitration that all the various arguments, analogies and policy issues began to be appreciated and seriously analysed. The literature of recent years has generally been more expansive and reasoned in its analysis.[4]

*

---

3 Article 5(b) provides: "In particular circumstances, members of an international organization may be liable for its obligations in accordance with a relevant general principle of international law, such as acquiescence or the abuse of rights." This proviso was never meant to suggest, and never was understood to suggest, that the failure of Members States to assume liability was of itself an abuse of rights.

4 *See, e.g.*, Amerasinghe, *Liability to Third Parties of Members States of International Organizations,* AJIL (1991) at 280; HARTWIG, DIE HAFTUNG DER MITGLIEDSTAATEN FÜR INTERNATIONALE ORGANISATIONEN (1993); HIRSCH, THE RESPONSIBILITY OF INTERNATIONAL ORGANIZATIONS TOWARDS THIRD PARTIES: SOME BASIC PRINCIPLES (1995); Wenckstein, *Die Haftung der Mitgliedstaaten für Internationale Organisationen,* ZEITSCHRIFT FÜR AUSL. UND INT. PRIVATRECHT (1997), at 93–114.

The second question on which I should like the chance to chat with Dr. Shihata, and which equally was not within our sights in the *Institut* in the early 90s, is this: can we be confident that the *lex lata* we identified in the *Institut*'s resolution hold good in the face of the hybrid forms of peacekeeping and enforcement that have been so rapidly evolving in the last few years? Ever since the *Reparation for Injuries* case, the responsibility of the United Nations, rather than that of their national State, for the welfare of its servants, has been insisted upon. Conversely, the United Nations has accepted the responsibility for defaults of and injury caused by those in its service, *vis-à-vis* third parties (even if complex bilateral arrangements have also evolved here between the UN and national States providing forces for UN peacekeeping, dealing, *inter alia,* with questions of discipline and of liability). However, the recent trends raise interesting questions. In resolution 678, the Security Council authorized any coalition of States that chose so to act to take "all necessary measures" (everywhere understood as an authorization to use force, though whether under Article 42 or 51 remains questionable) against Iraq to end its invasion of Kuwait. Unlike the Korean precedent, there was here no UN Unified Command — rather, a finding of a Chapter VII situation warranting the use of force, the authorization to States to use such force, and an establishment of the objectives and purposes for which such action should be undertaken. The strategic objectives stipulated by the Security Council were manifestly lawful. It has not been suggested, in these particular circumstances, that the United Nations should itself be responsible for any perceived illegal acts relating to tactical objectives, nor any theoretic claims of default on contract obligations with third parties. Any responsibility was that of the volunteering coalition nations. (This, incidentally, is in part a reply to those who suggest that recommendations to members might entail responsibility for the members, whereas decisions requiring action by States members are said to reserve the responsibility to the organization itself. Resolution 678 was clearly a decision — a decision to authorize volunteer action, and was thus a complex hybrid, the form of which cannot itself determine liability.)

What of the acts of certain western States, among the original coalition, who later patrolled no-fly zones, asserting such action to be "based on" the UN resolutions, which called for humanitarian support without in terms authorizing any such acts? *A fortiori* responsibility may be assumed to lie with the States concerned for any delicts, and not with the United Nations. But what are the implications, for the attribution of the responsibility, of the silence of the United Nations in the face of such action? Did the UN thereby take responsibility for what the States concerned said had anyway been implicitly authorized by it?

These matters became ever more complicated with the proposals for a "new complementarity" between the UN and regional organizations, proposals made in Boutros Ghali's *Agenda for Peace* and first realized in the former Yugoslavia. In 1992 the NATO Secretary General responded to the approach from Boutros Ghali by stating that NATO had determined to support "on a case by case basis and in accordance with our own procedures, peacekeeping operations under the authority of the UN Security Council, which has the primary responsibility for peace and Security."[5] Within a short period NATO was assisting in naval embargoes, the enforcement of a no-fly zone over Bosnia, the protection of UN personnel and the protection of "safe zones."

Here the issue presented itself not as one of allocating legal liability between the UN and its member States, but between the UN and another international organization, said to be acting "under its own procedures" but as agent for the Security Council in the fulfilment of UN objectives. Clearly very complex issues arise out of allocation of international responsibility *vis-à-vis* third parties, made no easier by the "dual request/dual key" system then in place for air strikes. Both NATO and the UN could call for airstrikes in support of UNPROFOR; and both had to agree.

In Kosovo there has been much written about whether NATO did or did not act lawfully in its aerial action against the former Yugoslavia, given both what was said and what was not said in Security Council resolutions 1160 and 1199. Whatever the answer to this difficult question, there is also present the less noted, but equally real, question of distribution of responsibility. NATO, while insisting that it has acted lawfully, has at no stage suggested that any responsibility for claimed delicts or defaults is that of the

5 *Communiqué*, NATO Press Service, Dec. 17, 1991.

UN, rather than of itself. But there are the beginnings of the classic "organization/States members" conundrum regarding responsibility. NATO is an organization which functions operationally upon the basis of consensus among the member States (though Article 5 of the North Atlantic Treaty provides treaty obligations in certain circumstances — circumstances not obtaining either in Bosnia nor in Kosovo, where the response of member States was voluntary). China has treated the United States, and not NATO, as responsible for the bombing of its Embassy in Kosovo, and diplomatic activity regarding that event has been on a bilateral basis.

In the case of *Yugoslavia v. Canada (Request for Interim Measures),* in the oral hearings of May 1999, Canada, in disputing the jurisdiction of the International Court of Justice, made the following observations:

> "No specific conduct — we said it two days ago — is alleged against Canada itself, as an independent sovereign State, or for that matter against any of the other Respondents. As a very poor substitute for the imputation of specific acts to any of the respondents, the applicant asserts broadly that joint and several liability can be imported to each one of the Respondents for acts it may not have committed because of the integrated command structure of NATO. Mr. President, it was for the Respondent to demonstrate a basis in international law for that proposition, and it has not done so. Joint and several liability for acts of an international organization, or for the acts of other States acting within such an organization, cannot be established unless the relevant treaty provides for such liability. Article 5 of the 1949 NATO Convention, cited in the first round, provides no such indication of an assumption of joint and several liability, and neither do the provisions of the Handbook respecting the integrated military structure of the organization. The separate liability of Australia in *Nauru* was of course based on the specific terms of the trust instruments in issue in that case, not on general principles on international organizations. The work of the International Law Commission on State Responsibility provides no more support for the joint and several concept. I note as well that these concepts were canvassed in the Tin Council litigation in the United Kingdom, and the outcome would not support the Applicant in the present case."[6]

6 *Yugoslavia v. Canada,* ICJ oral hearings of May 12, 1999 (CR 99/27).

The International Court of Justice did not pronounce upon this issue in rejecting Yugoslavia's request for the indication of provisional measures. Should matters proceed in this case (and in the seven comparable cases which remain on the Court's docket) it may yet be necessary to return to the question — in which case, many, many factors would need to be taken into consideration. The findings in Westland and Tin, and the formulations of the *Institut de Droit International,* all retain their relevance; but the configurations of fact to which they are to be applied become ever more complex.

Those of us who remain interested in questions of responsibility within international organizations have somehow to follow the developing detail of relevant practice while firmly keeping our eye on the larger picture. It is to be hoped that Ibrahim Shihata, freed from his heavy responsibilities as General Counsel for the World Bank, will continue to take an active interest in such matters.

FREEDOM OF ESTABLISHMENT, FREEDOM OF CAPITAL MOVEMENTS, AND FREEDOM OF INVESTMENT

Patrick Juillard

I. INTRODUCTION

The purpose of this paper is to add a footnote to the landmark contribution which Dr. Shihata has made on one knotty question, i.e., the question of "admission" of foreign investment.[1] More specifically, the paper purports to discuss the relationship between three concepts which are at the very center of that question. These three concepts are: (i) freedom of establishment; (ii) freedom of movement of capital; and (iii) freedom of investment.

Such a discussion seems logical, if for no other reason than that legal terminology is in this respect in a state of confusion. Definitional problems are not entirely resolved; and while there is some degree of agreement on the meaning of "freedom of establishment" as well as of "freedom of movement of capital," this is not yet the case with respect to the meaning of "freedom of investment." Furthermore, it is not clear how the three concepts interrelate. The term "freedom of investment," for instance, is sometimes taken as synonymous with the two others. While it is obvious that there is a close connection between the three, it should not be taken for granted, however, that they entirely coincide with one another.

In order to shed modest light on an obscure issue, this paper will try: (i) to define the concepts here under consideration; (ii) to

---

[1] Ibrahim F.I. Shihata, *Recent Trends Relating to Entry of Foreign Direct Investment,* 9 ICSID Review — Foreign Investment Law Journal 47 (1994).

determine the extent to which these definitions coincide with each other, and (iii) to offer some comments on the present state of the law on freedom of investment.

II. DEFINITIONS

Defining these three basic concepts is no small undertaking. Dr. Shihata has rightly pointed out that international customary law is of no help here. One therefore has to turn to other sources, such as international treaties or agreements, as well as to resolutions from international organizations. But then a problem of another kind arises: international instruments, which are quite numerous, do not necessarily correspond to each other because they use the same concepts in different contexts.

A. Freedom of Establishment

Freedom of establishment may be defined as the right for nationals of one country to set up a permanent presence within the territory of another country for the purpose of conducting economic activities other than activities of a salaried character.[2]

There is no international customary law on the freedom of establishment. Therefore, the "freedom of establishment" results solely from international treaties or agreements which are concluded between sovereign States. Earlier treaties or agreements used to be bilateral treaties — known in French practice as *Conventions d'établissement*. Later on, the pressure for more economic integration, which developed in a Europe devastated by war, caused the creation of common markets through multilateral instruments — the model of which remains to date the 1957 Rome Treaty.

Bilateral as well as multilateral instruments rest upon the *national treatment* clause. Under that clause, each of the Contracting

---

2 *See*, for instance, Article 52 of the Rome Treaty (now Art 42 under the new numeration): "La liberté d'établissement comporte l'accès aux *activités non-salariées* et leur exercice, ainsi que la constitution et la gestion d'entreprises, et notamment de sociétés au sens de 1'Article 58, deuxième alinéa, dans les conditions définies par la législation du pays d'établissement pour ses propres ressortissants, sous réserve des dispositions du chapitre relatif aux capitaux."(Emphasis added).

Parties undertakes to afford to nationals of the other Party or Parties the same treatment which it affords to its own nationals. Most instruments, in addition to the national treatment clause, also contain specific provisions which detail the rights covered by the freedom of establishment. These rights relate to the "pre-establishment" phase as well as to the "post-establishment" phase. Therefore, national treatment, as far as it refers to the pre-establishment phase, means that foreigners may engage in the same economic activities as nationals, and that foreigners may engage in these economic activities under the same conditions as nationals — provided, however, such economic activities will be conducted through a permanent establishment.

B. Freedom of Capital Movements

The freedom of movement of capital may be defined, *stricto sensu,* as the right of residents of one country, to transfer any currency amounts to another country for the purpose of financing capital operations, i.e., operations other than current transactions.

Here again, it must be stressed that customary international law does not offer any definition of capital movements. Thus, removal of restrictions on capital movements is basically achieved through international treaties or agreements, with the one major exception of the Organisation for Economic Co-operation and Development (OECD) Code,[3] which, over the years, has evolved from a non-binding agreement into a comprehensive instrument of a binding character. These treaties or agreements are multilateral in character:[4] while States, in the past, have often entered into bilateral conventions relating to payments connected with current transactions, they have consistently failed to do so with respect to payments connected with capital operations. This may be easily explained. States used to be concerned, above all, with the development of international trade. Hence, the conclusion of bilateral instruments, on the basis of reciprocity, in order to remove restrictions on payments connected with current transactions, satis-

---

3 Code of Liberalization of Capital Movements OECD / C (61) 96, adopted by the Council on Dec. 12, 1961.

4 *See Les instruments de l'O.C.D.E. pour la promotion de la libération de l'investissement direct étranger,* O.C.D.E. / GD (95) 36, 1995, and namely II, Principes et procédures, at 3.

fied their common goal. It was only at a later stage that certain States started to feel the need for economic integration, and undertook to enter into international agreements that called for the removal of barriers on payments connected with capital.

Under international financial practice, the terms "freedom of movement of capital or capital movements" have been interpreted either in a restrictive sense or in an extensive sense. It would seem that the restrictive interpretation is giving way to the extensive interpretation.

Under the restrictive interpretation, "freedom of movement of capital" covers solely the payment related to a given capital operation; it does not cover that given capital operation. Thus, the term "freedom of movement of capital" may not be the most accurate here. It might have been more accurate to use the term "freedom of payments related to capital movements." Under that restrictive interpretation, removal of barriers on payments related to capital operations would not necessarily mean removal of barriers on the related capital operation. To give an illustration, a given country might remove all restrictions on payments related to investments, while it might still maintain some degree of control on admission of foreign investments.[5]

Under the extensive interpretation, "freedom of movement of capital" covers at the same time the capital operation and the payment related to the capital operation. Thus, in that sense, removal of restrictions on the movements of capital means at the same time removal of restrictions on the underlying operation and on the payment relating to that operation. For instance, and always assuming an "investment" is a movement of capital, removal of restrictions on investment would at the same time mean removal of restrictions on the investment and on the payments related to that investment. The OECD. and the European Community (EC) instruments have adopted this extensive interpretation: they cover "operations which comprise transactions between residents of dif-

[5] France followed such a policy in the late sixties. At that time, Decree No. 67-78 of Jan. 27, 1967 (the "investment decree") subjected French direct investments outside France and foreign direct investments within France to preliminary control, though, at that time, no restriction was yet in force with respect to payments related to capital operations, whatever their nature. In other words, at that time France had an investment regulation, but no exchange regulation.

ferent countries as well as capital transfers resulting directly therefrom and envisaged thereunder by the parties concerned."[6]

Capital operations are to be distinguished from current transactions. The distinction is not easy to draw, and no general definition of capital operations which could be considered as satisfactory has been proposed to date. The Court of Justice of the European Communities certainly made a gallant effort; but that effort has been dismissed by most commentators.[7] Thus, the only definition of capital operations which actually remains in use is the enumeration which has evolved in the international financial practice and which is annexed to the relevant instruments (OECD Codes and EC Directives). This enumeration, again, is intended in both cases to cover at the same time the underlying operation and the payment relating to that operation.

C. Freedom of Investment

While there is some substantial degree of agreement on the definitions of freedom of establishment and freedom of capital movements, the same cannot be said about the definition of freedom of investment. The reason why the concept of freedom of investment is so difficult to articulate is that there is no accepted definition of freedom of investment. And there is no accepted definition of freedom of investment, because there is no accepted

---

[6] Annex D to the O.C.D.E. Code, Point 3. *See also* Annex 1 of the 1988 Directive: "les mouvements de capitaux énumérés dans la présente nomenclature [Annexe à la Directive] s'entendent comme couvrant l'ensemble des opérations nécessaires à la réalisation des mouvements de capitaux conclusion et exécution de la transaction et transferts y afférents. La transaction s'éfectue généralement entre résidents de différents Etats membres; il arrive, toutefois, que certains mouvements de capitaux soient éffectues par une seule personne pour son propre compte (car, par exemple, des transferts d'avoirs d'émigrants)."

[7] E.C.J. cases 286 / 82 & 26 / 83, Luisi & Carbone, Jan. 31, 1984. The Court in that case held that current payments are currency transfers which are caused by an underlying transaction, while movements of capital are financial operations which have for their prime purpose the placement or the investment of the relevant amounts. This case has been commented and / or criticized by G. DRUESNE, REVUE TRIMESTRIELLE DE DROIT EUROPÉEN 296 (1984); by J. DUTHEIL DE LA ROCHÈRE, DROIT ET PRATIQUE DU COMMERCE INTERNATIONAL 75 (1985); and L. FOSCANEANU, 11, JURISCLASSEURS PERIODIQUES 14 237(Ed. II).

definition of investment. A brief overview of certain of the relevant sources will easily support that view.

Once more, customary international law will be of no help in this connection. The word "investment," which comes from economics, has only recently found its way into international law, under pressure of political circumstances. It is not until the 1960s that the word has become of current use in United Nations (UN) resolutions as well as international treaties and agreements.[8] It has met instant success, however, and the number of instruments relating to international investment probably stands unequalled today — with the one exception of instruments relating to the elimination of double taxation. The proliferation of investment treaties and agreements, whether bilateral or multilateral, primarily accounts for the high legal density in this area.

It will come as no surprise to anyone that bilateral treaties or agreements constitute the most important group of international instruments in this respect . These instruments, which were originally oriented North-South — and still are in large part — were intended to promote investment by nationals of industrial countries into developing countries through the definition of principles and rules of treatment and protection which would be legally binding under international law. Hence their generic denomination — bilateral treaties or bilateral agreements for reciprocal *promotion and protection* of investments. It is interesting to note that these bilateral instruments were patterned after model conventions drafted by investment exporting States.[9] These models actually fall into two categories: the European models are deemed to be more sovereignty-oriented because they provide for control of admission by the investment importing States; the US model is deemed to be more tilted in favor of the freedom of investment, because it provides for national treatment in the pre-establishment phase, as well as in the post-establishment phase.[10]

---

8 *See* P. Juillard, *L'évolution des sources du droit des investissements,* 250, RECUEIL DES COURS DE L'ACADÉMIE DE DROIT INTERNATIONAL 5, 22 (1994-VI).

9 On the origin and notion of "Model Conventions," *see* P. Juillard, *supra* note 8, at 5, 120.

10 An overview of clauses in the European and US models will be found in the Survey by Mohamed L. Khalil, *Treatment of Foreign Investment in Bilateral Investment Treaties,* reprinted in IBRAHIM F.I. SHIHATA, LEGAL TREATMENT OF FOREIGN. INVESTMENTS, THE WORLD BANK GUIDELINES 221 (1993).

But bilateral treaties or agreements are not the only conventional instruments dealing with international investment. The United Nations Commission on Trade and Development (UNCTAD) has compiled a three-volume compendium on International Investment Instruments (IIIs) which lists an impressive number of treaties and agreements, both at the universal and the regional levels, dealing in whole or in part with international investments.[11] Among these treaties and agreements, special mention ought to be made of two multilateral conventions, because they are World Bank Conventions: the 1965 Washington Convention, creating the International Centre for Settlement of Investment Disputes (ICSID), and the 1985 Seoul Convention, creating the Multilateral Investment Guarantee Agency (MIGA). These are major achievements, and it is proper that special tribute should be paid here to Dr. Shihata, who played such an important role in the negotiation of the MIGA Convention.

These instruments have different purposes. As has been indicated, the bilateral agreements purport to promote and protect international investment. But the Washington and the Seoul Conventions pursue quite different goals. The Washington Convention sets up a mechanism for the settlement of investment disputes between investors and host countries; the Seoul Convention sets up a mechanism to guarantee investors from political risks arising in host countries. Given the variety of purposes, it is no wonder that the definition of investment which is given by these Conventions should be different so as to adjust to these purposes.

On one side, the ICSID Convention contains no definition whatsoever of investments, though Article 25 provides that the Centre has jurisdiction only over investment disputes.[12] The reason[13] for this lack of any definition is that the Parties in dispute

---

[11] Volume I: Multilateral instruments; Volume II: Regional instruments; Volume III: Regional Integration, Bilateral and Non-governmental Instruments (1996). The compendium uses the word instruments because (i) it comprises international law sources other than treaties and agreements, such as, for instance, Resolutions from International Organizations, and (ii) it also comprises instruments which may not be deemed to be sources of international law, such as instruments drafted by non-governmental institutions.

[12] *See* Article 25 (1): "The jurisdiction of the Center shall extend to any legal dispute arising directly of an investment.../..."

[13] *See* Report on the Convention, §27: Il n'a pas été jugé nécessaire de définir le terme "investissement" compte tenu du fait que le consentement des parties con-

should be left free to agree as to whether their particular dispute should be deemed to be covered by the Washington Convention. The result was that the notion of investment was extended to its outer limits, and may be even beyond.

On the other side, bilateral treaties and agreements on the promotion and protection of investments, though they claim to be reciprocal in character, are instruments that purport to afford the highest possible level of protection to investments by nationals of industrial countries in developing countries. Thus, the definitional clauses, be it in the European models or in the US model, give such a broad definition of investment as to completely dissolve it into the notion of assets. Assets are deemed to be investments in all kinds of property, whether immovable or movable; and, in the case of movable property, they may be in the form of tangible or intangible assets. In short, every kind of asset is covered, even though such assets clearly would not qualify as investments within the meaning of economics.

Somewhere in the middle, the MIGA Convention takes a more balanced approach. On the one hand, the Agency, because it has only limited resources[14] cannot guarantee each and every investment made by nationals of industrial countries within the territory of developing countries. Thus, the MIGA Convention opts for a definition of investment which is somewhat more restrictive than the very broad definition contained in bilateral treaties or agreements on the promotion and protection of investments. But, on the other hand, the Agency is clearly preoccupied with efficiency, in the sense that whatever the amounts involved, it will always favor "productive" over "unproductive" investments. Thus, Article 12 provides that, in order to benefit from the MIGA guarantee, investments should either be "direct" investments, whatever their form, or equity investments — whether "direct" or not "direct" investments. Investments other than direct investments or equity investments may still be declared admissible, provided such investments would be in the form of contributions in kind.[15]

---

stitue une condition essentielle et compte tenu du mécanisme par lequel les Etats contractants peuvent, s'ils le désirent, indiquer en avance les catégories de différends qu'ils seraient ou ne seraient pas prêts a soumettre au Centre [Article 25 (4)].

14 *See* Commentary on the Convention, §20, which states that, in order to spare its "limited resources," the Agency will issue no guarantee with respect to export credits.

15 *See* Commentary, §19, in fine.

Commercial contracts may be deemed in certain cases to constitute foreign investment and even foreign direct investment, provided the compensation of the contractor depends at least substantially on the income earned by that investment — a welcome illustration of the French saying: *"l'investisseur doit s'investir."*

Freedom of establishment as well as freedom of movement of capital are concepts which under international law and practice, have long enjoyed definitions that can be considered as well-settled. In contrast, freedom of investment remains a somewhat blurred concept, which seems susceptible of a multiplicity of definitions. As a consequence, while the terms "freedom of establishment" and/or "freedom of movement of capital" are of current use in legal terminology, the term "freedom of investment" is not, because it has not gained sufficient acceptance. International instruments, in order to deal with freedom of investments, thus revert to the most common concepts of freedom of establishment or freedom of movement of capital, as the case may be.

III. CORRELATIONS

Given the definitions of freedom of establishment, on the one hand, and of freedom of movement of capital, on the other hand, is it safe to conclude that freedom of investment coincides with either of them? In order to answer this question, it is necessary to determine how the freedom of establishment, the freedom of movement of capital and the freedom of investment interrelate.

A. Freedom of Investment and Freedom of Establishment

How do the freedom of investment and freedom of establishment interrelate with each other? The notion of a "permanent presence" is central to both investment and establishment. But does this really mean that freedom of investment and freedom of establishment just superimpose each other, and that, therefore, the two are synonymous? This question can be best answered by breaking it into two sub-questions. Sub-question One may be formulated as follows: Does the freedom of establishment require that freedom of investment be ensured? Sub-question Two may be formulated as follows: Does the freedom of investment require that freedom of establishment be ensured?

1. Does freedom of establishment require that freedom of investment be ensured?

This sub-question must clearly be answered in the affirmative. One fails to see how freedom of establishment can be ensured if restrictions on freedom of investment have not been lifted. Establishment assumes a permanent presence in order to carry out an economic activity. There can be no such permanent presence if the physical person or legal entity undertaking this economic activity is not allowed to operate from facilities located within the country of establishment. A German baker cannot establish his business in France if he is not authorized to buy or rent a bakery there. Similarly, a US car manufacturer cannot establish his business in France if he is not allowed to build or purchase an automobile plant there. Buying or renting a *"fonds de commerce"* such as a bakery, as well as building or purchasing a plant are transactions which, under French law, are deemed to constitute direct investments. Thus, the German baker or the US car manufacturer will not be able to establish their businesses in France if they are not permitted to make there the investments necessary to start and operate their respective businesses.

OECD law as well as EC law are at point here. Article 67, Section 1 of the Rome Treaty, namely, provides that Member States eliminate, as between themselves, restrictions relating to movements of capital, insofar as this elimination was "necessary for the proper functioning of the Common Market." These words were interpreted as meaning that restrictions on capital movements were to be eliminated only insofar as this elimination would be necessary in order to achieve the "fundamental freedoms" provided for by the Treaty — including the freedom of establishment.[16] This is the philosophy underlying the 1960 Directive,[17] the Preamble of which restated that the achievement of Community goals, such as provided by the Rome Treaty, necessitate that the

[16] Case 203 / 80, Regina v. Casati,-E.C.R. – (1981) Nov. 11, 1981.

[17] For the implementation of Article 67 of the Treaty, July 12, 1960, *see* OFFICIAL JOURNAL OF THE EUROPEAN ECONOMIC COMMUNITY, AT 921.

freedom of movement of capital be "as broad as possible." Therefore, it comes as no surprise that the first rubrics in the nomenclature of movements of capital annexed to the Directive related to those capital movements on which restrictions ought to he lifted in order to ensure the freedom of establishment. Moreover, Article 1 of the Directive provided that List A movements, i.e., movements on which all restrictions were to be lifted, contained: (i) direct investments; (ii) liquidation of direct investments; and (iii) investments in real property. Obviously, these are "movements of capital" which are ancillary to "establishment" in the sense that there can be no permanent presence if these "movements" do not enjoy full freedom.

This problem was at the core of the dispute between France and the Community in the late 1960s. By that time, France was very reluctant to permit free entry of US investments, and, as a consequence, had issued Decret No. 67.78 of January 27, 1967, which gave *"Direction du Trésor"* the power to postpone (*postponement/ajournement*) the making of any given direct investment (including those from other member states of the European Community), either within or outside France. The Commission took argument with the regulatory scheme on the grounds that the postponement mechanism amounted to a denial of (i) freedom of investment, such as provided by the 1960 Directive, and of (ii) freedom of establishment, such as provided by Article 58 of the Rome Treaty. Article 169 proceedings culminating in Case 66/69 were commenced by the Commission against the French Government. When it became clear to the French Government that it could not escape the imposition of sanctions by the European Court of Justice, it withdrew the regulatory scheme.[18] But the withdrawal did not result in a lifting of the restrictions, as one might have expected. Quite on the contrary, the postponement mechanism, which could be considered as a relatively mild form of control, was replaced by a much tougher system of exchange authorizations, which, for technical reasons, was upheld and remained in force for more than ten years. Case 66/69, however, clearly shows that in the mind of the Commission, freedom of investment was considered as a condition for freedom of establishment.

---

18 *See* Juillard, *supra* note 8 at 52.

2. Does the freedom of investment require that the freedom establishment be ensured under all circumstances?

This sub-question calls for a more complex answer. Of course, one fails to see how the freedom of investment could be achieved in case the freedom of establishment would not be guaranteed, if for no other reason than a number of investments call for a permanent presence, and that this permanent presence cannot be ensured in case there is no freedom of establishment. A French lawyer could not invest in the opening of legal offices in Germany, in case Community law, as combined with German law, would not permit French lawyers to establish offices in Germany, i.e., to set up a permanent establishment there in order to practice law, including German law. In that sense, the freedom of investment would be a totally empty shell, if it did not walk hand in hand with the freedom of establishment. Thus, it is clear that the freedom of investment could not be ensured if the freedom of establishment were not guaranteed.

But this is not true under all circumstances. As has been mentioned above, a distinction must be drawn between investments that require a permanent presence and investments that do not require a permanent presence. Certain investments, like the purchase by individuals of small businesses, or the acquisition by companies of a majority of the stock of large entities will suffice, by themselves, to establish a permanent presence. In that sense, direct investment, in most cases, requires freedom of establishment. But there are investments other than direct investments: such is the case, for instance, of portfolio investments. If a French national buys shares on some foreign market, he is making an investment. Indeed, each and every bilateral instrument on the promotion and protection of investments list the purchase of stock as an investment. But this kind of portfolio investment, which is passive in character, certainly does not make it necessary for the purchaser to establish a permanent presence within the country concerned, i.e., the country within which the company is listed. Clearly, the freedom of investment covers a broader range of operation than the freedom of establishment.

The Seoul Convention further illustrates that point in the sense that it implies that certain forms of direct investment would not even require any permanent presence. Paragraph 19 of the Commentary on the Convention, which is annexed thereto, states that the Board of Directors of the Agency may, in its discretion, consider as *"direct investment,"* for guarantee purposes, new forms of investments, such as commercial arrangements, which tie the compensation of the foreign party, i.e., the investor — with the "financial results" of the company concerned. For instance, a leasing agreement might be considered as a "direct investment," in case a substantial fraction of the compensation due from the lessee to lessor would depend upon the financial outcome of the operation. In that case, lessor, for guarantee purposes, could qualify as an investor under MIGA regulations, even though that investor might have no permanent presence in the country of operation.

The conclusion which may be drawn from the foregoing is that the freedom of investment and the freedom of establishment do not totally coincide with each other, if for no other reason than that all investments are not carried out through permanent establishments. Freedom of investment and freedom of establishment, therefore, should not be seen as synonymous.

B. Freedom of Investment and Freedom of Movements of Capital

There also is an obvious connection between the freedom of investment and the freedom of movement of capital. Indeed, that connection is so obvious that one is left to wonder whether there could be any freedom of investment at all as long as restrictions on the freedom movement of capital would not be lifted. But here again, legal analysis shows that there is no coincidence between the freedom of investment and the freedom of movement of capital, because (i) a number of movements of capital do not qualify as investments, and (ii) a number of investments can be carried out without any movements of capital.

1. A Number of Capital Movements Do Not Qualify as Investments

As has already been noted, there is no general definition of movements of capital which would be accepted by the international financial community. Movements of capital seem to be sort of a residual category which is defined by opposition to current payments: any and all financial transactions which would not qualify as current payments should be deemed to be movements of capital. To go one step further — as the European Court of Justice put it — current payments are transfers which are caused by some underlying transaction of a "current character," whereas capital operations may be defined as financial operations which essentially contemplate the placement or investment of the amount involved, rather than the compensation due by reason of some "current" transaction. While this definition has given rise to much criticism, it still shows that at the core of the matter lies the distinction between "current payments" and "capital operations."

The main instruments regulating the movements of capital do not undertake to propose a general definition the same. Rather, what they do is list what they consider to be movements of capital. This is the approach followed by OECD as well as EC instruments. For instance, the most elaborate of the then ECC Directives, i.e., Directive No. 88/361 of June 24, 1988, does not contain any general definition of movements of capital. Annex I to the 1988 Directive, however, lists no less than thirteen different categories of movements of capital, ranging from Category I, i.e., direct investments, to Category XIII, i.e., other movements of capital. Of these thirteen categories, only two, Category I, i.e., direct investments, and Category II, i.e., real estate investments relate to investments. The other eleven categories include movements of capital which may have nothing in common with investments, namely because they are short-term, "speculative" movements.

Hence, the notion of movements of capital cover a much broader range of financial operations than the notion of "investment." It is clear, nevertheless, that the removal of restrictions on capital movements entails at the very least removal of restrictions on payments connected with direct investments and/or real estate investments. Thus, members of the EC, under the 1988 Directive, which is still in force, could not possibly prohibit a German national from paying the price of the country house which he would have bought in Denmark. But this leaves one question open: can Denmark still issue a regulation prohibiting German nationals from buying real estate in Denmark? Under EC law, that particular question has been settled by a specific arrangement.[19] But, as

19 *See* the Protocol on Purchase of Real Estate Property in Denmark, attached to the Treaty of Maastricht.

stated above, and in a more general fashion, the notion of movements of capital may cover not only financial operations, but also the underlying transaction. Thus, under European Community law, removal of restrictions on movements of capital, such as payment by a non-resident of the purchase price of a country house on the domestic market, also entails removal of all restrictions on the purchase of that country house.

2. *Some Investments can be Carried out without any Capital Movements*

But it may well be that an investment does not call for any payment. For instance, the foreign investor will contribute in kind to the formation of a new company in the host country.There is no financial transfer whatsoever. Does this mean that, because there is no financial transfer, the "underlying transaction," i.e., the participation of the investor in the formation of the new company, can still be subject to some restrictions? Technically, the instruments here under consideration, such as the OECD Codes or the EC Directives, purport to remove restrictions on the financial transfers and on the investment itself whenever the latter is related to the former. But it does not purport to remove all controls on an investment whenever that investment does not call for any financial transfer.

Here again, the conclusion which may be drawn from the foregoing is that the freedom of investment and the freedom of movements of capital do not totally coincide with each other, if for no other reason than that all investments do not necessitate a capital movement, i.e., a payment associated with a capital transaction. Freedom of investment and freedom of movements of capital, therefore, should not be considered as synonymous.

III. CONCLUSIONS

International instruments have proliferated over the years and they certainly reflect a general tendency toward a relaxation of domestic controls over the admission of foreign investments. It may be argued, however, that none of these instruments, be they the bilateral protection instruments or the codes on free move-the bilateral protection instruments or the codes on free movement of capital, are adequate tools in order to achieve the goal of free admission.

The old opposition between the North (investment exporting countries) on the one hand, and the South (investment importing countries), on the other hand, with respect to protection of investments from the former into the latter seems to have faded away so as to become a thing of the past. The real problem is no longer protection: It is the admission or rather, the free admission of investment. And that problem seems to be one between North and North rather than one between North and South.

The failed Multilateral Agreement on Investment (MAI) has been interpreted, rightly or wrongly, as evidence of this shift in emphasis during the failed international negotiations. In a somewhat arbitrary fashion, some commentators have tried to show that OECD Member States did not all agree on the issue of admission, and that European and US practice, as expressed in bilateral protection instruments, were at odds with each other. In that connection, it was argued that the European models of bilateral instruments were tilted more in favor of protection of sovereign rights of the host State than the US model, which allegedly favored an open-door policy with respect to the entry of foreign investment.

To be sure, European models seem to abide by a somewhat protective view. To take one sole example, the Swiss model reflects the desire of federal authorities to maintain some kind of screening process with respect to the entry of foreign investments. The so-called "admission clause" in that model is worded as follows:

> "(i) Each Contracting Party shall in its territory promote as far as possible investments by investors of the other Contracting Party and admit such investments in *accordance with its laws and regulations*." (Emphasis added.)

This clause will be found, in more or less similar terms, within each and every European model. It is not an open-door clause: by reserving the application of domestic laws and regulations, which could close certain economic activities to foreign investment, the model preserves the sovereign rights of each Contracting Party with respect to the admission of foreign investment. Since the Swiss model does not recognize the freedom of investment, neither does it recognize the freedom of establishment nor the freedom of movement of capital.

The US model, by contrast, contains no admission clause. Rather, it contains a general provision on treatment, which covers at the same time the pre-investment phase and the post-investment phase. This clause is worded as follows:

> "With respect to the establishment, acquisition, expansion, management, conduct, operation and sale or other disposition of covered investments, each Party shall accord treatment no less favorable than that it accords, in like situations, to investments in its territory of its own nationals and companies (hereinafter national treatment) or to investments in its territory of nationals or companies of a third country (hereinafter most favored nation treatment) whichever is most favorable (hereinafter national and most favored nation treatment)."

This clause, though it has been slow in gaining acceptance, now appears in a number of bilateral instruments as well as multilateral instruments, and its influence is growing. It clearly calls for greater freedom of investment. It is not certain, however, that it is worded in such a way to ensure total freedom of investment. By linking freedom of investment to national treatment in both the pre-establishment phase and the post-establishment phase, the US model brings freedom of investment into alignment with freedom of establishment. There are investments, however, which do not call for any permanent presence, and which therefore fall outside the scope of the freedom of establishment. Are these investments covered by the national treatment clause in Article II of the US model?

While the network of bilateral protection instruments has been developing rapidly over the years, the instruments on free movements of capital still bind only a limited number of States, basically industrial countries. At this point in time, it seems that a universal instrument on removal of restrictions on the movements of capital is still far away.

It is true that the existing instruments, be they the OECD or the EC instruments, cover transfers of capital in both into and out of the respective countries, therefore, the establishment as well as the liquidation of investments. The OECD instruments are very clear on that point:

> "All international capital movements have two distinct aspects: the capital export from one country, and the corresponding capital import into another."

This, however, still does not close one major loophole. Some investments do not call for any capital movement and, therefore, do not fall within the removal of restrictions which may be found in the provisions of the relevant instruments. Thus, under the present state of international law, there is no multilateral instrument which would create a general obligation to remove restrictions on the freedom of investment. As a conclusion, it inescapably follows that these investments are still subject to national control.

Whether restrictions on free admission should or should not be lifted is a political question, the resolution of which lies with all those entrusted with the power to shape or make policy decisions. But the issue has a legal element. Assuming that a consensus would exist as to whether these restrictions should be lifted, it is not by relying upon inaccurate extrapolation that the law could ever give to that consensus its proper expression.

It may be that the freedom of investment is in order, and that international economic law, as it presently takes its new form, calls for no less than that. But if this is the case it must then be clearly stated, and the legal instruments should explicitly provide for it. It is suggested that this is not yet the case, because freedom of investment, be it in bilateral instruments or in multilateral instruments, has not yet found its proper expression.

A sound basis exists from which to start. This basis is afforded by Guideline II (Admission) of the World Bank Guidelines on the Legal Treatment of Foreign Investment. To be sure, Guideline II does not go so far as to recommend lifting any and all controls on admission of foreign investment, and, in that sense, it certainly is not an open-door policy instrument. But, at least, Guideline II has unquestionable merits: it clearly delineates the issues, and it tries to use the proper concepts which are adapted to their solution.

What are these concepts? Above all, an instrument which is intended to remove restrictions on the freedom of investments must express itself in terms of admission and, therefore, provide for free admission of investments, even though there might be exceptions to the general proposition. This means that drafters of investments instrument should not try to achieve freedom of investment through oblique ways. This is not to say, however, that such an instrument should not also provide for freedom of establishment, and even national treatment in both the pre- and post-establishment phase. But this is a different question, and since the freedom of investment and freedom of establishment do not coincide with one another, the latter should not be used in order to achieve the former. The same may be said of freedom of movements of capital, without which, in most instances, there could be no freedom of investment. Investment instruments, however, do not really provide for the freedom of movement of capital: rather, they provide for freedom of transfers between the investment importing and the investment exporting countries. But as far as admission is concerned, this type of provision is irrelevant. Instead, what would be relevant would be a provision which would authorize transfers from the capital exporting country into the capital importing country in the event these transfers would be necessary in order to achieve freedom of investment. It is thus suggested that only such a use of the three concepts of the freedom of establishment, the freedom of movements of capital and the freedom of investment would achieve an open-door policy. Whether such a policy is desirable is another question, to which this paper dare not submit an answer.

INTERNATIONAL FINANCE CORPORATION: FINANCING ENVIRONMENTALLY AND SOCIALLY SUSTAINABLE PRIVATE INVESTMENT

*Carol F. Lee**

I. INTRODUCTION

The International Finance Corporation (IFC) stands at the crossroads of the public sector and the private sector. As a member of the World Bank Group, IFC's mission is "to promote private sector investment in developing countries, which will reduce poverty and improve people's lives." Thus, IFC works with private investors who are motivated by return on their investments, with the objective of achieving IFC's public sector values. In recent years, IFC has adopted as a core commitment that the projects it supports will be environmentally and socially sound.

This article addresses the challenges facing IFC in its efforts to lead the way to environmentally and socially sustainable development in the private sector. Some private businesses have become increasingly aware of environmental issues and recognize the added value that improved environmental and social performance can bring to their activities. Others may start with the narrower perspective that environmental and social requirements are costs that they would prefer to avoid or minimize. In order to fulfill its objectives, IFC needs to recognize the four sources of "leverage" that may be brought to bear on financial institutions and private enterprises to encourage better environmental and social

* This article represents the personal views of the author and should not be attributed to the institution she works with.

performance. This article considers these types of leverage in the context of IFC's project finance work. It then summarizes the significant improvements that IFC has recently made in its environmental and social policies and procedures and the resources that it devotes to environmental and social issues in its project work.

II. IFC'S ROLE AT THE CROSSROADS OF THE PUBLIC AND PRIVATE SECTORS

IFC's position at the crossroads of the public sector and the private sector is fundamental to understanding its work. IFC is a *public sector* institution. Its shareholders are 174 governments from around the world.[1] IFC is accountable for its stewardship of public resources. And as a member of the World Bank Group, sharing the same President and the same Board of Directors, IFC is committed to following the same environmental and social safeguards in its project work as the World Bank itself.

At the same time, IFC's mandate is to work with the *private sector*, to share private sector risks, and thus to promote private sector development in its developing member countries.[2] To achieve this objective, IFC makes loan and equity investments in private enterprises — without government guarantee of repayment — as well as providing technical assistance and advice.[3]

---

1 Number of shareholders by 1999. *See* INTERNATIONAL FINANCE CORPORATION — ANNUAL REPORT (1999).

2 The Corporation's mandate is laid down in Article I of the IFC Articles of Agreement. Accordingly, the Corporation is "to further economic development by encouraging the growth of productive private enterprise in member countries, particularly in the less developed areas, thus supplementing the activities of the International Bank for Reconstruction and Development."

3 To achieve its mandate, the Corporation shall, according to Article I (i) of the IFC Articles of Agreement, "in association with private investors, assist in financing the establishment, improvement and expansion of productive private enterprises which would contribute to the development of its member countries by making investments, without guarantee of repayment by the member government concerned, in cases where sufficient private capital is not available on reasonable terms[.]"

III. LEVERAGE FOR THE ENVIRONMENT IN IFC'S PROJECTS

IFC is not able to do projects by itself. In fact, its charter — the Articles of Agreement — prohibits IFC from managing the projects in which it invests.[4] So it has to work with private sponsors who are in control of the construction and implementation of the projects for which it provides financing. And IFC frequently works in countries where the environmental standards are not very well developed or enforced. In this context, one has to think about how IFC can go about leveraging its influence in the private sector to promote better environmental and social performance in developing countries. More generally, one has to think about what the reasons are that a private entrepreneur or investor would be willing to consider environmental and social issues, and to take steps to improve its performance in these areas.

In answering this question, one may use the four categories presented in an interesting publication by the World Resources Institute (WRI), a Washington-based think tank and NGO. It is called "Leverage for the Environment."[5]

The first category is *bottom-line leverage*[6] — improved financial performance that results directly from taking environmental performance into account. On the one hand, environmental risks can cost time and money. On the other hand, environmental business opportunities can generate profits.

The second category is *policy leverage*[7] — legislation, regulation, and taxation that reward good environmental performance and penalize poor environmental performance.

---

4 Article 3, Section 3(iv) of the IFC Articles of Agreement states that "the Corporation shall not assume responsibility for managing any enterprise in which it has invested and shall not exercise voting rights for such purpose or for any other purpose which, in its opinion, properly is within the scope of managerial control[.]"

5 John Ganzi, Frances Seymour & Sandy Buffett, with Navroz K. Dubash, Leverage for the Environment — A Guide to the Private Financial Services Industry (1998).

6 *Ibid.* at 6.

7 *Ibid.*

The third category is *reputational leverage*[8] — the effects of good or poor environmental and social performance on the enterprise's public image (and thus perhaps indirectly on its bottom line). Actions that generate positive or adverse media attention are examples of reputational leverage. Firms that have a high level of brand name recognition — especially those in consumer goods or retail services — are, of course, more susceptible to reputational leverage.

The final category is *values-based leverage*[9] — the willingness of an entrepreneur or investor to promote environmental values even at the possible expense of financial value. In other words, this final type of motivation is essentially a moral one — taking actions that are environmentally and socially sound is the right thing to do.

As a public sector institution which deals with the private sector, IFC has been influenced by all of these types of leverage over the years, as it has developed environmental and social requirements and an institutional capacity to implement them. IFC also seeks to use these types of leverage to promote improved environmental and social performance in the projects it supports.

A. Bottom-line Leverage

Starting with *bottom-line leverage,* good environmental and social practice is, quite simply, good business. IFC's continuing ability to promote economic development depends on successful investments — loans which are repaid and equity investments which grow in value. Therefore, it is in its financial interest as well as that of project sponsors to enhance the eco-efficiency and reduce the environmental risks of the projects in which it invests.[10]

One example would be energy and raw materials that are important components of production costs in many manufacturing industries. Reducing the amount of these inputs utilized per unit of output is not only environmentally responsible; it is also a

---

8 *Ibid.*

9 *Ibid.*

10 For details, *see* STEPHAN SCHMIDHEINY & FEDERICO J. L. ZORRAQUÍN, FINANCING CHANGE — THE FINANCIAL COMMUNITY, ECO-EFFICIENCY, AND SUSTAINABLE DEVELOPMENT (1996).

source of competitive cost advantage.[11] IFC has a strong technical staff of experienced engineers who are part of every project team. One of their responsibilities is to help the project sponsor select technologies that meet environmental standards and are energy-efficient and cost-efficient.

To give another example of bottom-line leverage, political opposition or local social unrest can delay a major capital investment project and be extremely costly. On the other hand, public consultation and community outreach efforts, starting from the earliest stages of a project, can help build community understanding and support and resolve issues before they lead to conflict.[12] This is socially responsible as well as financially advantageous. Accordingly, depending on the extent of potential environmental and social impacts, IFC requires project sponsors to disclose information about the proposed project at an appropriate stage to the affected local people, to engage them in a dialogue and to take their concerns into account during project preparation and implementation.[13] This is now an important part of the project cycle for IFC-financed projects.

---

11 According to SCHMIDHEINY & ZORRAQUÍN, *supra* note 10, at 41, the idea of the environment being a source of competitive advantage requires business executives and financiers to develop new perspectives, concepts, operational tools. Furthermore, it requires governments to set up a regulatory system that does not make large-scale pollution a viable business option. In India, the new environmental policy announced in 1993 as part of the country's economic liberalization program places the emphasis of government tax incentives and regulations on cleaner production by industry.

According to SCHMIDHEINY & ZORRAQUÍN, *supra* note 10, at 42, investments, for example, in plant modernization generally lead to lower pollution intensities, since new processes and plants typically use fewer inputs, are more efficient, and rely on more materials recycling than older technologies. Clean technologies installed in new plants often pay for themselves in terms of both lower input costs and improved competitiveness in light of new product specifications.

12 *See generally* DOING BETTER BUSINESS THROUGH EFFECTIVE PUBLIC CONSULTATION AND DISCLOSURE — A GOOD PRACTICE MANUAL, INTERNATIONAL FINANCE CORPORATION (1998).

13 *See* IFC's Policy on Disclosure of Information (effective September 1, 1998). For further details *see* IFC's website at <www.ifc.org/enviro/index.html>.

B. Policy Leverage

Turning to the second form of leverage, *policy leverage,* IFC invests in projects that are fully subject to local laws and regulatory requirements. IFC requires the project sponsor to assure that the project satisfies all environmental requirements, both up front and during the life of the project.

As mentioned earlier, however, in many of the countries in which IFC does business, the environmental regulatory framework is still underdeveloped.[14] Within the World Bank Group, it is the role of the World Bank rather than IFC to work with governments to improve their environmental policies and regulatory capabilities. The Bank is currently carrying out a number of these projects worldwide.[15] There have been, however, some IFC projects that have helped to stimulate the development of an environmental regulatory framework in the country, where none had existed previously.[16]

C. Reputational Leverage

The third category of leverage is *reputational leverage,* that is, the harm to an institution's public image that results from visi-

---

14 Many countries lack an adequate legislative and regulatory framework for environmental protection and management. The World Bank provides assistance to those countries, in order to integrate environmental principles into development planning, and thus helps to develop tools and methodologies to protect people and natural resources from adverse impacts of development projects. For further details, *see* THE WORLD BANK ANNUAL REPORT 77 *et seq.* (1998).

15 For a current overview of the World Bank's environmental work during FY99, *see* ENVIRONMENT MATTERS AT THE WORLD BANK — ANNUAL REVIEW 1999 (1999). *See also* IBRAHIM F. I. SHIHATA, THE WORLD BANK IN A CHANGING WORLD, VOL. II (1995), especially Chapter 5 (*The World Bank and the Environment: Legal Instruments for Achieving Environmental Objectives*), and Chapter 17 (*Institutional Aspects of the Bank's Role with Respect to the Environment*); *id.*, THE WORLD BANK IN A CHANGING WORLD, VOL. III (2000), especially Chapter 15 (*The World Bank's Contribution to the Progressive Development of International Environmental Law*), and Chapter 16 (*Implementation, Enforcement and Compliance with International Environmental Agreements — Practical Suggestions in Light of the World Bank's Experience*).

16 One of these projects was the Pangue hydroelectric project in Chile, approved by IFC's Board in 1992 at a time when Chile did not yet have a framework for the government review and approval of environmental impact assessments for major projects.

ble environmental embarrassments. The environmental NGO movement very effectively used a set of big 'problem projects' to help pressure IFC's sister institution, the World Bank, into developing environmental policies and procedures starting around a decade ago. These included a large dam project in India, a road project through the tropical forest in northeast Brazil, and a transmigration project in Indonesia.[17]

It took longer for the environmental advocacy NGOs to discover IFC, since it is smaller and less visible than the World Bank. But as private sector capital flows grew dramatically in the 1990s to become several times as large as public sector capital flows,[18] the private sector activities of the World Bank Group also grew.[19] So the environmental NGOs turned their attention to IFC. IFC found itself under much closer scrutiny than ever before.[20] Similarly, the environmental movement has recently mobilized reputational leverage in order to try to influence the actions of multinational corporations.[21]

---

17 *See, e.g.*, BRUCE RICH, MORTGAGING THE EARTH: THE WORLD BANK, ENVIRONMENTAL IMPOVERISHMENT, AND THE CRISIS OF DEVELOPMENT (1994).

18 *See generally* Private Capital Flows to Developing Countries — The Road to Financial Integration 9 (World Bank Policy Research Report 1997) (stating that, by 1996, net private capital flows to developing countries were nearly six times greater than they were at the start of the decade), and *see* GLOBAL DEVELOPMENT FINANCE 24 (World Bank 1999) (in table 2.1 showing the huge discrepancy between the amount of private capital flows and public, i.e. official, capital flows).

19 IFC's total disbursed loan and equity portfolio for its own account reached in FY99 US$10.0 billion, compared to US$3.6 billion for IFC's total disbursed loan and equity portfolio for its own account in FY90. The financing approved for IFC's own account reached in FY99 US$3.5 billion, compared to US$1.5 billion net investments for IFC's own account in FY90. *See* INTERNATIONAL FINANCE CORPORATION — ANNUAL REPORT (1999), at 1999 Financial Highlights; *see also* INTERNATIONAL FINANCE CORPORATION — ANNUAL REPORT (1990), at Highlights of the Year.

20 For an example, *see* the article on the Pangue project in the FINANCIAL TIMES, August 8, 1997, with the headline *Chile Dam Row Shows IFC's Problems With Projects.*"

21 *See,* for example, the campaign of an NGO, Rainforest Action Network, to protect the U'wa, an indigenous community of 5000 people in the cloudforest of eastern Colombia, against Occidental Petroleum's oil development plans at <www.ran.org/ran_campaigns/beyond_oil/index.html>. Related articles can be found in the BOSTON HERALD, February 4th, 2000 entitled *Protesters Target Fidelity in Dispute Over Oil Drilling,* and the BOSTON GLOBE, February 4, 2000 entitled *Fidelity a Target in Oil Protest.* Another prominent example is Shell's problems with environmental NGOs

D. Values-based Leverage

Finally, *values-based leverage* should not be neglected. Although good environmental and social practices are good business, there are occasional situations in which there is a substantial cost to meeting IFC's environmental and social requirements.

Sometimes it is difficult to translate the additional cost of compliance into an immediate dollars-and-cents return. In fact, every once in a while, a project sponsor decides not to deal with IFC because of its environmental and social requirements. But IFC is committed to adhering to its standards, in every project, even if there is a financial cost. That is because IFC believes that, as a member of the World Bank Group, it has a moral responsibility to make sure that its projects are environmentally and socially sound.

Ultimately, IFC is in the business of promoting economic development and reducing poverty.[22] This means that IFC cannot ignore the impacts of the projects it finances on the physical environment and the local community. Perhaps it would be cheaper to operate a tannery without expensive waste water treatment facilities, and perhaps there is no applicable local regulation prohibiting waste water discharges. But IFC is not willing to put its money into a project that would foul the local water supplies and create a health hazard.

And perhaps it would be consistent with local law for a project developer to evict the people living on the site where a project is to be built, without taking responsibility for assuring that they have replacement housing and an opportunity to earn an equivalent livelihood. But, in the view of the World Bank Group, it would not be developmentally sound to build a project at the expense of those most immediately affected.[23]

---

arising from its proposal to dispose of the Brent Spar oil rig in the North Sea. For more information on controversies about Shell, *see* <www.sierraclub.org/_vti_script/search.html0.idq>.

22 *See* IFC's Mission Statement available at IFC's website address <http://www.ifc.org>.

23 *See,* Operational Directive (OD) 4.30 on Involuntary Resettlement (June 1990), to be replaced by Operational Policy (OP) 4.12 on Involuntary Resettlement.

IV. IFC's ENVIRONMENTAL AND SOCIAL POLICIES

Turning from the philosophical to the practical perspective, IFC's environmental and social commitments are embodied in a set of environmental and social safeguard policies and review procedures. In 1998, after extensive consultation with civil society and the private sector, IFC took important steps to improve its policies and procedures.

Starting first with the *environmental and social policies* applicable to IFC,[24] the major change in 1998 was to increase clarity, which is essential for accountability. In 1997, when Friends of the Earth said that "[i]t is not clear which policies apply to the private-sector lending arm" of the World Bank, they were right.[25] IFC had never clearly specified which World Bank policies applied to IFC projects.

IFC's very first environmental procedure issued in 1990 stated that "IFC projects will be subject to an environmental review process to ensure that they are consistent with the spirit and intent of the appropriate Bank guidelines and policies."[26] This formulation left IFC with a great deal of room for interpretation.

The next version, issued in 1993, left out "spirit and intent" but still said "IFC projects must comply with appropriate World Bank environmental policies and guidelines" without specifying which policies and guidelines were appropriate.[27] As a result, when IFC confronted public criticism on the Pangue hydroelectric project in Chile, some IFC staff maintained that the World Bank's policy on Dams and Reservoirs did not apply to IFC.

But IFC has learned its lesson. Today, IFC's environmental performance is under close scrutiny and IFC is being held ac-

---

24 *See* IFC's Procedure for Environmental and Social Review of Projects and Policy on Disclosure of Information (effective September 1, 1998 and available on IFC's website <www.ifc.org/enviro/index.html>).

25 *See* FINANCIAL TIMES, August 8, 1997, *supra* note 20.

26 Purpose of Review, paragraph 1, *in* Procedure for Environmental Review of IFC Projects (in effect from March 1990 to December 1992).

27 Procedure for Environmental Review of International Finance Corporation Projects, *in* International Finance Corporation — Environmental Analysis and Review of International Finance Corporation Projects, September 8, 1993.

countable by various external constituencies and interest groups. IFC simply cannot assert that "appropriate" World Bank policies are applicable, and reserve for itself the ability to decide which ones on a case-by-case basis.

At the same time, it is not simply possible to say that all World Bank environmental and social safeguard policies are applicable in their exact wording to IFC projects. The World Bank policies assume that the borrower is a government, and sometimes call on the borrower to do things that only governments can do. The World Bank environmental policies and procedures[28] also correspond to World Bank lending procedures which differ from those at IFC.

So, IFC engaged in a line-by-line analysis of the entire corpus of the World Bank environmental and social safeguard policies, and applied a simple principle: IFC would turn them into IFC policies conforming as closely as possible to the World Bank policies, with only the modifications necessary to reflect IFC's different client base, project cycle, and organizational structure. During an extensive public comment period, another innovation for IFC, IFC used its World Wide Web site to post side-by-side comparisons of the proposed IFC policies with the Bank policies on which they were based. IFC believes that the result is a major step forward. IFC has now spelled out clearly what policies it is required to live up to. They are harmonized with those of the World Bank, and they are adapted as necessary to fit IFC's operations.

V. IFC's ENVIRONMENTAL AND SOCIAL REVIEW PROCEDURE

Concerning the *environmental and social review procedure,*[29] IFC has also made significant advances. The new IFC environmental and social review procedure is too lengthy to summarize here. The procedures fill more than 50 densely-packed (but well in-

28 *See* <http://www.worldbank.org/environment/op-policies.html>.

29 *See* IFC's Procedure for Environmental and Social Review of Projects and Policy on Disclosure of Information (effective September 1, 1998 and available on IFC's website <www.ifc.org/enviro/index.html>).

dexed) pages and can be found on IFC's website.[30] However, a few of the highlights will be provided.

IFC has made a real effort to spell out exactly what has to be done at each stage of the project cycle.[31] This includes greater attention to incorporating environmental and social requirements into the legal documentation, and better project supervision and monitoring on an ongoing basis.

IFC has also specified the procedures and requirements applicable to different types of IFC investment projects.[32] In particular, IFC has given great attention to the wide range of investments that IFC makes through financial intermediaries, including commercial banks, venture capital funds, leasing companies, and others. IFC's objective here is to use its leverage so that financial sector borrowers apply sound environmental and social standards in their own lending and investment activities. At the same time, IFC recognizes that different types of financial intermediaries play different roles and have different degrees of leverage over their own clients.

The new procedure also gives more attention to the social aspects of IFC projects. This corresponds to IFC's realization in the past few years that the social impacts of projects — including involuntary resettlement and effects on indigenous peoples — are often the greatest challenge. Over time, business people have become accustomed to quantifiable environmental standards — air emission limits, water discharge standards, noise levels.[33] But it is

---

30 *See* <http://www.ifc.org/enviro/index.html>.

31 Information on the IFC Project Cycle can be found on IFC's environmental website <http://www.ifc.org/ifc/enviro/Review_Procedure_Main/Project_Cycle/project_cycle.html>.

32 *See* IFC's website <http://www.ifc.org/ifc/enviro/Review_Procedure_Main/Project_Cycle/project_cycle.html>. The requirements for Financial Intermediary (FI) projects are spelled out in Annex F of IFC's Environmental and Social Policies and Procedure available on IFC's website <http://www.ifc.org/ifc/enviro/Review_Procedue_Main/Review_Procedure/Anne.../annex_f.html>.

33 The Pollution Prevention and Abatement Handbook became effective in 1998. It applies to all projects directly financed by IFC. The Pollution Prevention and Abatement Handbook is founded on the principles of sustainable development, cleaner production processes and pollution prevention. Therefore, it provides pollution and abatement measures and emission levels that are normally acceptable to IFC, subject to project-specific analysis in the environmental assessment. The Pollution Prevention and Abatement Handbook contains three parts. Part I is a summary

more complicated and difficult to apply somewhat subjective criteria, such as assisting project-displaced peoples "to achieve the production levels, income-earning capacities, and living standards they are likely to have had without the project." In order to assist project sponsors in meeting these requirements, IFC has now added several social scientists to its staff.

The new procedures also significantly strengthen public consultation and disclosure in IFC projects.[34] This varies, of course, according to the magnitude of the project's environmental and social impacts. In the projects with the greatest impacts, so called Category A projects, earlier versions of IFC' s procedures did require public disclosure and consultation regarding environmental and social impacts; now IFC provides much more guidance to project sponsors on how to carry out effective, culturally appropriate consultation with the local community.[35]

In projects with less substantial impacts, so called Category B projects, IFC has previously required disclosure of project information in Washington, D.C., at the World Bank InfoShop (formerly called the Public Information Center). IFC is now requiring that the same information be disclosed locally — and translated into the local language — for the benefit of the affected communities.

VI. CONCLUSION

At a time of greatly increased private capital flows into developing countries, IFC's experience in integrating environmental and social concerns into private sector projects may serve as a model for other financial institutions and for private investors. Until recently, environmental NGOs have tended to concentrate their energies on the multilateral financial institutions, such as the World Bank and IFC. In "Leverage for the Environment," the World Re-

---

of key policy lessons in pollution management based on experience gained by the World Bank Group. Part II contains the enumeration of good practice notes on implementation of the policy objectives, and Part III sets forth the detailed provisions to be taken into account by project sponsors in designing and operating projects.

34 *See* IFC' s Policy on Disclosure of Information (effective September 1, 1998).

35 *See generally* DOING BETTER BUSINESS THROUGH EFFECTIVE PUBLIC CONSULTATION AND DISCLOSURE — A GOOD PRACTICE MANUAL, *supra* note 12.

sources Institute challenged the environmental movement to look beyond engagement with public sector financial institutions in order to influence development finance decisions that are increasingly made in the private sector.[36] In time, private financial institutions and their clients will face some of the same environmental challenges that IFC has recently confronted.

[36] *See* Ganzi, Seymour & Buffett, *supra* note 5.

THE ASIAN FINANCIAL CRISIS, CORRUPTION AND LEGAL REFORM

*Barry Metzger**

I. INTRODUCTION

The financial crisis in Asia is now more than three years old and each each of the crisis economies has now returned to economic growth. While the crisis may be "over," the process of economic adjustment which the crisis triggered continues. Corporate and financial institution restructuring and recapitalization is far from complete in Korea, Thailand and Indonesia, and each of these economies and their immediate neighbors remain economically vulnerable. The crisis has been a crisis of many parts. There was an important, underlying element of macroeconomic imbalance in the economies affected by the crisis, and errors in macroeconomic management. The tying of exchange rates to a rising US dollar, the deterioration of export competitiveness, a cyclical downturn in important sectors of the global semiconductor and consumer electronics markets, softening Japanese import demand and foreign investment, growing current account deficits, and a growing conservatism among some foreign lenders traditionally active in the region were all elements of this macroeconomic landscape.

The distinguishing characteristic of the crisis, however, was a series of structural, microeconomic problems in the financial sector and the corporate sector. In each country felled by the crisis, financial institutions were revealed to be fragile, undercapitalized, under-supervised, and poorly managed. High levels of non-performing loans, resulting in some cases from the legacy of

---

* The views expressed in this paper represent the opinion of the author and should not be attributed to the organization with which he was affiliated.

government policies and the politics of directed credit and in some cases from the collapse of real estate and share prices, forced many banks and financial institutions to close and undermined the viability of many others.

In the early days of the crisis, the withdrawal of inter-bank credit lines and the flight of portfolio investment in the Asian equity and bond markets were staggering in their speed and depth. In some cases the order of magnitude of this flight of credit and capital was approximately ten percent of the total size of the economies concerned — measured in GDP (Gross Domestic Product) terms. Investors viewed the problems of one Asian economy as the problem of all Asian economies, and institutional investors' capital flight turned from an orderly retreat from particular markets into broadly based, panicked selling.[1]

There was also a political dimension to this flight of credit and capital. At the time the crisis broke, political uncertainties existed in Thailand (which was engaged in a politically divisive debate over a new constitution): in Korea (with an impending presidential election in which Kim Dae-jung — viewed by some as an anti-business populist — was considered a possible winner); in Indonesia (with the impending re-election of President Suharto reminding observers of the uncertainty of his succession); and in the Philippines (where another candidate considered by many as an anti-business populist — now President "Erap" Estrada — was expected to win a landslide victory). A year-long speculation about the impact of China's resumption of sovereignty in Hong Kong made some analysts particularly sensitive to the political dimensions of economic analysis in the region. To the extent there was a political dimension to investors' decisions about their Asian exposures in the early days of what became the Asian financial crisis of 1997, there is an irony which is almost tragic. Investors who value open markets, market economy institutions, and the transparency and predictability of legal and regulatory rules, were reacting in part to political uncertainties which, in many markets, represented the ongoing evolution of more democratic political institutions and processes which had begun to emerge in the mid- to late-1980s.

---

1 *See, generally, Recovery from the Asian Crisis and the Role of the IMF*, International Monetary Fund Staff Paper (June 2000).

Many observers, particularly in the West and including a number on Capitol Hill, have emphasized the extent to which corruption in these countries and "crony capitalism" contributed to the crisis. These are problems about which American and other foreign investors have been concerned over many years. The view has been that poor governance — deficiencies in the transparency, predictability and accountability of governments in the region and the absence of "level playing field" opportunities for stakeholder participation — compromised economic performance, even during the years of dynamic economic growth in the region. This too is ironic, because most in-depth studies of the economic performance of Asia during the post-World War II period[2] attribute the successes of Japan, Korea, Taiwan, Singapore and Hong Kong in part to the relative efficiency of their governments and to the opportunities which these governments provided, at least to the domestic private sector, to make inputs into the economic policy-making process.

There is a tendency of many analysts — at times looking for simplistic, media "sound byte" explanations of complex situations — to place too great an emphasis on corruption and "crony capitalism" as the principal explanations of the Asian financial crisis. Corruption and "crony capitalism" certainly played a role, and they have been the focus of considerable attention in the reform process which we see unfolding in the region. It would be an error, however, to place such explanations at stage center. It is important to attempt to grasp and understand the other component parts of a complex crisis, particularly the macroeconomic policy mistakes of government and the structural weaknesses in the financial sector which were at the core of the crisis and are the principal focus of reforms. At the same time, the crisis undermined the credibility of the bureaucracy in many countries of the region and exposed deeply-seated (and previously little appreciated) opposition to corruption and "crony capitalism." These developments are contributing to a revolution of rising expectations about reforms in corporate governance and, more broadly, the accountability of governments.

---

2 See The World Bank's study, THE EAST ASIAN MIRACLE: ECONOMIC GROWTH AND PUBLIC POLICY (1993), and the Asian Development Bank's study, EMERGING ASIA: CHANGES AND CHALLENGES (1997).

As the complexity of their economies increased and as lessons were learned about the costs of inappropriate government industrial policies, many of these countries over the past ten years have deregulated or liberalized their domestic economies and permitted markets to play a far greater role in making allocative economic decisions. The market can be harsh in the judgments which it makes. Governments are finding their latitude for decision-making circumscribed by international rules to which they have subscribed — whether they be as a result of membership in the International Monetary Fund (IMF) or in the World Trade Organization (WTO) — and by the markets' swift and at times brutal punishment of errors in macroeconomic policy. Markets are also characterized by overreaction, and there can be no question that the depreciation of the baht, the won and the rupiah at the outset of the crisis far exceeded the economic fundamentals requiring rebalancing.

The prescription for cure from the IMF and the other multilateral institutions, as the traditional international economic doctors, involved more than a traditional macroeconomic adjustment program. It was a program of structural reform of institutions in the financial sector and of corporate governance.

II. THE RESPONSE TO THE CRISIS

In each of the crisis-affected countries the response to the crisis included major institutional, legal and regulatory reforms. The principal elements of such reforms can be identified as follows: (i) policy reforms for restructuring the financial sector, (ii) legal reforms for financial sector regulation and rehabilitation, (iii) legal reforms in corporate governance, (iv) a liberalized environment for foreign investment, and (v) anti-corruption measures.

A. Policy Reforms for Restructuring the Financial Sector

This has involved the closing of insolvent banks and non-bank financial institutions; changing prudential requirements regarding the treatment of non-performing loans, provisioning and capital adequacy, and changing prudential and public information disclosure and reporting requirements. The independence of regulators has been significantly enhanced and their regulatory, prudential oversight of financial institutions increased. Accounting standards applicable to financial institutions have been tightened, off-balance sheet transactions are being subjected to fuller disclosure, and derivatives transactions more closely monitored and regulated. Poorly capitalized banks have been forced to close or merge with stronger institutions. Non-bank financial institutions — whether they be finance companies in Thailand or investment and trust companies in China — are being subjected to new and particularly close regulatory oversight and, generally, their role in the financial system is being circumscribed. The task of recapitalizing such financial institutions has been staggering. For example, the level of non-performing loans in the Korean financial system exceeded US$50 billion equivalent; the final costs of recapitalization in most of the crisis-affected economies will run between ten percent and twenty-five percent of GDP. Significant quantities of public money have been required, in part because the private sector — itself devastated by the financial crisis — was not in a position in most of the economies to mobilize new capital for investment in these financial institutions. Foreign investment has also played an important role. For the first time, foreign investors can acquire controlling interests in financial institutions in many of the crisis-affected economies and attractively-priced investment opportunities in financial institutions are available (though many potential investors claim that too many putative sellers are still "in denial" and that asking prices still have a long way to move before deals can be struck). In addition to cash investment, a large element of human capital investment has been required. Training for regulators in crisis regulation and in the crisis management of financial institutions is taking place on an accelerated basis. Training of bankers is also a priority, in such areas as debt restructuring and debt recovery and in more rigorous credit analysis and monitoring. It is widely recognized that a "credit culture" and related skills must be established in banks and other financial institutions in the region which more rigorously analyzes, and bases lending decisions on, the corporate creditworthiness of borrowers.

B. Legal Reforms for Financial Sector Regulation and Rehabilitation

This financial sector restructuring and the rehabilitation of banks and non-bank financial institutions required major legal reforms. The legal powers of bank regulators to intervene in the affairs of troubled financial institutions and, where necessary, to assume management control or close such institutions have been enhanced in most jurisdictions. New bank restructuring agencies have been created, largely based on the Resolution Trust Company model from the United States and on the Mexican experience with that model during the Mexican financial crisis of 1994–95. Securitization of loan assets is being made possible through new laws, with corresponding changes in tax, corporate and bank regulatory legislation, in a number of the crisis-affected countries. Moreover, new insolvency regimes have been introduced that improve liquidation insolvencies and introduce reorganization procedures and, more generally, facilitate the reorganization and liquidation process. Foreclosure laws and auction procedures have been revised, and finally, collateral security regimes are being revisited, to provide a sounder basis for secured lending in the future.

C. Legal Reforms in Corporate Governance

Legal and regulatory reforms have been introduced into the corporate sector, particularly affecting the largest companies in the crisis-affected countries and most listed companies. Corporate reforms in Korea seek to reduce the dominance of the largest corporate groups — the *chaebols* — while recognizing their continuing importance to the economy. Government policies required abolition of the Office of the Chairman in most groups and reassert the legal importance of individual corporate boards of directors and directors' fiduciary obligations to their companies and their shareholders; a reduction in debt-equity ratios has been mandated; intra-group guarantees to support funding have been phased out; *chaebols* are being encouraged to focus on core businesses and to divest non-core businesses; selective consolidation is being encouraged and Korea's competition/anti-monopoly laws are being reinvigorated. An irony, with some history to it, is the

Korean government's desire to encourage group holding companies, ultimately to supplant the current structure of *chaebols* informally controlled by their founders with limited personal shareholdings. Holding companies have been illegal in Japan and Korea for decades, as part of the American-imposed legal reforms of the post-World War II occupation; the prohibition was part of the legal regime intended to prevent reconstruction of the pre-War *zaibatsu* in Japan and their dominance of the economy.

In all of the crisis-affected countries of the region, the manner in which large corporations conduct themselves and their accountability are today subject to unprecedented scrutiny. A broadly-based debate about corporate governance has emerged in many of the countries and regionally, in part through the Asia Pacific Economic Cooperation (APEC) forum. In all of the crisis-affected countries, changes are taking place in securities regulation and in the listing requirements applicable to publicly-traded companies. In some cases, greater representation of independent, "outside" directors is being required; audit and remuneration committees are being established; expanded disclosure of corporate information is being mandated; and new accounting standards and expanded minority shareholders protection are under consideration. The powers and independence of securities regulators are being enhanced; capitalization requirements for securities firms are being increased; and prudential supervision of such firms is being tightened (either directly or through greater industry self-regulation); investor protection regimes are being strengthened including increased regulation of investment funds. Foreign investment rules are being relaxed to permit higher levels of investment in listed companies by foreign investors and higher levels of foreign investment, including controlling interests, in the securities industry.[3]

D. Improved Environment for Foreign Investment

The relaxation of restrictions on foreign investment both generally and in particular, in the financial sector, is a development of

---

[3] *See* Ibrahim F. I. Shihata, *Law, Development and the Role of the World Bank,* in COMPLEMENTARY REFORM — ESSAYS ON LEGAL, JUDICIAL AND OTHER INSTITUTIONS REFORMS BY THE WORLD BANK, 3–30 (1997); *see also* KATHARINA PISTOR & PHILIP A. WELLONS, THE ROLE OF LAW AND LEGAL INSTITUTIONS IN ASIAN ECONOMIC DEVELOPMENT 1960–1995 (1998).

special significance. Foreign investment will not only serve to provide badly needed capital for the recapitalization of financial institutions and other private sector enterprises, it will also play an important role in accelerated programs of privatization of state enterprises in a number of countries. Equally important, especially in the financial sector, foreign investments that carry management control will contribute to standard-setting in financial institution management and credit controls in those markets. Foreign investments which carry with them management control, particularly in the financial sector, remain controversial but it is doubtful that such controversy will prevent foreign investment from playing an important role over the years immediately ahead in the process of financial sector reform.

E. Anti-corruption Reform

The crisis also brought corruption to the fore on the domestic agenda in the crisis countries. Domestically, corruption and crony capitalism are viewed as among the principal culprits of the crisis. The search for simplistic explanations for the crisis is by no means the exclusive domain of foreign commentators. For example, an anti-corruption campaign in Korea has resulted in the dismissal or disciplining of several thousand civil servants. In Thailand, the new constitution (drafted prior to the crisis but brought into effect only as a result of the broadly-based calls for political reform which the crisis engendered) mandates creation of a National Counter Corruption Commission, Ombudsmen and a system of administrative courts. In Indonesia, the government undertook as part of its US$1.5 billion Financial Governance Sector Development Program with the Asian Development Bank (ADB) to effect a comprehensive updating of its 1973 anti-corruption legislation and to develop and provide adequate resources for implementation of a national anti-corruption strategy. We know from experience in many countries that anti-corruption legislation and the creation of anti-corruption agencies are the "easy pieces" in fighting corruption, and that real progress requires political will and direction. In Thailand and Korea, there is clear evidence of such political will and direction, both "top down" from the current political leadership and "bottom up" from electorates that are demanding greater accountability of government, from a more vigorous press and media, and from civil society groups — nongovernmental organizations (NGOs) — dedicated to cleaner and more effective government. Such efforts are reinforced by the breadth and depth of current international attention to corruption as an issue in the developing world, including the work of international institutions such as the World Bank, IMF and the ADB, the new OECD-sponsored international convention criminalizing foreign bribery, and the activity of international NGOs such as Transparency International.[4]

III. THE INFORMAL CONSULTATION ON LEGAL PROBLEMS OF INVESTMENT AND FINANCE ARISING FROM THE ASIAN FINANCIAL CRISIS

Immediately before completing my service as General Counsel at the ADB, we brought together thirty prominent Asian and foreign lawyers practicing in the region, for what we called an "Informal Consultation on Legal Problems of Investment and Finance arising from the Asian Financial Crisis." The Informal Consultation focused on the crisis and the legal reform process in five countries — Thailand, Korea, Indonesia, Malaysia and the Philippines — and, from a regional perspective, on two subjects: (i) banking and financial sector reform, and (ii) on the impact of the crisis on private sector development of infrastructure. Our participants were drawn mostly from private practice but also included the general counsels of a number of the largest corporations operating in the region. Their messages were several-fold. First, they emphasized that the reform process in each of the crisis-affected countries remains incomplete. Many of the proposed reforms remain controversial, with significant political opposition and varying levels of continuing opposition within the bureaucracy and within the business communities. Second, it was repeatedly emphasized that the tendency of foreign analysts and many domestic opponents of reform to identify the reform process as foreign-imposed — as governments "doing what they are told to do" by

---

4 *See* Ibrahim F. I. Shihata, *Corruption — A General Review with an Emphasis on the Role of the World Bank,* 15 DICKINSON JOURNAL OF INTERNATIONAL LAW 451 (1997).

the IMF and by other international institutions (such as the ADB) — fails to recognize the important domestic roots of the reform process and the extent to which institutional reforms made possible by the crisis represent the realization of proposals for greater transparency and accountability in government which have been the subject of domestic debate over the past decade. This is probably most evident in the new constitution of the Kingdom of Thailand, largely written before the onset of the crisis. In many respects it is a remarkable political charter, which seeks to break the tradition of political interference in the bureaucracy by creating mechanisms for greater public participation in the political process and in executive (ministerial) decision-making. The third point made by participants at ADB's Informal Consultation was that the broadly-based legal reforms undertaken in response to the financial crisis cannot work in isolation from the effectiveness or ineffectiveness of the legal, regulatory and judicial infrastructure of the crisis countries. They emphasized the serious weaknesses in such infrastructure, including in particular the need to upgrade the skills base and the integrity of government legal services and the judiciary. They called upon the ADB and other donors to work with the governments concerned to address these serious weaknesses in the legal and judicial infrastructure.

IV. CONCLUSION

History teaches us that crisis is the anvil on which reform is forged. In the wake of the Asian financial crisis, a revolution in governance is emerging within the region. In corporate governance, financial institution governance, economic governance more generally and in the governance of public sector institutions, we are witnessing broadly-based demands for greater transparency and accountability. Those demands are being met with reforms. Twenty years ago within the region, economic adversity was generally associated with increased authority to governments to respond and, in such context, increased governmental discretion. Today, economic adversity is associated with reforms which increase the transparency and accountability of governments and which place greater reliance on legal rules and institutions. But, as noted at our Informal Consultation in Manila, the process is incomplete, and must be supported by broadly-based efforts to strengthen legal, regulatory and judicial institutions. It is only with such support that the emerging governance revolution in the region will become the lasting legacy of the Asian financial crisis.

CHARTER LIMITATIONS ON THE SCOPE OF INTER-AMERICAN DEVELOPMENT BANK ACTIVITIES

*John Niehuss**

I. INTRODUCTION

I am honored to have been asked to contribute to the *Liber Amicorum* for such an extraordinary man as Dr. Ibrahim F.I. Shihata. I have known Ibrahim in several capacities — briefly as a colleague at the World Bank, as a counterpart while I served as the General Counsel of the Inter-American Development Bank (IDB or Bank) and as a friend outside of work relations. I have been enormously enriched in my contacts with him in all of these capacities.

There is an informal network that exists among the general counsels of several international financial institutions to exchange information and advice on issues of common interest. Ibrahim Shihata was the center of this network from which most information flowed and to which all of the other general counsels were connected. His opinions, books and articles on development law issues were a key source of information for those of us who had to interpret our own charters and advise our management and boards. In addition to his written work, he was extremely generous in sharing orally his knowledge and experience. He guided me on difficult issues on many occasions as he did with the general counsels of the other multilateral development banks (MDBs). Ibrahim combines a superb intellect with wonderful human qual-

* The views expressed in this paper are the personal opinions of the author and should not be attributed to the institution he is or was affiliated with.

ities. He is not only the world's leading expert in the fields of development law and the law of development banks, but he is very accessible and willing to share his vast knowledge with others. When he retires, his presence will be missed by those who worked in his shadow in the field of development banking law.

My contribution to the *Liber Amicorum* focuses on factors involved in interpreting the Bank's mandate as set forth in the Agreement Establishing the IDB (The Charter). It also contains some brief reflections on development banking priorities, using the IDB as an example. In both areas, it draws on discussions with Ibrahim Shihata and advice received from him, although the opinions and conclusions are my own.

II. THE IDB'S MANDATE

Like the other development banks, the IDB is often asked to consider funding programs in areas which raise issues as to consistency with the purpose and functions of the institution as set forth in its Charter. Recent examples include such diverse areas as: crime prevention and law enforcement; anti-violence programs; training and support of police; criminal justice reform; penal reform and rehabilitation and construction of prisons; cultural activities; promotion of democracy; and support for peace initiatives within a country.

The paper's purpose is to (1) summarize the IDB's Charter provisions which establish limits on activities which can be funded by the Bank; and to (2) suggest a simple, four-part test which can be used by the Bank as it considers requests for operations in Charter-sensitive areas similar to those noted above.

A. Relevant Sections of the Charter

Several sections of the Charter need to be read together to establish the scope of activities that may be financed by the Bank. They are:

1) *Use of Resources:* The resources and facilities of the Bank must be used exclusively to implement the purpose and

functions of the Bank.[1] This means that the Bank cannot finance activities that fall outside the limits established by the Charter's language dealing with purpose and functions.

2) *Basic Purpose:* The Charter states that the Bank's purpose "shall be to contribute to the acceleration of the process of economic and social development[2] of the regional developing member countries, individually and collectively."[3]
3) *Key Functions:* In order to implement this basic purpose, Article I, Section 2 of the Charter gives the Bank the following functions:
    1. Promote investment for development purposes;
    2. Finance the development of member countries in a way that gives priority to loans that make the most effective contribution to economic growth;
    3. Encourage private investment;
    4. Help members orient their development policies toward a better utilization of resources consistent with the objectives of complimentary economies and growth of foreign trade; and
    5. Technical assistance for development plans and projects, including the study of priorities and formulation of specific proposals.
4) *Factors to Consider in Making Decisions:* Only economic considerations are to be relevant to the decisions of the Bank, and these considerations must be weighed impartially to achieve the basic purpose and functions of the Bank.[4]
5) *Non-Interference in Political Affairs:* Article VIII, Section 5(f) of the Charter states that the Bank "shall not interfere in the political affairs of any member" and that the Bank shall not "be influenced in (its) decisions by the political character of the member or members concerned."

---

1 Agreement Establishing the Inter-American Development Bank, art. III, sec. 1.

2 It should be noted that the IDB's basic purpose includes the concept of social as well as economic development. Arguably, this gives the IDB a slightly broader mandate than the World Bank whose Articles of Agreement do not include any reference to "social" development in the purpose section.

3 *Supra* note 1, art. 1, sec. 1.

4 *Ibid.* at art. VIII, sec. 5(f).

6) *Availability of Finance from Private Sources*: In considering a loan, the Bank is required to take into account the ability of the borrower to obtain finance from private sources on reasonable terms.[5]

B. The Charter Limits on Bank Activities

Although the mandate established in Article I of the Charter is drafted in broad terms, it is a limited mandate and does not give the IDB powers that exceed its defined purpose and functions. This means that the mere fact a country has a need or has made a request to the IDB for funding does not mean that the IDB can respond to that need. The loan or technical assistance must be for an activity that falls within the Bank's mandate as established in the Charter.

This raises the difficult issue of establishing the limits to the Bank's mandate. As IDB borrowers' economies develop and evolve, it is natural that their needs change and that the Bank will be asked for loans and technical assistance in new areas to help deal with emerging problems. To the extent possible, the Charter should be interpreted flexibly to enable the Bank to respond to changing circumstances and needs. On the other hand, the Charter does set limits and there are some activities which would be prohibited by the Charter.

To be consistent with the Charter and be eligible for Bank funding, an activity must meet all four basic tests established by the Charter provisions outlined above. These tests are:

1) *The Basic Purpose and Functions Test:* The activity must be used to implement the purpose and functions of the Bank. This means that the activity should (a) make a direct and foreseeable contribution to "the acceleration of the process of social and economic development . . ." and (b) implement the functions of the Bank, which are basically economic in nature and focus on activities that promote investment, economic growth, trade and better utilization of resources.

5 *Ibid.* at art. III, sec. 7(a)(ii).

2) *The Economic Considerations Test:* The Bank's decision with respect to the funding of an activity must be based solely on economic factors. Other factors are, under the Charter, irrelevant.
3) *The Non-Interference in Political Matters Test:* The activity to be funded should not have "political" dimensions which might be interpreted as interference in a member's political affairs, and the political nature of a member's government cannot influence the Bank's decision-making.
4) *The Availability of Private Finance Test:* The project must be one that cannot be funded from private sources of finance on reasonable terms. If private finance is available, the Charter suggests that the Bank should *not* proceed with a loan to the project.

Thus, before the Bank agrees to provide funding in new Charter-sensitive areas, it needs to analyze carefully each activity and ask: (1) does it make a significant, direct and foreseeable contribution to accelerating the process of social or economic development?; (2) can the Bank's decision be justified solely on economic factors?; (3) does it have aspects which are political (or potentially political) in nature?; and (4) can the project be funded from private sources on reasonable terms? As long as an activity meets all four of these tests, it would be eligible for funding by the Bank. However, if any of the four tests are not met, the Bank is not permitted to fund the activity in question.

Where the line between permissible and impermissible activities is drawn, is a matter of judgment on which reasonable persons may differ. For example, differences are likely to arise in answering such questions as: Is there sufficient economic impact to justify financing programs in such areas as culture, criminal justice and penal reform, construction of prisons, training of police and anti-violence? Does promotion of democracy or support for a peace initiative to end a civil war constitute impermissible political activity? The answers to these questions may vary from country to country and are certainly subject to variation depending on one's point of view. What the above analysis has suggested is that there are limits on the types of activities the MDBs can undertake. In the final analysis, those interpreting MDB Charters need to be creative and flexible so that the institutions can meet the changing needs of their borrowers while, at the same time, retaining the courage to say "no" when a proposed activity would be prohibited by the Charter.

III. SENSIBLE DEVELOPMENT FINANCE BEYOND THE STRICTLY LEGAL BORDERS OF AN MDB'S CHARTER

Even if a particular activity is legally permitted by the Charter, it may not always be justified as a policy matter. There is a tendency for the IDB, like other MDBs, to expand its activities into areas that are currently popular and politically, but not always developmentally, correct. By trying to undertake activities in many diverse sectors, any organization runs the risk of spreading itself too thin and diluting its long-term effectiveness. To avoid this risk, the IDB should have fewer, and not more lines of business. It should focus on basic, fundamental projects that create domestic capacity in borrowers which can be used by the country itself to promote development in all sectors.

Under this approach, the test for determining whether a particular activity should be funded would be: Does the project or program make a meaningful direct contribution to the creation of the *domestic* capacity for the borrower to achieve sustainable development without continuous external assistance? An increased focus on capacity building would implicitly accept the notion that, at some point in the future, the IDB would no longer be needed by some of its borrowers. The IDB's success over time would be judged by how many of its borrowers had graduated from reliance on IDB and other external assistance. In short, the long-run goal for the IDB, as well as other MDBs, should be to work itself out of existence — at least in some of its more advanced borrowers.

These capacity building programs require persistent and steady support and effort by both the IDB and its borrowers. The IDB and each borrower should identify a few key areas or sectors critical to create needed capacity and work to create long-term, multi-project programs. This would mean planning a series of loans in key sectors over an extended period. Too often the IDB funds a single project in a sector, proclaims victory and then moves on to other areas. To think of a major change in focus when there is unfinished business in a priority area means that the IDB risks spreading its resources too thinly. It is less glamorous to stay the course in a few traditional areas that it is to start initiatives in new, more politically correct areas. However, a steady approach concentrating on capacity building would, in most cases, contribute more to long-run development. The IDB needs to establish a better balance between staying the course in a few key areas and starting new initiatives.

Reasonable people can disagree on the priority sectors, and the areas for emphasis will vary from country to country. My own priority areas for IDB (and other MDB) activity can be grouped in four broad, overlapping areas:

1. *Favorable Private Sector Environment:* Creation of an environment for *domestic* private sector activity by creating a free, open market economy and by concentrating on the areas noted below.
2. *Human Capital:* Improvement in the quality of human capital with major programs in education, health and population control.
3. *Mobilization of Domestic Savings:* Promotion of the development of local savings and financial markets (including both banking and capital markets) which reduce dependence on external capital for development.
4. *Creation of Enduring Institutions:* Creation of both public and private autonomous institutions (including legal and judicial systems) that are efficient, transparent and stable and that endure through successive changes in government.

The basic rationale in selecting the above four broad groupings for core IDB activities is that they help create the tools or capacity for borrowers to assume full responsibility for their own development.

These priorities do not explicitly include many of the areas which are the focus of much current development thinking — e.g., poverty alleviation, social safety net programs, and the environment. This is intentional and reflects a view that programs that focus directly on these areas often merely mitigate symptoms of lack of development and do not attack the basic causes of underdevelopment (e.g., lack of education, lack of domestic capital, and lack of durable domestic institutions).

IV. CONCLUSION

If the IDB concentrated on the areas listed above and was able to help improve domestic capacity in these areas, it could make a more valuable contribution to long-run sustainable development in borrowers than it is doing through its current approach. The current emphasis seems to be directed more toward mitigating symptoms of underdevelopment than on creating the capacity within borrowers to deal with the root causes of poverty, social inequality and environmental degradation. In short, the mere fact that the Charter of the IDB permits the institution to fund an activity does not mean that the activity is a priority which *should* be financed from a long run development policy standpoint.

CHANGING APPROACHES TO THE NATIONALITY OF CLAIMS IN THE CONTEXT OF DIPLOMATIC PROTECTION AND INTERNATIONAL DISPUTE SETTLEMENT

*Francisco Orrego Vicuña**

The well deserved series of colloquiums and studies organized to honor Dr. Ibrahim F.I. Shihata on the occasion of his retirement as Vice President and General Counsel of the World Bank, have provided an important opportunity to examine the trends that international law has been following in the transition from the twentieth to the twenty-first century.

This contribution examines how the law relating to the nationality of claims has evolved in the context of diplomatic protection, and to what extent it is possible today to suggest new principles or approaches in this respect. The salient issues of the matter, the rules prevailing under traditional international law, and the changes that are intervening so as to establish trends, will be examined to this end and, where appropriate, new answers will be suggested. These thoughts are in part based on the work undertaken by the author for the Committee on Diplomatic Protection of the International Law Association.[1]

---

* The views expressed in this paper are the personal views of the author and should not be attributed to the organizations with which he is affiliated.

1 *See* First Report of the Committee on Diplomatic Protection, 69th Annual Conference of the International Law Association, London, 2000. Comments on the *Preliminary Report on Nationality of Claims* were made by Richard B. Bilder, David J. Bederman, Bozo Cerar, Lady Hazel Fox, Juliane Kokott, Vaughan Lowe and Torsten Stein, to whom the author is grateful for their contributions and views.

I. WHOSE RIGHTS ARE ASSERTED IN INTERNATIONAL CLAIMS?

The starting point of the discussion on the rules of nationality does not refer so much to nationality as such, but to a more fundamental issue, namely, the question of whose rights are asserted when bringing an international claim. Traditional rules on diplomatic protection undertaken by the State are confronted in this context with the increasing access of the individual to dispute settlement mechanisms.

The classic rule on the matter was well established in the *Mavrommatis Concessions* case, where the Permanent Court of International Justice ruled that "[b]y taking up the case of one of its subjects and by resorting to diplomatic action or international judicial proceedings on his behalf, a State is in reality asserting its own rights — its right to ensure, in the person of its subjects, respect for the rules of international law."[2] As rightly explained by Bennouna, this conceptual approach led to a "transformation" of the claim, which passed from the individual to the espousing State of nationality, but in so doing, the role of the State became paramount and eclipsed that of the individual which was at its origin.[3]

A number of consequences followed from this legal fiction, which responded to the time when the State was the single and most important subject of international law. Discretionary espousal of claims, disposition of the compensation by the State, introduction of a type of damage different from that suffered by the individual, and the influence of political power, are some of those consequences.[4]

A number of legal contradictions accompanied this approach since its outset. First, in cases where a direct injury to the State could be established, international law provided for different rules

---

[2] Mavrommatis Palestine Concessions (Greece v. Gr. Brit.), 1924 P.C.I.J. (ser. A) No. 30, at 6.

[3] Mohammed Bennouna (Special Rapporteur), *Preliminary Report on Diplomatic Protection,* International Law Commission, A/CN. 4/484, Feb. 4, 1998, at 5. *See also* Georges Scelle, *Droit de la Paix,* 46 RECUEIL DES COURS DE L'ACADEMIE DE DROIT INTERNATIONAL, No. IV, 660–661 (1933) as cited by Bennouna in note 18, at 8.

[4] *See* Bennouna, *supra* note 3, at 6-7.

of protection, such as measures of self-protection.[5] This included situations in which the affected individual was a high officer of the State.[6] The requirement of the continuity of nationality of the affected individual also involved a contradiction since "[i]t is also illogical to consider the State as the sole holder of the international claim, yet at the same time to prevent the State from pursuing this claim because the 'nationality' of the underlying individual claim has changed."[7] More importantly, while diplomatic protection was understood as the "procedural corollary to the legal responsibility of international law subjects,"[8] in many instances it does not appear to have followed the evolution that the law of state responsibility itself has experienced, particularly in respect of the operation of international mechanisms established to make states answerable to international wrongs.[9]

Besides the legal issues involved in this approach, there was a clear political connotation in the use of diplomatic protection as an instrument of power by States in international relations.[10] Reactions such as the "Calvo Clause,"[11] aimed at the elimination of the role of diplomatic protection, were the inevitable consequence of the abuse of this form of protection in the early part of the twentieth century.

Legal and political issues, however, were not enough to prevent the consolidation of the classic rules on the matter,[12] nor did considerations of equity and logic have much influence on State practice for a long period of time.[13] But this discussion also reveals that various issues appear not to have met the required standards of support by state practice and *opinio juris* so as to

---

5 *See* Wilhelm Karl Geck, *Diplomatic Protection, in* ENCYCLOPEDIA OF PUBLIC INTERNATIONAL LAW 1046 (Rudolf Bernhardt ed. 1992).

6 *See ibid.* at 1046.

7 *See ibid.* at 1056.

8 *See ibid.* at 1046.

9 *See* Resolution on Responsibility and Liability under International Law for Environmental Damage, *Institut de Droit International,* Sep. 4, 1997, in ANNUAIRE DE L'INSTITUT DE DROIT INTERNATIONAL, SESSION DE STRASBOURG, Vol. 67-II, 487 (1998).

10 *See* ENCYCLOPEDIA, *supra* note 5, at 1048.

11 The Calvo clause was named after the Argentine diplomat and international law writer, Carlos Calvo (1824–1906); *see* IBRAHIM F. I. SHIHATA, TOWARDS GREATER DEPOLITICIZATION OF INVESTMENT DISPUTES: THE ROLES OF ICSID AND MIGA 2 (1992).

12 *See* Bennouna, *supra* note 3, at 8–9.

13 *See* ENCYCLOPEDIA, *supra* note 5, at 1056.

become a rule of customary international law. One thing was the European and United States practice on diplomatic protection, but quite another was the view taken by many other countries that did not share the same legal understandings in this respect.

It would be the very structure of international law that prompted fundamental changes in the role of diplomatic protection. As the State lost its position of exclusivity in the international legal order, and both international organizations and individuals acquired specific, albeit still limited roles of their own, new alternatives emerged for the assertion of international claims. The law of human rights, on the one hand, and that relating to the protection of foreign investments, on the other hand, have opened up a clear path for the direct access of the individual to international mechanisms for the assertion of claims, following a number of specific precedents established during the twentieth century.[14] This trend is also present in a number of other developments taking place under contemporary international law in respect of the settlement of disputes.[15] In this new context, many times it is the right of the individual affected and no longer that of the State of nationality which is asserted. To that same extent, diplomatic protection is no longer required to intervene and, furthermore, as in the International Centre for Settlement of Investment Disputes (ICSID), it is expressly excluded to the extent that arbitration is resorted to and complied with.

The direct standing of the individual under international law will continue to expand for a variety of purposes, particularly in terms of access to dispute settlement mechanisms.[16] It can therefore be expected that claims will be increasingly handled outside of the operation of diplomatic protection. This does not mean that the role of the State has lost its significance. It will still be necessary for the state to espouse claims in the many areas where direct standing is not available: to enter into treaties and arrangements to ensure such direct access, to establish the legal framework under

---

14 *See* Marek St. Korowicz, *The Problem of the International Personality of Individuals,* 50 AMERICAN JOURNAL OF INTERNATIONAL LAW 533–562 (1956).

15 *See* Francisco Orrego Vicuña & Christopher Pinto, *Peaceful Settlement of Disputes, Prospects for the 21st Century* (Revised report prepared for the Centennial of the First International Peace Conference) *in* THE CENTENNIAL OF THE FIRST INTERNATIONAL PEACE CONFERENCE, 261-416 (F. Kalshoven ed., 2000).

16 *See ibid.*

which individuals will operate, and to make available its own judicial and administrative remedies for nationals and foreigners alike.

The essence of the evolution points toward the fact that in both the scenario of diplomatic protection and in that of direct standing of the individual, it is increasingly the right of the individual that is asserted in its own merits and no longer that of the sponsoring State. The State may still act as a conduit, an agent, or on behalf of the individual, but no longer in substitution of his rights. This is not to say that the State may not consider that a wrong done to one of its nationals affects its own interest, but the latter will be the consequence of the rights of the individual and not the State's own right. While the transition from a legal fiction to a different reality takes place, the interesting thought that a claim may actually have a "dual nature" and represent the interest of both the individual and the State has been advanced.[17]

Because the protection of human rights has advanced significantly under contemporary international law, the argument that this area of the law is different from that relating to diplomatic protection has also been suggested.[18] In this context diplomatic protection would rather be kept for the safeguard of the economic interests of the individual. While historically diplomatic protection has encompassed both the economic interests and the treatment of individuals abroad, it is quite true that the law of human rights has evolved beyond the framework of traditional diplomatic protection, following more liberal rules and allowing even for claims against the State of nationality. But it is also true that the same path is being followed by other areas of the law typically relating to economic interests, such as the case of investments, thereby evidencing that the evolution is not so much related to the nature of the rights but to the institution of diplomatic protection as a whole. Furthermore, economic rights are also considered today to be a part of human rights, thus also justifying liberal mechanisms of protection. This does not exclude, of course, that different areas of the law might follow different rules and requirements as to their protection, which are essentially embodied in new treaty

---

[17] *See* Comments by Kokott *in Preliminary Report, supra* note 1.

[18] *See* Comments by Bilder *in Preliminary Report, supra* note 1; *see also* Comments by Cerar *in Preliminary Report, supra* note 1.

regimes, but the underlying premise is always the same; that is, the assertion of the rights of the individual in their own merit. The fundamental changes taking place in this field have profound implications for the specific questions of nationality and the role of the State in the handling of claims.

II. ALTERNATIVES TO TRADITIONAL DIPLOMATIC PROTECTION

While the historic legal fiction underlying diplomatic protection might no longer always be necessary or justified, the key question, as has been aptly put by Lady Fox, seems to be which is the alternative solution to the traditional requirements of diplomatic protection.[19] The existing system has the advantage of an orderly administration of claims by the State of nationality, including the handling of multiple claims, the availability of diplomatic channels for negotiations and settlement, and the intervention of that State in the implementation of legal rules.[20] The disadvantages noted are also quite evident, particularly in terms of the political elements intervening in the governmental decision to espouse or not to espouse a claim, and the full discretionary nature that this decision has.

The option of abolishing diplomatic protection as a mechanism under international law, while justified in the context of specific treaty regimes, does not seem to be generally a reasonable one at the present time, since it would leave many individuals unprotected or left to their own action.

A residuary role for diplomatic protection seems more adequate to the extent that this mechanism might only intervene when there are no international procedures directly available to the affected individual.[21] It should be noted, however, that if direct access is available, diplomatic protection would be excluded altogether, except perhaps in order to ensure the enforcement of an award, or to secure compliance with a decision favoring that individual; in particular there would be no question of diplomatic pro-

---

19 *See* Comments by Lady Fox *in Preliminary Report, supra* note 1.

20 *See ibid.*

21 For a discussion of these options, *see* Comments by Lady Fox *in Preliminary Report, supra* note 1.

tection after the individual has resorted to international procedures, or in lieu thereof.

There is still the possibility of a parallel operation in which a State may espouse a claim at the same time that the individual pursues direct remedies,[22] but this alternative would result in various kinds of interference with the orderly conduct of the procedures and eventually with the outcome of the decision.

One other aspect that needs to be considered in the context of alternative options is how to ensure that the element of discretion in the governmental decision to espouse a claim is to some extent subject to legal scrutiny. On many occasions a government will simply refuse to accept the individual's request to have a claim espoused and no remedies will be available to this effect. An interesting historical solution to this problem is found in the Chilean legislation of the nineteenth century, where the request for diplomatic protection would be sent by the Ministry of Foreign Affairs to the Advocate General (Fiscal) of the Supreme Court for a legal opinion that was binding on the government.[23] Might a solution of this sort be adopted as an obligation under international law in the context of due process?[24]

III. AN EFFECTIVE LINK OF NATIONALITY

The requirement that claims may be brought by a State on condition that the affected person possesses its nationality has been well established under international law.[25] Moreover, the rule laid down by the International Court of Justice in the *Nottebohm* case[26] as to the requirements of a genuine and effective link of na-

---

22 *See ibid.*

23 *See* Francisco Orrego Vicuña, *Report on Chile, in* ELIHU LAUTERPACHT & JOHN G. COLLIER, INDIVIDUAL RIGHTS AND THE STATE IN FOREIGN AFFAIRS 123, 139–140 (1977).

24 For a suggestion in this respect *see* Comments by Lady Fox *in Preliminary Report, supra* note 1.

25 *See* Art. 23 of the Revised Draft Prepared by F. V. García-Amador, Special Rapporteur of the International Law Commission, 1961 [on State Responsibility] *in* F. V. GARCÍA-AMADOR, II THE CHANGING LAW OF INTERNATIONAL CLAIMS 784, 795 (1984); *see also* Art. 22 of the Draft Convention Prepared by Professors Louis B. Sohn & Richard R. Baxter (Harvard Law School) (1961) [on the international responsibility of states for injuries to aliens] *in* GARCÍA-AMADOR, *doc. cit.* note 25 at 841, 858.

26 *See* Nottebohm (Liech. v. Guat.) 1955 I.C.J. 23.

tionality with the sponsoring State, has kept its importance in present international law. A number of efforts have been undertaken in order to strengthen the effectiveness of nationality, as is evident, for example, in respect of the nationality of ships and, more recently, of fishing vessels.[27]

Notwithstanding the significance of this link, the very needs of the evolving legal order have led to changes in the rule to the extent that today a link of nationality is not always required to espouse an international claim. Departures from the rule agreed by treaty had allowed, in a number of cases, claims of persons who did not have the nationality of the claimant State, to be sponsored.[28] It has been also noted that since the claiming State had discretion as to the distribution of compensation, it can make payments to persons who did not meet the requirement of nationality.[29] A declaration of intention to acquire the nationality of the claiming State has also been considered enough to espouse the claim. Claims on behalf of non-nationals have not been unknown in the practice of international law.[30] Citizens of the European Union are entitled to diplomatic and consular protection by the authorities of any Member State in the territory of a third country in which the State of his nationality is not represented, although this type of protection is related more to consular or diplomatic assistance *in situ* than to the possibility of presenting an international claim.[31]

Two other situations need to be considered in this context. The first is the case of claims made on behalf of nationals of the defendant State. The early precedent set in this respect by the *I'm*

---

27 *See* United Nations Convention on the Law of the Sea, Dec. 10, 1982, art. 91; Agreement to Promote Compliance with International Conservation and Management Measures by Fishing Vessels on the High Seas, Nov. 24, 1993, 33 INTERNATIONAL LEGAL MATERIALS, 968 (1994), art. III. 3.

28 *See* L. OPPENHEIM, 1 OPPENHEIM'S INTERNATIONAL LAW 513 (Robert Jennings & Arthur Watts eds., 1992).

29 *See ibid.* at 513.

30 *See* Reparation for Injuries Suffered in the Service of the United Nations, 1949 I.C.J. 181, where the Court stated that there are "important exceptions to the rule, for there are cases in which protection may be exercised by a State on behalf of persons not having its nationality." For contemporary practice on diplomatic protection of foreign nationals *see* RUDOLF DOLZER, DIPLOMATIC PROTECTION OF FOREIGN NATIONALS, *in* Encyclopedia of Public International Law 1067–1070 (1992).

31 *See* Art. 8c of the European Community (EC) Treaty (now Art. 2c EC), as cited in Comments by Kokott *in Preliminary Report, supra* note 1.

Alone case, [32] has been recently expanded in the agreement between Chile and the United States in respect of the dispute concerning responsibility for the deaths of *Letelier and Moffitt*,[33] where "[t]he Chilean nationality or dual nationality of some of the persons protected by the United States Government was not raised as a bar to the disposition of the corresponding claims . . . what in actual fact means that the humanitarian concerns have prevailed over the traditional requirements [of diplomatic protection]."[34] One of the Chilean nationals on whose behalf the United States presented a claim was even a sitting member of the Chilean Congress. This last case also evidenced that the United States did not substitute its interest for that of the families protected, acting only on their behalf.[35] Consequently, it was the right of the individuals and not that of the claiming State that was enforced, the latter having been deprived of its discretion as to the handling of compensation and of its surrogate capacity.[36] While this case might be quite unique in contemporary practice,[37] it nonetheless evidences some of the new key features of diplomatic protection in practice.

Under the rules of the United Nations Compensation Commission (UNCC), a government may submit claims on behalf of its nationals and "at its discretion, of other persons resident in its territory."[38] The latter are evidently not its nationals but only its residents, and may have the nationality of another State.[39] Trusteeship arrangements are also used to extend protection to persons who are not in a position to have their claims submitted

---

32 *See* RIAA, iii, at 1609, and comments in L. Oppenheim, *supra* note 28, at 513.

33 *See* Agreement between Chile and the United States of June 11, 1990, 30 INTERNATIONAL LEGAL MATERIALS 412 (1991).

34 Decision of the Chile-United States Commission with regard to the dispute concerning responsibility for the deaths of Letelier and Moffitt, Jan. 11, 1992, Separate Concurrent Opinion of Commissioner Francisco Orrego Vicuña, 31 INTERNATIONAL LEGAL MATERIALS 17–18 (1992).

35 *See* Separate Concurrent Opinion, *supra* note 33, at 18.

36 *See ibid.* at 18.

37 *See* Comments by Stein *in Preliminary Report, supra* note 1.

38 *Provisional Rules for Claims Procedure,* art. 5, 1. a, United Nations Compensation Commission (1992).

39 It is also to be noted that United States law directs the President to afford the same protection to naturalized citizens as to native-born citizens, *see* 22 U.S.C. §1731; comment in 1 RESTATEMENT (THIRD) OF THE FOREIGN RELATIONS LAW OF THE UNITED STATES 123.

by a Government; under the UNCC rules, a person, authority or body may be appointed to this effect by the Governing Council.[40]

The second situation that must be considered is that the espousal of the State of nationality is not always required to submit a claim. Under the Rules of the UNCC, a corporation whose State of incorporation has failed to submit a claim on its behalf, may itself make a claim to the Commission, explaining why such claim was not submitted by a Government.[41] Also, many times a foreign national is allowed to claim before the courts of the defendant State or even in respect of claims against third States,[42] a policy that has been encouraged on non-discriminatory terms under the Organization for Economic Co-operation and Development (OECD).[43] In such cases, the State of nationality would probably not be allowed to sue in domestic courts on behalf of the individual, as it could not sue on its behalf in regional courts such as that of the European Union when direct access has been recognized.

Special forms of protection have also been recognized in the case of stateless persons,[44] and special rules have also been provided under the Convention on the Nationality of Women[45] for situations of change of nationality because of marriage; as in respect of military service; in cases of double nationality;[46] and other special situations.[47]

The situations examined evidence that the link of nationality has lost its rigor in the context of international claims. Moreover,

---

40 *See Provisional Rules, supra* note 38, art. 5. 2.

41 *See ibid.*, art. 5. 3.

42 *See* RESTATEMENT, *SUPRA* NOTE 39, AT 223.

43 *See* Recommendation of the Council for the Implementation of a Regime of Equal Right of Access and Non-discrimination in relation to Transfrontier Pollution, May 17, 1977 (OECD), 16 INTERNATIONAL LEGAL MATERIALS 977 (1977).

44 *See* Convention Relating to the Status of Stateless Persons, and Comments in RESTATEMENT, *supra* note 38, at 218.

45 *See* Convention on the Nationality of Women, T. S. No. 875 (1934), and Comments in RESTATEMENT, *supra* note 38, at 118.

46 *See* Protocol Relating to Military Obligations In Certain Cases of Double Nationality, 1930, T. S. No. 913.

47 *See* Convention Establishing the Status of Naturalized Persons Who Again Take Up Residence In The Country of Their Origin, T. S. No. 575 (1908) and Comments in RESTATEMENT, *supra* note 39, at 118.

to the extent that the intervention of the State is reduced or eliminated as a requirement for submission of international claims, the link of nationality will somewhat lose its relevance. This is particularly so in the field of human rights and related humanitarian concerns, where as noted direct access by the individual to international procedures is not only increasingly available but can also be exercised against its own State of nationality. While these trends cannot be taken to mean that the traditional requirements have been overturned, they certainly point toward a situation of greater flexibility and adaptation to changing needs.

IV. CONTINUANCE OF NATIONALITY

A second well-established rule in respect of diplomatic protection is that of continuance of nationality. As proposed by Garcia-Amador, the individual may be protected on condition that it possesses the nationality of the espousing State "at the time of sustaining the injury and conserves that nationality until the claim is adjudicated."[48] The continuance of nationality until the presentation of the claim has also been considered to meet the requirement of this rule,[49] an approach that seems to be favored by State practice.[50]

It was pointed out above that in the light of the State substituting its rights for those of the individual under the traditional approach to diplomatic protection, the requirement of continuance of nationality lacked legal logic. If the rights of the individual were no longer upheld after suffering the injury, and only those of the State prevailed thereafter, there was an inherent contradiction in requiring that the individual's nationality should continue. While it is true that the traditional rule provided criteria that were useful for the allocation of claims among various possible espousing

48 *See* Revised Draft, *supra* note 25, art. 23; and Draft Convention, *supra* note 25, art. 23. 7.

49 *See* L. OPPENHEIM, *supra* note 28, at 512. *See also* the discussion of the rule by G. SCHWARZENBERGER, INTERNATIONAL LAW: INTERNATIONAL LAW AS APPLIED BY INTERNATIONAL COURTS AND TRIBUNALS 597 (1957); and GARCÍA-AMADOR, *supra* note 25, at 504.

50 *See* ENCYCLOPEDIA, *supra* note 5, at 1055.

States and helped to avoid conflicts of interest,[51] thereby eliminating the uncertainties that otherwise could affect the practice of international claims,[52] these elements do not mean that a revision of the traditional rule should necessarily result in a situation of instability or uncertainty as to the handling of claims.

The important question is whether the rule is justified in the context of the new approach to diplomatic protection, where it is increasingly the right of the individual that is upheld and enforced and not that of the State acting on its behalf. While in the view of some scholars there are strong reasons to favor the continuance of nationality,[53] the opposite conclusion may be justified. In fact, if the right of the individual is affected, the relevant critical date is that of the wrong, and the situation should not change simply because there has been a change of nationality intervening thereafter; in this perspective, the wrong follows the affected individual.

As commented by Lowe, if the date of the injury is the critical date for questions of nationality, there is a good reason for this also to be so in respect of questions of jurisdiction of the tribunal.[54] Lowe also points out that the prevalence of the traditional rule might be explained by the view of States that dispute settlement procedures are as much about present engagements as about past wrongs, and therefore they regard the date at which the tribunal is seized as the critical date.[55] In this light, there is also the possibility that the nationality be required at the time of injury and at the time the tribunal is seized, irrespectively of what happens in between.[56] But this alternative might introduce more instability and encourage transfers of nationality for the sole purpose of securing diplomatic protection.

The need for stability and certainty might be ensured if the affected individual is given a choice that either the State of nationality at the time of the critical date or that of a later nationality could espouse his claim, since in both cases the State will be act-

51 *See* Comments by Lady Fox *in Preliminary Report, supra* note 1.

52 See Comments by Bederman *in Preliminary Report, supra* note 1.

53 *See supra* notes 51, 52.

54 *See* Comments by Lowe *in Preliminary Report, supra* note 1.

55 *See ibid.*

56 *See ibid.*

ing on behalf of the individual. It has also been suggested that only the "new" home State should be able to bring a claim but not the previous one.[57] Furthermore, it is quite evident that the new State of nationality should not be able to claim against the former State of nationality for wrongs that the individual might have suffered under the latter's jurisdiction. Moreover, if the individual has a direct access to international mechanisms for making a claim, the need for State intervention might no longer be needed.

These alternatives were already hinted at by the Sohn and Baxter Draft Convention of 1961 when stating that "[a] State shall not be precluded from presenting a claim on behalf of a person by reason of the fact that that person became a national of that State subsequent to that injury."[58] Also, a project prepared by the American Institute of International Law in 1925 had recognized the right of a State to accord diplomatic protection "to its native or naturalized citizens," it being possible that the latter might have been injured before their naturalization.[59] A practical application of this solution is found in the *Helms-Burton Act* of 1996, which not only allows claims by United States nationals deprived of property in Cuba but also by such nationals who at the time of the expropriations were Cuban citizens.[60] Not only is this an exception to the rule of continuance of nationality, but also to the availability of claims procedures to former nationals of the wrongdoing State, although the claims are directed in this context against governments, companies or individuals engaged in business relating to the confiscated properties.

The strict retention of the rule of continuance of nationality does not any longer seem to find justification in the light of the changing role of nationality as a requirement of diplomatic protection. There is here a need to revise, or at any rate, to adjust the operation of the rule to this new reality, a situation that becomes still more evident in the context of the transfer of rights and claims that will be discussed next.

---

57 *See* Comments by Stein *in Preliminary Report, supra* note 1.

58 Draft Convention, *supra* note 25, art. 23. 6.

59 Projects on State Responsibility of the American Institute of International Law (1925), art. II, *in* García-Amador, *supra* note 25, at 826.

60 *See* United States H.R. Report No. 104-202, at 31.

V. TRANSFERABILITY OF CLAIMS

As a consequence of the rule set out above, the continuance of nationality has been generally required in respect of the transferability or assignability of claims. To this end, transfer of claims can only be done between persons having the same nationality of the espousing State. This has been the approach to questions such as succession on death, assignment, and insurance subrogation.[61]

However, again the question must be asked whether this rule is always justified in the light of a new approach to diplomatic protection and the enforcement of claims. If the right of the individual prevails, it would seem enough that the right to a claim be established at a critical date, and changes of nationality intervening thereafter in the context of transfers or assignment should not be a bar to bringing a claim at a later point in time.

To some extent this situation was recognized in claims to property beneficially owned by one person, the nominal title to which is vested in another person of a different nationality; it was usually the nationality of the former that prevailed for the purposes of claims.[62] The question is still more relevant in the insurance business, where the rights of the insured may pass to the insurer by way of subrogation.[63] The continuance of nationality is probably not any longer justified in the light of a global market of insurance, in which the insured and the insurer will often have different nationalities. Investment insurance, such as that available under the Overseas Private Investment Corporation (OPIC) or the Multilateral Investment Guarantee Agency (MIGA), is also based on subrogation of rights.[64]

Although the traditional rule on this point is still regarded as accepted, there are solid grounds justifying departure from it in given matters, or in any event, for introducing necessary flexibility. The globalization of financial and service markets will probably require such a departure. In fact, in the context of globally structured financial markets where shares, bonds and other in-

---

61 *See* L. OPPENHEIM, *supra* note 28, at 514.

62 *See ibid.* at 514.

63 *See ibid.*

64 *See* RESTATEMENT, *supra* note 39, at 227.

struments change hands, and consequently nationality, constantly and speedily, the application of the traditional rule can only be regarded as an anachronism that could amount in given instances to depriving legitimate owners and investors of protection on the part of States of nationality. In a recent ICSID case the question of international transfer of promissory notes was considered, and the rules protecting a foreign investor as the transferee were upheld by the Tribunal in the light of the nature of global markets.[65]

To the extent that the requirement of continuance of nationality might be moderated in this context, it might be appropriate to ensure that transfer of claims be made *bona fide* so as to prevent that a claim be transferred to a national of a stronger State in order to strengthen diplomatic protection, a concern that has been often expressed.[66]

VI. QUESTIONS RELATING TO DOUBLE NATIONALITY

The traditional rules relating to double nationality have been well explained in Articles 4 and 5 of the 1930 Hague Convention on Certain Questions Relating to the Conflict of Nationality Laws.[67] These various situations have been aptly summarized in the following manner: (i) a State should not be allowed to present a claim on behalf of a national when such person is also a national of the respondent state and with which it is more closely connected; (ii) this claim should not be presented even where the national in question is more closely connected with the claimant State; (iii) if the national of the claimant State is also a national of a third State — not being the respondent — and is more closely connected with that State, the claim should not be allowed either; and, (iv) if in this last situation the national is more closely connected with the claimant State than with the third State in question, then the claim could be brought against the respondent.[68]

---

65 *See* ICSID: Fedax. N. V. v. Republic of Venezuela, July 11, 1997, 37 INTERNATIONAL LEGAL MATERIALS 1378 (1998).

66 *See* ENCYCLOPEDIA, *supra* note 5, at 1056.

67 For a discussion of these provisions, *see* ENCYCLOPEDIA, *supra* note 5, at 1050.

68 *See* L. OPPENHEIM, *supra* note 28, at 516–517.

Although it has been suggested that these rules probably reflect customary international law,[69] the situation does not appear today to be quite consolidated.[70] In fact, it has been shown above that in a number of cases, diplomatic protection has been exercised in respect of nationals of the defendant State or in respect of other non-nationals. The possibility that a State might accept by treaty the obligation to provide to all persons within its jurisdiction, regardless of nationality, a standard of protection required by that treaty has also been envisaged, a situation in which the issues of nationality will again lose significance, as often happens in treaties of economic integration or trade liberalization.[71] To the extent that these situations might reflect a trend, then the case explained in (i) above will also be subject to a greater degree of flexibility. The same holds true of the situation considered in (ii) above since here the closer connection is given with the claimant State, this latter departure from the rule has been accepted in international decisions.[72]

In (iii) and (iv) the issue concerns a dual nationality involving a third State. Again the rules explained rely on the effectiveness of the nationality link, depending on which criteria they are based, they point to different answers. However, flexibility or departure from the rule is allowed in cases involving the dual nationality of the respondent State, with even more reason, this should be the case of dual nationality involving third States. Also, when the person has direct access to international claims, the situation has been compared to that of a claim involving a dual nationality with a third State, so that the Tribunal may take into account the principle of "effective nationality."[73] The practice of the Iran-United States Claims Tribunal,

---

69 *See Ibid.* at 516.

70 In the Advisory Opinion on the Reparation for Injuries Suffered in the Service of the United Nations case, the International Court of Justice considered that the practice of a State not to protect a national against another State which also regards him as a national is "the ordinary practice," 1949 I.C.J. 174, 186, as cited *in* ENCYCLOPEDIA, *supra* note 5, at 1050.

71 *See* Comments by Lady Fox *in Preliminary Report, supra* note 1.

72 *See in particular* the *Mergé Claim,* 22 INTERNATIONAL LAW REPORTS 443 (1955), and discussion of this and other cases in L. OPPENHEIM, *supra* note 28, at 516; *see also* RESTATEMENT, *supra* note 39, at 218.

73 L. OPPENHEIM, *supra* note 28, at 516, with reference to the decision of the Iran-US Claims Tribunal in Esphahanian v. Bank Tejarat, 1983.

and the dissenting views expressed in that context, offer interesting insights into the new issues and problems relating to the rules on dual nationality.[74] The joint action by two States of nationality in respect of a third State has also been suggested as an alternative when both are willing to extend their diplomatic protection to the affected individual.[75]

Two trends seem to emerge from the above discussion. The first is that the traditional rules of the 1930 Convention are being applied with a greater degree of flexibility, which will become particularly clear in connection with the approach to diplomatic protection relying on the rights of the individual as the prevailing element. The second trend is that in this context, like in other matters pertaining to nationality, effectiveness offers an important guiding tool, particularly for decisions of tribunals. Criteria to evaluate effectiveness will depend on the circumstances of each case, where residence, family ties, property, taxation and many other elements will determine the "stronger social bond of attachment."[76]

VII. REVISING THE RULES ON NATIONALITY OF CORPORATIONS

Besides the obvious situation of a corporation incorporated under the laws of the claimant State and the majority of its shareholders being nationals of that State, in which case the entitlement to its diplomatic protection will not be questioned,[77] in every other conceivable situation, there will probably be difficulties with the traditional requirements of nationality. Precisely because of this,

---

74 For a discussion of the issue of effective nationality in the context of dual nationality in the practice of the Iran-US Claims Tribunal, *see* GEORGE H. ALDRICH, THE JURISPRUDENCE OF THE IRAN-UNITED STATES CLAIMS TRIBUNAL 54–79 (1996); and CHARLES N. BROWER & JASON D. BRUESCHKE, THE IRAN-UNITED STATES CLAIMS TRIBUNAL 32–42 (1998). *See also* the Comments by Lowe *in Preliminary Report, supra* note 1.

75 *See* Comments by Kokott *in Preliminary Report, supra* note 1, with reference to C. Warbrick, *Protection of Nationals Abroad: Current Legal Problems,* 37 INTERNATIONAL AND COMPARATIVE LAW QUARTERLY, 1003, 1006 (1988).

76 *See generally,* the *1965 Resolution of the Institut de Droit International,* 1965 ANNUAIRE DE L'INSTITUT DE DROIT INTERNATIONAL, Vol. 51 No. II, at 260.

77 L. OPPENHEIM, *supra* note 28, at 517–518.

the nationality of corporations has been assimilated to that of individuals only in a limited way under international law and, in addition to the State of incorporation, a number of other criteria have been used for the purpose of diplomatic protection, with particular reference to domicile, *siège social* or principal place of management and control.[78]

These additional criteria have been rightly described not as conferring nationality, but as creating an equivalent connection[79] which on occasion is considered to provide enough ground for the exercise of diplomatic protection.[80] Questions of the effectiveness of the connection will also arise in this context, particularly when a corporation having the nationality of the State of incorporation is owned by non-nationals of that State.

One of the most problematic aspects of the matter was that submitted to the International Court of Justice in the *Barcelona Traction* case,[81] regarding the right of a State to protect shareholders of its nationality in a foreign corporation affected by measures of a third State. While the *dictum* of the Court was in the negative and the right to diplomatic protection was recognized only in respect of the State of incorporation, criticism of this decision and subsequent practice evidence that the question was not really settled at that time.[82] A number of earlier precedents were also invoked but were considered by the Court to be rather exceptions to the rule upheld.[83] Some of the criticism of the holding in the *Barcelona Traction* case has been based on the fact that the Court applied a too rigid standard "owing to an exaggerated fear of competing claims, thus neglecting the economic realities and leaving the real losers without protection."[84]

As to the practice, it should be noted first that the Court itself recognized that a State may protect its shareholders in a foreign corporation when they have their rights as such directly infringed,

---

78 *See* García-Amador, *supra* note 25, at 508–512.

79 *See* Restatement, *supra* note 39, at 213.

80 On United States practice, *see* Restatement, *supra* note 39, at 126.

81 *See* Barcelona Traction Light and Power Company Limited (Belg. v. Spain), 1970 I.C.J. 3, 4.

82 For references to the legal literature on the decision, *see* L. Oppenheim, *supra* note 28, at 518, note 4.

83 *See* García-Amador, *supra* note 25, at 508.

84 *See* Encyclopedia, *supra* note 5, at 1053–1054.

independently from damage inflicted upon the company.[85] Also, the Court considered cases in which shareholders may be protected by their State of nationality if the foreign company has ceased to exist, or when the State of incorporation lacks the capacity to take action on its behalf, but it did not find such situations applicable in the light of the facts of the case.[86] The protection of shareholders who have suffered damage through damage to the company can always be agreed to between various States.[87] It has also been noted that agreements between States facilitating given forms of jurisdiction should not affect the rights and interests of a third State,[88] including therein the right to diplomatic protection of its nationals.

Recent practice is even more well-expressed in the *Elettronica Sicula* case,[89] in which the United States brought action before the International Court of Justice against Italy for damage suffered by an Italian company owned by two American companies. In this case, the shareholders of a foreign company were protected by their State of nationality against the State of incorporation.[90] It is also interesting to note that in a number of treaties and claims arrangements provision has been made for protection of shareholders in affected partnerships or companies. A fifty percent interest in the total capital was required to this effect in British claims against Mexico, as in US claims against Peru and Hungary; and twenty percent was required in US claims against the former Yugoslavia.[91]

Also, the Algiers Declaration on the Settlement of Iran-United States claims[92] includes as nationals corporations organized under the laws of one or the other country if citizens of such country directly or indirectly have an interest in the corporation equivalent to fifty percent or more of its capital stock; in respect of other corporations, the Declaration refers to an interest of such nationals

---

85 *See* L. OPPENHEIM, *supra* note 28, at 520.

86 *See ibid.* at 519.

87 *See* ENCYCLOPEDIA, *supra* note 5, at 1054.

88 *See* Comments by Lowe *in Preliminary Report, supra* note 1.

89 *See* Elettronica Sicula S.p.A (U.S. v. Italy) 1989 I.C.J. 15.

90 *See* L. OPPENHEIM, *supra* note 28, at 520; and *see* generally RESTATEMENT, *supra* note 39, at 127.

91 *See* the discussion of the cases and practice in L. OPPENHEIM, *supra* note 28, at 521–522.

92 *See* Algiers Declaration, 20 INTERNATIONAL LEGAL MATERIALS 230 (1981).

enough to control the corporation.[93] A 49.8 percent of the shares owned by a US company in a corporation organized in Iran, was considered sufficient for this purpose by the Iran-US Tribunal.[94] Proof of the controlling interest has also been evaluated with flexibility.[95] US practice on diplomatic protection also relies on the concept of incorporation and of being the company owned at least in a 50 percent by United States citizens.[96] Similarly, Switzerland grants diplomatic protection when a company is mainly owned by Swiss citizens.[97]

The control of a company is also reflected in the ICSID Convention for the purpose of foreign investments dispute settlement. In terms of its Article 25(2)(b), a juridical person which has the nationality of the State Party to the dispute may be a party to the proceedings if, because of foreign control, the parties have agreed that the juridical person should be treated as a national of another Contracting Party.[98] The practice under ICSID is, however, broader.[99] It has also been noted that under the Law of the Sea Convention, an entity applying for a contract for seabed mining may be sponsored not only by the State of nationality but also by the State whose nationals effectively control it.[100]

The rules governing the UNCC have also included interesting arrangements in respect of corporate claims. It was noted above that corporations whose claims are not submitted by the State of incorporation may submit their claims directly together with an explanation. Also, if the governments concerned agree, one government may submit claims in respect of joint ventures, corporations or other entities of other governments, on behalf of its nationals.[101] Most importantly, it is provided that shareholders of a corporation which is barred from making a claim because of its

---

93 *See* the discussion of these rules in the RESTATEMENT, *supra* note 39, at 127-128.

94 *See* Sedco Inc. v. National Iranian Oil Co., Iran-US Claims Tribunal, 1985, as commented in RESTATEMENT, *supra* note 38, at 128.

95 *See* RESTATEMENT, *supra* note 39, at 127–128.

96 *See* ENCYCLOPEDIA, *supra* note 5, at 1053.

97 *See Ibid.* at 1053.

98 *See* Convention on the Settlement of Investment Disputes Between States and Nationals of Other States, March 18, 1965, 575 U.N.T.S. 159, art. 25, para. 2(b).

99 On the ICSID practice *see generally* Christoph Schreuer, *Commentary on the ICSID Convention,* 11 ICSID REVIEW-FOREIGN INVESTMENT LAW JOURNAL 316 (1996).

100 *See* RESTATEMENT, *supra* note 39, at 128.

101 *See Provisional Rules, supra* note 38, art. 5. 1. b.

nationality, may claim the losses with respect to that corporation.[102] In the case of a partnership which has a separate legal personality and which, because of its nationality, is ineligible to claim for its losses, each of the eligible partners may claim *pro rata* his proportionate interest;[103] a similar rule is followed for partners in a partnership which has no separate legal personality.[104]

Questions of nationality of corporations are compounded in their difficulty when the corporation has a multinational character, allowing eventually for a number of States to act on its behalf, a situation which becomes increasingly more common in a globalized economy. The concept of control and of prevalent nationality is also useful in this context in order to determine the prevailing national interest in the assets of the company. This would eventually allow for action by the State holding the greater interest or it would establish an order of priority to this effect. International registration of such companies would also be a helpful measure to overcome problems of concurrent nationalities, as it is done in respect of trademarks or has been proposed in respect of a *societas europaea*.[105]

Even if a number of these arrangements are done by treaty or special agreement, the aggregate of the practice evidences quite forcefully that the criteria of the *Barcelona Traction* no longer prevail and that shareholders are increasingly entitled to protection or action based solely on their status of being shareholders. This trend is also strengthened by the development already noted that the right of the affected individual prevails over that of the State in the context of diplomatic protection.If the fiction of State intervention on its own right has been curtailed, similarly the fiction of corporate personality should not preclude the rights of individual shareholders to be protected.

---

[102] *See* Decision of the Governing Council on Business Losses of Individuals, United Nations Compensation Commission, S/AC. 26/1991/4, para. f. (Oct. 23 1991).

[103] *See ibid.* para. d.

[104] *See ibid.* para. e.

[105] In respect of the *societas europaea* and its international registration, *see* RESTATEMENT, *supra* note 39, at 131.

VIII. EMERGING TRENDS IN RESPECT OF NATIONALITY IN THE CONTEXT OF DIPLOMATIC PROTECTION AND INTERNATIONAL DISPUTE SETTLEMENT

In light of the above discussion, the following aspects may be summarized as reflecting current or prospective international trends in this matter.

1. The right of the individual as the prevalent interest affected by a wrong is increasingly asserted and enforced by means of diplomatic protection. A parallel right of the claimant State can also be asserted and enforced in this context but it is no longer usually substituted for the individual's own right.
2. The discretion exercised by a Government in refusing to espouse a claim on behalf of the individual might be appropriately subject to judicial review in the context of due process.
3. Direct access by the individual to international claim settlement arrangements and dispute settlement procedures is increasingly available as an expression of the assertion of his own rights.
4. In the context of such arrangements, the submission of claims by the State of nationality is increasingly dispensed with.
5. Diplomatic protection can always be exercised in a residual manner when direct access by the individual to international claim procedures is not available. The availability of such procedures generally excludes diplomatic protection, except for the enforcement of decisions.
6. The rule requiring that the link of nationality to the claimant State must be genuine and effective is well established.
7. In exceptional circumstances, claims are brought on behalf of non-nationals, of nationals of the defendant State, or under trusteeship arrangements. Such exceptional circumstances are particularly related to humanitarian concerns, or where the individual would have no other alternative to claim his rights.

8. Continuance of nationality may acquire greater flexibility in the context of global financial and service markets and operations related thereto or in other special circumstances.
9. Transferability of claims ought to be facilitated so as to meet the realities of such global markets.
10. Changes of nationality and transferability of claims should always be required to be made *bona fide*.
11. In cases of dual nationality the effectiveness of the link appears on occasions to prevail over other considerations, allowing when justified for claims against the State of which the individual is also a national.
12. Shareholders of a foreign company may be protected by the State of their nationality if their rights have been directly infringed, as well as in other special circumstances where they would otherwise be deprived of protection.
13. Shareholders of a foreign company may also be protected by the State of their nationality for wrongs affecting such company if the State of nationality of the company is unable or unwilling to exercise such protection or is the defendant State.
14. Control of a foreign company by shareholders of a different nationality, generally expressed in a fifty percent ownership of its capital stock or such other proportion needed to control the company, may entitle the State of nationality of such shareholders to exercise diplomatic protection on their behalf or otherwise to consider the company as having its nationality.
15. If a company or partnership is prevented from bringing a claim because of its nationality, shareholders or partners not so affected may claim a proportionate interest in such company or otherwise be entitled to diplomatic protection by the State of their nationality.

While some of these aspects are already part of current arrangements for dispute settlement, others seem to be emerging as prospective trends. As international dispute settlement develops in the years ahead, the law and practice relating to the requirements of nationality is likely to be one of those areas where major changes can be expected.

THE TIMOR GAP TREATY REVISITED TEN YEARS ON

*William T. Onorato**

This piece is written in appreciation of Dr. Ibrahim F.I. Shihata, whom I have been pleased to have as both a mentor and friend. In the fifteen years that I worked for him as our General Counsel, he always provided me with unparalleled intellectual leadership and his good and personal counsel. As I know that we share a special interest in joint development of offshore international petroleum reserves, I thought that this piece would be an appropriate addition to his *Liber Amicorum,* to which I am pleased and proud to have been asked to contribute.

I. INTRODUCTION

On December 11, 1989, Australia and Indonesia signed the Timor Gap Treaty[1] (Treaty) to establish a Zone of Cooperation (Zone) in the Timor Sea, south of what is now East Timor and north of Western Australia and Australia's Northern Territory. The main purpose of the Treaty was to allow exploration and production of the Zone's petroleum resources to proceed without delay, while efforts continued ultimately to reach agreement between the States involved on a permanent boundary on the continental shelf area in question. As will be seen herein, this desired result has been substantially achieved on an ongoing basis. Just over ten years later, on February 10, 2000, with both the pending independence

* This article presents the personal views of the author and should not be attributed to the organization he works with.

1 *Treaty Between Australia and the Republic of Indonesia on the Zone of Cooperation in an Area Between the Indonesian Province of East Timor and Northern Australia, Dec. 11, 1989,* 29 INTERNATIONAL LEGAL MATERIALS (I.L.M.) 469 (1990).

of East Timor and the discovery of significant hydrocarbon resources in the Zone as new stimuli, a new treaty between the United Nations Transitional Administration in East Timor (UNTAET), and the Government of Australia went into effect (New Treaty), providing practical arrangements for the continuity of the terms of the former Treaty.

Previous in-depth analysis of the Treaty may be found in William T. Onorato and Mark J. Valencia, "International Cooperation for Petroleum Development: The Timor Gap Treaty."[2] Accordingly, this paper needs only briefly to reprise the history and terms of the original Treaty and then move on fully to discuss activities under the two Treaties and their implications for the soon-to-be Republic of East Timor.

II. RECENT HISTORY

The creation of the Zone was some twenty years in the making. In 1971–72, Australia and Indonesia agreed to a seabed boundary between them in the Timor Sea which followed the northern edge of the continental shelf lying off Australia.[3] The sea area south of the eastern portion of the island of Timor — the "Timor Gap," (Gap) a distance of some 200 nautical miles (nm) — was excluded from that agreement because East Timor, at the time, was a colony of Portugal.

When East Timor was annexed by Indonesia,[4] Australia suggested settlement of the question of the boundary through the Gap by proposing a delimitation which would have joined the ends of the previously agreed seabed boundary on either side of the Gap. Indonesia, however, would not agree to this solution, maintaining, instead, that since the time of the earlier delimitation,

---

2 ICSID Review-Foreign Investment Law Journal, Vol. 5, Spring 1-29 (1990).

3 Agreements signed on May 18, 1971 and Oct. 9, 1972.

4 Despite the apparent annexation, however, the government of Portugal filed at the time an official protest with the UN Secretary-General over the signing of the Treaty. Subsequently, it filed an unsuccessful action in the International Court of Justice. *See infra* note 52, in this regard. The Portuguese still claim jurisdiction over East Timor and they maintain that the Treaty goes against previous Security Council and General Assembly Resolutions on the matter which failed to recognize Indonesian sovereignty over East Timor.

international law and practice had evolved towards such delimitation being fixed as the median line between opposite coastal States,[5] and, thus, that the boundary should be the line equidistant between the two States' territories. The disputed area measured some 12,000 square nm.

The Timor basin would have been completely within Indonesian jurisdiction if the equidistance line had become the agreed boundary. But if the middle of the Australian margin had been used as a guide to complete the Gap, a small portion of the core of the Timor basin would have accrued to Australia, which had already leased it for exploration. Former Portuguese Timor had also leased the area extending to the hypothetical Gap connection, being the bulk of the basin. Thus the Timor Gap area between Indonesia and Australia became a prime candidate for joint development. A number of factors influenced State decisions in this regard. Neither State was acutely short of petroleum resources, although new discoveries were certainly important to both parties, particularly Australia. Australia had unilaterally leased portions of the area. There were no islands involved in the claims to the Timor Gap and the claims of both States were based on *bona fide* legal principles. Nor were there any overriding security concerns in the area at the time to influence the outcome of the dispute. The presence of several potentially hydrocarbon-endowed structures in the area itself focused attention there and raised expectations in both countries.[6] Resolution of the dispute thus became more urgent and stimulated interest in adjacent areas that were claimed by both States.

---

5 *See* Continental Shelf Case (Libyan Arab Jamahiriya v. Malta),1985 I.C.J. 13 (June 3), wherein the Court substantially pre-empted Australia's probable arguments concerning both the importance of the Timor Trough and the principle of natural prolongation by rejecting Libya's argument that the boundary with Malta should follow a rift zone closer to the latter than to the former. The Court stated that international law on the topic had developed to the point where a State could claim that the continental shelf appertaining to it extends up to 200 miles from its coast, whatever the geological characteristics of the corresponding seabed and subsoil (e.g. an intervening trough) and that no criterion for delimitation of shelf areas can be derived from the principle of natural prolongation in the physical sense. The Timor Sea in the vicinity of the Timor Gap varies from 250 to 290 nautical miles in width between the closest points of the two coasts.

6 *See* Prescott, *Maritime Boundary Agreements; Australia and Australia-Solomon Islands,* I Marine Policy Report 37-45 (1989).

Eventually, it was the oil companies and the Australian state governments involved who pressed the Australian central government to come to terms with Indonesia over the East Timor issue, so that a boundary could be agreed and they could get on with petroleum exploration and exploitation. However, negotiations on a boundary would have amounted to *de jure* recognition by the Australian government of Indonesia's incorporation of East Timor. To avoid inordinate delays in the resolution of the boundary dispute and to maintain interest already shown by international oil companies in the Gap, Australia announced on January 20, 1979, that it would recognize *de facto* that East Timor was part of Indonesia. In 1985, agreement in principle was finally reached to create a provisional joint development regime to operate pending final and definitive agreement on a precise boundary through the Gap. This was duly accomplished by the signing of the Treaty in early December 1989.[7] Establishment of the Zone was viewed as a significant step in the development of closer relations between the two States.

The Zone is delineated on the northern side by a simplified bathymetric axis line; on the southern side by a 200 nm line measured from the Indonesian archipelagic baselines; and on the eastern and western sides by equidistance lines. Thus, both States conceded their extreme boundary claims and presumably the principles upon which they were based. These equidistant lines are determined by the former relationships between the coasts of Indonesia and then Portuguese Timor. The northern limit of the coffin-shaped Zone is a simplified line marking the axis of the Timor Trough. The southern limit line is 200 nm from the coast of Timor. The two other intermediate lines that separate the three areas are a straight line in the general vicinity of the 1,500 meter isobath and a median line between Australian and Indonesian territories. The only lines that cannot be definitely explained are the short lines that link the northern limit to the termini of the 1973 boundary. It is possible that these lines were placed on a convergent course to correspond to the convergence of the lines south of the 1972 boundary.

[7] Chronology of negotiations through to signing of the Treaty is set out in the Joint Statement dated Oct. 27, 1989, by Australia's Senators Gareth Evans, Minister for Foreign Affairs and Trade, and Peter Cook, Minister for Resources.

This arrangement means that the positions and interests of both States were preserved. Both the axis of the Timor Trough and the median line have been used. The structure with the most perceived hydrocarbon potential at the time — which subsequently proved to be dry — fell entirely within Area A. Thus, the settlement was an integrated solution to two problems. The shape of the overall area was determined by the extreme claims of both States and the focus of joint development on Area A was determined by a perceived distribution of hydrocarbon potential and the desire of both States to get on with exploration there.

III. THE FIRST TREATY

As earlier said, the Treaty was the foremost example at the time of a comprehensive and "classic" joint development regime. State practice to date has shown such a "classic" legal format for joint development of international common hydrocarbon reserves normally includes:

(i) a treaty between the interested States which establishes the area subject to the accord and the legal basis for such joint development;

(ii) the establishment under such treaty of some form of an International Joint Commission, of equal representation between the Contracting States, which acts as the administrative, supervisory and consultative overseer of the venture;

(iii) the grant of exploitation rights to licensees or concessionaires (rightsholders) — normally by the interested States but, possibly, also directly by the Joint Commission; and

(iv) the nomination by the rightsholders, subject to approval by the Joint Commission, of a single operator to conduct joint operations on their behalf.

While joint development arrangements antecedent to that created by the Treaty have had some or most of the elements of such a "classic" format, none has ever before incorporated all of them. The arrangements under the Treaty for Area A, however, would appear, clearly, to have accomplished this end in both a complete and thorough fashion. The Treaty, in comprehensive fashion, establishes both the area subject to the accord and the legal basis for joint development in Area A. As previously indicated, in respect of the latter, the Treaty goes far beyond any previous arrangements for joint development in that it also creates, in detail, a comprehensive, interlocking legislative, contractual and fiscal regime to govern joint development in the designated area. Other arrangements have selectively extended the applicable national laws, suitably adapted, of one or both interested States to a joint development area, but never before have contracting States purposefully negotiated in advance a complete and area-specific regime, solely for the purpose of setting the total parameters of their intended joint endeavor. Let us next examine briefly what are the essential elements of this novel Treaty regime.

A. The Zone

As previously noted, the Zone created under the Treaty, encompassing almost 61,000 square kilometers, has several unusual features, the most notable of which is that it is tripartite. It is subdivided into three areas (A, B and C), each of which has a different exploration and exploitation regime applicable to it.[8] The central and largest area, Area A, is the true joint development area in the "classic" sense.[9]

In Areas B and C — south and north of Area A, respectively — joint development *per se* does not occur. Rather, Indonesia administers Area B and Australia administers Area C. Nevertheless, the spirit of international cooperation pervades even the non-joint development areas of the Zone in that both partial sharing of revenues occurs and each State is obligated to take all necessary measures to ensure the timely and optimum utilization of the petroleum resources of the Area which it administers.[10]

Necessarily and predictably, however, the creation of the Zone was without prejudice to the positions of the two States as to the location of any permanent boundary between them on the continental shelf running through the Zone and, notwithstanding

8 *See* Treaty, *supra note* 1, art. 2, "The Zone," paras. 1& 2 (a)–(c).

9 *Ibid.* pt. I, art. 2, para. 2 (a).

10 *Ibid.* pt. II, art. 4, para. 6.

joint development and cooperation in the Zone, the two States undertook to continue to negotiate in good faith to reach agreement on such a permanent boundary.[11]

B. Management Structure for Joint Development

1. *The Ministerial Council*

For Area A, the management structure for joint development operations is two-tiered. The upper tier is the Ministerial Council (MC). The MC is composed of an equal number of ministers from each State.[12] Its primary purpose is to exercise overall responsibility and supervision over all matters relating to the exploration and exploitation of the petroleum resources of Area A of the Zone.[13] The MC has no formal voting procedure governing its decision making but, rather, acts, as one would expect, through consensus.[14]

2. *The Joint Authority*

The second tier of the joint development management structure for Area A is the Joint Authority (JA). Under the Treaty, the JA is granted juridical personality and such legal capacities under the laws of each Contracting State as are necessary for the exercise of its powers and the performance of its functions. Most notably, the JA has capacity to contract, as it is the party which directly grants exploration and production rights in Area A to potential Contractors. It does this by entering into Production Sharing Contracts (PSCs) with such parties, subject to prior approval by the MC.[15]

The JA has an equal number of Executive Directors nominated by each Contracting State.[16] It also has a Technical Directorate responsible for petroleum operations;[17] a Financial Directorate responsible for collecting fees and proceeds of sale of

---

11 *Ibid.* pt. I, art 2, paras. 3 & 4.

12 *Ibid.* pt. III, art. 5, "The Ministerial Council," para. 2.

13 *Ibid.* pt. III, art. 6, "Functions of the Ministerial Council," para. 1.

14 *Ibid.* pt. III, art. 6, para. 1(k)–(m), (o) & (r).

15 *Ibid.* pt. IV, art. 7, "The Joint Authority," para. 2.

16 *Ibid.* pt. IV, art. 8(b), "Functions of the Joint Authority."

17 *Ibid.* pt. IV, art. 9, "Structure of the Joint Authority," para. 1 (a).

the JA's production share;[18] a Legal Directorate responsible for advising on issues arising under the Petroleum Mining Code (PMC) or any PSCs;[19] and a Corporate Services Directorate to provide technical support to the JA's Directors and to the MC.[20] The Executive Directors and the directors of the four Directorates constitute the Executive Board of the JA.[21]

To discharge its responsibilities and exercise its supervisory, administrative and management functions over Area A, the JA is empowered, notably, to: subdivide Area A into contract areas and to offer them for tender;[22] enter into PSCs with contractors; supervise their performance; and terminate such PSCs if necessary, either for non-performance or through mutual agreement, with the prior approval of the MC;[23] directly handle other operational and administrative matters, including, of note, marketing of petroleum produced from Area A; preparation of the JA's annual budget; and collecting and distributing to the two Contracting States each of their portions of the JA's share of revenues derived from production under PSCs;[24] and issue Regulations under the PMC.

C. The Specified Joint Development Regime

The core components of the joint development regime agreed between the two States under the Treaty for Area A are the PMC, the PSC and the Tax Code (TC). Uniquely, the two States devised a complete, interlocking legislative, contractual and fiscal framework to govern joint development of the potential petroleum resources of the central, most prospective region of the Zone, Area A. The complete picture which is created by the interaction of these components may be better understood by brief examination of each of them in turn.

18 *Ibid.* pt. IV, art. 9, para. 1 (b)(i).
19 *Ibid.* pt. IV, art. 9, para. 1 (b)(ii).
20 *Ibid.* pt. IV, art. 9, para. 1 (b)(iii).
21 *Ibid.* pt. IV, art. 9, para. 1 (c).
22 *Ibid.* pt. IV, art. 8.
23 *Ibid.* pt. IV, art. 8.
24 *Ibid.* pt. IV, art. 8.

1. The Petroleum Mining Code

The PMC is the basic law which governs operational activities relating to exploration for and exploitation of the petroleum resources in Area A of the Zone.[25] It is a reasonably broad, generic, enabling law which leaves much detail to be negotiated in individual PSCs. However, on a non-exclusive basis, it specifies what PSCs concluded under the Code must, at minimum, contain.[26]

The JA is empowered to consider each qualified bid for acreage in Area, the principal criteria of which is the amount and quality of the exploration work proposed in the bid. If the JA is inclined to accept a particular bid, it will first seek the requisite MC approval and then communicate its intention to award and to negotiate a PSC with the successful applicant. If a discovery is subsequently made by the Contract Operator, a declaration of discovery will then be made by the JA if it and the Contract Operator agree that the discovery can be produced commercially.[27]

Subsequent to a declaration of commercial discovery, a contractor must have the JA's approval to construct production and transportation (pipeline) facilities. Production, when commenced, is subject to Regulations promulgated by the JA as to specific rates, consistent with good oilfield practices.

On a broad scale, the PMC also covers numerous general and customary arrangements normally to be concluded in standard exploration and production arrangements.

2. The Model Production Sharing Contract

The Treaty provides that the model PSC is the model format upon which basis all production sharing contracts for Area A shall be concluded.[28] As previously noted, the PMC specifies matters which, on a non-exclusive basis, must, as a minimum, be included and addressed in the model PSC.[29] Thus, the model PSC fully complies in content with the essential requirements of the PMC, substantially elaborating thereon, to produce a modern, state-of-

25 *Ibid.* pt. I, art. 1, "Definitions."

26 *Ibid.* pt. III, art. 5, "The Contract."

27 *Ibid.* pt. IV, art. 16, "Declaration of a Discovery Area."

28 *Ibid.* pt. I, art. 1, "Definitions."

29 *Ibid.* pt. III, art. 4, para. 4.

the-art, commercially attractive production sharing contractual mechanism.

The maximum term of a PSC is to be, normally, thirty years. The PSC further divides such term into incremental phases for exploration, appraisal and if a commercial discovery has been made, production. In the case of a significant natural gas discovery, an extension of the term will be granted until marketing arrangements and gas sales contracts can be completed. As regards relinquishment, the PMC requires a pattern of progressive surrender. Blocks containing discoveries are excluded from the relinquishment requirements.

The heart of any PSC is its work program and expenditures requirements. In the model PSC, these items are, of course, negotiable as to amounts, but quite structured as to sequence. The Contract Operator must agree with the JA to an annual minimum work program which, for each contract year, specifies minimum acceptable expenditures for data review, seismic surveys to be undertaken, number of exploratory wells to be drilled and overall exploration expenditures.[30] It must then submit, annually to the JA for approval an exploration and appraisal strategy, a work program and budget, and a development plan, if a discovery has been made.[31]

The Contract Operator and Contractor are afforded all usual and necessary rights and attendant obligations under the PSC, as derived from requirements under the PMC. For its part, the JA undertakes to discharge its responsibilities for the management of petroleum operations under the PSC, subject to obligations imposed on it under both the Treaty and the PMC, having due regard to the Contract Operator's responsibilities under the PSC for undertaking petroleum operations.[32]

If the heart of a PSC is its work program and expenditure requirements, the essence of it is its provisions for the sharing of production derived from successful exploration and development, carried out pursuant to the PSC. In this regard, the model PSC has detailed provisions equitably to achieve this end. Encompassed in

30 *Ibid.* Annex C, sec. 4, "Work Program and Expenditures," para. 4(2).

31 *Ibid.* Annex C, sec. 4, para. 4(7)-(9).

32 *Ibid.* Annex C, sec. 5, para. 5(5).

two central Sections of the PSC[33] are extensive rules and procedures which cover the identification of contractor's eligible costs, their recovery and the actual production sharing mechanism.

The basic principle of production sharing is that the JA owns all petroleum in Area A of the Zone, and on behalf of the two Contracting States, companies receive a share of the petroleum produced. The Contractor's portion of such petroleum is calculated according to a mechanism which takes into account First Tranche Petroleum at 20 percent of production, recovery of exploration and operating costs and depreciation of capital costs on a straight line basis and recovery of investment credits and all other allowable costs. The remaining quantity of petroleum produced is then shared according to a state-of-the-art sliding-scale production sharing formula. The JA however, receives a fifty percent share of natural gas production irrespective of production rates, after Contractor's recovery of investment credits and all costs.[34]

The remainder of the PSC deals with standard matters common to all exploration contracts. These include such general matters as applicable laws, notices, arbitration, *force majeure* and effectiveness.[35]

3. The Taxation Code

The last piece of the interlocking legislative, contractual and fiscal framework which governs joint development of the petroleum resources of Area A is the TC. Under the Treaty, the TC is the law which spells out provisions for the avoidance of double taxation in respect of activities connected with Area A of the Zone.[36]

To avoid exposure to double taxation, there are separate, detailed provisions spelling out the exact tax treatment of such items as: business profits (or losses) derived from activities by corporations operating in Area A;[37] dividends paid by companies from

---

33 *Ibid.* Annex C, sec. 6, "Operating Costs" and sec. 7, "Recovery of Operating Costs and Sharing of Petroleum Production."

34 *Ibid.* Annex C, sec. 7, para. 7(5).

35 *Ibid.* Annex C, sec. 12, "Consultation and Arbitration," sec. 15, "Other Provisions" & sec. 16, "Effectiveness."

36 *Ibid.* pt. 1, art. 1, "Definitions," para. 1(m).

37 *Ibid.* Annex D, art. 4, "Business Profits."

profits derived from activities in Area A;[38] interest paid by a Contractor to which a resident of one of the Contracting States is entitled;[39] royalties paid by contractors operating in Area A;[40] and capital gains (or losses) realized from property employed in Area A.[41]

Lastly, goods imported from outside of either Contracting State into Area A for petroleum operations are tax free, unless and until they are transferred permanently into one of the Contracting States, which may then tax them.[42]

As one would expect, the TC contains necessary provisions both for mutual consultation and exchange of information between the two Contracting States both to facilitate its enforcement and to remedy any potential inequities which its application might create.[43]

IV. ACTIVITIES IN AREA A TO DATE

Implementation and progress under the Treaty in the ten years since its inception has been fruitful. There have been six bidding rounds for acreage in Area A of the Zone,[44] of which eighteen awards were made by the JA and PSCs concluded accordingly. Currently, twelve of these PSCs are still under active implementation by Contractors. Over 209,473 kilometers of seismic have been shot in Area A and forty-five wells drilled through 1999. Total expenditures to date by Contractors for exploration, development and production activities have exceeded US$681 million.[45]

Over 475 service contracts have been let in support of petroleum operations in Area A. Their total value exceeds US$1.2 mil-

---

38 *Ibid.* Annex D, art. 5, "Dividends."

39 *Ibid.* Annex D, art. 6, "Interest."

40 *Ibid.* Annex D, art. 7, "Royalties."

41 *Ibid.* Annex D, art. 8, "Alienation of Property."

42 *Ibid.* Annex D, art. 13, "Goods Imported into Area A."

43 *Ibid.* Annex D, art. 14, "Mutual Agreement Procedure," and art. 15, "Exchange of Information."

44 In 1991, 1992, 1994, 1995, 1996 & 1998.

45 Information and data supplied to the author by Dr. Bona Situmorang, an Executive Director (Indonesia) of the JA, at the Second Meeting of the Study Group on Zones of Cooperation in the South China Sea, Bali; Indonesia, June 27–July 1, 1999.

lion. About sixty percent have been awarded to Australian Contractors, three percent to those from Indonesia and thirty-seven percent to third country Contractors. On a cumulative basis to date, mandays of labor performed in Area A on petroleum operations have been divided amongst Australian and Indonesian nationals 51–32 percent, with 17 percent being performed by third country nationals. This is all in furtherance of the Treaty requirement to give preference, where possible, to goods, services and labor from the two Contracting States when such are competitive in price, quality and timeliness.[46]

Seven oil discoveries have been made in Area A. Seven more discoveries of gas and condensate have also been made. Eight wells have shown residual oil columns and two have had significant shows of natural gas. Nine appraisal/delineation wells have been drilled. Only eight of the wells drilled to date have been completely dry.[47]

The first oil discoveries in Area A were made in 1994.[48] In 1995 two gas condensate discoveries were made, including the very significant Bayu-Undan gas/ condensate field.[49] Subsequent oil and gas discoveries were made in 1996, 1997 and 1998.[50] Currently under production are the Elang, Kakatua and Kakatua North oilfields which Phillips Petroleum Corporation acquired in 1999 from Australia's BHP. The annual revenue from these fields is only in the range of US$1.9–3.2 million a year.

The Bayu-Undan field, however, discovered by Contractor Phillips Petroleum Corporation in 1995, has now been fully appraised and has received approval for production of significant quantities of gas and condensate to begin in 2004. Bayu-Undan contains proven reserves of 3.6 TCF of gas and condensate or about one billion barrels of oil equivalent. Last October, following written assurances of support from leaders of the Counsel for East Timorese Resistance (CNRT), Phillips announced that it would proceed with its $1.4 billion, twenty-year project. There are two

---

46 *See* Treaty, *supra* note 1, pt. VI, art. 24, para.1 *et seq.*

47 *See supra* note 54.

48 The Elang -1 well, followed by the Kakatua -1 well.

49 Bayu -1 and Undan -1.

50 Kakatua North -1A (oil), Hingkip -1 (oil), Krill -1 (oil), Sunset -1 & West -1 (gas/condensate), Bard -1 (gas/condensate), Chuditch -1 (gas/condensate).

other potential oil fields and one gas field in Area A. As earlier noted, only about forty-five wells have been drilled to date, indicating that the Area is still relatively unexplored.

V. THE NEW TIMOR GAP TREATY

A. The 1999 UNTAET — Australia Agreements[51]

The United Nations has the authority to conclude any international agreement with States and international organizations as may be necessary for the carrying out of the functions of UNTAET in East Timor.[52] Accordingly, UNTAET determined that an agreement between it, acting on behalf of East Timor, and Australia, providing practical arrangements for the continuity of the terms of the Treaty in the transitional period, would benefit the people of East Timor and would assist UNTAET in carrying out its functions entrusted to it under Security Council Resolution 1272 (1999). The conclusion of such an agreement, however, had to be without prejudice to the position of the future government of an independent East Timor with regard to the Treaty.

UNTAET, on behalf of East Timor, therefore assumed all rights and obligations under the Treaty previously exercised by Indonesia until the independence of East Timor. By agreement, UNTAET and Australia can enter into subsidiary arrangements or agreements relating to the continued operation of the terms of the Treaty. But the United Nations was careful not to give any validity to the "integration" of East Timor into Indonesia. Indeed, both UNTAET and Australia confirmed that UNTAET will exercise its rights and obligations under the Treaty in close consultation and cooperation with representatives of the East Timorese people.

---

51 Exchange of Notes constituting an Agreement between the Government of Australia and the United Nations Transitional Administration in East Timor (UNTAET) concerning the continued Operation of the Treaty between Australia and the Republic of Indonesia on the Zone of Cooperation in an Area between the Indonesian Province of East Timor and Northern Australia of Dec. 11, 1989. (Dili, Feb. 10, 2000); Entry into force: Feb. 10, 2000 (with effect from Oct. 25, 1999). Australian Treaty Series, 2000 No.9.

52 Pursuant to United Nations Security Council resolution 1272 (1999) of 25 Oct. 1999, and in accordance with para. 35 of the Report of the Secretary–General; (S/1999/1024).

According to the UNTAET–Australia agreement (New Treaty), the following provisions of the legal regime of the former Treaty continue to be applicable:

(a) in accordance with UNTAET Regulation 1999/1, the laws applied in East Timor prior to October 25, 1999, to the extent necessary to give effect to the Treaty;
(b) all rules, regulations directions, decisions, guidelines, procedures, approvals, authorizations and other determinations made by either the MC for the Zone or the JA for Area A of the Zone before October 25, 1999; and
(c) all existing PSCs under the Treaty.

Amendments to the New Treaty may be made at any time by an arrangement in writing between the Government of Australia and UNTAET. The New Treaty applies as of October 25, 1999, and continues in effect for the duration of the transitional period. The Government of Australia and UNTAET each recognized that it will be important to facilitate, as a matter of priority, training and employment opportunities for East Timorese national and permanent residents. UNTAET agreed to designate its representative on the MC as soon as possible. It will also nominate for appointment by the MC a person as Executive Director in the head office of the JA as soon as possible. Pending the appointment of the Executive Director by the MC, in order to ensure the continued efficient operation of the JA, UNTAET agreed to appoint an acting Executive Director. UNTAET also undertook to nominate persons for appointment as Technical Director, Finance Director and as Senior Technical Officer on the JA without delay.

The New Treaty provides that the head office of the JA will be established in East Timor as soon as possible, having regard to ensuring the continued efficient operation of the JA. Pending the establishment of the head office of the JA in East Timor, both of its present offices will be consolidated in Darwin on a temporary basis. In addition, the JA will pay East Timor's share of the proceeds collected from PSCs under the Treaty, from October 25, 1999, into a bank account to be advised by UNTAET. The JA will also close its bank account in Jakarta and consolidate all of its funds into its existing bank accounts in Darwin. UNTAET undertook to advise Contractors of details of a bank account into which all taxes payable to UNTAET pursuant to petroleum operations under the Treaty should be deposited.

B. Legal and Political Implications

UNTAET has now officially replaced Indonesia as Australia's partner in exploiting the reserves in the Gap, valued at between US$11 billion and US$19 billion.[53] Effectively, UNTAET and the Australia government will share control over petroleum operations in the Timor Sea, with the royalties to be split between them. The UN's share of the royalties will be backdated to October 25, 1999, when Indonesia formally relinquished its claim to East Timor, but the use of the money has yet to be determined. UNTAET's royalties will go into a trust fund for the duration of its administration, but no decision has yet been made on whether to use them to defray the costs of running the administration.

There are several possible complications at this point. The leaders of CNRT and UN officials are still negotiating the distribution of the hundreds of millions of dollars in revenue expected over the next three years. East Timor, or even Portugal, may ask for Indonesia's portion of the revenues from the date of the Indonesia-Australia Treaty. East Timor might also prefer a royalty system which, unlike production-sharing, would provide a steady stream of payments over time.[54]

The first public announcement that a new Treaty was about to be signed came at an international workshop held in Dili from January 15 to 18, 2000, to discuss the exploitation of the seabed between Timor and Australia. About fifty geologists, lawyers, engineers, economists, oil executives and officials from Australia, the UN, Portugal, Mozambique and East Timor were present. CNRT leaders were also on hand, including vice president Jose Ramos-Horta, Timor Gap spokesman Mari Alkateri and members of the UN administration's appointed National Consultative Council. Expectations were high. The CNRT's Alkateri stated that East Timor

---

53 Mike Head, *Australian Government Secures New East Timor Oil Treaty*, World Socialist Web Site <www.wsws.org>, *Feb. 15, 2000.*

54 John McBeth, *Timor's Inheritance,* Far Eastern Economic Review, Sept. 9, 1999, at 83-84.

and Australia stand to share US$800 million in royalties over the next twenty years. A half share of royalties, being twenty million US dollars a year, would be a very significant contribution to a fledgling state with only 800,000 people.

On January 19, 1999, at a press briefing, UNTAET's principal legal advisor, Hansjoerg Strohmeyer, gave some indication of the intense diplomacy behind the New Treaty. He said that the Dili workshop was the last point in a series of four meetings initiated by Australia and the CNRT leaders. He emphasized that the New Treaty was a fresh legal instrument between UNTAET and Australia. The practical arrangements would remain the same — with UNTAET replacing Indonesia as a party — but it was not a revised version of the 1989 Treaty. This was necessary, he stated, to avoid giving any retrospective legitimacy to the 1989 document.

Indeed, one of the major problems facing Canberra with regard to the 1989 Treaty had been its possible illegality under international law. Australia was the only western country to formally recognize the Indonesian takeover of East Timor. Portugal had acquiesced in the Indonesian invasion but kept its colonial interests alive by sponsoring various UN resolutions that recognized East Timor as a "non-self-governing territory," with Portugal designated as the "administrative power."

In 1991, following new major discoveries in the Timor Sea, Portugal revived its formal claim to sovereignty. It launched proceedings against Australia in the International Court of Justice (ICJ), charging that the Timor Gap Treaty was illegal, damaged the material interest of both Portugal and the people of East Timor, and abrogated the right of the East Timorese people to self-determination.[55]

In June 1995, the ICJ ruled that it could not make a decision on the legality of the Indonesian annexation because Indonesia did not recognize the court's authority. But the ICJ did find certain of Portugal's claims to be "irreproachable." Thus, when East Timor gains independence, the Treaty might have to be renegotiated. Portugal could still continue to claim a share or compensation.

There are potential jurisdictional problems as well. Before the Treaty could be signed, Indonesia had to agree that the area covered by the Treaty was outside Indonesian jurisdiction. This it did,

[55] East Timor Case (Portugal v. Australia), 1995 I.C.J. 90 (June 30).

but it is still possible that the people of West Timor (East Nusa Tenggara) may argue that some of the oil and gas potential falls within the jurisdiction of West Timor, which is part of Indonesia.[56] Or East Timor may try to renegotiate the boundary to be the median line between its coast and that of Australia. That would put much of the known potential under sole East Timor jurisdiction. But if Australia agrees to this renegotiation, Indonesia is likely to want to renegotiate its boundaries with Australia as well.[57]

The next task will be to hold the interest of and to attract further foreign direct investment from international oil companies. Major oil companies from the United States, Australia, Japan, Britain and the Netherlands have much at stake in the Timor Sea. Last year Robert Mollah, the Australian Executive Director of the JA for the Gap, noted that twenty seven companies had spent more than half a billion dollars on exploration and development in the Zone.

Although current Zone revenues of about US$3 million per year are negligible by world standards, they are expected to rise dramatically in 2004, when the Bayu-Undan gas/condensate field comes on stream. Phillips has a 50.3 percent stake in the Bayu-Undan project. Santos, an Australian oil and gas producer and Japan's Index each hold an 11.8 percent interest. Kerr-McGee Corp of the United States has 11.2 percent, followed by Australia's Petroz (8.3) and British Borneo Oil & Gas (6.7). Phillips also operates the smaller Eland and Kakatua fields in the Gap, having bought Australian company BP's 42 percent stake in April, 1999.

Another Australian oil and gas company, Woodside Petroleum, underscored the potential value of the Timor Sea when, on January 20, it announced higher-then-expected oil production from its new half-owned Laminaria/Corallina oil project, which lies in Australian waters just outside the Treaty's Zone. Royal Dutch/Shell owns 34 percent of Woodside, and has its own 25 percent share in the Laminaria/Corallina project, as does BHP.

UN officials said that the CNRT leaders had been consulted, and that they appreciated the requirements of foreign investors.

---

56 *Indonesia: East Nusa Tenggara has more rights to Timor Gap.* ANTARA, Jakarta, Dec.22, 1999.

57 Nawaz Sharif, *Indonesia Calls for Border Talks,* CHINA DAILY, Feb.18, 2000.

Stohmeyer said the extension of the old arrangements reflected "the declared opinion of the CNRT to give the investors the planning security that they need." In Australia, Foreign Minister Downer told reporters: "These arrangements are important to politically convince investors already making investments in the context of the Timor Gap Cooperation Zone."

The recent dramatic rise in world oil price has increased the potential profits from the Gap. Phillips, for example, announced last month that higher crude oil prices boosted its global revenue in the final quarter of 1999 by about 60 percent to US$4.3 billion. While the known reserves in the Gap are in the Treaty's Area A, which is now jointly operated by Australia and UNTAET, current higher prices will probably encourage test drilling in two zones that have not been extensively explored — Area B, controlled exclusively by Canberra, and Area C, now under UNTAET jurisdiction.

VI. CONCLUSION

As first said, the main purpose of concluding the Treaty was to allow petroleum exploration and production to proceed in the Zone without delay while continuing good faith efforts to reach agreement on a permanent delimitation of the continental shelf lying between the two Contracting States. We may safely conclude from all of the foregoing that this primary objective has been fully met. Significant foreign direct investment has flowed into the Zone under the politically settled and comprehensive development regime put in place by the Treaty. Joint development, as was wisely chosen in this instance, assures that development goes forward without interruption and often strengthens further cooperative approaches over time. Indeed, in some cases, it proves to be a useful prelude to a final agreement on offshore boundaries between the States involved.

Another test of the success of a joint development regime is whether it can stand the tests both of time and political change. In the current situation, the change of a sovereign party to the Treaty is a very significant one. Yet it would appear that the transition to

East Timor as the new State party may be a smooth one. There are, indeed, precedents to draw on for such seamless transitions in the face of significant change of circumstances.[58] This would appear, thus far, to be an additional such precedent in the making.

All of the above said, however, any renegotiations of the Treaty terms or the maritime jurisdictional boundaries will still be quite problematic. It took twenty years for Australia and Indonesia to reach agreement, in part because of the use of different principles underlying their boundary claims — natural prolongation of the continental shelf versus equidistance. We do not know yet which such principles will be adopted by East Timor, although they seem to have moved, preliminarily, towards the equidistance principle. Indeed, if the boundary were to be renegotiated today, equidistance would probably eventually prevail.

As East Timor moves closer to independence, its leaders, such as Jose Ramos-Horta, have begun openly to call on Australia to renegotiate the Treaty on the principle of equidistance, which would enable East Timor to receive almost twice the benefit it would otherwise under the current *status quo* State succession. An alternative, however, to a renegotiation of the offshore boundary might be merely to renegotiate the shares of Zone revenues payable to each State under the joint development regime. While classic joint development is predicated on equal sharing of resources and revenues between the Contracting States, there are a few examples of State practice based on unequal sharing. These have been motivated primarily by disproportionate wealth and development capabilities between friendly, neighboring States — one granting a favor to the other by taking a lesser share, as some have suggested that Australia should do for East Timor. Indeed, in the early stages of negotiation between Australia and UNTAET for East Timor, Australia has hinted that it would consider a greater than fifty percent share of revenues and royalties for East Timor

[58] For example, in the case of joint development of the Neutral Zone between Saudi Arabia and Kuwait, when a boundary was subsequently agreed between the States to partition the Neutral Zone, joint development of the Zone's petroleum resources continued, uninterrupted, despite this significant change in circumstances. For full details, *see* Onorato, *A Case Study in Joint Development: The Saudi Arabia-Kuwait Partitioned Neutral Zone, in* Geology and Hydrocarbon Potential of the South China Sea and Possibilities of Joint Development 539 (M. Valencia ed., 1985).

as part of an overall aid package, but it would *not* consider renegotiating either the Zone or any permanent boundaries in the Timor Gap.

Also posing difficulties for any renegotiation of the Treaty are its purpose-built legal regimes which are grounded in a harmonization of Indonesia and Australian legal precepts and therefore would be difficult to unwind. Renegotiation of boundaries or terms would also be a deterrent to continued or new investment in the area for exploration and development, which, of course, is the primary purpose of a joint development regime in the first place. Thus, only time will tell whether the regime in place will stand the long-term tests of both time and significant change.

SIGNING AND RATIFYING INTERNATIONAL AGREEMENTS IN EASTERN EUROPE AND CENTRAL ASIA: THE KYRGYZ AND ROMANIAN LAWS ON INTERNATIONAL TREATIES

Maurizio Ragazzi[*]

For Dr. Ibrahim F.I. Shihata, the law of treaties has been a constant area of intellectual and practical interest. In one of his early writings, he explored the question of treaties as evidence of general rules of international law;[1] in the last volume of his series on the World Bank in a Changing World, he addressed another fundamental issue of the law of treaties, namely the interpretation and amendment of the constituent instrument of an international organization.[2] In his professional capacity as General Counsel of the World Bank, i.e., the International Bank for Reconstruction and Development (IBRD) and the International Development Association (IDA), Shihata participated, for example, in the United Nations Conference on the Law of Treaties Between States and International Organizations or Between International Organizations,[3] and presided over the preparation and conclusion of thou-

[*] The opinions expressed by the writer in this article are those of the writer alone, and should not be attributed to the institutions with which he is associated.

[1] Ibrahim F. I. Shihata, *The Treaty as a Law-Declaring and Custom-Making Instrument,* 22 Revue Égyptienne de Droit International 51–90 (1966).

[2] Ibrahim F. I. Shihata, The World Bank in a Changing World, Vol. III, 3–19 (2000), Introductory Chapter (*Interpretation and Amendment of the IBRD Articles of Agreement*).

[3] The conference took place in Vienna, between February 18 & March 21, 1986. The official records have been published, in two volumes, in 1995.

sands of international agreements to which IBRD and/or IDA are parties.

In consideration of the foregoing, the present writer thought it appropriate to contribute to this collection of essays in Shihata's honor with a note on international treaties. His main purpose is to present an English translation of the 1999 law on international treaties of the Kyrgyz Republic, and the 1991 law on the conclusion and ratification of treaties of Romania. No English translation of either law is available (at least to the writer's knowledge) to the general public. Apart from a desire to make them accessible to English-speaking academics and practitioners alike, the ground for selecting these laws is eminently practical. From 1994 to 1999, the present writer was the lawyer in charge of almost all the operations regarding the Kyrgyz Republic and Romania,[4] with the consequence that the laws on treaties of these two countries were obviously relevant to his work on IBRD loan agreements and IDA credit agreements with the Kyrgyz Republic and Romania.[5]

However, in addition to these pragmatic reasons, the joint presentation of the treaty laws of the Kyrgyz Republic and Romania offers a new perspective on the variety of ways in which the former socialist States have addressed, over the last decade, the need for legislative changes that would ease the transition of these States to new economic relations. Much has been written on constitutional reform in these countries, and its impact on the re-

[4] The qualification "almost" is necessary, because the present writer exercised his natural right of conscientious objection to working on operations connected with voluntary abortion or contraception, and was therefore exempted from work on such operations.

[5] For the purposes of this contribution, the international legal nature of IBRD loan agreements and IDA credit agreements will be assumed without additional discussion. On the World Bank's international financial agreements, *see* Aron Broches, *International Legal Aspects of the Operations of the World Bank*, 98 RECUEIL DES COURS DE L'ACADÉMIE DE DROIT INTERNATIONAL DE L'HAYE NO. III, 297–409 (1959). *See also* Jean Salmon, *Banque Internationale pour la Reconstruction et le Développement — Les Contrats de la Banque Internationale pour la Reconstruction et le Développement*, 2 ANNUAIRE FRANÇAIS DE DROIT INTERNATIONAL 635–42 (1956). On international financial agreements, more generally, *see* JEAN SALMON, LE RÔLE DES ORGANISATIONS INTERNATIONALES EN MATIÈRE DE PRÊTS ET D'EMPRUNTS – PROBLÈMES JURIDIQUES (1958); Antoine Brédimas, *Les accords de Prêt et de Garantie Interétatique*, 29 REVUE HELLÉNIQUE DE DROIT INTERNATIONAL 74–150 (1976); Hugo J. Hahn, *International Loan and Guarantee Agreements*, 4 SRI LANKA JOURNAL OF INTERNATIONAL LAW 55–77 (1992).

lationship between international law and domestic law.[6] There is no need to revisit these issues here. Rather, the relevant point for the present purposes is this: the World Bank and its borrowers have a joint interest in a prompt declaration of effectiveness of loan and credit agreements after their signing, because, among other reasons, this facilitates the timely performance of the activities to be undertaken by the borrower in compliance with the agreement, and because (at least in the case of IBRD loans) the commitment charge on the unwithdrawn amount starts accruing sixty days after the date of signing, irrespective of whether the loan agreement in question has or has not entered into force.

This need for a prompt completion of the internal procedures of approval or ratification of financial agreements is probably at the origin of the amendment to the Kyrgyz Constitution (introduced in 1996), whereby, if they have not been signed by the President but by another authority, international financial treaties and credit agreements are internally ratified by presidential decree instead of parliamentary law.[7] This solution is ingenious but not immune from difficulties. In the internal Kyrgyz order, does an international provision ratified by presidential decree have the same hierarchical value of a provision ratified by parliamentary

---

6 *See, for example,* Eric Stein, *International Law and Internal Law in the New Constitutions of Central-Eastern Europe, in* RECHT ZWISCHEN UMBRUCH UND BEWAHRUNG. VÖLKERRECHT, EUROPARECHT, STAATSRECHT. FESTSCHRIFT FÜR RUDOLF BERNHARDT 865–84 (Ulrich Beyerlin et al eds., 1995); Vladlen S. Vereshchetin, *New Constitutions and the Old Problem of the Relationship Between International Law and National Law,* 7 EUROPEAN JOURNAL OF INTERNATIONAL LAW 29-41 (1996); Theodor Schweisfurth & Ralf Alleweldt, *The Position of International Law in the Domestic Legal Orders of Central and Eastern European Countries,* 40 GERMAN YEARBOOK OF INTERNATIONAL LAW 164–80 (1997); CONSTITUTIONAL REFORM AND INTERNATIONAL LAW IN CENTRAL AND EASTERN EUROPE (Rein Müllerson et al eds., 1998). Within the abundant literature on the issue regarding, in particular, Russia, *see* A. N. Talalaev, *Sootnoshenie Mezhdunarodnogo i Vnutrigosudarstvennogo Prava i Konstitutsiia Rossiiskoi Federatsii,* MOSCOW JOURNAL OF INTERNATIONAL LAW No. 4, 3-15 (1994); O. N. Khlestov, *Mezhdunarodnoe Pravo i Rossiia, ibid.,* at 52–9; E. T. Usenko, *Sootnoshenie i Vzaimodeistvie Mezhdunarodnogo i Natsional'nogo Prava i Rossiiskaia Konstitutsiia,* MOSCOW JOURNAL OF INTERNATIONAL LAW No. 2, 13–28 (1995); I. I. Lukashuk, *Konstitutsiia Rossii i Mezhdunarodnoe Pravo, ibid.,* at 29–41; *Id., Treaties in the Legal System of Russia,* 40 GERMAN YEARBOOK OF INTERNATIONAL LAW 141–63 (1997).

7 *See* Article 48 of the Kyrgyz Constitution. *See also* Article 13(2) of the Kyrgyz law on international treaties.

law? In other words, does the rule contained in the Kyrgyz civil code,[8] whereby, in case of conflict with an internal law, an international treaty ratified by parliamentary law prevails extend to international financial agreements ratified by presidential decree?

The case of Romania is different. Under its Constitution, there is no separate procedure for the ratification of international financial agreements. There is, however, the possibility of ratifying an international treaty such as an IBRD loan agreement not only by parliamentary law but also by governmental order pursuant to an enabling law previously adopted by Parliament, or by emergency order.[9] In the first case, the enabling law may provide that the order be subsequently submitted to Parliament for approval, lest the order be discontinued or lose its effectiveness. In the second case, parliamentary approval is a requirement for the coming into force of the order. Each of the three procedures has been followed, at one time or another, in the internal ratification of IBRD loan agreements concluded by Romania.

8 *See* Article 6 of the Kyrgyz civil code.

9 *See* Article 114 of the Romanian Constitution.

APPENDIX 1

KYRGYZ REPUBLIC

Law No. 89

ON INTERNATIONAL TREATIES OF THE KYRGYZ REPUBLIC*

(dated July 21, 1999)

International treaties are the legal basis of the international relations of the Kyrgyz Republic.

The international treaties of the Kyrgyz Republic, in accordance with the Constitution of the Kyrgyz Republic, are a constituent and integral component of the legislation of the Kyrgyz Republic.

The Kyrgyz Republic supports the strict observance of the norms of international law and confirms its adherence to a basic principle of international law, namely the principle of the fulfillment of international obligations in good faith.

I. GENERAL PROVISIONS

ARTICLE 1
OBJECTIVES AND SCOPE OF THIS LAW

1. This law establishes the procedure for the conclusion, implementation, termination, suspension and denunciation of the international treaties of the Kyrgyz Republic. The international treaties of the Kyrgyz Republic are concluded, im-

* *Zakon Kyrgyzskoi Respubliki o Mezhdunarodnykh Dogovorakh Kyrgyzskoi Respubliki*. The English translation from the Russian version, *reproduced here,* reflects an extensive revision by the present writer of an earlier draft provided by the World Bank's country directorate and resident mission for the Kyrgyz Republic.

plemented, suspended, terminated and denounced in accordance with generally recognized principles and norms of international law, the Constitution of the Kyrgyz Republic, as well as this law and provisions of the treaties in question.

2. The procedure for the conclusion, implementation, termination, suspension and denunciation of the international treaties of the Kyrgyz Republic, established in the present law, apply to all the international treaties of the Kyrgyz Republic, irrespective of their type, form and denomination.

ARTICLE II
USE OF TERMS

For the purposes of this law, the following terms are used:

"international treaty of the Kyrgyz Republic" means an equal and voluntary agreement of the Kyrgyz Republic with one or more States, international organizations or other subjects of international law, with respect to rights and obligations in the area of international relations;

"conclusion" means the expression of consent of the Kyrgyz Republic to be bound by an international treaty;

"signature" means either a phase in the conclusion of a treaty or a means of expressing the consent of the Kyrgyz Republic to be bound by an international treaty, unless the treaty is subject to subsequent ratification or approval;

"internal procedures" means ratification or approval of an international treaty;

"ratification, approval and accession" means, as the case may be, the form expressing the consent of the Kyrgyz Republic to be bound by an international treaty;

"full powers" means a document emanating from the competent authority of the Kyrgyz Republic, designating a person or a number of persons to represent the Kyrgyz Republic for negotiating, adopting or authenticating the text of a treaty, for expressing the consent of the Kyrgyz Republic to be bound by a treaty, or for accomplishing any other act with respect to a treaty;

"initialing" means the certification of the final agreement on the text of an international treaty by the parties, expressed by the authorized representatives of the contracting States by writing their initials on the text of the treaty;

"authentic texts" means the texts of one and the same international treaty made in different languages but having the same legal effect;

"reservation" means a unilateral statement of the authorized representatives or competent authority of a State, made when signing, ratifying, accepting or approving a treaty, or acceding to it, purporting to exclude or modify the legal effect of certain provisions of a treaty in their application to that State;

"international organization" means an inter-state, intergovernmental organization;

"depositary" means a State, an international organization or its chief executive officer, who keeps custody of the original text of an international treaty and who performs, with respect to the treaty in question, the functions specified under international law;

"denunciation" means the repudiation by the Kyrgyz Republic of an international treaty it had concluded, by notice given in accordance with the procedure and the terms established in the same treaty; and

"instrument of ratification" means the special document, attesting that the Jogorku Kenesh of the Kyrgyz Republic has considered an international treaty, and expressing consent to the binding force of the international treaty for the Kyrgyz Republic.

ARTICLE III
DENOMINATION AND TYPES OF INTERNATIONAL TREATIES

1. International treaties may be called and concluded as treaties, agreements, conventions, protocols, memoranda, exchanges of letters and notes, and may also be called in other ways.
2. By the number of subjects that are parties to them, international treaties are subdivided into bilateral and multilateral. By their contents, international treaties can be: economic, political, financial, legal, and can also be con-

cluded on other issues. By their duration, treaties are subdivided into those lasting for a definite and those lasting for an indefinite period of time. International treaties can also be concluded according to other types.

3. The international treaties of the Kyrgyz Republic are concluded with foreign States, as well as with international organizations on behalf of:
   - the Kyrgyz Republic (inter-state treaties);
   - the Government of the Kyrgyz Republic (inter-governmental treaties);
   - the Jogorku Kenesh of the Kyrgyz Republic (inter-parliamentary treaties);
   - ministries, State committees and administrative departments of the Kyrgyz Republic (inter-departmental treaties).

ARTICLE IV
LANGUAGE AND FORM OF AN INTERNATIONAL TREATY

The language of an international treaty of the Kyrgyz Republic is the Kyrgyz language, but in certain cases it may be the Russian language and the language of the other contracting party (or parties).

By agreement with the other party to an international treaty some other language can be chosen as the language of the treaty.

The language in which the text of an international treaty is written is identified in the treaty, where its authenticity and official status are established. International treaties are concluded in written form.

ARTICLE V
EXPRESSION OF CONSENT OF THE KYRGYZ REPUBLIC TO BE BOUND BY AN INTERNATIONAL TREATY

1. The consent of the Kyrgyz Republic to be bound by an international treaty can be expressed by:
   - signing the treaty;
   - exchanging notes or letters forming the treaty;
   - ratifying the treaty;
   - approving the treaty;

- acceding to the treaty;
- using any other means expressing consent, on which the contracting parties have agreed.

2. Decisions on the consent to the binding effect of international treaties for the Kyrgyz Republic are taken by the State authorities of the Kyrgyz Republic, in conformity with their competence established by the Constitution of the Kyrgyz Republic, by this law, and by other normative legal acts of the Kyrgyz Republic.

II. PROCEDURE FOR THE CONCLUSION AND ENTRY INTO FORCE OF INTERNATIONAL TREATIES OF THE KYRGYZ REPUBLIC

SECTION 1. PROPOSALS ON THE CONCLUSION OF INTERATIONAL TREATIES, CONDUCT OF NEGOTIATIONS, AND SIGNATURE OF INTERNATIONAL TREATIES

ARTICLE VI
PROPOSALS ON THE CONCLUSION OF INTERNATIONAL TREATIES

1. Proposals on the conclusion of international treaties on behalf of the Kyrgyz Republic are submitted to the President of the Kyrgyz Republic, while proposals on the conclusion of international treaties on behalf of the Kyrgyz Republic, with respect to issues within the sphere of authority of the Government of the Kyrgyz Republic, are submitted to the Government of the Kyrgyz Republic.
2. Proposals on the conclusion of international treaties on behalf of the Kyrgyz Republic are submitted to the President of the Kyrgyz Republic by the Ministry of Foreign Affairs of the Kyrgyz Republic.

   Other ministries, State committees and administrative departments submit to the President of the Kyrgyz Republic proposals on the conclusion of international treaties on behalf of the Kyrgyz Republic with respect to issues within their sphere of authority, with the concurrence of the Ministry of Foreign Affairs of the Kyrgyz Republic.
3. Proposals on the conclusion of inter-parliamentary treaties are submitted by the Toraga of the Legislative Assembly,

the Toraga of the Assembly of People's Representatives of the Jogorku Kenesh of the Kyrgyz Republic, or members of the Jogorku Kenesh of the Kyrgyz Republic, to the consideration of the chambers of the Jogorku Kenesh of the Kyrgyz Republic.

4. Proposals on the conclusion of international treaties of the Kyrgyz Republic on behalf of the Government of the Kyrgyz Republic are submitted to the Government of the Kyrgyz Republic by the Ministry of Foreign Affairs of the Kyrgyz Republic.

   Other ministries, State committees and administrative departments submit to the Government of the Kyrgyz Republic proposals on the conclusion of international treaties on behalf of the Government of the Kyrgyz Republic, with the concurrence of the Ministry of Foreign Affairs of the Kyrgyz Republic.

5. Proposals on the conclusion of international treaties of the Kyrgyz Republic having an inter-departmental character are submitted to the Government of the Kyrgyz Republic, for approval, by the ministries, State committees and administrative departments with respect to issues within their sphere of authority, with the concurrence of the Ministry of Foreign Affairs of the Kyrgyz Republic.

6. Proposal on the conclusion of an international treaty must be accompanied by a draft of that treaty, the substantiation of the reasons for its conclusion, the mechanism of implementation of the treaty, the conclusions on the conformity between the draft of the treaty and the legislation of the Kyrgyz Republic, as well as the assessment made by the competent ministries, State committees and administrative departments of the Kyrgyz Republic of the financial, economic and other consequences that may derive from the conclusion of the treaty.

ARTICLE VII
CONSENT TO THE PROPOSAL ON THE CONCLUSION OF INTERNATIONAL TREATIES BY THE MINISTRIES, STATE COMMITTEES AND ADMINISTRATIVE DEPARTMENTS CONCERNED

1. Proposals on the conclusion of international treaties of the Kyrgyz Republic are agreed upon, before their submission to the President of the Kyrgyz Republic or the Government of the Kyrgyz Republic, by the ministries, State committees and administrative departments concerned.

   Drafts of the treaties subject to ratification by the Jogorku Kenesh of the Kyrgyz Republic are submitted to the concerned committees of the Legislative Assembly of the Jogorku Kenesh of the Kyrgyz Republic, for their concurrence.

   Drafts of the treaties are submitted to the examination of the Ministry of Justice of the Kyrgyz Republic regarding their conformity with the legislation of the Republic, and of the Ministry of Finance of the Kyrgyz Republic regarding the financial obligations reflected in the draft treaties, and are agreed upon by the Ministry of Foreign Affairs of the Kyrgyz Republic.
2. The ministries, State committees and administrative departments of the Kyrgyz Republic have the right to have consultations, subject to the concurrence of the Ministry of Foreign Affairs of the Kyrgyz Republic, with their counterparts in foreign States or international organizations, regarding the preparation of draft international treaties, the proposals for the conclusion of which are submitted, in accordance with the procedure established in Article 6 of this law and the present Article, to the President of the Kyrgyz Republic or the Government of the Kyrgyz Republic.

ARTICLE VIII
DECISIONS ON THE SIGNATURE OF INTERNATIONAL TREATIES

1. Decisions on the signature of international treaties of the Kyrgyz Republic are taken:
   a) by the President of the Kyrgyz Republic, with respect to treaties to be concluded on behalf of the Kyrgyz Republic, and by the Government of the Kyrgyz Republic, with respect to treaties to be concluded on behalf of the Kyrgyz Republic on issues within the sphere of authority of the Government of the Kyrgyz Republic;
   b) by the Government of the Kyrgyz Republic, with respect to treaties to be concluded on behalf of the Government of the Kyrgyz Republic.
2. Decisions on the signature of inter-parliamentary treaties of the Kyrgyz Republic are taken by the chambers of the Jogorku Kenesh of the Kyrgyz Republic.
3. Decisions on the signature of inter-departmental treaties are taken, subject to the concurrence of the Government of the Kyrgyz Republic, by the ministries, State committees and administrative departments of the Kyrgyz Republic whose authority extends to the issues regulated by these treaties.
4. Decisions on the signature of international treaties of an inter-departmental character are taken by the Government of the Kyrgyz Republic whenever the issues in question are of great significance to the State interest of the Kyrgyz Republic.

ARTICLE IX
CONDUCTING NEGOTIATIONS AND SIGNING INTERNATIONAL TREATIES OF THE KYRGYZ REPUBLIC WITHOUT SPECIAL FULL POWERS

1. The President of the Kyrgyz Republic, as the head of the State, represents the Kyrgyz Republic in international relations and, in conformity with international law and the

Constitution of the Kyrgyz Republic, conducts negotiations and signs international treaties of the Kyrgyz Republic without special full powers.

2. The Toraga of the Legislative Assembly and the Toraga of the Assembly of People's Representatives of the Jogorku Kenesh of the Kyrgyz Republic have the right to conduct negotiations and sign, on behalf of the Jogorku Kenesh of the Kyrgyz Republic, inter-parliamentary treaties of the Kyrgyz Republic without special full powers.
3. The Prime Minister of the Kyrgyz Republic, as the head of the Government of the Kyrgyz Republic, in conformity with international law, conducts negotiations and signs international treaties of the Kyrgyz Republic without special full powers.
4. The Minister of Foreign Affairs of the Kyrgyz Republic, in virtue of his or her full powers and in conformity with international law, conducts negotiations and signs international treaties of the Kyrgyz Republic without special full powers.
5. The head of the diplomatic mission of the Kyrgyz Republic to a foreign State, or the head of the mission of the Kyrgyz Republic to an international organization, has the right to conduct negotiations on the conclusion of an international treaty of the Kyrgyz Republic with the State or international organization to which he or she is accredited, without special full powers, pursuant to instructions received from Ministry of Foreign Affairs of the Kyrgyz Republic.
6. A minister, a president of a State committee or a head of an administrative department has the right, within the limits of his or her authority, to conduct negotiations and sign international treaties of an inter-departmental character without special full powers.

ARTICLE X
FULL POWERS TO CONDUCT NEGOTIATIONS AND SIGN INTERNATIONAL TREATIES OF THE KYRGYZ REPUBLIC

Full powers to conduct negotiations and sign international treaties of the Kyrgyz Republic are conferred:

- by the President of the Kyrgyz Republic, with respect to treaties to be concluded on behalf of the Kyrgyz Republic, and by the Government of the Kyrgyz Republic, with respect to treaties to be concluded on behalf of the Kyrgyz Republic regarding issues within the sphere of authority of the Government of the Kyrgyz Republic. Full powers to conduct of negotiations and sign these treaties are formalized and conferred by the Ministry of Foreign Affairs of the Kyrgyz Republic, pursuant to a decision of the President of the Kyrgyz Republic or the Government of the Kyrgyz Republic;
- by the Toraga of the Legislative Assembly, or the Toraga of the Assembly of People's representatives of the Jogorku Kenesh of the Kyrgyz Republic, with respect to treaties to be concluded on behalf of the Jogorku Kenesh of the Kyrgyz Republic;
- by the Government of the Kyrgyz Republic, with respect to treaties to be concluded on behalf of the Government of the Kyrgyz Republic. Full powers to conduct negotiations and sign these treaties are formalized by Ministry of Foreign Affairs of the Kyrgyz Republic on behalf of the Government of the Kyrgyz Republic;
- by the concerned minister, president of State committee or head of administrative department of the Kyrgyz Republic, with respect to inter-departmental treaties.

SECTION 2. INTERNAL PROCEDURES OF THE KYRGYZ REPUBLIC

ARTICLE XI
INTERNATIONAL TREATIES OF THE KYRGYZ REPUBLIC SUBJECT TO RATIFICATION

1. The following treaties are subject to ratification:
   - international treaties of the Kyrgyz Republic on friendship, cooperation and mutual assistance, and treaties on the foundations of inter-state relations;
   - treaties on matters related to the defense of the State;
   - treaties on disarmament matters;

- treaties on the maintenance of international peace and security;
- treaties on collective security;
- treaties on the boarders and the territorial delimitation of the Kyrgyz Republic with other States;
- treaties on the extension of State loans, economic and other assistance by the Kyrgyz Republic to foreign States;
- investment treaties;
- treaties on the fundamental human and civil rights and freedoms;
- treaties on the participation of the Kyrgyz Republic in inter-state unions, international organizations and other inter-state associations, if these treaties provide for the transfer to such entities of the execution of some of the full powers of the Kyrgyz Republic or establish that the decisions taken by the organs of these entities are legally binding on the Kyrgyz Republic;
- treaties on the use of natural resources by other subjects of international law and by foreign companies;
- treaties on the extension of credits to the Kyrgyz Republic, and treaties providing for financial obligations of the Kyrgyz Republic;
- treaties establishing other rules than those contained in the legislation of the Kyrgyz Republic.

2. The international treaties of the Kyrgyz Republic upon the conclusion of which the parties have agreed on subsequent ratification are likewise subject to ratification.
3. The President of the Kyrgyz Republic ratifies financial treaties and credit agreements signed, pursuant to his or her instruction, by the Prime Minister of the Kyrgyz Republic, members of the Government or other officials.

ARTICLE XII
PROPOSALS ON THE RATIFICATION OF INTERNATIONAL TREATIES OF THE KYRGYZ REPUBLIC

1. Proposals on the ratification of international treaties, the decisions on the signing of which have been taken by the

President of the Kyrgyz Republic, are submitted by the President of the Kyrgyz Republic to the Jogorku Kenesh of the Kyrgyz Republic for ratification.

2. Proposals on the ratification of international treaties, the decisions on the signing of which have been taken by the Government of the Kyrgyz Republic, are submitted by the Government of the Kyrgyz Republic to the Jogorku Kenesh of the Kyrgyz Republic for ratification.
3. Proposals on the ratification of international financial treaties and credit agreements are submitted by the Government of the Kyrgyz Republic to the President of the Kyrgyz Republic, in accordance with the Constitution of the Kyrgyz Republic.
4. Proposals on the submission to ratification of international treaties of the Kyrgyz Republic are submitted to the President of the Kyrgyz Republic or, respectively, the Government of the Kyrgyz Republic by ministries, State committees and administrative departments, with respect to treaties within their sphere of authority, with the concurrence of the Ministry of Foreign Affairs of the Kyrgyz Republic.

   International treaties that are presented to the President of the Kyrgyz Republic for submission to ratification, the carrying out of which requires prior consideration by the Government of the Kyrgyz Republic, are submitted to the Government of the Kyrgyz Republic.

   The proposal on ratification of an international treaty must contain a certified copy of the official text of the international treaty, a substantiation of the advisability of ratification, the concurrence of the ministries, State committees and administrative departments concerned, as well as the assessment of the possible financial, economic and other consequences of ratification, with special regard to those leading to a change in the legislation of the Kyrgyz Republic.
5. Decisions of the Government of the Kyrgyz Republic on the approval, or on the submission to ratification, of international treaties are taken in the form of a resolution.

ARTICLE XIII
DECISION ON THE RATIFICATION OF INTERNATIONAL TREATIES OF THE KYRGYZ REPUBLIC

1. The decision on ratification of international treaties of the Kyrgyz Republic (including financial treaties and credit agreements) is taken by the Legislative Assembly of the Jogorku Kenesh of the Kyrgyz Republic in the form of a law, which is approved by the Assembly of People's Representatives of the Jogorku Kenesh of the Kyrgyz Republic and signed by the President of the Kyrgyz Republic.
2. The decision on ratification of financial treaties and credit agreements of the Kyrgyz Republic is taken by the President of the Kyrgyz Republic in the form of a decree, only when the President has transferred his or her full powers to sign the same.

ARTICLE XIV
INSTRUMENT OF RATIFICATION

Pursuant to the law on ratification of an international treaty, the President of the Kyrgyz Republic signs an instrument of ratification, which is accompanied by his or her seal and is signed by the Minister of Foreign Affairs of the Kyrgyz Republic.

ARTICLE XV
EXCHANGE OF THE INSTRUMENTS OF RATIFICATION AND DEPOSIT FOR THEIR CUSTODY

The exchange of the instruments of ratification, and the deposit of the instruments of ratification of international treaties of the Kyrgyz Republic for custody by depositaries, are made by the Ministry of Foreign Affairs of the Kyrgyz Republic or, pursuant to its instruction, by a diplomatic mission of the Kyrgyz Republic or a permanent mission of the Kyrgyz Republic to an international organization.

ARTICLE XVI
APPROVAL OF INTERNATIONAL TREATIES OF THE KYRGYZ REPUBLIC THAT ARE NOT SUBJECT TO RATIFICATION

1. The approval of international treaties of the Kyrgyz Republic that are not subject to ratification, but are subject to approval, is made:
   a) by the President of the Kyrgyz Republic, in the form of a decree, with respect to treaties to be concluded on behalf of the Kyrgyz Republic, and by the Government of the Kyrgyz Republic, in the form of a resolution, with respect to treaties to be concluded on behalf of the Kyrgyz Republic regarding matters within the sphere of authority of the Government of the Kyrgyz Republic;
   b) by the Government of the Kyrgyz Republic, in the form of a resolution, with respect to treaties to be concluded on behalf of the Government of the Kyrgyz Republic;
   c) by the ministry, State committee or administrative department on whose behalf the treaties have been signed, in the form of orders, with respect to inter-departmental treaties coming into force after their approval.
2. Proposals on the approval of international treaties of the Kyrgyz Republic are submitted in accordance with the procedure established in Article 6 of this law.

ARTICLE XVII
ACCESSION OF THE KYRGYZ REPUBLIC TO INTERNATIONAL TREATIES

1. The decision on the accession of the Kyrgyz Republic to international treaties is made:
   a) by the Jogorku Kenesh of the Kyrgyz Republic, in accordance with the procedure established in Article 12 of this law, with respect to treaties subject to ratification;
   b) by the President of the Kyrgyz Republic, with respect to treaties that are not subject to ratification, accession to which is made on behalf of the Kyrgyz Republic,

and by the Government of the Kyrgyz Republic, with respect to treaties that are not subject to ratification, accession to which is made on behalf of the Kyrgyz Republic, regarding matters within the sphere of authority of the Government of the Kyrgyz Republic;

c) by the Government of the Kyrgyz Republic, with respect to treaties accession to which is made on behalf of the Government of the Kyrgyz Republic.

2. Decisions on the accession to inter-parliamentary treaties are made by the Legislative Assembly and the Assembly of the People's Representatives of the Jogorku Kenesh of the Kyrgyz Republic.
3. Accession to international treaties of an inter-departmental character is made in accordance with the procedure established in Article 8, paragraphs 3 and 4, of this law.
4. Proposals on the accession to international treaties implemented in the form of a law are submitted in accordance with the procedure established in Article 12 of this law, and in the other cases in accordance with the procedure provided for in Articles 6, 7 and 16 of this law.

ARTICLE XVIII
PROPOSALS ON THE INTRODUCTION OF AMENDMENTS AND SUPPLEMENTARY PROVISIONS TO THE LEGISLATION OF THE KYRGYZ REPUBLIC IN CONNECTION WITH THE CONCLUSION OF INTERNATIONAL TREATIES OF THE KYRGYZ REPUBLIC

In those cases in which it is necessary to eliminate existing conflicts between the norms of an international treaty and the legislation of the Republic, or to adopt a law or another act with a view to implementing an international treaty of the Kyrgyz Republic, the concerned ministries, State committees and administrative departments of the Kyrgyz Republic submit the relevant drafts of normative legal acts to the President of the Kyrgyz Republic or the Government of the Kyrgyz Republic, in accordance with the established procedure.

ARTICLE XIX
SPECIAL PROCEDURE OF EXPRESSING THE CONSENT TO THE BINDING FORCE OF INTERNATIONAL TREATIES OF THE KYRGYZ REPUBLIC

If an international treaty contains rules requiring an amendment of certain provisions of the Constitution of the Kyrgyz Republic, the decision on the consent to its binding force for the Kyrgyz Republic is made in the form of a law only after the introduction of the corresponding amendments to the Constitution of the Kyrgyz Republic, or the review of the provisions of the Constitution in accordance with the established procedure.

ARTICLE XX
TEMPORARY APPLICATION OF AN INTERNATIONAL TREATY BY THE KYRGYZ REPUBLIC

1. An international treaty or part of it may temporarily be applied by the Kyrgyz Republic, before the treaty enters into force, if this is provided for in the treaty or has been agreed upon by the parties which had signed the treaty.
2. The decision on the temporary application by the Kyrgyz Republic of an international treaty or a part of it is made by the organ that has made the decision on the signature of the international treaty.

ARTICLE XXI
ENTRY INTO FORCE AND TIME OF OPERATION OF INTERNATIONAL TREATIES OF THE KYRGYZ REPUBLIC

1. International treaties enter into force for the Kyrgyz Republic, in accordance with this law, pursuant to the procedure and at the time provided for in the treaty or agreed upon by the contracting parties.
2. Official notices by the Ministry of Foreign Affairs of the Kyrgyz Republic, with respect to the entry into force of international treaties of the Kyrgyz Republic concluded on

behalf of the Kyrgyz Republic and on behalf of the Government of the Kyrgyz Republic, are published in accordance with the procedure provided for in Article 23 of this law.

ARTICLE XXII RESERVATIONS TO INTERNATIONAL TREATIES OF THE KYRGYZ REPUBLIC

1. When signing, ratifying, approving (adopting) international treaties of the Kyrgyz Republic, or acceding to treaties, reservations may be formulated in conformity with the terms of the treaty and the relevant norms of international law.
2. Reservations may be withdrawn at any time, in accordance with the same procedure in which they have been formulated.
3. The acceptance of a reservation formulated by another contracting State to an international treaty of the Kyrgyz Republic, or the objection to a reservation, is made in accordance with the terms of the treaty and the norms of international law by the organ that has made the decision on the consent to the binding force of the international treaty for the Kyrgyz Republic.

    Proposals on the acceptance of reservations to international treaties requiring ratification are submitted in accordance with the procedure established in Article 12 of this law and, for the other cases, in accordance with the procedure provided for in Article 6 of this law.

III. PUBLICATION AND REGISTRATION OF INTERNATIONAL TREATIES OF THE KYRGYZ REPUBLIC

ARTICLE XXIII PUBLICATION OF INTERNATIONAL TREATIES OF THE KYRGYZ REPUBLIC

1. International treaties entering into force for the Kyrgyz Republic (with the exception of treaties of an interdepartmental character) are officially published in *Vedo-*

mosti of the Jogorku Kenesh of the Kyrgyz Republic, in the collection of acts and laws of the President of the Kyrgyz Republic, and in the official publications of the Government of the Kyrgyz Republic, in accordance with the laws of the Kyrgyz Republic *On Normative Legal Acts of the Kyrgyz Republic* and *On the Procedure for the Publication of Laws of the Kyrgyz Republic.*

2. International treaties of the Kyrgyz Republic of an interdepartmental character are published pursuant to a decision of the concerned ministries, State committees and administrative departments on whose behalf the treaties in question have been concluded, in the official publications of these organs or in the official publications of the Government of the Kyrgyz Republic.
3. International treaties of the Kyrgyz Republic, the authentic texts of which are written in foreign languages, are published in the State language. International treaties of the Kyrgyz Republic may also be published in other languages.

ARTICLE XXIV
UNIFORM STATE SYSTEM OF REGISTRATION AND TRACKING OF INTERNATIONAL TREATIES OF THE KYRGYZ REPUBLIC

A uniform State system of registration and tracking of international treaties of the Kyrgyz Republic is accomplished by the Ministry of Foreign Affairs of the Kyrgyz Republic.

ARTICLE XXV
REGISTRATION OF INTERNATIONAL TREATIES OF THE KYRGYZ REPUBLIC WITH INTERNATIONAL ORGANIZATIONS

The registration of international treaties of the Kyrgyz Republic with the Secretariat of the United Nations Organization and with the corresponding organs of other international organizations is accomplished by the Ministry of Foreign Affairs of the Kyrgyz Republic.

ARTICLE XXVI
CUSTODY OF THE TEXTS OF INTERNATIONAL TREATIES OF THE KYRGYZ REPUBLIC

1. The originals (or certified copies and official translations) of international treaties of the Kyrgyz Republic, concluded on behalf of the Kyrgyz Republic and on behalf of the Government of the Kyrgyz Republic, are given for custody to the Ministry of Foreign Affairs of the Kyrgyz Republic within a period of two weeks from the day of their signature (or receipt from the depositary of certified copies and official translations), while copies of these treaties are distributed to the ministries, State committees and administrative departments concerned, within a period of two weeks from the day of their entry into force.
2. The originals of international inter-departmental treaties of the Kyrgyz Republic are kept in custody in the archives of the concerned ministries, State committees and administrative departments of the Kyrgyz Republic, while certified copies of these treaties are transmitted to the Ministry of Foreign Affairs of the Kyrgyz Republic within a period of two weeks from the day of their signature (or receipt from the depositary of certified copies and official translations).
3. The procedure for the custody of the originals of international treaties of the Kyrgyz Republic is approved by the Minister of Foreign Affairs of the Kyrgyz Republic.

ARTICLE XXVII
PERFORMANCE OF THE FUNCTIONS OF DEPOSITARY

The Ministry of Foreign Affairs of the Kyrgyz Republic performs the functions of depositary of international multilateral treaties, if in accordance with the terms of these treaties such functions are entrusted to the Kyrgyz Republic.

1. The correspondence with organs of foreign States, international organizations or their chief executive officers, performing the functions of depositary of international multilateral treaties, is maintained by the Ministry of Foreign Affairs of the Kyrgyz Republic.

IV. IMPLEMENTATION OF INTERNATIONAL TREATIES OF THE KYRGYZ REPUBLIC

ARTICLE XXVIII
OBSERVANCE OF INTERNATIONAL TREATIES OF THE KYRGYZ REPUBLIC

1. International treaties of the Kyrgyz Republic are subject to strict and mandatory observance by the Kyrgyz Republic, in accordance with the norms of international law and the legislation of the Kyrgyz Republic.
2. An international treaty must be performed by the Kyrgyz Republic from the moment of its entry into force for the Kyrgyz Republic. The Kyrgyz Republic, before the entry into force of an international treaty for the Kyrgyz Republic, is obliged, with due regard to the relevant norms of international law, to refrain from acts that would deprive the treaty of its object and purpose.

ARTICLE XXIX
PERFORMANCE OF OBLIGATIONS UNDER INTERNATIONAL TREATIES OF THE KYRGYZ REPUBLIC

1. The President of the Kyrgyz Republic, in accordance with the Constitution of the Kyrgyz Republic, guarantees the observance of the treaties concluded, and the obligations accepted, by the Republic.
2. The Government of the Kyrgyz Republic elaborates the measures to implement the international treaties of the Kyrgyz Republic and identifies the ministries, State committees, administrative departments, and officials who are responsible for the implementation of the obligations under international treaties of the Kyrgyz Republic.

3. The Government of the Kyrgyz Republic, ministries, State committees, administrative departments, and other State organs having authority over matters regulated by international treaties of the Kyrgyz Republic ensure the performance of the obligations that the Kyrgyz Republic has accepted by treaty, and monitor the exercise of the rights of the Kyrgyz Republic arising from these treaties as well as the performance by the other parties to the treaty of their obligations.
4. The Government of the Kyrgyz Republic controls the performance of the obligations of the Kyrgyz Republic under international treaties.

ARTICLE XXX
CONTROL OVER THE IMPLEMENTATION OF INTERNATIONAL TREATIES OF THE KYRGYZ REPUBLIC

1. Overall control over the implementation of international treaties of the Kyrgyz Republic is exercised by the Ministry of Foreign Affairs of the Kyrgyz Republic.
2. Overall control over the implementation of international financial treaties of the Kyrgyz Republic, credit agreements and grant agreements is exercised by the Ministry of Finance of the Kyrgyz Republic.

ARTICLE XXXI
MEASURES TAKEN IN CASE OF BREACH OF AN INTERNATIONAL TREATY OF THE KYRGYZ REPUBLIC BY OTHER PARTIES

In case of breach, by other parties, of obligations of the Kyrgyz Republic under an international treaty, the Ministry of Foreign Affairs of the Kyrgyz Republic or other ministries, State committees and administrative departments concerned, with the concurrence of the Ministry of Foreign Affairs of the Kyrgyz Republic, submit to the President of the Kyrgyz Republic or the Government of the Kyrgyz Republic proposals on the adoption of necessary measures, in accordance with the norms of international law and the terms of the treaty in question.

V. INVALIDITY, TERMINATION, DENUNCIATION, AND SUSPENSION OF THE OPERATION OF INTERNATIONAL TREATIES OF THE KYRGYZ REPUBLIC

ARTICLE XXXII INVALIDITY OF INTERNATIONAL TREATIES OF THE KYRGYZ REPUBLIC

1. An international treaty of the Kyrgyz Republic may be considered invalid in accordance with the norms of international law.
2. If there are grounds, provided for in norms of international law, for considering an international treaty to be invalid, the Ministry of Foreign Affairs of the Kyrgyz Republic or other concerned ministries, State committees and administrative departments, with the concurrence of the Ministry of Foreign Affairs of the Kyrgyz Republic, submit to the President of the Kyrgyz Republic (in the case of inter-state treaties) or to the Government of the Kyrgyz Republic (in the case of inter-governmental treaties) proposals on the consideration of the treaty as being invalid.

ARTICLE XXXIII TERMINATION OF OR WITHDRAWAL FROM AN INTERNATIONAL TREATY

Termination of an international treaty or withdrawal from it by the Kyrgyz Republic may take place:

a) in conformity with the provisions of the treaty;
b) at any time after consultation with the other parties to the treaty.

ARTICLE XXXIV
DENUNCIATION OF AN INTERNATIONAL TREATY OF THE KYRGYZ REPUBLIC

1. Proposals on the denunciation of international treaties of the Kyrgyz Republic, concluded on behalf of the Kyrgyz Republic and on behalf of the Government of the Kyrgyz Republic, are submitted to the President of the Kyrgyz Republic or the Government of the Kyrgyz Republic, depending on who has made the decision expressing consent to the binding force of the treaty for the Kyrgyz Republic, by the Ministry of Foreign Affairs of the Kyrgyz Republic, on its own initiative or with the concurrence of other ministries, State committees and administrative departments of the Kyrgyz Republic.
2. Proposals on the denunciation of international treaties of the Kyrgyz Republic, the decisions on the binding force of which, for the Kyrgyz Republic, have been taken in the form of a law, are submitted to the Jogorku Kenesh of the Kyrgyz Republic by the President of the Kyrgyz Republic or the Government of the Kyrgyz Republic, depending on who had introduced the proposal on the basis of which the Jogorku Kenesh of the Kyrgyz Republic ratified the international treaty.

   The Government of the Kyrgyz Republic has the authority, in case of necessity, to propose to the President of the Kyrgyz Republic to submit a proposal to the Jogorku Kenesh of the Kyrgyz Republic regarding the denunciation of an international treaty of the Kyrgyz Republic, the decision expressing consent to the binding force of which, for the Kyrgyz Republic, has been taken in the form of a law upon submission by the Government of the Kyrgyz Republic.
3. Proposals on the denunciation of international treaties of the Kyrgyz Republic must contain a certified copy of the official text of the international treaty, the substantiation of the reasons for its denunciation, as well as the assessment of the possible financial, economic, and other consequences of terminating the operation of the international treaty.

ARTICLE XXXV
SUSPENSION OF THE OPERATION OF AN INTERNATIONAL TREATY OF THE KYRGYZ REPUBLIC

1. Suspension of the operation of an international treaty of the Kyrgyz Republic with respect to all the parties to the treaty or to a particular party to the treaty may take place:
   a) in conformity with the provisions of the treaty;
   b) at any time after consultation with the other parties to the treaty.
2. Proposals on the suspension of an international treaty of the Kyrgyz Republic are submitted in accordance with Article 34 of this law.

ARTICLE XXXVI
TERMINATION AND SUSPENSION OF THE OPERATION OF INTERNATIONAL TREATIES OF THE KYRGYZ REPUBLIC

1. Termination and suspension of the operation of international treaties of the Kyrgyz Republic are made in accordance with the provisions of the treaty in question and the norms of international law, by the organ that has made the decision expressing consent to the binding force of the international treaty for the Kyrgyz Republic.
2. Proposals on the suspension of the operation of an international treaty is submitted by the Ministry of Foreign Affairs of the Kyrgyz Republic to the President of the Kyrgyz Republic, with respect to inter-state treaties, and to the Government of the Kyrgyz Republic, with respect to intergovernmental treaties.

   Proposals on the suspension of international treaties of the Kyrgyz Republic, the decisions expressing consent to the binding force of which, for the Kyrgyz Republic, has been made in the form of a law, are submitted to the Jogorku Kenesh of the Kyrgyz Republic by the President of the Kyrgyz Republic or the Government of the Kyrgyz Republic, depending on who had submitted the proposal pursuant to which the Jogorku Kenesh of the Kyrgyz Republic ratified the international treaty.

3. Termination and suspension of the operation of international treaties of the Kyrgyz Republic are accomplished by the ministries, State committees and administrative departments on whose behalf these treaties have been concluded, with the concurrence of the Ministry of Foreign Affairs of the Kyrgyz Republic, other concerned State organs of the Kyrgyz Republic, and upon authorization by the Government of the Kyrgyz Republic.

ARTICLE XXXVII
CONSEQUENCES OF TERMINATION OF AN INTERNATIONAL TREATY OF THE KYRGYZ REPUBLIC

Termination of an international treaty of the Kyrgyz Republic, unless otherwise provided for in the treaty or otherwise agreed with the other parties to the treaty, releases the Kyrgyz Republic from any obligation to implement the treaty further and does not affect the rights, obligations or legal status of the Kyrgyz Republic resulting from the implementation of the treaty before its termination.

ARTICLE XXXVIII
CONSEQUENCES OF SUSPENSION OF THE OPERATION OF AN INTERNATIONAL TREATY

1. Suspension of the operation of an international treaty of the Kyrgyz Republic, unless otherwise provided for in the treaty or otherwise agreed with the other parties to the treaty, releases the Kyrgyz Republic from the obligation to implement the provisions of the treaty during the period of suspension of the treaty, regarding its relations with those parties with respect to which the operation of the treaty has been suspended, and does not affect in other respects the legal relations, established by the treaty, of the Kyrgyz Republic with the other parties to it.
2. During the time the operation of an international treaty of the Kyrgyz Republic is suspended, the State authorities of the Kyrgyz Republic refrain from actions that could interfere with the resumption of the operation of the treaty.

ARTICLE XXXIX
OFFICIAL NOTICES ON TERMINATION OR SUSPENSION OF INTERNATIONAL TREATIES

Official notices of the Ministry of Foreign Affairs of the Kyrgyz Republic on termination or suspension of the operation of international treaties of the Kyrgyz Republic, concluded on behalf of the Kyrgyz Republic and on behalf of the Government of the Kyrgyz Republic, are published pursuant to the procedure established in Article 23 of this law.

VI. FINAL PROVISIONS

ARTICLE XL
ENTRY INTO FORCE OF THIS LAW

1. This law enters into force on the day of its publication.
2. The following laws are repealed:
   - Law of the Kyrgyz Republic *On the Conclusion, Ratification, Implementation and Denunciation of International Treaties of the Kyrgyz Republic* (*Vedomosti of the Jogorku Kenesh of the Kyrgyz Republic*, 1994, No. 7, p. 230);
   - Law of the Kyrgyz Republic *On the Introduction of Amendments and Supplementary Provisions to the Law of the Kyrgyz Republic "On the Conclusion, Ratification, Implementation and Denunciation of International Treaties of the Kyrgyz Republic"* (No. 54 of September 7, 1996).
3. The Government of the Kyrgyz Republic must bring its decisions into accord with this law.

The President of the Kyrgyz Republic: A. Akaev.

Adopted by the Legislative Assembly of the Jogorku Kenesh of the Kyrgyz Republic on June 22, 1999.

Bishkek, July 21, 1999.

APPENDIX II

ROMANIA

LAW No. 4/1991

ON THE CONCLUSION AND RATIFICATION OF TREATIES

(dated January 11, 1991)

(published in the Official Gazette No. 5 of January 12, 1991)*
The Romanian Parliament adopts the present law.

ARTICLE I

The President of Romania represents the State in international relations and, in this capacity, concludes treaties in the name of Romania or, for this purpose, can authorize the Prime Minister, the Minister of Foreign Affairs, another member of the Government, or a diplomatic representative of Romania.

Pursuant to the authorization given by the President of Romania, the Government can initiate and negotiate international treaties that are concluded in the name of Romania.

ARTICLE II

The Government can negotiate and sign agreements, conventions and other international understandings at the governmental

---

* *Lege Privind Incheierea si Ratificarea Tratatelor.* The English translation, *reproduced here*, reflects an extensive revision by the present writer of an earlier draft provided by the World Bank's resident mission in Bucharest. For the Romanian text of, and a commentary on, the law, *see* DUMITRA POPESCU & ADRIAN NASTASE, DREPT INTERNATIONAL PUBLIC 219–53 & 423–6 (1997).

level. It approves the conclusion of agreements, conventions and other understandings at the departmental level.

ARTICLE III

The negotiation and signature of international treaties concluded in the name of Romania are carried out, pursuant to presidential authorization, by the representatives authorized by the President.

The negotiation and signature of agreements, conventions and other international understandings at the governmental level or departmental level are carried out pursuant to authorization given to the representatives identified for this purpose.

ARTICLE IV

The international treaties signed in the name of Romania, as well as the agreements, conventions and understandings signed at the governmental level that pertain to political or military cooperation, those that require the adoption of new laws or the revision of existing ones, those that imply political or financial arrangements or that affect the political or territorial regime of the State, the status of persons, their rights and freedoms, or the participation in an international organization, as well as those expressly providing therefore, are submitted to parliamentary ratification by law.

The provisions of paragraph 1 regarding parliamentary ratification apply also in the case of accession to the international treaties referred to in that paragraph.

The denunciation of the international treaties referred to in paragraphs 1 and 2 is subject to the same procedure.

ARTICLE V

The agreements, conventions and other international understandings which, by reason of their subject matter, do not fall under the provisions of Article 4 are within the authority of the Government. After their negotiation and signature, they are submitted to the Government for its approval.

The Government notifies the President of Romania and the Parliament of any agreement, convention or other international understanding which has been concluded and is not subject to ratification.

ARTICLE VI

The agreements and understandings in simplified form, concluded by the Ministry of Foreign Affairs pursuant to an exchange of notes or letters, can enter into force on the date of their conclusion, without being further subject to ratification or approval.

The provisions of paragraph 1 do not apply to the agreements, conventions and international understandings which, pursuant to the provisions of Article 4, require the adoption of a law.

ARTICLE VII

The initiation, negotiation and signature of treaties, agreements, conventions and other international understandings, in the name of Romania or at governmental level, are carried out, in accordance with the provisions of Article 3, by the Ministry of Foreign Affairs. They can also be carried out by the ministries and central bodies empowered and authorized for this purpose, in cooperation with the Ministry of Foreign Affairs, which is the specialized body through which the Government ensures coordination and a unified policy in this domain.

The Ministry of Foreign Affairs, alone or jointly with other ministries as the case may be, submits to the Government the proposals regarding the signature, ratification and approval of the treaties, agreements, conventions and other understandings, or regarding the accession thereto or denunciation thereof.

ARTICLE VIII

The authorization to sign treaties, agreements, conventions and other understandings at the governmental level is reflected in the instrument of full powers issued by the Ministry of Foreign Affairs and is signed by the Minister of Foreign Affairs, in accordance with international rules and practice.

The President of Romania, the Prime Minister of the Government and the Minister of Foreign Affairs can negotiate and sign treaties, agreements, conventions and other international understandings, without having to produce their full powers.

ARTICLE IX

The ratification, accession or denunciation of treaties concluded in the name of Romania is reflected in the instruments of ratification, accession or denunciation signed by the President of Romania, endowed with the State seal and counter-signed by the Minister of Foreign Affairs.

The above-mentioned instruments are to be exchanged between the parties or delivered to a depositary, in accordance with the norms of international law and international practice.

The approval of agreements, conventions and understandings concluded at the governmental level is notified, through diplomatic channels, to the other contracting parties or the depositary.

ARTICLE X

The Government takes the necessary measures for the application of treaties, agreements, conventions and other international understandings, and monitors their implementation.

The Government periodically notifies the President of Romania and the Parliament of the issues arising from the application of certain treaties, agreements, conventions and other international understandings, with a view to finding the appropriate solution to these issues, in full conformity with the principles of international law and the interest of the Romanian party.

ARTICLE XI

The laws of ratification of international treaties, and the decrees regarding the approval of agreements, conventions and other international understandings, together with their texts, are published in the Official Gazette.

The Parliament or the Government, as the case may be, can decide that certain treaties, agreements, conventions or other international understandings are not to be published.

The Ministry of Foreign Affairs ensures the publication, in the Official Gazette, of the data and information concerning the main treaties, agreements, conventions and other international understandings to which Romania is a party, and their registration with the United Nations Organization.

This law was adopted by the Senate at its session of January 4, 1991.

The President of the Senate: Academician Alexandru Birladeanu

This law was adopted by the Chamber of Deputies at its session of January 8, 1991.

The President of the Chamber of Deputies: Martian Dan

Pursuant to Article 82(m) of decree-law No. 92/1990 on the election of the Parliament and the President of Romania, I hereby promulgate the law on the conclusion and ratification of treaties, and order that it be published in the Official Gazette of Romania.

The President of Romania: Ion Iliescu

Bucharest, January 11, 1991

No. 4.

THE REGIME FOR *LACUNAE* IN THE ICSID CHOICE OF LAW PROVISION AND THE QUESTION OF ITS THRESHOLD

*W. Michael Reisman**

I. ARTICLE 42(1) OF THE ICSID CONVENTION:

Article 42(1) of the Washington, or ICSID, Convention[1] provides:

> "The Tribunal shall decide a dispute in accordance with such rules of law as may be agreed by the parties. In the absence of such agreement, the Tribunal shall apply the law of the Contracting State party to the dispute (including its rules on the conflict of laws) and such rules of international law as may be applicable."

The French text provides:

> "Le Tribunal statue sur le différend conformément aux règles de droit adoptées par les parties. Faute d'accord entre les parties, le Tribunal applique le droit de l'Etat contractant partie au différend y compris les règles relatives aux conflits de lois ainsi que les principes de droit international en la matière."

The Spanish text provides:

* This Article dedicated to Dr. Ibrahim Shihata takes up a number of points he and Mr. Antonio Parra raised in their landmark, *Applicable Substantive Law in Disputes Between States and Private Foreign Parties: The Case of Arbitration Under the ICSID Convention*, 9 ICSID REVIEW-FOREIGN INVESTMENT LAW JOURNAL 183 (1994).

1 Convention on the Settlement of Investment Disputes Between States and Nationals of Other States, *opened for signature* Mar. 18, 1965, art. 42(1), 17 U.S.T. 1270, 1286, 575 U.N.T.S. 159, 186.

> "El Tribunal decidirá la diferencia de acuerdo con las normas de derecho acordadas por las partes. A falta de acuerdo, el Tribunal aplicará la legislacion del Estado que sea parte en la diferencia, incluyendo sus normas de derecho internacional privado, y aquellas normas de derecho internacional que pudieren ser aplicables."

All the texts give primacy to the parties' choice of law and the dispositive operation of host State law in the absence of another explicit choice of law by the parties. But there are minor textual divergences with regard to the role of international law. The English and Spanish texts use the same term for parties' choice of law and international law (*rules* in the English text and *normas* in Spanish) while the French text uses *règles* for the choice of law and *principes* for international law. The difference, though subtle, may be pertinent, as we will see below.

Although the progression of drafts that culminated in Article 42(1), has, like all *travaux,* some inconsistent strands, I am persuaded that it makes clear that the intention of the majority was one of a default choice of law of the host State, unless the parties agreed otherwise. The legislative history certainly does not demonstrate an intent for a disguised superordination of international law in all cases. This specific regime was the result of a conscious decision, as the evolution of the provision in the *travaux* indicates. In the earliest drafts, choice of law was to have been assigned to the Tribunal itself. A 1962 working paper provided that: "In the absence of any agreement between the parties concerning the law to be applied . . . the Arbitral Tribunal shall decide the dispute submitted to it in accordance with such rules of law, whether national or international, as it shall determine to be applicable."[2] In the preliminary draft,[3] the language of the working paper was reproduced verbatim. This same formula was reiterated in the first draft, with the addition of a specification of international law by

---

2 Working Paper in the Form of a Draft Convention (June 5, 1962), *in* 2 Convention on the Settlement of Investment Disputes Between States and Nationals of Other States: Documents Concerning the Origin and the Formulation of the Convention 19, 21 (International Center For Settlement of Investment Disputes 1968) [hereinafter ICSID Documents].

3 Preliminary Draft Convention, *in* 2 ICSID DOCUMENTS, *supra* note 2, at 184, 214.

reference to Article 38 of the Statute of the International Court of Justice.[4]

But in the Revised Draft,[5] a major policy change emerges, and is confirmed in the final version of Article 42(1). Whereas all the previous drafts assigned to the Tribunal the initial competence to decide whether national or international rules of law were applicable, the version that became the final text substantially reduced the competence of the Tribunal, in the absence of agreement, to choose so freely. Based on the Revised Draft, the final version of the Convention provides, "[i]n the absence of such agreement, the Tribunal shall apply the law of the Contracting State party to the dispute (including its rules on the conflict of laws) and such rules of international law as may be applicable."

In the earlier drafts, the Tribunal, in the absence of agreement by the parties, was accorded considerable discretion: [it was to choose between national and international law as it shall determine to be applicable]. In the final version, two textual changes, whose clear purport allows no mistake about the drafters' intentions, withdrew such a competence from the Tribunal: "The Tribunal shall apply the law of the Contracting State party to the dispute." This is a mandatory injunction which is common to all three language texts. The Tribunal may apply such rules of international law as may be applicable, in language in which the French text diverges slightly from its English and Spanish counterparts. Thus, the rules to be applied are not selected at the discretion of a tribunal, as in the earlier drafts, but are henceforth determined by operation of law.

The *travaux* are less instructive on the contingencies for the application of international law in Article 42(1) situations and, in particular, whether and when the role of international law is corrective or supplemental (or both) and on which contingencies. As Professor Fatouros has shown in his minute examination of the succession of *projets,* the English, French, and Spanish drafts diverged and often changed, using *termini* such as "rules," *règles,* "principles," *principes, reglas, principios,* and *normas.* He finds:

---

4 Draft Convention: Working Paper for the Legal Committee, *in* 2 ICSID DOCUMENTS, *supra* note 2, at 610, 630.

5 Revised Draft of the Convention, *in* 2 ICSID DOCUMENTS, *supra* note 2, at 911, 939.

> "Les travaux préparatoires semblent indiquer que le terme principes de la version française, avec toutes ses connotations, est plus près du sens voulu par les membres du comité . . ."[6]

Principes, in this context, suggests a corrective function. But the final English and Spanish texts concur in adopting a term suggesting a supplemental role. In any case, Professor Fatouros notes that because the content of international economic law is not precise, the practical difference between it and international public policy may not be great. In effect, there may not be much to supplement with.

Professor Phillipe Kahn remarks on ambiguities in the provision but concludes:

> "The text in its present formulation would indicate if taken literally, simultaneous application of the two laws, but the reference to the law of the State should counsel prudence to arbitrators and guide them to call on the more general rules of international law only where the State law is not well adapted to settlement of the dispute or in case of flagrant violation of the law of nations."[7]

The late Professor Berthold Goldman, known for his exposition of *lex mercatoria* as the inherently proper law for international contracts and transactions, would interpret the word and in the final phrase of Article 42(1) as superordinating. In the words of one of his critics at the colloquium at which he presented his thesis, *ainsi que* would be read as *avant tout.*[8] This is plainly a very free reading of the text. As Sir Elihu Lauterpacht has observed, the phrase in question is introduced by the word *and.*[9] If, as Sir Elihu points out, the intention had been to subordinate in-

---

6 Fatouros, *Investissements étrangers et arbitrage-entre Etats et personnes privés,* LIX Revue critique de droit international privé 580, 594 (1970).

7 Phillipe Kahn, *The Law Applicable to Foreign Investments: The Contribution of the World Bank Convention on the Settlement of Investment Disputes,* 44 Indiana Law Journal 28 (1968).

8 *See* A. Pedone, Investissements Etrangers et Arbitrage Entre etats et personnes privées 133-160, 157 (1969).

9 Elihu Lauterpacht, *The World Bank Convention on the Settlement of International Investment Disputes,* Recueil d'Etudes de Droit International: En Hommage À Paul Guggenheim 642, 660 (Imprimerie de la Tribune de Genève 1968) (italics in original).

ternational law, the text would have been written as *including*. By the same token, if the text had intended to superordinate international law, it would have said *avant tout*.

There is, nonetheless, a role for international law here. The text of Article 42(1) contemplates both supplemental and corrective functions for international law. But because there is a prior reference to the law of the contracting State, the critical question is how choice of law is viewed from the perspective of public international law. Article 42(1) directs ICSID tribunals to relate two different bodies of law. Involved here is both a choice of law and, for certain matters, the contingent exercise of certain supplementations and legal controls by one system of law over another. This is especially complex, because, for example, the juridical exercise of choice of law does not involve a qualitative choice between competing systems, but the juridical exercise of control does. Hence it may be useful to consider the international legal basis of choice of law, so that the two mandates of Article 42(1) can be applied properly, without one displacing the other.

II. CHOICE OF LAW UNDER PUBLIC INTERNATIONAL LAW

The final part of Article 42(1) is a choice of law clause in which all signatories to the ICSID Convention have agreed that, absent agreement to the contrary by the parties to a particular contract, the formula expressed there ("the law of the Contracting State party to the dispute . . . and such rules of public international law as may be applicable") applies.

Choice of law must be understood in the context of public international law, for the reality of international politics and the policies of international law are the necessary predicates of the operation of choice of law. A basic postulate of public international law is that every territorial community may organize itself as a State and, within certain basic limits prescribed by international law, organize its social and economic affairs in ways consistent with its own national values. The Declaration on Principles of International Law Concerning Friendly Relations and Co-operation Among States in Accordance with the Charter of the United Nations[10] (Friendly Relations) provides that "[e]ach State has the right freely to choose and develop its political, social, economic and cultural systems."[11] Article 1 of the Charter of Economic Rights and Duties of States provides that:

> "Every State has the sovereign and inalienable right to choose its economic system as well as its political, social and cultural systems in accordance with the will of its people, without outside interference, coercion or threat in any form whatsoever."[12]

This public international law principle has a direct relation to private international choice of law. As an expression of and implementation of the basic right expressed in Friendly Relations, the content of the various legal codes of each state may be expected to vary, quite legitimately, reflecting the diversity of national political, economic, social, and cultural values that the international system permits and even encourages. As a reflection of those different values and social preferences, the various parts of the law of each community may vary with regard to the distribution of benefits and burdens in economic and social relationships and, in particular, in the allocation of risk for various commercial contingencies. The point of emphasis here is that the legislative expression of these variations in the law of different states is internationally lawful and entitled to respect.

In transactions that are, factually, transnational and may be subject simultaneously or sequentially to the law of different states, parties frequently anticipate the dissonance (and economic risks) that may result from the uncertainty as to which law will be applied by explicitly selecting one particular law from the various competitors to govern their contractual relations. That choice by the parties will be honored by international law and most advanced municipal systems as a contractual option. In the *Caltex* case, the sole arbitrator, the late Professor René Jean Dupuy,

---

10 G.A. Res. 2625, U.N. GAOR, 25th Sess., Supp. No. 28, at 121, U.N. Doc. A/8028 (1970).

11 *Ibid.* at 124.

12 Charter of Economic Rights and Duties of States art. 1, G.A. Res. 3281 (XXIX), U.N. GAOR, 29th Sess., Agenda Item 48, U.N. Doc. A/RES/3281 (1974).

posed the question of the availability of such choices to parties in international law:

> "Did the parties have the right to choose the law or system of law which was to govern this contract?
>
> . . .
>
> The answer to this first question is beyond any doubt: all legal systems, whatever they are, apply the principle of the autonomy of the will of the parties to international contracts."[13]

Where the choice of law option obtains, it necessarily becomes a matter for negotiation between the parties, for parties well appreciate that different legal systems are likely to benefit or prejudice one or the other party. Hence various concessions and trade-offs may be made in return for one party's acceding to the choice of law preference of the other. All of this is based on the recognition that the social and economic arrangements of that law may discriminate in favor of one party in regard to certain aspects or contingencies of the transaction.Where such choices of law are made by the parties, third-party decision-makers are obliged, as an international legal matter, to give effect to the decision of the parties as to which set of norms or which legal system is to be incorporated within their contract. Respect for the contractual choice of law is no less mandatory than respect for any other term of the contract.

But international law itself has juridical values, which are not necessarily the same as those expressed in domestic or municipal legal systems. How are they accommodated? When do they override national legal arrangements? From the public international choice of law perspective, the answer is clear. As long as the various national arrangements do not violate principles such as *pacta sunt servanda* or other peremptory international human rights norms, which I will treat below, there is no ground for saying that one national arrangement is better than another or that international law, insofar as it regulates certain matters, is better than domestic law. Such comparisons are not only invidious and essentially parochial, but they are inconsistent with a basic premise of international law, for they deny the internationally guaranteed

---

13 Texaco Overseas Petroleum Co. and Cal. Asiatic Co. v. Libyan Arab Republic, 17 INTERNATIONAL LEGAL MATERIALS 11, at paras. 24-25 (1978).

right of each community to be itself and to be different, and they render the notion of choice of law meaningless.

III. ARBITRAL IMPLICATIONS

In every choice of law, a double burden is imposed on the arbitrators. First, they must identify, with fidelity, the law the parties have chosen. Second, they must determine, in good faith, what that law holds with regard to the matter that may be in dispute. This involves more than a perusal of some of the major texts of the legal system in question. In the *ELSI* case, the Chamber of the International Court, citing with approval *Brazilian Loans,* said:

> "Where the determination of a question of municipal law is essential to the Court's decision in a case, the Court will have to weigh the jurisprudence of the municipal courts, and if this is uncertain or divided, it will rest with the Court to select the interpretation which it considers most in conformity with the law."[14]

Since this second task of exploration of the law may involve substantial investigation into a legal system with which the arbitrators have no training, first-hand experience, or even basic language facility, the burden may be great. But the difficulty of the task is no excuse for avoiding it.

Not all arbitrators have discharged this obligation as they should have. In the *Abu Dhabi* case, the arbitrator, Lord Asquith of Bishopstone, presented an object lesson of what not to do, when he said:

> "What is the Proper Law applicable in construing this contract? This is a contract made in Abu Dhabi and wholly to be performed in that country. If any municipal system of law were applicable, it would *prima facie* be that of Abu Dhabi. But no such law can reasonably be said to exist. The Sheikh administers a purely discretionary justice with the assistance of the Koran; and it would be fanciful to suggest that in this very primitive region there is any set-

[14] Case Concerning Elettronica Sicula S.p.A. (ELSI) (United States of America v. Italy), 1989 I.C.J. 15, 47 (July 20) (citing Brazilian Loans, 1929 P.C.I.J. (ser. A) Nos. 20/21, at 124).

tled body of legal principles applicable to the construction of modern commercial instruments. Nor can I see any basis on which the municipal law of England could apply. On the contrary, Clause 17 of the Agreement, cited above, repels the notion that the municipal Law of any country, as such, could be appropriate. The terms of that Clause invite, indeed prescribe, the application of principles rooted in the good sense and common practice of the generality of civilised nations — a sort of "modern law of nature." I do not think that on this point there is any conflict between the parties.

But, albeit English Municipal Law is inapplicable *as such,* some of its rules are in my view so firmly grounded in reason, as to form part of this broad body of jurisprudence — this "modern law of nature." For instance, while in this case evidence has been admitted as to the nature of the negotiations leading up to, and of the correspondence both preceding and following the conclusion of the Agreement, which evidence as material for construing the contract might, according to domestic English Law be largely inadmissible, and to this extent the rigid English rules have been disregarded; yet on the other hand the English rule which attributes paramount importance to the actual language of the written instrument in which the negotiations result seems to me no mere idiosyncrasy of our system, but a principle of ecumenical validity. Chaos may obviously result if that rule is widely departed from: and if, instead of asking what the words used mean, the inquiry extends at large to what each of the parties meant them to mean, and how and why each phrase came to be inserted."[15]

Neither Islamic nor common law had an explicit and developed notion of continental shelf. But Islamic law has a written history and complex literature in jurisprudence that is older and at least as rich as that of common law; its fundamental principles could be used, in the familiar pattern of judicial analogizing, to generate answers to new doctrines such as the continental shelf, in much the same way that the principles of common law could be applied to that task. But rather than undertake this difficult endeavor, Lord Asquith, through a transparent stratagem, assured himself, by *ipse dixit,* that rules of English municipal law formed a part of the "modern law of nature" and proceeded to apply them. The *Abu*

---

15 In the Matter of an Arbitration Between Petroleum Dev. (Trucial Coast) Ltd., and the Sheikh of Abu Dhabi, 1 INTERNATIONAL AND COMPARATIVE LAW QUARTERLY 247, 250-251 (1952), *also in* 18 INTERNATIONAL LAW REPORTS, 144 (1951).

Dhabi case cannot serve as a model for the way that the choice of law function should be performed.

ICSID Article 42(1), as we have seen, is an obligatory choice of law clause and a central feature of the ICSID Convention. In the distribution of concessions, burdens, and benefits among developing countries, as frequent hosts to foreign investment, on the one hand, and foreign investors, on the other, the Convention determines that in the absence of agreement to the contrary, a host State may be assured that its law is and will be applied as the choice of law. That does not mean that the foreign investor may not yield some of the concessions it receives under the Convention in order to effect a change in this *jus dispositivum* and thereby secure the full application of, say, international law or some system of national law. But it does mean that a Tribunal that, itself, refuses to honor the default choice of law made by the Convention and confirmed by the parties, has exceeded its power by application of the incorrect law.

The dispositive choice of host State law in all cases in which ICSID is incorporated and the parties do not make a different explicit choice of law under Article 42(1), requires a careful examination of the law of the Contracting State party with regard to the issue in dispute. The law of the State, host to the foreign investment, must be understood broadly to include its statutory as well as judicially illuminated law. In each case, the question is not whether the host State's law provides the remedies sought by the claimant or, indeed, whether any remedy provided by the host State approximates a remedy that might be granted by international law in comparable circumstances. Were that the case, the mechanism in Article 42(1) would be rendered meaningless, for international law would always govern.

The question is whether or not the law of the host State addresses the issue at hand. If it does and, as part of its law, has decided not to grant remedies in such matters then there is no remedy, as none is provided in the law that must be applied. The notion of addressing a problem must be understood broadly. Even the most developed of legal systems and even the most articulated code cannot anticipate and provide for every contingency and every possible legal dispute. Thus, the question for an ICSID tribunal under Article 42(1) is not whether the host State law provides a pre-packaged answer. If the host State's law provides a general analytical framework, it is up to the Tribunal to apply that framework to the statutes, judicial precedents, and general principles of that system, in the manner followed by the Permanent Court in *Brazilian Loans* and the Chamber of the International Court in the *ELSI* case.

The point bears emphasis. If an ICSID tribunal takes the claimant's demand for a remedy as the framework of inquiry and assumes that if that remedy is not provided by the host State's law, the Tribunal must then proceed to search for it in international law, the Tribunal will subvert the purpose of the dispositive choice of law in Article 42(1) and create a new regime: national law is applied insofar as it provides a particular remedy, but if it does not, international law is then searched for the remedy.

I emphasize once again that the absence of a remedy is not necessarily a *lacuna*; it may represent a decision not to regulate a certain matter or to regulate it in a different way. A *lacuna*, or gap, in the law of a particular State may be said to exist only when the State engages in certain transactions for which its legal system has not yet considered regulations or remedies. In short, it exists in those circumstances in which there is a socio-legal lag.

The national law that has been selected as the choice of law by operation of Article 42(1) may already incorporate the law of another advanced industrial system for *lacunae*. Consider, for example, the very complex regime of Article 46 of the 1922 Palestine Order in Council, which states:

> "46. The jurisdiction of the Civil Courts shall be exercised in conformity with the Ottoman Law in force in Palestine on 1st November, 1914, and such later Ottoman Laws as have been or may be declared to be in force by Public Notice, and such Orders in Council, Ordinances and regulations as are in force in Palestine at the date of the commencement of this Order, or may hereafter be applied or enacted; and subject thereto, and so far as the same shall not extend or apply, shall be exercised in conformity with the substance of the common law, and the doctrines of equity in force in England, and with the powers vested in and according to the procedure and practice observed by or before Courts of Justice and Justices of the Peace in England, according to their respective jurisdictions and authorities at that date, save in so far as the said powers, procedure and practice may have been or may hereafter be modified, amended or replaced by any other provisions.

> Provided always that the said common law and doctrines of equity shall be in force in Palestine so far only as the circumstances of Palestine and its inhabitants and the limits of His Majesty's jurisdiction permit and subject to such qualification as local circumstances render necessary."[16]

This technique of what we might call "progressive supplementation"[17] was used by the British Empire in its colonial and mandatory territories, and analogues have been used by other imperial powers. In many circumstances, such supplementation by reference to the law of the Metropolitan survived the termination of colonial status and continued to be a part of local law.

In private international law, a *lacuna* may be said to exist only in those circumstances of socio-legal lag, in which the local law allows or encourages certain activities but has plainly not yet provided for any regulation of them and does not incorporate a progressive supplementation mechanism. Where the local law does regulate those activities, but in a way different from that of competing legal systems, no *lacuna* can be said to exist. To characterize such regulation as a *lacuna* is to displace local law without acknowledging what is being done.

IV. SPECIFIC CONDITIONS FOR THE INTRODUCTION OF INTERNATIONAL LAW

The continuing contingent role for international law, even when the Tribunal must apply the law of the Contracting State, is supplemental and corrective. Article 42(1) instructs that the Tribunal shall apply the law of the Contracting State to the dispute (including its rules on the conflict of laws) *and* such rules of international law as may be applicable.[18] Note the markedly different degrees of reference here. The reference to the comprehensive law of the Contracting State is much broader than the reference to only "such rules of international law as may be applicable," *les*

---

16 The Palestine Order in Council, 1922, *reprinted in* 3 The Laws of Palestine 2580 (Waterlow & Sons Ltd., rev. ed. 1934), art. 46.

17 I am not using the term "progressive" here in a qualitative sense.

18 (Italics supplied).

principes de droit international en la matière, or *aquellas normas de derecho internacional que pudieren ser aplicables.* All latter versions contain a much more precise and restricted reference.

International law rules may become applicable in a number of ways. If the Contracting State's law includes a *renvoi* to international law, the ICSID tribunal must apply that rule of international law in accordance with the Contracting State's law.[19] Rules of international law might also become applicable because of a treaty relationship. For example, if a State such as Egypt passes legislation purporting to consent to ICSID jurisdiction, a mode of consent that is permissible in the ICSID system, it is plain that that expression of consent, must be interpreted *vis-à-vis* all other States parties to the Convention. This would be consistent with the rules of interpretation of the Vienna Convention on the Law of Treaties, which provide a consistent mode of construction for all parties to the Convention rather than by the idiosyncratic interpretation rules of a particular State party.[20] The point of emphasis here is that Article 42(1), by its own terms, provides for a limited and contingent application of particular rules of international law. International law may be applied in another limited way: by ensuring that the result does not violate peremptory rules of international law, a matter which I will treat below.

V. SUPPLEMENTING

Article 42(1) does not provide, by its own terms, a broader dominating and displacing role for international law. If there is a *lacuna* in the host State's law (and it must be borne in mind that the failure to provide a remedy for a particular matter is not necessarily a *lacuna*), Article 42(1) does not thereupon authorize a Tribunal promptly or automatically to resort to international law. The law of the Contracting State may itself provide for a method for dealing with *lacunae.* In Swiss law, for example, a judge, encountering an authentic *lacuna,* is instructed to respond as he thinks the legislator would have: *selon les règles qu'il établirait s'il*

---

19 *See, e.g.,* Shihata & Parra, *supra* note *, at 192.

20 Vienna Convention on the Law of Treaties, *opened for signature* May 23, 1969, 1155 U.N.T.S. 331, *reprinted in* 8 INTERNATIONAL LEGAL MATERIALS 679 (1969).

avait à faire acte de législateur.[21] If Swiss law had been the choice of law, it would be inappropriate for an international arbitrator to respond to a relevant *lacuna* in Swiss law by applying international law.

In many colonial systems, as we have seen, the law of the Metropolitan was available, in the case of a *lacuna,* for supplementary purposes, usually with the proviso that this would be accomplished only insofar as it was feasible. In some systems, judicial supplementation is accomplished by reference to an earlier, more general system of law, such as Roman law. Even if a genuine *lacuna* is found in the law applicable by virtue of Article 42(1) or by other choice of the parties, an ICSID tribunal cannot simply turn to international law. It is still obliged to examine the Contracting State's law to see what procedures it provides for dealing with *lacunae.* The Tribunal is not simply looking for a rule in a mechanical fashion. It must explore the analytical framework for decision that the designated legal system has developed for the particular issue, and address the issues within that framework.

VI. CORRECTING: INTERNATIONAL JUS COGENS

International law plays an important role under Article 42(1), but if it is wielded incautiously, it can defeat other parts of this provision. Where there is a genuine *lacuna,* i.e., one for which host State law does not provide a method for filling, the Tribunal may turn to international law. In addition, international law may perform a corrective function, but the contingency for correction must be more than a mere difference between international and host State law. What is required is a veritable collision. This standard allows an effective role for the law of the host State, yet ensures the foreign investor that domestic arrangements that *violate* fundamental international norms will not be given effect. It is plain that mere inconsistencies between the Contracting State's law and international law cannot mean *ipso facto* that international law prevails. If that were the case, the choice of law component of Article 42(1) would lose all of its meaning. It is to be expected that in any system in which different laws may be se-

---

21 *See* Code Civil Suisse (Cc) art. 1 (Switz.).

lected, their provisions and solutions to different types of social and economic problems will themselves be different. A demonstration of a violation, and not mere inconsistency, is required. To characterize inconsistencies that are only different as violations would simply mean that international law would often be the Tribunal's choice of law and key parts of Article 42(1) would be defeated. The test, then, is not inconsistency, but whether applying the Contracting State's law would constitute a violation of something fundamental to international law.

Cognate examples of this may be found in international treaty law. Article 53 of the Vienna Convention on the Law of Treaties defines a peremptory norm of general international law, or *jus cogens,* as a norm accepted and recognized by the international community of States as a whole as a norm from which no derogation is permitted and which can be modified only by a subsequent norm of general international law having the same character.[22] The commentary of the International Law Commission (ILC) to the draft articles explained:

> "(3) The emergence of rules having the character of *jus cogens* is comparatively recent, while international law is in process of rapid development. The Commission considered the right course to be to provide in general terms that a treaty is void if it conflicts with a rule of *jus cogens* and to leave the full content of this rule to be worked out in State practice and in the jurisprudence of international tribunals. Some members of the Commission felt that there might be advantage in specifying, by way of illustration, some of the most obvious and best settled rules of *jus cogens* in order to indicate by these examples the general nature and scope of the rule contained in the article. Examples suggested included *(a)* a treaty contemplating an unlawful use of force contrary to the principles of the Charter, *(b)* a treaty contemplating the performance of any other act criminal under international law, and *(c)* a treaty contemplating or conniving at the commission of acts, such as trade in slaves, piracy or genocide, in the suppression of which every State is called upon to co-operate. Other mem-

22 Vienna Convention on the Law of Treaties, *supra* note 20, art. 53.

> bers expressed the view that, if examples were given, it would be undesirable to appear to limit the scope of the article to cases involving acts which constitute crimes under international law; treaties violating human rights, the equality of States or the principle of self-determination were mentioned as other possible examples. The Commission decided against including any examples of rules of *jus cogens* in the article for two reasons. First, the mention of some cases of treaties void for conflict with a rule of *jus cogens* might, even with the most careful drafting, lead to misunderstanding as to the position concerning other cases not mentioned in the article. Secondly, if the Commission were to attempt to draw up, even on a selective basis, a list of the rules of international law which are to be regarded as having the character of *jus cogens,* it might find itself engaged in a prolonged study of matters which fall outside the scope of the present articles.
>
> (4) Accordingly, the article simply provides that a treaty is void if it conflicts with a peremptory norm of general international law from which no derogation is permitted and which can be modified only by a subsequent norm of general international law having the same character. This provision makes it plain that nullity attaches to a treaty under the article only if the rule with which it conflicts is a peremptory norm of general international law from which no derogation is permitted, even by agreement between particular States."[23]

It is significant that the ILC did not suggest that all inconsistencies be struck down — only those that collided with rights that derived from non-derogable norms. Authoritative examples of this dynamic are available in basic human rights documents: Article 4(2) of the International Covenant on Civil and Political Rights, with its references to Articles 6, 7, 8(1), 8(2), 11, 15, 16, and 18, would qualify in this context as a class of peremptory norms.[24]

---

23 UNITED NATIONS CONFERENCE ON THE LAW OF TREATIES, OFFICIAL RECORDS, DOCUMENTS OF THE CONFERENCE, 67-68, UN Doc.A/CONF.39/11/ Add. 2 (1971).

24 International Covenant on Civil and Political Rights, *adopted* Dec. 19, 1966, art. 4(2), 999 U.N.T.S. 171 (entered into force Mar. 23, 1976).

The consequence of ICSID Article 42(1), then, is not that every arrangement in national law will always be given effect. An ICSID Tribunal, operating under an international treaty, is an organ of international law, and it cannot be imagined that it would give effect to arrangements or procedures that violate fundamental international law, norms or shock the conscience of the world. For example, a domestic remedy providing for a form of enslavement could hardly be given effect by an international tribunal.

The ICSID *travaux* may shed some light on what is contemplated by Article 42(1) in this regard. At a meeting of the legal committee on December 7, 1964, discussing what was then Article 45, Chairman Broches defended his draft:

> "It was quite clear that the laws of the host country would be of primary importance and that international law itself would in the first place refer to them. The principles of international law which might be brought into play would be such as *pacta sunt servanda*."[25]

After considerable debate, largely on the question of under what circumstances, if any, should international law be applicable,[26] Chairman Broches proposed the language that became Article 42(1). This draft was unsatisfactory to the delegate from China who wanted to limit the application of international law to cases where it was inconsistent with national law, introduced after the investment was made.[27] This was, of course, not the point the conference was discussing and it was not incorporated in the subsequent votes. Indeed, that part of the Broches proposal was then adopted by a vote of 24 to 6, apparently over the Chinese proposed amendment. Some confusion arises in the record here, for the *précis* writer indicates:

> "*Mr. BROCHES* (Chairman) then submitted the redraft for a vote. The first sentence dealing with an express choice of law agreement

[25] Summary Proceedings of the Legal Committee Meeting, December 7, Morning, *in* 2 ICSID DOCUMENTS, *supra* note 3, at 799, 800. *See also ibid.* at 801; UNITED NATIONS CONFERENCE ON THE LAW OF TREATIES, *supra* note 23, at 801.

[26] Summary Proceedings of the Legal Committee Meeting, *supra* note 25, at 804 (per Chairman Broches).

[27] *Ibid. at* 804.

was approved by a majority of 35 to one. The first part of the second sentence referring to the 'national' law applicable was adopted by a majority of 31 to one. The final provision relating to international law (which would bring it into play both in the case of a *lacuna* in domestic law as well as in the case of inconsistency between the two) was adopted by a majority of 24 to 6."[28]

The French version renders "in case of inconsistency" as *en cas de incompatibilité*.[29] The Spanish version refers to *incompatibilidad*.[30] In all of these versions, this section appears in parentheses and does not seem to reflect Dr. Broches' own words. Indeed, one paragraph later, the record attributes to Chairman Broches a further response to the delegate from China: "*Mr. BROCHES* (Chairman) then re-stated the principle adopted and explained the advantages of the present draft over a text couched in terms whereby international law would become applicable where the domestic legislation of the host State was inconsistent with it."[31]

The French and Spanish texts correspond. I would speculate that the description of the second part of the second sentence was an editorial attempt at clarification by the *précis* writer. Hence it is written with parentheses. Chairman Broches' *rejection* of the inconsistency test a paragraph later and his statement that the vote had not adopted the description expressed in the parenthetical statement represented both his own and the views of the majority.[32]

Compelling evidence of this is offered by Dr. Broches in two publications. In an article published shortly after the conclusion of the conference, which appeared in a *Festschrift* for the late Martin Domke, Dr. Broches reviewed the applicable law regime in the Convention in terms of *textual* analysis and legislative history. He concluded:

"I believe that the final text achieves all the objectives that could be reasonably pursued within the framework of the Convention:

---

28 *Ibid.* at 804.

29 3 ICSID DOCUMENTS, *supra* note 2, at 631.

30 4 ICSID DOCUMENTS, *supra* note 2, at 420.

31 2 ICSID DOCUMENTS, *supra* note 2, at 804.

32 *Ibid.*

(a) Article 42(1) clearly establishes party autonomy as the basic principle governing the law to be applied by the tribunal.

(b) The remainder of Article 42(1) gives subsidiary rules for the case where the parties have failed to prescribe the applicable law. Under these subsidiary rules the tribunal may apply both national and international law. The history of the provision leaves no doubt, in my opinion, that the tribunal may apply international law (i) where national law calls for its application, (ii) where the subject matter is directly regulated by international law (a case which may not be easily distinguishable in practice from (i)) and (iii) where national law or action taken thereunder violates international law."[33]

Dr. Broches confirmed his view in more detail in his respected Hague Lectures in 1972, where he set out at length his conception of the role of international law under Article 42(1):

"My submission as to the relationship between the law of the host State and international law in the second sentence of 42(1) is as follows. The Tribunal will first look at the law of the host State and that law will in the first instance be applied to the merits of the dispute. Then the result will be tested against international law. That process will not involve the confirmation or denial of the validity of the host State's law, but may result in not applying it where that law, or action taken under that law, violates international law. In that sense, as I suggested earlier, international law is hierarchically superior to national law under Article 42(1)."[34]

In sum, I submit that there are four situations in which an ICSID tribunal will have occasion to apply international law:

(i) where the parties have so agreed;

(ii) where the law of the Contracting State party to the dispute calls for the application of international law, including customary international law;

---

[33] *See* A. Broches, *The Convention on the Settlement of Investment Disputes Between States and the Nationals of Other States: Applicable Law and Default Procedure, in* INTERNATIONAL ARBITRATION, LIBER AMICORUM FOR MARTIN DOMKE 12, 16-17 (Pieter Sanders ed., 1967).

[34] *See* Aron Broches, *The Convention on the Settlement of Investment Disputes Between States and Nationals of Other States,* 136 RECUEIL DES COURS DE L'ACADEMIE DE DROIT INTERNATIONAL 331, 392 (1972).

(iii) where the subject matter or issue is directly regulated by international law, such as treaty between the states party to the dispute; and, finally,

(iv) where the law of the Contracting State party to the dispute, or action taken under that law, violates international law. In this last situation, international law operates as a corrective to national law.

VII. CONSEQUENCES

What are the consequences of a misapplication of Article 42 of the Washington Convention? Traditionally, *excès de pouvoir* has resulted from the failure of a tribunal to apply the law prescribed by the *compromis*. Carlston, reviewing a wide variety of doctrinal views and case law, states: "A decision which manifestly fails properly to apply a rule for decision laid down in the *compromis* or an applicable rule of international law having a material bearing upon the outcome of the case involves an excess of jurisdiction and is therefore void."[35]

The legislative history of the ICSID Convention indicates that the drafters took a comparable view. The representative of China, referring to an early version of what became Article 52, suggested that the clause "the tribunal exceeded its power" could be improved if the words "including failure to apply the proper law" were added. As the parties were entitled to agree on the applicable law, failure of the tribunal to apply that law would frustrate that agreement.[36]

The representative of Lebanon opined that if the parties had agreed to the application of a particular law and the tribunal had in fact applied a different law, the award would be *ultra petita* and could therefore be validly challenged.[37] The representative of the Philippines felt that this ground was included within the requirement of reasons (which ultimately became Article 52(1)(e)).

35 CARLSTON, THE PROCESS OF INTERNATIONAL ARBITRATION 140 (1946).

36 2 ICSID DOCUMENTS, *supra* note 2, at 517.

37 *Ibid.* at 518.

The uncertainty as to where the requirement of motivation should be placed is understandable for it is a polymorphous pathology. A failure to state reasons defeats the parties' ability to determine what law (if any) was applied and thus to ensure that the prescribed law was indeed applied.

PROBING PROBITY: A DISCOURSE ON THE DARK SIDE OF DEVELOPMENT

Barry A. K. Rider

I. INTRODUCTION

Dr. Ibrahim Shihata has played such a significant role, at so many levels, in promoting and fostering the development and stability of the international legal order, that it is almost disparaging to focus on a single issue, let alone be arrogant enough to do so from a somewhat personal perspective. Nonetheless, those of us who do not have such breadth of vision or depth of learning have little choice but to focus on the parochial. Therefore, with trepidation, let the present author attempt to take up, but one issue — that of the dark side of economic development and stability, illustrated by organized economic crime. Let me say at the outset, that my interest in this topic, like Dr. Shihata's concern about the dark forces at work in promoting economic insecurity and destabilization, has not been primarily as an academic. Consequently, the reader of this paper will search more or less in vain, for discussion let alone citation of the more scholarly deliberations, of those who have had the privilege of being able to devote themselves to the study of criminology, international affairs, economics and all the other pertinent disciplines, that can, in varying measures, contribute to the debate. Rather, the approach of this paper is to concentrate on those particular factors and issues, which the present writer became to a greater or lesser degree acquainted with during his own time as an international civil servant. Indeed, it was in this context and more recently in Dr. Shihata's 'crusade'[1] against

1 *See,* for example, Ibrahim F.I. Shihata, *Corruption — A General Review with an Emphasis on the Role of the World Bank,* in CORRUPTION: THE ENEMY WITHIN (B. Rider

corruption, while at the World Bank, that the author had the privilege to meet and admire him.

II. ORGANIZED ECONOMIC CRIME — A THREAT?

When the time comes to look back at the last two decades of the Twentieth Century, a future historian would be forgiven for thinking we were almost obsessed with organized crime, corruption and money laundering. Of course, when one considers the ignominious fall from favour of so many world leaders, in circumstances where serious corruption was at least alleged, if not self-evident, the exposure of rampant financial malpractice in intergovernmental organizations, the penetration of entire economic and political structures by, for want of a better notion, what we describe as organized crime, then perhaps our historian's impression might not be too far from the truth. Although it is possible to find the odd comment in international meetings, about the serious implications of economic crime and the like before the 1980s, these were few and far between.[2] Most related to complaints from developing countries about the unwillingness of developed countries to assist in the enforcement of exchange control laws. In fact, it was not until November 1980 that the Commonwealth, an organization or rather association of states, whose justification has increasingly been based on its ability to recognize and address problems related to small and relatively fragile economies, began to concern itself, at the governmental level, with the implications of what appeared to be a growth in serious economic abuse.[3] At the Commonwealth Law Ministers' Meeting in Barbados in that year, the ministers accepted the recommendations of a report, commissioned a year earlier by the then Director of the Commonwealth Secretariat's Legal Division, Mr. Kutlu Fuad and written by the present author, which led to the instigation of a Commonwealth pro-

---

ed., 1997), also *published in* 5 Journal of Financial Crime 12 (1997). *See also id.*, The World Bank in a Changing World, Vol. I (1991), Chapter Two (*Issues Of "Governance" in Borrowing Countries*).

2 For example, Communiqué of the Commonwealth Law Ministers' Meeting in Winnipeg, Canada, 1977.

3 For example, Communiqué of the Commonwealth Law Ministers' Meeting in Barbados, April 28–May 2, 1980.

gramme against serious economic crime.[4] It is interesting to note that certain Commonwealth governments had expressed concern during the 1970s not so much about abusive conduct on the part of conventional criminals, but on the part of those seeking to 'bust' the economic sanctions that had been imposed on Rhodesia and later South Africa. Indeed, it was claimed by some that, for example, South Africa was attempting to deliberately destabilize the economies of the 'front line states' through a programme of economic sabotage and crime. In those days, there was little talk, even in such organizations as ICPO-Interpol about the threat of organized crime. Terrorism, whether by individuals or by state agencies, was then considered to be a matter almost beyond the ambit of traditional law enforcement agencies. It was much later that, most came to recognize that organized crime and terrorist organizations may well be one and the same.

III. A NEW THREAT?

Some have argued that organized crime is a problem of the last quarter of the twentieth century and in the case of most states is a new phenomenon. Of course, so much depends upon what is meant by organized crime. Groups of individuals, formed and managed to perpetrate acts against the law, is nothing new. Nor is it novel that the primary motivation of such enterprises is economic gain — spurred on by "plain old fashioned" greed and corruption. Banditry, smuggling, racketeering and piracy, were just as much a problem for the praetors and the vigils of ancient Rome as they are today for the Italian authorities. What has changed is the criminals' ability to operate beyond the reach of the domestic legal system and, therefore, be able to conduct an enterprise in crime that is not so amenable to the traditional criminal justice system and its agents. Of course, in truth, thinking criminals have always sought to place themselves beyond the reach of the law

---

4 B. Rider, *The Promotion and Development of International Co-operation to Combat Commercial and Economic Crime,* Memoranda, 1980 Meeting of Commonwealth Law Ministers, Barbados, Com. Sec. London. *See also id., Combating International Commercial Crime — a Commonwealth Perspective,* LLOYDS MARITIME AND COMMERCIAL LAW QUARTERLY 217 (1985); and A. Shipman & B. Rider, *Organised Crime International, in* SECURITY AND DEFENCE REFERENCE BOOK 9 (1987).

and it was not just a matter of having a faster horse! Corruption of officials and the patronage of powerful individuals whose interests, for whatever reason, might be at variance with those of the state, are tried and tested tools. It has always been recognized that even if, as a matter of theory, jurisdiction was unfettered, the practicalities are such as to render enforcement parochial. Thus, when Henry II of England was asked towards the end of the twelfth century how far his writ ran, he responded — "as far as my arrows reach."[5] While developments in ballistic technology might render this a relatively useful approach to dealing with the international criminal, in the vast majority of cases the criminal law in its application or at least administration, will be confined within domestic borders. Developments in technology, communication, travel and the liberalization of movement, whether of persons, things or wealth, have all combined to give the criminal enterprise of today, the same ability as any other business to move from one jurisdiction to another, or involve in a single act two or more different jurisdictions.

In addition, to these factors, which criminals have exploited no less imaginatively than legitimate businessmen, there is another and perhaps crucial consideration. This is the profitability of smuggling, and in particular the illicit trade in drugs, psychotropic substances and other narcotics. The enterprise of smuggling is a natural and predictable consequence of the imposition of restrictions or other costs, on the supply of a commodity for which there is a greater market. History records that highly developed illicit operations developed not just to evade the imposition of taxes, but also to avoid tariffs and other market controls. Indeed, by creating situations where otherwise law abiding members of society see advantage in resorting to secret and illicit suppliers of goods or services, we foster the existence and long term viability, of criminal and subversive structures. For example, when certain 'blocking laws' were introduced in Zimbabwe to prevent the transfer of valuable securities outside the country, some individuals were tempted to deal with 'financial advisers' outside the country who could arrange for these securities to be replaced by external financial paper, which appeared to be of equivalent value. The Reserve

---

5 *See* B. Rider, *Policing the International Financial Markets: An English Perspective,* XVI Brooklyn Journal of International Law 179 (1990).

Bank was then misled into releasing the blocked certificates in return for the deposit of securities of highly dubious worth. Many of these 'investors' were horrified to then discover that they were, as a consequence of these transactions, susceptible to threats of blackmail and extortion by their 'advisers,' who turned out to be gangsters based in New York. The horrendous trade that has developed in immigrant workers, has also enabled organized crime to retain influence and control over those poor men and women that it has placed in, or assisted in finding, work for. Although the illicit trade in weapons and cultural and heritage property is vast, it is the illicit market in drugs that has given organized crime its almost incomprehensible resources and capital. Attitudes to the utility and acceptability of commodities do change, and this is perhaps no more dramatically illustrated than in regard to drugs. Within the space of little more than three decades, opiate-based drugs became widely recognized, throughout the developed world as requiring strict control and supervision. Of course, less than a century before this, certain western governments and in particular Britain were ready and willing to contemplate military action in protection of the opium trade — at least with and in China. Commentators of a cynical disposition might well find it easy to find other examples, such as the expedient widely used by some European nations in the sixteenth and seventeenth centuries of licensing criminals to engage in what would have otherwise have been acts of piracy and pillage — also in the interest of trade!

IV. DRUGS — THE CATALYST

Unlike arms and works of art, the illicit drugs trade has a commodity which can be relatively easily smuggled and for which there is a more or less uniform, discreet and insatiable market. In the early days of what might be termed the modern trade, those areas of the world which were in a position to supply the raw material were not particularly amenable to external supervision, let alone control. To what extent some of the states that became 'victims' of this cancerous trade, almost facilitated the existence and growth of the criminal enterprises that subsequently took advantage of these opportunities, is a matter for debate. It is true, or at least reasonably well documented, that some criminal groups that had been almost suppressed prior to and during the Second World War were 'allowed' to revive and even strengthen themselves, as a bulwark against the threat of communism. It is said, that such a strategy was defensible on the basis that these organizations tended to have local concerns and were not at the time a viable threat to other societies. An allegation of naiveté is always easier to assert with the privilege of hindsight, and perhaps the 'planners' really did believe that the Sicilian gangs thought drugs were immoral! On the other hand, we should not forget the consistent inability of those that inform and advise the 'planners' to predict even quite fundamental changes. The developments, to which we have already referred, in technology and mobility were much more profound and quicker than perhaps anticipated. Furthermore, even the most alarmist predictions of the growth of the illicit market and trade in drugs and narcotics, proved to be conservative. Drugs became, during the seventies, just far too a profitable and easy trade for even traditional and 'conservative' organized crime groups to ignore. Within a decade, even terrorist groups, that conventional wisdom considered unwilling to risk the taint of drugs, entered into the market, and by so doing became virtually indistinguishable from 'ordinary' organized crime. It might be thought perverse that notwithstanding the 'corruption,' or at least seduction, of traditional organized crime, certain Western powers still found it necessary and efficacious to 'dance with the devil' in Latin America and Asia Minor, well into the seventies if not early eighties. However, it must always be remembered that covert channels and underground systems are not cheap to replicate and can seemingly have a real value in the pursuit of national interests. Whatever the rights and wrongs were of the Bank of Credit and Commerce International (BCCI) debacle,[6] the fact is that despite relatively widespread knowledge in governments as to what was or might be taking place within this extraordinary group, the intelligence and security agencies of several countries, apparently saw value in its services and networks. While there may not be particularly convincing evidence supporting the allegation that such agencies deliberately kept the BCCI alive for their own ends, it is clear that

6 *See generally,* The Rt. Hon Lord Justice Bingham, *Inquiry into the Supervision of the Bank of Credit and Commerce International,* Oct. 22, 1992, House of Commons, HMSO.

some did not feel it appropriate to 'blow the whistle' with the vehemence that they should have. Although the BCCI saga is both well known and well documented, there are other, perhaps even more illustrative examples of government agencies allowing essentially criminal operations to continue in furtherance of some other, presumably higher policy. Indeed, there may well come a point, when to intervene through the criminal justice system could be unduly disruptive and even counter-productive.

V. THE ROAD TO LEGITIMACY

It has been said that one of the reasons why certain elements within the Provisional Irish Republican Army (IRA) are prepared to countenance peace in Northern Ireland is because, at least, some have come to enjoy their lifestyles as relatively successful businessmen. The interruption of funding from sympathetic overseas sources led the Provisional Irish Republican Army into activities which were indistinguishable from organized crime. The profitability of their rackets and the stability and even respectability that came to some, as a result of running clubs, bars and taxi services, contributed to their desire to, if not become legitimate, at least protect their new positions. The legitimacy that comes through the possession and accumulation of wealth, is a phenomenon that can be observed in a number of places. It has been said that organized crime is essentially a conservative force, and is therefore concerned — in the main, to provide a degree of stability. Businessmen, whether running a legitimate enterprise or not, prefer certainty and stability. It was said that this distinguished crime from terrorism. Terrorists were not, by definition, a conservative and stabilizing factor. However, this view, while no doubt true in regard to many such groups, does not give sufficient weight to the tendency of subversive organizations to move into conventional forms of criminal activity if for no other reason than to raise money. Once such a process is initiated and individuals start to accumulate personal wealth, the aspirations of the terrorist group may become very different.

Legitimacy is perhaps at best an equivocal concept in law and is notoriously difficult to define. It involves rather more than merely ceasing to be at risk from adverse legal sanctions. It suggests at least some degree of justification and even respect. While the creation and disposal of wealth can hardly itself justify the mantle of legitimacy, it is a significant factor. We see this in Central and Eastern Europe. The downward slide of blackmarketeers and smugglers into organized crime, and the creation of essentially ethnically based, almost traditional, organized crime groups within, in particular the former Soviet Union, have inevitably had a powerful influence on the way in which business is carried out, both domestically and internationally. Organized crime impacts on and even gives effect to, business activity at almost every level of the economy whether it is simply a matter of providing protection or facilitating corruption, to actually providing a viable business partner. The Russian Mafia is a reality, although far more complex in its structures and aspirations than might be imagined from the often sensationalized reports that may be read in the Western press. Given the roots of many criminal organizations within this region and their historical involvement with the black market economy, they are an important element within the pervading Russian underground economy.[7] Consequently, to a very real extent, they become almost indistinguishable, at least in economic terms, from what is left of the economy.

Control and interdiction of organized crime and its effects, on this scale is in practical terms impossible. Containment within what were the borders of the USSR has also proved to be a naive strategy. The level of interdependence, integration and penetration by organized crime throughout the regional economy and sub-political structures are such as to render such a policy both unacceptable and impractical. On the other hand, it is almost certain that the resources within the state, within a political framework that the West would wish to contemplate, could not be made available to control and eradicate organized crime. The resources that have been made available by Western nations and international organizations to assist law enforcement, within the region, are not such as to convince anyone who has a grasp of the extent of the problem, that the West is convinced the traditional processes of interdiction and control are viable. To proceed further than the provision of cosmetics, might well involve consider-

---

7 *See* Alena V. Ledenova, *Practices of Exchange and Networking in Russia,* 6 JOURNAL OF FINANCIAL CRIME 234 (1999); and *id.*, RUSSIA'S ECONOMY OF FAVOURS (1998).

ation of strategies that would be unacceptable in terms of their implications for human rights and the pursuit of democracy. As one senior Chinese judge recently observed, we have been successful in controlling the activities of organized crime groups because we are able to, and often do, execute their leaders. Whether the Chinese have been as successful in this campaign as the judge maintained might be debated, but the message is clear. Indeed, in the days when the Soviet state was effectively indistinguishable from the economy, more people were executed for economic crime than any other form of criminal activity. The message was then quite clear — economic crime is a crime against the state, because the state is the economy.

Unless a strategy, that would be so extreme as to unnerve our liberal democracies, could be executed, then it would appear that ordinary notions of crime control in regard to this level of organized crime are bound to failure. Does this really matter? Perhaps, the two countries which have at least in popular perception, a long history of organized crime, namely Italy and Japan, provide if not an answer at least some guidance. In both countries it would appear that the role of organized crime, other than at a very parochial level, has not been, by any standard, beneficial. While it may be true that low level street crime is, within the territories of particular gangs and families, far less a problem than it is on the streets of London or New York, the costs — in financial and other respects to local businesses in terms of protection — in its various forms, is not inconsiderable. Organized crime is also predatory and often tends to monopolistic practices. The business activities that it engages in, whether directly or indirectly through investment and penetration, are able to compete on an unfair basis. Otherwise law abiding and tax paying businessmen, to maintain their enterprise in the face of such competition, will be encouraged to slide down the "slippery slope" to corruption and illegality. Organized crime given its adverse moral values and perfidious nature will tend to spread its taint, like a cancer, through society. It operates, survives and protects itself through corruption and intimidation. It, by its nature, creates and sustains structures that are at odds with the values and ethics of the society within which it operates. Despite the attempts by film-makers to glamorize gangsters and emphasize their 'traditional' values, the reality is very different. One of the reasons that some traditional organized crime families, have been superseded by new criminal formations, has been their reluctance to depart from traditional areas of influence and business. Furthermore, the desire of such criminals to be respected and well regarded in their neighborhood does not inhibit their true nature when they are away from home! It may well be that some of the families objected to and still object to the sale of drugs on the streets of Palermo, but they have no such scruples in facilitating its sale on the streets of Milan, let alone London or Chicago.

VI. A NEW ORDER OF LEGITIMACY?

When the level of taint or degree of corruption becomes pervasive, then perhaps it is too late to confine the discussion to the traditional strategies of control and interdiction. For example, it has been said that in one country within the region, most of its banks are, if not controlled by organized crime, susceptible to its influence. If this is anywhere near the mark, the implications for that country's well-being should be a matter of concern for everyone. To isolate that banking system, even if such a strategy was feasible in operational let alone legal terms, would not be constructive. Therefore, in effect we either have to live with the *de facto* threat of penetration of the global banking system or perhaps revise our notions of what is acceptable, or even legitimate. Perhaps by allowing the concentration of wealth to take place and then mature, within these jurisdictions, we will achieve a class of businessmen who can not only deliver in real terms, but who have a direct personal interest in creating and maintaining a degree of stability. The 'robber barons' maturing into a new aristocracy. Perhaps in the modern world, where it is easier to purchase the trappings of respectability — at least at an international level, this process might occur quicker than it has in the past. The somewhat romanticized 'laundering' of the new generation into respectable lawyers, accountants and bankers, in such movies as the Godfather, do in fact reflect reality. Some have argued that this process is being and should be speeded up, within those economies where change has effectively necessitated the identification of a new business class.

Indeed, there are those who contend that it is in the interests of the West to foster this process and not seek to inhibit it, through ill conceived and disruptive law enforcement action. Whether this is a strategy that commends itself or not in regard to Central and Eastern Europe, there are those who contend — with some vigor, that this is what is happening in parts of Southern Africa and perhaps even in Northern Ireland. The truth is, however, much more likely to be far less conspiratorial. While there is evidence that the British and for that matter Irish governments have been prepared to adopt a 'softer' approach to enforcement, and some have alleged that over several years the full force of the law allowing for the interdiction of funds associated with terrorist activity has not always been strictly applied, it is quite another thing to accept that there is or was a deliberate policy to foster such a process of self-interested withdrawal from crime. Indeed, much of what has or has not taken place, is more referable to the desire to prosecute a negotiated solution to "The Troubles" and, very occasionally, the protection of those sympathetic to such a process. The commentator should always be wary in discovering conspiracies — with the benefit of hindsight.

Having said this, however, it would be equally naïve to assume that there is anything approaching a uniform and integrated policy, even on the part of the developed western nations, to many of these issues. In fact, there has been resistance, until relatively recently within many countries to the recognition that organized crime does present a real risk to world stability. In Britain, until just a decade or so ago, those who contended that these organized crime existed in Britain or was at least using the facilities of the City of London, were invariably dismissed as ill-informed Cassandras. Whether this was a result of just ignorance on the part of traditional law enforcement agencies or a well rehearsed response modeled on the ostrich, who it is said, when faced with a problem, pushes its head into the nearest available sandpit, but nevertheless remains to be seen! It is true, that until the "cooling" of the Cold War and the freeing of intelligence and related resources, little if any real intelligence capability existed in most traditional police agencies — at least in Europe. It is even more recent, that the ability to perceive flows of funds associated with criminal and subversive activity, has given a picture of the size and disposition of criminal enterprises that would have been thought sensational even for the plot of a 'James Bond' thriller. Traditional law enforcement agencies, for a variety of reasons, associated with resources, perceptions, priorities and jurisdiction, invariably focus, and perhaps rightly, on the more manifest aspects of criminal conduct. Therefore, it was not surprising that police agencies, seeing things as they appeared from the street, were generally not in a position to perceive, let alone engage activity that took place elsewhere. It was not until resources became available to examine structure and organization that Europe's police began to appreciate the real extent of the problem. A key factor in this process was the development and use of financial intelligence. By looking at how money moves within an organization, a much better picture of its structure, operations and weaknesses can be discovered, as compared with external observation, no matter how competent and well executed. The availability of this vitally important and essentially new resource, became available to traditional law enforcement agencies increasingly during the last decade and is today if not commonplace, fast becoming so. The analysis of the financial and economic aspects of criminal and subversive organizations is of importance not only from a strategic standpoint, but also tactically. Governments place considerable reliance in the fight against many forms of serious crime on laws permitting the courts to seize and eventually confiscate the proceeds of criminal conduct. Good financial based intelligence, allows law enforcement agencies to more efficiently collect evidence which may result in an effective forfeiture order or at least disruption of the criminal enterprise.

VII. A SYMBIOTIC RELATIONSHIP?

Before we look at this important strategy, which has been endorsed by all major international organizations, including the World Bank, let us return, albeit briefly to the vexed and no doubt controversial relationship of governments to criminal and subversive conduct. We have already touched upon the use that intelligence and other agents of the state may make of the networks that have been developed by criminal and even subversive organizations. Such facilities may not only be more efficient and discreet, even in terms of accountability, to other organs and operations of the relevant government, but also they are deniable and ultimately expendable. There is, however, another, albeit less intriguing, dimension to the relationship between government agencies and crime. This has manifested itself again in the case of banks and financial stability. There have been occasions where strict enforcement of the law would bring into peril the stability of a bank or other financial institution, and possibly have much wider repercussions. Law enforcement agencies sometimes complain that commercial and financial enterprises are coy in drawing attention to frauds and other abuses perpetrated by their own employees or customers, because disclosure of the facts might well provoke a loss of confidence in the integrity and, or competence of management. Whether there are many instances of serious fraud that are 'brushed under the carpet' or not, can only be a matter of conjecture. It is certainly the case, that there is much anecdotal evidence which indicates that banks would rather suffer in silence and get rid of the person concerned, even to another institution, rather than become involved in a protracted legal process with embarrassing disclosures. The practical reasons which might be thought to justify such an approach, are evidently not confined to the private and commercial sectors.

What is, perhaps, of more concern is when government agencies condone criminal conduct that they are aware of. For example, in February 1980 the Commissioner of Banking for Hong Kong entered into an agreement with the then Government, pursuant to which he was authorized not to report to the Attorney General offences under the banking laws, save where, in the Commissioner's view they were deliberate or for some other reason he felt he should do so. In other words, the Commissioner was relieved from the general 'duty' to report offences for prosecution. The Commissioner justified this on the basis that ". . . bearing in mind our aim to protect depositors, we are really more concerned in getting things put right in the bank or deposit-taking company than in considering a prosecution, which could, and probably would, lead to a loss of public confidence in the bank or deposit-taking company, and could even start a run on that institution which might spread to others." While no one could argue with the need for sensitivity in administering the relevant law and regulations, and this approach was by no means confined to Hong Kong, it is a dangerous precedent, to relieve a regulator of the basic responsibility to inform the Attorney General that crimes have been committed. Although there is no evidence that this agreement was abused in Hong Kong, similar arrangements or understandings have led to extraordinary states of affairs in other countries. Nor is it confined to the banking sector. For example, in one instance in Britain, it was claimed that the relevant authority permitted an investment company, which was known to be engaged in fraudulent activity, to continue to operate so that it could earn money to pay its tax bills! In all these cases, however, we are not talking about corruption, at least in the conventional sense, on the part of officials. Their conduct is dictated by what they consider to be in the greater public interest.

Perhaps, this is not too unlike the situation, at least in institutional terms, of where a crime is perpetrated or allowed to continue, so as to expose or provide evidence in regard to a more serious offence. Obviously, such conduct throws up a host of legal issues, not least those pertaining to entrapment. It is interesting in this regard to see the different attitudes of the American and English governments in regard to Operation De Niro.[8] This undercover operation took place in the Caribbean in 1994. The British Government agreed to be agents of various US Federal agencies — setting up an offshore bank in a British dependency and then offering essentially money laundering services. The bank was run by convicted criminals paroled for the purpose under the supervision of Federal agents. This operation resulted in indictments being brought against a number of individuals in the United States, although none in the country concerned or for that matter elsewhere. On the other hand, the ability to permit suspected cases of money laundering to continue, under police monitoring, is specifically provided for in the British anti-money laundering laws, as it is in the laws of most countries. While this is something very different from entrapment, there is in some cases a fine, although very important line that needs to be drawn.

Before we focus rather more on the laundering of dirty money and before we leave the relationship of governments and criminals, there is another issue that should be mentioned, albeit perhaps not labored. This is the apparent willingness of some states to service or at least turn a blind eye to the activities of criminal organizations. While there are examples of states being pre-

---

8 *See* Wilmer Parker III, *Nowhere to Run; Nowhere to Hide — The Long Arm of the US Law Enforcement,* in MONEY LAUNDERING CONTROL 304 *et seq*. (B. Rider & M. Ashe eds., 1996).

pared to provide safe havens for organizations that assume the mantle, no matter how ill fitting, of dissidents or liberators, but which in reality engage in international crime, what the present writer has particularly in mind, in the context of our present discussion, is those who are prepared to prostitute their legal sovereignty. Too many states, often susceptible to outside influence because of their size, economic vulnerability or lack of infrastructure, have been prepared to become so called 'offshore financial centres' offering not just secrecy and confidentiality for financial transactions, but much more.[9] Some have compounded their inability to supervise and monitor the activity that they permit or encourage to take place within or through their jurisdiction, by corruption.[10] Most have enacted legislation that accords those engaged in financial and commercial activity, through or with a legal entity registered in their jurisdiction, a high degree of secrecy.[11] Indeed, some have imposed additional legal devices which effectively block all inquiries from overseas, or for that matter even domestic, regulators and agencies. While the provision of tax efficient services are unobjectionable[12] and there is justification for many of the facilities offered on an 'offshore' basis, there can be no doubt that too many of these jurisdictions have become complicit or at least involved in money laundering activities. In some, ministers and senior officials have been corrupted with serious consequences for the integrity of their governments. While these problems were recognized by the late 1970s[13] and discussed in

---

9 M. Findlay, *Corruption in Small States; Case Studies in Compromise,* in CORRUPTION: THE ENEMY WITHIN (B. Rider ed., 1997) .

10 *See* B. Rider, *The Practical and Legal Aspects of Interdicting the Flow of Dirty Money,* 3 JOURNAL OF FINANCIAL CRIME 234, 236 (1996), and *see generally,* R. BLUM, OFFSHORE HAVEN BANKS, TRUSTS AND COMPANIES: THE BUSINESS OF CRIME IN THE EUROMARKET (1984).

11 *See* M. GRUNDY, TAX HAVENS, OFFSHORE BUSINESS CENTRES: A WORLD SURVEY (1993).

12 In *Inland Revenue v. Duke of Westminster* (1936) HL (E) 1, Lord Tamlin observed:

> "Every man is entitled, if he can, to order his affairs so that the tax attaching under the appropriate Acts is less than it otherwise would be. If he succeeds in ordering them so as to secure this result, then, however, unappreciative the Commissioner of Inland Revenue or his fellow taxpayers may be of his ingenuity, he cannot be compelled to pay an increased tax."

13 *See* Rider, *supra* note 4.

many international meetings, during the 1980s,[14] it has only been recently that significant pressure has been brought to bear upon these states to 'clean up their acts.'[15] Of course, many have made very determined and genuine efforts themselves to improve their laws and their administration, in an attempt to discourage bad business and dirty money.[16] Others have, however, not been so willing or perhaps able to take responsibility. The suggestion that such states should be 'cold shouldered' by the international financial community is not new,[17] albeit it is now being much more seriously considered by international organizations. The problem with such a policy is that it is susceptible to political considerations which can render the process apparently partisan.[18] Furthermore, it remains to be seen whether it is practical to place a jurisdiction in a state of purdah. Developments in technology require rather more for an effective blockade than a few 'gun boats.' It must also be remembered that it is not just Caribbean and South Sea islands that offer the services that those so concerned with

---

14 *See,* for example, B. Rider, *Commercial Crime Co-operation in the Commonwealth,* in PROCEEDINGS AND PAPERS OF THE 7TH Commonwealth Law Conference, HONG KONG, SEPTEMBER 18–23, 1983.

15 *Note,* for example, the notice to financial institutions issued by the UK Treasury warning about the deficiencies in the anti-money laundering system in Antigua, April 19, 1999. Commenting on the notice the Economic Secretary at the Treasury, Ms. Patricia Hewitt stated:

> "The UK is determined to take a global approach to combat money laundering. As part of the G7 initiative on financial crime, we have signalled our willingness to identify jurisdictions which fail to meet minimum standards. In doing so, we also help protect UK financial institutions from corruption by criminal money, as well as helping to address the insidious influence of global organised crime."

Reference should also be made to FINANCIAL HAVENS, BANKING SECRECY AND MONEY LAUNDERING (UNDCP Report, May 1998).

16 *See generally,* A. EDWARDS, REVIEW OF FINANCIAL REGULATION IN THE CROWN DEPENDENCIES (UK Home Office 1998); and by way of example, D. Harris & S. Hellman, *Cayman Islands: Anti-Money Laundering Legislation — The Proceeds of Criminal Conduct Law 1996*, 1 JOURNAL OF MONEY LAUNDERING CONTROL 104 (1997); and M. L. Alberga, *Cayman Islands: Privacy — A Balancing Act in Changing Times*, 6 JOURNAL OF FINANCIAL CRIME 176 (1998) .

17 *See,* for example, the statement of Mr. Saul Froomkin QC, Attorney General of Bermuda at *The White House Conference for a Drug Free America,* Mar. 3, 1988, Washington D.C.

18 *See generally,* K. Alexander, *Trafficking in Confiscated Cuban Property: Lender Liability Under the Helms-Burton Act*, 5 JOURNAL OF FINANCIAL CRIME 207 (1988).

these issues consider objectionable.[19] In the modern world physical location is becoming increasingly irrelevant.

Of course, to some extent similar considerations apply to the position of states which are prepared to engage in dubious activity, financial and otherwise, in the name of development. There are examples, where governments have been willing to receive money for development or at least government sponsored projects from sources that would not bear a great deal of scrutiny.[20] These states are not, as some would no doubt assume, confined to the African continent. Indeed, there are examples, of regional and local governments in developed countries exhibiting an equivalent disregard for probity, or perhaps to be charitable, the same degree of naïveté. While the inability to secure funds in the case of developing countries, might in the minds of some excuse at least gullibility, in the case of countries such as Australia, Malaysia, Japan and Italy this is less convincing. The level of organized crime involvement both proffering funds, as part of a laundering cycle, or in 'penetrating' through investment, the economic and political structures of developing and vulnerable societies should not be under-estimated. There is very compelling evidence of transnational organized crime regarding certain jurisdictions as not only a source of profit, but as an attractive venue for establishing activities which can be 'protected' by either grateful or corrupt officials. The ability of, in particular, organized crime that has a common ethnic 'origin', to reach into countries where there is already a presence of those sympathetic to its cultural and ethnic characteristics is also well documented. It must also be remembered that in societies which have developed alternative banking or underground financial networks, the ability of such criminal groups to influence and adapt such facilities to their own purposes is so much greater.

VIII. Dirty Money

Let us now return to the now almost universal crusade against money laundering, particularly where it involves wealth that repre-

---

19 *See*, for another perspective, M. Findlay, *Crime as a Force in Globalisation*, 6 JOURNAL OF FINANCIAL CRIME 103 (1998).

20 *See* L. Camerer, *Derailing the Gravy Train — Controlling Corruption*, 4 JOURNAL OF FINANCIAL CRIME 364 (1997).

sents the proceeds of illicit drug trafficking. The wish to hide a source of wealth is nothing new, or necessarily objectionable.[21] The desire to sever the product of an activity from the enterprise from which it is produced is perhaps of more recent origin. Secrecy as to one's financial affairs may be justified on a number of grounds, some socially and morally more justified than others. While the contention that strict bank secrecy was introduced, to provide a safe haven for those subject to Nazi oppression, has some merit although perhaps in the light of experience less than it did.[22] The general view in most developed jurisdictions, until relatively recently, was that it is perfectly acceptable for individuals and even business organizations to order their affairs as they choose and provided they remain within the law, the state of their finances is a matter for them.[23] If they wish to keep it hidden under the bed or in the name of a nominee, that was their business. Indeed, the law of trusts even aided discretion in the holding of property.[24] There are, of course, a variety of legal obligations to reveal at least the quantity of wealth, such as in insolvency and matrimonial proceedings or in certain cases under tax law.[25] Furthermore, when exchange control was far more common, controls were also imposed on the actual location of wealth. Now, such laws are rare and becoming rarer. Although in most common law countries, secrecy of financial information is not protected by specific statutes as it is in most civil law countries, the general law of confidentiality has been well used to provide a significant degree of protection albeit through the civil law.[26] Indeed, such is the protection afforded to banking information by the common law, that some have won-

---

21 *See* B. Rider, *The Practical and Legal Aspects of Interdicting the Flow of Dirty Money,* 3 JOURNAL OF FINANCIAL CRIME 234 (1996). *See also* D. CAMPBELL, INTERNATIONAL BANK SECRECY (1992), at vii.

22 *See* T. BOWER, BLOOD MONEY: THE SWISS, THE NAZIS AND THE LOOTED BILLIONS 46 *et seq.* (1997).

23 B. RIDER & H.L. FFRENCH, THE REGULATION OF INSIDER TRADING, 420 *et seq.* (1979); *see also* Hans Peter Friedrich, *The Anonymous Bank Account in Switzerland,* JOURNAL OF BUSINESS LAW 15 (1962); and R. T. NAYLER, HOT MONEY AND THE POLITICS OF DEBT (1987).

24 *See,* for example, M.S. Kenny, *The Penetration of Asset Protection Trusts,* 6 JOURNAL OF FINANCIAL CRIME 111 (1998).

25 *See generally,* M. ASHE & B. RIDER, INTERNATIONAL TRACING OF ASSETS, Vol. 1 (1998).

26 *See* Campbell, *supra* at note 21; and *see generally,* MONEY LAUNDERING AND BANKING SECRECY (P. Bernascerni ed., 1996).

dered what possible justification there can be for common law jurisdictions, such as Singapore, Malaysia and some of the Caribbean countries to reinforce their law by enacting specific secrecy provisions. Somewhat paradoxically at a time when many seem to advocate greater transparency as almost a universal cure to our social and moral ills, there is, at least in Britain, increasing concern to protect privacy including that of financial and business information, as a human right. It is also sadly the case that, as in the past, the world for many is not and will not in their life time be a safe place. Without the ability to protect their wealth, particularly, that which is more liquid, they and their loved ones will remain even more at risk from greedy dictators, corrupt tyrants and racist thugs masquerading as governments.

Hiding money is one thing, but as we have already indicated, attempting to disassociate wealth from its actual source, smacks of something rather more sinister. Why, at least in a country where the rule of law is a meaningful concept, if the wealth has been legitimately acquired, should anyone be concerned to frustrate anyone inquiring into its source? By contrast, those that have obtained their wealth through, perhaps rather disreputable methods have, no doubt, always preferred their neighbors and admirers to remain in ignorance. Furthermore, it is true that unexplained wealth might draw suspicion and unwanted interest — from both sides of the law. However, until very recently there was little risk to those assets as a consequence of legal procedures, other than those associated with taxation. Although it is possible to find in many ancient systems of law provisions which allow the state or ruler to forfeit the instruments of crime, and even the proceeds of crime, and in extreme cases all the criminal's property, there are few contemporary examples of such laws enduring. It is much more recently that governments have realized, that where criminal conduct is motivated by economic gain, it makes a great deal of sense to attack the profits of crime. To hit the criminal in his pocket! Furthermore, where the criminal conduct involves a continuing criminal enterprise, taking away, or otherwise interdicting, the proceeds of crime might well prevent the re-investment of this wealth back into the criminal operation, thus causing serious liquidity problems. US agencies have been particularly attracted by the logic of this approach, the more so because in the main those assets that are seized remain within the possession and use of law enforcement.

Furthermore, the law as it has developed in the USA, particularly in regard to civil enforcement actions *in rem*[27] has proved to be relatively effective. Indeed, given the manifest failure, viewed from the USA, of various programs based on drug supply and demand reduction, attacking the assets of the drug barons has appeared increasingly attractive. The significance of this strategy has been elevated by obtaining the support of other jurisdictions, and in particular inter-governmental organizations, to almost that of a crusade. A series of international conventions and agreements[28] have, directly or indirectly, obliged countries to enact legislation, which enables their authorities to seize and then, on conviction for a drug related offence, confiscate property which represents the proceeds of that crime. Most states have extended these laws to cover property which can be shown to be directly, or even indirectly, the proceeds of such a crime, even though it took place in another jurisdiction. More recently, this approach has been sensibly extended so as to encompass the proceeds of all serious crime, whether drugs related or not. These provisions are also reinforced by laws which facilitate financial investigations and mutual legal co-operation. Indeed, discussion of such laws has dominated international meetings for the last decade and there is every sign that this will continue well into the next millennium.

In the case of crime that is motivated by economic gain it does make sense for the legal system to focus attention on the 'profit' that the criminal hopes to make from his illicit conduct. We recognize today that far more crimes than those that might be described as 'economic crimes' are motivated by greed and the prospect of financial gain. For example, the motivation driving most drug trafficking operations will be the prospect of financial rewards disproportionate to the risks involved. Organized crime given its character and often its structures, will be particularly focussed on the ability to generate income. Its purpose is to 'wring exorbitant profits from . . . society, by whatever means, legal or

---

27 *See,* for example, Fletcher Baldwin Jr., *All Funds and International Seizure Cooperation of the USA and UK,* 5 JOURNAL OF FINANCIAL CRIME 111 (1997).

28 *See* B. RIDER & C. NAKAJIMA, CCH ANTI-MONEY LAUNDERING GUIDE (1999), at paras. 80-000–82-850, and W. C. GILMORE, DIRTY MONEY, (Council of Europe, 1995), Chapter III; and BASIC DOCUMENTS ON INTERNATIONAL EFFORTS TO COMBAT MONEY LAUNDERING (1991), Commonwealth Secretariat.

illegal, fair or foul. . . .'[29] It also needs money as well as the prospect of disproportionate rewards, to retain and foster its operational efficacy and the loyalty of its members. Because economic and commercial crime constitute relatively high reward and low risk activities, organized crime groups have become increasingly attracted to this sort of activity. Interdicting the proceeds of crime can also provide a useful mechanism for undermining the ability of criminals to invest in other criminal activities or their own enterprises. Although there is little evidence, other than on an anecdotal basis, as to the effect of such strategies, it stands to reason that inhibiting the flow of funds into such activities, must have a disrupting effect on the enterprise. This is particularly so, when liquidity is at a premium, as it is in drug related crime, where a high proportion of transactions are spot and in cash and yet retention of large amounts of cash is both impractical and high risk for the criminal.

IX. TAKING THE PROFIT OUT OF CRIME

A profound weakness of the strategy of attacking criminal enterprises through the confiscature and forfeiture of ill-gotten wealth is that the law has proved to be exceedingly difficult to apply. Outside the USA, the value of property and money actually confiscated is very small when compared with even conservative estimates as to the amount of wealth that is likely to be flowing through the criminal pipeline. Of course, estimates or rather "guesstimates" as to what this figure might be vary greatly depending upon the perspective of those concerned. There are no really reliable figures and although various attempts have been made to quantify the amount of dirty money that may at any one point in time be flowing through the pipeline, at the end of the day, it comes down to speculation and informed guess work. The situation is complicated by the presence in the systems of money and wealth, which, al-

[29] Statement of Conference of State Attornies-General on Organized Crime, USA 1966; and *see* B. Rider, *The Financial World at Risk; The Dangers of Organised Crime, Money Laundering and Corruption*, 8 MANAGERIAL AUDITING JOURNAL 3 (1993).

though not directly the product of crime, is for some reason or another susceptible to the same processes of laundering.

In 1995, a former senior official in the Legal Directorate of the British intelligence and security service was reported in a newspaper as expressing the view that £200 billion a year of narcotics related money passes through the City of London.[30] Whether such an astronomical amount is anywhere near the truth remains to be seen. While some have 'confirmed' the accuracy of this "guesstimate," others have been somewhat more conservative. The truth is that so little work has been done on this question in Britain, or for that matter anywhere outside the USA, no one really knows the extent of the problem. Ms. Elisabeth Bresee, Assistant Secretary (Enforcement) in the US Department of the Treasury, in giving evidence to the Sub-Committees on Financial Institutions and General Oversight and Investigations of the House of Representatives' Committee on Banking and Financial Services, was asked to quantify the amount of money being laundered through the USA.[31] She stated: "partial figures can give one some idea of the problem. The Office of National Drug Control Policy estimates that approximately US$60 billion is now expended in the purchase of illegal narcotics each year. If eighty percent of that represents profit, the sales generate US$48 billion to be laundered each year, simply on account of narcotics sales without taking into account all of the other crimes whose proceeds require laundering. And even a fraction of that number, reinvested year after year, generates a sizeable and frightening war chest of criminal capital."

Ms. Bresee then pointed out that, if one sought to obtain a picture of the total amount of wealth being laundered in the USA, then one had to add the profits from crimes committed outside the USA that were laundered through the USA, or by utilizing US currency or US institutions, and also the repatriation, either permanently or as part of the laundering cycle, of wealth generated by US criminals at sometime in the past, that had been held out-

---

30 J. Adams, *£200 bn in Drugs Cash Heads for London Markets*, SUNDAY TIMES, Nov. 19, 1995; and *see generally* B. Rider, *Organised Crime in the United Kingdom: A Personal Perspective,* (Memorandum 15), *in* ORGANISED CRIME, MINUTES OF EVIDENCE AND MEMORANDA, Home Affairs Committee, Nov. 16, 1994, House of Commons, HMSO.

31 April 15, 1999, and *see* B. Rider, *What Do We Mean By 'Dirty' Money?,* MONEY LAUNDERING MONITOR, June 1999.

side the USA. When one takes all this into account, perhaps the comment reported in the British press in 1995 was not as preposterous as some have made out.

What is manifest and indisputable is that the amount of money that would, in theory, be susceptible to the application of legal forfeiture laws is vast. In Britain, however, the recently published Third Report of the Home Office Working Group on Confiscation,[32] discloses that since the relevant law came into force in 1987, the authorities in England and Wales have been able to confiscate only £37,261,600 of drug-related wealth. Under legislation designed to take the profit out of all serious crime, whether drugs related or not, the amount, since the law came into force in 1989, is just £4,484,659. If even a conservative estimate of the amount of wealth liable to confiscation during this period was compared with these figures, the results obtained would, if the matter was not so serious, be laughable. Of course, there are mitigating factors: the law is relatively new, financial investigations are always difficult, time consuming and often complex; it is only recently that law enforcement agencies have been able and willing to commit the necessary resources to this strategy and the courts and prosecutors have yet to become entirely comfortable with this body of the law. On the other hand, the world community is heralding this strategy as the way ahead, and Britain is not in anyway coy about 'advising' if not 'encouraging' other states to follow it down this path. At one recent meeting, organized at a senior diplomatic level, at which several British agencies offered technical assistance to judicial and police authorities of certain countries in Latin America, embarrassment was caused when it was pointed out that the municipal police authority of a city in one of these countries had seized drugs' related wealth in a single case, in excess of the total national seizures in Britain over a decade. In evaluating the efficacy of this strategy, however, it is most important to remember that the criminal law is only one weapon and much can be achieved, as it has in Britain, under tax law and the civil law.[33]

---

32 UK Home Office (1998), at 12 and 13. *See also* B. Rider, *Taking the Gloves Off*, 2 JOURNAL OF MONEY LAUNDERING CONTROL 196 (1999).

33 *See* in a different, although related context, B. Rider, *Civilising the Law — the Use of Civil and Administrative Proceedings to Explore Financial Services Law*, 3 JOURNAL OF FINANCIAL CRIME (1995) II; and also LAUNDERING AND TRACING (P. B. H. Birks ed., 1995).

It might also be argued that the very presence of confiscature and anti-money laundering laws discourage criminal organizations from placing their wealth in the relevant jurisdiction, either as part of the laundering process or by way of investment. The presence of such laws is an unnecessary risk and the regulatory obligations that the laws impose on those who handle other peoples' wealth imposes an additional cost on the criminal doing business in that jurisdiction. While it is true that money laundering as an economic activity is susceptible to being influenced by cost considerations, it is not necessarily the case that even a high level of control — and effective control at that — will render the jurisdiction unattractive to the criminal enterprise. The organization will require a place in which to hold its wealth which is secure and well respected. The "end-deposit" country must be reputable so that the organization's laundered and now 'clean' money can be deployed as it sees fit with the minimum of suspicion. Countries, such as the Bahamas and the Cayman Islands that have made a real effort to improve their surveillance and control over the grosser forms of money laundering, may well have discouraged criminal organizations attempting to use them as entry points into the financial system. However, they would be rash to think that they are no longer at real risk from being involved in laundering. Their efforts to improve the probity of their reputations, have earned them promotion along the money laundering cycle nearer that favored position as an "end-deposit" country. The implications of this process, which cynically mirrors the process of legitimization itself, have yet to be fully appreciated within and, indeed, outside these states.

There are still those, albeit a diminishing band, who advocate the 'intelligence' advantages of retaining 'soft' entry points to the financial system, where those with an interest in monitoring flow of funds can operate in a way less circumscribed by law and due process. According to this view, the crusade to convince every jurisdiction to put in place legal constraints on laundering, and to provide legal mechanisms for co-operation, in practice has imposed a level of legal control and bureaucracy which can only help the criminal and provide new opportunities for corrupt officials. A not too dissimilar argument was used by some Scotland Yard detectives in regard to the enactment of confiscature laws in Britain. Their concern was that the law would drive the funding of crime underground, which would render it even more difficult to monitor, and 'tactically' disruptive. Such views when articulated by the agents of traditional law enforcement are perhaps less easy to accommodate, than when advocated by intelligence officers and those concerned with the interdiction of activity which politicians perceive as "subversive" rather than merely criminal. Certainly, the authorities in Northern Ireland were more receptive to such arguments! The retention of 'soft' financial centres and 'corrupt' organizations that can be manipulated and controlled for the benefit of other societies is at best a difficult policy to contemplate — let alone defend. Those who were prepared to countenance the survival of the BCCI on this basis, although not publicly pursued, have paid a heavy price albeit behind closed doors. This sort of policy only works if you do not get caught!

X. THE COST OF PROBITY

Perhaps a more serious issue is the price that the financial and banking system is required to pay for the strategy of taking the profit out of crime. It is not an exaggeration to claim that the impact of anti-money laundering law on the way in which business is carried out in the British financial sector is greater than that of legislation, such as the Financial Services Act 1986, which is directly aimed at the conduct of financial business.[34] The costs involved in establishing, maintaining and demonstrating compliance are considerable by any standard. It is also clear that in many jurisdictions, even dedicated attention to compliance will only serve in mitigation should an offence actually occur.[35] The total cost of compliance, training, and supervision in regard to the control of money laundering in Britain can only be a very rough "guesstimate," like so much in this discussion. It has been put at £600 million a year. Of course, there are those who would wish to add on

---

[34] *See* N. Clark, *The Impact of Recent Money Laundering Legalisation on Financial Intermediaries*, in MONEY LAUNDERING CONTROL (B. Rider & M. Ashe eds., 1996); and also B. RIDER, C. ABRAMS & M. ASHE, GUIDE TO FINANCIAL SERVICES REGULATION 268 (CCH 3rd ed. 1997); and R. BOSWORTH-DAVIES & G. SALTMARSH, MONEY LAUNDERING (1994) Chapter 3.

[35] *See*, for example, *Re: Supply of Ready Mixed Concrete (no. 2)* (1995) IAC 456, and CHIZU NAKAJIMA, CONFLICTS OF INTEREST AND DUTY: A COMPARATIVE ANALYSIS IN ANGLO-JAPANESE LAW (1999).

the cost of 'loss of opportunity,' whether they have in mind the business that they cannot undertake because their resources are otherwise employed in compliance, or the loss of 'good' money laundering business remains to be seen. What is clear is that policing the anti-money laundering laws and their regulations represents a considerable in-house cost within the financial services and banking industry. There is also the important issue, which has yet to be fully grasped in many countries, of the impact of anti-money laundering laws on other areas of legal responsibility. For example, little thought has been given to the relationship, if any, of the obligation cast upon financial intermediaries to know more about their clients and the responsibility on certain intermediaries to ensure that their advice and management is suitable to the circumstances of their clients.[36] In other words, does the 'know your customer rule' impact on the duty of care and suitability of advice? Furthermore, while most legal systems protect intermediaries from direct legal liability to their customer when they report their suspicions to the authorities, few protect against defamation suits or collateral and transactional liability to third parties. There is also, at least in some common law jurisdictions, a possibility of a conflict between the law pertaining to the protection of fiduciary interests and the offence of disclosing that an anti-money laundering investigation is imminent.[37] All these and many other issues, represent a real risk to those who handle other peoples' wealth, which needs to be placed in the balance when evaluating the "cost-benefit" of the strategy we have all so enthusiastically adopted — and imposed on those who want to join the West's global economy.

The present author would not wish to create the impression that he considers that focussing upon the assets of criminal organizations has not played, and will not continue to play, a significant role in the control of organized and serious crime. Indeed, he was one of the first to advocate such a strategy and has been a staunch supporter of it over the years.[38] However, he is convinced that it is no panacea. There is a real danger that the understandable desire

36 *See* B. Rider, *The Limits of the Law: An Analysis of the Interrelationship of the Criminal and Civil Law in the Control of Money Laundering,* 2 JOURNAL OF MONEY LAUNDERING CONTROL 209 (1999).

37 *See* NAKAJIMA, *supra* note 35, at chapter 8.

38 *See* Rider, *supra* note 4; and *Combating Organised Crime,* Memorandum by B. Rider to the Meeting of Commonwealth Law Ministers, Zimbabwe, July 26, 1986 to

on the part of leaders and politicians to come up with a 'solution' to the problem of organized crime has rendered them too willing to seize upon, what is no doubt a good weapon, when used with others, but in no way a solution. To some extent those responsible for the management of law enforcement have also found it convenient to espouse this strategy, and promote perhaps an unrealistic level of expectation. The inability of the traditional criminal justice system in most countries to deal effectively with transnational and serious economic crime, has placed tremendous pressure on those charged with protecting the integrity of the economy and state to come up with a viable policy.[39] The attention of the media and the political implications of the nature of the problem, have underlined the need for prompt action which can be at least represented as directly attacking the primary threat. Furthermore, newspapers tend to report the value of seizures and do not often follow the story through until confiscature of the proceeds of the crime on subsequent conviction. Thus, in the mind of the public the law does appear to be far more effective than in fact it is, judged purely in terms of the amount of money that has been taken out of the criminal pipeline.[40]

Mention has already been made of the various international and regional initiatives which require or at least encourage states to adopt more or less uniform laws providing for the confiscature of the proceeds of serious crime, or at least those associated with the illicit trade in drugs, the investigation and interdiction of the proceeds of such offences, the criminalization of money laundering, the reporting of suspicious transactions, the imposition of reporting and due diligence requirements on those most likely to confront money laundering and the facilitation of international mutual legal assistance. All this is highly commendable. However, as in other areas, the laws and legal procedures of one jurisdiction are not always easily transported, without significant adaptation,

---

Aug. 1, 1986, Com. Sec, London; and MARITIME FRAUD — THE FEASIBILITY OF IMPROVING THE ADMINISTRATION AND LEGAL PROCEDURES OF PROSECUTING AUTHORITIES IN CASES OF MARITIME FRAUD, Report by UNCTAD Secretariat, Aug. 12, 1985, Geneva.

39 *See,* for example, B. Rider, *Policing the City — Combating Fraud and Other Abuses in the Corporate Securities Industry,* 41 CURRENT LEGAL PROBLEMS 47 (1988); and B. RIDER & M. ASHE, INSIDER CRIME 86 *et seq.* (1993).

40 For a similar discussion in regard to insider dealing and securities fraud, *see* B. RIDER, THE CONTROL OF INSIDER TRADING — SMOKE AND MIRRORS (1999).

to the legal system of another, with quite different traditions and structures.[41] If more than cosmetic surgery is to be achieved, considerable attention needs to be given to a host of issues — legal, procedural, evidentiary, institutional and cultural. There are innumerable examples in financial law, where devices that have proved effective in, for example, the US Federal Courts, have looked very much out of place in a wholly alien environment. The present writer is not advocating a parochial attitude to the reception of experience, legal and otherwise, from foreign jurisdictions, indeed, there is much to be gained. What he is concerned about is the almost imposition of alien concepts and mechanisms without due regard to the particular sensitivities and needs of the jurisdiction concerned. In many areas of financial regulation, it is as though cadres of international legal consultants have sprung from the earth to serve the gods of legal homogeneity or at least standardization. The same rules and mechanisms will be commended as almost a 'take it or leave it' product, regardless of whether they suit the very different circumstances of a legal system struggling out of the shadows of European communism, or awaking from the nightmare of new civil war and apartheid. The author was on one occasion invited to give oral evidence before an expert committee on financial law in South Africa, which had already devoted a great deal of time and resources to crafting a law against insider dealing.[42] When the author expressed the view that the ordinary criminal law would be unlikely to work and consequently wondered whether it would not be better for the committee to focus on more pressing issues relating to the markets, he was told in no uncertain terms, that the South African Government had been informed that such laws were necessary if South Africa's was to meet the 'international standard.'[43] That business travelers stand a much greater chance of being mugged, or even murdered on the streets, than being seriously prejudiced by insider dealing, ap-

---

[41] *See* B. Rider, *Blindman's Bluff — A Model for Securities Regulation?*, in EMERGING FINANCIAL MARKETS AND THE ROLE OF INTERNATIONAL FINANCIAL ORGANISATIONS (J.J. Norton & M. Andenas eds., 1997).

[42] Of course, South Africa has long had laws on insider dealing — although they have proved to be unenforceable. *See* B. Rider, *The Regulation of Insider Trading in the Republic of South Africa*, 94 SOUTH AFRICAN LAW JOURNAL 437 (1977).

[43] This is not a new 'obsession.' *See* B. RIDER & H. L. FFRENCH, THE REGULATION OF INSIDER TRADING (1979).

pears to be almost irrelevant.[44] By the same token, it is seemingly justifiable to pour resources into policing such 'cosmetic offences,' when only half of the officers in the South African Police Services can drive! In fashioning the laws and procedures we need to be able to effectively discourage the international criminal, we need to look rather more at substance and place rather less emphasis on form.[45]

If we are going to make a significant attack on corruption and criminal organizations, more radical strategies will be required than those we have adopted, or perhaps dared to contemplate in the past. It appears increasingly obvious that any strategy based on the ability of a prosecutor to prove, to the satisfaction of the court, that wealth represents the proceeds of a crime or even a pattern of criminal activity can be expected to have only minimal impact on the totality of criminal and subversive assets. Although it may be possible to facilitate law enforcement by providing more and more resources, fostering meaningful international co-operation, improving training and by even lowering thresholds of proof, the need to establish a nexus between wealth and a specific crime will result in the vast majority of criminal assets remaining well beyond the reach of the law. While the costs to criminals of using their ill-gotten gains may also be increased through taxation, regulatory laws and requirements, and even by law enforcement adopting a strategy of disruption, the impact is likely to still fall far short of that required. Consequently, the present author is convinced that governments will need to devise a much more radical approach to this problem. The notion of taxing unaccountable wealth is not novel. Furthermore, there are many examples around the world of laws which attach certain presumptions to the holding of wealth that cannot be satisfacto-

---

44 The author has long maintained that it is the market that is 'harmed,' if anything, in the insider's abusing privileged information. *See* RIDER, *supra* at note 40, and H. L. Ffrench & B. Rider, *Insider Trading — Some Initial Considerations,* 95 SOUTH AFRICAN LAW JOURNAL 79 (1978); THE FIDUCIARY, THE INSIDER AND THE CONFLICT (B. Rider & M. Ashe eds., 1995), Chapter 12; and DEVELOPMENTS IN EUROPEAN COMPANY LAW (B. Rider & M. Andenas eds., 1998), Chapter 2.

45 *See* B. Rider, *Policing Insider Dealing in Britain,* in EUROPEAN INSIDER DEALING (K. Hopt & E. Wymeersch eds., 1991); *id., Fraud in the Financial Markets,* in THE REGULATION OF FINANCIAL AND CAPITAL MARKETS (C. Lye & R. Lazar eds., 1990) Singapore Academy of Law; and B. Rider, *Insider Trading — A Crime of Our Times,* in CURRENT DEVELOPMENTS IN BANKING AND FINANCE (D. A. Kingsford Smith ed., 1989).

rily explained. Thus, in Hong Kong,[46] if a public servant is in possession of wealth beyond his salary, there is a legal obligation on him to explain its source. The possession of unaccountable wealth is presumptive of corruption. In Britain, the prosecution may request, on a second conviction for a serious offence, within a period of six years, that the court regards that any property in the possession of the defendant, that has been acquired during the last six years and the source of which he cannot properly explain, be presumed to be the proceeds of his criminal life style.[47] Now, there are obviously a host of legal, evidentiary and human rights issues that arise in regard to such legal devices. Focussing on the accumulation of wealth in this manner, might not make a great deal of sense in the case of the 'new economies,' but the author remains convinced that over the next decade, more and more legal systems will move over to imposing obligations on those in possession of significant amounts of wealth, the source of which cannot be publicly justified. These obligations may range across a spectrum, from mere transparency to effective confiscature. It will be for the society in question to determine the appropriate balance. What this new strategy will require, however, is a very different approach by law enforcement where the skills of the tax investigator and financial intelligence officer will be placed at a premium.

XI. AN INDULGENCE?

This discussion, of a very narrow, but with respect important issue facing those charged with maintaining and promoting the integrity of our financial order is, as was indicated at the outset a very personal one and does not pretend to do more than raise the sort of issues that have been in the minds of those concerned about the integrity of the world in which we live. Dr. Shihata's writings on, for example, the control of corruption, particularly at the international level, indicate a clear concern for not just the law, but its administration and the importance of being alert to such matters as human rights and good governance. Now that the World Bank has

---

46 *See,* for example, § 10 of the Prevention of Bribery Ordinance CAP 201.

47 Proceeds of Crime Act 1995.

become such an authoritative voice on many issues of direct concern to the integrity of the global financial system, it is even more important that, in framing policies, the opportunity is taken to assess efficacy in terms wider than might be appropriate for a purely commercial or financial programme.

The challenge for the future is to ensure that the steps we take to promote probity and stability do not stifle the very enterprise which drives our economies or trespass too much on the very ideals which remain so precious to civilization. The ability to balance these counter weights rightly will determine the very character of the world we leave to future generations.

DIRECT FOREIGN INVESTMENT AND THE LAW IN DEVELOPING COUNTRIES

Jeswald W. Salacuse

I. INTRODUCTION

One of the most significant changes affecting the developing world during the last decade has been the enormous expansion in private foreign investment. In 1987, developing countries received total direct foreign investment (valued in 1996 dollars) of less than US$20 billion. In 1996, they received nearly US$120 billion, a six-fold increase.[1] Foreign investment has grown in importance not only in absolute terms but also in its relation to other forms of development finance. Whereas in 1982 direct foreign investment in developing countries accounted for only about eight percent of total external capital flows (with portfolio investment at an insignificant 0.1 per cent), in 1996, out of all external financial flows to developing countries, nearly forty percent consisted of direct foreign investment, with portfolio investment accounting for an additional sixteen percent.[2] By the following year, 1997, nearly fifty percent of all capital flows to developing countries consisted of direct foreign investment.[3] Direct foreign investment has thus become the largest single source of external development finance for

---

1 FOREIGN DIRECT INVESTMENT — LESSONS OF EXPERIENCE NO. 5, 10 (INTERNATIONAL FINANCE CORPORATION 1997) (hereinafter LESSONS OF EXPERIENCE).

2 *Ibid.* at 15.

3 ENTERING THE TWENTY-FIRST CENTURY: WORLD DEVELOPMENT REPORT 1999/2000, 72 (WORLD BANK 1999) (hereinafter ENTERING THE TWENTY-FIRST CENTURY).

developing countries. By contrast, in 1996 official development finance had fallen to only fourteen percent of the total.[4]

The impact of direct foreign investment has meant much more than money to host countries. It has meant the transfer of technology, the introduction of new management skills, and the creation of links to world market. It has also meant increased productive capacity, employment, and the provision of new goods and services, among other things. Foreign direct investment has thus become a powerful force for development throughout the world. At the global level, it is also a dynamic force for the integration of economies. It is an engine of globalization.

Many factors explain the enormous growth of foreign investment in developing countries. One important though often neglected element is the role of law and legal institutions, both international and domestic, in facilitating the flow of private capital from one country to another.

II. THE WORK OF DR. IBRAHIM F.I. SHIHATA IN LAW AND FOREIGN INVESTMENT

An important area of endeavor in Ibrahim Shihata's distinguished and multi-faceted career has been his work in helping to shape an appropriate legal framework for foreign direct investment in developing countries. In one of my first meetings with him while he was a Professor of Law at Ain Shams University in Cairo about thirty years ago, he spoke insightfully of the important link between law and foreign investment, a link that was often overlooked by development economists of that period. Dr. Shihata would continue to make this point eloquently in his articles and lectures over the next three decades.[5]

As Legal Advisor to the Kuwait Fund for Arab Economic Development, then the leading development bank in the Middle

---

4 LESSONS OF EXPERIENCE, *supra* note 1, at 15.

5 *See, e.g.*, IBRAHIM F. I. SHIHATA, THE WORLD BANK IN A CHANGING WORLD, Vol. II, 127–145 (1995), Chapter Three (*Legal Framework for Development and the Role of The World Bank in Legal Technical Assistance*). "The role of law in economic development has not always been recognized . . . law plays a key role in the development process." *Ibid.* at 127.

East, he applied his ideas and creative legal talents in designing instruments and institutions, such as the Inter-Arab Investment Guarantee Corporation,[6] to facilitate the flow of funds from the oil-rich Arab states such as Kuwait and Saudi Arabia, to states such as Egypt and the Sudan, with immense financial needs. Not only did he help the Kuwait Fund play a leading role as a developmental institution, but he would also assist through advice and example the other development banks in the Middle East that were emerging during the era of the petro-dollar boom.[7] Though created by public funds, their presence and activities served to support and encourage the flow of private capital to developing countries.

It was of course as General Counsel and Vice President of the World Bank, an institution whose basic purposes include ". . . facilitating the investment of private capital for productive purposes . . ." and promoting ". . . private foreign investment . . ."[8] that Dr. Shihata achieved some of his most significant accomplishments in creating a new legal framework to facilitate the flow of private capital to developing countries. Under his leadership, the Multilateral Investment Guarantee Agency (MIGA)[9] came into existence; the International Centre For Settlement of Investment Disputes (ICSID)[10] became genuinely established as a leading arbitral institution with a truly global membership for resolving disputes between investors and host countries; and the Legal Framework for

---

6 *See* Ibrahim F. I. Shihata, *Arab Investment Guarantee Program: A Regional Investment Guarantee Project,* 6 JOURNAL OF WORLD TRADE LAW 185–202 (1972).

7 *See generally,* Jeswald W. Salacuse, *Arab Capital and Middle Eastern Development Finance: The Emerging Institutional Framework,* 14 JOURNAL OF WORLD TRADE LAW 283–309 (1980); IBRAHIM F. I. SHIHATA, THE OTHER FACE OF OPEC: FINANCIAL ASSISTANCE TO THE THIRD WORLD (1982).

8 Art. 1 of the Articles of Agreement of the International Bank for Reconstruction and Development, *opened for signature* Dec. 27, 1945, 2 U.N.T.S. 134.

9 IBRAHIM F. I. SHIHATA, MIGA AND FOREIGN INVESTMENT— ORIGINS, OPERATIONS, POLICIES AND BASIC DOCUMENTS OF THE MULTILATERAL INVESTMENT GUARANTEE AGENCY (1988); and *id., The Multilateral Investment Guarantee Agency,* 20, NO. 2 THE INTERNATIONAL LAWYER 485 (1986).

10 *See* IBRAHIM F. I. SHIHATA, *ICSID Arbitration: The Institution's Point of View,* 36 PRIVATE INVESTMENT ABROAD 16.1–16.25 (1993); *id.,* THE WORLD BANK IN A CHANGING WORLD, Vol. II, 425–453 (1995), Chapter Eleven (*ICSID's Role in the Resolution of Investment Disputes*).

the Treatment of Foreign Investment[11] was elaborated as a statement of universal standards for the treatment of international investments, a document that has influenced the policies of host governments and will surely become the basis for an eventual global treaty on the subject. In addition to these achievements at the international level, the World Bank, through the leadership of Dr. Ibrahim F.I. Shihata, devoted increased attention and resources to assisting individual developing countries to create national legal systems that would foster and use effectively foreign private capital within their territories.[12] While carrying out these significant achievements in the realm of international policy and legal practice, Dr. Ibrahim F.I. Shihata, in the best traditions of the scholar *engagé,* has also written extensively on the legal requirements for foreign investment, thus making an important contribution to scholarship in the field of law and development.[13]

III. LAW, FOREIGN INVESTMENT AND THE FUTURE

Although foreign direct investment in developing countries has grown in magnitude and force and although many new laws and institutions, both at the national and the international level, have emerged to facilitate this flow, host country governments and international agencies still need to be concerned with overcoming law-related obstacles to investment in developing countries for several reasons. First, the bulk of foreign direct investment has tended to concentrate in a relatively limited number of countries.[14] In 1997, for example, eight countries received two-third of all the

---

11 LEGAL FRAMEWORK FOR THE TREATMENT OF FOREIGN INVESTMENT, 2 VOLUMES (INTERNATIONAL BANK FOR RECONSTRUCTION AND DEVELOPMENT 1992). For details, *see* IBRAHIM F.I SHIHATA, LEGAL TREATMENT OF FOREIGN INVESTMENT: THE WORLD BANK GUIDELINES (1993). For a summary of the issues dealt with in the World Bank Guidelines, *see* Sabine Schlemmer-Schulte, *The World Bank Guidelines on the Treatment of Foreign Direct Investment,* in LEGAL ASPECTS OF FOREIGN DIRECT INVESTMENT (Daniel D. Bradlow & Alfred Escher eds., 1999).

12 *See* SHIHATA, *supra* note 5, at 127–145.

13 *See, e.g.,* IBRAHIM F. I. SHIHATA, THE WORLD BANK IN A CHANGING WORLD, Vol. I (1991) of which one half of the volume is devoted to the subject *The World Bank and the Promotion of Private Foreign Investment.*

14 ENTERING THE TWENTY-FIRST CENTURY, *supra* note 2, at 72–73.

foreign direct investment flowing to the developing world.[15] Second, financial demands of development remain great and the type of finance that is most likely to grow in the future is private foreign investment. Third, throughout the developing world, one can ask whether countries receiving foreign direct investment maximize its potential — whether better laws and policies will not only increase the amount of foreign investment received but will also enable host countries to use what is received to greater effect, thereby achieving increased benefits from that investment for both the investor and the host country. In short, all developing countries need to ask themselves two fundamental questions about foreign direct investment: (1) How can they get more?; and (2) How can they maximize the benefits and minimize the costs of the foreign investment they receive?

With regard to the first question, one must make a preliminary inquiry: What influences flows of direct foreign investment to developing countries? Certainly, the natural attributes of a given country, including the size of its market, the quality of its infrastructure and educated work force, and its geographic location, among others, are powerful factors that attract foreign investment to particular host countries. But there is equally strong evidence, as Dr. Shihata has long argued, that legal and administrative structures can also influence the nature, direction, and use of investment flows. The International Finance Corporation (IFC), in a 1997 publication entitled *Direct Foreign Investment: Lessons of Experience*, stated one important lesson:

> "The flow and direction of FDI flows respond to the national and international policy environment."[16]

The term "national policy environment" is a somewhat vague concept. But whatever else is included within in it, certainly the legal system is a vital part. Law and the legal system are the means by which policy is made real and applied. Policy without law to support it is a mere academic exercise.

---

15 *Ibid.* at 72.

16 *See* LESSONS OF EXPERIENCE, *supra* note 1, at 20.

IV. THE LINK BETWEEN LAW AND INVESTMENT

What then is the link between law and investment? Host country governments need to understand that fundamental link as they go about creating their policy environments and developing their legal and administrative systems. The link lies in two concepts that are basic to the investment decision: *risk* and *return*. Investors will commit funds to a project when in their judgment the project will yield a satisfactory return at an acceptable level of risk. They will refuse to invest when the reward is insufficient in view of the expected risk.

Laws, legal institutions, administrative structures, indeed whole legal systems may have either a positive or a negative impact on an investor's evaluation of the risks and returns of a potential investment in a developing country. For example, a host country's high tax regime, lengthy and cumbersome governmental procedures, and prohibitive foreign exchange controls reduce returns to the investor and thus serve to deter investment. Similarly, an independent judiciary strongly committed to the sanctity of business contracts and their expeditious enforcement creates a less risky and therefore a more investment-friendly environment than does a corrupt system of courts characterized by ten-year backlogs of cases and decisions that are invariably influenced by the country's governing elite.

Faced with an environment of heightened risk, an investor may do one of two things: (1) abstain from investing in that country; or (2) structure the investment in such a way as to increase returns to offset the risk created by the environment. Thus, in the end, the legal and policy environment may deny a potential host country foreign investment or force it to pay more for investment capital than would a more effective legal system. Similarly, laws and regulations which raise transactions costs, such as lengthy and cumbersome business licensing requirements, may also force the investor to seek higher returns on its investment than it would otherwise require.

During the last fifteen years, many developing countries, with the help of the World Bank and other agencies, have engaged in law reform that has served to reduce the costs and risks of foreign investment to investors and thereby encouraged the flow of private foreign capital. At the same time, they have participated in a variety of international measures such as bilateral investment treaties,[17] international arbitration conventions,[18] the Multilateral Investment Guarantee Agency,[19] and the International Centre for Settlement of Investment Disputes,[20] all of whose fundamental purposes have been to reduce the risk of international investment and thereby encourage private capital flows to developing countries. Nonetheless, certain law-related obstacles to investment do remain. It is therefore important to understand them and to determine the extent to which they may be reduced.

V. THE NATURE OF LAW-RELATED OBSTACLES TO INVESTMENT

What precisely are law-related obstacles? Bearing in mind the crucial importance of investor perception of return and risk on the

---

[17] As of the end of 1996, 1300 bilateral investment treaties had been signed, all of which involved at least one developing country. Two thirds of this number had been concluded in the 1990's. Kenneth J. Vandevelde, *Investment Liberalization and Economic Development: The Role of Bilateral Investment Treaties,* 36 COLUMBIA JOURNAL OF TRANSNATIONAL LAW 500, 503 (1998). *See also* Jeswald W. Salacuse, *BIT by BIT: The Growth of Bilateral Treaties and Their Impact on Foreign Investment in Developing Countries*, 24 THE INTERNATIONAL LAWYER 655–675 (1990).

[18] *See, e.g.,* Convention on the Recognition and Enforcement of Foreign Arbitral Awards, June 10, 1958, 21 U.S.T. 2517, T.I.A.S. No. 6997, 330 U.N.T.S. 3. As of December 1, 1998, 119 states had ratified the Convention. INSTITUTE OF TRANSNATIONAL ARBITRATION , SCOREBOARD OF ADHERENCE TO TRANSNATIONAL ARBITRATION TREATIES (as of Dec. 1, 1998) (1999). By contrast, in 1987, only 77 countries had ratified the Convention. *Ibid.,* as of July 1, 1987 (1987). The increase in membership came largely from the ranks of Third World Countries.

[19] Convention Establishing the Multilateral Investment Guarantee Agency, October 11, 1985, *reprinted in* 24 INTERNATIONAL LEGAL MATERIALS 1599, 1605 (1985). *See also* Shihata, *supra* note 10.

[20] Convention on the Settlement of Investment Disputes Between States and Nationals of Other States, *done* at Washington, D.C., Mar. 18, 1965, [1965] 17 U.S.T. 1270, T.I.A.S. No. 6090, 575 U.N.T.S. 159. As of 1998, 144 states had signed the Convention and 129 had ratified it. ICSID, 1998 ANNUAL REPORT 4 (1998). In 1984, by contrast, 90 countries had signed and 86 countries had ratified the Convention. ICSID, 1984 ANNUAL REPORT 6 (1984). The increase in membership is largely attributable to developing countries. Of particular interest is that the 1990s witnessed many Latin American countries, such as Argentina, Chile, Columbia, Peru and Venezuela join ICSID, thus overcoming the strictures of the Calvo doctrine (yet another manifestation of the drive for economic independence) which had previously caused them to refrain from participating in international arbitration arrangements.

size and direction of foreign investment flows, one needs to give this term a broad and comprehensive definition. Law-related obstacles mean much more than the provisions found in individual laws and regulations, for example the tax rate on profits or the documentary requirements to obtain a license to open a factory. Law-related obstacles to foreign investment are to be found at three levels: (1) the level of individual legal provisions that create obstacles by unreasonably raising risks or reducing returns to investment in developing countries (the legislative level); (2) legal and administrative institutions which function in such a way as to impede investment (the institutional level); and (3) systemic factors — i.e., fundamental problems in the functioning of the legal system as a whole. Let us address the obstacles at each of these three levels in turn. As one makes this survey, it is important to underscore the fact that all developing countries are not alike, that their laws and legal systems demonstrate great variety, and that some have relatively few significant law-related obstacles while others have a great many.

VI. LEVEL 1: LEGISLATIVE AND REGULATORY PROVISIONS

Many individual laws and regulations serve to impede foreign investment because they unreasonably increase risks or reduce returns to the investor. These provisions can be grouped into six basic categories: (a) restrictions on foreign investment entry into the country; (b) licensing requirements and administrative approvals; (c) limits on foreign exchange transfers; (d) operational requirements; (e) limitations on the use and ownership of land and natural resources; and (f) onerous taxation requirements. Let us look briefly at each of these and their impact on foreign investment in developing countries.

A. Restrictions On Foreign Investment Entry

Probably no country today imposes an outright ban on the entry of all foreign investment. Nonetheless one can find throughout the developing world a variety of lesser restrictions on entry.

Some of these bans are sectoral. That is, legislation limits or prohibits foreign investment from acquiring interests in certain sectors, such as retail trade, electrical power generation, or shipping. The justification for the sectoral bans are often stated in grandiose, but vague terms: "national security," "protection of strategic industries," or the need to control the "commanding heights of the economy." Upon close analysis, one sometimes finds that such justifications are pretexts for protecting the interests of certain elites, rather than the public interest in general.

Many of these sectoral bans are falling. India, for example, which had made electrical power generation a virtual state monopoly since the 1950s, lifted the ban in the early 1990's to encourage foreign direct investment to enter this sector as a means to alleviate the country's desperate shortage of electricity.[21] Countries should examine carefully their sectoral bans and ask certain hard questions: Precisely what national interests are being advanced by bans on foreign investment in specified sectors? What has been the record of national capital, public and private, in developing those sectors? What positive contribution could FDI make to such sectors in the current circumstances? New devices, such as the Build-Operate-Transfer (BOT) concept, have facilitated the lifting of certain sectoral restrictions while still permitting governments to assert that they have not turned over vital sectors permanently to foreign interests.

In addition to sectoral bans are two other relatively common, but questionable legal provisions on foreign investment: joint venture requirements and performance requirements.

Joint venture requirements, sometimes referred to as equity restrictions, provide that foreign investment may not enter the country or a particular sector unless it includes the participation of local capital. Laws often limit the permissible amount of foreign equity participation in the project to a maximum percentage, sometimes to less than fifty percent. Many justifications are advanced for this requirement: to prevent control of the national economy by foreigners, to facilitate the transfer of technology and management skills to nationals, to develop national capital, to increase the like-

---

21 *See, e.g.*, R. P. Teisch & W. A. Stoever, *Enron in India — Lessons From a Renegotiation*, 35 THE MID-ATLANTIC JOURNAL OF BUSINESS 51–62 (1999).

lihood that the project will be managed in accordance with national interests.[22] It is not clear that these justifications are always valid or realistic. Here too, the time has come for developing countries to reevaluate the purpose and record of joint venture requirements and equity restrictions. They should examine their experience carefully to determine whether they have derived the benefits desired and whether the benefits achieved outweigh the costs incurred by the host country.

Strong arguments exist that these restrictions raise the cost of private capital to the host country and may prevent it from using the investment received to maximum advantage. For example, there is evidence that foreign investors in joint ventures tend to transfer less advanced technology to joint ventures than to wholly owned subsidiaries which give them greater assurance of protecting their technology from appropriation by local partners and others. Also, in such imposed joint ventures, the investor's commitment to the future development of the project may be less than optimum; consequently, it may focus on gaining revenues through its contractual arrangements with the project (for example as a supplier of technology) rather than as a project owner. Further, the project's potential for growth may be limited by the joint venture requirement because the foreign investor is saddled with a local partner who does not have the financial or managerial resources to build and develop the enterprise or take advantage of new opportunities after it has been established.

Performance requirements, a second entry restriction, are conditions imposed by law or administrative regulation that mandate, as a condition for entry, that the foreign investment project function in a particular way, for example that it export a minimum percentage of its production or that it purchase a minimum amount of locally produced inputs. Rather than let market factors determine such production decisions, host countries seek to compel them by law, often with perverse results. Performance requirements generally raise the cost of production, which in turn increases the price of goods sold to consumers in the host country and the level of return required by the investor. Here too, countries should examine the utility of these requirements. The World Trade Organization

---

22 *See* STRENG & SALACUSE, INTERNATIONAL BUSINESS PLANNING: LAW AND TAXATION s. 19.09 (1986).

(WTO) Agreement on Trade Related Investment Measures (TRIMS), which emerged from the Uruguay General Agreement on Tariffs and Trade (GATT) Negotiations, has made many of these performance requirements illegal when applied by one WTO member against another.

B. Licensing Requirements and Administrative Approvals

Many developing countries have created elaborate systems requiring government screening and approval before an investment can be made. These systems are ostensibly designed to protect national interests and to make sure that investments comply with the law. On the other hand, in practice one finds that approval requirements increase the expense and time required to implement an investment project. Such delays can extend up to two years. It is therefore time for developing countries to weigh the costs and benefits of their investment approval systems and procedures.

Beyond the special approvals required for foreign investors are the many approvals that all business enterprises, both foreign and domestic, in the host country must secure in order to operate. As a result of colonial legacies and post-independence emphasis on centralized state planning, many if not most developing countries have created pervasive systems of regulation to control and sometimes curtail the private sector. In order to direct the private sector toward the achievement of developmental goals, third-world governments subjected private enterprises to pervasive regulation on such fundamental matters as investment, product prices, currency exchange, trading operations, business formations, technology transfers, and wages and salaries of workers. The systems that emerged seemed based on a fundamental legal principle: no economic activity is permitted unless the state has specifically approved it.[23] The pervasiveness of regulation was so great in India, for example, that business executives called the country the "License Raj."

---

[23] *See generally,* J. W. Salacuse, *From Developing Countries to Emerging Markets: A New Role For Law in the Third World,* 33 THE INTERNATIONAL LAWYER (Winter, 1999).

These regulatory systems have a variety of negative consequences: they discourage investment, both foreign and local; they raise the costs of investment that is made; and they often force local businesses to operate outside the law in the so-called "informal sector." Government officials, administrators, and even academics can always offer facile justifications for the importance of regulation — especially if they earn their salaries by enforcing or explaining them. But rather than remain in the abstract realm of speculation, host country governments should examine the actual experience of foreign investors in dealing with them. They should adopt the approach of the Peruvian economist Hernando De Soto, described in his book *The Other Path,*[24] who carefully documented the time and cost necessary for a small business enterprise to comply with all the regulations necessary to do business in Peru. His conclusion was that the regulatory burden was so heavy and expensive that it forced many small businesses to act illegally and to become part of the "informal sector." For De Soto and others who studied the problem, regulation has been a brake on development. Not only has it thwarted economic initiative, but it also permitted elites and oligarchies to exploit the poor, and it created significant opportunities for governmental corruption by bureaucrats who had gained a valuable monopoly on awarding permits, licenses and authorizations.[25]

As developing countries proceed with the task of examining actual business experience with their regulatory systems, they would seek to determine the real, rather than hypothetical benefits and costs — not only to specific businesses but to the country as a whole. They should ask, for example, the extent to which regulation has contributed to corruption in the civil service by giving bureaucrats discretionary power over the allocation of scarce resources and opportunities. They should also seek to determine whether and how they can convert the old basic principle that "nothing is permitted unless specifically approved" to a new principle: every economic activity is permitted unless specifically prohibited.

---

24 HERNANDO DE SOTO, THE OTHER PATH— THE INVISIBLE REVOLUTION IN THE THIRD WORLD (1989).

25 *See generally*, ROBERT G. KLITGAARD, CONTROLLING CORRUPTION (1988).

C. Foreign Exchange Restrictions

For virtually all foreign investors, restrictions on repatriation of capital and profits and on the ability to secure foreign exchange for the purchase of raw materials and to service foreign debts are major barriers to investment in relevant host countries. For example, in 1986 an IFC Foreign Investment Advisory Service survey of almost 100 actual and potential investors in China found that their biggest impediment to investment was China's foreign exchange system. It is interesting to note that the great inflow of foreign investment to China dates from the time after China reformed that system, particularly when it did away with a strict application of the rule that a foreign investor could only repatriate funds to the extent that it earned foreign exchange.[26] Foreign exchange regulations are therefore yet another law-related obstacle that needs to be addressed.

D. Operational Requirements

Once an enterprise obtains the necessary licenses and approvals and actually begins business, it often faces a host of complex, costly legal requirements on its operations whose effect is to reduce returns or increase risks to the investor. These operational requirements include price controls, restrictions on the use of expatriate personnel in the enterprise, and customs clearing procedures, among hundreds of others.

In many cases, as with licensing requirements, such legal obstacles to foreign investment are necessary to protect vital public interests, such as the environment and the health and safety of workers. The point here is that host governments should examine the actual experience with these operational requirements to see whether in fact they are achieving their intended purposes and at what cost.

---

26 LESSONS OF EXPERIENCE, *supra* note 1, at 35–36.

E. Restrictions on Access to and Use of Land and Natural Resources

The acquisition by foreigners of rights in land and natural resources is in many countries a sensitive and emotional issue. Even in the United States, which has traditionally had an open-door policy to foreign investment, large foreign investments in land, for example the purchase by Arab interests of agricultural land in the West and mid-west and the acquisition by the Japanese of Rockefeller Center in New York, provoked outcries about the need to protect the national patrimony from foreigners.

In response, many countries have adopted restrictions that prevent foreigners from acquiring rights in land. In others, the land law system is so inadequate that it cannot assure investors of clear defensible rights in land or the natural resources necessary for their operations. These phenomena also constitute law-related obstacles to foreign investment. No firm wants to invest without secure tenure of the land on which its facilities are located or the natural resources that are essential for its operations. Faced with the increased risks entailed by inadequate or insecure tenure, the investor will either avoid the investment or demand a high rate of return to compensate for the added risk. For example, Indonesia had traditionally allowed foreign investors in the production of tropical tree products to obtain a long-term lease on land for this purpose. In 1980, a presidential degree provided that a foreign company or a joint venture in which a foreign company was a partner could no longer hold such a long-term lease. Instead, the Indonesian partner could obtain the lease and convey a right of use to the joint venture. Foreign investment in the sector virtually ceased as a result. No investor was willing to commit substantial funds to a venture to plant trees requiring at least eight years to mature without long-term control of the land on which those trees were planted.[27]

F. Taxation

Taxation law, including customs duties and fiscal charges of all sorts, constitute a final set of barriers at the legislative level.

---

27 *Ibid.* at 37.

Taxes that are too high are without question an obstacle to investment.

In addition to examining individual taxes required of the investor, developing countries need to study the investor's total effective tax burden, levied from all sources, to begin to understand its effect on inward investment flows. Many developing countries have maintained high tax rates while granting tax exemptions and incentives of all sorts to selected, approved investments. This approach should be questioned. First, governments may be giving incentives to firms that do not need them, thus needlessly forgoing tax revenue. Second, special tax incentives often raise issues of discrimination between local firms and foreign firms. Third, they sometimes cause distortion in business decision making. Fourth, the discretion in granting them sometimes leads to corruption. For these reasons, a moderate tax system with few special investment incentives is preferable to a high tax rate system with many incentives and exemptions.

VII. LEVEL 2: INSTITUTIONS

One can not talk about law-related obstacles to investment by reference to legislative provisions alone. It is also important to examine the institutions that apply and enforce those laws. Institutions give laws their reality.

A. Foreign Investment Agencies

Many, if not most, developing countries have created agencies to apply their foreign investment laws. Their authorizing legislation usually states that such agencies are to do three things: to promote, to screen and to monitor foreign investments. In reality, most agencies see their primary function as screening foreign investment proposals; consequently, they sometimes become one more obstacle in the foreign investment process. They are often slow to approve investment, impose costly requirements, and often try to renegotiate arrangements that have already been decided.

Some investment agencies claim to be "one-stop shops," in that they provide a single office that grants all the approvals necessary. In fact, that usually does not happen, since other ministries and government agencies may refuse to give up their power to grant approvals.

A fundamental issue is how to turn such agencies into true investment promotion organizations that will really bring investment to the country and genuinely help foreign investors in getting started. Their change of mission begins with engaging the right personnel, persons with knowledge of, and sympathy for business and investment, rather than merely civil servants who have served time in some economic-related ministry. For example, an investment banker may be a more appropriate person to lead such an agency than a former central bank foreign exchange controller whose basic instinct in reviewing any proposal is to say "no."

B. Other Executive Agencies and Organizations

A foreign investor will come into contact with a host of other governmental agencies and organizations in developing countries, just as it would in any country. But here too, the principal issue is whether these agencies and organizations really function in accordance with the legislative scheme. Various approvals, such as those concerning environmental protection and the health and safety of workers, are necessary to protect the public interest, but to what extent is the approval process carried out efficiently, effectively, and fairly? Or to what extent is it an occasion for delay, increased costs, and corrupt payments? For example, the legal formation of a company in many countries can be accomplished within a few days, a week at most. In some countries, however, it takes much longer. Why? Because the request to form a company is used by the company registrar to review the business plan of the proposed company, something that had already been done by the investment agency.

C. The Courts

Another institution of key importance is the judiciary. It is the judiciary that resolves business disputes, enforces the laws as written, protects property rights, and assures the sanctity of contract —

matters of key importance for all investors, both national and foreign. By performing judicial functions properly, the courts can reduce political and commercial risk to investors, thereby contributing to an environment favorable to investment.

In many countries which have gone through an era of heavy state planning, of the domination of the public sector over the private sector, and of the overwhelming control of the executive over the other two branches, the courts have been relegated to a very subordinate role in economic life. Indeed, during that period, many developing country governments sought constantly to strengthen their powers in the name of development and to weaken the judiciary which might thwart them. Although most developing countries have today shifted their macro-economic orientation away from state planning, a command economy, and heavy regulation, and are trying to strengthen the private sector, they need to remember the key role that a judiciary plays in supporting the private sector.

Many countries, as part of economic transformation and with the help of international agencies such as the World Bank (another area in which Dr. Shihata has played a vital role),[28] have undertaken judicial reform programs to improve the training of judges and court personnel, to provide courts with the material resources necessary for their new role, to modernize the judicial process, and to develop alternative methods of dispute resolution. The specific goals of judicial reform efforts include increased efficiency and dispatch in handling cases, a reduction in levels of corruption among judges and judicial personnel, and heightened knowledge to understand the sophisticated transactions of a private enterprise economy and to judge disputes that may arise in connection with them.[29] Similarly, private attorneys in those countries are having to assume new and expanded roles to serve the new players in private sector. More than ever before, the imperatives of a market economy require them to have the skills to plan, negotiate, and structure transactions on behalf of clients.

---

[28] *See* IBRAHIM F. I. SHIHATA, THE WORLD BANK IN A CHANGING WORLD, Vol. II, 147–182 (1995), Chapter Four (*Judicial Reform In Developing Countries and the Role of the World Bank*).

[29] *See, e.g.*, Maria Dakolias, *A Strategy For Judicial Reform: The Experience of Latin America*, 36 VIRGINIA JOURNAL OF INTERNATIONAL LAW 53–231 (1995).

VIII. LEVEL 3: SYSTEMIC ISSUES

Beyond legislative provisions and the functioning of institutions are issues related to the legal system as a whole. Three of the most important systemic issues which have concerned the World Bank and its legal department under Dr. Shihata have included:

A. Respect for Property Rights and the Sanctity of Contract

During an era of command economies and autocratic governments, many developing countries had either allowed private law to languish or had actively sought to limit its application, particularly with respect to private property rights and the sanctity of contract. Thus, the developing world witnessed wide spread expropriations of private property, both foreign and nationally owned, as well as laws that placed increasing limitations on freedom of contract.

Private rights and the sanctity of contract are legal elements that underlie the market system and foreign investment. To the extent that they are strengthened, a more favorable investment climate is created. Expropriation in developing countries has declined in recent years, and many developing countries, through more than 1300 bilateral investment treaties, have sought to guarantee foreign investment against expropriation. A few developing countries have placed somewhat less emphasis on the respect for contracts. But a climate in which contracts may not be respected is one which impedes investment. For example, in 1995 when the state of Maharashtra in India cancelled its long-term contract to purchase electricity from a power project being constructed by Enron, an American company, that action, ultimately resolved through negotiation, had a chilling effect for a time on other investors contemplating India as a site for investment.

In addition, many developing countries' systems of private law need modernization and reform to meet the demands of private enterprise at the end of the twentieth century. Thus with the advent of market economies, developing countries, sometimes with the help of foreign advisers, have undertaken law reform programs to write new commercial codes, company laws, land laws, and legislation on secured transactions, bankruptcy, stock exchanges and taxation.[30]

In addition to the development of private law, countries seeking foreign investment must develop a new approach to regulation. While current policies may favor "deregulation," this does not mean that all regulation should end. Regulation of markets and private transactions is necessary to be sure that the rules of the game are clear and that the private players abide by those rules and play fairly. Markets as a means for allocating society's resources require a minimum level of regulation not only to protect participants but to maintain society's confidence in those markets as fair and efficient allocators of resources. Whereas the essential role of regulation in command economies was to direct transactions in particular ways that the government judged necessary, the role of regulation in market economies is to protect participants in the market from fraud, coercion, and abuse by other participants.

B. The Rule of Law

A major law-related obstacle to investment in many countries is the absence or weakness of the rule of law.[31] The rule of law is of course vital for democracy, but one can also argue that it is equally important for investment because it reduces risks — the risks of arbitrary governmental action. For foreign investors, the rule of law in the host country is a risk-reduction device, and it also saves on transaction costs.

An effective rule of law means that actions by the governmental authorities are in accordance with rules known to all. The basic requirements for the rule of law include: (1) that the law is known to all those to whom it applies (i.e., transparency); (2) that the law is applied equally and even-handedly to those for whom it is intended; (3) that governmental action is done only in accor-

---

30 *See, e.g.*, Thomas W. Wälde & James L. Gunderson, *Legislative Reform in Transition Economies: Western Transplants-A Short-Cut to Social Market Economy Status?*, 43 INTERNATIONAL & COMPARATIVE LAW QUARTERLY 347–378 (1994).

31 *See generally*, Thomas Carothers, *The Rule of Law Revival*, 77 FOREIGN AFFAIRS 95–106 (March/April 1998).

dance with stipulated and known rules of law; and (4) that governmental authorities are accountable through legal process for their actions.[32] Investors who know the law can plan. In this respect, it is well to remember the work of the great German legal sociologist Max Weber who sought to understand why capitalism grew up in Europe. He attributed it in part to European law, one of whose important attributes was that it gave "predictability" to human transactions, thus facilitating the kinds of long-term economic transactions necessary for productive investment.[33] An effective rule of law helps to provide predictability for investors in developing countries and thus facilitates investment.

C. Corruption

The final systemic issue of note is corruption, specifically governmental corruption, which one may define as "the abuse of public office for private gain." Although it is found throughout the world, corruption in developing countries can be a significant obstacle to foreign investment because it raises the costs of doing business, thereby reducing returns to the investor.[34] Given its unpredictable nature, substantial governmental corruption also increases investor risks. It raises the cost of capital to host countries, facilitates unproductive or inappropriate investment projects, and leads to a general lowering of standards.[35] While corruption is by no means a purely legal problem calling for a purely legal solution, there is little doubt that effective strategies to reduce corruption begin with an effective legal framework.[36]

---

32 *See generally,* IBRAHIM F.I. SHIHATA, COMPLEMENTARY REFORM: ESSAYS ON LEGAL, JUDICIAL AND OTHER INSTITUTIONAL REFORMS SUPPORTED BY THE WORLD BANK 3–30 (1997), Chapter One (*Law, Development And The Role Of The World Bank*).

33 *See generally,* David Trubeck, *Towards a Social Theory of Law: An Essay on the Study of Law and Development,* 82 YALE LAW JOURNAL 1, 50 (1972).

34 *See generally,* Paolo Mauro, *Corruption and Growth,* 110 QUARTERLY JOURNAL OF ECONOMICS 681 (1995).

35 *See* CURBING CORRUPTION: TOWARD A MODEL FOR BUILDING NATIONAL INTEGRITY 3–4 (Rick Stapenhurst & Sahr J. Kpunedeh eds., 1999).

36 *See generally,* W. PAATI OFOSU-AMAAH, RAJ SOOPRAMANIEN & KISHOR UPRETY, COMBATING CORRUPTION: A COMPARATIVE REVIEW OF SELECTED LEGAL ASPECTS OF STATE PRACTICE AND MAJOR INTERNATIONAL INITIATIVES (1999).

IX. CONCLUSION: ONE PERSON'S LEGAL OBSTACLE IS ANOTHER PERSON'S PROTECTION

Key issues affecting foreign investment in developing countries are legislative, institutional, and systemic. A variety of mechanisms exist to address them. They include treaties to establish investor-friendly standards and law reform programs. On the other hand, it is well to remember that all law-related obstacles to investment may not necessarily be bad. Many of them exist to protect important national interests such as the environment, health and safety of workers, and indigenous cultures. One person's obstacle is another person's protection. Consequently, in any program of reform aimed at these obstacles, it is important to balance the benefits and costs of retaining them against the benefits and costs to be derived from new investment. Such balancing of interests is of course the traditional job of the law.

THE PRECAUTIONARY PRINCIPLE: NEW BATTLEGROUND FOR ENVIRONMENT AND DEVELOPMENT?

Peter H. Sand

This paper will address a focal issue of contemporary global environmental policy, an area which has long been among the topics of personal interest to Dr. Ibrahim Shihata — both in his professional work at the World Bank, and in his active contributions to legal theory, such as the 1997 Strasbourg resolutions on environmental law by the *Institut de Droit International.* The 'precautionary principle' has indeed been described as "the most important new policy approach in international environmental cooperation."[1] After making its debut in a number of 'soft law' declarations in the 1980s,[2] it has since found its way into at least fourteen 'hard'

[1] D. Freestone, *The Precautionary Principle, in* INTERNATIONAL LAW AND GLOBAL CLIMATE CHANGE 36 (R. Churchill & D. Freestone eds., 1991); *see also* J. Cameron & J. Abouchar, *The Precautionary Principle: A Fundamental Principle of Law and Policy for the Protection of the Global Environment*, 14 BOSTON COLLEGE INTERNATIONAL AND COMPARATIVE LAW REVIEW 1,1 (1991); E. Hey, *The Precautionary Concept in Environmental Policy and Law: Institutionalizing Caution*, 4 GEORGETOWN INTERNATIONAL ENVIRONMENTAL LAW REVIEW 303, 303 (1992); H. HOHMANN, PRECAUTIONARY LEGAL DUTIES AND PRINCIPLES OF MODERN INTERNATIONAL ENVIRONMENTAL LAW: THE PRECAUTIONARY PRINCIPLE (1994); THE PRECAUTIONARY PRINCIPLE AND INTERNATIONAL LAW: THE CHALLENGE OF IMPLEMENTATION (D. Freestone & E. Hey eds., 1995); F.G. Primosch, *Das Vorsorgeprinzip im Internationalen Umweltrecht*, 51 AUSTRIAN JOURNAL OF PUBLIC AND INTERNATIONAL LAW 227, 227(1996); O. McIntyre & T. Mosedale, *The Precautionary Principle as a Norm of Customary International Law*, 9 JOURNAL OF ENVIRONMENTAL LAW (1997), at 221; P. Martin-Bidou, *Le Principe de Précaution en Droit International de l'Environnement*, 103 REVUE GÉNÉRALE DE DROIT INTERNATIONAL PUBLIC 631,631 (1999).

[2] *E.g.*, the 1982 World Charter for Nature, UN General Assembly Resolution 37/7, principle 11; the Ministerial Declarations of the International Conferences on the Protection of the North Sea (Bremen 1984, London 1987); and decision 15/27 (1989) of the Governing Council of the UN Environment Programmme.

multilateral agreements.[3] Yet, its invocation remains controversial — sometimes explosively so: witness the collapse of negotiations for a biosafety protocol at the Cartagena meeting in February 1999, where disagreement on 'precautionary' draft provisions was a contributing factor.[4]

To avoid some of the confusion surrounding the debate,[5] let us take, as a starting point, the core definition as formulated in Principle 15 of the 1992 *Rio Declaration on Environment and Development*:[6] "Where there are threats of serious or irreversible

---

3 The 1991 Bamako Convention on the Ban of Import into Africa and the Control of Transboundary Movement and Management of Hazardous Wastes Within Africa, art. 4(3)(f); the 1992 UN Framework Convention on Climate Change, art. 3(3); the 1992 Convention on Biological Diversity, preamble; the 1992 UN/ECE Convention on the Protection and Use of Transboundary Watercourses and International Lakes, art. 2(5)(a), and its 1999 London Protocol on Water and Health, art. 5(a); the 1992 Paris Convention for the Protection of the Marine Environment of the North-East Atlantic, art. 2(2)(a); the 1992 Helsinki Convention for the Protection of the Baltic Sea Area, art. 3(2); the 1994 Oslo Protocol (on sulphur emission reductions); the 1998 Aarhus Protocols (on heavy metals, and on persistent organic pollutants) and the 1999 Gothenburg Protocol (on acidification, eutrophication and ground-level ozone) to the Convention on Long-Range Transboundary Air Pollution, preambles; the 1995 Straddling Fish Stocks Agreement implementing the UN Convention on the Law of the Sea, art. 6(2); the 1996 Syracuse Amendment Protocol for the Protection of the Mediterranean Sea Against Pollution from Land-Based Sources, preamble; and the 1996 London Amendment Protocol to the Convention on the Prevention of Marine Pollution by Dumping of Wastes and Other Matter, art. 1(3). According to a 1996 decision by the Indian Supreme Court, the precautionary principle has already become part of customary international law; *see* Vellore, *Citizens Welfare Forum vs. Union of India*, ALL INDIA REPORTER [1996] SC 2715, 9 JOURNAL OF ENVIRONMENTAL LAW (1997), at 387.

4 Meeting summary, *in* 9 EARTH NEGOTIATIONS BULLETIN No. 117, Feb.26, 1999, at 3, 11, <http://www.iisd.ca/linkages/biodiv/bswg6>. The controversy was only partly resolved by a compromise formula in the final text of the protocol adopted in Montreal on Jan. 29, 2000 (art. 10).

5 *See* the critical comments by L. Gündling, *The Status in International Law of the Principle of Precautionary Action*, 5 INTERNATIONAL JOURNAL OF ESTUARINE AND COASTAL LAW (1990), at 26; and D. Bodansky, *Scientific Uncertainty and the Precautionary Principle*, 33 ENVIRONMENT No. 7 (1991), at 4.

6 Report of the UN Conference on Environment and Development (Rio de Janeiro, June 3-14, 1992), UN Doc. A/CONF,151/26/Rev.1, Vol. I (1993), at 6. On the drafting of the declaration (by Working Group III of the UNCED Preparatory Committee, mainly during the 3rd and 4th PrepCom sessions in Aug. 1991 and Mar. 1992), *see* H. Mann, *The Rio Declaration*, *in* PROCEEDINGS OF THE 86TH Meeting of the American Society of International Law (1992), AT 405; AND T.T. KOH, *UNCED Leadership: A Personal Perspective*, *in* NEGOTIATING INTERNATIONAL REGIMES: LESSONS LEARNED FROM

damage, lack of full scientific certainty shall not be used as a reason for postponing cost-effective measures to prevent environmental degradation." Save for the not-so-innocuous rider 'cost-effective' — which originated in the 1990 World Climate Conference,[7] and which was slipped into the Rio text by the US delegation, over the objections of the European Union and Japan,[8] — that sentence in Principle 15 was a *verbatim* quote from the 1990 Bergen Declaration by thirty-four environment ministers from Europe and North America.[9]

Predictably, therefore, the principle was eyed with some suspicion by Third World countries (the so-called 'Group of 77'), who always considered it a typical 'Northern' demand and who swallowed it without enthusiasm at the time, and only in return for the

---

THE UNITED NATIONS CONFERENCE ON ENVIRONMENT AND DEVELOPMENT (UNCED) (B.I. Spector, G. Sjostedt & I.W. Zartman eds., 1994), at 168. It has been pointed out that negotiations for the Rio Declaration "were — except perhaps those on the financial resources chapter of the UNCED action plan, *Agenda 21* — the most overtly political of the UNCED process," I.M. Porras, *The Rio Declaration: A New Basis for International Cooperation*, in GREENING INTERNATIONAL LAW (P. Sands ed., 1994), at 22. *See also* P.H. Sand, *UNCED and the Development of International Environmental Law*, 3 YEARBOOK OF INTERNATIONAL ENVIRONMENTAL LAW 3, 8 (1992).

7 Ministerial Declaration of the Second World Climate Conference (Geneva, Nov. 7, 1990), art. 7, 1 YEARBOOK OF INTERNATIONAL ENVIRONMENTAL LAW (1990), at 475; *see* J.D. Kovar, *A Short Guide to the Rio Declaration*, 4 COLORADO JOURNAL OF INTERNATIONAL ENVIRONMENTAL LAW AND POLICY 119, 134 (1993).

8 While the prefix 'cost-' had not been part of the original US draft proposal submitted to the 4th PrepCom session in New York (A/CONF.151/PC/WG.III/L.21 of Mar. 4, 1992, principle 6), it was added as an oral 'correction' by the US delegate, State Department lawyer Jeffrey D. Kovar, Mar. 12, 1992. Even though both the delegates of Portugal (on behalf of the European Union) and of Japan, Mar. 24,1992, proposed to delete the rider, Working Group III retained it [within square brackets] in the Chairman's draft of Mar. 31, 1992 (A/CONF.151/PC/WG.III/L.33, principle 12) which served as the basis for Tommy Koh's final re-draft forwarded to the Rio Conference (A/CONF.151/PC/WG.III/L.33/Rev.1, principle 15).

9 Ministerial Declaration on Sustainable Development in the [UN] ECE Region (Bergen/Norway, May 16, 1990), art. 7, 1 YEARBOOK OF INTERNATIONAL ENVIRONMENTAL LAW (1990), at 431; also incorporated in art. 3(3) of the UN Framework Convention on Climate Change, 1992. Inclusion of that same sentence, with only minor variations, was formally proposed in the pre-Rio negotiations by the USA (*see* note 8), by the European Union (A/CONF.151/PC/WG.III/L.25 of Mar. 6, 1992, principle 6, revising an earlier proposal submitted at the 3rd PrepCom session, and replacing 'should' by 'shall'), and by the Scandinavian countries (A/CONF.151/PC/WG.III/L.27 of Mar. 9, 1992, principle 11).

acceptance of other 'Southern' points in the bargain.[10] It is all the more ironic now, eight years after Rio, to see the United States and its 'Miami group' in the biosafety negotiations *opposing* the precautionary principle — and the Group of 77 (now called the 'like-minded group') *defending* it, with diplomatic support from the European Union.

Not that the Europeans have been all that unanimous about it all this time. In 1995, when the precautionary principle was for the first time invoked before the International Court of Justice — in the *Nuclear Tests* case brought by New Zealand against France — the French Government responded that the legal status of the principle was 'uncertain.'[11] And not so long ago, the UK Government had even less kind things to say about the principle when it was invoked by the European Commission as a reason for precautionary trade restrictions against the risk of BSE ('mad cow' disease).[12] Principles are principles — alas, the French bomb is the French bomb; and British beef is British beef.

From the point of view of comparative law, a country-by-country study commissioned by the German Federal Environmental Agency in 1990 came to the conclusion that there are indeed two distinct camps in the modern industrialized world: 'precaution countries' (including Germany, the Netherlands, Sweden, and Switzerland, along with the United States); and 'protection coun-

---

10 The original proposal submitted on Mar. 4, 1992 by China and by Pakistan (on behalf of the Group of 77, A/CONF.151/PC/WG.III/L.20) made no reference to the precautionary principle, but eventually took it on board — albeit with a rider reserving the special socio-economic situation of developing countries, again drawn from the ministerial declaration of the Second World Climate Conference (*see* note 7) — in a revised compromise draft on Mar. 19, 1992 (A/CONF.151/PC/WG.III/L.20/Rev.1, principle 12). The United States reserved its position on some of the 'Southern' points (by way of an 'interpretative statement' at the time of adoption of the Rio Declaration, A/CONF.151/26, vol. IV, para. 16, but did *not* object to principle 15; Kovar, *see* note 7, at 122.

11 International Court of Justice (The Hague, Sept. 12, 1995), *Verbatim Record* CR 995/20, at 56; *see* M. Bothe, *Challenging French Nuclear Tests: A Role for Legal Remedies?*, 5 Review of European Community and International Environmental Law 253, 253 (1996).

12 A. Giddens, *Risk and Responsibility*, 62 Modern Law Review 1, 9 (1999); *id.*, *Risk Society: The Context of British Politics, in* The Politics of Risk Society 29 (J. Franklin ed., 1998).

tries' (including France and the UK, along with Japan).[13] Historically, to be sure, the precautionary principle in Europe goes back much further than the often-quoted German Environment Report of 1976,[14] or the Swiss Federal Environmental Protection Act of 1983.[15] There is what sociologists have diagnosed as 'the crisis of the provident state'[16] Europe had come to know in the 19th and early 20th century. François Ewald, long-time collaborator of Michel Foucault at the *Collège de France,* notes a transformation from traditional social security to 'insurance society'[17] in the new welfare state which Tony Giddens, of the London School of Economics, now sees as 'a form of collective risk management.'[18] Ulrich Beck, at the University of Munich (and former member of the German Government's 'Commission on the Future'), comes to the opposite conclusion: What he calls 'risk society'[19] (or 'world risk society,'[20]

---

13 E. REHBINDER, DAS VORSORGEPRINZIP IM INTERNATIONALEN VERGLEICH [THE PRECAUTIONARY PRINCIPLE COMPARED INTERNATIONALLY] (1991), at 237.

14 *Umweltbericht 1976*, submitted to the Federal Parliament on July 14, 1976, BTD [parliamentary document] 7/5684; implemented by specific federal legislation and supplemented in 1986 by 'Guidelines on Environmental Precaution' (*Leitlinien zur Umweltvorsorge*), BTD 10/6028; English summaries in K. von Moltke, *The Vorsorgeprinzip in West German Environmental Policy, in* TWELFTH REPORT OF THE ROYAL COMMISSION ON ENVIRONMENTAL POLLUTION (London 1987), Annex 3, at 57; and S. Boehmer-Christiansen, *The Precautionary Principle in Germany: Enabling Government, in* INTERPRETING THE PRECAUTIONARY PRINCIPLE 38 (T. O'Riordan & J. Cameron eds., 1994).

15 Federal Act of Oct. 7, 1983 on Environmental Protection (*Bundesgesetz über den Umweltschutz*), SR 814 No.1, art.1(2) of which provides that "with a view to precaution, impacts that are potentially harmful or potential nuisances must be curtailed at an early stage," *see* D. KOECHLIN, DAS VORSORGEPRINZIP IM UMWELTSCHUTZGESETZ UNTER BESONDERER BERÜCKSICHTIGUNG DER EMISSIONS- UND IMMISSIONS-GRENZWERTE (1989).

16 P. ROSANVALLON, LA CRISE DE L'ETAT PROVIDENCE (2nd ed. 1984).

17 F. EWALD, L'ETAT PROVIDENCE 16 (1986); *id., Die Versicherungs-Gesellschaft*, KRITISCHE JUSTIZ No. 4 (1989), at 22.

18 A. Giddens, *see supra* note 12 , at 9.

19 U. BECK, RISIKOGESELLSCHAFT: AUF DEM WEG IN EINE ANDERE MODERNE (9th ed. 1992); *English transl.*: RISK SOCIETY: TOWARDS A NEW MODERNITY (1992); *id., Modern Society as a Risk Society, in* THE CULTURE AND POWER OF KNOWLEDGE: INQUIRIES INTO CONTEMPORARY SOCIETIES (N. Stehr & R. Ericson eds., 1992). *See also* P. LAGADEC, LA CIVILISATION DU RISQUE: CATASTROPHES TECHNOLOGIQUES ET RESPONSABILITÉ SOCIALE (1981); *English transl.:* MAJOR TECHNOLOGICAL RISKS: AN ASSESSMENT OF INDUSTRIAL DISASTERS (1982).

20 U. Beck, *Weltrisikogesellschaft: Zur Politischen Dynamik Globaler Gefahren*, INTERNATIONALE POLITIK No.8 (1995); *id., World Risk Society as Cosmopolitan Society? Ecological Questions in a Framework of Manufactured Uncertainties, in* THEORY, CULTURE AND SOCIETY, No.4 (1996), at 13.

in the wake of globalization) is actually un-insured (*versicherungslos*), he says; for paradoxically, post-modern society's insurance coverage seems to decrease as the risks increase.[21]

Be that as it may — it was in Scandinavia, at the peak of that region's own experiment with the welfare state, where the precautionary principle was first translated into a general legal rule: The Swedish Environment Protection Act of 1969[22] — enacted half a year before the US National Environmental Policy Act[23] — introduced the concept of 'environmentally hazardous activities' (*miljöfarlig verksamheter*),[24] for which the burden of proof is flatly reversed; i.e., the regulatory authorities "do not have to demonstrate that a certain impact will occur; instead, the mere risk (if not remote) is to be deemed enough to warrant protective measures or a ban on the activity."[25] That, of course, is nothing else than what international legal experts today define as the most radical variant of the precautionary principle.[26] It has been the law in Sweden for the past thirty years,[27] and is also reflected in the legislation of other Nordic countries.[28]

---

21 U. Beck, *Überlebensfragen, Sozialstrukturen und Ökologische Aufklärung, in* POLITIK IN DER RISIKOGESELLSCHAFT (U. Beck ed., 1991), at 122; *English transl.: Risk Society and the Provident State, in* RISK, ENVIRONMENT AND MODERNITY: TOWARDS A NEW ECOLOGY (S. Lash, B. Szerszynski & B. Wynne eds., 1996), at 31.

22 *Miljöskyddslag* of May 29, 1969, and related Environment Protection Ordinance, SVENSK FÖRFATTNINGS-SAMLING Nos. 387–88 (1969); *English transl. in* 21 INTERNATIONAL DIGEST OF HEALTH LEGISLATION (1971), at 180.

23 Public Law No. 91-190, enacted on Jan. 1, 1970, 83 STAT. 852; for a comparative survey, *see* P.H. Sand, *Legal Systems for Environment Protection: Japan, Sweden, United States*, FAO LEGISLATIVE STUDIES, NO. 4 (Food and Agriculture Organization of the United Nations, 1972).

24 S. WESTERLUND, MILJÖFARLIG VERKSAMHET (1975); *id., The Legal Control of Land Use and Environmental Quality in Sweden, in* EUROPEAN ENVIRONMENTAL LAW: LEGAL AND ECONOMIC APPRAISAL (S. Ercman ed., 1977), at 392.

25 S. Westerlund, *Legal Antipollution Standards in Sweden*, 25 SCANDINAVIAN STUDIES IN LAW 225, 231 (1981).

26 Report of the Expert Meeting on Identification of Principles of International Law for Sustainable Development, Background Paper No.3 for the 4th Sess. of the UN Commission on Sustainable Development 18 (N.Y. 1996).

27 *See* the Swedish National Report to the 1992 United Nations Conference on Environment and Development (Ministry of the Environment, 1991), at 23.

28 *E.g.*, Denmark's 1973 Environment Protection Act, Norway's 1981 Pollution Control Act, and Finland's 1992 Environmental Permits Act; *see The Precautionary Principle,* ENVIRONMENTAL NEWS NO. 35 (E. Lindgard ed., Danish Environmental Protection Agency, 1998). The idea of subjecting hazardous activities to precautionary

In less radical garb, precautionary policies also made their appearance in the emerging quasi-federal law of the European Union, starting with some early environmental 'directives' adopted in the wake of the 1976 Seveso accident,[29] and culminating in more recent ones in areas such as genetically modified organisms (GMOs, 1990), 'novel foods' (1997), and biotechnology (1998),[30] where EU law-making — because of trade prerogatives in the intra-European common market — has to a large extent superseded national regulatory powers. The 1992 Maastricht treaty amendment, which may be said to have elevated the precautionary principle to the rank of European constitutional goal,[31] was merely a logical consequence and formal recognition of that trend. There is no doubt that its impact will be felt well beyond the geographical scope of the EU, as the latest row over 'hormone-beef' imports from the United States illustrates.[32] Indeed, the precautionary principle "seems to loom as a major new controversial issue on

---

permit conditions can, of course, be traced much further back in European environmental law, including the 1906 Alkali and Other Works Regulation Act in the UK, 19th century French legislation on *'installations classées'*, and Prussia's *Gewerbe-Ordnung* of 1845.

[29] *E.g.*, Council Directive 82/501 ('Seveso Directive') on Major Accident Hazards of Certain Industrial Activities, OFFICIAL JOURNAL OF THE EUROPEAN COMMUNITIES (OJEC) (1982) L 230/1, as amended by Directives 88/610 and 96/82, OJEC (1988) L 336/14 and (1997) L10/13; L. Hancher, *EC Environmental Policy: A Precautionary Tale?*, *in* THE PRECAUTIONARY PRINCIPLE AND INTERNATIONAL LAW, *see supra* note 1, at 187.

[30] Council Directives 90/219 and 90/220 of Apr. 23, 1990, OJEC (1990) L 117/1 and 117/15, as amended in OJEC (1994) L103/20 and OJEC (1997) L169/72; Council Regulation 258/97, OJEC (1997) L 43/1; and Directive 98/44, OJEC (1998) L 213/13; *see* E. Rehbinder, *Das Konzept des Anlage- und Produkt-bezogenen EG-Gentechnikrechts: Die Freisetzungs-Richtlinie und die Novel-Foods-Verordnung*, 7 ZEITSCHRIFT FÜR UMWELTRECHT (1999), at 6.

[31] Art. 130(r)(2), stipulating that EU environmental policy "shall be based on the precautionary principle," 31 INTERNATIONAL LEGAL MATERIALS (I.L.M.) (1992), at 247; *see* A. Epiney, UMWELTRECHT IN DER EUROPÄISCHEN UNION (1997), at 98; A. Doyle & T. Carney, *Precaution and Prevention: Giving Effect to Article 130(r) Without Direct Effect*, 8 EUROPEAN ENVIRONMENTAL LAW REVIEW (1999), at 44. EU guidelines on implementation of the principle are in preparation. Following the 1997 Amsterdam consolidation of the Treaty, art. 130(r) has been renumbered art. 174; *see* OJEC (1997) C 340/145.

[32] After the WTO Appellate Body on Feb. 13, 1998 found the EU ban on US 'hormone beef' imports contrary to the WTO Agreement on Sanitary and Phytosanitary Measures (SPS, in force since 1995), the EU submitted new scientific evidence in May 1999 to maintain the ban, which now faces countervailing trade measures by the United States.

the trade and environment horizon" in negotiations in the World Trade Organization (WTO),[33] with the European Union pleading for a clarification and expansion of the principle, and the US calling for sanitary and phytosanitary measures to be based on 'sound science.'

Mind you, as we say in German, "we never eat our soup as hot as we boil it." Political and even legislative pronouncements of the precautionary principle are one thing, application by courts and administrative authorities is quite another. So far, the European Court of Justice has sanctioned the principle only implicitly, in the 1993 *Mondiet* case confirming the validity of EU regulations on driftnet fishing, which had been challenged in a French court.[34] In Sweden, "even if the principle is well and explicitly founded in law, the authorities are often reluctant to make use of it — even though in theory they are obliged to do so."[35] In the United Kingdom, where the principle was endorsed by a 1990 Government White Paper,[36] attempts at establishing it in the courts have been notoriously unsuccessful in at least two cases,[37] and inconclusive in others.[38] In the Netherlands, the two *Wadden Sea* cases involving wastewater discharges and offshore drilling permits, respectively,[39] did invoke the

---

33 Special report on the WTO High-Level Symposium on Trade and Environment in Mar. 1999, by the NGO International Centre for Trade and Sustainable Development, 3 BRIDGES No. 2 (1999), at 8.

34 Council Regulation 345/92, OJEC (1992) L 42/15, upheld by the Court (Luxembourg, 24 November 1993), I EUROPEAN COURT REPORTS 6133 (1993); *see* E. Hey, *The European Community's Courts and International Environmental Agreements,* 7 REVIEW OF EUROPEAN COMMUNITY AND INTERNATIONAL ENVIRONMENTAL LAW 4, 6 (1998).

35 Westerlund, *see supra* note 25.

36 Department of the Environment, *This Common Inheritance,* WHITE PAPER ON ENVIRONMENTAL POLICY (London 1990), at 7.

37 R. vs. Secretary of State for Trade and Industry *ex parte* Duddridge and others (Queen's Bench), ENVIRONMENTAL LAW REPORTER (1994), at 151; 7 JOURNAL OF ENVIRONMENTAL LAW (1995), at 224; and Gateshead Metropolitan Borough Council vs. Secretary of State for the Environment and Northumbrian Water Group plc. (High Court), 7 PROPERTY AND COMPENSATION REPORTS (1996), at 355; *see* D. Bodansky & J. Brunnée, *The Role of National Courts in the Field of International Environmental Law,* 7 REVIEW OF EUROPEAN COMMUNITY AND INTERNATIONAL ENVIRONMENTAL LAW 11, 16 (1998).

38 Alfred McAlpine Homes (North) Ltd. vs. Secretary of State for the Environment (Queen's Bench), NEW PROPERTY CASES 138 (1994); Bodansky & Brunnée, *see supra* note 37, at 20 n. 78.

39 Landelijke Vereniging tot Behout van de Waddenzee et al. vs. Minister of Transport and Public Works (Council of State, Judicial Division), MILIEU EN RECHT

precautionary principle but may also be founded on other existing rules of Dutch environmental legislation and administrative due process.[40] The French Council of State, in the 1997 *Superphénix* case involving closure of a nuclear power plant on the Swiss border (in Creys-Malville near Geneva),[41] initially refused to consider the precautionary principle formulated in the Maastricht amendment[42] as self-executing in the member states of the European Union,[43] but has since accepted it in the 1998 *Transgenic Corn* case as "serious ground" to justify suspension of a ministerial permit for the cultivation and marketing in France of bio-engineered corn (by a Swiss corporation, tit for tat).[44] However, what remains of the principle after it was transformed into French national law by the 1995 *Loi Barnier*[45] reads rather different from the original Rio text: "Lack of certainty, taking into account scientific and technical knowledge at the time, shall not delay effective *and commensurate* measures, *at economically acceptable cost*, to prevent the threat of

(1996), at 243; and Landelijke Vereniging tot Behout van de Waddenzee et al. vs. Minister of Economics (Leeuwarden District Court, Apr. 28, 1997), MILIEU EN RECHT (1997), at 99.

40 *See* A. Nollkaemper, *Judicial Application of International Environmental Law in the Netherlands*, 7 REVIEW OF EUROPEAN COMMUNITY AND INTERNATIONAL ENVIRONMENTAL LAW 40, 42 & 44 (1998); *See also* C. W. Backes & J.M. Verschuuren, *The Precautionary Principle in International, European, and Dutch Wildlife Law,* 9 COLORADO JOURNAL OF INTERNATIONAL ENVIRONMENTAL LAW AND POLICY 43, 43 (1998).

41 WWF Geneva et al. vs. French Republic, *Conseil d'Etat* (Paris, Feb. 28, 1997), CAHIERS JURIDIQUES DE L'ELECTRICITÉ ET DU GAS (1997), at 217.

42 *See supra* note 31.

43 Conclusions by Commissioner Ms. Denis-Linton, CAHIERS JURIDIQUES DE L'ELECTRICITÉ ET DU GAS, *see supra* note 41, at 229; *see* the case comment by J.P. Colson, *Superphénix et le Droit*, 23 REVUE JURIDIQUE DE L'ENVIRONNEMENT (1998), at 163 ("short shrift for the precautionary principle").

44 Association Greenpeace France et al. vs. French Republic, Novartis Seed SA and Monsanto Europe SA, *Conseil d'Etat* (Paris, Sept. 25, 1998), RECUEIL DALLOZ (1998) 2/IR, at 240. Final judgment on the merits has been postponed, pending a request to the European Court of Justice for determination of compatibility with applicable EU law, in light of earlier decisions (97/98/EEC and 98/294) by the EU Commission to legalize genetically modified corn, *OJEC* (1997) L 31/69 and (1998) L 131/33. *See* D. Bojic Bultrini, *La Directive Européenne sur la Protection Juridique des Inventions Biotechnologiques: La Vie Enfin Dans le "Filet" Communautaire?*, 23 REVUE JURIDIQUE DE L'ENVIRONNEMENT (1998), at 484.

45 Act No. 95-101 of Feb. 2, 1995 on the further strengthening of environmental law, JOURNAL OFFICIEL , Feb. 3, 1995, at 1840.

serious *and* irreversible damage to the environment."[46] The focus of the precaution debate in France has thus shifted to legal definitions of 'irreversibility,' as a criterion for distinguishing tolerable from intolerable risks — so far with less than conclusive results.[47]

Germany has had the largest share of court cases involving the precautionary principle, in response to the plethora of federal legislation enacted since the 1970s on different environmental topics, much of it sector-specific and anything but uniform or consistent.[48] The overriding tendency of the courts has been to limit the margin of administrative discretion which the principle inevitably confers and which critics see as potentially 'boundless' (*uferlos*).[49] E.g., as regards operating permits for nuclear reactors, both the leading 1978 *Kalkar* decision by the Federal Constitutional Court[50] and the 1985 *Wyhl* decision by the Federal Administrative Court[51] ostensibly confirm the executive's power to take precautionary measures against identified 'dangers' as well as against as yet unidentified 'risks,' but then go on to define a lower-level 'residual risk' (*Restrisiko*) which the public (and the plaintiffs adjoining the power plant) will have to tolerate; and in the 1998 *Krümmel* case, the Federal Administrative Court considered leukemia risks in the power plant's neighborhood too remote to warrant revocation of a lower court's permit approval.[52] Similarly, in several appellate decisions

---

46 *Ibid.* art. 1(1)(3) [my translation and emphasis]. Curiously, the authentic French text of Principle 15 of the 1992 Rio Declaration did not contain the 'cost-effective' US rider (*see* note 8), an omission for which the 1995 French statute more than compensates.

47 *See, e.g.*, M. Fritz-Legendre, *Biodiversité et Irreversibilité*, REVUE JURIDIQUE DE L'ENVIRONNEMENT (1998 special issue), at 79; and M. Prieur, *L'irreversibilité et la Gestion des Déchets Radioactifs Dans la Loi du 30 Décembre 1991*, REVUE JURIDIQUE DE L'ENVIRONNEMENT (1998 special issue), at 125; *see also* LE PRINCIPE DE PRÉCAUTION DANS LA CONDUITE DES AFFAIRES HUMAINES (O. Godard ed., 1997).

48 In particular, art. 5(1) of the Federal Act for Protection Against Pollution (*Bundes-Immissions-Schutz-Gesetz*) enacted in 1974, as consolidated on May 14, 1995, I BUNDESGESETZBLATT (1995), at 930; and art. 6(2) of the 1990 Biotechnology Act (*Gen-Technik-Gesetz*), I BUNDESGESETZBLATT (1990), at 1080.

49 Rehbinder, *see supra* note 13, at 11.

50 *Bundes-Verfassungs-Gericht* (Karlsruhe, Aug. 8, 1978), 49 ENTSCHEIDUNGEN (1979), at 137.

51 *Bundes-Verwaltungs-Gericht* (Berlin, Dec. 19, 1985), 72 ENTSCHEIDUNGEN (1986), at 315.

52 *Bundes-Verwaltungs-Gericht* (Berlin, Feb. 16, 1998), 17 NEUE ZEITSCHRIFT FÜR VERWALTUNGSRECHT (1998), at 631. (After the federal court on Aug. 21, 1996 had

concerning electro-magnetic fields of mobile phone networks, actionable health risks were distinguished from mere 'concerns' (*Besorgnis*) deemed insufficient to invalidate operating permits.[53] In the 1992 *EPO-Mouse* case, the Administrative District Court of Giessen held that precautionary measures with regard to genetically modified organisms were warranted only "up to a degree which in light of risk assessment on the basis of the best available scientific and technological information is sufficient to ensure control of the risks."[54] And in the famous *Waldsterben* case (forest damage attributed to acid rain), the Federal Supreme Court had in 1987 already dismissed attempts at invoking the precautionary principle as a basis for holding the federal government liable for 'legislative inaction.'[55] There is indeed a wide range of legal and procedural constraints on precautionary action — including the Administration's duty to make full use of all available information; the duty to undertake benefit-risk assessments; the duty to motivate and disclose assessments; and general due process rules such as the requirement that precautionary measures be commensurate with the risk, and not excessive.[56]

---

granted an appeal on precautionary grounds, the case was sent back to the *Ober-Verwaltungs-Gericht* Schleswig, which again reviewed the permit but re-confirmed it on Oct. 29, 1997.)

53 *See, e.g., Ober-Verwaltungs-Gericht Münster* (May 18, 1993), 12 NEUE ZEITSCHRIFT FÜR VERWALTUNGSRECHT (1993), at 1115; and two further cases reported, *ibid.*, at 1116-1119; case comments by U. Di Fabio, *Rechtsfragen zu Unerkannten Gesundheitsrisiken Elektromagnetischer Felder*, 48 DIE ÖFFENTLICHE VERWALTUNG 1,1 (1995). On recent developments following the 1996 federal regulations on electro-magnetic fields *(Verordnung über Elektromagnetische Felder)*, I BUNDESGESETZBLATT (1996); *see* C. Kirchberg, *Elektrosmog — und (k)ein Ende?*, 17 NEUE ZEITSCHRIFT FÜR VERWALTUNGSRECHT (1998), at 375.

54 *Verwaltungs-Gericht Giessen* (Sept. 2, 1992), 12 NEUE ZEITSCHRIFT FÜR VERWALTUNGSRECHT: RR 6 (1993 case reports), at 534. Plaintiff successfully sued the Federal Health Agency for refusing her, on precautionary grounds, a licence to produce erythropoietin (EPO hormone) from genetically modified mouse cells. For comments on further biosafety cases, *see* I. Appel, *Stufen der Risikoabwehr*, 18 NATUR UND RECHT (1996), at 235; M. Jörgensen & G. Winter, *Rechtliche Probleme der Freisetzung von Gentechnisch Veränderten Organismen*, 4 ZEITSCHRIFT FÜR UMWELTRECHT (1996), at 293.

55 City of Augsburg et al. vs. Federal Republic of Germany, Federal Supreme Court (*Bundesgerichtshof Karlsruhe*, Dec. 10, 1987), 103 DEUTSCHES VERWALTUNGSBLATT (1988), at 232; *see* A. Rest, *International Environmental Law in German Courts*, 27 ENVIRONMENTAL POLICY AND LAW 409, 414 (1997).

56 Von Moltke, *see supra* note 14; Rehbinder, *see supra* note 13, at 253; K.H. LADEUR,

That being said, the precautionary principle is alive and well in Germany. It is perhaps worth recalling that the principle was introduced by a Social-Democrat Government in the 1970s, and the Social-Democrats are now back in power in coalition with the Greens. One of their first long-term policy decisions — to phase out nuclear power production — was crucially dependent on the *Vorsorgeprinzip* as a legal basis to terminate existing operating permits.[57] Whether the principle will also serve to terminate Germany's existing long-term contracts for nuclear waste re-processing in France and Britain remains to be seen.[58] Significantly, though, the need to preserve sufficient flexibility for executive action in transnational nuclear relations was already part of the rationale for the precautionary principle as interpreted by the Federal Constitutional Court in the 1978 *Kalkar* case.[59]

The legal ramifications of the precautionary principle are probably most significant when it comes to information access. It was Peter Bernstein, in his fascinating book *Against the Gods,* who said that "risk is not fate, it is choice."[60] If that is so — and his point seems to be borne out by anthropologists[61] — it follows that those

---

Das Umweltrecht der Wissensgesellschaft: Von der Gefahrenabwehr zum Risikomanagement 99 (1995); and U. Di Fabio, *Gefahr, Vorsorge, Risiko: Die Gefahrenabwehr unter dem Einfluss des Vorsorgeprinzips*, 18 Jura (1996), at 572–74.

57 As already pointed out in the 1978 Kalkar case, *see supra* note 50, at 145, art. 7(2)(3) of the 1976 German Nuclear Energy Act provides for 'conditionally suspended injunctions' *(Verbot mit Erlaubnis-Vorbehalt)* rather than conditional permits, thereby shifting the burden of proof to the operator; *Atom-Gesetz* of Dec. 23, 1959, as revised in 1976, I Bundesgesetzblatt (1976), at 3053.

58 The bilateral agreements concluded in 1990 between the German Nuclear Fuel Re-Processing Corporation *(DWK)* and its French and British counterparts (*Compagnie Générale des Matières Nucléaires* & *British Nuclear Fuels plc.*), though backstopped by joint governmental declarations, contain saving clauses in the event of 'act or restraint of government' ('*Gesetze oder Einschränkende Massnahmen der Regierung*' in the German text). *See* R. Wahl & G. Hermes, Nationale Kernenergiepolitik und Gemeinschaftsrecht (1995), at 34–39.

59 *See supra* note 50, at 147.

60 P.L. Bernstein, Against the Gods: The Remarkable Story of Risk 8 (1996). I owe this reference to Sylvia A. Earle.

61 According to M. Douglas & A. Wildawsky, Risk and Culture: An Essay on the Selection of Technical and Environmental Dangers 8 (1982), "we choose the risks in the same package as we choose our social institutions," and "if the selection of risk is a matter of social organization, the management of risk is an organizational problem," at 198. *See also* M. Douglas, Risk Acceptability According to the Social Sciences (1985).

who take the risk (and who will potentially suffer the consequences) should be given equal access to all information enabling them to know what their choices are. Hence, information about risk of harm should never be monopolized, whether by public or private knowledge-holders, and should by definition be common property.

A number of mechanisms are becoming available for this purpose — from precautionary labeling and life-cycle product information, to new methods of public and private risk disclosure. In this regard, most parts of the world still have a lot to learn from the American experience. Munich sociologist Ulrich Beck actually considers civil society 'disenfranchised in risk matters.'[62] Except for Scandinavia, European legal systems have no equivalent to the 1966 US Freedom of Information Act[63] or the 1983 Canadian Access to Information Act,[64] which make government-held knowledge generally accessible to concerned citizens. The European Union's timid 1990 Directive on Freedom of Access to Information on the Environment[65] has yet to be transformed into actual administrative practice in most member states of the EU;[66] and the more progressive 1998 Aarhus Convention of the UN Economic Commission for Europe[67] has yet to enter into force. There is even

---

62 *"Entmündigt in Sachen Gefahr."* U. Beck, *Der Anthropologische Schock: Tschernobyl und die Konturen der Risikogesellschaft, in* POLITIK IN DER RISIKOGESELLSCHAFT, *see supra* note 21, at 68; *English transl. in* ECOLOGICAL ENLIGHTENMENT: ESSAYS ON THE POLITICS OF RISK SOCIETY (U. Beck ed., 1995).

63 5 U.S.C. 552, as supplemented by the 1996 Electronic Freedom of Information Act Amendments, and parallel legislation at the state level; *e.g.*, the Ohio Public Records Act.

64 *R.S.C.* 1985, c. A-1, and parallel legislation at the provincial level; *e.g.*, the British Columbia Freedom of Information and Protection of Privacy Act. For a comparative survey, *see* Commission for Environmental Cooperation, *Public Access to Government-Held Environmental Information: Report on North American Law, Policy and Practice, in* NORTH AMERICAN ENVIRONMENTAL LAW AND POLICY (1999), at 65.

65 Council Directive 90/313 of June 7, 1990, OJEC (1990) L 158/56; and the related code of conduct approved by the EU Council and Commission, OJEC (1993) L 340/41.

66 For a comparative survey, *see* ACCESS TO ENVIRONMENTAL INFORMATION IN EUROPE (R.E. Hallo ed., 1996); *see also* C.J.M. Kimber & F. Eckardt, *Zugang zu Umwelt-Informationen in Grossbritannien und Deutschland,* 21 NATUR UND RECHT (1999), at 268.

67 Convention on Access to Information, Public Participation in Decision-Making and Access to Justice in Environmental Matters, adopted at Aarhus/Denmark on June 25, 1998; 38 INTERNATIONAL LEGAL MATERIALS (I.L.M.) (1999), at 517.

less international experience with rules on access to privately-held risk information, by way of community 'right-to-know' and 'duty-to-warn' statutes. Communities outside North America can only dream of the kind of geographically specific and user-friendly data now available from the US Toxics Release Inventory (TRI)[68] — or its Canadian equivalent, the National Pollutant Release Inventory (NPRI)[69] — which anybody can download from the Internet.[70] Efforts to extend this type of risk communication across political boundaries — possibly through voluntary commitments or 'codes of conduct' by responsible multinational corporations — should be a priority in making the precautionary principle work transnationally.[71] Rather than the 'provident state,' it is the provident citizen and the provident consumer who must be empowered to take informed precautionary action[72] — so as to exercise the choice of risks which we are told we have.

Let me conclude here with a tribute to Ibrahim Shihata. Long before 'knowledge management' became fashionable in World

---

68 Pursuant to the Emergency Planning and Community Right-to-Know Act, enacted as part of the Superfund Amendments and Reauthorization Act of 1986, Public Law No. 99-499, 100 *Stat.* 1613; *see* G.D. Bass & A. MacLean, *Enhancing the Public's Right-to-Know About Environmental Issues*, 4 VILLANOVA ENVIRONMENTAL LAW JOURNAL (1993), at 287. Parallel legislation exists at the state level, *e.g.*, the New Jersey Worker and Community Right-to-Know Act.

69 Environment Canada, <http://www.ec.gc.ca/pdb/npri/index.html> (Ottawa 1997); for a summary of both inventories, *see* UN Environment Programme, GLOBAL ENVIRONMENT OUTLOOK 2000 (1999), at 309.

70 In addition to the information available directly from the US Environmental Protection Agency, <http://www.epa.gov/opptintr/tri/national.html> (Washington, D.C. 1998), *see* the *Chemical Scorecard* mapped by the NGO Environmental Defense Fund, <http://www.scorecard.org> (N.Y. 1998).

71 Articles 5(6), 5(8) & 5(9) of the 1998 Aarhus Convention, *see supra* note 67, call on each member state to encourage voluntary public information by operators, to develop product information mechanisms, and to establish nation-wide pollution inventories "taking into account international processes where appropriate." *See also* the proceedings of the 1998 OECD International Conference on Pollutant Release and Transfer Registers, <http://www.oecd.org/ehs/prtr/index.htm>.

72 *See* the plea for freedom of risk information as 'The New Magna Charta of Ecological Democracy' (citing the US Freedom of Information Act) by J. Fischer, *in* POLITIK IN DER RISIKOGESELLSCHAFT, *see supra* note 21, at 324, *reprinted from* FISCHER, DER UMBAU DER INDUSTRIEGESELLSCHAFT: PLÄDOYER WIDER DIE HERRSCHENDE UMWELTLÜGE 152 (1989); *English transl. in* ECOLOGICAL ENLIGHTENMENT: ESSAYS ON THE POLITICS OF RISK SOCIETY (U. Beck ed., 1995). (Joschka Fischer, prominent German *Green*, is now the Federal Minister of Foreign Affairs.)

Bank jargon, he was instrumental in engineering a revision of the Bank's policy on information disclosure,[73] against apprehensions and considerable internal resistance from management staff at the time. The results of those efforts — in conjunction with the Inspection Panel, for the architecture of which he was primarily responsible — illustrate the crucial link between transparency of decision-making and accountability, in national and international institutions alike.

73 BANK PROCEDURES 17.50 (SEPT. 1993) ON DISCLOSURE OF OPERATIONAL INFORMATION, *in* IBRAHIM F.I. SHIHATA, THE WORLD BANK INSPECTION PANEL (1994), at 28 & 357.

THE WORLD BANK'S ROLE IN THE PROMOTION OF THE RULE OF LAW IN DEVELOPING COUNTRIES

*Sabine Schlemmer-Schulte**

I. INTRODUCTION

The history of civilization and political, economic, social, and cultural progress of mankind is also a history of law. Wherever in the world the era of hunter-gatherer cultures ended and society began to organize itself in a more civilized way, the development of a *rule of law* (in the broad sense of some societal order) stood at the center of mankind's endeavor to shape society's life and well-being. At the heights of cultures, law was the means through which rulers governed, by which the relationships among citizens in society were regulated, and through which safeguards against the ruler's or the government's influence were introduced.

Ancient cultures testify to the struggle in establishing a *rule of law,* its varying contents over centuries, as well as acceptance of it or skepticism *vis-à-vis* it by the people. Thus, the *Egyptian civilization* blossomed in the first six Pharaoh dynasties when a state administration, court rituals, and a fixed legal practice plus religious doctrine were established.[1] In *ancient Greece,* Athens' polis prospered when its tyrants were overthrown and Athenians achieved the establishment of a *rule of law* through codification of rules, a process for the amendment of these rules, and a separa-

---

* The views expressed in this paper are those of the author and should not be attributed to the institutions with which she is affiliated. The author wishes to thank Nara Beginyan, Rowena M. Gorospe, and Hege E. Kjos for valuable research assistance.

1 *See* MAX RODENBECK, CAIRO — THE CITY VICTORIOUS 10 (1999).

tion of the judiciary power from other powers to build a system of justice.[2] The *Roman empire* rested on the principle *justitia fundamentum regnorum,* including, among others, the codification of the law (*jus civile*), i.e. the rules containing the rights and duties of individual citizens, to safeguard the small man against the arbitrary behavior of the patrician nobility and to ensure the administration of justice.[3]

Like today, the law either was a static pillar lending continuity to rules that had proven to be beneficial for a society's development and the individuals in this society, as well as a dynamic tool for change where the circumstances of the time required an adjustment. In this combination, the *rule of law* was praised as a guarantor for the well-being of the state and its citizens.[4] Or, the law's twofold characteristics, i.e. its static and dynamic nature, kept provisions that were due for an overhaul from a political, economic, or social point of view unchanged, and proceeded only to adopt new provisions adversely affecting the state and its citizens. In that situation, the law was criticized, resort sought to non-legal means of organization, and the *rule of law* was qualified as "harsh" whereas the *rule of men* was considered moral and more tolerant.[5]

---

[2] *See* RAPHAEL SEALEY, THE ATHENIAN REPUBLIC: DEMOCRACY OR THE RULE OF LAW? 146 *et seq.* (1997).

[3] *See* WOLFGANG KUNKEL, AN INTRODUCTION TO ROMAN LEGAL AND CONSTITUTIONAL HISTORY 24 *et seq.* (Translation by J.M. Kelly 1966).

[4] This rather ideal situation was circumscribed by the International Commission of Jurists as follows: "The state is subject to the law. The rule of law is a dynamic concept for the expansion and fulfillment of which jurists are primarily responsible and which should be employed not only to safeguard and advance the civil and political rights of the individual in a free society, but also to establish social, economic, educational and cultural conditions under which his legitimate aspirations and dignity may be realized." *See* HOWARD B. TOLLEY JR., THE INTERNATIONAL COMMISSION OF JURISTS – GLOBAL ADVOCATES FOR HUMAN RIGHTS 68 (1994). For further literature on how an adequate model of law can contribute to the process of development, *see* L. Friedman, *Legal Rules and the Process of Social Change,* 19 STANFORD LAW REVIEW 791 (1967); and R. SEIDMAN, THE STATE, LAW, AND DEVELOPMENT (1978).

[5] Such a situation apparently existed to some degree in China in the 18th and 19th century. *See* PHILIP C.C. HUANG, CIVIL JUSTICE IN CHINA — REPRESENTATION AND PRACTICE IN THE QING 2 (1996) (further stating that Qing civil law must have been more like the arbitrary "Kadi justice" based on magisterial whims than "rational" modern law). Also discussing some difficulties in the use of law as an instrument to promote development, P. Bondzi-Simpson, *Dilemmas of Development Through Law, in* THE LAW AND ECONOMIC DEVELOPMENT IN THE THIRD WORLD (P. Bondzi-Simpson ed., 1992).

Mankind's struggle over the "right" *rule of law* continues to date despite of the fact that worldwide consensus over the essential elements of the modern concept of the *rule of law* is increasing as a result of historical developments since the 19th century, including in particular the most recent political and economic changes that took place when the Berlin wall fell in 1989 and democracy and the market economy became the leading political and economic models for many more states in the world than before 1989.[6]

While a general trend towards a common definition of the modern *rule of law* may be discerned, local differences in, as well as different actors' different approaches to, the *rule of law* should neither be down-played nor in principle looked at as of evil because no *rule of law* concept has yet proven to be the single superior solution to the organization of modern society in general, or in developing countries in particular. It should be kept in mind that the *rule of law* belongs to the category of open-ended concepts which are subject to permanent debate and have to be constantly redefined to meet the need of an ever-changing political, economic, social, and cultural, thus also changing legal, environment.

The modern concept of the *rule of law* emerged in England and the United States. Its most prominent parallels in the European continental traditions are the *Rechtsstaat* (commonly, but incorrectly, translated as *rule of law*), and *l'état de droit*. None of these concepts are identical. In the past, they have varied consid-

---

[6] The *rule of law* is a prerequisite for the attainment and preservation of the basic conditions for the proper functioning of a market economy. *See,* in particular, IBRAHIM F.I. SHIHATA, THE WORLD BANK IN A CHANGING WORLD, VOL. III (2000), Chapter 6 (*Relevant Issues in the Establishment of a Sound Legal Framework for a Market Economy*). For early writings on the relevance of the rule of law to capitalism, *see, e.g.*, ADAM SMITH, INQUIRY INTO THE NATURE AND CAUSES OF THE WEALTH OF NATIONS (1776); D. RICARDO, ON THE PRINCIPLES OF POLITICAL ECONOMY AND TAXATION (1817); and MAX WEBER, ECONOMY AND SOCIETY (G. Roth & C. Witlich eds., modern edition 1978) (all stressing that a stable and predictable legal environment and free competition in a state represent the bases for a functioning market) . For more recent writings on the *rule of law* after the fall of the Berlin wall, *see* Thomas Carothers, *The Rule of Law Revival,* 77 FOREIGN AFFAIRS 95, Issue 2 (1998); MAKING DEVELOPMENT WORK: LEGISLATIVE REFORM FOR INSTITUTIONAL TRANSFORMATION AND GOOD GOVERNANCE (A. Seidman et al eds., 1999); and Materials and Papers of the 5th Meeting of the Economic Forum of the Organization for Security and Cooperation in Europe (OSCE), held in Prague, Czech Republic, on June 11–13, 1997.

erably from one country to another, while a convergence among them is a more recent phenomenon.

In *England,* the *rule of law* translates in the first place into supremacy of the law enacted by Parliament which is implicitly democratically elected and based on a multi-party system. It is parliamentary sovereignty guaranteeing the separation of powers by restraining the monarch and government and creating the positive law through which the rights and liberties of the individuals are protected.[7] The *rule of law* in the form of common law complements acts of Parliament, limiting the monarch's and the government's powers and securing the "Englishman's primary rights," i.e. personal security, personal liberty, and private property.[8]

The situation was fundamentally different in the *United States (US)* where the earlier British colonies in the 18th century had been confronted with a British Parliament imposing financial burdens on them without taking properly into account their legitimate interests since the settlers in America were not represented in the British Parliament. As a result, acts of the British Parliament started in the colonies being considered as void if they were against natural equity. From there, the idea developed that the legislature was bound by some higher law in the exercise of its powers, a feature that remained a cornerstone of the evolving US constitutional law doctrine, to be officially adopted later on by the US Supreme Court.[9] Central to the US concept of the *rule of law* was the idea of a written constitution as a valid and legally binding statement of the sovereign on the structure of the country's institutions and the fundamental liberties to be enjoyed by its

---

7 *See* ALBERT VENN DICEY, INTRODUCTION TO THE STUDY OF THE LAW OF THE CONSTITUTION (10th ed. 1959), Chapter IV. According to Dicey, while Parliament was free to make or unmake any law whatever and no body outside Parliament had the right to override a Parliamentary Statute, the law protected individuals as the law-making process remained subject to the control of the different groups and interests represented in Parliament.

8 *See* SIR WILLIAM BLACKSTONE, COMMENTARIES ON THE LAWS OF ENGLAND (1765–69).

9 *See* Marbury v. Madison, 5 U.S. 137 (1803). *See* also the Massachusetts Constitution (Part of the First, Article XXX) of 1780 which spelled out the principle of separation of powers "to the end [the government] may be a government of laws, and not of men." *See* further Rainer Grote, *Rule of Law, État de Droit, and Rechtsstaat — The Origins of the Different National Traditions and the Prospects for their Convergence in the Light of Recent Constitutional Developments,* found on the web at <http://www.eur.nl/frg/iacl/papers/grote.html>.

citizens. This concept implied in particular separation of powers, checks and balances among them, and a fundamental rights catalogue, the latter specifically to be ensured by the judiciary.

The *Rechtsstaat* in *Germany* evolved as a solution to unchecked powers not only by an absolute monarch and his/her administrative authorities, but also by parliaments that, politically, did not stand on the people's side as they had initially little legislative powers and, worse, were not democratically elected.[10] Checks and balances, and safeguards against encroachments on individuals' rights had to be built into the constitution. The constitution, not parliamentary sovereignty (as in England), became the directing normative principle since rights of individuals could only be protected effectively *vis-à-vis* state authority once the latter's competences had been systematized at that level and courts had been entrusted the power to review administrative and legislative measures for their constitutionality.[11]

---

10 The origins of the German concept of *Rechtsstaat* can be found in the philosophy of the Enlightenment ("Aufklärung"), notably in the theory of the state formulated by Immanuel Kant. According to Kant, a lawful state (or *Rechtsstaat*) had to be based on three principles: (i) the freedom of every member of society as a human being, (ii) the equality of each with all the others as a subject, and (iii) the independence of each member of a commonwealth as a citizen. In order to assure observance of these principles, the monarch, his legislature, his government, and his administration had to be bound by the constitution. *See* IMMANUEL KANT, IDEE ZU EINER ALLGEMEINEN GESCHICHTE IN WELTBÜRGERLICHER ABSICHT, *first published in* 1784, *reprinted in* SÄMMTLICHE WERKE (G. Hartenstein ed., 1867), Vol IV, at 141 *et seq. See also* GEORG JELLINEK, ALLGEMEINE STAATSLEHRE (1900).

11 *See generally* KLAUS STERN, DAS STAATSRECHT DER BUNDESREPUBLIK DEUTSCHLAND Vol. I, 602 *et seq.* (1977); and MARTIN KRIELE, EINFÜHRUNG IN DIE STAATSLEHRE — DIE GESCHICHTLICHEN LEGITIMITÄTSGRUNDLAGEN DES DEMOKRATISCHEN VERFASSUNGSTAATES 96 *et seq.* (5th ed. 1994) (outlining the differences between the historical roots of the *rule of law* and the *Rechtsstaat*). It is apparent that in order to realize the constitution's safeguards, a strong constitutional judiciary is needed. The conviction that protection of individuals' rights against abuses by the legislature and the executive is only safely guaranteed when embodied in the constitution and enforced through a special constitutional court is reflected in the German Constitutions of 1849, 1919, and 1949. The 1849 Constitution adopted by the National Assembly at St. Paul's church in Frankfurt/Main provided, *inter alia,* for an elaborate catalogue of fundamental rights and for an extensive constitutional jurisdiction of the Imperial Supreme Court which was to review the constitutionality of any exercise of public power. While the 1849 Constitution never became effective as a result of the failure of the 1848/49 revolution, its aspirations in terms of *Rechtsstaat* elements left their mark on legislation adopted in the Bismarck era and the development of a special administrative jurisdiction to provide the individual with a sufficient measure of protection against an abuse of powers by administrative authorities which might have

In *France, l'état de droit* developed in several stages. The revolution of 1789 introduced the idea of the supremacy of the constitution and respect for fundamental rights listed in the Declaration of the Rights of Man and of the Citizen.[12] Unlike US constitutionalism, however, French constitutional theory and practice did, for a long time, not manage to develop effective mechanisms to defend this supremacy of the constitution and this respect for fundamental rights. Firmly established became soon instead the principle of legality, which left the implementation of the various individual rights to the law. Solely, on the basis of the latter was the administration allowed to act. As a result of suspicion against judicial powers, controversies between individuals and the administration were, for a long time, entrusted to the administrative bodies themselves. It was only at the end of the 19th century that a stricter control of the legality of administrative action was introduced with the new concept of "*service public.*" After World War I, the *Conseil d'État* further strengthened the concept of legality by recognizing certain "*principes généraux du droit*" derived from tradition and general principles of legislation and including constitutional documents such as the 1789 Declaration on fundamental rights to fill gaps left by the legislature. Protection of rights and liberties of the citizens matured not further by binding government in judicial reviews (beyond mere gap filling) until a control of constitutionality of parliamentary laws was established in the 1970s.[13]

---

been provided had the review of administrative measures been left to the adjudication by ordinary courts. Civil rights provisions and the idea of judicial review of legislative measures resurfaced visibly in the 1919 Constitution and played an even more eminent role in the 1949 Constitution, the latter making unsusceptible for amendment the core elements of the *Rechtsstaat,* including fundamental rights, and establishing, with the *Bundesverfassungsgericht,* a constitutional court with an extraordinary wide range of review powers, surpassing those of the US Supreme Court.

12 For a historical overview of the development of *l'état de droit* in France, *see* Luc Heuschling, *État de Droit, Rechtsstaat, Rule of Law — Quelques réfleions sur les mots et les choses,* looked up on the web at <*http://www.eur.nl/frg/iacl/papers/heuschling.html. See also* on the same web site the paper *Rule of Law, État de Droit and Rechtsstaat — The Origins of the Different National Traditions and the Prospects for their Convergence in the Light of Recent Constitutional Developments,* by Rainer Grote. *See further* DICTIONNAIRE CONSTITUTIONNEL 415 (Oliver Duhamel & Yves Mény eds., 1992), at entry *"état de droit,"* and PIERRE AVRIL & JEAN GICQUEL, LEXIQUE DU DROIT CONSTITUTIONNEL 49 (1986), also at entry for "ÉTAT DE DROIT."

13 Such control of the constitutionality of laws had long been asked for by Carré de Malberg, in whose view without such control the concept of *état de droit* was

The differences between the four concepts resulting from the different historic contexts in which they emerged also explain why there is much emphasis on the positive law and great reliance on judge made common law under the *rule of law,* while the center of gravity under the *Rechtsstaat* and *état de droit* concepts rests on a pre-determined and well-designed constitution, in which natural law principles are embedded, as well as in comprehensive codes.[14]

Specifically in Britain, and, to a great extent, also in France in the earlier phase, confidence existed in the Parliament's function to protect the rights of those who placed its members in office through the adoption of appropriate laws. Similarly, it was believed in the British tradition and, to a great degree, also in the US tradition, that individual freedom could be best secured by legal recourse to private law made by judges. By contrast, distrust in parliament and the monarch in Germany resulted in the call for explicit provisions and guarantees of individual and political freedom at the highest level, in their core aspects enshrined best in Germany's 1949 Constitution.[15] At a lower level, trust exists in a comprehensive legal framework for both public and private law matters including predictable solutions to problems by having sought to anticipate most possible problems and designed solutions for them in the code, leaving little room for a judge's interpretation.

The differences between the four concepts may also be explained by the struggle between two ideas that have, to a lesser or greater degree, been part of the evolution of the *rule of law, Rechtsstaat,* and *état de droit* in the history of the different coun-

---

doomed to be incomplete. *See* R. CARRÉ DE MALBERG, CONTRIBUTION À LA THÉORIE GÉNÉRALE DE L'ÉTAT, VOL. I (1920-22). *See also* DICTIONNAIRE CONSTITUTIONNEL 417 (Oliver Duhamel & Yves Mény eds., 1992). While the Conseil Constitutionnel developed from a watchdog of the legislative branch of government primarily checking on the Parliament's keeping within its formal boundaries of powers into a mechanism which would also review the constitutionality of parliamentary laws, it may be noted that such review of constitutionality can only take place before the laws have been promulgated. Furthermore, individual citizens have no legal possibility to bring cases before the Conseil on the ground that laws violate their fundamental rights.

14 For a more detailed analysis of the *rule of law* and the *Rechtsstaatsprinzip, see* Loammi C. Blaau, *The Rechtsstaat Idea Compared with the Rule of Law as a Paradigm for Protecting Rights,* 107 SOUTH AFRICAN LAW JOURNAL 76 (1990).

15 It may be noted that these core aspects of fundamental rights under the German Constitution are unsusceptible to amendment. They are considered to reflect eternal natural law principles to safeguard against abuses of powers based on positive law adopted by the Parliament or the government.

tries itself or have been part of parallel phenomena: (i) the democratic ideal of law, and (ii) the liberal theory of fundamental rights as inherent limit even to the democratically legitimized exercise of legislative power. It goes without saying that where democracy's history went smoothly, the fundamental rights question did receive little attention, while where the development of democracy was problematic or democracy developed later than the sense for the protection of individual rights, the fundamental rights question moved to the center of discussion.

Today, a convergence between the various modern Western concepts of the *rule of law,* as they have expanded and developed in practice, may be noticed, especially when one looks at the substance of the concepts. All translate, to a varying degree of intensity, into the principles of separation of powers, law-abiding governmental powers, independent courts, transparency of legislation, judicial review of the constitutionality of laws and other norms of lower order, and the protection of fundamental rights.[16] One of the major remaining differences is that the *rule of law* implies democracy and a multi-party system, while the *Rechtsstaat* does not include the latter.[17]

---

16 *See* INTERNATIONAL ENCYCLOPEDIA OF THE SOCIAL SCIENCES, Vol. 7, 283, 304 (David L. Sills ed. 1972). It may be noted that the idea of the supremacy of law is not a creation of the modern concepts of the *rule of law, Rechtsstaat* or *état de droit.* The idea of supremacy of law existed before the latter concepts emerged. For example, in the Europe of the Middle Ages, when the State as abstract political entity did not yet exist and political authority was entirely vested in the king or emperor, it was stressed that law derived its binding force from the fact that king and people willingly accepted it. When popes and kings began to claim the power not only to interpret the existing God-given, rules, but also to make new law, they did so as deputies of God. The idea of some sort of higher, immutable law, the law of God and of nature, pervaded the Middle Ages. Similarly, in the Arab world, Islam introduced the idea of supremacy of law (*siyadat al-qanun*) into *Shari'a* in the 7th century. A complimentary concept introduced in parallel under *Shari'a* law is the principle of legality, or *ibāhah*. These concepts meant that, in the criminal realm, no punishment would be allowed without a clear legal justification. In the civil realm, property rights would be protected and infringements on property would not be allowed without clear legal basis. Authority would operate on the basis of fixed, identifiable, and predictable legal provisions rather than unlimited personal discretion. An independent judiciary, free from executive interference would apply the law in concrete disputes. Courts would be equally accessible to all. Rulers are fully subject to the text of the law (religiously mandated) just as ordinary citizens. For details on the supremacy of law under *Shari'a, see generally* NATHAN J.BROWN, THE RULE OF LAW IN THE ARAB WORLD (1997). *See also* MOHAMMAD HASHIM KAMALI, PRINCIPLES OF ISLAMIC JURISPRUDENCE 301 (revised edition 1989).

Despite of a great overlap of the concepts of the *rule of law*, the *Rechtsstaat*, and *l'état de droit*, the operation of these concepts rests still on different conceptual cultures. While, in the era of globalization, all cultures are in flux, it may be said that, to a great extent, the following considerations inherent in the British and US approaches to law are: (i) There is confidence in social automatism backing the law (through Parliament and/or judges). The law is able to organize itself and its own operation; (ii) the law will organize whatever it deems necessary for its operation; (iii) the law need not be provoked or forced to provide answers. It will, through an organic process, generate conclusions.[18] From the German and other continental European cultures, however, it may be inferred that: (i) a belief exists that only a written constitution and code can provide guarantees of law. The lack of such a code would often result in insecurity, disorder and perhaps even chaos; (ii) the written constitution and code spells out the rules of the game that men is supposed to follow. They represent the sole and exclusive basis for the social contract on which social order rests; and (iii) any updating or modification of this contract can only be implemented through an amendment of the constitution or code, with some principles having *a priori* been determined as unchangeable because they are considered to be eternally indispensable for a society.[19]

II. THE RULE OF LAW AND DEVELOPMENT

In the 1960s, the *rule of law*, which had until then only been a prominent part of the debate on appropriate legal frameworks in

---

17 In Germany, democracy, as not included in the *Rechtsstaatsprinzip*, is a second, separate pillar of the modern German state. In terms of the chronological history of the German Constitution, that pillar was introduced later than the *Rechtsstaat*.

18 *See* Csaba Varga, *Varieties of Law and Rule of Law*, 82 ARCHIV FÜR RECHTS — UND SOZIALPHILOSOPHIE (Archives for Philosophy of Law and Social Philosophy) 61, 62 (1996). For a discussion on the pros and cons of different legal systems under the pressures of globalization , *see, e.g.*, W.E. Scheuerman, *Economic Globalization and the Rule of Law*, *in* LEGAL CULTURE OF GLOBAL BUSINESS TRANSACTIONS (Appelbaum et al eds., 2000).

19 *See* Csaba Varga, *Varieties of Law and Rule of Law*, 82 ARCHIV FÜR RECHTS — UND SOZIAL — PHILOSOPHIE (ARCHIVES FOR PHILOSOPHY OF LAW AND SOCIAL PHILOSOPHY) 62 (1996).

developed states, became part of the discussion on development. A vivid and controversial discussion began about the place of the *rule of law* in countries which were, first and foremost, in the process of economic development. That the *rule of law* in the modern sense of democracy, separation of powers, and protection of fundamental rights is among the goals of development is to date largely uncontested. Whether it must and can be achieved simultaneously with, or even before, economic development is, however, still heavily disputed.[20]

Interest in the *rule of law* in the context of development from the 1960s until today varied in form and substance, and depending on the actor involved.

In the *US*, private foundations, and the United States Agency for International Development (USAID) helped in the 1960s, the so-called "Law and Development Decade," develop faculties of law in African, Asian, and Latin American countries. US law schools received professors and students from developing countries. These foreign lawyers were expected to spearhead the political and economic modernization process in their countries. These programs came to an end by the mid-1970s as a result of heavy criticism from within and outside the programs that they were imperious and ethnocentric in their efforts to transplant Western notions of law into non-Western settings.[21] From the mid-1970s until the mid-1980s, US foundations and USAID supported projects alleviating poverty by meeting the basic needs and giving the poor a larger voice in the development process, e.g. by mak-

20 *See*, e.g., Jon Elster, *The Necessity and Impossibility of Simultaneous Economic and Political Reform, in* CONSTITUTIONALISM AND DEMOCRACY — TRANSITIONS IN THE CONTEMPORARY WORLD 267 (Douglas Greenberg, Stanley N. Katz, Melanie Beth Olivero & Steven C. Wheatley eds. 1993) (arguing that democracy is an obstacle for ownership reform/privatization as well as market price reform because the latter both enhance inequalities that are unacceptable to large segments of the population which would thus rather prevent those reforms).

21 *See* Weighing in on the Scales of Justice – Strategic Approaches for Donor-Supported Rule of Law Programs 3 (USAID 1994). *See also* Abdullai Ahmed Abu-Na'im, *Law and Development: The Rule of Law in Developing Countries,* THIRD WORLD LEGAL STUDIES 33 (1986) (pointing out that, while colonial experience of most developing countries had effectively destroyed or at least severely disrupted preexisting traditional structures and mechanisms for political organization, the replacement of indigenous structures with Western models was in most cases not successful as the latter were insensitive to general culture in developing countries and were not negotiated with the population in these countries).

ing legal services accessible to the poor. In the 1980s, USAID investment in the legal sectors began focusing on court reform efforts in Central America, starting the era of "administration of justice" programs. In the early 1990s, USAID broadened the geographic and analytic perspectives of its law programs. Support for democracy is today emerging as USAID's major objective, moving with these "rule of law" programs into a fourth generation of legal programs.

Other *bilateral Western aid agencies,*[22] the *European Union (EU), private foundations,* and *non-governmental organizations* involved in development assistance have followed a similar path to the extent that they were engaged in legal programs or programs which included a human rights dimension, as have *United Nations (UN)* programmes such as the *United Nations Development Programme (UNDP).*[23] It may be noted for all that the great revival of their interest in legal programs came with the changes taking place in Eastern Europe and Central Asia after the fall of the Berlin wall when the former communist countries transformed

---

22 *See, e.g.,* Bundesministerium für Wirtschaftliche Zusammenarbeit und Entwicklung (BMZ) (German Ministry for Economic Cooperation and Development), BMZ Aktuell No. 90 (April 1998) (highlighting the promotion of human rights as a task of German development policy on which German aid through BMZ is based); Zentrum für Entwicklungsforschung (ZEF) (Center for Development Research) of the University of Bonn, Germany, Questionnaire on Human Rights Policies of [Bilateral] Donors and Businesses (2000) (compiling data from European bilateral donors and businesses showing that, while most European bilateral donors have not established a human rights department as such, most give prominence to selected human rights concerns and have started thinking about mainstreaming human rights into their development assistance program); Michael Doucin, *Droits de l'homme et développment,* Abstract of statement as panelist at the Workshop "Putting Human Rights First?" — Rethinking Development and Trade Policies" held at the ZEF in Bonn, Germany, on November 9–10, 2000 (noting that France's aid policy shifted in 1998 to pay attention to human rights concerns on a regular basis); and Tania Järvinen, *On the Role of Human Rights in Finnish Development Cooperation,* Statement as panelist at the Workshop "Putting Human Rights First?- Rethinking Development and Trade Policies" held at the ZEF in Bonn, Germany, on November 9–10, 2000 (noting that human rights concerns have been part of the policy aid since the mid-1990s).

23 *See* UNDP Today — Introducing the Organization 3, 5-7 (September 1998) (noting the UNDP's mandate was reshaped in 1995 to focus UNDP's mission on the most important development needs, including rule of law and human rights dimensions such as poverty eradication, creation of livelihoods for the poor, good governance, public resource management for sustainable human development, and environmental resources and food securing). *See also, generally,* Human Development Report (UNDP Publication 2000).

into democracies and their planned economies turned into market economies.[24] The parallel pressures of globalization on other developing countries and the ensuing move towards market reform evoked also needs for market-oriented laws as well as some political, i.e. human rights oriented, changes.[25]

Even *private corporations,* especially the multinational ones, which originally would be primarily, if not exclusively, concerned with profits, have started to consider the social and human dimensions of development on a voluntary basis,[26] and to establish codes of conduct guiding their own behavior, while it is, by far and large, not the private business's genuine task to design its own legal framework and standards to which it would be subject. The latter are normally imposed on private companies by local law enacted by the host country's government. Nevertheless for example, voluntary codes of conduct for the respect of environmental and social values have been adopted by numerous companies for their business in developing countries.[27]

Other multilateral development banks (*MDBs*) have, depending on the changing needs of the time and their mandate, also been engaged in the strengthening of the *rule of law* in their client countries through legal technical assistance, encompassing legal, judicial, and civil service programs and emphasizing economic, social, and environmental human rights dimensions of their aid.[28]

---

24 *See* Shaping a Market Economy Legal System - A Report of the EC/CIS Joint Task Force on Law Reform in the Independent States, Report No. 2 (1993) (listing the areas in which a great need for law reform exists in order to make the market economy work in the Eastern European and Central Asian transition economies).

25 For an overview of the legal changes necessary as a result of changes in the economic system in Asian Countries, *see* Discussion Materials of the Roundtable Meeting of Chief Justices and Ministers of Justice on Legal and Judicial Reform in Asia: Agenda for the New Millennium held under the Auspices of the Asian Development Bank (ADB) in Manila, Philippines, on August 25, 1997.

26 *See, e.g.,* Profits and Principles — Does there have to be a choice? (Shell Report 1998).

27 Firms that have established such codes of conduct include Dayton Hudson Corporation, The Dress Barn Inc., The Gap, JC Penney Company, Ikea, K-Mart Corporation, Nike, Nordstrom, and Woolworth Corporation. For an analysis of such developments in modern corporations, *See* MICHAEL NOVAK, ON CORPORATE GOVERNANCE — THE CORPORATION AS IT OUGHT TO BE (1997).

28 For example, the Inter-American Development Bank (IDB) worked on many fronts in FY1999 and, besides infrastructure, it focused greatly on the social sectors (education, water and sanitation, health, social investments, urban development, mi-

Among them, the *European Bank for Reconstruction and Development (EBRD)* stands out as it is the only MDB the charter of which explicitly commits it to the principles of "multi-party democracy, democratic institutions, the *rule of law,* respect for human rights, and market economics."[29] EBRD's charter authorizes not only the support of general economic development in Central and Eastern European countries but, first and foremost, the support for the economic transition to markets and the political transition to multi-party democracy. EBRD's special political mandate results from the special circumstances which motivated EBRD's creation to facilitate the Central and Eastern European countries' move from communist regimes and command economies to democratic systems and market economies.[30]

---

croenterprises, and the environment) and on the public sector (to strengthen institutions in the legislative, public administration, judiciary, and civil society). *See* IDB Annual Report 9–13 (1999). The Asian Development Bank (ADB) promoted economic growth through both investment in brick and mortar projects and reforms to ensure equitable access to and use of land, capital, knowledge, and labor. It financed education, health, population planning, social protection, urban development, improvement of women's status, protection of environment, regional cooperation, good governance, and law and policy programs. *See* ADB Annual Report 27 *et seq.* (1999).

[29] *See* Preamble of the Agreement Establishing the EBRD. (Emphasis added.) It may be noted that the fact that the *rule of law* and democracy are both mentioned, while the UK notion of the *rule of law* already implicitly includes democracy, may be explained by the intention of the drafters of the EBRD Charter to avoid confusion by those who would have seen the *Rechtsstaatsprinzip* in the rule of law.

[30] *See,* for more details on the broad mandate of EBRD, IBRAHIM F.I. SHIHATA, THE EUROPEAN BANK FOR RECONSTRUCTION AND DEVELOPMENT — A COMPARATIVE ANALYSIS OF THE CONSTITUENT AGREEMENT (1990). *See also* Article 1 of EBRD's charter defining the purpose of EBRD as to foster the "transition towards open market-oriented economies and to promote private and entrepreneurial initiative in the Central and Eastern European countries committed to and applying the principles of multi-party democracy, pluralism and market economies." It may be, however, noted that not even the EBRD's charter asks for direct financing of democracy-building in its client countries. Rather it calls for financing of market reforms and private sector business in countries that commit to a transition to democracy. As a result, even EBRD thus finances democracy only indirectly or makes such financing dependent on a commitment to democracy. This view is confirmed when looking at EBRD's lending portfolio in which no democracy-building program, has ever appeared. *See* consecutive EBRD Annual Reports (1995–1999). *For example,* in the last years, EBRD's activities have focused on the financial sector, the promotion of small-and medium-size enterprises, infrastructure and environment, and the creation of a sound investment climate in which corruption and poor governance has no place. *See* EBRD Annual Report 4–7 (1999).

MDBs (such as the Inter-American Development Bank (IDB), the Asian Development Bank (ADB), and the African Development Bank (AfDB)) other than EBRD, the charters of which are constructed similar to the World Bank with a focus on economic development, have mainly followed the World Bank's approach in their provision of legal technical assistance and general assistance with a human rights dimension.[31] Legal technical assistance is generally seen as part of the broader objective of improving the governance capacity of recipient governments, a concern that grew when MDBs started realizing that economic and social development projects increasingly fail to achieve their objectives because of inadequate, or even lack of, institutional and legal frameworks.

III. THE RULE OF LAW AND THE WORLD BANK

A. Overview of the Bank's Concern for the Rule of Law and Human Rights as It Developed Historically

As mentioned earlier and in contrast to EBRD, the World Bank's[32] charter does not include specific provisions on the *rule of law,* nor does it include provisions on specific aspects of the *rule of law* such as multi-party democracy, democratic institutions, political human rights, or similar political goals. On the contrary,

---

31 For more detailed information on assistance for legal and judicial reform by other MDBs, *see, e.g.*, for the EBRD, the issues of the journal LAW IN TRANSITION of the years 1997-2000; for the IDB, JUSTICE DELAYED: JUDICIAL REFORM IN LATIN-AMERICA (Edmundo Jarquin & Fernando Carrillo eds., 1998); and KATHARINA PISTOR & PHILIP WELLONGS, THE ROLE OF LAW AND LEGAL INSTITUTIONS IN ASIAN ECONOMIC DEVELOPMENT 1960–1995 (1998) (including information on ADB's efforts to finance appropriate legal reforms in its borrowing members). For further information on other MDBs, *see also* in this LIBER AMICORUM the contributions by Barry Metzger, *The Asian Financial Crisis, Corruption and Legal Reform*; John Niehuss, *Charter Limitations on the Scope of Inter-American Development Bank Activities*; and Francis Ssekandi, *Law and Development — An Empirical Study of the Evolution of the Legal Framework for Delivery of Multilateral Development Assistance: National Execution*.

32 For the purposes of this paper, references to the World Bank (or Bank) include the International Bank for Reconstruction and Development (IBRD) and the International Development Association (IDA) unless specified otherwise.

the World Bank's charter includes a specific provision prohibiting it from engaging in political activities or from being influenced by the political character of its members in its decision-making.[33] The World Bank's charter requires the Bank to take "only economic considerations" into account in its decisions.[34] The World Bank's range of activities is thus limited. Assistance of a political nature or based on political grounds cannot be rendered by the Bank.

In the affirmative, the Bank's charter specifically asks it "to facilitate the investment of capital for productive purposes," "to promote private foreign investment by guarantees and loans . . . for productive purposes," and "to encourage international investment for the development of the productive resources of members, thereby assisting in raising productivity, the standard of living and conditions of labor in their territories."[35] In other words, the Bank's objective is to promote reconstruction, economic growth and development in its borrowing countries.

Despite the absence of a reference to the *rule of law* in its charter, the World Bank nevertheless managed to integrate *rule of law* concerns into its development finance activities. It may be safely stated that the promotion of the *rule of law* has increasingly played an important role in the Bank's development assistance, as it evolved over the years. The promotion of the *rule of law* by the Bank was evoked by the changing needs in developing countries. The Bank responded to it through a balanced revision of its practice, supported by a creative but legally sound interpretation of its charter by the Bank's Board of Executive Directors, the organ of the Bank that has the power to interpret the charter.[36] Incorporation of the *rule of law* concerns into the Bank's work through interpretation rests on two pillars: (i) *rule of law* concerns proper in

---

33 *See* Article IV, Section 10, first sentence of IBRD's Articles of Agreement providing that "[t]he Bank and its officers shall not interfere in the political affairs of any member; nor shall they be influenced in their decisions by the political character of the member or members concerned. *See also* Article V, Section 6, first sentence of IDA's Articles of Agreement containing the same statement.

34 *See* IBRD's Arts., *id.*, second sentence, and IDA's Arts., *id.*, second sentence.

35 *See* Article I (i, ii, iii) of IBRD's Articles of Agreement. *Compare* also Article I of IDA's Articles of Agreement which, to a certain degree, uses similar language.

36 For details on the interpretation of the Bank's Charter, *see* IBRAHIM F.I. SHIHATA, THE WORLD BANK IN A CHANGING WORLD, Vol. III (2000), Chapter 1 (*The Dynamic Evolution of the World Bank Within Its Original Legal Framework*).

conjunction with concerns for good governance, and (ii) *human rights* concerns as they relate to the Bank's economic and social development mission. Historically, the *rule of law* was explicitly referred to only in the context of the concern for good governance although that concern developed historically later than the concern for human rights.

Under a literal reading of the Bank's charter, the Bank's financial assistance to its members related initially to the financing of productive investments in furtherance of economic growth and development.[37] Over time, the Bank's financial assistance evolved so that social development was also referred to as a chief development goal. This extension was accepted in the late 1960s when the Bank started making loans for education projects. The latter were by then considered to meet the "productive purposes" requirement although such projects were only indirectly productive by contrast to industrial projects, the initial type of project financed by the Bank that generated revenues directly. Similarly, today's operations of the Bank cover numerous diverse issues, including population, education, health, women in development, social security (concerns which were added when it became clear in the 1970s that the provision of these services was essential to promote growth in incomes), environment (a concern which was introduced in the 1980s when it was seen that economic development was only sustainable if it was environmentally sound), macro-economic policy and structural reform (a component in the Bank's development strategy that responded to the problems of global recession and debt crises in the 1980s), and governance.

Through the financing of programs and projects promoting its member countries' economic and social development, the Bank contributes to the promotion and protection of a broad array of *human rights* of an economic, social and cultural character. Its work may in this respect be described as a continuous attempt to help its less developed members exercise their "right to development," a right proclaimed by the United Nations in 1986[38] as a

---

37 For an overview of the evolution of the Bank's development assistance over the last five decades, *see* IBRAHIM F.I. SHIHATA, THE WORLD BANK IN A CHANGING WORLD, Vol. III(2000), Chapter 3 (*Major Changes in the Bank's Activities*).

38 *See* UN Declaration on the Right to Development of 1986, G.A. Res. No. 41/128 (Annex), UN GAOR, 41st Sess., Supp. No. 53, at 186, UN Doc. A/41/53 (1987).

basic human right that was reaffirmed in the 1993 Vienna Declaration of the World Conference on Human Rights.[39]

As *Ibrahim Shihata* put it, "the Bank *transforms* many ideals of the UN declarations and covenants regarding *economic, social and cultural human rights* through its lending operations, its policy dialogue with its borrowing members, and through its research, publications and cooperation with governments and other agencies into realities."[40]

It should, however, be emphasized that the Bank's promotion of economic, social and cultural human rights, unlike the activities of other international agencies, does not take place from the point of view of a general standard setter and enforcer of human rights, but from the point of view of a development finance institution. Thus, if the Bank effectively promotes the right of development and various economic and social rights, it does so because this is what, in its view, needs to be done to fulfill its broad economic and social development mandate. The Bank does not engage in development activities because the promotion of peoples' rights to development or the realization of an individual's economic and social rights would be its immediate purpose. In other words, the Bank's contribution to the achievement of economic, social and cultural human rights is a by-product, (a very welcome by-product but) not an immediate or direct goal. It is part of its agenda on social development but there exists no obligation on it to realize these rights for the benefit of the rightholders.[41]

---

39 *See* Vienna Declaration and Programme of Action, adopted by the UN World Conference on Human Rights on June 25, 1993, UN Doc. A/CONF. 157/24 (Part I) (October 13, 1993), at 20–46, 32 I.L.M. 1661 (1993).

40 *See* IBRAHIM F.I. SHIHATA, THE WORLD BANK IN A CHANGING WORLD, Vol. II, 567, at 568 (1995), Chapter Nineteen (The World Bank and Human Rights) (emphasis added); *see also id.*, THE WORLD BANK IN A CHANGING WORLD, VOL. I, 97, at 109 (1991), Chapter Three (*The World Bank and Human Rights*); *id.*, THE WORLD BANK IN A CHANGING WORLD, Vol. II 553, at 558 (1995), Chapter Eighteen (*Human Rights, Development, and International Financial Institutions*), and *id.*, *The World Bank and Human Rights*, *in* THE UNIVERSAL PROTECTION OF HUMAN RIGHTS: TRANSLATING INTERNATIONAL COMMITMENTS INTO NATIONAL ACTION — PROCEEDINGS OF THE 40TH INTERNATIONAL SEMINAR FOR DIPLOMATS held in Salzburg, Austria, on July 28–August 1, 1997, SPECIAL ISSUE OF THE ÖSTERREICHISCHE AUßENPOLITISCHE DOKUMENTATION (1997). (Emphasis in the quote above added.) *See also* Development and Human Rights — The Role of the World Bank (World Bank Publication 1998).

41 It may be noted that the Bank's situation is thus contrary to the situation in which states are parties to international human rights treaties.

According to its purposes under its Articles of Agreement, the Bank has to look after its member countries' economic and social development as a whole. That may require both a selection and a sequencing in the development assistance that does not allow for paying attention to all economic, social and cultural human rights equally and at the same time.[42] Also, not necessarily every Bank-financed project leads to the direct improvement of an individual's economic, social and cultural human rights. There are projects and programs targeting public and/or private sectors as a whole and whose direct positive effects on an individual's economic, social and cultural rights are difficult to see, to measure or quantify.[43]

While the Bank had long been concerned with issues of institutional development and public sector management in its borrowing member countries and long recognized that political stability and sound economic management are basic prerequisites for economic development, it had not given these issues a major priority in its work until the late 1980s when the economic performance in many developing countries started to decline dramatically or defied improvement. Major studies identified *governance* as a basic issue in the development strategy of the countries that were performing poorly. The most important among these studies was the Sub-Saharan Africa study of 1989.[44] The 1989 study provided a more comprehensive treatment of development issues in Sub-Saharan Africa and, for the first time, spelled out the question of governance as a central issue to be addressed and corrected.[45]

---

42 The selection and sequencing of development assistance by the Bank is discussed with the borrower in the so-called policy dialogue the results of which and the Bank's conclusions thereupon are recorded in the Country Assistance Strategy (CAS) documents. The CAS is discussed later together with other operational tools used by the Bank in its development assistance.

43 That Bank operations may generate both positive and negative effects on individuals' economic situation is particularly true in the context of adjustment programs. The latter's macroeconomic reforms are often accompanied by negative effects on large segments of the population, e.g. the unemployment resulting from privatization measures or the downsizing of a country's civil service. While the Bank tries to mitigate these effects through additional social programs, they may not always be completely avoided. However, the reforms are intended to ultimately strengthen a country's economy and increase job opportunities in the future.

44 *See* Sub-Saharan Africa — From Crisis to Sustainable Growth — A Long-term Perspective Study (World Bank November 1989).

45 *Ibid.* at 3 (noting that many governments are wracked by corruption and are increasingly unable to command the confidence of the population at large).

It proposed a strategic agenda for Africa in the 1990s, but predicted that "none of [the proposed strategic] measures will go far, nor will much external aid be forthcoming, *unless governance in Africa improves*."[46] The study emphasized as relevant aspects in this improvement process the accountability of leaders to their principles, the transparency of transactions, the proper administration of public funds and the overhauling of procurement procedures. It called for respect of due process, cautioned against the proliferation of administrative regulations, and emphasized the importance of reforming the civil service. The study further explained that a simple and transparent legal framework properly enforced is indispensable for the long-term success of an enterprise. It pointed out the importance of establishing the *rule of law*, rehabilitating the judicial system, ensuring independence for the judiciary, scrupulous respect for the law and *human rights* at every level of government, transparent accountability of public monies, and independent public auditors responsible to a representative legislature, not to an executive.

In his introduction to the 1989 study, the Bank's then President highlighted in general terms the importance of *good governance*, defining it in terms of "a public service that is efficient, a judicial system that is reliable and an administration that is accountable to its public." Following this study's discussion in the Bank's Board of Executive Directors, the Bank decided to pay closer attention to governance issues as defined in a legal opinion prepared by *Ibrahim Shihata*, the Bank's then General Counsel, and approved by the Bank's Board of Executive Directors.[47]

B. Promotion of the Rule of Law/Good Governance and Human Rights in Practice

In the Bank's practice, the notion of the *rule of law* had rarely (and certainly never as guiding theme) been used before the Bank endorsed the focus on governance issues at the end of the 1980s.

---

46 *Ibid.* at 15. (Emphasis added.)

47 *See* Legal Opinion of the Vice President and General Counsel endorsed by the Bank's Board of Executive Directors and published in IBRAHIM F.I. SHIHATA, THE WORLD BANK IN A CHANGING WORLD, Vol. I, 85 (1991), Chapter 2 (*The World Bank and "Governance" Issues in its Borrowing Members*).

Since then, however, the importance of law for development, specifically the *rule of law* as core element of good governance, gained prominence in the Bank's development assistance activities. As will be explained below, the governance related *rule of law* aspect in the Bank's development assistance has been defined for Bank purposes in a fairly value neutral way. Where values are embedded in the Bank's *rule of law* notion, they are broad, leaving ample choices for countries without being at risk to lose Bank support. Partially as a result of the Bank's special mandate (in particular the prohibition for it to take political considerations into account) and partially as a result of its conviction from practical experience that some flexibility to allow for country-sensitive approaches is appropriate, the Bank's definition of the *rule of law* does not imply it being tied to any political system, or particular economic, social, cultural, or moral systems and objectives. Yet, it is inherently incompatible with some systems and objectives, and gives preference to a wide range of others. The Bank's *rule of law's* incompatibility with some systems and objectives, and favoritism of others, stems to some degree from the rather value neutral elements of the *rule of law* and the value oriented elements of the *rule of law* that set broad economic and social frameworks, as defined for the purposes of the Bank's work on governance issues.

In addition, they stem from a body of more value oriented, or content based, guidelines which evolved throughout the years of Bank experience with development assistance. This body of guidelines (some of them mandatory) is contained in Bank policies and procedures and further strategy tools used in the Bank's development assistance. While not explicitly stating so, the values embodied in these guidelines for development assistance reflect also development specific standards of a broad range of economic, social, environmental, and cultural human rights. The latter have been referred to in the context of the Bank's first governance paper as part of the *rule of law*. They will thus, in addition to the explicit definition by the Bank of the *rule of law* for development purposes, be laid out here, together with the way the Bank promotes them.

The two major areas in which the Bank promotes the *rule of law* in a broader encompassing sense include: (i) the Bank's work under the rubric of *governance*; and (ii) the part of the Bank's work which actively promotes a broad range of economic, social and cultural human rights.

1. Promotion of Good Governance

Under the rubric of *governance,* the Bank finances efforts to improve public sector management, to reform the civil service, to strengthen legal, regulatory and judicial frameworks, and to reduce corruption. For its purposes, the Bank has defined *governance* as "the manner in which power is exercised in the management of a country's economic and social resources for development," thus limiting its concern for good *governance* to issues which have undisputed economic implications.[48]

The *rule of law* represents the legal dimension of good *governance* by a country. To guide its support for enhancement and/or establishment of good *governance* in its client countries, the Bank established its own definition of a *rule of law*. *Ibrahim Shihata* defined the *rule of law* for purposes of the Bank's work on *governance* issues as "a system [which] assumes that: (i) there is a set of rules which are known in advance; (ii) such rules are actually in force; (iii) mechanisms exist to ensure the proper application of the rules and to allow for departure from them as needed according to established procedures; (iv) conflicts in the application of rules can be resolved through binding decisions of an independent judicial or arbitral body; and (v) there are known procedures for amending the rules when they no longer serve their purpose."[49]

In a nutshell, it may be said that, the *rule of law* for Bank purposes consists of: (i) legally binding *rules*; (ii) appropriate *pro-*

---

48 *See* Governance: The World Bank Experience 58 (World Bank 1994).

49 This definition was formulated by Ibrahim F.I. Shihata in a legal opinion requested for by the Bank's Board of Executive Directors in support of the endorsement of a new development assistance strategy by the Bank to overcome a shortcoming in its assistance to developing countries that had long been unidentified but recognized in the 1989 Governance Study on Sub-Saharan Africa. The definition of the *rule of law* proposed in the legal opinion was endorsed by the Bank's Board. *See* Legal Opinion of the Vice President and General Counsel, *published in* IBRAHIM F.I. SHIHATA, THE WORLD BANK IN A CHANGING WORLD, VOL. I, 85 (1991), Chapter 2 (*The World Bank and "Governance" Issues in its Borrowing Members*).

cesses through which these rules are made, enforced and changed; and (iii) well-functioning public *institutions* to apply and enforce these rules.[50]

This definition of the *rule of law* for Bank purposes represents in the first place a formal (or content-neutral) concept. The content-oriented part of the Bank's *rule of law* definition becomes clear, however, when studied together with the concrete projects and programs which the Bank finances with a view of assisting a country in the establishment or improvement of a sound legal framework. It is Bank practice that shows that its notion of the *rule of law* has also a substantive content, albeit its notion is not tied to a single particular economic and social system. The substantive content comprises a broad range of economic, social and justice related, environmental, and cultural aspects.

From a *formal point of view,* the *rule of law* as defined by the Bank for development purposes requires that *legal norms* are the supreme authority in a society binding all powers, and that these norms are public, clear, impartial, general, prospective, and stable.[51] In other words, decisions should be made by the application of known principles or laws without the intervention of arbitrariness or excessive discretion in their application.[52]

From a *substantive point of view,* the rules promoted by Bank-financed projects and programs relate to the regulation of commercial and financial activities in a market economy or one that is on the road of transformation into such an economy. They cover broadly or partially laws on movable, immovable, and intellectual property, contract law, tort liability law, companies partnership and cooperatives laws, central banking, commercial and investment banking laws, capital market and securities laws, collateral security laws, taxation laws, insolvency laws, labor safety laws, competition laws, anti-corruption and fraud laws, foreign investment laws, cross-boarder sales laws, and commercial arbitra-

---

50 *See,* for details, IBRAHIM F.I. SHIHATA, COMPLEMENTARY REFORM — ESSAYS ON LEGAL, JUDICIAL AND OTHER INSTITUTIONAL REFORMS SUPPORTED BY THE WORLD BANK (1997), Chapter 1 (*Law, Development and the Role of the World Bank*).

51 *See* IBRAHIM F.I. SHIHATA, THE WORLD BANK IN A CHANGING WORLD, Vol. III (2000), Chapter 6 (*Relevant Issues in the Establishment of a Sound Legal Framework for a Market Economy*) .

52 *See* BLACK'S LAW DICTIONARY 1332 (6th ed. 1990).

tion.[53] They also cover a broad range of social aspects including pension and social security laws, health insurance laws, education laws, and environmental legislation.

For the aspects of *processes of law-making, application and enforcement,* the Bank's assistance, while staying away from referring to a special political system, asks for non-arbitrary processes based on a system of consultation with the people affected by the law, transparency of these processes, and accountability of the public officials involved in them. Although these requirements fall largely short of what would be required from legislative, executive, and judicial processes in a democracy (i.e. in the sense of the Western countries' modern notion of the *rule of law*), they represent requirements which do not allow for any political system in a country, especially not a strictly totalitarian system. Moreover, while these requirements contain primarily formal elements, they also include some substantive aspects in a broader sense such as justice and fairness.

As to the *public institutions applying and enforcing the law,* the Bank sees, in a combination of formal and substantive elements that make up the respective institutions, an efficient civil service and independent and fair judiciary as well as other complementary alternative dispute resolution mechanisms as greatly important for the functioning of the economic and social order in a country. The list of institutions contributing to this functioning is not limited to the executive and judiciary. It includes further parts of civil society, e.g. bar associations, law schools, consumer rights groups, NGOs, business associations, labor unions as far as they enhance the application and enforcement of the law.[54]

---

53 For brief reference purposes, it may be said that the market-friendly substance of the Bank's *rule of law* notion covers the following main five areas: property, contract, company, bankruptcy, and competition.

54 The promotion of processes in the Bank's jargon is often referred to as furtherance of the social dialogue. The promotion of institutions is called "capacity-building." The focus on capacity-building tries to make good for earlier weaknesses in the way development assistance was given, particularly to increase aid effectiveness. Thus, instead to the quantity of financial and technical assistance, attention was given to sustainable development outcomes. Furthermore, assistance is being turned into a more "client-driven" process as opposed to a "donor-driven" one. In order to ensure the latter, new programs such as the "Learning and Innovations Loans" and the "Adaptable Program Loan" have been introduced under which the Bank and the

The following examples of Bank projects and programs financed under the rubric *governance* assistance illustrate the Bank's activities in promoting the *rule of law*.[55]

Legal Reform Projects

Angola

The Financial Institutions Modernization Project[56] intends to improve Angola's financial legal and regulatory framework, including the following activities: (i) application of banking legislation through design, publication and distribution of a banking operational manual; (ii) compilation, harmonization, publication and dissemination of the banking legal and regulatory framework; (iii) strengthening of legal and technical capabilities of banking institutions' staff; (iv) strengthening of the National Directorate of Registries and Notarial Services; and (v) review and development of modern banking regulations.

China

The Bank's first freestanding legal reform project, the IDA-financed Economic Law Reform Project for China,[57] supports technical assistance in drafting key economic legislation, training in new economic laws, and institutional strengthening of key agencies, such as the National People's Congress (NPC) Commission on Legislative Affairs; the NPC Economic and Finance Committee; the State Council's Office on Legislative Affairs; and the Ministry of Justice.

The project consists of three components: (i) legal drafting; (ii) training; and (iii) institutional support. The legal drafting component currently supports a wide range of sub-projects in such areas as enterprise reform, corporate restructuring, competition policy, tax, trade, legal profession, procurement, intellectual property, etc. The project also finances innovative training programs prepared by law faculties. The Office of Legislative Affairs has a program to establish

---

borrower agree on long-term goals without committing to a final project design and implementation plan but for allowing the design and implementation to be adjusted as a result of learning in the capacity building process.

55 *See also* Initiatives in Legal and Judicial Reform (World Bank, Legal Department, Legal and Judicial Reform Unit 2000).

56 *See* Credit No. 2421 ANG, September 15, 1992 for US$21 million equivalent.

57 *See* Credit No. 2654-CN, October 18, 1994, for US$10.0 million equivalent.

a legal information system accessible to all national and regional government agencies (and eventually to the public at large).

Russian Federation

The overall objective of the Legal Reform Project for the Russian Federation[58] is to improve the performance of the Russian legal system in areas key to the effective functioning of market institutions. The project's specific objectives are to (i) improve the quality of drafting of economic laws, decrees, and regulations; (ii) assist the government of Russia in designing the appropriate classification of legislation (including legislation in electronic format); (iii) identify the appropriate methods of codifying Russian legislation; (iv) introduce innovative teaching methods and materials in the legal education system, with particular emphasis on increased exchange between legal academia and practice; (v) improve teacher training; and (vi) improve the quality of judicial training for courts of general jurisdiction and arbitrage courts.

The project comprises four inter-related components consisting of technical assistance to support: (i) legal drafting; (ii) collection and dissemination of legal information; (iii) legal education, including public education campaigns; and (iv) judicial reform, including support for alternative dispute resolution.

Judicial Reform Projects

Ecuador

The Judicial Reform Project for Ecuador[59] is part of the government's overall legal and judicial reform strategy which had been formulated on the bases of broad consultation with all stakeholders. The project has eight components: (i) case administration and information support to be piloted at the first instance level courts in three main cities; (ii) court-annexed Alternative Dispute Resolution (ADR) mechanisms to be piloted and ADR training; (iii) a program for law and justice, including among other things, a special fund for law and justice to support activities initiated by civil society and innovation by courts; (iv) a professional development program for law professors; (v) a study on the state of legal education; (vi) research and

58 *See* Loan No. 4036-RU, June 13, 1996, for US$58.0 million equivalent.

59 *See* Loan No. 4066-EC, April 13, 1995, for US$10.7 million equivalent.

evaluation of ADR pilot programs; (vii) legal service pilots for poor women; and (viii) infrastructure remodeling and development of court infrastructure standards.

Peru

In 1999, the Bank approved an Institutional Development Fund (IDF) Grant for the Institutional Development of the Ombudsman's Office in Peru.[60] The objective of this grant is to enhance the citizen's access to the Office's services, and improve the efficiency of the internal processing of complaints against other state agencies. The project's objectives include: (i) modernization of the administrative structure and operation of the Ombudsman's Office; (ii) improvement of the overall performance of the Ombudsman's national and regional offices; (iii) enhancement of the coordination between state authorities and the civil society; and (iv) improvement in the users' knowledge of, and access to, the Ombudsman's services.

Mixed Legal and Judicial Reform Projects

Republic of Yemen

Until unification in 1990, the People's Democratic Republic of Yemen (North) and the Arab Republic of Yemen (South) had different legal regimes. While the People's Democratic Republic's legal system drew heavily on the legal traditions of the Ottoman system, the Arab Republic's system had a distinct common law influence resulting from decades of British mandate. The Reunification Constitution of the Republic of Yemen (approved by referendum in 1991) established the principle of independence of the judiciary. Under the Republic's Constitution of 1994, the judicial branch was established as an autonomous financial and administrative entity.

The legal and judicial reform project, approved in June 1999, is a Learning and Innovation Loan.[61] The project has three components: (i) a judicial reform component, which includes training for the judiciary and arbitrators, an assessment of court administration and judgement execution regulations and practices, and the rehabilitation of infrastructure; (ii) a legal reform component, comprised of institutional strengthening for the Ministry of Legal and Parliamentary Affairs and assessments of the legal frame-

60 IDF Grant for US$500,000.

61 Credit No. 3274-RY approved June 28, 1999, for US$2.5 million equivalent.

works governing business, economic, and financial activities, as well as the legal framework for land tenure, transfer, titling, and registration; and (iii) and a public awareness campaign.

Civil Service Reform Projects

Burkina Faso

The objective of the Public Institutional Development Project[62] is to support the borrower's efforts to reinforce the major public institutions charged with economic and sector management. The project intends to: (i) improve the current state of knowledge regarding the civil service through systematic data collection and analysis, including building or rebuilding of personnel system files through census and computerization; (ii) rationalize payroll systems; (iii) undertake organizational audits or functional reviews of selected agencies, mainly to justify retrenchment policies; and (iv) provide limited training to facilitate redeployment.

Anti-Corruption Project

Since September 1997, the Bank has started addressing corruption explicitly as a grave governance problem in borrowing countries.[63] In recognition that systemic corruption is a symptom of public sector breakdown, the Bank is focusing on addressing corruption as part of a broad strategy for improving public sector performance and economic and sector policies in a country.

Bolivia

The Bolivia Financial Decentralization and Accountability Project addresses the issue of corruption through a variety of measures.[64] The development objectives for the project are: (i) implementing a sustainable process of self-management in financial administration while instituting sound financial management standards and systems in a critical mass of public entities; and (ii) build-

---

62 Credit No. C-2378 approved June 29, 1992, for US$11 million equivalent.

63 *See* Report of the Corruption Action Plan Working Group — Helping Countries Combat Corruption: The Role of the World Bank Group (SecM97-548), dated June 25, 1997. *See also* Helping Countries Combat Corruption: The Role of the World Bank (R97-201), dated August 13, 1997, a paper prepared by the Poverty Reduction and Economic Management Network (PREM) which is based on the report of the CAPWG amending it in order to reflect the discussion on the Executive Directors' seminar on July 15, 1997.

64 *See* Credit No. N033 approved September 5, 1997, for US$15 million equivalent.

ing up a strong public auditing function able to collaborate with private sector auditing firms to continuously review and evaluate financial performance and integrity of operations conducted by public sector entities. The project's components are: (i) implementing decentralized integrated financial management systems (IFMS), developing institutional capacity to improve project auditing, accounting, and reporting; (ii) IFMS public sector-wide integration through installing telecom links, linking both the decentralized and centralized financial and budget reporting systems; (iii) modernizing the budget transactions payments systems *via* a private sector banking network; (iv) disseminating integrated financial management operation and implementing public financial regulations; (v) project operating costs covering administrative and project management staff, travel, materials, and equipment; (vi) strengthening government auditing and decentralized sector evaluations; (vii) implementing audit capability for operational and special audits; (viii) anti-corruption auditing techniques and public sector ethics dissemination; (ix) training in accounting, auditing, and financial management; and (x) contingencies and project preparation facilities refinancing.

2. *Promotion of Economic, Social, and Cultural Human Rights*

While the Bank's promotion of a broad array of human rights of an economic, social, environmental, and cultural character[65] emanates from its economic and social development mandate as

---

[65] It may be noted that the prohibition of political activities of the Bank's charter have been interpreted by the Bank's Executive Directors, in addition to not borrow for political reform (e.g. for the purposes of establishing a democracy), to in principle not be concerned with the status of political rights in a borrowing country, especially the borrowing country's record of political human rights violations. However, the Bank may take into account pervasive violations of such rights to the extent that they have obvious and significant adverse effects on the economy of the country it assists. Another exceptional case where attention to the treatment of political human rights by a borrower is allowed is the case of the Bank's duty to pay due regard to the binding decisions of the UN Security Council taken under Article 41 and 42 of the UN Charter. These decisions may be based on political grounds and may require the Bank not to deal with a certain country. In their respect, the Bank is bound by virtue of its Relationship Agreement with the UN. It may be noted that, where the Bank requires participation of affected people in the design and implementation of projects it finances, this does not mean that it asks the borrowing country, on the territory of which the project financed by the Bank is located, to introduce the freedom of free expression or assembly as a general matter. Participation of affected people is geographically limited to the project

a development finance institution and not from a mission of a general standard setter for or enforcement agency of human rights,[66] the Bank's contribution to the realization of these rights in developing countries is by no means smaller because of the special angle of the Bank and its being a facilitator rather than a world government or world policeman for human rights.

The Bank's combined development assistance of helping its borrowing members to create macroeconomic frameworks conducive to growth such as the expansion of production and trade, financing human resource development, infrastructure etc. contributes to the *reduction of poverty* in borrowing countries. Altogether, the Bank's assistance is geared towards establishing a situation in which people in its borrowing countries can enjoy freedom from poverty, i.e. a basic economic freedom from which still 1.3 billion people are deprived in the world.[67] The Bank ad-

---

area and time wise also bound to the project stages where Bank policies require such participation. For further details, *see* IBRAHIM F.I. SHIHATA, THE WORLD BANK IN A CHANGING WORLD, Vol. III (2000), Chapter 4 (*Democracy, Development and The World Bank*) and Chapter 5 (*Political Limitations on the Bank's Work*).

[66] It must be emphasized that the Bank does not engage in development activities because the promotion of peoples' rights to development or an individual's economic and social rights would be its immediate purpose. It also does not engage in these activities based on the numerous existing international human rights treaties. The Bank itself is not bound by these treaties because it is not a party to them. Only the Bank's members are, to a varying degree, bound by these treaties. The Bank's assistance in areas that concern economic, social and human rights, however, helps its members to implement their treaty obligations and is thus both consistent and complementary with the international human rights framework without the Bank having the role to enforce these rights. *See* Ibrahim F.I. Shihata, The World Bank in a Changing World, Vol. I, 97, 109 (1991), Chapter 3 (The World Bank and Human Rights), and *id.*, The World Bank in a Changing World, Vol. II, 567, 568 (1995), Chapter 19 (The World Bank and Human Rights). More recently, *see also* Sabine Schlemmer-Schulte, *The World Bank and Human Rights,* 4 AUSTRIAN REVIEW OF INTERNATIONAL AND EUROPEAN LAW (ARIEL) 230 (1999).

[67] *See* World Bank Atlas 15 (1998) and World Development Indicators 66 *et seq.* (World Bank Publication, 1999). While over the past decades living standards in developing countries have much improved, infant mortality has on average been reduced by half, people's life expectancy risen, and average incomes per person in the developing world have doubled, a number of other figures still speak of frightening poverty in many regions. Every year, nearly 8 million children die from diseases caused by dirty water and poisoned air, 50 million children are mentally or physically damaged because of inadequate nutrition, and 130 million — 80 percent of them girls — do not have the chance to go to school.

dresses poverty in its borrowing member countries through its poverty assessments.[68]

Another contribution to the Bank's general efforts to reduce poverty in its borrowing member countries is its *special debt relief program*. In a number of developing countries, official debt owed to bilateral and multilateral creditors has grown so high that governments are finding it difficult to both service their debt and make important investments in health care and education. In light of the magnitude of the problem and among other initiatives, the Bank decided (together with the International Monetary Fund) in September 1996 to establish the Heavily Indebted Poor Countries (HIPC) Debt Initiative Trust Fund.[69]

The Bank is increasingly concerned with the development of human capital. Over the past three years, total Bank lending for financing *education, health, nutrition and population* projects and programs has averaged about 15 percent.[70] The Bank's lending in health, population and nutrition in FY1998 amounted to about US$ 2 billion, in FY1999 to about US$1.1 billion, and in FY2000 to about US$1.04 billion.[71] The Bank is also one of the leading financiers of HIV/AIDS prevention and control activities.[72] Furthermore, it is the single largest external source of finance for education in the developing world.[73] In the past three years, Bank lending for education has averaged US$1.7 billion annually.[74] The Bank's lending for education, health, nutrition and population

68 *See* Development and Human Rights — The Role of the World Bank (World Bank Publication 1998) (hereinafter Development and Human Rights).

69 For details regarding this initiative, *see* Ibrahim F.I. Shihata, *Introductory Note on the Resolution on the Establishment of the Heavily Indebted Poor Countries (HPIC) Debt Initiative Trust Fund,* 36 I.L.M. 990 (1997).

70 *See* World Bank Annual Report 33 (2000).

71 *See* World Bank Annual Report 67 (1998), World Bank Annual Report 10 (1999), and World Bank Annual Report 33 (2000).

72 *See* Development and Human Rights – The Role of the World Bank 7 (World Bank Publication 1998). To date, the Bank has committed more than US$ 800 million to more than 70 HIV/AIDS related projects.

73 *Ibid.* at 69. During the past 35 years, the Bank has loaned US$ 24billion for education, supporting nearly 600 projects in more than 100 countries. *See also* World Bank Annual Report 10 (1999) (including the figures for FY 1999), and World Bank Annual Report 33 (2000)(for the FY2000 figures). *See also* the contribution by Louis B. Sohn, *The World Bank and the Human Right to Education,* to this LIBER AMICORUM.

74 *See* World Bank Annual Report 33 (2000).

contributes to people's enjoyment of their rights to education and health services.[75]

The Bank also provides advice, technical assistance and financing to strengthen borrowing members' systems of *"governance."* As was mentioned before, strengthening the "governance" systems of countries, in the terminology of the Bank, means, the improvement of the efficient management of a borrowing member's human and economic resources. In this vein, the Bank is lending for legal, judicial and civil service reform to help improve the rules of the countries' legal framework, the processes of the elaboration of these rules, and the working of the institutions which apply and enforce these rules.[76] The Bank's assistance tries in particular to enhance coherence, transparency, and accountability in the set up of the legal framework.[77] Its support of the countries' judiciary improves people's access to legal remedies.[78] Institutional reforms financed by it, help people realize their property rights, an essential prerequisite for an efficient economic use of land.[79] The Bank also seeks to combat corruption.[80] While these efforts do not address

---

75 For a detailed analysis of how Bank lending for education and health specifically promotes children's rights, *see* Ibrahim F.I. Shihata, *The World Bank's Protection and Promotion of Children's Rights,* 4 INTERNATIONAL JOURNAL OF CHILDREN'S RIGHTS 383 (1996). *See also* Sabine Schlemmer-Schulte, *The World Bank and Children's Rights, in* UNDERSTANDING CHILDREN'S RIGHTS — PROCEEDINGS OF THE THIRD INTERNATIONAL INTER-DISCIPLINARY COURSE ON CHILDREN'S RIGHTS 317–327 (Eugen Verhellen ed. 1998).

76 For more details on the Bank's financing of the establishment of legal institutions and the "rule of law" in transition economies, *see* World Development Report — From Plan to Market 87-97 (World Bank Publication 1996). For the Bank's search for an optimal role of the state to ensure sustainable and widely shared development, *see* World Development Report — The State in a Changing World (World Bank Publication 1997). *See also* IBRAHIM F.I. SHIHATA, COMPLEMENTARY REFORM — ESSAYS ON LEGAL, JUDICIAL AND OTHER INSTITUTIONAL REFORM SUPPORTED BY THE WORLD BANK (1997).

77 *See* Governance: The World Bank's Experience, (World Bank Publication 1994).

78 *See,* e.g., IBRAHIM F.I. SHIHATA, COMPLEMENTARY REFORM- ESSAYS ON LEGAL, JUDICIAL AND OTHER INSTITUTIONAL REFORM SUPPORTED BY THE WORLD BANK (1997); and Maria Dakolias & Javier Said, *Judicial Reform: A Process of Change Through Pilot Courts,* 2 EUROPEAN JOURNAL OF LAW REFORM 95 (2000).

79 *See* ALEX F. MCCALLA, RURAL DEVELOPMENT: FROM VISION TO ACTION (1997).

80 *See* Helping Countries Combat Corruption: The Role of the World Bank (World Bank Publication 1997). *See also* Ibrahim F.I. Shihata, *Corruption — A General Re-*

specific human rights, they do, however, further the enjoyment of all such rights, including political rights.

The Bank encourages and requires the *participation* of affected people and local NGOs in the design and implementation of the projects it finances.[81] Non-Governmental organizations (NGOs) are now directly involved in half of all Bank-financed projects.[82] Such participation helps meet people's real needs and priorities. While limited to Bank-supported projects, this participatory approach to development demonstrates the advantages of consultations with people and may have a catalyst effect to introduce participation beyond Bank-financed projects in other affairs of the state.[83]

Environmental protection has become an integral part in the Bank's development assistance.[84] The projects the Bank finances

---

view with an Emphasis on the Role of the World Bank, in CORRUPTION: THE ENEMY WITHIN 255 (Barry Rider ed., 1997).

81 The Bank's policies on environmental assessment, involuntary resettlement, and indigenous people include participation procedures. *See* Operational Policy (OP) 4.01 Environmental Assessment (1999), Operational Directive (OD) 4.30 Involuntary Resettlement (1990), now being converted into Operational Policy (OP) 4.12, and Operational Directive (OD) 4.20 Indigenous People (1991), being converted into Operational Policy (OP) 4.10. World Bank policies are important internal instruments underlying each Bank-financed project. They are available on the World Bank's webpage at *http://wbln0011.worldbank.org/Inst*. For a general overview of the Bank's participatory approach, *see* The World Bank Participation Source-Book (World Bank Publication 1996). *See* further Christopher Gibbs, Claudia Fumo & Thomas Kuby, Non-governmental Organizations in World Bank-supported Projects: A Review by OED (World Bank Publication 1999). On the legal framework for the involvement of NGOs in the preparation and implementation of Bank-financed projects, *see* IBRAHIM F.I. SHIHATA, THE WORLD BANK IN A CHANGING WORLD, Vol. II (1995), Chapter Six (*The World Bank and Non-Governmental Organizations*).

82 *See* World Bank Annual Report 73 (1998), World Bank Annual Report 139 (1999),and World Bank Annual Report 29 (2000). *See also* The Bank's Relations with NGOs — Issues and Directions (World Bank Publication 1998), and World Bank — Civil Society Relations — Fiscal Year 1999 Progress Report (World Bank Publication 2000).

83 For a more detailed description of the role of civil society and NGOs in the Bank's activities, *see* World Bank — Civil Society Relations — Fiscal Year 1999 Progress Report (World Bank publication 2000). For a legal analysis of the issue, *see* IBRAHIM F.I. SHIHATA, THE WORLD BANK IN A CHANGING WORLD, Vol. II (1995), Chapter Six (THE WORLD BANK AND NGOS), and, more recently, Sabine Schlemmer-Schulte, *The Impact of Civil Society on the World Bank, The International Monetary Fund, and the World Trade Organization — The Case of the World Bank,* ILSA JOURNAL OF INTERNATIONAL AND COMPARATIVE LAW (2001) (forthcoming).

84 *See generally* Environment Matters (World Bank Publication 1998), and Main-

help ensure that as many people as possible have access to basic facilities such as clean air and water and basic sanitation facilities.[85] Through the trust funds it administers, especially the Global Environment Facility (GEF), the Bank also addresses issues such as ozone depletion and global warming.[86]

The Bank has long emphasized the crucial role of *women* in development. It supports a great number of projects aimed at giving women full access to education, health and credit services, thereby reducing any existing gender discrimination.[87] Bank research pointed out that persistent inequality between women and men constrains a society's productivity and, ultimately, slows its economic growth.[88] Since then, the Bank has increased its efforts to formulate further strategies for promoting gender equality and, consequently, enhancing economic efficiency.

---

streaming the Environment - The World Bank Group and the Environment since the Rio Earth Summit (World Bank Publication 1995). *See also* Ibrahim F.I. Shihata, *The World Bank's Contribution to the Development of International Environmental Law, in* FESTSCHRIFT FÜR IGNAZ SEIDL-HOHENVELDERN 631 (1998) (comprehensively describing the Bank's framework ensuring that environmental concerns, whenever the environment is at stake, are part of the Bank's development assistance approach).

85 *See* World Bank Annual Report 76 *et seq.* (1998), World Bank Annual Report 113 *et seq.* (1999), and World Bank Annual Report 33 and 92 *et seq.* (2000) for figures on Bank-financed environmental projects. *See also* Charles di Leva, *International Environmental Law and Development,* 10 GEORGETOWN INTERNATIONAL ENVIRONMENTAL LAW REVIEW 501 (1998), and Salman M.A. Salman, ed., Groundwater: Legal and Policy Perspectives (World Bank Technical Paper No. 456).

86 On general environmental trust funds as well as the GEF, *see* IBRAHIM F.I. SHIHATA, THE WORLD BANK IN A CHANGING WORLD, Vol. II (1995), Chapter Five (*The World Bank and the Environment: Legal Instruments for Achieving Environmental Objectives*); *id., The World Bank's Contribution to the Development of International Environmental Law, in* FESTSCHRIFT FÜR IGNAZ SEIDL-HOHENVELDERN 631 (1998); and Laurence Boisson de Chazournes, *Le fond pour l'Environnement Mondial: Recherche et Conquête de son Identité,* XLI ANNUAIRE FRANÇAIS DE DROIT INTERNATIOINAL 612 (1995). *See also* the contributions by Rudolf Dolzer, *The World Bank and the Global Environment: Novel Frontiers?,* and David Freestone, *The World Bank 's Prototype Carbon Fund,* to this LIBER AMICORUM.

87 *See generally* Caroline O.N. Moser, Annika Tornqvist & Bernice van Bronkhorst, Mainstreaming Gender and Development in the World Bank (World Bank Paper 1999); Lawrence H. Summers, Investing in all the People: Educating Women in Developing Countries (World Bank Paper 1994); Enhancing Women's Participation in Economic Development (World Bank Policy Paper No. 1014-8124, 1994); Anjana Bushan, Advancing Gender Equality: From Concept to Action (World Bank Paper 1995).

88 *See* Towards Gender Equality: The Role of Public Policy vii (World Bank Development in Practice Series 1995).

The Bank's policies on *resettlement of people involuntarily displaced* by projects it finances attempt to ensure that development is not achieved at the expense of people who are resettled in order to pave way for the construction of an infrastructure project.[89] The Bank requires that displaced persons must regain, if not improve, their standard of living. It requires that displaced people, including the landless, receive full compensation and rehabilitation and share in the project's benefits.

The Bank has a *policy on indigenous and tribal people* and advocates the recognition, demarcation and protection of indigenous lands and the provisions of "culturally appropriate" services.[90]

The Bank is taking measures to reduce the harmful forms of *child labor* by mainstreaming child labor concerns into its activities. It has thus been devising new lending and non-lending strategies addressing the exploitative aspects of child work.[91] It is also reviewing old projects in light of child labor concerns, sensitizing staff to these issues and working closely together with UNICEF and ILO in this respect.

In recent years, the Bank has strongly advocated, and supported through its lending, the *liberalization of investment and trade* and the transition to open economies.[92] It has called for a

---

89 *See* Operational Directive (OD) 4.30 Involuntary Resettlement (1990), currently being converted into Operational Policy (OP) 4.12 (establishing procedures to ensure that the population displaced by a project receives benefits from it by compensating them for their losses, assisting them with the move and their efforts to improve their former living standards, income earning capacity, and production levels, or at least to restore them).

90 *See* Operational Directive (OD) 4.20 Indigenous People (1991), currently being converted into Operational Policy (OP) 4.10 (describing Bank policies and processing procedures for projects that affect indigenous people to ensure that the latter do not suffer adverse effects during the development process).

91 *See* Peter Fallon & Zafiris Tzannatos, Child Labor – Issues and Directions for the World Bank (World Bank, Social Protection Human Development Network, 1998) (summarizing the Bank's new approach to child labor issues which was endorsed by the Bank's Board of Executive Directors in May 1997). *See also* Ibrahim F.I. Shihata, *The World Bank's Protection and Promotion of Children's Rights*, 4 INTERNATIONAL JOURNAL OF CHILDREN'S RIGHTS 383, at 403–405 (1996), and Sabine Schlemmer-Schulte, *The World Bank's Role in Fighting Child Labor, in* UNDERSTANDING CHILDREN'S RIGHTS- PROCEEDINGS OF THE FOURTH INTERNATIONAL INTER-DISCIPLINARY COURSE ON CHILDREN'S RIGHTS 441 (Eugen Verhellen ed., 1999).

92 *See* Private Capital Flows to Developing Countries: The Road to Financial Integration (World Bank Publication 1997).

freer flow of services, goods and information across borders in its borrowing countries. Over time, the changes called for will help create more open societies. They contribute to the creation of an enabling environment in which gradually all human rights may be fully enjoyed, including political rights.[93]

The Bank has been useful to assist in the *alleviation of the social cost of economic adjustment* it supports through its structural adjustment and other loans by financing of social funds and safety nets.[94]

The World Bank recognizes that *culture* is fundamental for development. Bank policies prevent projects financed by it from injuring cultural heritage sites and attempt to protect indigenous cultures.[95] In order to further contribute to the preservation and advancement of culture, the Bank has intensified its efforts to identify the role of culture in society, in enhancing and limiting people's social and economic contributions.[96] It is also starting programs designed to safeguard important cultural heritage. It is further helping to create cultural partnerships with governments, the private sector, and civil society as well as UNESCO and other development institutions to strengthen its overall concern for culture in its development assistance. Altogether, these efforts contribute to the attainment of peoples' cultural human rights.

---

93 *See* Ibrahim F.I. Shihata, *Democracy and Development,* 46 INTERNATIONAL AND COMPARATIVE LAW QUARTERLY 635 (1997) (discussing the difficult processes of countries towards development and democracy and suggesting in reference to empirical studies that economic liberalization is conducive to political liberalization).

94 *See* in particular the social supplements in the Bank's assistance to countries affected by the East Asian Crisis described in Warwick NcKibbin, The East Asian Crisis: Investigating Causes and Policy Responses (World Bank Paper 1998); Steven Radelet, The East Asian Financial Crisis: Diagnosis, Remedies, Prospects (World Bank Paper 1998); and Kalpana Kochher, Prakash Loungani & Mark R. Stone, The East Asian Crisis: Macroeconomic Developments and Policy Lessons (World Bank Paper 1998). World Bank lending for social protection has increased considerably over the last three years compared to figures from 1992-1997. *See* World Bank Annual Report 33 (2000) (noting that the bank spent US$2,240 in FY1998, US$2,678 in FY1999, and US$1,517 in FY2000 on social protection projects).

95 *See* Operation Policy Note (OPN) 11.03 on Cultural Property (1986), being converted into Operational Policy (OP) 4.11, and Operational Directive (OD) 4.20 on Indigenous Peoples (1991), being converted into Operational Policy (OP) 4.10.

96 *See* CULTURE AND DEVELOPMENT IN AFRICA – PROCEEDINGS OF AN INTERNATIONAL CONFERENCE SPONSORED BY THE WORLD BANK (Ismail Serageldin & June Taboroff eds., 1994).

Recently, the Bank has realized the importance of *knowledge and information* for development. In the era of globalization, commercial and social prosperity of a society depends largely on how well-informed the people in it are. Poor countries do not only have less capital than rich ones; they have in particular less knowledge and information.[97] The Bank is increasing its efforts to assist borrowing members to fill their technology knowledge gaps and address their problems regarding information crucial to effective markets such as the quality of a product, the diligence of a worker, the creditworthiness of a firm etc. Especially, in connection with its interventions in the East Asian crisis, the Bank is emphasizing the need for transparent and adequate information for all market players and advising countries in crisis to bring their accounting and auditing practices in line with international standards, strengthen corporate governance structures and the power of supervisory authorities of financial institutions.[98] These Bank efforts contribute directly to the achievement of people's economic and social human rights. They also help indirectly create the environment for the enjoyment of further freedoms such as the freedom of expression, the freedom of press, and the freedom of informed participation in the state's affairs.

The enormous increase in civil conflicts in the post-Cold War world has tested the Bank's ability to address unprecedented devastation of human and social capital. Since 1980, the volume of Bank *lending to post-conflict countries and territories* has increased over 800 percent, to US$6.2 billion, and touched every region and economic sector.[99] In the past, the Bank has addressed the special needs posed by civil conflict on an *ad hoc* basis. But recently, it has endorsed a comprehensive policy framework to guide its actions in post-conflict situations.[100] That framework calls for Bank intervention in the early stages of post-conflict reconstruction by coordinating external aid to the countries con-

---

97 *See* World Development Report — Knowledge for Development (World Bank Publication 1998/99).

98 *See* East Asia: The Road to Recovery (World Bank Publication 1998).

99 *See* Post Conflict Reconstruction — The Role of the World Bank (World Bank Publication 1998).

100 *Ibid. See also* The World Bank's Experience with Post-Conflict Reconstruction (World Bank Publication 1998), and Security, Poverty Reduction and Sustainable Development — Challenges for the New Millennium (World Bank Publication 1999).

cerned, effectively contributing to the understanding of the economic and social implications of peace negotiations, and later supporting macroeconomic stabilization and rebuilding physical infrastructure. In particular, the Bank has played a significant role in financing demining, and restoring human and social capital. These efforts contribute directly to people's ability to resume enjoyment of economic and social rights disrupted by the conflict and help also create the societal prerequisites for the enjoyment of further human rights.

The Inspection Panel, an independent mechanism created in 1994 to receive complaints of groups of people adversely affected by Bank-financed projects, is reinforcing and complementing the Bank's role of a transformer of human rights through the enhancement of Bank compliance with its policies and procedures, in particular those that contribute to the protection of environmental and social rights.[101]

C. Operationalizing the Rule of Law in the Bank's Development Assistance

1. The Bank's Policies and Procedures

The Bank's financial support in some *rule of law* or *governance* areas and most human rights areas builds on its *policies and procedures,* i.e. standards for sustainable development which the Bank has developed over the years of experience in financing development.[102] These standards have invariably been inspired by

---

[101] For details on the Bank's Inspection Panel, *see* IBRAHIM F.I. SHIHATA, THE WORLD BANK INSPECTION PANEL: IN PRACTICE (2nd ed. 2000). *See also* Sabine Schlemmer-Schulte, *The World Bank's Experience with Its Inspection Panel,* 58 ZEITSCHRIFT FÜR AUSLÄNDISCHES ÖFFENTLICHES RECHT UND VÖLKERRECHT (ZAÖRV) (HEIDELBERG JOURNAL OF INTERNATIONAL LAW) 353 (1998), *id., The World Bank, Its Operations and Its Inspection Panel,* RECHT DER INTERNATIONALEN WIRTSCHAFT (RIW) 175 (1999), and *id., The World Bank Inspection Panel: A Record of the First International Accountability Mechanism and its Role for Human Rights,* 6 AMERICAN UNIVERSITY HUMAN RIGHTS BRIEF, Issue No. 2, 1,6-6, 20 (1998).

[102] The Bank's policies and procedures have been streamlined and simplified within the last eight years in a process called conversion. They are contained in the Operational Manual which consists of two volumes. Volume I of the Manual includes all policies and procedures regarding strategies and financial products. It covers the thematic areas of country focus, sector strategies, financial products and instruments and partnership arrangements (in particular co-financing and trust funds). Volume II

international standards, including human rights standards, but, very often, have also gone beyond the latter.[103] Sample areas in which Bank standards represent model standards are the Bank's standards for resettlement, indigenous peoples, environmental assessment and participation.[104]

In several instances, the Bank's financial support has a catalytic effect for the development of standards in its borrowing member countries in that it establishes new standards through the incorporation of the Bank's policies in loan agreements in coun-

---

contains those policies and procedures that relate to project requirements. It includes safeguard policies (e.g. environmental aspects, indigenous peoples, involuntary resettlement and international waterways), economic project analysis, fiduciary aspects of Bank operations (e.g. procurement guidelines), financial aspects and "management" of operations (i.e. project supervision, monitoring and evaluation), and contractual aspects of the financial agreements. The Operational manual can be accessed through the World Bank's web site, at *<http://wbln0018.WorldBank.org/institutional/manuals/opmanual.nsf>*.

103 In this context, it may be noted that it has been Bank policy since 1984 to not finance (i) "projects that contravene any international environmental agreement" to which the country on whose territory the project is located is a party, and (ii) "projects which would significantly modify natural areas designated by international conventions as World Heritage Sites or Biosphere Reserves. This language appeared first in Operational Manual Statement (OMS) 2.36 on Environmental Aspects of Bank Work, para. 9(e) (1984). Operational Policy (OP) 4.01 on Environmental Assessment (1999) contains a similar provision. The Bank's Operational Policy (OP) 4.36 on Forestry (1993) contains a similar statement to the effect that "[t]he Bank does not finance projects that contravene applicable international environmental agreements."

104 It may be also noted that the Bank refers to general international treaty standards in its loan and grant agreements in the context of special financing mechanisms. Such financing mechanisms include in particular the Global Environment Facility (GEF). The GEF was first created in 1991 as a pilot program to which the Bank served as trustee. *See* Documents Concerning the Establishment of the Global Environment Facility, November 1991, 30 I.L.M. 1739. It was restructured in 1994 as "interim" financial mechanism of the Convention on Climate Changes and the Convention on Biological Diversity. *See* Instrument for the Establishment of the Restructured Global Environment Facility, March 1995, 33 I.L.M. 1273. *See also* Ibrahim F.I. Shihata, The World Bank in a Changing World, Vol. II (1995), Chapter Five (*The World Bank and the Environment: Legal Instruments for Achieving Environmental Objectives*), at 223 *et seq*. Participation in certain international environmental conventions by the recipient country of Bank financing is a pre-condition for eligibility to benefit from GEF-funds. The relevant international conventions relate to the following matters: (1) protection of the Ozone Layer; (2) limitation of the emission of greenhouse gases; (3) protection of Biodiversity; and (4) protection of International Waters. In the context of development assistance under the GEF, the Bank is, therefore, devising and monitoring international environment standards.

tries whose national law standards are lower than Bank standards.[105] Experience with Bank-financed projects may encourage these countries to accept higher standards beyond the narrow context of Bank-financed projects applicable throughout the entire territory of these countries.

From the point of view of the legal implications of standards in the Bank's policies, it must be emphasized that these standards do not create substantive rights for individuals in the borrowing countries. They do not give these individuals a legal claim against the Bank in the context of its operations. The Bank's policies are internal instructions by Bank Management to staff issued for their guidance in the preparation, negotiation, appraisal, implementation, and supervision of Bank-financed projects. They are binding on staff.[106] The standards embodied in the policies create a duty for staff to exert their best efforts to achieve them, while their actual achievement depends mostly on the action of other parties, notably the borrower. These policies become binding on the Bank's borrowing member countries when they are incorporated in the relevant loan documentation. They do not, however, give the people potentially affected by the Bank-financed project enforceable rights against the Bank as there is no legal relationship between the Bank and potentially affected people.[107] Their participation and their consultation in the project's design and implementation is ensured *via* the borrower.

---

[105] *See* Ibrahim F.I. Shihata, *The World Bank's Contribution to the Development of International Environmental Law*, *in* FESTSCHRIFT FÜR IGNAZ SEIDL-HOHENVELDERN 631 (1998) at 655–57.

[106] *See* IBRAHIM F.I. SHIHATA, THE WORLD BANK INSPECTION PANEL 42–47 (1994) (discussing the legal nature and function of Bank policies and procedures), and *id.*, THE WORLD BANK INSPECTION PANEL: IN PRACTICE (2nd ed. 2000), at 41–46.

[107] The Bank does not enter into any contractual relationship with potentially affected people in borrowing countries. *See* Sabine Schlemmer-Schulte, *The World Bank, Its Operations and Its Inspection Panel*, 3 RECHT DER INTERNATIONALEN WIRTSCHAFT (RIW) 175–181 (1999) (describing in detail the relationship between the Bank, the borrower, and the affected people in the context of the project cycle of Bank-financed projects). For an analysis of the issue whether Bank policies could develop a binding force similar to administrative norms under German law resulting in "subjektive öffentliche Rechte" giving rights to people in exceptional cases while originally only internally but not externally binding, *see* Sabine Schlemmer-Schulte, *The World Bank and Human Rights*, 4 AUSTRIAN REVIEW OF INTERNATIONAL AND EUROPEAN LAW (ARIEL) 230 (1999).

The implementation of standards of Bank policies in the project involved is the duty of the borrowers as stipulated in the loan agreements. It is thus in an indirect way that standards of Bank policies and procedures contribute to the promotion of economic, social, and cultural rights of people in the Bank's borrowing countries as well standards that would qualify as elements of the *rule of law* as defined by the Bank for developmental purposes.

2. CAS and CDF

Operational tools in which a concern for the rule of law and human rights is visibly embedded and which the Bank developed as its experience with development assistance grew include, in addition to its policies and procedures, two country specific instruments used in the policy dialogue with its borrowers, the *Country Assistance Strategy* (*CAS*) document and the *Comprehensive Development Framework* (*CDF*). Unlike the Bank's policies which contain general guidelines Bank staff have to follow (unless the policies themselves allow for deviation) in designing, appraising, and supervising the implementation of every Bank-financed project and program notwithstanding the country on the territory of which these projects and programs are implemented, the CAS and CDF consist of essentially country specific outlines of development assistance strategies and frameworks. Both CAS and CDF determine, as a result of discussions between the Bank and borrowers, the priorities and focus of development assistance primarily in terms of the timing of that assistance and the selection of subject-matters for that assistance over a longer period of time for respective borrowers.

CAS and CDF set specific countries' future development agenda. They contain the broad development assistance picture, listing future projects and programs of and general focuses for the development of respective borrowers. CAS and CDF, while possibly different in their contents country-by-country, do not override Bank policies or side step them. They imply their validity and full-fledged application for any project and program they list to be taken on in the future.

Within the broad agenda of CAS and CDF, however, the decisions by policy-makers of the different countries in their dialogue with the Bank on the type of projects and programs that have priority and deserve greater attention reflect also a decision on which *rule of law* elements and which human rights will have priority and receive greater attention in the next years of development finance by the Bank in the country.[108] Especially the CDF stands for the Bank's recently reinvigorated sensitivity for the *rule of law* and the promotion of economic, social, and cultural human rights through generally greater consideration of people's needs in the decision on the development assistance framework for a country, the country's ownership of the new development agenda (particularly the agenda's flexibility in being able to respond to special needs of the country), the longer time frame for it, and the inclusion of all stake holders in the setting up of the agenda, in particular civil society and business. From the general, long-term and holistic framework of the CDF, however, the *rule of law* and *human rights* visions therein will have to trickle down through the medium-term CAS with its list of targeted projects to the individual lending to a country. This lending is based on broad country specific CDF and CAS goals as well as on uniform standards of Bank policies, which, as mentioned earlier, are the tool that actually help transform many human rights ideals as well as *rule of law* concerns into realities.

The *CAS*, a formalized tool for Bank operations, developed in the 1980s. The first reviews of specific countries' development problems and responses to these problems were discussed in the Board of Executive Directors on the basis of a comprehensive economic report on the country concerned during the early 1970s. However, these reviews were soon discontinued. At regular intervals of around 5 years per country review, they began to become a regular feature in the Bank's operations separate from individual lending operations from the mid-1980s on; the periodic country reviews were later introduced in recognition of the fact that discussions of the Bank's assistance strategy for each borrower would increase the efficiency of individual lending operations because they provided an overall context for individual lending operations. These discussions of specific countries' needs in the Bank's Board allow for a determination of an appropriate Bank lending strategy in each country in relation to the local poli-

[108] For an earlier discussion of the manner in which and extent to which CAS and CDF stand for human rights concerns in the Bank's work, *see* Sabine Schlemmer-Schulte, *The World Bank and Human Rights*, 4 AUSTRIAN REVIEW OF INTERNATIONAL AND EUROPEAN LAW (ARIEL) 230 (1999).

cies and priorities of the country concerned. The CAS essentially facilitates later evaluation and appraisal of not only the technical and financial aspects of individual projects but also of the relative urgency and comparative value of each project in accelerating a country's economic development.

The *CDF* was introduced by *James D. Wolfensohn* in January 1999. Earlier in his annual speech before the Bank's Board of Governors in October 1998, *Wolfensohn* had, in the aftermath of the global financial crisis, called for a new development framework "where the fate of the poor would no longer take a back seat to market stability."[109] With reference to the fact that the International Monetary Fund (IMF) has an overall framework which it reviews annually with its client countries to evaluate the macroeconomic performance of each country, *Wolfensohn* stressed the need for a second framework covering "the overall structure that is required in a country to allow it to develop in an integrated fashion."[110] *Wolfensohn* called specifically for a better assessment of the linkages among all elements of development and moving beyond typical indicators of economic performance to include "fundamental long-term issues of the structure, scope and substance of social development"[111] in the Bank's approach to a country's development assistance.

The CDF is a concept that takes a holistic approach to development.[112] It seeks a better balance in poverty alleviation and promotion of sustainable development by highlighting the interdependence of two intrinsically linked pillars: sound macroeconomics and finances on the one hand and a sound structural and social framework on the other. Based on this recognition, the CDF argues that closer integration of all aspects than in the Bank's past approach is necessary. For the implementation of the newly defined approach, the CDF formulates a comprehensive, holistic framework for each borrowing country to include strategies about the sequencing and timing of policies, programs and projects in all areas beyond the linear approach of the CAS in a multi-

---

109 *See* James D. Wolfensohn, The Other Crisis, Address to the Board of Governors, Annual Meetings of the IMF and the World Bank, October 6, 1998, at 5.

110 *Ibid.*

111 *Ibid.*

112 For more information on the CDF, *see* the Bank's website at <*http://www.worldbank.org/cdf/cdf-faq.htm*>.

dimensional way to achieve stable, equitable, and sustainable development.

The new holistic framework for development includes structural, human, physical and specific strategic aspects. Elements of the structural aspects include a good and clean government, an effective legal and justice system, a well-organized and supervised financial system, and a social safety net and social programs. The human aspects of the framework consist of education, knowledge institutions, health services and population measures. Elements addressing the physical needs of each developing country look after issues of water and sewerage, energy, roads, transportation and telecommunications, environment and culture. Specific strategies relate to rural, urban, and private sector development issues. The CDF is particularly sensitive to a country's special national considerations with an in-built flexibility to accommodate special needs. Besides timing and substance-related selectivity as first and second dimensions of the CDF, the third dimension of the Bank's new approach to development assistance includes consultation with all stakeholders and other players concerned with development in the country involved, specifying the roles to be played by each with respect to each element in the framework. The country itself prepares a matrix including all dimensions of its development agenda. The role of each multilateral and bilateral development aid agency, the country's civil society, and the private sector are identified in concerted discussions with the government to ensure appropriate implementation of the CDF's goals. The Bank is testing the CDF in 12 countries[113] and the West Bank and Gaza. The pilot efforts are moving forward, although it is too early for results, given the inherently long-term nature of the CDF.[114]

3. PRSP: A Special CDF Principles Based Tool For Heavily-Indebted Poor Countries (HIPC)

At the September 1999 joint meeting of the Development and Interim Committees, the Finance Ministers decided to link the special debt relief provided to heavily indebted poor countries

113 Countries involved in CDF pilots include Bolivia, Cote d'Ivoire, the Dominican Republic, Eritrea, Ethiopia, Ghana, the Kyrgyz Republic, Morocco, Romania, Uganda, and Vietnam.

114 *See* World Bank Annual Report 26 (2000).

(HIPC) under the joint Bank/(International Monetary) Fund HIPC trust fund program directly to poverty reduction. It was determined that countries being considered under the HIPC trust fund program should have in place a poverty-reduction strategy that appropriately balances financial/macroeconomic and structural/social considerations. The ministers further decided that poverty reduction strategies should provide the basis for all World Bank and IMF (International Monetary Fund) concessional lending.

As a result of the Ministers' decision, the country poverty reduction strategies are, for the purposes of HIPC and IMF/Bank concessional lending, assessed in a Poverty Reduction Strategy Paper (PRSP).[115] The PRSP[116] serves as the operational document that defines a country's poverty reduction objectives, and its specific strategy to meet these objectives. PRSPs are prepared according to the principles upon which the CDF is based. They translate the Bank's CDF principles into a concrete plan of action. Like the CDF, the PRSP promotes poverty reduction strategies that are: (i) country-driven; (ii) results-oriented; (iii) comprehensive; (iv) partnership–based; and (v) framed within a long-term perspective.

The PRSP will be submitted to the Boards of both the Bank and the Fund, together with a joint Bank-Fund Assessment. The latter presents the management's views on the poverty challenges facing the country, the proposed strategy, the risks, and summarizes the quality of the contents and the participatory process that went into the preparation of the PRSP. Each institution will endorse the PRSP in so far as it relates to the polices and programs respectively supported by it. The Bank takes the lead on structural and social issues, including poverty assessments, monitoring of progress against poverty, social policy, and social safety nets. In the public sector, the Bank has primary responsibility for assistance on public enterprise reform, the composition and efficiency

115 The PRSP replaces the Policy Framework Paper (PFP) which has served as the basis for the former Enhanced Structural Adjustment Facility (ESAF) at the IMF. PRSPs will serve as the basis for the Poverty Reduction and Growth Facility (PRGF), which has replaced the ESAF in the IMF. It may be noted that in middle-income countries Social and Structural Reviews (SSRs) are used. SSRs are similarly structured as PRSPs from an operational view.

116 For countries that are not ready to prepare a PRSP at the time of their HIPC decision point, or at the time of the Fund Board approval of a new PRGF or its annual review programs, the government will be asked to prepare an interim PRSP (I-PRSP).

of public expenditure, and administrative and civil reform. The Bank also has primary responsibility for assistance on the corporate sector, which includes restructuring, accounting, auditing and disclosure, governance, judicial reform, environment, social protection and development. The Fund takes the lead on macroeconomic issues, assistance on the aggregate aspects of public sector spending and revenues. Overlapping areas of responsibility/concern are tax policy and administration, issues of transparency and governance, corruption and legislative reform, trade policy, debt and financial sector work.

The Bank, the Fund, the country's other development partners, in consultation with the government, will assess how and to what extent they will provide technical assistance, policy advice and financial assistance. For the Bank, the PRSP will guide decisions on overall and individual lending as summarized in the Country Assistance Strategy (CAS), including support through the IDA, HIPC facilities, International Finance Corporation (IFC), and Multilateral Investment Guarantee Agency (MIGA). For the Fund, the PRSP will guide the decision on the Poverty Reduction and Growth Facility (PRGF) and HIPC.

The promotion of the *rule of law* and of economic and social human rights finds formulation in the relationship between poverty, governance, economic and social concerns. In each of the poverty concerns (empowering the poor; improving the reach, efficiency and sustainability of basic services, and increasing access to markets; and providing security from economic shocks and from corruption, crime and violence), there are corresponding governance and human rights issues (such as, providing rules for fair, transparent national electoral processes; providing transparent budget processes, capable civil service, equal access to the judiciary, and government accountability; improving the legal and regulatory framework; recognition of property rights, ensuring efficient enforcement mechanisms). Thus, designing a PRSP against these broad framework objectives promotes the *rule of law* and economic and social human rights by means of improving citizen's opportunities for involvement in the mainstream of economic and social life.

IV. CONCLUSION

From the outside, the World Bank's approach to the *rule of law* may seem fragmented. From the Bank's perspective, however, it is a consistent and coherent concept, albeit complex in its operation, that has evolved from the Bank's perspective of its economic and social development mandate and its experience in realizing the goals assigned to it in its mandate. The Bank's concept may, in a nutshell, be referred to as including formal (or content/value-neutral) aspects (i.e. the formal parts of the trio of consistent and unambiguous rules, similar processes for rule-making, rule-application, and rule-enforcement, and strong institutions ensuring rule-application, and rule-enforcement), and material (or substantive or content/value-loaded) aspects (i.e. the focus on market-friendly, socially considerate, justice oriented, environmentally sustainable and culturally sensitive rules both in legal, institutional governance focused reform, and as components of other project-and-non-project lending).

The Bank's concept of the *rule of law* is unique and suits the realization of the Bank's goals of development assistance under the changing circumstances in the world and the changing needs of developing countries well. The concept has three major advantages:

(i) With the *rule of law's* substantive focus on economic, social, environmental, and cultural subject matters for the building of rules, processes, and institutions in its client countries, the Bank is focusing on its area of comparative advantage. Bilateral donors and others may, on a country's request, add to the Bank's *rule of law* agenda an explicit democratic and political component.[117] Any Bank activities enhancing the economic, social, environmental and cultural development of a client country will, at the same time, however, be indirectly conducive to political development in the sense that poverty reduction and general capacity-building contribute to the creation of an enabling environment for political reform.

---

117 *See also* Julio Faundez, *Introduction – Legal Technical Assistance, in* GOOD GOVERNMENT AND LAW – LEGAL AND INSTITUTIONAL REFORM 1, 6 (Julio Faundez ed. 1997).

(ii) The Bank's *rule of law* concept with its substance-orientation towards economic, social, environmental, and cultural matters responds constructively to a major difficulty that globalization creates for all countries, in particular for developing countries. Globalization is creating a tension between the market-driven forms of globalization and the people-driven modes of resistance as exhibited by movements to protect the environment, promote human rights, challenge the oppression of women and the destruction of indigenous peoples. The Bank's *rule of law* oriented assistance attempts to address this dilemma and, with a careful design and discussion of its projects and programs with all relevant players, to promote economic development as well as ensure human development.

(iii) The Bank's *rule of law* notion pays special respect to the law as a cultural phenomenon. It recognizes that law is value-oriented and that values may differ from country to country and over time, as the brief initial references to the *rule of law* as developed in modern times in different Western societies show. The Bank's concept of the *rule of law* is more basic and less sophisticated than its modern Western counterparts of the UK or US *rule of law*, the German *Rechtsstaat* concept, and the French *état de droit*. It is, however, not without teeth as formal as well as material standards exist. The flexibilities which are nevertheless inherent in the Bank's *rule of law* concept allow for being sensitive to each client country's individual structures, values, and stage of development.[118]

A special reference to the Bank's Comprehensive Development Framework (CDF) should be made before concluding. The CDF, as tool for Bank assistance, introduced by the Bank's President *James D. Wolfensohn* in early 1999, is a means particularly susceptible to transmit the Bank's *rule of law* idea. Like the Bank's *rule of law* concept itself, the CDF recognizes the holistic nature of development in looking at the market-related structural aspects of development projects and programs (all not only *governance* oriented ones) as well as the social aspects of projects and pro-

118 The Bank should, based on the greater flexibility of the *rule of law* concept, be able to avoid the mistakes of the USAID Law and Development program in the 1960s.

grams, always reaching for a balance or complementarity between the two poles. Also, the CDF stresses the client countries' ownership of projects and programs, an idea that the Bank's *rule of law* concept reflects through its culture sensitivity. It may be said that the Bank's *rule of law* notion conceptualized for countries' legal frameworks, what, from an operational perspective, the CDF now does for all Bank assistance. The CDF thus reinforces the Bank's *rule of law* concept.[119]

The Bank promotes the rule of law in its own way. Its notion of the *rule of law* is constantly evolving. There is certainly much room for further expansion, be it in the human rights area or the rules and institution building area. Thanks to *Ibrahim Shihata*'s ground work in the formulation of the Bank's notion of the *rule of law,* the Bank has been able to pay due respect to both the limitations under the Bank's own charter, and to the complexities of development and cultural differences of the Bank's client countries.[120] Thanks further to the way *Ibrahim Shihata* defined the

---

119 A recent Bank study, Voices of the Poor, which was conducted as background for the World Development Report 2000/2001 reviewed participatory poverty studies in 50 countries involving about 40,000 poor people and completed a new comparative study in 1999 in 23 countries engaging about 20,000 poor people, showed that poor people are active agents in their lives, but are often powerless to influence the social and economic factors that determine their well-being. As a result, the World Bank Development Report 2000/2001 recommends action in three complementary areas which draw together from the perspective of the rule of law and human rights as these notions were defined by the Bank and keep evolving in the Bank's work. The three areas include: (i) *promoting opportunity:* expanding economic opportunity for poor people by stimulating overall growth and by building up their assets (such as land and education) and increasing the returns on these assets, through a combination of market and nonmarket actions; (ii) *facilitating empowerment*: making state institutions more accountable and responsive to poor people, strengthening the participation of poor people in political processes and local decision-making, and removing the social barriers that result from distinctions of gender, ethnicity, race, religion, and social status; and (iii) *enhancing security*: reducing poor people's vulnerability to ill health, economic shocks, crop failure, policy-induced dislocations, natural disasters, and violence, as well as helping them cope with adverse shocks when they occur. A big part of this is ensuring that effective safety nets are in place to mitigate that impact of personal and national calamities. *See* World Development Report — Attacking Poverty vi (World Bank Publication 2000/2001).

120 It may be noted that, both from a formal and substantive point of view, the future evolution of the Bank's *rule of law* notion may actually mean a narrowing down of concepts as a result of experience with medicines for development to that one may see a trend of convergence, similar (but not the same) to the one the world

notion *rule of law* for Bank purposes, there is a great potential for the notion's further evolution and expansion. The Bank will continue paying attention to its charter and, at the same time, expand its promotion of the *rule of law* in its client countries further and, thereby, contribute to the building of the *new international development architecture of the future.*[121] It is hoped that the further evolution of the Bank's *rule of law* notion will be brought to fruition in the context of the *Law and Justice Network* which is currently being built under the Bank's new General Counsel, *Ko-Yung Tung.*[122]

---

could witness with the modern Western *rule of law* models, outlining more systems as incompatible with it and being more specific in what features and systems it favors, while maturing as developmental concept.

121 The need for keeping this vision of building a new future for development .in mind has been emphasized by James D. Wolfensohn at one of the last joint Bank-Fund Annual Meetings. *See* James D. Wolfensohn, Coalitions for Change, Address to the Board of Governors, given on September 28, 1999 at the joint Bank-Fund Annual Meetings.

122 In conjunction with the *Law and Justice Network* efforts, the Bank's Legal Department is in the process of writing two major strategy papers which will outline Ko-Yung Tung's strategic vision for the Bank's future support to developing countries which wish to strengthen their *rule of law* and *human rights* frameworks.

LIABILITY OF MEMBER STATES FOR ACTS OR OMISSIONS OF AN INTERNATIONAL ORGANIZATION

Ignaz Seidl-Hohenveldern

As far as liability of member States for acts or omissions of an International Organization is concerned the wisdom of the conclusion drawn long ago by our friend and colleague Ibrahim Shihata[1] has been confirmed again and again. To establish such liability "all relevant provisions and circumstances must be studied to ascertain what was intended by the parties in this respect and the extent to which their intention was made known to third parties dealing with the enterprise." Shihata's article dealt with international public ventures rather than with international organizations. However, the above quotation applies also to international organizations *stricto sensu.* By an *a fortiori* conclusion, doctrine has understood it in this way.[2] What has changed over the years, mainly owing to the debates in the Institut de Droit International on the liability of common inter-State enterprises[3] and of international organizations,[4] was the development of a larger consensus on the significance and weight to be given to certain of these circumstances, especially in the light of the litiga-

---

1 Ibrahim F.I. Shihata, *Role of Law in Economic Development: The Legal Problems of International Public Ventures,* 25 REVUE ÉGYPTIENNE DE DROIT INTERNATIONAL 119, 125 (1969).

2 *Cf.* R. Higgins, *Provisional Report on the Legal Consequences for Member States of the Non-Fulfilment by International Organizations of Their Obligations Towards Third Parties,* 66-I ANNUAIRE DE L'INSTITUT DE DROIT INTERNATIONAL 251, 373, 401 (1995).

3 Report by I. Seidl-Hohenveldern, *Le droit applicable aux entreprises internationles communes, étatiques ou para- étatiques,* 60-I ANNUAIRE DE L'INSTITUT DE DROIT INTERNATIONAL 1, 106 (1983).

4 Report by R. Higgins, *supra* note 2.

tion concerning the bankruptcy of the International Tin Council (ITC)[5] and of the European Molecular Biology Laboratory (EMBL) award.[6]

It does not seem to be a mere co-incidence that Dr. Shihata as well as myself, prior to the research by the Institut de Droit International and prior to the ITC bankruptcy, developed our views as to the liability of member States of international entities in respect to common inter-State enterprises rather than to international organizations *stricto sensu*. Such enterprises, by their very nature, will much more frequently be confronted with situations involving liabilities, mainly of a financial nature, than such organizations. Apart from Shihata's statement mentioned above — applicable to the enterprises as well as to organizations — such enterprises should be distinguished. Actually, the Institut de Droit International dealt with enterprises as a separate topic.[7]

We are quite ready to admit that there are difficulties in keeping the two notions apart.[8] Nobody would qualify, e.g., the Council of Europe as an enterprise, or Air Afrique, an airline enterprise jointly established by several African States, as an international organization *stricto sensu*. On the one hand, commercial transactions by the Council of Europe would be limited to those which, like, e.g., the purchase of office equipment, would have to be made in support of the Council's *jure imperii* activities. On the other hand, the activities of the airline will, by their nature, be *jure gestionis* questions — except where the airline would serve, e.g., to transport armed intervention forces. However, there are the cases in between. In part, at least, the activities of the World Bank family of organizations are commercial in nature. The main activities of the ITC were its operations on the international tin market, side by side with other traders in this commodity. Yet, all these en-

---

5 A vast amount of literature has been published on the ITC. For a recent publication, *cf.* Ignaz Seidl-Hohenveldern, *Failure of Controls in the Sixth International Tin Agreement, in* ESSAYS IN HONOR OF HENRY G. SCHERMERS, Vol. I, 255–74 (N. Blokker & S. Muller eds., 1994).

6 Award of June 29, 1990, European Molecular Biology Laboratory (EMBL) v. Germany, 105 ILR, at 1.

7 *See supra* note 3.

8 In his reply to the questionnaire by R. Higgins, K. Zemanek is in favor of making such a distinction *de lege ferenda, see supra* note 2, at 327.

tities are usually considered to be international organizations rather than common inter-State enterprises, as their acts, which are *jure gestionis* questions by nature, appear to have been undertaken for *jure imperii* purposes, e.g., IMF (International Monetary Fund) stand-by agreements to fend off a speculative attack on a country's currency or the ITC's purchase or sale of tin in order to protect the national economies of the member countries against excessive fluctuation of commodity prices.

Recourse to the purpose rather than to the nature of the act test in order to qualify an act as *jure imperii* is rejected in the international practice concerning State immunities[9] — but for a timid effort in this direction by the International Law Commission (ILC) in the course of its codification and progressive development of the law of State immunities.[10] The purpose test clearly led to qualify OPEC (Organization of Petroleum Exporting Countries) as an international organization rather than as a cartel in an anti-trust suit brought before US courts.[11] No venue could be established for OPEC, but there remained the charge against the OPEC member States to have participated in OPEC, allegedly an international cartel. The suit failed, as OPEC's restrictions on production were held to be made not so much to drive prices up for individual profit but to protect the national economy of the member States and, at least partly, also to prevent the depletion of scarce resources.

Common inter-State enterprises frequently are established as companies under some municipal law, usually that of the seat

---

9 Austrian Supreme Court, Feb. 10, 1961, *Collision with Foreign Government-Owned Motor Car Case (Austria)*, 40 ILR, at 75 *et seq*.

10 Draft Articles on Jurisdictional Immunities of States and Their Property, YEARBOOK OF THE INTERNATIONAL LAW COMMISSION, Vol. II, 1554 (1991). *Contra* B. Heß, *The International Law Commission's Draft Convention on Jurisdictional Immunities of States and of Their Property*, 4 EURPOPEAN JOURNAL OF INTERNATIONAL LAW 274 (1993), V. Balas & M. Pauknerova, *The Czechoslovak Approach to the Draft Convention on Jurisdictional Immunities of States and Their Property*, 12 MICHIGAN JOURNAL OF INTERNATIONAL LAW 886 (1991). *Cf. also* Chr. Tomuschat, *Jurisdictional Immunities of States and Their Property, in* FESTSCHRIFT FÜR IGNAZ SEIDL-HOHENVELDERN (K.H. Böckstiegel et al. eds., 1988), at 612–13 (commenting on the identical provision of the 1986 draft).

11 International Association of Machinists and Aerospace Workers v. OPEC, 477 F. Supp. 533 (C.D. Cal. 1979), 76 AMERICAN JOURNAL OF INTERNATIONAL LAW 160 (1982).

State.[12] In these cases, what liability might exist for the member States of such an enterprise will be determined by this municipal law. However, some such enterprises are established by a treaty, the latter not providing for the full[13] application of any municipal law. These enterprises thus are established under international law, as they owe their existence to a rule of international law, *viz.*, to a treaty. They thus are persons under international law. However, it does not follow from there that they are also persons in international law, i.e., bearers of rights and obligations to be exercised in international law. Actually, such an enterprise acting *jure gestionis* will not become an actor in the field of public international law. It therefore does not need to have a personality in international law — and, indeed, we do not believe that it has such a personality. However, it is inconceivable that either enterprises or organizations lack personality in municipal law. Otherwise, how would they be able to function? They would be unable to hire staff or office space and could not even open a bank account.

All activities of enterprises will be governed by the municipal law which the courts of the forum will hold applicable to the transaction concerned, either directly or by the detour via the law of the seat State.[14] The latter — and not international law — will govern also the liability, if any, of the member States for the enterprise concerned. If, for the reasons just indicated, we deny that such enterprises enjoy a personality in international law, it does not follow that, therefore, we hold their member States liable for the acts or omissions of the enterprise. My answer to the questionnaire by Higgins[15] may not have made this sufficiently clear. The liability, if any, of member States for a common inter-State enterprise will depend on its national law. No problem arises if the

---

[12] *E.g.*, the Moselle Canal Company. *Cf.* D. Ruzié, *Le Régime Juridique de la Moselle,* 10 ANNUAIRE FRANÇAIS DE DROIT INTERNATIONAL 792 (1964).

[13] According to the Statutes of some enterprises a municipal law may be applied in a subsidiary manner, *e.g.*, *in* Eurochemic. *Cf.* H. Adam, *Convention of Dec. 20, 1957 on the Establishment of Eurochemic,* LES ORGANISMES INTERNATIONAUX SPÉCIALISÉS VOL. II, 154 (1965).

[14] Arab Monetary Fund v. Hashim and Others No. 3, 2 WLR 729 (1991), 85 ILR, at 1.

[15] Higgins, *supra* note 2, at 399 (comenting on IGNAZ SEIDL-HOHENVELDERN, CORPORATIONS IN AND UNDER INTERNATIONAL LAW 119–120 (1987)).

enterprise is established under the municipal law of a State, e.g., as a corporation under its law. However, a rivalry between member States sometimes leads to the establishment of such an entity as a person under international law. The latter thus would be deemed to be the national law of the enterprise. Yet, international law does not contain any clear rules on such liability. An ingenuous way out of this dilemma has been found by the House of Lords in the Arab Monetary Fund case. According to the will of its founding fathers, the Fund is a person under international law. However, according to its Statute, the Fund enjoys legal personality in the municipal law of its member States. The House of Lords therefore held that the Fund was a person under the law of its seat State. It may be objected to this solution that it betrays the intentions pursued by the founding fathers of the Fund.[16] However, it has the great advantage of leading to practicable solutions.[17] Should the issue of the liability of member States of such an enterprise arise, the forum State will use this detour via its conflict of law rules to determine the scope, if any, of such liability in accordance with the municipal law of the seat State. This leaves us to deal with this problem exclusively in relation to international organizations *stricto sensu,* however wide or strict this notion is to be defined.

Today, there appears to be general agreement on the issue of the legal personality of international organizations in and under international law as well as in the municipal law of their member States.[18] They are held to have a legal personality of their own, with a will of their own.[19] The latter will not necessarily coincide

---

16 I. Seidl-Hohenveldern, Corporations in and Under International Law 108 (1987); and D. Vignes in his reply to the questionnaire by R. Higgins, *supra* note 2, at 304.

17 F.A.Mann, *International Organizations as National Corporations,* 107 Law Quarterly Review 358–59 (1991).

18 According to J.E.Carroz & A.G. Roche, *The Proposed International Commission for the Conservation of Atlantic Tunas*, 61 American Journal of International Law 673, 698 (1967). Canadian authorities had refused to recognize the personality under international law of the International Commission for the Northwest Atlantic Fisheries, as far as Canadian municipal law was concerned. However, this appears illogical. An organization needs to have personality in municipal law, already in order to open a bank account or to rent a house. *See* Seidl-Hohenveldern, *supra* note 15, at 102.

with the sum of the wills of all the member States.[20] Hence, the personality of an international organization cannot be simply seen as a patchwork, i.e., an aggregate of the personalities of its member States. Would that be the case, the liability of any such State for the organization would be an outcome of this State's own personality. In the past, this patchwork theory sometimes had led to a deduction of an organization's immunity from that granted to its member States.[21] The latter, likewise, would then remain liable for the organization's acts or omissions.

However, this patchwork theory is generally rejected. Member States thus could hide behind the distinct personality of the organization. Would that be possible also in respect to non-member States? We do not hold such personality opposable to third States.[22] An organization will be established by a treaty or other act of international law. A general rule of treaty law provides that such acts cannot create either obligations or rights for a third State without its consent.[23] Could the legal personality of the organization, distinct from those of its member States, be opposed to a non-member country, the latter would thus suffer a disadvantage. It would have to accept a worse debtor than the member States, which, hitherto would have been liable to the non-member. It seems obvious that the aggregate wealth of the member States will be considerably higher than that of even an affluent organization. It is true that the Advisory Opinion of the International Court of Justice (ICJ) concerning the murder of Count Berna-

---

19 Advocate General Darmon in his conclusions in case 241/87, Société Maclaine Watson & Co, Ltd v. Conseil des Communautés Européenes et Commission des Communautés Européennes, 1990 ECR V 1798.

20 Seidl-Hohenveldern, *supra* note 16, at 72.

21 Judicial Decisions, *John H. Chapman v. Commissioner of Internal Revenue*, 42 AMERICAN JOURNAL OF INTERNATIONAL LAW 229 (1948) (League of Nations) and Landesarbeitsgericht Rheinland-Pfalz Feb. 23, 1960 (NATO), *discussed in* Seidl-Hohenveldern, *see supra* note 19, at 70–71.

22 *See also* J. Salmon in his reply to Mrs. Higgins' questionnaire, 66-I ANNUAIRE DE L'INSTITUT DE DROIT INTERNATIONAL 336, 342 (1995), *but see* F. Seyersted, *ibid.* No. 2, at 331.

23 *See* Art. 34 of the Vienna Convention on the Law of Treaties, providing that "[a] treaty does not create either obligations or rights for a third State without its consent." For the Vienna Convention on the Law of Treaties, *see* 8 INTERNATIONAL LEGAL MATERIALS 679 (1969).

dotte[24] comes out in favor of an *erga omnes* personality, i.e., objective personality, of the United Nations. However, we deem that this rule applies only to the United Nations on account of their near-universal membership and because their activities cover all possible areas of international concern.[25] In practice, the problem is more or less moot. By entering into transactions with an organization, a non-member State *eo ipso* recognizes the latter's personality.[26]

The very status, enjoyed by international organizations in general international law is different from that of States. Thus, the embassy of a Foreign State in Austria failed to convince the Austrian Supreme Court that reasons of equality before the law would entitle the embassy to a privileged position granted to international organizations by the Austrian Law on the Employment of Handicapped Persons.[27] The embassy claimed that States and organizations should enjoy identical privileges and immunities, if not under the Austrian law concerned, then according to general customary international law. However, the Court found their situation to be different. Such privileges and immunities are granted to organizations in order to ensure their impartiality.[28] Moreover, they dispel the envy of non-seat States in respect of financial advantages, which, but for these privileges, e.g., exemption from taxation, would accrue to the seat State. Moreover, organizations usually provide for the settlement of disputes, either by arbitration or by the submission of staff disputes to an international administrative tribunal. Acceptance of such dispute settlement clauses are corollary to the grant of immunity.[29] Otherwise, such immunity

---

24 Advisory Opinion, Reparation for Injuries Suffered in the Service of the United Nations, Apr. 11, 1949 ICJ Reports, at 174.

25 Seidl-Hohenveldern, *supra* note 16, at 87–88.

26 *See supra* note 2, at 337.

27 Austrian Bundesgesetzblatt No. 111 (1979).

28 Decision of Nov. 21, 1990, 63 ENTSCHEIDUNGEN DES ÖSTERREICHISCHEN OBERSTEN GERICHTSHOFES IN ZIVIL-UND JUSTIZVERWALTUNGSSACHEN, No. 206, 395, 120 (1993), at 388.

29 Heltzel v. EUROCONTROL, German Federal Constitutional Court (Nov. 10, 1981), 59 BVERFGE 63, Eur.Ct.H.R. (Feb. 18, 1999); Waite & Kennedy v. Germany (Application No. 26083/94) and Beer & Regan v. Germany (Application No. 28934/95) and Groupement d' Entreprises Fougerolle v. CERN, Swiss Federal Tribunal (Dec. 21, 1992) 118 I b BGE 562, at 565 and Malek v. Ligue des Etats Arabes (Jan. 25, 1999) ZI. 4 C 518, 1996, 19 Iprax (1999), with note by I. Seidl-Hohenveldern, *ibid.*

would lead to a denial of justice,[30] as, in contrast to States, organizations do not possess a territory of their own.[31]

Today, it appears to be generally admitted that international organizations do enjoy legal personality in and under international law, albeit of a different nature from that of States. However, the mere fact that an entity composed of several persons enjoys a personality of its own does not by itself exclude that these persons could become liable for acts or omissions of this entity. In other words, may the corporate veil be lifted? As there exists no clear rule of international law to this effect, the ICJ, in the *Barcelona Traction* case, had to recur to private law analogies.[32] Higgins[33] deems this approach understandable in this specific case which dealt with problems of a company established under municipal law. However, international organizations are created by international law. Private law analogies may be less appropriate in such cases. Moreover, such analogies may be adduced for as well as against lifting the corporate veil. There are, after all, certain legal persons under municipal law which hold the members of such an entity liable for the latter's acts or omissions, e.g., *sociétés en nom collectif*. Yet, this is not a general rule. Most forms of commercial companies limit the liabilities of the participants therein for the acts or omissions of the company to the amount of their participation in the company. No such limiting rules can be found in international law. Schermers[34] had thus drawn the conclusion that, therefore, the States forming an organization remain fully liable for the acts or omissions of the latter. It may be objected to Schermers that, if we were to admit private law analogies in this field, preference should go to the rules restricting the lia-

---

30 I. Seidl-Hohenveldern, *Functional Immunity of International Organizations and Human Rights, in* ESSAYS IN HONOUR OF KONRAD GINTHER (R. Kicker et al. eds., 1999).

31 *See* the Swiss Federal Tribunal in the Fougerolle case, *supra* note 29.

32 Barcelona Traction Light and Power Co. Ltd. (Belgium v. Spain) 1970 ICJ, at 33–34.

33 *See supra* note 2, at 417.

34 H.G. SCHERMERS, INTERNATIONAL INSTITUTIONAL LAW 780 (2nd ed., Sijthoff Noordhoff & Alphen eds., 1980); *id., Liability of International Organizations,* 1 LEIDEN JOURNAL OF INTERNATIONAL LAW (1988), at 3–14; H.G. SCHERMERS & N.M. BLOCKKER, INTERNATIONAL INSTITUTIONAL LAW (3rd ed., 1995), at 994 (describes the situation as uncertain).

bilities.[35] After all, in municipal law, the vast majority of business is done by companies limiting the liabilities of their members. Yet, the bankruptcy of the ITC constitutes a warning against admitting that, in all circumstances, the members of an organization should incur only such restricted liability. An uneasiness remains when we see how, for reasons which were never fully disclosed, the affluent member States of the ITC availed themselves of all conceivable procedural tricks to escape liability for the latter's debts. Ebenroth went so far as to consider the member States' reliance on the separate legal personality of the ITC to constitute an *abus de droit*.[36] We would not go so far. We fully approve the opinion of Shihata, that, in solving the problem of liability, all circumstances ought to be taken into account.

Obviously, there exists no problem where the organization concerned and its member States have clearly stated that the latter will not assume any liabilities for acts or omissions of the former, and where third parties had been made aware of this statement or should have become aware of it.[37] Such is not only the practice of the World Bank. In the ITC case, Judge Kerr,[38] after examining the constituent documents of sixty-four organizations, found that sixteen among them contained rules excluding the liability of member States. Yet, here as always,[39] we refuse to draw an *a contrario* conclusion from the fact that a specific rule appears in numerous treaties, while likewise rejecting the view that such rules are mere *clauses de style*, declaratory of existing customary international law.[40]

However, in the absence of such specific provisions, what considerations should prevail at least *de lege ferenda*.[41] Prior to

---

[35] D. Vignes and C.F. Amerasinghe in their replies to the questiannaire by Higgins, *supra* note 2, at 293, 297 & 352.

[36] C.T. Ebenroth, *Shareholders' Liability in International Organizations: The Settlement of the International Tin Council Case,* 4 LEIDEN JOURNAL OF INTERNATIONAL LAW (1991), at 178.

[37] J. Crawford in his reply to the questionnaire by R. Higgins, *supra* note 2, at 333.

[38] Maclaine Watson v. Department of Trade (Kerr, J.) (1988) 3 WLR 1033, at 1058, 80 ILR, at 67.

[39] I. SEIDL-HOHENVELDERN, INTERNATIONAL ECONOMIC LAW (2nd ed. 1992).

[40] *See also* C.F. Amerasinghe, *supra* note 2, at 358.

[41] R. Higgins, *supra* note 2, at 418 *et seq.*

the ITC bankruptcy, creditors, when entering into business relations with an international organization, were justified to assume that, should the organization come into financial difficulties, its member States would come to its rescue by providing sufficient new funds to allow it to escape bankruptcy.[42] Actually, there have been at least two precedents to this effect.[43] The circumstances of the near bankruptcy of Eurochemic were such that any other course would have been a crass injustice to its creditors. The managers of Eurochemic actually had warned the member States that, owing to dramatic changes on the nuclear energy market, Eurochemic would never be able to make the profits anticipated by its founders and that, therefore, Eurochemic should be wound up. Yet, for political reasons, the member States insisted that Eurochemic should continue its activities, thus running deeper and deeper into debt.[44] Eurochemic was established as a common inter-State enterprise at least subsidiarily governed by Belgian law. If we would have to pursue private law analogies to their bitter end, and if we would ignore the immunity the member States might feel entitled to invoke, the latter would have become civilly and even criminally liable for fraudulent bankruptcy. The International Institute for Management of Technology in Milan was established as an international organization *stricto sensu,* established for a purpose held to be *jure imperii,* i.e., the formation of European management élites in an international school free of US influence. The Statutes of the Institute thus were published, e.g., in the Austrian Official Law Collection.[45] The mismanagement of the Institute was less blatant than that of Eurochemic. However, the creditors of the institute were small traders having worked to transform an ancient monastery into a boarding school. These

---

42 Although Crawford denies a liability of member States for the organization, he would, if at all, prefer this solution to a direct claim by the creditors against the States, *supra* note 2, at 364.

43 Amerasinghe challenges the value of these precedents. The member States may not have felt legally obliged to act as they did, *supra* note 2, at 354.

44 Ministère (Belge) des Affaires Économiques, *Eléments pour une nouvelle politique énergétique,* Brussels, Government Printing Office (1979), at 301; P. Strohl, *Les aspects internationaux de la liquidation de la société Eurochemic,* 36 Annuaire Français de Droit International 728, 730 (1990).

45 Convention of Oct. 6, 1971, Austrian Bundesgesetzblatt 516 (1975).

traders and craftsmen could hardly be assumed to be aware that, from a strictly legalistic point of view, the member States of OECD (Organisation for Economic Co-operation and Development), having established the Institute, might rely on the latter's distinct personality in order to escape liability for its debts.

Circumstances may appear different in the ITC case. Traders in tin are a relatively small group of well-advised specialists. They certainly were aware of the distinct personality of the ITC and of the rapidly growing risk incurred by the reckless purchasing policy of the ITC's buffer stock manager. Could they really hold a reasonable expectation that the member States would come to the rescue of the ITC? The States themselves did not give any outright promise to the tin traders and it is doubtful, whether the traders could imply such a promise from the attitude of the member States. Yet, we have seen that, in international oil concession disputes, even a firm promise of the State concerned to claim a fixed percentage of royalties for an extended period of time does not establish a legitimate expectation that the State will abide by its promise.[46] A worldwide tin trader should not have placed so much reliance on the ethical considerations which should compel the member States to come to the rescue of the ITC, even in the absence of a firm promise to do so.[47]

Apart from ethical considerations, another factor also would support a secondary liability of the member States of an organization for the latter's debts. Such a rule would greatly enhance the credit-worthiness of the organization concerned. The ethical consideration that the member States, as the real beneficiaries of the activities of the organization,[48] should become liable subsidiarily for its debts as well as the credit-worthiness argument had led me to maintain up to the debate of the Institut de Droit International that member States should assume jointly and severally such subsidiary liability towards third parties. As among themselves, they should be liable according to the rate of their participation to the

---

46 Government of Kuwait v. Aminoil, Award of Mar. 24, 1982, 66 ILR, at 603.

47 P-M. Eisemann, *L'Épilogue de la crise du Conseil de l'Étain,* 36 ANNUAIRE FRANÇAIS DE DROIT INTERNATIONAL 679, 701 n. 40 (1990).

48 *See also* M. Waelbroeck in his reply to the questionnaire by R. Higgins, *supra* note 2, at 322.

expenses of the organization.[49] However, Higgins has convinced me that should such liability become binding in international law, the more affluent member States would insist even more strongly than they do today, e.g., in the United Nations by means of the Committee for Programme and Coordination (CPC),[50] to obtain a corresponding right to influence the activities of the organization having financial implications. Who pays the piper, calls the tune. In this way, the most precious asset of any international organization, the belief in its impartiality, would be jeopardized. We can console ourselves for having tuned down our ethical objections. After all the publicity given to the ITC case, only a fool would believe that, in future, member States would be willing to assume liability for the debts of an organization. Organizations will have to learn to live with a reduced creditworthiness.

Shihata rightly sees that there may be circumstances which nevertheless may justify the lifting of the corporate veil in favor of "innocent" third parties.[51] He also holds that the denial of immunity to international legal persons which perform commercial acts may offer such protection. For some time, Italian courts have come out in favor of extending this restrictive immunity theory to international organizations. While present-day international law grants to States only such restricted immunity, international organizations continue to enjoy immunity also for their commercial transactions. This latter rule is justified by the fact that any act by an organization must be done to promote the purpose of the organization. The organization enjoys its personality in and under international law only so as to enable it to fulfil its functions and purpose. Commercial acts of organizations thus remain so closely connected with its official functions as State commercial activities were with sovereign acts of the State in the nineteenth century. The reasons which, then, justified the grant of absolute immunity also to States[52] continue to exist even today, as far as international

---

49 I. Seidl-Hohenveldern in his reply to Mrs. Higgins' questionnaire, 66-I ANNUAIRE DE L'INSTITUT DE DROIT INTERNATIONAL 367, 371 (1995). *See also* Crawford, *ibid.*, 332, 334.

50 I. Seidl-Hohenveldern, *Die mißliche Finanzlage der Vereinten Nationen, in* FESTSCHRIFT FÜR HUGO J. HAHN (A. Weber ed., 1997), at 562.

51 I.Shihata, *see supra* note 2, at 315.

52 Prussian Tribunal for the Settlement of Conflicts of Jurisdiction, June 25, 1920, 5 JAHRBUCH DES ÖFFENTLICHEN RECHTS 252 (1911) *et seq.*; E. Thomas, *Hellfeld Fall, in*

organizations are concerned. Recently, the EMBL award[53] has followed this Italian example by restricting the immunity from taxation of this Laboratory to activities connected with its official purposes. No German tax was held to be due, where a guesthouse built by EMBL was used to accommodate research scholars to the Laboratory. However, where EMBL let the house be used by third parties, EMBL became liable to German tax. The grant of restrictive immunity rather than full immunity to organizations may allow the protection of "innocent" creditors under certain circumstances, but not always. The purchase of the tin by the ITC certainly was a commercial transaction. If we apply the nature of the act test for the grant or refusal of immunity the ITC therefore would no more enjoy immunity in this case than, e.g., a State purchasing armored vehicles for its army.[54] This rule, however, would have benefited the creditors of ITC only, if the counter-argument could have been overcome, that the purchase of tin, commercial in nature as it was, nevertheless did serve a public purpose.

To sum up:

Shihata's suggestion to take all relevant provisions and circumstances into account, when establishing the liability, if any, of member States for acts or omissions of an international organization will enable us to arrive at a solution appropriate to the case at hand. The factors to be considered are not exclusively of an ethical character — or else, such liability could hardly be denied. After all, the member States are the ones, who profit from the organization's activities. Political and pragmatic considerations militate in favor of non-liability — or, else, the organization risks to be seen as a mere tool of its more affluent members. Shihata's formula allows the decision-maker to draw a balance between these rival factors and, thus, to come to an equitable solution of the case concerned.

K. STRUPP & H.J. SCHLOCHAUER, WÖRTERBUCH DES VÖLKERRECHTS (1960) Vol. I, at 786 *et seq.*

53 *See supra* note 6.

54 Oberlandesgericht Koblenz, Oct. 10, 1972, Arms Sales Commission Agreement Case, 65 ILR, at 119.

THE WORLD BANK AND THE HUMAN RIGHT TO EDUCATION

Louis B. Sohn

INTRODUCTION

Dr. Ibrahim Shihata was my student at the Harvard Law School in 1960–63, and participated in my classes on World Order and on International Law and International Organizations. He prepared an interesting paper in 1963 on "The Treaty as a Law-Declaring and Custom-Making Organization," which dealt with a topic that the International Court of Justice considered for the first time in the Continental Shelf Case in 1969, and finally clarified in the two Libyan Continental Shelf Cases in 1982–1985.

Similarly anticipating, in his doctoral dissertation on "The Power of the International Court to Determine Its Own Jurisdiction" (published in 1965), he pointed out that the Court was developing a distinction between having jurisdiction over the parties and the admissibility of a claim. Others were surprised, however, when the Court in the South West Africa case first accepted in 1962 jurisdiction over the case submitted by Ethiopia and Liberia, but later declared it inadmissible. I proudly showed then to my colleagues that one of my students anticipated it. I have noticed also recently that this issue was raised again in 1998 by Nigeria in a case brought against it by Cameroon.

There was also another person that already in 1965 became interested in Dr. Shihata after reading his book. Aron Broches, who was then the General Counsel of the World Bank, called me, asking for Shihata's address, as he wanted to offer him a job at the Bank. I gave him Shihata's address in Egypt, but Shihata told him that he would like to do it some day, but he wanted to spend some time in his home country from which he had been away for too long. After a few years of teaching international law in Egypt, Dr. Shihata became first a legal adviser to the Kuwait Fund for Arab Economic Development, and later a director of the OPEC Fund for International Development and the executive director for International Fund for Agriculture Development in Rome. Finally he came back to the United States as Vice-President and General Counsel for the World Bank. The Broches wish was thus realized.

It is quite clear that throughout this period, Dr. Shihata continued to have a strong interest in economical and social development and the need to develop some better approach to the treatment of a billion of people in the world who, because of lack of adequate education, are unable to earn enough for themselves and their families.

In 1991, Dr. Shihata included in his first volume of essays on *The World Bank in a Changing World,* a chapter on the World Bank and human rights.[1] One section of that essay dealt with the special problem of the right to education, which was first introduced into international law in 1948 by Article 26 of the Universal Declaration of Human Rights.[2] That provision reads as follows:

> "1. Everyone has the right to education. Education shall be free, at least in the elementary and fundamental stages. Elementary education shall be compulsory. Technical and professional education shall be made generally available and higher education shall be equally accessible to all on the basis of merit.
>
> 2. Education shall be directed to the full development of the human personality and to the strengthening of respect for human rights and fundamental freedoms. It shall promote understanding,

---

1 IBRAHIM F. I. SHIHATA, THE WORLD BANK IN A CHANGING WORLD, Vol. I (1991), Chapter Three (*The World Bank and Human Rights*), at 97–134. An earlier, shorter, version of this article was published under the title *The World Bank and Human Rights: An Analysis of the Legal Issues and the Record of Achievement,* 17 DENVER JOURNAL OF INTERNATIONAL LAW AND POLICY 39–66 (1988).

2 Universal Declaration of Human Rights, approved on 10 December 1948 by Resolution 217A (III) of the General Assembly, reprinted in THE UNITED NATIONS, HUMAN RIGHTS: A COMPILATION OF INTERNATIONAL INSTRUMENTS (1994 ed.) [hereinafter HUMAN RIGHTS COMPILATION], Vol. I, p. 1, at 6. In 1968, the First United Nations Conference on Human Rights, held at Teheran, adopted a Proclamation which declared, in paragraph 2, that the1948 Universal Declaration "states a common understanding of the peoples of the world concerning the inalienable and inviolable rights of all members of the human family and constitutes an obligation for the international community." HUMAN RIGHTS COMPILATION, *supra,* Vol. I, p. 51, at 52.

tolerance and friendship among all nations, racial or religious groups, and shall further the activities of the United Nations for the maintenance of peace.

3. Parents have a prior right to choose the kind of education that shall be given to their children."

1. PROLOGUE

The importance of education is, of course, not a new idea. In both Europe and the United States it can be traced back more than 150 years, but only one person was able to prepare detailed proposals showing how it can and should be done. Among the personalities that, together, were responsible for the establishment of the United States of America, Thomas Jefferson was the one especially interested in the need to provide appropriate education for the population of the new state. His *Notes on the State of Virginia,* were a response to queries by a "Foreigner of Distinction."[3] In response to Query 14, relating to the proposed administration of justice and the necessary laws, Jefferson described first the laws inherited from England, and added that the first Assembly of the Commonwealth of Virginia appointed a committee of three experts to prepare a more satisfactory new code. This committee presented a detailed draft to the Assembly which put it aside "till the restoration of peace."[4]

According to Jefferson, the committee decided that some of the parts of the English law had to be drastically revised. Among the proposed "revisals" was a draft bill prepared by him, "to defuse knowledge more generally through the mass of the people." Jefferson summarized this bill as follows:

> "Another object of the revisal is, to diffuse knowledge more generally through the mass of people. This bill proposes to lay off [divide] every county into small districts of five or six miles square,

---

[3] These notes were written in 1781–82, and were first published anonymously in Paris in 1785, and first printed in the United States in Philadelphia in 1788. This pamphlet was reprinted in THE COMPLETE JEFFERSON (assembled and arranged by Saul K. Padover, and published by the Tudor Publishing Company, New York, in 1943), at 567–697).

[4] THE COMPLETE JEFFERSON, *supra* note 3, at 660.

called hundreds, and in each of them to establish a school for teaching, reading, writing, and arithmetic. The tutor to be supported by the hundred, and every person in it entitled to send their children three years gratis, and as much longer as they please, paying for it. These schools to be under a visitor who is annually to choose the boy of best genius in the school, of those whose parents are too poor to give them further education, and to send him forward to one of the grammar schools, of which twenty are proposed to be erected in different parts of the country, for teaching Greek, Latin, geography, and the higher branches of the numerical arithmetic. Of the boys thus sent in one year, trial is to be made at the grammar schools [after] one or two years, and the best genius of the whole selected, and continued six years, and the residue dismissed. By this means twenty of the best geniuses will be raked from the rubbish annually, and be instructed, at the public expense, so far as the grammar schools go. At the end of six years instruction, one half are to be discontinued (from among whom the grammar schools will probably be supplied with future masters); and the other half, who are to be chosen for the superiority of their parts and disposition, are to be sent and continued three years in the study of such sciences as they shall choose, at William and Mary college, the plan of which is proposed to be enlarged, as will be hereafter explained, and extended to all the useful sciences. The ultimate result of the whole scheme of education would be the teaching all the children of the State [of Virginia] reading, writing, and common arithmetic; turning out ten annually, of superior genius, well taught in Greek, Latin, geography, and the higher branches of arithmetic; turning out ten others annually, of still superior parts, who, to those branches of learning, shall have added such of the sciences as their genius shall have led them to; the furnishing to the wealthier part of the people convenient schools at which their children may be educated at their own expense. The general objects of this law are to provide an education adapted to the years, to the capacity, and the condition of everyone, and directed to their freedom and happiness. Specific details were not proper for the law. These must be the business of the visitors entrusted with its execution. The first stage of this education being the schools of the hundreds, wherein the great mass of the people will receive their instruction, the principal foundations of future order will be laid here. Instead, therefore, of putting the Bible and Testament into the hands of the children at an age when their judgments are not sufficiently matured for religious inquiries, their memories may here be stored with the most useful facts from Grecian, Roman, European, and American history. The first elements of morality too may be instilled into their minds; such as, when further developed as their judgments advance in strength, may teach them how to work out their own greatest happiness, by showing them that it does not depend on the condition of life in which chance has placed them, but is always the result of a good conscience, good health, occupation, and freedom in all just pursuits. Those whom either the wealth of their parents or the adoption of the State shall destine to higher degrees of learning, will go on to the grammar schools, which constitute the next stage, there to be instructed in the languages. The learning of Greek and Latin, I am told, is going into disuse in Europe. I know not what their manners and occupations may call for; but it would be very ill-judged in us to follow their example in this instance. There is a certain period of life, say from eight to fifteen or sixteen years of age, when the mind like the body is not yet firm enough for laborious and close operations. If applied to such, it falls an early victim to premature exertion; exhibiting, indeed, at first, in these young and tender subjects, the flattering appearance of their being men while they are yet children, but ending in reducing them to be children when they should be men. The memory is then most susceptible and tenacious of impressions; and the learning of languages being chiefly a work of memory, it seems precisely fitted to the powers of this period, which is long enough too for acquiring the most useful languages, ancient and modern. I do not pretend that language is science. It is only an instrument for the attainment of science. But that time is not lost which is employed in providing tools for future operation; more especially as in this case the books put into the hands of the youth for this purpose may be such as will at the same time impress their minds with useful facts and good principles. If this period be suffered to pass in idleness, the mind becomes lethargic and impotent, as would the body it inhabits if unexercised during the same time. The sympathy between body and mind during their rise, progress and decline, is too strict and obvious to endanger our being missed while we reason from the one to the other. As soon as they are of sufficient age, it is supposed they will be sent on from the grammar schools to the university, which constitutes our third and last stage, there to study those sciences which may be adapted to their views. By that part of our plan which prescribes the selection of the youths of genius from among the classes of the poor, we hope to avail the State of those talents which nature has sown as liberally among the poor as the rich, but which perish without use, if not sought for and cultivated. But of the views of this law none is more important, none more legitimate, than that of rendering the people the safe, as they are the ultimate, guardians of their own liberty. For this purpose the reading in the first stage, where they will receive their whole education, is proposed, as has been said, to be chiefly historical. History, by apprizing them of the past, will enable them to judge of the future; it will qualify them as judges of the actions and designs of men; it will enable them to know ambition under every disguise it may assume; and knowing it, to defeat its views. In every government on earth is some trace of human weakness, some germ of corruption and degeneracy, which cunning will discover, and wickedness insensibly open, cultivate and improve. Every government degenerates when trusted to the rulers of the people alone. The people themselves therefore are its only safe depositories. And to render even them safe, their minds must be improved to a certain degree. This indeed is not all that is necessary, though it be essentially necessary. An amendment of our constitution must here come in aid of the public education. The influence over government must be shared among all the people. If every individual which composes their mass participates of the ultimate authority, the government will be safe; because the corrupting the whole mass will exceed any private resources of wealth; and public ones cannot be provided but by levies on the people. In this case every man would have to pay his own price. The government of Great Britain has been corrupted, because but one man in ten has a right to vote for members of parliament. The sellers of the government, therefore, get nine-tenths of their price clear. It has been thought that corruption is restrained by confining the right of suffrage to a few of the wealthier of the people; but it would be effectually restrained by an extension of that right to such numbers as would bid defiance to the means of corruption."[5]

A few years later, Jefferson returned to this topic in a commentary on the Federal Constitution. He expressed the view that in a country the peace is best preserved, not "by giving energy to the government," but by giving "information to the people." He explained that to "[e]ducate and inform the whole mass of the people" is the "most legitimate engine of government." It would "[e]nable them to see that it is their interest to preserve peace and

5 *Ibid.* at 667–69.

6 Letter to James Madison, December 20, 1787. *Ibid.* at 120, 123. This was only a modest beginning. Thereafter, Jefferson returned frequently to this topic, preparing

order, and they will preserve them." He added that "it requires no high degree of education to convince them of this."[6]

Jefferson's ideas about the importance of education as a basis for other human rights were not realized in his time, but they were not completely forgotten. One of his admirers, President Franklin Delano Roosevelt, decided to apply them at the end of the Second World War. His advisers were working on various benefits, bonuses or rewards for returning war veterans: mustering out pay; broad medical care, including building more veterans' hospitals; death and disability pensions; re-employment rights; and a guarantee of half of the amount of loans made to veterans to buy or build homes, farms or business properties. President Roosevelt did not consider that all these temporary devices were sufficient, and decided to include in the GI Bill of Rights[7] the right to education, one of the rights previously included in his second Bill of Rights.[8] He proposed, therefore, that all the returning soldiers should be offered a chance to education, the amount of it depending on their length of military service, hard work, and ability to move up. The approved plan provided for education and training at any level from primary grades to postgraduate level. Each serviceman would be entitled to receive an educational grant

---

special legislation on various educational stages for Virginia or the United States, and writing to various friends about his endeavors. His proposals were usually very detailed, and culminated with his plans for the ideal university, which were realized when the University of Virginia was built in accordance with his plans. *See ibid.* at 1043–1115.

7 The expression "GI" came from "government issue" of military clothing, and became generally applicable to anything connected with the soldiers and veterans of WWII, including even a GI Haircut.

8 Already in January 1941, in his "Four Freedoms" message to Congress, President Roosevelt mentioned the "freedom from want" that would "secure to every nation a healthy peacetime life for its inhabitants — everywhere in the world." *See* THE PUBLIC PAPERS AND ADDRESSES OF FRANKLIN D. ROOSEVELT, 1940 (Macmillan, N. Y., 1941), p. 663, at 672. Later he revised several times the list of the "rights" encompassed in the "freedom from want," and in his 1944 message to Congress he pointed out that "true individual freedom cannot exist without economic security," and presented "a second Bill of Rights under which a new basis of security and prosperity can be established for all — regardless of station or race and creed." Among the eight rights listed in that bill was "the right to a good education." THE PUBLIC PAPERS, *supra, 1944–1945* (Samuel I. Rosenman ed., 1950), p. 32, at 41. The Congress refused to pay any attention to the President's Bill of Rights, but was persuaded to accept, almost unanimously, the GI Bill of Rights.

for one year plus the time served in the armed forces, up to a total of four years. The Administrator of Veterans' Affairs was authorized to pay the veteran's tuition at an educational or training institution, including laboratory, library, health and infirmary fees, and to pay for books, supplies and equipment, and other necessary expenses generally required for the successful pursuit and completion of the course by other students in the institution. There was also a subsistence allowance for the veteran and one dependent.[9]

It was really a miracle that Congress actually passed the law that worked even better than expected, and really changed America.[10] Taking advantage of these arrangements, in the fall of 1946, more than 1 million veterans enrolled in colleges and universities all over the United States.[11] With the help of other assistance programs, such as the loans for mortgage financing, not only the schools were busy, but also the building industry, and suburbs sprang like mushrooms around every sizable city.[12] Suddenly, for the first time in its history, the United States had a large middle class. In addition, the GI Bill was a pioneering example of America's color-blind social legislation, and enabled many Afro-Americans to go to college, and some became leaders of the civil rights movement.[13] Instead of a post-war crisis, the GI Bill made possible bringing millions of customers for supermarkets and a variety of new merchandise. Both Jefferson and Roosevelt were right that an educated population can contribute more to the "pursuit of happiness," and to promoting "general welfare," as promised by the US Declaration of Independence and the preamble to the Constitution of the United States, as well as to "social progress and better standards of life in larger freedom," that was promised by the Charter of the United Nations.[14]

---

9 *See* Servicemen's Readjustment Act of 1944, Title II, Chapter IV (Education of Veterans), June 22, 1944, 58 Stat. 284, at 287–91.

10 MICHAEL J. BENNETT, WHEN DREAMS COME TRUE: THE GI BILL AND THE MAKING OF MODERN AMERICA (1996), at 22.

11 *Ibid.* at 18.

12 *Ibid.* at 24

13 *Ibid.* at 26.

14 Preamble to the UN Charter, para. 4. In addition, Article 35 (a) provides that the United Nations shall promote "higher standards of living, full employment, and conditions of economic and social progress and development."

2. THE WORLD BANK AND THE RIGHT TO EDUCATION

During the fifty years after the Second World War the World Bank and other international institutions have discovered that money spent on education can provide better results than great projects that often have unexpected negative effects.

When Dr. Shihata joined the World Bank's Counsel office in 1983, the Bank's role in assisting the reconstruction of the countries damaged by the Second World War was terminated, and the emphasis could be put on its second major goal — to encourage "international investment for the development of the productive resources of members, thereby assisting in raising productivity, the standard of living and conditions of labor in their territories."[15]

In the introduction to his second volume of essays, Dr. Shihata pointed out that in the second half of the 1980s the World Bank has started increasing its "investment" in "people," a people-oriented approach to development.

By 1994, the Bank's lending for this purpose increased to 17 percent of total lending. In particular, the lending for education exceeded US$2 billion. In this work, the Bank is working closely with various NGOs in both developed and developing countries.[16] Under the heading "Investing in People: Human Resource Development," Dr. Shihata notes that the World Bank and other development institutions have found that "the optimal mix of development projects includes both programs directed at economic growth and programs targeted directly to the poor." He believes that in this way "the poor have a greater chance of being able to participate in and benefit from economic growth."[17] Four issues are intertwined in these programs: education, gender policy, population and health. In particular, "education increases the economic productivity of the poor and enables them to participate more effectively in and benefit from economic growth."[18]

---

15 Articles of Agreement of the International Bank for Reconstruction and Development, December 27, 1945, 2 United Nations Treaty Series, at 134. *See* article 1 (III).

16 *See* Introduction, IBRAHIM F. I. SHIHATA, THE WORLD BANK IN A CHANGING WORLD, Vol. II (1995), at 10.

17 *Ibid.* Chapter One (*Development Policies and Strategies — with Emphasis on the World Bank Group*), at 48.

18 *Ibid.* For instance, World Bank studies in Africa have found that the mortality

While many governments grant priority to the political and civil rights and consider the economic and social rights as mere "entitlements," the World Bank, in its basic constitutional document, or Articles of Agreement, and in its constant practice grants priority to the economic and social rights, and interprets quite strictly its constitutional injunction that "[t]he Bank and its officers shall not interfere in the political affairs of any member; nor shall they be influenced in their decisions by the political character of the member or members concerned."[19]

Dr. Shihata explains his views on the subject, which are accepted also by other officers of the World Bank, in chapter 19 of the second volume of his essays, which deals with "The World Bank and Human Rights."[20] He makes clear that the World Bank in all its activities contributes "to the promotion and protection of a broad array of human rights of economic, social and cultural character." The Bank has made a special effort to assist its less developed members in the exercise of their "right to development."[21]

Dr. Shihata makes clear further that the Bank's "overriding objective" is "to enable people in its borrowing countries to enjoy freedom from poverty," and that this is "a basic freedom which is needed in fact for the full enjoyment of other human rights and is still denied to more than one billion people."[22] In particular, the Bank uses its lending power for "human resources development," concentrating as far as possible on enabling people in the borrowing countries "to have better opportunities for education and health services which are not only human rights themselves, but also prerequisites for the full attainment of other human rights."[23]

While some experts have been suggesting that the Articles of Agreement should be amended to give to the World Bank a clear political role in enforcing political human rights and in supporting democratization, Dr. Shihata points out that such an amendment would require an approval by 60 percent of the members having

---

rate of children under five is only half if the mothers have had more than seven years of education. *Ibid*, at 48–49.

19 Articles of Agreement, *supra* note 15, Art. IV, Sec. 10.

20 Ibrahim F. Shihata, The World Bank in a Changing World, Vol. II (1995), Chapter Nineteen (*The World Bank and Human Rights*), at 567–578.

21 This right has been proclaimed by the UN General Assembly in 1986 as a basic human right, and was strongly reiterated by the 1993 Vienna Declaration of the World Conference on Human Rights. *Ibid*. at 568.

22 *Ibid*.

23 *Ibid*. at 569.

at least 85 percent of the total vote (which is based on the number of shares of the capital stock possessed by each member; for instance, the United States always has had the percentage of votes that was needed to block an amendment). It would be very difficult to obtain such a majority for politicizing the Bank's decisions.

Instead, Dr. Shihata believes that necessary changes can come by the Bank concentrating its efforts on assisting the borrowing members in fulfilling their obligations concerning the socio-economic development, the reduction of poverty, more efficient management of resources, and universal education. Perhaps, by continuing to promote economic and social rights, the Bank would, indirectly, lay the foundations for the promotion of political rights.

The remedies suggested by Dr. Shihata might not be liked by some governments, but would benefit the people not only of the developing countries but even those of the United States and the European Union, as in both of them there are many millions of unemployed who need the education that would enable them or their children to obtain jobs good enough to give them a better life. The United States was able to do it for the soldiers coming back from World War II, and the Marshall Plan did it later for Western Europe. It can be done also in the next millennium and the World Bank might be able to help. By now, all human beings are entitled to all generally accepted human rights. The right to education has become such a right.

As the President of the World Bank, Barber B. Conable announced hopefully at the beginning of the last decade:

> "In the new century, the dividends from knowledge will grow as dramatically as the penalties of ignorance increase. Much of the gulf between misery and opportunity, squalor and hope, can be bridged by education, by investing in the bright inquisitiveness of children [. . .]. Education, and human resource development more broadly, must be a central focus of the development effort in the 1990s."

In doing that, both the Bank and the developing countries might find that some ideas of Jefferson that were appropriate for the new United States might fit their needs better than some modern ideas.

LAW AND DEVELOPMENT AN EMPIRICAL STUDY OF THE EVOLUTION OF THE LEGAL FRAMEWORK FOR DELIVERY OF MULTILATERAL DEVELOPMENT ASSISTANCE: NATIONAL EXECUTION

*Francis M. Ssekandi & Peri Lynne Johnson**

I. INTRODUCTION

The study of Public International Law today would not be complete without an examination of the legal instruments establishing the multitude of international agencies devoted to social, economic and sustainable development. These agencies vary not only in terms of their mandates but also in the manner in which they deliver development assistance to recipient countries. The Bretton Woods Institutions, now including the International Monetary Fund (IMF) and the World Bank Group, i.e., International Bank Reconstruction & Development (IBRD), International Development Association (IDA), International Finance Corporation (IFC), Multilateral Investment Guarantee Agency (MIGA), and International Centre for Settlement of Investment Disputes (ICSID), together with the regional finance institutions, the European bank for Reconstruction and Development (EBRD), African Development Bank (AfDB), Asian Development Bank (ADB) and the Inter-American Development Bank (IADB), provide assistance

* The views expressed herein are the views of the authors and do not necessarily represent the views of the United Nations, the United Nations Development Programme (UNDP), or the African Development Bank (AfDB).

through a combination of loans and grants. However, apart from the United Nations Capital Development Fund, the United Nations Agencies give assistance largely through grants. The challenge for these agencies was how to maximize the use of the resources they place at the disposal of the beneficiary Governments. In order to do this effectively, a variety of legal modalities were devised over time to control not only the methods of disbursements but also the rules for the procurement of goods and services for the funded projects. This paper analyzes the establishment of instruments governing the United Nations Development Programme and its Executing Agencies, including the World Bank, and the evolution of the National or Government Execution modality as an alternative to use of the Executing Agencies. As will be demonstrated, the National Execution modality was an attempt at providing empowerment of the countries receiving assistance over not only the design of assisted programmes but also of the process of their implementation. The relative success of this noble objective still remains to be assessed, but suffice it to say that full empowerment over the implementation of programmes in developing countries continues to be plagued by the endemic lack of accountability and mal-administration, which hamper full donor confidence that development aid will be put to proper use by these countries. This lack of confidence has resulted in the institution of restrictive conditionalities for the release of development assistance funds and rigid application of procurement rules to the extent sometimes of negating the achievement of the very objectives of such assistance: in aid of the poor, the sick and disadvantaged in these countries. There is, therefore, a need — it is argued — for capacity building and institutional reforms, to instill Good Governance, so as to restore donor confidence.

There is no doubt that implementation of projects funded with donor aid by local institutions can be done at reduced overhead costs.

II. THE UNITED NATIONS DEVELOPMENT PROGRAMME

United Nations Development Programme (UNDP) is the cornerstone of the United Nations efforts in the field of international development cooperation and operates as the central funding and catalytic mechanism of the United Nations development system. From its origins in the Expanded Programme of Technical Assistance and Special Fund to the present, UNDP has continually adapted itself to the changing needs of programme countries and the evolving nature of international development.

Development cooperation in the 1960s and early 1970s was largely perceived as technical assistance: the transfer of skills technology and knowledge from the advanced and rich countries to the poor countries of the third world. In keeping with the times, UNDP used Specialized Agencies,[1] such as Food and Agriculture Organization of the United Nations (FAO) and United Nations Educational, Scientific and Cultural Organization (UNESCO), largely staffed by people from developed countries, to provide technical assistance.

It is widely accepted today that a more cooperative approach to the provision of development assistance is necessary,[2] one where there is partnership among people and active participation by those in the programme country in the design and implementation of development programmes and projects.[3] In UNDP, the main instrument to convey this approach to the provision of development assistance is known as national execution.

This paper documents UNDP's transition from the traditional model of providing development assistance referred to above (which used Specialized Agencies as UNDP's technical and managerial agents) known as the tripartite relationship among UNDP, the Specialized Agencies and programme country governments, or agency execution, to national execution, where governments assume overall responsibility for such management.

In order to understand UNDP and the significance of this transition, the first section describes UNDP's origins in the Expanded Programme of Technical Assistance and the Special Fund, as well as the subsequent merger of these two programmes to form UNDP. The second section traces the institutionalization of national execution in UNDP as the norm for the provision of de-

---

1 Organizations brought into relationship with the United Nations under Article 63 of the U.N. Charter.

2 OUR GLOBAL NEIGHBORHOOD 189 (The Commission on Global Governance, 1995).

3 *See Ibid.* at 191–192.

velopment assistance. Finally, the third section gives an overview of the promises and challenges of national execution.

A. The Expanded Programme of Technical Assistance

The Expanded Programme of Technical Assistance was approved by the General Assembly in its resolution 304 (IV) of November 16, 1949, on recommendation by the Economic and Social Council (ECOSOC), with the primary objective of helping underdeveloped countries to "strengthen their national economies through the development of their industries and agriculture, with a view to promoting their economic and political independence in the spirit of the Charter of the United Nations, and to ensure the attainment of higher levels of economic and social welfare for their entire populations."[4] It was the first attempt by the United Nations to provide technical assistance on a large scale.[5] An analysis of the principles on which the Expanded Programme was based and the manner in which it functioned can help to understand UNDP today — and the significance of the shift to national execution.

The origins of the Expanded Programme can be traced to an earlier General Assembly resolution, resolution 200 (III), of December 4, 1948, in which the General Assembly considered that "the promotion of conditions of economic and social progress and development [was] one of the principal objectives of the Charter of the United Nations" and that the lack of "expert personnel" and "technical organization" were among the factors impeding the economic development of underdeveloped countries.[6] The General Assembly considered further that the United Nations could extend "efficacious and timely help" and requested the Secretary-General to arrange the following:

4 *See* U.N. ECOSOC resolution 222 (IX) of Aug. 14 and 15, 1949, and Annex 1 (para. 1).

5 *See* Mahyar Nashat, National Interests and Bureaucracy Versus Development Aid 1 (1978).

6 *See* U.N. General Assembly resolution 200 (III) of Dec. 4, 1948, para. 2 (a) and (b).

(a) international teams of experts to advise Governments on their economic development programmes;
(b) facilities for the training of experts from under-developed countries through fellowships for study;
(c) facilities for the training of local technicians within the under-developed countries themselves; and
(d) facilities to assist Governments obtain technical personnel, equipment and supplies.[7]

The General Assembly requested the Secretary-General to report at each session on measures taken to implement the resolution and to formulate recommendations.[8]

In resolution 180 (VIII) of March 4, 1949, ECOSOC requested the Secretary-General, taking into account, *inter alia,* General Assembly resolution 200 (III) and the Secretary-General's first report in response thereto,[9] to prepare a report in consultation with the executive heads of the interested specialized agencies setting forth:

1. A comprehensive plan for an expanded cooperative programme of technical assistance for economic development through the United Nations and its specialized agencies, paying due attention to questions of a social nature which directly condition economic development;
2. Methods of financing such a programme including special budgets; and
3. Ways of coordinating the planning and execution of the programme.[10]

In response to ECOSOC's request, the Secretary-General consulted with the executive heads of the International Labour Organization (ILO), the Food and Agriculture Organization (FAO),

---

7 *Ibid.* at para. 2(c) and 3 (a) to (d).

8 *Ibid.* at para. 6.

9 Creation of a Central Publication for the Promotion of and Advising on Development Projects, E/1083/Add.1 dated Feb. 2, 1949.

10 *See* U.N. ECOSOC resolution 180 (VIII) of March 4, 1949, preamble and paras. 1–3.

UNESCO, the World Health Organization (WHO), the International Civil Aviation Organization (ICAO), IBRD, IMF and the International Refugee Organization (IRO); input was also received from a number of Member Governments and the Organization of American States (OAS).[11] The Secretary-General's Report in response to ECOSOC resolution 180 provided an overview of the objectives and nature of the programme, the fields of work, forms of technical assistance, organization, finance, and included detailed proposals by the above-referenced organizations, except the IMF and IRO which prepared statements instead along with the, at the time, still contemplated, International Trade Organization (ITO).[12]

In June 1949, the Secretary-General proposed that "ECOSOC give consideration to the expansion of the scope of the technical assistance programme."[13] Notably, the Secretary-General proposed comprehensive missions, advisory services by experts, training, seminars and publications, for a total increase in the 1950 budget for such activities to US$676,000 from US$307,750 appropriated for such purposes in 1949.[14]

The Secretary-General's March and June 1949 Reports provided the basis for ECOSOC resolution 222 (IX), which set out the Observations and Guiding Principles of the Expanded Programme.

The Observations and Guiding Principles of the Expanded Programme contained in Annex I of ECOSOC resolution 222 (IX) were recommended by ECOSOC to serve as guides to the United Nations and the specialized agencies participating in the Expanded Programme (hereinafter collectively called "Participating Organizations") and addressed the following areas: General Principles,[15] Standards of Work and Personnel, Participation of Re-

---

11 *See* U.N. Secretary-General Report to ECOSOC, E/1327/Add.1, May 1949, at page vii and viii.

12 The negotiations to create an International Trade Organization (ITO) was concluded in Havana, Cuba in 1948, but the ITO was never established, due to the refusal of the US Congress to ratify the agreement.

13 Addendum to Second Report by the Secretary-General, E/1335/Add.1 dated June 7, 1949, at 2.

14 *Ibid.* at 5, para. (f).

15 The general principles for the provision of technical assistance are taken from General Assembly resolution 200 (III) and are as follows:

> "(a) Technical assistance for economic development of under-developed countries shall be rendered by the participating organizations only in agree-

questing Governments,[16] Coordination of Effort, Concentration and Economy, and Selection of Projects.

ECOSOC resolution 222 (IX) also set out the administrative and governing structure for the Expanded Programme. The Programme was governed by both a Technical Assistance Board (TAB) and a Technical Assistance Committee (TAC), both of which were to be guided by the Observations and Guiding Principles of the Expanded Programme.[17]

The TAB consisted of the executive heads of the Participating Organizations chaired by the Secretary-General or his representative, and included the United Nations, ILO, FAO, UNESCO, ICAO, and WHO.[18] The TAB provided a forum through which the Participating Organizations could come together and share information on new requests for assistance and ongoing activities. Each

---

ment with the Governments concerned and on the basis of requests received from them;

(b) The kinds of services to be rendered to each country shall be decided by the Government concerned;

(c) The countries desiring assistance should perform, in advance, as much of the work as possible in order to define the nature and scope of the problem involved;

(d) The technical assistance furnished shall:

(i) Not be a means of foreign economic and political interference in the internal affairs of the country concerned and not be accompanied by any considerations of a political nature;

(ii) Be given only to or through Governments;

(iii) Be designed to meet the needs of the country concerned; and

(iv) Be provided as far as possible in the form which that country desires."

ECOSOC resolution 222 (IX), Annex I, paras. 1–3.

16 Governments were, *inter alia,* to facilitate the activities requested from the Participating Organizations, to undertake sustained efforts required for economic development, including "progressive assumption of financial responsibility for the administration of projects initiated at their request under international auspices." *Ibid.* at Annex 1, paras.1 and 5.

17 *Ibid.* at 7, para. 7.

18 Although not Participating Organizations, the IBRD, IMF and IRO regularly attended and participated in the meetings of the TAB and pledged the fullest cooperation for the promotion of the objectives of the Programme. *See* Report of the Technical Assistance Board, E/1742 dated July 4, 1950, para 7. In addition, the International Telecommunications Union (ITU) and the World Meteorological Organization (WMO) became Participating Organizations on August 30, 1951 by U.N. ECOSOC resolution 400 (XIII), and the International Atomic Energy Association (IAEA) on Oct. 23, 1958 by U.N. ECOSOC resolution 704 (XXVI) of the same date.

Participating Organization was required to present annual reports to the TAB on its proposed programme for the next year and the TAB was to make recommendations concerning the proposals and the overall programme to ECOSOC through the TAC. The Secretary-General was authorized to designate the Executive Secretary of the TAB, in consultation with the Participating Organizations, whose responsibility was to service the TAB.[19]

The TAC was proposed as a standing committee of ECOSOC, consisting of the members of ECOSOC. The terms of reference for the TAC were as follows: to critically examine activities undertaken by the Programme and the results achieved; to examine each year's programme; to interpret ECOSOC resolution 222 (IX) in the event of conflicts; to receive reports from the TAB; and to review the working relationships between the Participating Organizations.[20]

At the first meeting of the TAB, a draft basic Agreement was prepared to be used in negotiating with the recipient countries regarding the provision of the technical assistance. The Agreement was based on the Observations and Guiding Principles contained in ECOSOC resolution 222 (IX), Annex I, and the experience of a number of international organizations.[21] The Agreement set out the basic terms and conditions under which the Participating Agencies would provide technical assistance to the recipient countries and addressed issues relating to the type of assistance to be provided, administrative and financial arrangements and the privileges and immunities to be accorded to the Participating Agencies and their personnel.[22] The clauses in this early agreement are similar to those still being used today in UNDP's Standard Basic Assistance Agreement (SBAA).[23]

As has been shown, the Expanded Programme was truly a joint initiative of the United Nations and the Specialized Agencies.

---

19 *Ibid.* at 5, paras. 3–4.

20 *Ibid.* at 6, para. 6.

21 *Ibid.* at para. 16.

22 Articles in the agreement addressed: Furnishing of Technical Assistance; Co-operation of the Government with Respect to the Provision of Technical Assistance; Administrative and Financial Obligations of the Parties; Facilities, Privileges and Immunities; Publication of Findings; Modification of Agreement, Supplemental Agreements and Termination. *Ibid.* at Annex I.

23 *See* discussion of SBAA below.

The Specialized Agencies were deeply involved in establishing the principles upon which technical assistance would be provided to Governments under the Expanded Programme. From the earliest efforts of the United Nations in the field of development cooperation, the Specialized Agencies assumed the role of providing and managing such assistance.

B. The Special Fund

The Special Fund was established following a number of years of study by special committees of the General Assembly and ECOSOC on ways of enhancing urgent assistance to developing countries, as complementary to the work already done by the United Nations, the specialized agencies and the Expanded Programme.[24] The purpose was to "advance the process of technical, economic and social development of the less developed countries, and, in particular, [. . .to] facilitate new capital investments of all types — private and public, national and international — by creating conditions which would make such investments either feasible or more effective."[25]

By its resolution 1219 (XII), and on the basis of the reports prepared by the Ad Hoc Committee on the Question of the Establishment of a Special United Nations Fund for Economic Development, the General Assembly established the basic conditions for the establishment of the Special Fund and the terms of reference of a Preparatory Committee, composed of representatives of sixteen Governments and appointed by the General Assembly.[26]

The Special Fund was intended to establish a new administrative and operational machinery to spearhead the enlargement of the scope of technical assistance available from the United Nations and the Specialized Agencies, to include such activities as "intensive surveys of water, mineral and potential power resources, the establishment — including staffing and equipping — of training institutes in public administration, statistics and tech-

---

[24] *See* U.N. General Assembly resolutions 923 (X) of Dec. 9, 1955, and 1030 (XI) of Feb. 26, 1957.

[25] Financing Of Economic Development, *see* U.N. General Assembly resolution 1219 (XII).

[26] U.N. General Assembly resolution 1219 (XII) was adopted on Dec. 14, 1957.

nology, and agricultural and industrial research and productivity centers."[27]

The establishment of the Special Fund was accomplished in October 1958, by General Assembly resolution 1240 (XIII), entitled "Establishment of the Special Fund." The resolution was adopted on the recommendation of ECOSOC, which by its resolution 692 (XXVI) of July 31, 1958 had set out the basic principles and structure of the Fund, following review of the recommendations of the Preparatory Committee.[28]

The realization of the Special Fund was a unique accomplishment of the United Nations in the field of development. Many of the institutions until that time had been, by and large, inherited from the League of Nations, so this was one of the new structures under the Charter of the United Nations. The Fund was provided a separate inter-governmental governing body, known as the Governing Council.[29] The Council was to exercise inter-governmental control of the policies and operations of the Fund, with final authority for the approval of the projects and programmes recommended by the Managing Director. It was to provide "general policy guidance on the administration and operations of the Special Fund." The management of the Fund was to be entrusted to a Management Director appointed by the Secretary-General after consultation with the Governing Council and subject to confirmation by the General Assembly. The Management Director was to be advised by a Consultative Board consisting of the Secretary-General of the United Nations, the Executive Chairman of the Technical Assistance Board and the President of the IBRD or their designated representatives.[30]

Immediately following the Governing Council's second session in May of 1959, action was taken towards establishing the legal framework of Special Fund projects.[31] The Governing Coun-

---

27 *Ibid.* at paras. 1–2.

28 *See Ibid.*, paragraph 2, which reads: "Establishes a Special fund in accordance with the provisions set forth in part B below."

29 The Governing Council was transformed into the Executive Board in 1994 as a result of U.N. General Assembly resolution 48/162 dated December 20, 1993.

30 The Consultative Board would *seem* to be the precursor of the modern day Management Committee established by the UNDP Executive Board for UNOPS.

31 *See* Implementation of the Programme Approved By the Governing Council at its Second Session, Report by the Managing Director, SF/L.22, 3rd Session, page 1, para. 2.

cil prepared standard agreements designed to govern the relations between the Special Fund on the one hand, and the recipient governments and executing agencies on the other.[32] These agreements were similar to those used by the Expanded Programme and embodied the conditions under which the Fund would provide each government with assistance. The Agreement specified the nature of participation of the government in the execution of projects, its counterpart contribution (provision of materials, equipment, supplies, etc.) as well as the provision of local facilities. The Agreement also dealt with the provision of privileges and immunities to be accorded to the Special Fund and the executing agencies, their property, funds and assets, and their personnel.[33]

The Standard Agreement with the Specialized Agencies, the UN or the International Atomic Energy Agency (IAEA) when acting as Executing Agency, known as the Executing Agency Agreement, specified the respective responsibilities for the execution of projects and outlined the financial and reporting arrangements.[34] Pursuant to this agreement, the role of the Specialized Agencies under the Special Fund remained much the same as in the Expanded Programme — the Managing Director of the Fund was to rely on the assistance of the Specialized Agencies when evaluating project requests and to use the services available within the Expanded Programme, moreover such Agencies along with the UN and IAEA were responsible for the execution of the projects.

In addition to the two aforementioned sets of agreements which constituted the basic legal framework for co-operation, a

---

[32] SF/L.28. page 14 para. 28.

[33] *Ibid.* at para. 29. The articles of agreement addressed the following: Assistance to be provided by the Special Fund, Execution of Projects, Information Concerning Project, Co-operation of Government in Execution of Project, Local Facilities to be Provided by the Government to the Special Fund and the Executing Agency, Relation to Assistance from other Sources, Use of Assistance, Facilities — Privileges and Immunities, Settlements of Disputes, and General Provisions. *See*, e.g., Draft Standard Agreement with Governments, SF/L.12/Add.14/Rev.1.

[34] SF/L.28 at para. 30. The agreement included articles on the following: Performance of Work by Executing Agency, Conclusion of Agreement with Governments, Executing Agency Status in Carrying out Projects, Information Regarding projects, Cost of Projects, Manner of Payment, Records-Accounts-Vouchers, Expenses of Preparation, Currency and Rates of Exchange, Revision of Financial Arrangements, Immunities of Subcontractor, and General Provisions. *See, e.g., Draft Standard Agreement with Executing Agency,* SF/L.12/Add.15/Rev.1.

Plan of Operation was signed by the three parties concerned, for each individual project. A typical Plan of Operation, as a tripartite agreement between the Government, the Special Fund and the Executing Agency concerned, contained a description of the project; a detailed work plan for its execution including particulars concerning experts; fellowships and equipment to be provided; a timetable showing sequence of operation; and a detailed budget of the costs to be borne by the government and the Special Fund.[35] Today, the Plan of Operation is known as the programme support or project document.

The other salient features of the Fund were that projects were to be undertaken only at the request of a Government or group of Governments (as with the Expanded Programme); the execution of projects was to be carried out by the United Nations, by the Specialized Agencies and the IAEA; and the Managing Director was authorized to contract services of "other agencies, private firms or individual experts" where the services of the executing agencies were "wholly or partly unavailable or inadequate."

C. The Consolidation of the Expanded Programme Of Technical Assistance and The Special Fund into the United Nations Development Programme (UNDP)

UNDP was established by General Assembly resolution 2029(XX) of November 22, 1965 by merging the Expanded Programme of Technical Assistance and the Special Fund, on the understanding that the special characteristics and operations of the two programmes, as well as two separate funds, were to be maintained and that contributions would be pledged to the two programmes separately.[36] The justifications for the merger were to, *inter alia,* streamline the activities of the two programmes and provide a "more solid basis for the future growth and evolution of UN assistance programmes."[37]

35 SF/L.28, page 15, para. 31.

36 U.N. General Assembly resolution 2029(XX) of Nov. 22, 1965, para. 1.

37 *Ibid.* at Preamble.

A single inter-governmental committee of thirty-seven members known as the Governing Council of UNDP was established to perform the functions previously exercised by the Governing Council of the Special Fund and the TAC, including the consideration and approval of projects and programmes and allocation of funds. In addition, the Governing Council was to provide general policy guidance and direction for the United Nations Development Programme as a whole, as well as for the United Nations regular programmes of technical assistance.[38]

In place of the TAB of the Expanded Programme and the Consultative Board of the Special Fund, an advisory committee known as the Inter-Agency Consultative Board of UNDP was established. The Board was to meet under the chairmanship of the Administrator or Co-Administrator and was to include the Secretary-General of the United Nations and the executive heads of the specialized agencies and of the IAEA or their representatives. The Board was to be consulted on all significant aspects of the United Nations Development Programme, in particular on the programmes and projects submitted by governments prior to their submission to the Governing Council; the selection of agencies for the execution of specific projects; and the appointment of the Resident Representative.[39]

In 1969, a few years following the consolidation of the Expanded Programme and the Special Fund, the United Nations commissioned a Study on the Capacity of the United Nations Development System (hereafter Study).[40] The purpose of the Study was to assess the capacity of the United Nations system to effectively use UNDP's resources and its capacity to handle a programme twice the size of the operations at that time.[41] The Study criticized the problems experienced in the UN development system, in quantitative and qualitative terms, and made recommendations for the future.

With respect to the qualitative aspects of UN development programmes relevant to the present paper, the Study pointed out that a donor bias existed whereby initiative came from specialized

---

38 *Ibid.* at para. 4.

39 *Ibid.* at para. 6.

40 DP/5, 1969 (Vols. I and II).

41 *Ibid.* at para. 1.

agencies and not from the country itself, that there was a failure to recognize the need for a comprehensive approach to development problems and insufficient emphasis on training.[42] The Study further noted that development projects resulted from the "salesmanship of specialized agencies rather than the priority needs of recipient governments, that specialized agencies had heavy operational burdens which resulted in delays in programme delivery as well as a decline in quality."[43] Included in the Study's recommendations to address the problems was the need to broaden the concept of development to take into account the changing political, economic and social conditions, noting that international development is made up of individual national goals and reaffirming the country approach to development.[44] With respect to the specialized agencies, the Study recommended that, in cases where specialized agencies were over-burdened, projects should be contracted outside the system, noting that the legislative authority already existed, whereby the Administrator could specify that the Agency subcontract on his behalf when assigning a project to it for execution.[45]

Following the recommendations contained in the Study, the General Assembly adopted resolution 2688(XXV) of December 11,1970, which sets out UNDP's methods of operation, excluding the subsequent changes relating, *inter alia,* to national execution discussed below.[46] In accordance with this resolution, distinctions between the Technical Assistance and Special Fund components have been eliminated.[47] UNDP was to operate under the "United

---

42 *Ibid.* at para. 21.

43 *Ibid.* at para. 23 (a) and (b).

44 *Ibid.* at. para. 34.

45 *Ibid.* at para. 72.

46 Other significant changes since the Consensus relate to the introduction of the programming approach which seeks to integrate projects into a coordinated programme or programmes within the country (E/1993/73, Annex III; E/1995/98, para. 69) and the shift from the use of the Indicative Planning Figure (IPF) for the allocation of programme resources which was essentially guaranteed funding for the country programme to TRAC resources which is based on the premise that governments get only a percentage of designated funding and that the remainder is contingent upon minimum performance indicators. Executive Board decision 95/23 of June 16, 1995.

47 *See* General Assembly resolution 2688 (XXV) of 11 Dec.1970, Annex, para. 13.

Nations Development Co-Operation Cycle," which included the following phases: country programme formulation, project formulation, appraisal and approval, implementation, evaluation and follow-up.[48] The Cycle also included periodic reviews.[49]

Pursuant to resolution 2688, country programming, the first phase of the Cycle, is based on individual national development plans, or where they do not exist, on national development priorities or objectives. The Government of the country concerned retains the exclusive responsibility for formulating its national development plan.[50] The total resources available for programming are divided between country programming on the one hand and inter-country programming (consisting of sub-regional, regional, inter-regional, and global projects) on the other.[51]

The implementation of UNDP assistance is overseen by the Governing Council and the Administrator. The Governing Council is empowered to approve projects submitted by programmes for consideration. However, the Governing Council, while retaining this authority, delegates to the Administrator for three years the authority to approve projects within country programmes.[52] The Governing Council has over-all responsibility for ensuring that the resources of the Programme are employed with maximum efficiency and effectiveness in assisting the development of the developing countries.[53] In particular, the Council's responsibilities include: considering and approving country programmes, approving certain projects included in the programmes, exercising operational control (including periodic reviews of the country programmes), making broad allocations of resources and controlling their use. [54]

In addition to the responsibilities delegated to him by the Governing Council, the Administrator is fully responsible and accountable to the Governing Council for all phases and aspects of

48 *See Ibid.* at para.1. New developments concerning UNDP programming arrangements are reflected in Executive Board decision 95/23, paras. 11-14.

49 *Ibid.* at para. 1.

50 *Ibid.* at paras. 4 and 5.

51 *Ibid.* at para. 24.

52 *Ibid.* at para. 20.

53 *Ibid.* at para. 35.

54 *Ibid.* at para. 36.

the implementation of the Programme.[55] The application of the twin principle of the Administrator's full accountability for the Programme and the decentralization to the country level envisaged in General Assembly resolution 2688 required modifications in the existing structures and procedures of the Programme. At the headquarters level, regional bureaus were established to provide a direct link between the Administrator and the resident representative in all matters concerning field activities.[56] In addition, in order to analyze the main trends in the evolution of the Programme, a small long-term planning staff was established at the headquarters level under the direction of a senior official.[57] And, at the country level, the resident representative was re-designated resident director.[58] There was the maximum possible delegation of authority to the resident director; he was to have full over-all responsibility for the programme in the country concerned.[59]

Under General Assembly resolution 2688, the role of the specialized agencies in the provision of development assistance is preserved. The resolution stipulates that the role of such Agencies is to be that of partners, and their advice available to the Administrator in the implementation of all projects, whether executed by them or not.[60] The resolution further stipulates that such specialized agencies shall have first consideration as executing agents for the implementation of the programme assistance.[61]

Following the consolidation of UNDP, the Administrator commenced preparation of a new standard agreement with a view to reflecting the "unitary concept" of UNDP and to incorporating certain provisions from the project documents in order to simplify negotiations with the recipient countries on such project documents.[62] Today, over 130 governments have signed the new basic agreement, referred to as the SBAA. It continues to be the basic agreement between UNDP and programme country governments

---

55 *Ibid.* at para. 37.
56 *Ibid.* at para. 57.
57 *Ibid.* at para. 58.
58 *Ibid.* at para. 62.
59 *Ibid.* at para. 63.
60 *Ibid.* at para. 38.
61 *Ibid.* at paras. 39–40.
62 Note by the Administrator, DP/86, of Nov. 29, 1974, para. 3.

that sets out the terms and conditions of UNDP's support to such countries.

III. NEW DIMENSIONS IN TECHNICAL COOPERATION

A. The Transition to Government Execution

Throughout the period up to 1974, development theory, policy and practice remained largely unchanged. The persistence of underdevelopment was explained by the lack of technical skills, shortage of managerial capacity and dearth of capital.[63] The injection of technical assistance and capital from more advanced countries was the logical solution.

However, by the Second United Nations Development Decade, developing countries expressed the desire for a new international economic order, in part a manifestation of the declining validity of the traditional approach to development. The General Assembly adopted the International Strategy for the Decade on October 24, 1970, wherein the General Assembly confirmed that the ultimate objective of development must be to bring about sustained improvement in the well-being of the individual and bestow benefits on all.[64] By 1974, the General Assembly had proclaimed a "New International Economic Order," declaring that the greatest achievement during the last decades had been the independence from colonial domination and that the present international economic order was in direct conflict with developments in international political and economic relations.[65] The General Assembly further declared that changes in the international economy necessitated full and equal participation of developing countries in all decisions concerning the international community.[66]

These dramatic changes in the international economic order forced UNDP to consider new dimensions in technical coopera-

---

63 Harrod/Domar growth model.

64 International Development Strategy for the Second United Nations Development Decade, U.N. General Assembly resolution 2626(XXV), preamble, para. 7.

65 *See* U.N. General Assembly resolution 3201 (S-VI) of May 1, 1974.

66 *Ibid.* at paras. 1–3.

tion. UNDP recognized that the increased emphasis placed on self-reliance by developing countries required a re-thinking of the automatic dependence on external inputs in technical assistance.[67] It is against this backdrop that UNDP declared for the first time that governments and institutions in recipient countries should be increasingly entrusted with the responsibility for executing UNDP projects.[68] This view was supported by a group of experts selected by the Secretary-General, at the request of the General Assembly in resolution 3343 (XXIX) of December 17, 1974, to recommend proposals on structural changes within the United Nations system to ensure that it is fully capable of dealing with problems of international economic cooperation in a comprehensive manner. In this respect, the experts recommended that responsibility for execution of projects need not be automatically assigned to specialized agencies but that it could be entrusted to, *inter alia,* "the recipient Government itself; institutions in the recipient country; appropriate consultants, universities, contracting agencies or firms, etc., institutions of other developed or developing countries."[69]

Consistent with UNDP's consideration of new dimensions in technical cooperation, and the recommendations of the group of experts convened by the General Assembly, in June and November 1975, the Governing Council and the General Assembly decided that "Governments and institutions in programme countries should be increasingly entrusted with the responsibility for executing projects assisted by UNDP."[70] The decision by the Governing Council and the General Assembly constituted the first major legal step towards government execution and represents a significant progression from General Assembly resolution 2688, which gave first consideration for the execution of projects to organizations of the United Nations system.[71]

---

67 Report of the Administrator on the Future Role of UNDP in World Development in the Context of the Preparations for the Seventh Special Session of the General Assembly, DP/114 dated March 24, 1975.

68 *Ibid.* at para. 53.

69 Report of the Group of Experts on the Structure of the United Nations System, E/AC.62/9 dated May 28, 1975, para. 150.

70 Decision of the Governing Council taken at its 487th meeting on June 25, 1975 and endorsed by the General Assembly in resolution 3405 (XXX) of Nov. 28, 1975, Annex (e)(i, ii, vii).

71 U.N. General Assembly resolution 2688, para. 40. Under resolution 2688, however, the Administrator was authorized to make use of "suitable services" from gov-

Shortly after the adoption of resolution 3405 by the General Assembly, the UNDP Administrator issued guidelines on the execution of UNDP-assisted projects by governments and institutions of developing countries.[72] In the introduction to the guidelines, the Administrator explained that government execution would constitute "an important aspect of the move towards decentralization, and a means of economizing on overheads, enhancing the capabilities of local expertise and institutions, and thereby promoting self-reliance."[73] The Administrator further explained that government execution would strengthen the indispensable role of governments in their development, diversify the supply base for UNDP and facilitate the delivery of an expanding programme.[74] In accordance with the guidelines, governments were to nominate themselves or other national agencies, organizations or institutions as the "Government Executing Agency with full responsibility for the preparation, implementation and follow-up of a project assisted by UNDP."[75] Thus, the new partnership with governments under this modality was to be that of a bipartite relationship between UNDP and the government.[76]

Upon the request of a government to execute a project, UNDP would carry out an assessment of the government's capacity to determine whether the proposed government executing agency had sufficient managerial and technical capability to fulfill its obligations as executing agency. In order to assess capacity, governments were requested to provide information on:

"(a) the experience of the institution in executing similar projects, whether financed from domestic or external sources;
(b) the depth of technical experience and know-how of the institution and its access to, and links with, national and international sources of expertise and know-how;

---

ernmental and non-governmental institutions and firms, through competitive bidding. The provision of such services would be on the basis of a contract and are, thus, distinguished from execution which implied a larger role in the management of the project.

72 UNDP/PROG/51;UNDP/PROG/FIELD/72;UNDP/PROG/HQTRS/91 of May 5, 1976.

73 *Ibid.* at 1.

74 *Ibid.*

75 *Ibid.* at 3.

76 *Ibid.* at 2.

(c) the ability of the institution to exercise adequate managerial and administrative supervision over the project; and
(d) the internal budgetary, accounting and audit arrangements of the institution . . . [as well as] a copy of the financial rules and regulations of the institution."[77]

When UNDP determined that the government executing agency had sufficient capacity to execute the project under the government execution guidelines, that entity would be responsible for carrying out the project as it would if it were a government project. Thus, the government executing agency would be responsible for the engagement of international and national project staff, who were responsible to the government; the procurement, transport and installation of equipment under the rules and procedures of the government; awarding of sub-contracts, which would be entered into directly between the government and subcontractor; and placement of fellows in training institutions and carrying out other training activities.[78]

Although government execution was largely a bilateral arrangement between UNDP and the government, provision was made for the involvement of specialized agencies and other agencies of the UN system in all stages of the project cycle. However, the involvement of such agencies was subject to the specific request of the government and their role under government-executed projects was limited to providing technical and substantive backstopping and not the direct delivery of inputs, such as procurement.[79]

Following the issuance of the guidelines for execution of projects by governments and institutions, on July 2, 1976, the Governing Council began to restrict the Administrator's use of government execution by only authorizing him to initiate government execution projects on a "carefully selected basis pending submission of a detailed report to the Council . . . on the criteria, evaluation and administrative procedures and changes in the financial rules necessary for the implementation of that new dimension on a regular basis."[80] Thus, although the guidelines on government

---

77 *Ibid.* at para. 8.

78 *Ibid.* at para. 23.

79 *Ibid.* at. paras. 49–51.

80 *See* Governing Council decision 76/57 of July 2, 1976, para. (e).

execution were issued in May of 1976 to field offices and participating/executing agencies, just two months following their issuance, the Governing Council in its decision 76/57 appeared to slow down the move towards government execution.

In 1978, the Joint Inspection Unit (JIU) prepared a report on the Role of Experts in Development Cooperation (hereafter Report).[81] The 1978 Report included an assessment of the government execution modality. In particular, the Report noted that implementation problems arise in projects when there is a "failure to recognize government responsibility at the project identification and formulation stages."[82] The inspectors found that governments which were not involved at the early stages of project formulation felt that the project activities did not relate to what they actually wanted and, consequently, expressed little sense of commitment towards the project.[83] The JIU recommended a "fresh approach to government execution where each new project supported by UNDP would be under full government management."[84] Under the JIU proposal, although the government management authority would be exercised over all aspects of project implementation, the government could seek the cooperation of one or more of the agencies of the United Nations system in any aspect of project preparation or implementation, such as recruitment and procurement of international project components.[85]

In preparing the Report, the JIU sent questionnaires to governments, UNDP resident representatives and agencies to elicit views on the applicability and feasibility of government execution. An analysis of the responses showed that four-fifths of the seventy-two responding governments felt that government execution was appropriate for use in their countries, with half giving it

---

81 JIU/REP/78/3 of March 1978. In accordance with the Statute of the Joint Inspection Unit (JIU), approved by the General Assembly in resolution 31/192 of December 22, 1976, the JIU consists of not more than 11 inspectors chosen among members of national supervision or inspection bodies who serve in their personal capacity. The JIU is charged with the responsibility of investigating all matters bearing on the efficiency of the services and proper use of funds, including evaluation of programmes and activities. The inspectors may propose reforms or make recommendations which are contained in reports drawn up under their signature.

82 *Ibid.* at para. 44.

83 *Ibid.*

84 *Ibid.* at para. 45.

85 *Ibid.*

a high priority ranking.[86] Resident Representatives and Agencies took a more conservative position than governments in assessing the suitability of government execution.[87] The JIU further found that many governments had gained experience in recruitment and procurement through implementation of their own development programmes and established systematized procedures and machinery for these purposes.[88] The JIU concluded, as follows:

> "Government project management is an essential step in the direction of self-reliant development, and it is equally imperative in order to clear up the existing uncertainty as to where the management authority for UNDP-assisted projects really lies. The present system not only divides responsibility and authority — thus contradicting one of the fundamental principles of good management by setting up dual chains of command — but it does so in a way which places actual decision-making powers in large measure beyond the reach of national authorities, who are nevertheless most vitally concerned. By the same token, the present system partly diverts the Agencies of the United Nations system from their proper preoccupation with the transmission of technical knowledge and skills, by involving them in numerous management and administrative tasks which should not be their primary concern. For all these reasons, the present system contributes to difficulties in project identification, planning and implementation in which there is insufficient government participation, and hence leads to large, if as yet unquantified, wastage in the use of both national and international resources. By accepting government management as standard procedures for the UNDP programme, an energetic start can be made towards rectifying this situation and reducing the inefficiencies and diseconomies which characterize it."[89]

The response of UNDP and the UN Agencies to the JIU Report was one of caution. In joint comments prepared by UNDP and the UN Agencies, they indicated that the proposals made by the JIU required the "most careful assessment by the Council."[90]

---

[86] *Ibid.* at 47.1.

[87] *Ibid.* at 48.

[88] *Ibid.* at 52.

[89] *Ibid.* at para. 54.

[90] Joint Comments of UNDP and the Organizations of the United Nations System on JIU's Report on the Role of Experts in Development Assistance, DP/334/Add.2 of May 16, 1978.

Following the JIU report, new guidelines on government execution were issued on January 18, 1979.[91] The major difference in the 1979 procedures as compared to the 1976 procedures is the prominence of the role of the UN agencies. The 1976 procedures indicated that under government execution, UNDP and the government would essentially have a bilateral relationship, with UN agencies providing technical support at the specific request of the government. In the 1979 procedures, however, the close association of the UN agencies with UNDP using the government execution modality is affirmed, as follows:

> "Government execution calls for constant awareness on the part of UNDP and Agencies of Governments primary responsibility for all management aspects of projects, and careful judgement in each case of how to derive the greatest benefit from the technical experience and knowledge available with the organizations of the United Nations system. The interdependence of UNDP and the Agencies in their support of countries development efforts and UNDP's reliance on Agencies technical judgement in the planning and implementation of projects and in the assessment of their results call for constant and close cooperation in all aspects of government execution."[92]

Consistent with the maintenance of the role of the UN agencies under government execution, the 1979 procedures introduced the term "Cooperating Agency" whereby a UN agency could participate in project execution along with the Government agency concerned, to assist the government in the utilization of UNDP-financed inputs.[93] In addition, in Annex 1 to the procedures, government execution is defined as an "arrangement whereby UNDP entrusts to a government the responsibility for the mobilization of UNDP-financed inputs and their effective application, in combination with the government's own and other available resources, towards the project's objectives."[94] In accordance with the 1979 procedures, governments were invited to designate one central authority to represent the government in dealing with UNDP,

---

91 UNDP/PROG/69;UNDP/PROG/HQTRS/116; UNDP/PROG/FIELD/101 of Jan. 18, 1979.

92 *Ibid.* at. para. 2.

93 *Ibid.* at para. 43.

94 *Ibid.* at Annex 1, para. 7.

however, the central authority did not have to be the same entity actually carrying out project activities.[95]

In his report to the Governing Council in DP/558 of March 12, 1981, the Administrator proposed a reversal of the cautious and selective approach to implementing government execution previously adopted by the Governing Council. While the debate on the Report reflected a range of views, with some member states fully endorsing the approach and others arguing for a continuation of the cautious approach, the Governing Council requested, in its decision 81/21, that the Administrator give full consideration to implementation of UNDP assistance by the host governments and that the Administrator, along with representatives of the UN agencies, should review and analyze in greater detail the reasons for the lack of progress in implementing government execution.[96]

In response to decision 81/21, the Administrator submitted a report to the Governing Council wherein he stated that the experience with government execution had generally been positive, with a "slow but steady progress in its use."[97] Findings contained in the report indicated that most governments felt that, through government execution, they were closer to realizing self-reliance in their development efforts. Others felt that through assuming full responsibility in project design and implementation, the projects would be more likely to "respond to specific requirements determined by local norms, values and conditions."[98] However, the Report also noted that some governments preferred the traditional modality of providing assistance through the use of the UN agencies.[99] The Report concluded that while many governments saw the concept of government execution in a favorable light, they did not see immediate large-scale implementation of government execution.[100]

---

95 *Ibid.* at Annex 1, para. 9.

96 Governing Council decision 81/21 of June 27, 1981.

97 *Government Execution,* Report of the Administrator, DP/1982/11 of March 22, 1982, para. 8. For example, in 1976, two projects were under government execution for a total UNDP contribution of US$1,630,230; by 1981, 40 projects were under government execution for a total contribution of US$12,298,538 (*See,* e.g. DP/1982/11/Add.11 of March 22, 1982, para. 13.

98 *Ibid.* at paras. 13 and 15.

99 *Ibid.* at para. 17.

100 *Ibid.* at paras. 20–21.

In April 1987, the Administrator again reviewed the impact of government execution.[101] In his report to the Governing Council, the Administrator noted that since its inception, government execution had grown in importance and complexity. By the end of 1986, some 600 projects had been executed by governments for a total of US$150 million.[102] The Asia and Pacific region utilized the government execution modality more than any other region, with China executing the highest number (forty) of projects.[103] At the end of 1986, the four sectors with the largest number of government executed projects were general development issues, policy and planning; agriculture, forestry and fisheries; natural resources; and industry.[104]

With respect to the impact of government execution, the Administrator indicated that an evaluation exercise was underway to make detailed assessments of the successes and failures of government execution. The Administrator further explained that preliminary replies from Resident Representatives indicated that a high proportion of the government executed projects appeared successful.[105] However, the Administrator pointed out that some problems had been experienced with government execution, including low rates of delivery.[106] The reasons for the low delivery were being investigated but it appeared that it was related to delays in recruiting experts and slow reporting.[107] In addition, the Administrator indicated that cost-effectiveness was to be measured by the evaluation exercise underway. It was noted in this respect that the UNDP field offices and headquarters had expended considerable resources in supporting government execution, largely in the area of administrative and financial/accounting support. The reason for this was not the inability of governments to carry out administrative, financial and accounting procedures, but was due to the difficulty in getting governments to comply with extraneous

[101] DP/1987/16 of April 8, 1987.

[102] *Ibid.* at para. 45.

[103] *Ibid.* at paras. 46–47.

[104] *Ibid.* at para. 48.

[105] *Ibid.* at para. 52.

[106] *E.g.*, in 1981, the total programme delivery rate was 77.6 percent but only 61.6 for percent government executed projects; in 1985, the total programme delivery rate was 69.1 percent but only 50.1 percent for government executed projects. *Ibid.* at para. 57.

[107] *Ibid.* at para. 58.

administrative and accounting procedures for projects which were considered relatively small in relation to governmental budgets.[108] The Administrator concluded that the general assessment of government execution was that much progress had been made.[109] The detailed evaluation was submitted to the Governing Council on March 4, 1988.[110] The response of the Governing Council was positive, with the Council, in its decision 88/18, encouraging governments to "continue the expansion of government execution."[111]

B. National Execution

By 1990, the term "government execution" was replaced with "national execution" to better reflect the variety of ways in which projects are implemented.[112] At the same time, UNDP began referring to national execution as the "ultimate modality for activities supported by UNDP."[113] UNDP defined national execution, as follows:

> "National execution is a cooperative operational arrangement whereby the Government assumes responsibility for the effective management of all aspects of its UNDP-financed technical assistance projects and programmes as requested by it and agreed to by the United Nations Development Programme (UNDP). National execution recognizes the wide range of technical support possibilities, and encourages implementation arrangements that draw upon outside technical expertise and in particular, the specialized agencies of the United Nations. Under national execution, Governments are responsible for the conduct of all project and programme activities including those implemented by the specialized agencies of the United Nations, the Office of Personnel Services (OPS) of UNDP, or other organizations or institutions on their behalf. Governments are accountable to the Administrator of UNDP for ensuring the most appropriate implementation arrangements, the quality

108 *Ibid.* at paras. 63, 68.

109 *Ibid.* at para. 79.

110 *See* DP/1988/19/A.2 of March 4, 1988.

111 Governing Council decision 88/12 of July 1, 1988, para. 1.

112 Report of the Administrator, DP/1990/33 of May 14, 1990, para. 7.

113 *Ibid.* at para. 3.

of technical cooperation funded by UNDP and its judicious financial management."[114]

With respect to the role of the specialized agencies in national execution, UNDP saw the effective use and association of the specialized agencies as a major challenge.[115] In this respect, the Administrator pointed out in his report to the Governing Council that the specialized agencies had been used only to a very limited extent in national execution. One reason for this trend suggested by the Administrator is the appearance of new implementation agents on the international development scene — non-governmental organizations, private sector firms and national institutions.[116] Notwithstanding the limited involvement of specialized agencies and the appearance of new actors in the development area, the Administrator concluded that there is still a "significant continuing role for United Nations specialized agencies."[117]

At the request of the Governing Council, UNDP issued guidelines for field offices on national execution in 1992, which defined key terminology such as execution and implementation, and the roles of the government, specialized agencies and UNDP in national execution. However, in 1993, the General Assembly, in resolution 47/199 — while affirming that national execution should be the norm for programmes and projects supported by the UN system — taking into account the needs and capacities of recipient countries, again requested that the United Nations development system agree on a common interpretation of national execution. Thus, the Consultative Committee on Programme and Operational Questions (CCPOQ), under the authority of the Secretary-General, agreed that national execution is a "cooperative operational arrangement entailing, *inter alia,* overall responsibility for the formulation and management of programmes and projects by the recipient country, as well as the recipient country's assumption of

---

114 *Ibid.* at para. 8. The Governing Council of UNDP took note of the Administrator's report containing the proposed definition of national execution (Governing Council decision 90/21 of June 22, 1990, para. 1.).

115 *See* Report of the Administrator to the Governing Council, DP/1991/23 of May 13, 1991, para. 36.

116 *Ibid.* at para. 37.

117 *Ibid.*

accountability for them."[118] The CCPOQ also agreed on the objectives and guiding principles for national execution, including, *inter alia,* the recognition of the central role, ownership, direction and control of the Government, and the enhancement of capacity building, self-reliance and sustainability.[119]

Thus, by 1993, after almost 20 years since the first legislation on government execution, the General Assembly had endorsed national execution as the norm for the provision of development assistance by the United Nations development system, with UNDP at the center of that system. Through this progression to national execution, UNDP attempted to adapt itself to respond to the needs of programme country governments and their desire to be in charge of their national development programmes. UNDP's willingness to make national execution the norm was a recognition of the fact that empowerment of and control by national governments was the only way to lead to real impact and results.

IV. EVALUATION OF NATIONAL EXECUTION

A. Initial Assessment of National Execution

In 1995, a team of experts carried out an independent evaluation of national execution, an abridged and edited version of which was published by UNDP under the title National Execution: Promise and Challenges.[120] The evaluation is based on a field study of 11 countries, Chile, China, Burkina Faso, Egypt, Ethiopia, Malawi, Nicaragua, Peru, Sri Lanka, Thailand and Zimbabwe.

The study noted that seventy-five percent of all UNDP projects were carried out through national execution.[121] The evaluators found that national execution had both positive and negative attributes. On the positive side, national execution (1) improved and expanded the sense of ownership of programmes; (2) increased self-reliance; (3) contributed to capacity building and (4) increased cost-effectiveness. On the negative side, national execu-

---

118 *See* E/1993/73, Annex 4.

119 *Ibid.*

120 The team consisted of the following experts: Mr. Fuat Andic, Mr. Richard Huntington, and Mr. Ralf Maurer with support from Mr. Abdenour Benbouali.

121 National Execution: Promises and Challenges, 7.

tion has led to (1) delays in implementation due to the participatory nature of the modality; and (2) weak public sector institutions have necessitated short-term compromises such as national execution support units and parallel salary scales which jeopardize the long-term objective of institutional capacity building. In this respect, the study noted that in Latin America, national execution was used to bypass normal government institutions to ensure that programme activities are completed on time and to ensure that the funds are properly utilized.[122]

The study was inconclusive on the cost-effectiveness of national execution. An analysis of project budgets showed a modest decline in the number of work months assigned to international personnel, with a large increase in work months delivered by national personnel.[123] However, evidence did not show that greater use of national personnel affected performance, either positively or negatively. Moreover, a full analysis of cost-effectiveness would have to take into account costs related to the increased workload of UNDP country offices.

The study was inconclusive on whether national execution led to increased sustainability of programmes and projects. The evaluators noted that national execution should lead to increased sustainability because the programmes are more fully integrated into national structures, the greater use of national personnel reduces technical discontinuity at the completion of projects, and the sense of ownership enhances the possibility that governments will continue supporting project activities in the future.[124]

The evaluators noted that the tripartite relationship among UNDP, governments and specialized agencies no longer applies in its traditional form as governments increasingly assume functions relating to ownership, oversight, execution and implementation while the role of the specialized agencies is to provide technical support. Thus, the evaluators recommended the adoption of a new conceptual framework for national execution with more clearly defined roles for UNDP, Government, and Specialized Agencies. The new model suggested by the evaluators envisages UNDP and Government as partners, who would select a manage-

---

122 *Ibid.* at 24.

123 *Ibid.* at 25.

124 *Ibid.* at 27 and 28.

ment team which would normally be a national entity, but could be a specialized agency if agreed by the partners that using such an agency was the optimal way to proceed.[125]

In addition to the 1995 evaluation, national execution has been regularly reviewed internally by the Board of Auditors. Recommendations of the Board of Auditors on the 1994–95 biennium included that UNDP should re-emphasize the need to assess the government's capacity to undertake national execution; the objectives of national execution should be clearly defined to provide closer link to UNDP's aims; and that UNDP should issue new guidance on national execution to reflect all relevant legislation.[126]

In order to address some of the issues raised in the 1995 evaluation of national execution and periodic comments of the Board of Auditors, UNDP revised the procedures for national execution which were finalized following guidance from the UNDP Executive Board in 1998. The procedures define national execution, consistent with the definition used by the CCPOQ in 1993, as a "cooperative operational arrangement entailing, among other things, overall responsibility and assumption of accountability of the formulation and management by the programme country of UNDP supported programmes and projects." The key principles of national execution are the use of government rules and procedures where they are consistent with internationally recognized practices, government accountability for effective use of UNDP resources, and adherence to UNDP rules and regulations when the UNDP country office provides services.

The procedures stipulate that national execution is based on an expression of government's interest and willingness to assume management responsibilities for the programme or project as well as national capacities. The procedures set out key considerations for execution to guide country offices in determining where national capacities need to be strengthened. Such considerations fall within the areas of technical, managerial, administrative and financial capacity of the national entity.

The procedures describe the roles of the various actors in nationally-executed programmes and projects. The Government Co-

125 *Ibid.* at 9.

126 A/51/5/Add.1.

ordinating Authority, the focal point for all communications with UNDP, assumes ultimate responsibility for the overall management of the programme or project on behalf of the Government. The Government Coordinating Authority in consultation with UNDP designates the national entity which will serve as the executing agent primarily responsible for the planning and overall management of programme and project activities, reporting, accounting, monitoring and evaluation, and audit. The executing agent can be a Ministry, a department within a Ministry; any other national entity, such as a central bank, a university, regional and local authorities and municipalities. The implementing agent, which provides services or carries out activities under the supervision of the executing agent, including procurement activities, can be the executing agent itself, another government entity, a United Nations executing agency (i.e., a specialized agency or other UN entity authorized to execute projects) or an outside entity such as an NGO, a private company, a consulting firm or a university. In addition to acting in the capacity of an implementing agent, the procedures specify that UN agencies can provide support to policy and programme development (policy for the formulation of strategies and programmes, advisory services and sectoral advice, technical assistance needs assessment, sectoral or multi-disciplinary studies) as well as technical support at all stages of the programme or project cycle (formulation and appraisal, technical support and monitoring of activities during implementation, evaluation).

The procedures provide that in addition to the assistance that UNDP normally provides to UNDP-supported programmes and projects, the UNDP country office may provide further support to the executing and implementing agents including assistance with UNDP reporting requirements and making direct payments.

One of the most important sections of the new procedures deals with the provision of support services, including recruitment of personnel, facilitation of training activities, and procurement of goods and services by the country office. UNDP sought confirmation of its mandate from the Executive Board to provide such services, which some delegations argued were tantamount to direct execution, outside of UNDP's mandate. In a hotly debated session of the Executive Board in January 1998, the Executive Board reaffirmed UNDP's mandate to provide support services under the following conditions, which are reflected in the national execution procedures: the services can only be provided at the request of the Government and for activities within the country cooperation framework; the services must be in support of the implementation of activities described in the annex to the programme support or project document; the support must be provided based on a capacity assessment and be accompanied by capacity building measures, including an exit strategy to ensure that long-term capacity building objectives are not jeopardized; and the nature of the must support will take into account services which can be provided by other UN agencies.[127] In order to placate those delegations which were concerned that country office support services were in fact direct execution, namely Germany, France, Belgium, and Switzerland (only an observer), the Executive Board also specified that direct execution activities of UNDP should be limited to countries in special circumstances and be applicable only when it is essential to safeguard the full responsibility and accountability of the Administrator for effective programme and project delivery.[128]

The procedures also stipulate that the costs of providing such services by the country office must be detailed in the annex to the programme support or project document and recovered by UNDP.

In addition to direct country office support, the procedures describe support services provided by management support units, which carry out administrative work such as procurement, payment, contracting, as well as reporting, programme management training and capacity building activities. The procedures stipulate that such units can only be supported or funded by UNDP when UNDP has assessed these units based on the criteria of sustainability, cost-effectiveness, and capacity building. Clear responsibilities must be assigned to the unit and described in the programme support or project document. The support provided by such units is supposed to be temporary, clearly defined and accompanied by capacity building measures. The unit is supposed to function within a government structure and under government supervision. Finally, UNDP cannot employ or remunerate civil servants

---

127 Decision 98/2 of Jan. 23, 1998.

128 Decision 98/2, para. 8(g).

working within such a unit and such units cannot be established with the UNDP country office.

The procedures also give detailed guidance on monitoring and evaluation, financial management, reporting and auditing requirements.

With respect to the legal framework for national execution, UNDP has not pursued the conclusion of the government execution agreement prepared in 1989. Instead, the national execution procedures provide for the conclusion of a letter agreement with governments to address the support services provided by UNDP field offices. The agreement extends the privileges and immunities accorded to UNDP under the SBAA to the support services provided by UNDP field offices under national execution. Thus, the SBAA continues to set out the basic conditions of UNDP's support to programme country governments. Under that overall agreement, the details concerning national execution are reflected in annexes to the project documents and in the letter agreements on support services provided by the UNDP field offices.

B. The Future Direction of UNDP and National Execution

After twenty-three years, national execution is now legally and actually the preferred modality for the execution of UNDP programmes and projects. During the twenty-three years leading up to the 1998 national execution procedures, the tension between giving responsibility to the Governments and taking such responsibility away from specialized agencies is evident. Clearly, the donors and member states of such agencies have been aware of the impact that national execution would have on the involvement of such agencies in UNDP programmes and projects: that the role of specialized agencies would be marginalized and their use in such programmes and projects reduced.

What has also become clear in the transition to national execution is that as the role of the specialized agencies has become less significant, the role of the UNDP country office has become more prominent. With the 1998 decision of the UNDP Executive Board, the country office role in providing support services has been reaffirmed. These activities, which include procurement and recruitment, are activities which were formally provided by specialized agencies. Under national execution, these activities should in principle be carried out by the national entities responsible for the programmes and projects. Thus, the role of the country office in national execution will have to be monitored carefully to ensure that governments are empowered to manage and carry out all aspects of the programmes and projects, including the procurement and recruitment activities. The true challenge to UNDP, if it is sincerely committed to the capacity building of national institutions and the development of programme countries, is not to allow national execution to become in effect direct execution by the UNDP country office. There is already evidence of UNDP country offices assuming far too large a role in national execution, notably in Latin America. Thus, the international community, donor and programme countries will have to watch and see if UNDP stays true to its mandate, in the hope that UNDP will meet one of its biggest challenges of the twenty-first century.

V. THE INTERNATIONAL FINANCE INSTITUTIONS (IFIs) — PROJECT IMPLEMENTATION UNDER THE AFRICAN DEVELOPMENT BANK FINANCING

A. Operating Procedures of the IFIs

The International Finance Institutions, in particular the African Development Bank (AfDB), provide funding for projects, essentially designed and originated by the Borrower, which contribute to the sustainable economic development and social progress of the Country.[129] The Bank uses two types of resources for this purpose: a) The subscriptions to the share capital of the Bank by its members, periodically supplemented by General or Special Capital Increases, and b) Concessionary resources contributed by countries that subscribe to the African Development Fund (ADF), mostly non-regional member countries. The Fund is replenished at three year intervals, the most recent of which was the ADF VIII Replenishment, approved in 1999. For the AfDB, the most recent Capital Increase (the Fifth General Capital Increase)

---

129 *See* Article 1 of the Agreement Establishing the African Development Bank (AfDB), August 4, 1963 510 U.N.T.S. 3 (as amended).

was approved by the Board of Governors in 1998. In addition, the Bank raises funds on the capital markets through floating of Bonds, borrowed at market interest rates. The concessionary resources are on-lent to qualifying Borrowers at low interest rates over longer-term periods. A small percentage of these resources are also made available for Grants. The Bank resources from capital subscriptions and borrowings from capital markets are on-lent at market rates to eligible countries.

The borrowing members of the AfDB, which include virtually all African regional countries, are grouped into three categories: Category A countries, which borrow from the concessionary window;[130] Category B countries, which are blend countries, borrowing both at market rates from the Bank and from the concessionary resources of the Fund; and Category C countries, which only borrow at market rates from the Bank. Thus, unlike UNDP which receives contributions from member countries for allocation to finance development assistance programmes on a grant basis, AfDB as well as other international finance institutions (IFIs), has to manage its available resources on a revolving basis to maximize the capital base from which further lending can be made. Furthermore, while UNDP finances projects and programmes of the recipient government, in the public sector, the international finance institutions are expressly authorized to provide financing not only to governments, but also to "political subdivisions or any agency thereof or for any institution or undertaking in the territory" of the borrowing country.[131] This formulation has permitted the international finance institutions to provide loans to private sector institutions and companies as well as other public sector institutions, such as parastatal bodies and local government administrations.[132]

---

130 Except for limited AfDB lending for enclave and private sector projects.

131 *See, e.g.*, AfDB Agreement, *supra* note 129, Article 14.

132 The lending to non-governmental institutions, such as private companies, pose serious problems for multilateral institutions which operate essentially as international persons with privileges and immunities not accorded to private companies. Thus recovery of loans to these companies through the normal judicial mechanisms to which the international financial institutions are immune has proved problematic both for the institutions and the member Governments. The remaining mode for resolution of disputes through arbitration is equally unsatisfactory, especially where foreclosure on secured assets, such as real property, is involved. Lending to parastatal bodies has traditionally been effected with guarantees from the Government.

The basic lending instrument used by the AfDB is the Loan Agreement signed between the Bank and the Borrower. Each loan is covered by an agreement, which is a formal document subject to ratification by the borrower to ensure that the debt obligation is assumed with full approval of all the organs of the borrowing government.[133] The signed Loan Agreement is supplemented by standard General Conditions approved by the Board of Directors. These general conditions form an integral part of the Agreement. In addition, the Agreement Establishing the Bank now provides that Loan Agreements constitute obligations to the Bank for purposes of imposing sanctions on Members for non-observance of the terms of the Articles of Agreement, including suspension of voting rights, suspension of membership and outright expulsion from membership.[134]

However, unlike UNDP which was initially established as a funding agency, but is operating through the Specialized Agencies of the United Nations, the IFIs generally use no outside intermediaries in the implementation of projects financed by them. In the case of UNDP, the Specialized Agencies provided the technical know-how for the project and advised Governments on its design and implementation. Quite often, the Specialized Agency as the Executing Agency provided the procurement services for equipment and personnel. UNDP was insulated from the problems of misuse of funds, for which it was content to hold the Executing Agency accountable. This accountability was established not without difficulty, since the Executing Agencies viewed themselves as

---

Increasingly, Governments are reluctant to provide these Guarantees as the borrowed funds then constitute part of the public debt, which reduces the level of a country's borrowing capacity for essential services.

133 In the case of private sector loans, the Bank insists that the Company obtains the approval of its Board and care is taken to secure the loan with assets of the company. In this context, the move to non-guaranteed public sector loans is troubling since the parastatal body would not have total ownership over its assets, being a Governmental entity and without a commitment from the Government, selling such assets could pose problems. Furthermore, the public sector institutions cannot give the same sanctity to the Loan Agreement as the Government, since the approving Board serves at the pleasure of the Government. One hopes, therefore, that if this move is approved, the loans to this sector will be marginal, otherwise the resulting debt would not be secured and could result in a call on the unpaid capital of the Members.

134 AfDB Agreement, *supra* note 129, Article 44 (as amended).

mere agents. However, in the face of losses due to failure to exercise adequate controls by the Executing Agencies, the UN Legal Office successfully obtained an agreement from the Executing Agencies to adjudicate cases of losses, and where responsibility was attributable to the Executing Agency, to make good any loss incurred. This was the case in at least two cases, one in Syria, executed by FAO, and in Gabon, executed by ICAO. As the execution of projects moved from the larger and financially self-sufficient Specialized Agencies to smaller subsidiary organs of the UN, and to execution by UNDP acting through its Office for Project Services (OPS), accountability proved difficult. Thus, in a clear case of loss due to mismanagement in Argentina, for example, responsibility for the loss on a project had to be borne internally through shared costs between UNDP and its OPS, which by the time of decision, had become a separate entity known as the United Nations Office for Project Services (UNOPS). It would prove even more difficult to attribute responsibility for loss resulting from lack of due care, if the project was entirely executed by a UNDP field office, as has been suggested in recent decisions.

The multilateral development banks do use executing agencies but these differ in material respects from those used by UNDP. The executing agencies of the Banks are normally sectoral institutions of the Government responsible for the project. These institutions do not sign any agreement with the Bank and execute the project not on behalf of the Bank, but on behalf of the Borrower, which remains accountable to the Bank for the utilization of the loan resources and proper implementation of the project. The procurement of goods and services for the project is carried out by the Borrower or its executing agency but under the procurement rules of the Bank. The Loan Agreement requires the Borrower to procure the goods and services on the basis, essentially, of international competitive bidding from enterprises in the member states of the Bank.

The Bank maintains a list of approved consulting firms to which bidding documents are submitted and from which the successful bidder is selected. This arrangement has not been without consequences. Consulting firms on the Bank-approved list consider that such an approval creates a relationship with the Bank, so that in case of the Borrower's failure to pay, they may look to the Bank for satisfaction. However, this is not the case. The Bank has thus successfully defended lawsuits instituted by disgruntled contractors on Bank projects who seek direct payment from the Bank. Using an array of defenses, including assertion of the Bank's immunities, the Bank has succeeded in Switzerland and France to show that the suit is without merit for lack of a contractual nexus between the Bank and the plaintiff contractor.

Major problems, which the IFIs may face, may result from the concerted efforts by the banks, quite rightly taken, to fight corrupt practices in the procurement of goods and services in bank funded projects. The banks now include in their rules and in the Loan Conditions, a provision which authorizes the bank to suspend or cancel a loan in case of established corruption in the execution of the project. Indeed, the AfDB has on a number of occasions suspended disbursements on projects where corruption is alleged while investigations are carried out, and, in at least one case, a consulting firm has been barred from further participation in Bank funded projects as contractor based on evidence of having engaged in corruption. The challenge for the IFIs is to establish transparent procedures for determination and subsequent imposition of sanctions in alleged corruption cases. Furthermore, the banks need to show *locus standi* in pursuit of these cases, since the consultant under suspicion of corruption would have been hired not by the Bank but by the borrower.

However, in view of the seriousness of the allegations of corruption and their consequences on the proper implementation of projects and the realization of their objectives, under the Articles of Agreement of the banks, in order to foster sustainable economic development and social progress of member countries, it is not difficult to establish a clear interest for the banks to sanction offending companies. As for the procedures leading to such sanctions, IFIs need to adopt uniform rules for conducting investigations, and to establish independent juridical or arbitration machinery for review of allegations of corruption and to make recommendations for appropriate action.

The United Nations has established the Office of the Internal Oversight Services, with wide powers of investigation and prosecution of offenders. IFIs could pull resources and establish a similar function under the umbrella of the World Bank, which could allow for recruitment of competent investigators and panels of judges with jurisdiction over cases of corruption. These could be given mandates by each of the banks under their internal rules so that there are shared facilities and services for efficiency.

B. Good Governance

It is apparent from this review that a lot needs to be done to instill a sense of accountability, responsibility, transparency and respect of law and property, if donors are to be assured that funds released for development can be used for their intended purposes. If this is done, we can then urge that conditionalities to development assistance must be eliminated and that Governments be empowered to administer available resources for programmes beneficial to their populations, without undue external interference.

The current moves to promote Good Governance are important steps in the right direction. However, we have to agree on the content and process for achieving such a noble objective. First of all, Good Governance should not be another prescription for promotion of an ideological agenda. It has to be recognized that individual societies and individual countries can achieve Good Governance at different paces and through different means. For example, multi-party politics as demonstrated in some countries is not a universal solution to Good Governance. The case of Uganda makes this point. Furthermore, the Westminster model of parliamentary democracy based on a two-party system, with one in power and another in the opposition, is also not ideal for all countries.

In Africa, for instance, governance by consensus between opposing social and other groups is traditional and seems to be most suited for populations plagued by poverty and illiteracy and thus susceptible to manipulation. Proportional Governance, with a Government composed of all participating political groups in proportion to their popular mandate, and proportional representation have been tried in South Africa and Namibia with some success and could be used as models. In countries where the public sector represents the main source of power and distribution of resources, it is vital that representatives of all shades of groupings have a voice in the governing of the country, for the benefit of their constituents.

In order to establish accountability and responsibility in government, institutional reforms are necessary. Firstly, the education system needs total reformation so that from at least the age of ten, a child is taught skills that can be used later to earn a living. Reading and languages alone are not enough. The child should learn how to type, how to sew, how to establish and run a business, and at every level these skills should be built upon until University level. Secondly, the process of money management at all levels should be part of the instilled skills at the individual and institutional level.

Governments in developing countries borrow money when in fact enough resources could be raised locally through revenue generation and tax collection. Revenues are lost through corruption and inadequate assessment of private sector operators by officials without a stake in the revenue collected. Public officials should be paid a living wage tied on performance, if loyalty to the country is to be promoted. It is scandalous that a revenue tax collector expected to realize up to one or two million dollars a month is paid less than twenty dollars a month, totally inadequate to buy a meal for a family of six in a week. Finally, attention should be paid to establish and maintain a well-trained, disciplined and well-paid police force, as well as a credible judicial system, free of corruption from all quarters. A judiciary compliant to the wishes of the Government is as much corrupt as that serving the personal interests of individual litigants willing to pay for a favorable decision. The Rule of Law, properly so called, is a necessary condition *sine qua non* for Good Governance and therefore, economic growth and development.

THE WORLD BANK AND TOBACCO

Paul C. Szasz

I. INTRODUCTION

History does repeat itself — though never in a plain circle but rather as a spiral. Although there may be an illusion of mere reiteration, along another axis there are considerable advances. In 1970, this author, along with other World Bank staff, had to be escorted by Danish police in Copenhagen to the locale of the Annual Meeting, past a mob of protesters against the then policies and practices of the World Bank and the International Monetary Fund (IMF). Now similar scenes appeared from Prague — which at the time of the earlier protests was still part of "Eastern Europe" looking from the outside at the institutions of which it was to have become a founding member.

One wonders how many of the new protesters — most of whom were not yet alive at the time of the Copenhagen meetings — are aware of the World Bank's 1999 report: "Curbing the Epidemic: Governments and the Economics of Tobacco Control,"[1] and of the tremendous evolution in the Bank's policies and practices that this publication represents.

The International Bank for Reconstruction and Development (IBRD), true to the first part of its formal title, spent its initial years assisting in the reconstruction of war-destroyed Europe, and it did so largely through the financing of large infrastructure projects. The substantial success of that operation then (mis)led it to try a similar approach in fulfilling the second part of its mandate: the development of territories and countries that were economically far backward. It soon became evident that, in spite of some su-

---

1 Issued in the World Bank's *Development in Practice* Series, 1999 [hereinafter the "Epidemic Report"].

perficial similarities, development was quite different from and ultimately far more difficult than reconstruction — an enterprise with which not just the World Bank but the entire international community is still struggling.

In particular, the infrastructure approach to development had two faults. Several of the projects financed had, in spite of the extensive studies that preceded each, a number of faults that negated or even entirely cancelled out the anticipated advantages; in this connection one need only mention certain dam projects. At the same time, these projects neglected the more immediate needs of the people of the developing countries, most of whom continued to live in abject poverty, without adequate education and health care and without opportunities to earn a decent living.

Whether shaken up by the 1970 demonstrations or by the insights of then World Bank President Robert S. McNamara, the Bank soon shifted gears to the financing of more people-oriented projects — ones that would impact directly on the population, in particular the neediest elements, while at the same time trying to observe the prime principle of the Hippocratic Oath: "In the first place, do no harm!"

More recently, however, the Bank has taken further steps. Instead of focusing its formidable machinery for economic analysis simply on the fiscal soundness of its projects, it is also addressing other types of questions that some decades earlier would have been considered entirely outside of its then more narrowly conceived mandate. Indeed, it would probably have been argued that these questions come perilously close to violating the prohibition against the engagement of the Bank in domestic political affairs.[2] For example, the 1998 study on *Child Labor and Health: Quantifying the Global Health Impacts of Child Labor*[3] evidently addresses questions of domestic labor and social standards on which governments might or might not welcome the Bank's advice.

---

2 Articles of Agreement of the International Bank for Reconstruction and Development, art. 4, sec. 10.

3 By Philip L. Graitcer and Leonard B. Lerer, published in the *Education* Series of the World Bank, Nov. 1998. *See also* PETER FALLON & ZAFIRIS TZANNATOS, CHILD LABOR — ISSUES AND DIRECTIONS FOR THE WORLD BANK (World Bank 1998), and Sabine Schlemmer-Schulte, *The World Bank's Role in Fighting Child Labor, in* PROCEEDINGS OF THE FOURTH INTERNATIONAL INTER-DISCIPLINARY COURSE ON CHILDREN'S RIGHTS 327–342 (Engen Verhellen ed., 2000).

However, it follows logically from the Bank's conclusion in its *World Development Report 1993: Investing in Health* that there is a crucial link between health and human capital formation. In this report, the Bank called attention, for the first time, to the specific dangers and burdens of tobacco and the need for public health intervention.[4]

II. THE WORLD BANK'S TOBACCO POLICY

Once the World Bank began supporting agricultural projects in developing countries, in the normal course some of these related to the growing or processing of tobacco — a significant crop in a number of these states. A 1991 study estimated that taking account of all such projects since 1974, the incremental tobacco production thus stimulated amounted to about 80,000 tons in 1990, or about one percent of the world's annual production. Presumably reacting to the growing international pressure against tobacco driven by the World Health Organization (WHO), the number of such projects declined during the 1980s to just five Bank loans and IDA credits; thereafter, no further ones were initiated.

Apparently the first time the Bank gave general consideration to the question of whether or not it should finance tobacco projects was in 1987.Then it supported a study on *Tobacco in Developing Countries: An Economic Approach to Policy Formulation.*[5] The need for such a policy arose out of the consideration that tobacco consumption can be an important cause of illness and premature death, that the market for tobacco products might not function adequately due to incomplete information about these dangers and due to the distorting effects of taxes, tariffs and subsidies. The principal conclusion of the study was that, from an economic point of view and taking the above factors into consideration, there was little justification for encouraging tobacco production; in addition, it was suggested that high priority be assigned, *inter alia,* to studies of the impact of tobacco use on health and on health care costs in less developed countries.

4 World Development Report 1993 at 87–88 (1993).

5 Study by Eugene M. Lewit, a consultant to the World Bank and commissioned by the Population, Health and Nutrition Department of the Bank (PHN Technical Note 87-15, June 1987).

In October 1991, the Bank's Executive Directors received a study on "Policy on Tobacco," in which the President recommended that:

> "(a) The Bank Group's activities in the health sector should encourage a reduction in the use of tobacco products;
> (b) The Bank Group should not directly financially support tobacco production, processing, imports or marketing, either for domestic consumption or for export; and
> (c) Tobacco processing machinery, equipment or services should be added to the negative lists of imports in adjustment loan and credit agreements."

In a meeting at the end of November 1991, the Executive Directors considered the paper and generally supported the recommendations.

To implement the new policy, in March 1994 an "Operational Policy on Tobacco" was issued, which was recently replaced by a revised version reading as follows:

> "1. The Bank does not lend directly for, invest in, or guarantee investments or loans for tobacco production, processing, or marketing. Exceptions, which must be approved by the Vice President, Operations Policy and Strategy, may be allowed for countries that are heavily dependent on tobacco as a source of income (especially for poor farmers and farm workers) and foreign exchange earnings (i.e., those where tobacco accounts for more than 10 per cent of exports). The Bank seeks to help these countries diversify away from tobacco.
> 2. To the extent practicable, the Bank does not lend indirectly for tobacco production activities, although some indirect support of the tobacco economy may occur as an inseparable part of a project that has a broader set of objectives and outcomes (i.e., rural roads).
> 3. Unmanufactured and manufactured tobacco, tobacco processing machinery and equipment, and related services are included in the negative list of imports in Loan Agreements.

4. Tobacco and tobacco-related producer and consumer imports may be exempt from borrowers' agreements with the Bank to liberalize trade and reduce tariff levels.
5. Bank activities in the health sector — including sector work, policy dialogue, and lending — discourage the use of tobacco products."[6]

All the above studies and decisions related directly to the Bank's own operations. In May 1999 however, the Bank issued what is essentially a free-standing study, the previously mentioned Epidemic Report. The Foreword to that study indicates its purpose: given that tobacco use is a major and growing health hazard, but also given that the production and trade in tobacco is a significant economic activity, "[t]he economic aspects of tobacco use are therefore critical to the debate on its control." In other words, the question that the report endeavors to answer is whether, disregarding for the nonce the moral aspects of furthering or controlling tobacco because of its effects on health, whether it makes economic sense to take a pro- or anti-tobacco stance.

The reason this question must be asked at all is because the production, processing and trade in tobacco are economic activities that affect many people in many countries, and because governments typically earn considerable revenues from taxes and tariffs on tobacco or from operating tobacco monopolies. It is clear that against these immediate economic and fiscal benefits there are some offsets: the health costs incurred by those sickened or disabled by using tobacco or by being involuntarily exposed to it, as well as their reduced productivity through disease or premature death. The question is: how do these countervailing factors balance out purely as an economic matter?

The World Bank considered it useful to address this question because of increasing pressures, both domestically and internationally, for the control of tobacco for medical and ultimately, moral reasons. These pressures come from the private and public health community and are gradually achieving some success do-

---

6 OP 4.76, Oct.1999 (Introductory Note and footnotes omitted).

mestically, in many of the developed countries, and internationally through efforts to control tobacco by treaties (see below). However, arrayed against these forces are those that see the immediate benefits of the tobacco trade in the form of not inconsiderable financial flows; these include ministries of agriculture, industry, and most importantly of finance — offices and policy-makers that typically are more influential than their counterparts dealing with health.

What the World Bank's report clearly demonstrates is that "tobacco control is highly cost-effective as part of a basic public health package in low- and middle-income countries."[7] In other words, one need not be economically soft-headed to adopt a number of strategies, discussed at some length in the report, designed to reduce smoking over-all and particularly on the part of children and youths.[8]

III. THE COORDINATION OF THE BANK'S EFFORTS WITH THOSE OF OTHER INTERNATIONAL ORGANIZATIONS

It should be noted that this latest initiative of the World Bank was not taken in isolation from other international efforts designed to control the use of tobacco. Indeed, the Bank, as well as the International Monetary Fund (IMF), have joined the UN System's Ad Hoc Inter-Agency Task Force on Tobacco Control, which was established in 1998 by the UN Secretary-General, at the request of the WHO Director-General, within the framework of the Administrative Committee on Co-ordination (ACC).[9]

---

[7] Epidemic Report, *supra* note 1 at 9. *See also* Prabhat Jha, Joy de Beyer & Peter S. Heller, *Death and Taxes: Economics of Tobacco Control,* FINANCE & DEVELOPMENT 46–49 (Dec. 1999).

[8] The Epidemic Report has a visually striking cover showing a child, three to five years old, puffing away at a cigarette.

[9] *See Origins of the Ad Hoc Inter-Agency Task Force on Tobacco Control, in* REPORT OF THE SECRETARY-GENERAL TO ECOSOC ON THE TASK FORCE, E/2000/21 (May 1, 2000), part I. The Annex to the SG's report lists as "collaborating organizations" 18 UN System organizations and organs, including the World Bank and IMF.

Although the Task Force operates under the general leadership of WHO, the World Bank has been designated as the lead agency on the economics of tobacco, in which other collaborators — besides WHO's Tobacco Free Initiative (TFI) — are the IMF, the Food and Agriculture Organization of the United Nations (FAO), the United Nations Foundation (UNF), and the US Centers for Disease Control and Prevention. As the Secretary-General's report indicates, "[g]iven the World Bank's comparative advantage in economics and policy dialogue, the Bank's efforts are focused on the economics of tobacco control, including taxation, the economic and social impact of tobacco control measures, including the impact on the poor, and the cost-effectiveness of interventions."[10] The dissemination of the Epidemic Report is one of a number of specific measures listed, which also mentions twelve Bank-funded projects in eleven countries (with more under preparation) that include tobacco control activities.

Special mention should be made here of the timing of the original release of the Epidemic Report: in mid-May 1999, just at the opening of the 52nd session of the World Health Assembly (WHA). It was at that session that the WHA adopted its resolution 52.18 by which the preparation of the proposed Framework Convention on Tobacco Control (FCTC) was formally launched. This release gave an important psychological boost to the participants in the WHA, for the most part Ministers of Health, by assuring them that the world's prime financial institution was addressing their Finance Ministers and specifically endorsing the FCTC initiative as one part of an economically sound approach to tobacco control[11].

Most recently, the Bank published, on behalf of itself and WHO, an extensive study on *Tobacco Control in Developing Countries,* which also contains an endorsement of the FCTC as a strategic priority for international agencies to help tobacco control activities beyond the reach of national governments.[12]

---

10 *Ibid.* at part III. A.

11 Epidemic Report, *supra* note 1 at 83-84. WHO subsequently republished the *Summary of the Report for the First Session of the FCTC Working Group,* A/FCTC/WG1/2 (Aug. 20, 1999).

12 Tobacco Control in Developing Countries 456 (Prabhat Jha & Frank Chaloupka eds., 2000).

IV. THE PROPOSED FRAMEWORK CONVENTION ON TOBACCO CONTROL[13]

The WHO has, of course, long been concerned with the health effects of smoking, and as early as 1970 the WHA adopted the first of what became nearly a score of resolutions on the subject.[14] For a quarter of a century these resolutions mainly appealed for voluntary action by member states and by international organizations, until in 1995 the possibility of adopting an "international convention on tobacco control" was first mentioned.[15] This step was one of considerable significance for the Organization, for it constituted the first time that it was proposed to utilize Article 19 of the WHO Constitution authorizing the WHA to adopt and to propose to member states international conventions. The long hesitation to resort to the device of treaty-making — one which many international organizations have long practiced — presumably reflected the general disinclination of the medical community to resort to legal instruments, such as treaties, laws and regulations, to resolve problems primarily in the medical domain.

The device that WHO chose to address the problem of tobacco control on an international level, was that of a "framework convention" (sometimes called an "umbrella" or "skeleton" treaty) — a form of treaty that has in recent years become quite popular in tackling various international issues, in particular in the area of environmental controls. In such conventions' states interested in addressing a particular international problem, especially one as to which no solution can be agreed to immediately and that in any event is likely to require adjustments on the basis of new technical developments, first merely negotiate a text that generally records their joint objective to deal with the indicated issue, without, however, committing the participating states to take any

---

13 For more detailed descriptions of the FCTC, *see* P.C. Szasz, *WHO Tackles the Tobacco Pandemic,* TRANSNATIONAL LAW EXCHANGE 1–5 (March 2000); and Allyn L. Taylor & Douglas W. Bettcher, *WHO Framework Convention On Tobacco Control: A Global 'Good' For Public Health, in* 78:7 BULLETIN OF THE WORLD HEALTH ORGANIZATION: THE INTERNATIONAL JOURNAL OF PUBLIC HEALTH 920–29 (2000).

14 WHO Resolution, WHA23.32 (May 19,1970).

15 WHO Resolution, WHA48.11 (May 12, 1995).

particular immediate actions, aside from conducting and coordinating studies and gathering pertinent data. However, the treaty does establish a mechanism for its further development, perhaps by episodic amendments or the addition of annexes, but most often by the conclusion of subsidiary treaties, usually referred to as "protocols." These treaties, which are open to participation by all parties to the framework convention but generally without any compulsion that these must do so (the protocols are therefore sometimes referred to as "optional"), contain substantive undertakings designed to address one or more aspects of the subject dealt with by the basic convention. There are various patterns by which this may be done: a framework convention implemented by a single subsequent protocol, which itself might be amended from time to time;[16] a framework convention initially accompanied by one or more protocols, to which others, or amendments, might be added later;[17] a framework convention that is followed by a series of protocols, each addressing a different sub-issue;[18] or even a convention that in itself sets out important substantive obligations, which are then supplemented by subsequent protocols.[19]

With reference to the proposed FCTC, preliminary soundings have indicated a number of possible subjects as to which protocols might be concluded, either simultaneously with the convention or subsequent thereto.[20] In the first place, certain general

---

16 *See, e.g.*, 1985 Vienna Convention for the Protection of the Ozone Layer, March 22, 1985 (1513 UNTS 293) and the 1987 Montreal Protocol on Substances that Deplete the Ozone Layer, Sept.16, 1987 (1522 U.N.T.S. 3).

17 *See, e.g.*, 1980 Convention on Prohibitions or Restrictions on the Use of Certain Conventional Weapons which may be deemed to be Excessively Injurious or to have Indiscriminate Effects, Oct. 10, 1980 (1342 U.N.T.S.137), with three 1980 Protocols I, II and III, 1995 Protocol IV, and 1996 Amended Protocol II.

18 *See, e.g.*, 1979 [Economic Commission for Europe] Convention on Long-Range Transboundary Air Pollution, Nov. 13, 1979 (U.N.T.S. Reg. No. 21623), to which seven Protocols have been added in the years 1984 to 1998.

19 *See, e.g.*, the 1950 [Council of Europe] Convention for the Protection of Human Rights and Fundamental Freedoms, which has since been supplemented by 11 substantive and procedural Protocols.

20 For a relatively complete list of potential protocols to the FCTC, *see Subjects Of Possible Protocols And Their Relation To The Framework Convention On Tobacco Control*, A/FCTC/WG1/3 (Sept. 3, 1999) and *Possible Subjects of Initial Protocols*, A/FCTC/WG2/4 (Feb. 15, 2000).

obligations, such as education, training and the fostering of public awareness, exchange of information and the systematic gathering of certain basic data, might be included in the framework convention itself. One of the protocols on which it is hoped that early agreement might be reached would be one banning any transboundary advertising of tobacco products — such as now frequently occurs in the broadcasting of sports events sponsored or supported by tobacco companies. Another priority protocol would be one to ban the smuggling of tobacco products — whether to evade high duties or taxes, or requirements to affix warning labels; such smuggling may also encourage smoking by young people to whom popular brands might thus be made available at especially low prices. There is also likely to be a protocol that would encourage cooperation in dealing with tobacco dependence, i.e., ways to overcome the effects of nicotine addiction. A protocol may provide for the creation of smoke-free environments, particularly in international areas such as airplanes, ships, airports, harbors, etc.; the same or another protocol might ban the sale of tobacco products on a "tax-free" basis.

It is also foreseen that the FCTC itself, and/or some of its protocols, will provide for the monitoring of the fulfillment of at least certain of the obligations undertaken by states in becoming parties to these instruments. In addition, there is likely to be some mechanism for the transfer of resources to the poorer states that become parties, to assist them in carrying out their respective obligations.

In launching the preparation of the FCTC, the World Health Assembly in 1999 provided for a carefully structured multi-stage process. The first stage was the establishment of an open-ended Working Group, to meet in the fall of 1999 and the spring of 2000 to prepare proposed draft elements of the FCTC. As many as 142 member states, plus observers, participated in the second session, which submitted to the 53rd WHA in May 2000 a lengthy "Provisional Texts of Proposed Draft Elements for a WHO Framework Convention on Tobacco Control with Comments of the Working Group."[21] Automatically following that preparatory work, an open-ended Intergovernmental Negotiating Body (INB) was con-

---

[21] WHA A53/12 (April 26, 2000), reissued as a document of the Intergovernmental Negotiating Group as A/FCTC/INB1/2 (July 26, 2000).

vened, meeting first for one week in October 2000,[22] then to meet for another week in April 2001, and for yet another in autumn 2001 and possibly again in the spring of 2002; the present schedule foresees that the INB will be able to present to the 55th WHA, in May 2002, the complete text of a FCTC, for adoption by the Assembly as provided in Article 19 of the WHO Constitution; possibly at the same time one or more protocols would also be submitted to the WHA.[23]

Once the FCTC is adopted by the WHA, it will be submitted to ratification by the member states of WHO; entry into force will require action by the number of states to be specified in the Convention. If one or more protocols are submitted to and adopted by the WHA at the same time, then action will be required by states with respect to these. Once the Convention itself has entered into force, it is foreseen that a mechanism built into that instrument will provide for its further development: by amendment, by the addition or amendment of annexes, and above all by the development and amendment of protocols. Thus, the FCTC is to become, as many similar instruments already have, a "living treaty". Not only will there be periodic meetings of political and expert organs to carry out or to review the results of monitoring and to decide on resource transfers, but these organs will also use the data gathered to develop the FCTC by the means just indicated.

V. CONCLUSION

The World Bank has come a long way from its initial indifference to tobacco and then its moderate support thereof as an agricultural crop of interest to some member states; to its later decision to withhold such support from any tobacco-related project, and to the current financing of more and more tobacco control projects.

---

22 At the first INB session, the representative of the World Bank, as an observer, intervened helpfully in the general debate (A/FCTC/INB1), as well as conducting a separate briefing for delegates on the economics of tobacco control.

23 It should be noted that Resolution WHA52.18 foresaw the possibility that the INB would continue its work until the 56th WHA in 2003, but current projections are that this will not be necessary.

Even more interesting is the evolution of the Bank from a purely financing institution that often went its solitary way without much coordination with other international institutions, to its current solid and important involvement with the UN System, especially with the WHO, in fighting the world-wide health scourge of tobacco and, in particular, in the Bank's active encouragement in developing the most promising international legal device for this purpose: WHO's proposed Framework Convention on Tobacco Control.

SOME PERSONAL REFLECTIONS ON CREATING THE LEGAL DEPARTMENT AND FORMING THE JURISPRUDENCE OF A NEW INTERNATIONAL FINANCIAL INSTITUTION

*John L. Taylor**

I. INTRODUCTION

When I was asked to write this essay for a book dedicated to Ibrahim F.I. Shihata, I was both delighted and diffident. The delight sprang from the opportunity to record, in a tangible form, my gratitude for the friendship and professional collaboration that I have shared with Ibrahim for more than twenty years. The diffidence resulted from a concern that whatever I was to write might trivialize that gratitude, when measured against the depth of scholarship and breadth of experience that has characterized Ibrahim's own extensive writings on the practice and theory of international financial law.

My diffidence was, however, set aside when it was accepted that I might like to share some of the experience that I had in helping to create the legal department and the jurisprudence of a new international financial institution. Since this topic was close to my heart, I decided that it would be fitting for a dedication to Ibrahim, not so much for what it could add to his own learning or experience, but in the expectation that it will be of interest to him and instructive for other readers.

---

* The views expressed in this Chapter are the personal views of the author and do not necessarily reflect the views of EBRD or any other organization.

II. THE ESTABLISHMENT OF A NEW INTERNATIONAL FINANCIAL INSTITUTION

In the spring of 1989, the formal regimes of communism in Central and Eastern Europe and the then Soviet Union were crumbling fast and the visible manifestation of the end came with the dismantling of the Berlin Wall in November of that year. Far-sighted leaders in Western Europe, North America and other parts of the world realized that many countries whose economies and forms of governance had been dominated by Soviet communism would need a great deal of assistance in rebuilding (and in many instances building) multi-party democracies and market-oriented economies. Many Western governments were re-orienting, or planning the re-orientation of their bilateral aid programs to help in this effort of building democracies and democratic institutions, establishing the rule of law and respect for human rights and bringing about fundamental changes in political and economic governance.

Almost immediately after the fall of the Berlin Wall, the French Government, on the initiative of President Mittérrand, went one step further by proposing the establishment of a new international financial institution dedicated especially for these purposes. And so it came to be, in record-breaking time, that the European Bank for Reconstruction and Development (EBRD) was established by an international treaty, entitled Agreement Establishing the European Bank for Reconstruction and Development (the EBRD Agreement) signed in Paris on May 29, 1990.

EBRD has two purposes: (i) to foster the transition to market-oriented economies; and (ii) to promote private and entrepreneurial initiative in member countries in Central and Eastern Europe and the former Soviet Union committed to and applying the principles of multi-party democracy, pluralism and market economics.[1] Unlike some of the other International Financial Institutions (IFIs), particularly the International Monetary Fund (IMF) and the International Bank for Reconstruction and Devel-

---

[1] Agreement Establishing the European Bank for Reconstruction and Development, May 29, 1990, Art. 1, 29 ILM 1077 (1990).

opment (IBRD), EBRD's activities center upon the financing of specific projects, not on the financing of balance of payments or policy based macro economic reform packages. In carrying out its project financing, EBRD must apply "sound banking principles to all its operations." It has the capacity to employ a wide variety of financing techniques, and was the first IFI whose founding Agreement directs it to promote environmentally sound and sustainable development in all of its activities.

EBRD formally commenced operations and opened its doors for business on April 15, 1991. From the signing of the EBRD Agreement at the end of May 1990 until April 15, 1991, a large amount of work was undertaken to prepare the EBRD for its opening, including the selection of most of the initial senior management team and a number of staff. In October 1990, Andre Newburg, a seasoned American lawyer with extensive international experience and knowledge of the then Soviet Union and of Central and Eastern Europe, was invited to become the first General Counsel of EBRD. Andre asked me to become his Deputy in this new and exciting venture. We worked together in these capacities until the end of July 1995, when Andre retired, and I was promoted to General Counsel, a position that I held until the end of October 1998 when I returned to the private sector.

It is impossible in the space available in this Chapter to describe all the activities undertaken and challenges confronted, by Andre and/or me during the years of our involvement with EBRD. To my mind, however, there were two major tasks that stood out above all others, namely: (i) the formation and evolution of the legal department (known as the Office of the General Counsel); and (ii) the development of the basic jurisprudence of the EBRD. I would like to share some personal reflections on these two topics.

III. FORMING THE LEGAL DEPARTMENT OF EBRD

As the first General Counsel of EBRD, Andre Newburg had been given the task of establishing the legal service functions from scratch. One of the first questions that he and I therefore had to consider was: what sort of legal department should we establish and what role did we envisage for ourselves and for the lawyers who would come to join us?

A preliminary step in answering these questions was to anticipate the main activities of the EBRD that would require the services of lawyers. In early November 1990, we identified the following four main activities:

1. Most of the legal services required by EBRD would be needed to assist the operational staff (or "bankers" as they were called) in structuring, negotiating, documenting and monitoring the financial investments that the EBRD would make in the countries of Central and Eastern Europe and the former Soviet Union, that comprised EBRD's "countries of operations;"

2. Legal services would also be needed to assist the EBRD in its own funding activities. The funding for EBRD was envisaged to come from its shareholders (in the form of payments for subscribed capital), from borrowings on the world's capital markets and from income and repayments/returns of capital on its investments;

3. Legal input would be needed for the vast array of institutional and administrative matters that the EBRD would have to address. This work included relationships with shareholders, assisting with corporate secretarial and internal governance issues, and the legal aspects of personnel and administration of what would, during our tenure, become a medium sized (about 1,100 personnel), multinational organization with offices in many countries;and

4. Legal advice would be required by the EBRD's countries of operations in their efforts to transform their economies into appropriately regulated market-oriented economies.

The identification of the first three activities mentioned above was not very creative because the legal departments of most of the then existing international financial organizations (e.g., the IBRD, the Inter-American Development Bank (IDB), the Asian Development Bank (ADB) among others) were providing legal services in these areas. Common sense and experience led Andre and me to conclude that EBRD would need these services as well. However, there were a number of choices that we made in designing the delivery of these services that were distinctive, as explained in the following paragraphs. The fourth category of legal service, namely law reform services offered by the legal department of an IFI to its member countries, was at that time, innovative (although it has today become an accepted part of the mainstream activities of the legal departments of the IBRD and the ADB).

Some of the distinctive ways in which we shaped the Office of the General Counsel were:

A. Law Firm Type "Pooling" Approach

From the beginning of EBRD's operations, we were determined that lawyers working on the EBRD's investments in, and loans for, projects in its countries of operations should not be assigned to specific countries or to specific sectors or types of operations. Rather, lawyers should be assigned to particular transactions having regard to their specific skills and experience, as well as their availability at the time. This enabled us to treat the lawyers handling these transactions as a resource pool and to manage the assignment, and re-assignment, of transactions in the most flexible way possible. The alternative would have been to assign specific lawyers to handle projects only in certain countries or designated sectors or types of transactions. This alternative had been adopted for the provision of legal services in many of the other IFIs and, indeed, would have mirrored the way in which the banking services of EBRD had been structured in the early years, where there were separate banking departments for public sector operations (so called Development Banking) on the one hand and private sector operations (so called Investment Banking) on the other. However, we maintained that the approach that we adopted was more flexible and cost effective for EBRD and gave our lawyers a more diverse range of work across different sectors and countries to keep them challenged and interested. It also reflected the practice of most large law firms, from which we expected to draw our legal team, and we believed that this would facilitate our efforts to recruit the lawyers with the most appropriate skills.

The experience of EBRD has generally borne out the wisdom of the approach that we instituted. It is still in use today, notwithstanding the fact that EBRD in general, and the Office of the General Counsel in particular, experienced substantial growth in its early years and has undergone many organizational and personnel changes. A potential downside of the approach we adopted was that, at times, the EBRD's banking staff complained that a lawyer assigned to their transaction was not knowledgeable enough about a particular country or sector. However, this complaint can often be addressed by taking greater care in choosing the lawyer to be assigned to a given transaction and particularly by consulting the lead banker when assigning a lawyer to a new transaction.

B. Recruiting of Skilled International Project Financing Lawyers

The pooling approach that we adopted with respect to the assignment of lawyers to banking transactions had a direct and profound influence on the criteria that we used to recruit lawyers. While country or sector specialization in any lawyer was not a disadvantage, we favored candidates who had diverse corporate, commercial and international financial experience, especially the legal skills developed in handling corporate and project financing transactions. We sought lawyers who had a track record of adaptability and flexibility and had sufficient experience to be able to manage the legal aspects of a diverse range of financing transactions, largely without direct supervision. This ensured that the "pool" approach would work.[2] It also resulted in us attracting and recruiting lawyers mainly from private law firms, who valued the importance of a constructive "client-oriented" approach to providing legal services. While urging our lawyers to protect the legal interests of EBRD, we wanted them to find ways in which to get a

2 As the work of the Office of the General Counsel grew, and the need for more junior lawyers emerged, we instituted a program under which we recruited well-educated but less experienced lawyers from the EBRD's countries of operations on fixed term contracts of up to two years. This program proved to be beneficial for EBRD and also for the young lawyers who gained invaluable experience during their time in the Office of the General Counsel.

job done, not simply to identify the legal restrictions or impediments.

C. The Value of a Diverse Multi-Cultural Department

An important consideration in building the Office of the General Counsel was to ensure a diverse spread of nationalities and language skills among lawyers. The Agreement Establishing the EBRD, like the Charters of most IFIs, requires that "subject to the paramount importance of efficiency and technical competence, [...]due regard [be paid] to recruitment on a wide geographical basis among" member countries.[3] For us, geographical diversity in the Office of the General Counsel was not seen as the mere fulfillment of this legal requirement, but as vital to our efforts to provide the skills needed to service the Bank's operational needs. On numerous occasions we witnessed the value that was delivered by lawyers who knew the local language, customs and legal systems of the countries in which we were operating.

As part of the skill diversification effort, we also sought to keep a balance in recruiting lawyers from both civil law and common law backgrounds. This practice, too, was driven more by common sense than for other reasons. It was obvious that, since EBRD was operating in civil law countries, we needed good civil law trained lawyers. However since most of our work involved international financing, where the techniques had mainly been developed in the common law centers of London and New York, we also needed lawyers with common law skills. The presence of a majority of lawyers from a civil law background was thought by some Directors of EBRD to be of great importance, lest the EBRD become overly "Anglo-Saxon" in its lawyering, a criticism occasionally leveled by disgruntled businessmen who thought that the EBRD's conditions of financing were too harsh. In reality, however, for the type of international financing work that our lawyers were called up to perform, the distinction between civil law and common law approaches is much less important than might at first be thought.

---

3 EBRD Agreement, *supra* note 1, Art. 30.5

D. Size Counts, Especially in the Private Sector

From the outset of EBRD, we had to address the question of how many lawyers we would need in the Office of the General Counsel and how much of the legal work would be assigned to outside counsel. We took the view that we should try to do as much of EBRD's legal work in-house, believing that this was much more efficient and cost effective.

All IFIs have a wide range of peculiar features, driven by their inter-governmental ownership and the special characteristics of the treaties under which each IFI is formed. To disregard these aspects is both politically and legally perilous. But it takes time to get to know the peculiarities. In-house lawyers are better placed to do so and also to translate those peculiarities into practice in the context of specific transactions. In addition, for many reasons, in-house lawyers are much less costly for IFIs than external counsel so that there are usually sound budgetary reasons to develop a sizeable in-house team of lawyers. Over the first four years of EBRD, we therefore built a team of more than twenty in-house lawyers who were devoted full time to the banking operations of EBRD.[4] However, for the reasons explained below, we also realized that the EBRD would need assistance from external counsel in EBRD's project financing activities.

Unlike most international financial institutions, EBRD was mandated to operate in both the public sector and the private sector. In particular, EBRD was designed to support the public sector in its transition from state-owned, centralized control to a competitive environment characterized by de-monopolization, decentralization and privatization. However, it was made abundantly clear in the EBRD Agreement and associated documents that the focus and bulk of EBRD's activities should promote the establishment, improvement and expansion of a productive and competitive private sector. This dual mandate to operate in both the

---

4 In later years, on more than one occasion, efforts were made by some senior officers of EBRD to press for the reduction in the size of the Office of the General Counsel and to shift a greater proportion of the legal work to external lawyers. There are many sound reasons why these efforts were strenuously and successfully, resisted by me. On a personal note, I can say that this was one task as a General Counsel that I had not anticipated and that I found particularly irksome and wasteful of senior management time and resources.

private and the public sectors meant that, at least initially, we had to recruit lawyers with experience in financing of both sectors. But we took a different approach to the use of external counsel in each sector, as follows:

- **Public sector financing.** This category of international financing is usually accomplished through relatively straightforward financing instruments namely loans by EBRD to, or guaranteed by, sovereign states (or, occasionally, EBRD guarantees of such loans counter-guaranteed by sovereign states). The loan documentation for, and the legal issues raised by, such sovereign lending from an IFI like EBRD can be complex and demanding.[5] But it is normally far less time consuming and complicated than the documentation for, and legal issues presented by, financing for the private sector. This is because sovereign lending from an IFI like EBRD is normally unsecured (thereby presenting no issues of securing or perfecting collateral), is preferred (i.e., excluded as a matter of long-standing international practice from debt rescheduling), and is reflected in agreements that take the form of international treaties governed by public international law, whose terms and conditions ought therefore to govern, to the exclusion of any local law that might otherwise apply. Public sector lending, however, has a high "policy" and sometimes highly charged "political," content in which the unique policy objectives of an IFI must be reconciled with the political environment in the borrowing country. All of these factors suggested to us that public sector lending was normally best handled entirely by lawyers in the Office of the General Counsel and that this legal work should not be assigned to outside counsel.
- **Private sector financing.** EBRD's financing of the private sector is a much more legally complex and diverse topic. In the first place, EBRD has many more instruments at its disposal to finance the private sector including the provision of equity, quasi-equity, loans, guarantees and underwriting facil-

[5] For a good summary of the issues in, and of EBRD's innovative approaches towards, public sector financing, *see* J. Head, *Evolution of the Governing Law for Loan Agreements of the World Bank and Other Multilateral Development Banks*, 90 AMERICAN JOURNAL OF INTERNATIONAL LAW 214 (1996).

ities.[6] Frequently EBRD's financing of a private sector transaction uses more than one of these instruments, thereby increasing the complexity of a given transaction. Secondly, the EBRD Agreement and the policies adopted by its Board of Directors discouraged the use of state guarantees for loans to private sector borrowers. It was therefore necessary in each case to more closely assess the creditworthiness of each borrower and, in many instances, EBRD has sought some form of collateral for its loans. The need for secured lending in transition economies with weak legal environments added a very substantial layer of legal complexity to EBRD's work. Thirdly, for a variety of reasons explored in detail elsewhere,[7] we decided that EBRD's documentation should be governed either by English law (wherever possible) or, in the case of security documentation, by the local law of the place where the security could be enforced.

These choice of law issues necessitated the engagement of outside counsel within the country where the private sector entity and/or security was located so that EBRD would have the comfort of a satisfactory (or, at the least, adequate) legal opinion that the transaction would be binding under local law. In addition, a significant part of EBRD's lending was structured as non, or partial, recourse project financing where the repayment of the loans and the payment of interest is secured on the revenues and assets of the borrowing entity or project. This financing technique can be one of the most complex to structure and document and required much more legal resources than could ever have been available in-house. This was a key factor driving the engagement of external specialist legal services, often from large UK or US law firms where the technique of non-recourse project financing had been

---

6 For a summary of these, and the other, facilities that EBRD offers to private sector clients, *see* John L Taylor, *What a Multilateral Financial Institution Can Bring to a Project — The Experience of EBRD, in* PROJECT FINANCING IN EMERGING MARKETS 1998, 49-61 (1998).

7 *See* John L. Taylor, *The Governing Law in Legal Agreements Used by the European Bank for Reconstruction and Development in its Banking Operations, in* INTERNATIONAL MONETARY LAW ISSUES FOR THE NEW MILLENNIUM 479-492 (Mario Giovanoli ed., 2000).

developed and refined. Fourthly, equity or quasi-equity investments in private sector enterprises in transition economies that had archaic, and sometimes no, legal infrastructure to accommodate such financing presented additional legal challenges that require time-consuming, sophisticated and creative lawyering that was necessary to hire from external law firms. The same could be said for some of EBRD's guarantee and underwriting operations.

These factors combined to make it necessary for the lawyers in the Office of the General Counsel who were assigned to the EBRD's project financing activities to possess two main characteristics. The first was to have had experience in a broad range of international financial transactions before joining EBRD so that they could properly assist the bankers in structuring the deals to accomplish EBRD's objectives and to protect EBRD's interests if the deals turned sour. The second was to be excellent project managers of outside counsel so as to guide them wisely and to minimize the amount of external counsel time, and, therefore, the costs, on each transaction. This has proved to be a very demanding role for EBRD's in-house lawyers and has provoked continuous examination of ways in which the necessary external legal services can be acquired at reasonable cost.[8]

E. Different Approaches for Other Legal Services

A significant part of this chapter has been devoted to the way in which we developed non-sector and subject matter specific legal services for EBRD's banking operations. In the three other areas of the work of the Office of the General Counsel, namely, the EBRD's own financing, personnel and administration, and law reform services, we took a different approach. In particular, we recruited and developed teams of specialists to handle each of these areas. There were three main reasons for this:

---

8 EBRD has always sought to use its prestigious position and its relative purchasing power to acquire external legal services at relatively low cost. At one stage during my time as General Counsel it was believed that a panel of law firms, selected after a competitive bidding process, would provide the bulk of external legal services in the most professional and cost-effective manner. However, experience has since shown this not to be the case and that it is better to allow all law firms who are keen to do so to bid for, and then provide, the legal work on individual projects.

- Each of these areas required specialized, and different, skills from those that were needed in EBRD's banking operations.
- The pace and demand for legal services for EBRD's banking operations meant that our early efforts to assign some of the work in these three areas to the lawyers handling the banking operations resulted in neither tasks being done satisfactorily. To give an example, a lawyer handling seven to ten current banking operations, and having as a result to travel at a moment's notice to faraway places, simply could not handle a pressing personnel issue at headquarters, the lease of new premises in another location, or the conclusion of a bond issue or sophisticated swap transaction where time was of the essence.
- Efficiency in providing the legal services for these specialized areas prompted us to conclude that they should be handled by specialist teams of lawyers who would develop an institutional memory that was particularly important in areas such as the Bank's own financing activities and its internal personnel and administration practices.

As far as the law reform services were concerned, we faced a particular challenge in their development. The Board of Directors of EBRD and some of the senior management were, quite correctly, eager that EBRD should assist its countries of operations in developing sound business laws and legal institutions. However, almost from its inception, EBRD had developed a "deal" culture that over-emphasized the value of deals in bringing about the transition process, and under-emphasized the worth of institution building. As a result EBRD severely restricted the amount of budget that could be devoted to the law reform effort. This meant that we had to strictly limit the topics of law reform that we could undertake[9] and had to rely far too heavily on the generosity of discretionary grant funding from external donors. The collapse of the financial system in Russia in 1998, and the consequent losses suffered by EBRD as well as the broader financial community,

9 We focused the law reform effort on the reform of secured transactions laws, concession laws, bankruptcy, capital markets and some corporate law. We also supported the broader effort of the international community to urge EBRD's countries of operations to tackle corrupt practices and money laundering.

proved the short-sightedness of this approach. It is reported that EBRD is now pursuing a more active law reform effort. Much more needs to be done in this area.

F. Strong Management and Quality Control

A final observation that I would like to make on the formation and evolution of the Office of the General Counsel was that at all times Andre Newburg and I placed great emphasis on strong management and quality control. At the very beginning, we recruited senior and experienced lawyers whom we judged would be ideally suited to handle specific legal assignments when the Office was very small and, just as importantly, who would grow into middle and later senior management roles as the Office grew larger. This was designed so that we could delegate the task of quality control and encourage internal growth and promotion which, in turn, we anticipated would strengthen the morale of the Office. History has shown that this was largely successful but what may not have been so apparent at the time was that this was a carefully conceived and deliberate process.

IV. FORMING THE "JURISPRUDENCE" OF THE EBRD

Like other international organizations at their beginnings, when EBRD opened its doors for business on April 15, 1991, it possessed a mere skeleton of the "jurisprudence" within which to conduct its activities. Established by a relatively short international treaty covering a wide range of topics, it was left for the persons who would occupy EBRD's governing bodies and its management to develop that "jurisprudence." The General Counsel played, and continues to play, a central role in that process.

The central — and prevailing — document around which the "jurisprudence" of EBRD is built is the EBRD Agreement, including a "Chairman's Report" on the EBRD Agreement and "Explanatory Notes" that were intended "for future reference in interpreting" the Agreement. Other sources of the "jurisprudence" of EBRD are the By-laws of the EBRD, adopted by the Board of Governors on April 15, 1991, and various substantive and procedural rules and regulations adopted pursuant to the Agreement.

Beyond the written text of these documents lies an expanse of international "law" and the "practice," including especially the law and practice of other international organizations, where guidance or analogies are sought, or from which distinctions are drawn, in the continuous process of developing EBRD's own "jurisprudence."[10]

The EBRD Agreement consists of only sixty-three, relatively succinct, "Articles" or clauses that cover such diverse topics as:

- membership in, and capital and other resources of, EBRD;
- its purpose, functions, methods and principles of operations;
- the terms of its loans, guarantees, borrowings and other operational matters;
- the organization and powers of its governing bodies and management;
- its status, privileges, immunities and exemptions;
- the withdrawal and suspension of membership and suspension and termination of operations;
- amendments, interpretation and dispute settlement; and
- miscellaneous provisions.

The text of virtually all of the Articles on the above topics had been the subject of extensive discussion and negotiation among the forty-two founding countries of EBRD. Many Articles reflected political compromises that had been reached during the course of these deliberations. As a result, numerous Articles contained text that was either intentionally susceptible to diverse interpretation, or simply omitted to give explicit direction in important respects. Indeed, in some instances, a plain reading of the text could have lead to absurd results, running contrary to the stated purposes of the EBRD.

---

10 In this connection, Andre Newburg and I benefited particularly from one of the comparative works of IBRAHIM SHIHATA, THE EUROPEAN BANK FOR RECONSTRUCTION AND DEVELOPMENT — A COMPARATIVE ANALYSIS OF THE CONSTITUENT AGREEMENT (1990). This publication contained a wealth of useful information on the practice of the other IFIs, even though in some instances the approaches that were taken in EBRD differed over time from these practices.

For EBRD to function effectively, it was essential to develop a shared understanding among its shareholding countries as to a proper, or acceptable, meaning for these Articles of the EBRD Agreement and for the management of EBRD then to implement this shared understanding. Without such a shared understanding, the day to day work of EBRD would be pulled in conflicting directions, leading to operational paralysis or worse. The challenge from the legal perspective in the early days of EBRD was to contribute positively to the development of the process by which such shared understandings could be developed and accepted and thereafter observed. In short, it became a key task for the General Counsel to lay the framework for the way in which the jurisprudence of EBRD could be formed and evolve.

Preliminary questions of jurisprudence that had to be addressed were:

- How were interpretations of the Agreement to be arrived at? In particular, who has the power to propose interpretations of the EBRD Agreement and which entity in EBRD has the power to make those interpretations?
- What is meant by "interpretation"? In particular, were some topics where a shared meaning was needed so "fundamental" or "extensive" in their content or impact that they could no longer be characterized as an interpretation of the EBRD Agreement, but would have to be regarded as amending that Agreement? This latter question was very important legally because, as explained below, the Agreement provided a different, and much more flexible, procedure for its "interpretation" than for its "amendment."

The answers to these questions evolved along the lines described below.

A. The Amendment Process

In keeping with many other international financial institutions, the EBRD Agreement provides for an organizational structure consisting of a hierarchy of organs, in the following descending order: "a Board of Governors, a Board of Directors, a

President, one or more Vice-Presidents and such other officers and staff as may be considered necessary."[11]

The Board of Governors, consisting of one Governor (normally the Minister of Finance or equivalent) and one Alternate appointed by each member, i.e., each shareholding country (initially forty two and now totaling sixty one), was vested by the EBRD Agreement with "[a]ll the powers of " EBRD[12]. Standing alone this provision would clearly have empowered the Board of Governors to propose and make interpretations of the Agreement. However, the process of obtaining the decisions of the Board of Governors is cumbersome and many topics on which interpretation was needed were not of such moment to be of concern to Ministers of Finance. Fortunately the framers of the EBRD Agreement recognized this and, consistent with many other IFIs, provided for interpretations to be made at a lower level in the organizational hierarchy of EBRD.

The Board of Directors consists of twenty three persons elected by Governors and a further twenty three Alternates, each being appointed by a Director. The delegates representing the founding countries of EBRD "agreed that Directors and their Alternates should be resident at the headquarters" of EBRD and should "normally function at" that office.[13] And so it is that the Board of Directors of EBRD is present in the London headquarters and most of the twenty three Board members and their Alternates spend their full time working there. Article 24, paragraph 2 of the EBRD Articles empowers the Board of Governors to delegate to the Board of Directors any of its powers, with the exception of certain expressly reserved powers. By Section 8(a) of the By-Laws of EBRD, the Board of Governors exercised this power of delegation in favor of the Board of Directors. Since the Board of Governors would have had the power to propose and make interpretations of the EBRD Agreement, it follows that the Board of Directors was given the delegated power to do likewise. However, the legal analysis relating to the power to propose and make interpretations of the EBRD Agreement does not end there.

---

11 EBRD Agreement, *supra* note 1, Art. 22.

12 EBRD Agreement, *supra* note 1, Art. 24 para.1.

13 EBRD Agreement, *supra* note 1, Art. 28, para. 1.

This is because Article 57 of the EBRD Agreement specifically addresses the question of interpretation. In summary, Article 57 provides that any question of interpretation or application of the provisions of the EBRD Agreement arising between any member and EBRD, or between any members of EBRD, "shall be submitted to the Board of Directors for its decision." It also provides that in any case where the Board of Directors has made such a decision, any shareholding country may require that the question be referred to the Board of Governors, whose decision shall be final (and this latter decision making power is one of the few powers of the Board of Governors that is non-delegable[14]). The question of the entity to which interpretations should be submitted, and by whom decisions could be made, was thus specifically addressed in the EBRD Agreement and the General Counsel often had the need in the early days of EBRD to advise the Board of Directors and senior management accordingly.

Having established that the Board of Directors was the principal organ to interpret the EBRD Agreement, the question that was often asked of the General Counsel was "by what procedure and by what majority?" Since Directors and their Alternates were mostly full time at the headquarters of the EBRD, there was little difficulty to convene meetings of the Board. Under pressure from the Directors themselves (who, in the early days of the EBRD were not very busy and in any event were anxious to keep a close watch on the early evolution of the EBRD), the practice developed that formal Board Meetings would be held at least every two weeks and informal sessions and "workshops" of the Board would occur even more frequently. Consequently, there were more than adequate occasions on which the views of Directors on the interpretation of the Agreement could be sought. With respect to the voting majority needed for the Board to decide on an interpretation, Article 29 paragraph 3 of the Agreement states that, except for certain types of decisions,[15] "all matters before the

---

[14] EBRD Agreement, *supra* note 1, Art. 24, para.2 (iv).

[15] The exceptions are matters where special voting majorities are expressly provided in the Agreement and "general policy decisions in which cases such policy decisions shall be taken by a majority of not less than two-thirds of the total voting power of the members voting." The General Counsel was given a special role in the process of determining what constituted a "general policy" since the Explanatory

Board of Directors shall be decided by a majority of the voting power of the members voting." This meant that, for most decisions on interpretation, a simple majority of the votes cast was all that was needed, so long as a quorum (i.e., a simple majority of the Directors, representing not less than two-thirds of the total voting power of the members [16]) was present.

The EBRD Agreement is silent on the issue of who should submit interpretations for decision by the Board of Directors. Were interpretations only to be submitted by the members, i.e., the shareholding countries, themselves, or could others submit interpretations?

Logic demanded that the necessity for most interpretations would arise out of the day-to-day operations of EBRD, and it was the management and staff of EBRD, not its shareholders or the Board of Directors, who were mainly involved in the day-to-day operations. In fact, Article 30 paragraph 6 of the EBRD Agreement obliged the "President" of EBRD to conduct the current business of the Bank under the direction of the Board of Directors. It was not for the Board of Directors to conduct that business. The General Counsel from the outset considered that it was within the powers of the President to submit matters for interpretation to the Board of Directors. To have done otherwise would have frustrated the business of the Bank and also would not have been consistent with practice in other comparable IFIs.

In the light of the foregoing, the jurisprudence was established that the management of EBRD, with advice and guidance from the General Counsel, would first consider and decide upon the most appropriate meaning or interpretation of the Articles of the EBRD. The President would then formally recommend to the Board of Directors a policy or course of action (including, for example, a particular type of project) based on that meaning or interpretation. The Board of Directors would consider the recommendation and, if they agreed with it, the interpretation underpinning the proposal would be regarded as accepted, and therefore "decided," by the Board of Directors under its powers of interpretation conferred by Article 57 of the Agreement.

Notes to Article 29 of the EBRD Agreement required that, in case of differing views on the question, the decision would be made by the Board of Directors "on the basis of advice from the Legal Counsel."

16 EBRD Agreement, *supra* note 1, Art. 28, para. 2.

In practice, the Board of Directors frequently accepted the proposals made by management and therefore the interpretations on which those proposals were based. On occasions, however, individual Directors or groups of Directors would challenge the interpretation proposed by the President and lively discussions occurred both within and outside the Board before a meaning was arrived at that commanded the approval of the Board. The Board often requested the legal opinion of the General Counsel before giving its approval. Once accepted, however, that interpretation or meaning would then become part of the "internal law" of the EBRD, to be observed by the President and staff in their day-to-day running of the business of the EBRD. In this way, EBRD arrived at a defined and relatively smooth procedure for the interpretation and application of the EBRD Agreement and a key part of the jurisprudential process of the organization was established.

B. Interpretation or Amendment?

An important question remained: were some topics so "fundamental" or "extensive" in their content or impact that they could no longer be characterized as an interpretation of the EBRD Agreement, but would have to be regarded as amending that Agreement? This question arose because Article 56 of the Agreement dealt specifically with amendments and provided a cumbersome procedure (involving approval by the Board of Governors followed by acceptance by a special majority[17] of the shareholding countries) before an amendment was made. Apart from Article 56, the internal constitutional processes of some of the shareholding countries of EBRD would have required legislative or other approval for any amendments to a treaty such as the EBRD Agreement. Therefore amending the EBRD Agreement could be a lengthy and politically uncertain process. In contrast, as explained above, the interpretation process was relatively simple and speedy and fitted well with the day-to-day operational needs of EBRD. If a decision as to the meaning of the EBRD Agreement

[17] The special majority required for amendments of the EBRD Agreement is "not less than three-fourths of the members (including at least two countries from ... [the countries of operations]), having not less than four-fifths of the total voting power of the members." *See* EBRD Agreement, *supra* note 1, Art. 56, para. 1.

were characterized as "amending" the text, and therefore required the application of the procedures of Article 56, the EBRD's scope of action could be severely frustrated.

As a matter of law, it is obvious that a distinction can be drawn between an amendment that changes the text of an agreement and an interpretation that ascribes meaning to an existing text. There is also little doubt that certain proposals couched as interpretations should properly be characterized as amendments. However, as a matter of practice to date, no decisions that were requested of EBRD's decision-making organs were made as formal amendments to the EBRD Agreement, despite the fact that some of these decisions were profound and altered the course of EBRD in very significant respects. For example:

- When the EBRD Agreement was signed in 1990 there were only eight countries of operations, namely, Bulgaria, Czechoslovakia, German Democratic Republic, Hungary, Poland, Romania, Union of Soviet Socialist Republics (USSR) and Yugoslavia. Within two years after EBRD opened its doors for business, the eight countries had become twenty-six[18] countries of operations (and the GDR and what was left of Yugoslavia were no longer members). However, most of these changes were accomplished by the process of interpretation or decision-making under Article 57 and not through the formal process for amending the Agreement or for admitting new countries to membership.
- Article 8, paragraph 4 of the EBRD Agreement and a related letter from the USSR imposed severe limits on the ability of EBRD to finance operations in the former USSR until April 1994. Following the dissolution of the USSR, this limitation was removed in 1992 by the application of the powers of interpretation under Article 57 and not through an amendment of the EBRD Agreement under Article 56. At the same time, a policy was adopted that, for the period from April 1, 1992

[18] Albania, Armenia, Azerbaijan, Belarus, Bosnia and Herzegovina, Bulgaria, Croatia, Czech Republic, Estonia, Georgia, Hungary, Kazakhstan, Kyrgyzstan, Latvia, Lithuania, FYR Macedonia, Moldova, Poland, Romania, Russia, Slovak Republic, Slovenia, Tajikistan, Turkmenistan, Ukraine and Uzbekistan. In 1999, Mongolia became the twenty-seventh country of operations of EBRD.

until the end of 1994, at least 60 percent of the EBRD's committed investments would be made in those countries of operations that had not been part of the USSR (excluding Estonia, Latvia and Lithuania). This policy, which was not part of the original EBRD Agreement, was also not adopted through the process of amendment.

- In 1996, a policy on graduation of countries from EBRD operations, whereby certain types of projects in qualifying countries would no longer be eligible for EBRD financing, was adopted through the process of interpretation and decision making by the Board of Directors and not through a formal amendment to the EBRD Agreement.

In each of the above cases, and in many other instances where the EBRD Agreement was interpreted by the Board of Directors, sound legal and policy advice was advanced by the General Counsel and supported by the President of the Bank to justify the approach that was taken. In rare instances, some shareholding countries questioned the legality of using the technique of interpretation rather than amendment, and, on at least one occasion, the decision concerning interpretation was appealed to and finally decided by the Board of Governors. From a practical point of view, the difficult and time-consuming process that is prescribed by the EBRD Agreement for its amendment meant that the less cumbersome procedure of interpretation was in all cases to date the preferred course of action by EBRD's management, its Board of Directors and its shareholding countries.

In the eyes of a layman, it could be said that the distinction between an amendment on the one hand and interpretation on the other has become blurred in the practice of EBRD. To the General Counsel of EBRD, there were sound legal and policy reasons for adopting one approach rather than the other. Given the dynamics of the organization and its processes, in my view it is unlikely that this situation will change in the future.

CREATING LAW IN CHANGING SOCIETIES: THE CASE OF LAW FOR PRIVATELY FINANCED INFRASTRUCTURE PROJECTS

Don Wallace, Jr.

I. INTRODUCTION

Privately financed infrastructure (PFI) projects and the contracts they entail can be complicated, as Dr. Ibrahim F.I. Shihata has written.[1] The effort to create a suitable legal infrastructure or framework for such projects may be even more so.[2] It is that effort, and the ambition that it reveals about law reform and harmonization, which is the subject of this contribution to this volume in honor of my much admired friend. As I know something of his many writings and achievements, and his splendid and patient character, I believe an essay about a subject with many sides and a legal and legislative project of considerable ambition, whose success will test the patience, may not be inappropriate.

Let me briefly parse the title of my essay before I embark on its substance, and let me acknowledge that, as an American, not all my views of my title may be shared by everyone.[3] As for the in-

---

1 IBRAHIM F.I. SHIHATA, COMPLEMENTARY REFORM: ESSAYS ON LEGAL, JUDICIAL AND OTHER INSTITUTIONAL REFORMS SUPPORTED BY THE WORLD BANK 139-165 (1997), Chapter Six (*Institutional Aspects of the Financing of Infrastructure*).

2 *Privately Financed Infrastructure Projects: Draft Chapters of a Legislative Guide on Privately Financed Infrastructure (PFI) Projects,* United Nations Commission on International Trade Law (UNCITRAL), A/CN.[9/444, March, 1999]. It may be noted that reference goes to the version of the UN document of March 1999 when this contribution to the Liber Amicorum was finished.

3 I should also note that while I have been a United States delegate to UNCITRAL for many years, most recently engaged with its privately finance infrastructure (PFI)

vestment economics of infrastructure, there is something of a consensus — probably shared by investors and host countries — even if sometimes reluctantly by the latter. It is this: economic development is indispensable to the achievement of a satisfactory modern life; various forms of infrastructure — electric power, telecommunications, transportation — are indispensable precursors to fuller development; internal taxation and government borrowing are constrained; and private sector innovation and efficiency often exceed that of the public sector. And increasingly, host countries are realizing that their legal institutions must possess certain characteristics if investors and lenders, whether foreign or domestic, are to commit their money and energies to projects for such infrastructure. In most countries, indeed if not all, changes in law are required if private participation in infrastructure projects is to proceed more expeditiously and on optimum terms; in some countries such changes are required if it is to proceed at all.

The parsing will be more contested by some when we talk of "creating law;" that "societies" are "changing" is presumably a given, certainly if we accept the 'consensus' premise that economic development is inevitable, whether desired or not, that it is taking place and will probably accelerate, and that such development is never exclusively limited to the 'economic' sphere. So it is "creating law," both its "creating" and "law" components, on which we wish to dwell.

Some countries will be forming relevant law for the first time; others reforming existing law; in most some new law will be made; in many there will be questions of its full acceptance by the public, the political classes, the legislature, the bureaucracy and the courts. We will see distinctions between common law and civil law; see that the subject straddles public and private law, embracing high public policy but also technical legalities (e.g., questions of applicable law), that there are countries quite at sea about the matter. At the end of the day, we will be applying 'best practices' (increasingly derived, some may say happily or otherwise — for example, one thinks of the increased length of documents — from

---

work (both as delegate and 'expert'), the views expressed in this essay are mine and not necessarily those of the United States government, or of UNCITRAL or its secretariat.

the work of London and New York solicitors and lawyers) to the 'inevitable,' i.e., the need to finance infrastructure.

A colleague of Ibrahim Shihata, Daoud Khairallah,[4] has expressed the view that foreign direct investment — which will often be central to PFI — is a most excellent window through which to consider a country's legal condition: this may well be true, but our perspective is different, from the 'inside out': what must a country do to make possible PFI on sound and fair terms? A suitable legal framework must exist or be created — so that government may act, investors be attracted and lenders feel secure; law and regulation must be well drafted. Jurisprudential questions of the 'reception' of foreign law may be beside the point; the fine point of the law's formality ignored. The World Bank now promotes such 'law reform.'[5] Societies do change and such reform will indeed contribute to such change. Many countries are now addressing the most basic legal topics of this era: civil service reform and administrative law, companies law and competition policy, and so forth. But we must here be more specific.

What law particularly needs to be created (or to exist) for success in PFI? This is the question we ask ourselves in UNCITRAL as we proceed with our work. It is the question that each country must ask itself.[6]

The law that we create is essentially a law that should *enable* governments to act. It must address a constellation of conditions and problems.

---

4 Acting Vice President and General Counsel, World Bank, 1998-1999.

5 IBRAHIM F.I. SHIHATA, THE WORLD BANK IN A CHANGING WORLD, Vol. II, 127-128 (1995), Chapter Three *(Legal Framework for Development and the Role of the World Bank in Legal Technical Assistance)*.

6 I write about a law to deal with the central problems to be solved if there are to be successful PFI projects. Inevitably there must also be laws dealing with many supporting subjects in place, in addition to the 'basic legal topics' just referred to in the text: laws dealing with security interests and foreign direct investments come immediately to mind; these and other areas of law are touched on in the UNCITRAL draft, *supra* note 2, Chapter VII.

II. TABULA RASA

There are countries of which it might be said that they are disabled to act. Why so? The reasons may be several. A country may not have crossed the policy Rubicon, may be unreconciled to the necessity of having private, including foreign, capital and personnel involved in infrastructure sectors. Given this situation, the process of enacting a general enabling law may in particular societies be the soundest way to engage professional, political and/or general public opinion so as to reach a national decision about proceeding with PFI projects.

In turn, the absence of clear legal authority, of an enabling framework, may further paralyze a country. The government's lawyers lack footholds, rungs to work from; investors and lenders are similarly at a loss. If efforts are made to proceed, the experience may be bad, negotiations drag on and transaction costs mount. If there is no competition in selecting a concessionaire the government is criticized; if there is and evaluation criteria are unclear, a proper result may not be reached and future projects may be discouraged.

Enabling legislation should deal with such matters of procurement law and selection of the concessionaire; with issues of a 'one stop shop' to facilitate action; with government authority to give guaranties and assurances (if deemed advisable) with respect to 'take or pay' contracts, fuel supply, shadow tolls and a host of other matters; to make project sites available; to admit foreign and domestic investors into infrastructure sectors.

As we shall see, the enabling law should reserve to the government the power to grant concessions on an exclusive or non-exclusive basis, and for a duration to be determined, whether for a term or in perpetuity.

III. ETATISM

The inability to act just discussed may be hidden under a different, although sometimes related, set of problems and difficulties. A country's constitution may bar private participation in infrastructure and the provision of public services, or there may be a national tradition of equal weight. Many countries have seen the provision by the state of roads and railways, the post, radio and telephone, electric power, gas pipelines and airline service as a matter of great pride; some have come to see the functions as 'inherently governmental.' Post, telephone and (when it was still used) telegraph were exclusively for the *Postes, Télégraphs et Téléphones* (PTT); roads for the *Ponts et Chaussées*. Socialism reinforced these phenomena, and its laws sanctified state monopolies in infrastructure sectors.

A related and more widespread difficulty for UNCITRAL's work is the existence in many countries of law which deals with PFI, but does so in a way that is too narrow or otherwise outdated. Here, law must be reformed or even dismantled. This seems to be especially the case in some civil law countries, those that have a separate body of law, and possibly courts, governing contracts with government, called the administrative law. This law tends to reserve to government control of public services, does not countenance sufficiently free bargaining between government and investor, but is more 'interventionist.' To be sure governments wish to ensure universal service (although many have failed to so do; which may be one reason why private participation is attractive to them) and consumer protection; but the administrative law (reserving to government unilateral power to vary contract terms in such a way as to deter private investment) seems like 'overkill' to many. Changing such law means grappling with trade unions, nationalist and socialist traditions and vested interests — the kinds of 'complementary' problems in law reform of which Ibrahim Shihata has written.[7] Where administrative law and courts are exclusive, a choice of any other law or forum, let alone a foreign law or international commercial arbitration, the latter often a condition *sine qua non* of foreign investment, is impossible.

IV. SOME NEW PUBLIC LAW

Governments must look before they leap into PFI projects. As one writer has noted,[8] a country should not replace a public monopoly with a private one, especially one that is unregulated. Policies

---

7 *See* Shihata, *supra* note 1.

8 Pierre Guislain, The Privatization Challenge: A Strategic, Legal and Institutional Analysis of International Experience (1997).

with respect to the economic structure of the sector of infrastructure should be propounded, a competition policy for the country or sector should probably be in place, and machinery of regulation — as to price, safety, quality and consumer protection — of the sector devised.[9] Such independent regulation has not been required of a PTT when it provides the services — it would be judging itself. However, were it to be the regulator when parts of the service is 'privatized,' it would be judging its competitor — hence the need for independent regulators.

V. SOME OLD RISKS REVEALED

Let me digress for a little from law *in stricto sensu*. Whenever PFI, or build-operate-transfer (BOT) as it has been known and called, comes up, so does the discussion of 'risk' or even more frequently the 'allocation of risks.'[10] Why is this so? It is, in a way, inherent in the shift from government operation to private. When the government has a road or power plant built for its own operation it absorbs all risks (except those assigned to the construction contractor, subcontractors, *et al.*, during the construction phase); indeed, there may be no conscious identification of risks. The case is, and must be, quite different with PFI. For one thing, whereas in the conventional case of government ownership and operation there are two parties — government and contractor — in PFI there will typically be at least four — government, concessionaire, contractor (not to mention others: e.g., operator, supplier of fuel, customer for, e.g., power) and lender(s). And each will wish to know

9 These are intricate matters; *see ibid. See also generally,* SHIHATA, *supra* note 1.

10 *See,* for example, UNCITRAL draft, *supra* note 1, Chapter II, and UNITED NATIONS INDUSTRIAL DEVELOPMENT ORGANIZATION, GUIDELINES FOR INFRASTRUCTURE DEVELOPMENT THROUGH BUILD-OPERATE-TRANSFER (BOT) PROJECTS (1996). Along the spectrum of public-private partnerships, BOT is one possible arrangement, signifying that the concessionaire of the project will not only construct, but operate (and maintain, and assure financial viability, and subject itself to government monitoring and, regulatory requirements during the term of the concession) and eventually transfer the project and its assets back to the government. Among other possibilities along the spectrum might be a 'build-operate-own' (BOO) arrangement: there the concessionaire 'owns' the project in perpetuity; in 'build-operate-own-transfer' (BOOT), the concessionaire at the end of the prescribed term of the concession transfers it back to the government. As readers will know, there are other possible arrangements and acronyms.

which risks it is to bear — e.g., delays during construction, failure of the completed road to generate enough toll revenues to cover loans, etc. — before agreeing to participate in the PFI project and on what terms. To be precise, as we shall see, it is the 'allocation of obligations,' rather than 'risks,' in the project agreement and other contracts making up the 'contractual matrix' of a typical PFI project, with which lawyers will be concerned.

VI. SELECTION OF THE PROJECT COMPANY

Here we come to another important aspect of law creation with respect to PFI, the need to have a proper law in place in the host country to govern the selection of the project company (concessionaire). UNCITRAL has previously promulgated its highly successful — in that it has served many countries — Model Law for the Procurement of Goods, Construction and Services.[11] Its possible application to PFI is a bit complex,[12] in part because there has been a tendency on the part of some to characterize — mischaracterize — the BOT and similar arrangements as, what I would call, "construction plus." But the subject of PFI is really, in procurement law terms, much more like a service, a "super-service," consisting of development (putting it all together), finance and investment, construction, operation, maintenance and transfer back in some cases, dealing with regulators, than it is a construction or equipment supply contract. Hence, the more discretionary, less objective methods of service procurement must be adapted to PFI. These methods are not as evolved as the simpler 'lowest responsive bidder' goods and construction procurement method. The more discretionary, more negotiation laden services methods can of course lend themselves more readily to abuse. This is a real possibility: many countries do not yet have enough experience to avoid problems; and because large amounts may be involved, the consequences of an inadequate legal framework may be costly. Here, as so often elsewhere with respect to PFI and other economic areas, law reform means law creation, and the work of an

---

11 United Nations, New York, 1995.

12 THE WORLD BANK'S GUIDELINES: PROCUREMENT UNDER IBRD LOANS AND IDA CREDITS, paragraph 3.13 (revised through August 1996) deal with BOO/BOT/BOOT arrangements.

UNCITRAL is not law harmonization but the development of models, embodying best practices where available, to assist such law creation.

Good procurement practice means competition; it means trying to compare apples and apples, if possible, to get the best apple at a price one can afford; not buying the first apple one sees; not comparing apples and chocolate candy and deciding what to eat. Selection of concessionaires must deal with some special problems. There is the matter of the unsolicited proposal; how to deal with it and yet have a competitive selection. Because 'negotiations' can take so long, and some potential concessionaires are unwilling to spend the time and lay out the funds if they might lose a bid, there is pressure for sole source procurement, which must be resisted. Then there is the matter of domestic preference; but can one calibrate that in a multi-billion dollar project; does a few pennies less (with respect to what aspect of a project) have any possible bearing on the choice to be made? Mischaracterization is not limited to 'construction plus:' the term 'negotiation' itself, almost always used to describe the process that takes too long and creates the excessive transaction costs attributed to 'BOT' is, or should be, something of a misnomer. For if a government has a proper law and procedure in place, there will be preparation of solicitation documents, possible clarification of them, submission of proposals, comparison of proposals, evaluation, selection (and then possibly some negotiation with the 'preferred' proposer) — hardly a mere negotiation, and certainly not with just one would-be concessionaire. And the solicitation documents package should include as much as possible of the ultimate project agreement with the concessionaire as the government can possibly produce in advance — this to increase the likelihood that all bidders will be offering 'apples' and not something else.

VII. "THE CONTRACTUAL MATRIX"[13]

Law creation should not extend to prescribing the terms of contracts. But a proper legal framework for PFI will have contracts very much in mind, and will have to deal with aspects of the mat-

13 SHIHATA, *supra* note 1, at 153.

ter. This should be plain from the prior discussions of *Tabula Rasa* and *Etatism.* The legal framework must enable host countries to enter into sound PFI/BOT arrangements; and must enable them to do so on terms which concessionaires will in fact be willing to agree to. A proper law must therefore 'unblock' government, must eliminate obstacles which may not merely impede and make arrangements more costly, but may in fact prevent them — as seems to be the case in at least some civil law countries with strict administrative law regimes. A proper law should allow 'free bargaining' between government and potential concessionaire (subject to the caveat above that there is more to the selection process than mere 'negotiation' — in fact a good deal of the 'bargaining' will come during the preparation of solicitation documents and their clarification during an 'iterative' process with potential proposers/bidders). Incidentally, the resultant arrangements and project agreement may be quite long; not a short form prescribed by a long statute (containing many mandatory provisions), but rather a long contract allowed by a short statute. This reflects a deeper reality governing much law reform in the economic and commercial area, the area of private, international business transactions, and reflected in much best practice, namely the rise of market oriented bargaining between parties, at the 'expense' of the solution of problems by detailed legislation reflecting the more 'interventionist' traditions of some countries. With this may come a growth of court/arbitration jurisprudence based on contract interpretation, again at the 'expense' of academic 'commentaries' addressed to codes and statutes.

The contractual matrix of a PFI project of course includes a lot more than the project agreement (concession agreement) although that is basic; there will be loan agreements, agreements among the members of the project company, construction, operation and maintenance arrangements, fuel and other supply agreements, power purchase agreements, arrangements with regulators, guaranties and insurance and so on and so on: a veritable matrix; it is good work for lawyers. And these agreements must deal with some sticky issues: the definition and allocation of obligations with respect to *force majeure* during the construction (and operations) phase; the rights of lenders to have a project assigned to them and 'step-in' in case of a concessionaire's default; termination of the project at the end of the concession term as contemplated and termination (not to be encouraged and as a last resort) for breach; transfer of assets in these various events; buy-outs; re-tendering of the concession in some events and so on. There is a matrix of contracts and a matrix of issues. And for the purposes of this essay and the discussion of law creation, the point remains that a proper law must permit all this.

VIII. THE LAWYERS' FAVORITES: GOVERNING LAW AND DISPUTE SETTLEMENT

No contract is complete without a governing law clause (or clauses) and provision for the settlement of disputes (a forum selection clause). A sound enabling law for PFI will also deal with these issues for the entire contractual matrix.

Governing law may prove vexatious — at least for the project agreement or other agreements to which the government is a party or which are otherwise deemed integral to the provision of a 'public service,' at least in those civil law countries with a separate body of administrative law and especially if they have a separate system of administrative courts (a number of countries have a Council of State (*Conseil d'Etat*) and lower administrative tribunals as most eminently does France). In this latter case if the application of administrative law is mandatory, there is in effect no scope for a choice of law, let alone foreign law; private international law 'need — and will — not apply.' A consequence of this regime, if strictly applied, is that the parties (e.g., government and concessionaire) may not agree even to the application of the domestic commercial law otherwise applicable in the host country to the transaction in question: e.g., sale of electricity, cell telephone services (which commercial law typically permits parties to bargain over a host of issues whether quantities, liquidated damages and other remedies, dispute settlement or what have you, in a way that the administrative law may not). So too, no choice of forum, whether of local or foreign court, or arbitration, whether foreign or domestic, will be allowed (some commentators in some countries argue that international treaties providing for international arbitration of various sorts may override the exclusive jurisdiction of the administrative law courts, but to my knowledge this is as yet nowhere established).

Of course some countries do permit choice of forums. But some points need to be noted. PFI disputes will be various, arising during different phases of the life of a project, and no single provision will accommodate them all. Thus during the selection phase disputes may be handled through challenge procedures, possibly involving domestic courts as well (in the rare case of an unsolicited proposal, one could envision a dispute as to whether a contract existed, which might take one to a court more directly); during the construction phase, various mechanisms exist (review board; consulting engineer as adjudicator, etc.; there may be a question as to who the relevant parties to a dispute are — e.g., contractor and concessionaire, or also government and lenders); during the operations phase, disputes may be with a regulatory body with jurisdiction over them, but with judicial review possible. It is to be seen how commercial arbitration, domestic or international, often favored by lawyers, fits into all this.

IX. CREATING THE LAW

A few final words on the creation of law, the theme of this essay's approach to PFI. The Commission (UNCITRAL) has directed its secretariat (officially the International Trade Law Branch of the Legal Department of the United Nations) to draft 'concise legislative principles' and where possible, 'model [law] provisions' for its legislative guide. I strongly favor the closest approximation possible to a model law — and there will be difficulties, alternative provisions, and inevitable gaps — which might be used as a checklist by a country to review its present laws or to prepare a new law to deal with the central problems of PFI, to be supplemented or not for particular sectors of infrastructure. Here another word about the recent UNCITRAL method with respect to model laws: we not only prepare a draft law but also a so-called 'guide to enactment,' which indicates the pluses and minuses of proposed legislative solutions and the considerations that have gone into them. This guide can be used by both executive and legislative branches in the host country in deliberating on legislation; indeed, it might even be of value to interested members of the public and media at the time of that process. Between model and guide, UNCITRAL provides both tight language to facilitate the mechanics of legislative drafting (recognizing that individual country conditions and solutions can vary widely), and an 'educational' text so that the legislative deliberations can be just that — deliberate and informed with respect to what otherwise might be an exotic, detailed and/or rumor filled area of public policy.

As I have noted, creation of law models (not just harmonization, as there are not enough proven national examples for that) at the international level, and creation of law within societies and nations undergoing accelerating change, is taking place. It will do so in a significant way with respect to the privately financed infrastructure projects which have been the subject of this essay. This development is, in my view, of a piece with the large works of Ibrahim Shihata and his career — both so admirable — to this date.

THE STATE, THE FOREIGN INVESTOR, AND INTERNATIONAL LAW: THE NO LONGER STORMY RELATIONSHIP OF A *MÉNAGE À TROIS*

Prosper Weil

The scenario itself is not new: a company has been authorized by the Government of a foreign country to develop the country's petroleum or mineral resources or build infrastructure or factories over an extended period of time, with guarantees ensuring that the undertaking will be profitable. True, the political and economic context in which such scenarios have unfolded has varied over the years, as have the legal concepts and the terminology used — from the mining concessions secured by European and North American companies during the nineteenth century in Latin America, Africa, and Asia to the economic development contracts and State contracts typical of the post-war "new economic order" and to the large-scale private investment operations within the framework of the "global economy" so typical of this late twentieth century. These differences aside, however, a common thread runs through all these phenomena, namely the controversy over what role international law plays, or should play, in relations between host States and foreign private investors.[1]

Ibrahim F.I. Shihata, through his decisive efforts at the World Bank and his remarkable scholarly writings, has done more than anyone else to legitimize the concept of international foreign investment law and to lay down its major substantive rules. We owe

1 For the sake of convenience, the words "foreign private investor/investment" will be used throughout this paper, even when speaking of earlier times when these concepts were yet to be recognized.

him a debt of gratitude for the fact that it is no longer considered politically incorrect or a legal oxymoron to assert the relevance of international law to relations between host States and foreign private investors. To pay tribute to him is a special pleasure and a particular honor to the author of this paper, who remembers his own efforts during the 1970s to win acceptance for the theory of the internationalization of State contracts and the concept of an international law of contracts.

The purpose of this article is to present an overview of the stages in the remarkable process whereby international law has metamorphosed from a controversial and unwanted intruder in the relationship between the couple formed by the host State and the foreign private investor into a most welcome partner in a no longer stormy, but now peaceful, *ménage à trois*.

ACT I — THE FOREIGN INVESTOR AND THE HOST STATE: A CLASSIC, EXCLUSIVE LEGAL *MÉNAGE*

During the initial stage, which continued well into the second half of the twentieth century, the host State and the foreign investor formed a classic legal *ménage:* the investor operated in the legal environment of the host State, was bound by its legislation, and was subject to the jurisdiction of its courts. How could international law have elbowed its way in when one of the partners was not a subject of international law, so that neither its rights nor its obligations arose out of, or could be given effect under, international law?

This situation applied particularly when the legal relationship between the State and the foreign investor was contractual in nature. It was the law of the contracting State which governed the implementation of the contract as well as the consequences of any breach of contract. The most refined statement of this concept was handed down in 1929 by the Permanent Court of International Justice in the *Serbian Loans* case:

> "Any contract which is not a contract between States in their capacity as subjects of international law is based on the municipal law of some country. The question as to which this law is forms part of

that branch of law which is at the present day usually described as private international law or the doctrine of the conflict of laws."[2]

Accordingly, what we would today call investment contracts were subject to the national law of the host State, since in the Court's words "... a sovereign State ... cannot be presumed to have made ... the validity of its obligations ... subject to any law other than its own."[3]

The State-investor relationship was admittedly not an entirely exclusive one, for a suitor was already waiting in the wings, so to speak, watching but never becoming involved directly. Such was the essence of what was known as diplomatic protection. If the investor was harassed by its State partner, the investor's home State had the right to intervene; the principle, however, was that the State "retains in this respect a discretionary power."[4] As the Permanent Court of International Justice repeatedly stated, the investor first had to exhaust internal remedies available, and if a Government decided to "tak(e) up the case of one of its subjects ... by resorting to diplomatic action or international judicial proceedings on his behalf," it was "in reality asserting its own rights — its right to ensure, in the person of its subjects, respect for the rules of international law."[5] In other words, when the investor's home State exercised diplomatic protection, it did so not on the grounds that the rights of its national had been violated, but rather on the grounds that the host State had violated its obligations *vis-à-vis* the investor's home State. The relationship between the investor and the host State were one thing, and the relationship between the host State and the investor's home State were another.

The idea underlying this concept was that compliance by the host State with its contractual obligations did not constitute an international obligation. A violation by the host State of its contractual obligations *vis-à-vis* a foreign contracting party was in the realm of *inter partes* relations, and the breach of contract did not

2 Serbian Loans, 1929 PCIJ (ser. A) No. 20/21, at 41.

3 *Ibid.* at 42.

4 Barcelona Traction Light and Power Company Limited (Belg. v. Spain), 1970 I.C.J. 3, 44 (para. 79).

5 The Mavrommatis Palestine Concessions, 1924 PCIJ (ser.A) No. 2, at 12.

per se constitute an internationally wrongful act. The investor enjoyed protection as a foreigner, not as a contracting party. The trigger establishing the international responsibility of the host State toward the investor's home State had to be a tort, that is to say, something other, and more serious, than a simple breach of contract, for instance, a breach of a minimum standard for the treatment of a foreigner, unjustifiable discrimination, the confiscatory nature of an act, or a denial of justice. The State did not incur international responsibility for having violated the contractual rights of the investor, but for having committed an internationally wrongful act *vis-à-vis* the investor's home State.

The rare attempts to treat a breach of contract by the host State as constituting *per se* an internationally wrongful act *vis-à-vis* the foreign contracting party's home State on the basis of the so-called principle of the sanctity of contracts proved unsuccessful. The prevailing wisdom was that contractual relations between an investor and a host State and relations between the host State and the investor's home State were on different planes. International law, it was maintained, had no bearing on relations between the host State and the foreign investor, its application being limited to relations between the host State and the foreign contracting party's home State. Given this approach, an international law of contracts or an international investment law could hardly enter into play.

ACT II — INTERNATIONAL LAW BURSTS IN: THE DRAMA IS UNFOLDING

The situation changed radically following World War II, particularly during the 1970s. On the one hand, an increasing number of countries, often former colonies, had become new sovereign States, but lacked the financial resources and technological know-how to build their infrastructure and develop their natural resources. On the other hand, companies from industrialized countries saw an opportunity to reap high profits by developing those resources, building infrastructure, and modernizing the countries of the Third World. However, each partner mistrusted the other: the host State worried that it would be at a disadvantage in an unequal economic relationship, while the foreign investor was concerned about entering an unequal legal relationship in which it would have to contend with state sovereignty. This was the era of the ideology of the new world economic order, which was hostile to the economic domination of Third World countries, described as the South, by multinational corporations from Western countries, described as the North. As misunderstanding bred suspicion, and suspicion bred prejudiced assumptions, relations between sometimes weak Governments and often powerful foreign investors became mired in mistrust. In order to guard against legislative changes or other governmental actions likely to upset the contractual balance, foreign investors sought to include stabilization and inviolability clauses in their contracts. States, on their part, endeavored to protect their sovereignty from such contractual restrictions. This was the era of massive nationalizations, claims to "permanent sovereignty" of States over their natural resources, and the Charter of Economic Rights and Duties of States.

As far as procedural matters were concerned, this climate prompted investors to favor some kind of denationalized arbitration mechanism that would shield them from the presumed partiality of the host State's courts. While this approach did not meet with much resistance from host States, on substantive matters, however, the opposing positions proved difficult to reconcile. Investors worried about being caught in a trap if the domestic law of the host State were to prevail, not only because of its possible deficiencies but, more importantly, because of its suspected bias against foreigners or foreign investment. In some instances, investors succeeded in including in their contracts a clause calling explicitly for the application of a law other than the domestic law of the host State. In other cases, they maintained that the very absence of a choice-of-law clause automatically required that application be made of a law other than the domestic law of the host State. On the exact nature of such law, however, there was no agreement. To some, it was transnational law; to others, it was *lex mercatoria,* which, since it covered the entire spectrum of international trade relations, was also deemed to cover relations between investors and States. Still others preferred *lex contractus,* according to which contractual relations were not bound by any legal system and constituted a self-contained and self-sufficient legal environment. The Third World countries, on the other hand, vehemently opposed any such attempt to "denationalize" State contracts and to strip them of the prerogatives inherent in state sovereignty. In their view, their national law, and that alone, should govern their relations with foreign investors.

It was against this background that the suggestion was put forward to bring investment contracts under international law. While shielding contracts from possible uncertainties under the domestic law of the host State, recourse to international law should, so it was thought, make it possible to establish a balance between Third World Governments and Western investors by ensuring that their relationship was to be governed by a legal system based on the principle of sovereign equality.

For most writers, such internationalization was admissible only where the parties had themselves endorsed it by an explicit choice-of-law clause. International law would then become applicable by giving effect to the will of the parties as rooted in the domestic law of the host State. In other words, it was the application of the domestic law of the host State which would make international law applicable. Similarly, it was easily accepted that international law could be applicable when incorporated into the domestic law of the host State by the latter's Constitution or — as rarely happened in those days — where the contract was covered by an umbrella agreement between the host State and the home State of the investor.[6] These situations aside, most scholars denied international law any governing role.

For the author of the present article, quite to the contrary, the investment contract had its roots, its *Grundlegung,* directly in the international legal order. It was not, he maintained, an internationalized contract solely by virtue of the will of the parties or the domestic legal order; it was by its very nature an international contract, that is to say, an international legal act. This assessment was based on economic and political realities. Many investments have their "center of gravity" in inter-State relations: indeed, it is hardly unusual for Western Heads of State traveling abroad to be accompanied by a group of businessmen, nor is it unusual for investments to evolve from the prevailing political relations be-

---

6 *See* for instance F. Rigaux, *Les situations juridiques individuelles dans un système de relativité générale, Cour général de droit international privé,* 213/9 RECUEIL DES COURS DE L'ACADÉMIE DE DROIT INTERNATIONAL 229–231 (1989).

tween a host State and the home State of the investors. Whether the application of international law is based on the will of the parties or the constitutional system of the host State, or whether one considers it to be a reflection of reality, the actual outcome is the same: the legal relationship arising out of an investment and the law governing the relationship are matters within the international legal order.[7]

By and large, this theory of the internationalization of State contracts was not well-received. Some pointed to the theoretical difficulty raised by submitting to international law a legal relationship in which one of the parties was not a subject of international law. Others noted the scarcity, if not the absence, of rules of international law specifically governing relations, especially contractual relations, between a State and a foreign private law entity. Still others maintained that to apply the rules governing international treaties to investment contracts, and to apply the rules governing inter-State relations to legal relationships arising out of investments, would be tantamount to conferring on a foreign private investor the status of a subject of international law equal to that of the host State. This led to the major accusation that the ulterior motive underlying the theory of the internationalization of State contracts was to grant to Western private investors *vis-à-vis* Third World countries the high level of protection that States enjoy under international law.

This Manichean vision was no doubt fundamentally flawed. Far from systematically favoring foreign investors to the detriment of host States, the theory that investment relations, especially those of a contractual nature, should be made subject to an international law of contracts, that is to say, to a branch of international law, represents, quite to the contrary, a way to establish a proper balance between the interests of the host State and those of the foreign investor. It is, indeed, of the very essence of international law to foster cooperation between entities which, although unequal in size and power, are deemed juridically equal. As to the

[7] *See* P. Weil, *Les problèmes relatifs aux contrats passés entre un Etat et un particulier,* 128/1 Recueil des Cours de l'Académie de Droit International (1969); *id. Les clauses de stabilisation ou d'intangibilité dans les accords de développement économique, in* La Communauté Internationale. Mélanges offerts à Charles Rousseau 301(1974); and *id. Droit international et contrats d'Etat, in* Le Droit International: Unité et Diversité. Mélanges offerts à Paul Reuter 549 (1981).

argument that international law incorporates only few rules on foreign investment, this is the case with most new branches of international law. It is a temporary deficiency which, like youth, vanishes with the passage of time.

However this may be, the internationalization of investment relations was not viewed favorably by Third World States and was widely criticized in the literature as a legal weapon wielded by companies from "rich" countries against the sovereignty of "poor" countries. To many only application of the domestic law of the host State was acceptable. Thus, the legal debate gradually became an exercise in prejudiced assumptions, and those who supported the application of international law to investment relations were accused of sacrificing the interests of the Third World countries to Western multinational corporations.

Hostility to the idea of making relations between States and investors subject to international law found its most telling expression in the efforts of many writers and arbitration tribunals to minimize the scope of the explicit reference to international law contained in the 1965 Washington Convention on the Settlement of Investment Disputes between States and Nationals of Other States.

This most important instrument — which was to win increasing support as time went by — bypassed the diplomatic protection process in favor of specific dispute settlement mechanisms. In so doing, it did not merely recall, in Article 42(1), the classic principle that

> "The Tribunal shall decide a dispute in accordance with such rules . . . as may be agreed by the parties,"

but immediately added that

> "In the absence of such agreement, the Tribunal shall apply the law of the Contracting State Party to the dispute (including its rules on the conflict of laws) and such rules of international law as may be applicable."

Whatever the exact interpretation to be given to these two provisions, this meant, at the very least, that, in certain circumstances, rules of international law are to govern the legal relations between a State and a foreign investor. Quite significantly, the Report of the World Bank Executive Directors on the Convention pointed out that

> "The term 'international law' as used in this context should be understood in the sense given to it by Article 38(1) of the Statute of the International Court of Justice, allowance being made for the fact that Article 38 was designed to apply to inter-States disputes."[8]

The drafting history of Article 42 shows that "this phrase is not designed to limit the rules of international law by declaring some of them inapplicable. It simply means that the relevant rules of international law are to be applied."[9] The idea underlying this provision was that notwithstanding certain concerns about the paucity of applicable rules in international law, "international law . . . is sufficiently complete to provide a legal answer to every dispute."[10]

The fact that the second sentence of Article 42 refers not to international law alone, but to both domestic law *and* international law, prompted some ICSID tribunals and writers to seek a solution whereby the two sources could be combined — in other words, to prevent international law from serving as the sole governing law. Various options were suggested: parallel application of domestic law and international law where they could be considered compatible; international law as an alternative where domestic law did not adequately address the issue at hand; and the corrective role of international law — in other words, application of domestic law where it was consistent with international law and application of international law where it was not.[11]

However complex and multifaceted, these attempts are actually futile, for no matter how domestic law and international law

---

8 Doc. ICSID/2, para. 40; 1 ICSID REPORTS 31.

9 C. Schreuer, *Commentary on the ICSID Convention,* 12 ICSID REV. — FILJ 365, 477 (1997).

10 I.F.I. Shihata & A.R. Parra, *Applicable Substantive Law in Disputes Between States and Private Foreign Parties: the Case of Arbitration Under the ICSID Convention,* 9 ICSID REV. — FILJ 183, 194 (1994).

11 Regarding these various options, *see* Schreuer, *supra* note 9, at 477–487.

are combined, under the second sentence of Article 42(1), international law always gains the upper hand and ultimately prevails. It prevails indirectly through the application of domestic law where the latter is deemed consistent with international law or incorporates it. It prevails directly where domestic law is deemed deficient or contrary to international law. Thus, under the second sentence of Article 42(1) international law has the last word in all circumstances: "international law is fully applicable and to classify its role as 'only' 'supplemental and corrective' seems a distinction without a difference."[12] As Sir Elihu Lauterpacht rightly observed, "[t]he assumption which appears to underlie the wording employed (in Article 42) is that, as a matter of established doctrine, international law is already effective to govern directly the relationship between States and foreign investors."[13] The reference to the domestic law of the host State, even if designed only to ascertain whether it is, or is not, compatible with international law, is indeed a pointless exercise, the sole *raison d'être* of which is to avoid offending the sensibilities of the host State.

By refusing to face this truth squarely, the tribunals and writers hostile to the internationalization of investment relations, and in particular of State contracts, demonstrated the extent to which they were still influenced by the criticism leveled against the very concept of an international law of international investment. If opposition to this concept could make itself felt so forcefully within

---

12 *Amco v. Indonesia,* resubmitted case, award of June 5, 1990, 1 *ICSID Rep.* 569, 580 (1993). C.Leben, *Retour sur la notion de contrat d'Etat et sur le droit applicable à celui-ci, in* MÉLANGES OFFERTS À HUBERT THIERRY 247, 261 (1998) (*si aucun choix n'a été opéré, le droit international devient la référence ultime des arbitres*). The same holds true where, under the first sentence of Article 42 (1), a choice of law clause refers at the same time to domestic and international law. In Sir Elihu Lauterpacht's view, Article 42(1) does not only mandate, in its second sentence, the application of international law in the absence of an express choice of law clause, but its first sentence could be read as calling for the application of international law even where an express choice of law clause exists without referring to international law, because "to pass upon such questions . . . is inherent in (an ICSID tribunal's) very status as a tribunal set up to dispose of issues under international investment contracts. . . ." *See* E. Lauterpacht, *The World Bank Convention on the Settlement of International Investment Disputes, in* RECUEIL D'ETUDES DE DROIT INTERNATIONAL EN HOMMAGE À PAUL GUGGENHEIM 642,658 (1968).

13 *See* Lauterpacht, *supra* note 12, at 664.

the context of ICSID arbitration, where Article 42 of the ICSID Convention is governing, it is no wonder that such resistance could hold sway in matters outside the ICSID arena. This shows just how ingrained the reluctance to introduce international law in investment relations had become,[14] and explains that even in recent years any suggestion of a *ménage à trois* incorporating international law continued to be met with mistrust and skepticism.

ACT III — INTERNATIONAL LAW FINDS ITS PLACE: THE *MÉNAGE À TROIS* SETTLES DOWN

Over the past few years, however, matters have again begun to change. International law, once brushed aside by legal nationalism and accused of being deficient and irrelevant, is in the process of making a resounding comeback.

This recovery may be attributed to two factors. The first is the increasing number of multilateral conventions containing provisions for the settlement of disputes between investors and host States that expressly call for the application of international law to disputes between a private investor and the host State. The prime example, of course, is the ICSID mechanism, already referred to, the novelty of which, despite the narrow interpretation initially put on it, grew increasingly impossible to ignore.[15] This, however, was not to remain an isolated example, for the ICSID Convention was to serve as the point of departure for a number of multilateral conventions that ascribed an increasingly important role to international law. The Colonia Investment Protocol of Mercosur (1994), for instance, stipulates that the arbitrators shall decide the dispute in accordance with the Protocol, the law of the State party to the dispute, any contracts relating to the investment, and the applica-

---

14 "[A]rbitral tribunals have not shown a particular eagerness to rely on international law. In most cases, the tribunals elected to resolve the dispute on the basis of domestic law either because it was felt that there was no need to apply international law or because it was found that the local law was in harmony with international law." *See* G.R Delaume, *The Proper Law of State Contracts Revisited*, 12 ICSID Rev. — FILJ 1,5 (1997). The author even points to a trend, in practice, toward the "relocalization of State contracts." *Ibid* at 11.

15 *See* Schreuer, *supra* note 9, at 463–487.

ble principles of international law. More remarkably, the North American Free Trade Agreement (NAFTA) (1992) states in Article 1131 that

> "A Tribunal established under this Section shall decide the issues in dispute in accordance with this Agreement and applicable rules of international law."[16]

Similar provisions may be found in the Cartagena Free Trade Agreement (1994) and the Energy Charter Treaty (1994).[17]

The criticism leveled not so very long ago against all theories favoring the internationalization of State contracts and, more generally, the internationalization of legal investment relations, are thus swept aside by major multilateral agreements.[18]

The second factor underlying the growing role of international law is the proliferation of bilateral investment treaties (BITs), a phenomenon which sheds an entirely new light on the matter.[19]

The very fact that certain rights and obligations of the host State and the foreign investor are set out in an international treaty confers an international character on those rights and obligations. Even where the investment instrument — be it a contract or a unilateral act — provides that the relationship between the host State

---

16 32 I.L.M 605, 645 (1993).

17 *See* A.R. Parra, *Provisions on the Settlement of Investment Disputes in Modern Investment Laws, Bilateral Investment Treaties and Multilateral Instruments on Investment,* 12 ICSID Rev. — FILJ 287, 347 (1997); *See also* Schreuer, *supra* note 9, at 434–5. *But cf.* F. Poirat, *L'article 26 du Traité relatif à la Charte de l'énergie,* 102 Revue Générale de Droit International Public 45 (1998).

18 The draft OECD Multilateral Agreement on Investment (1998) — now abandoned — similarly provided that disputes between investors and host States would be dealt with under the terms of the Agreement, which was to be interpreted and implemented in accordance with the applicable rules of international law.

19 *See* in particular Parra, *supra* note 17, at 322; Rudolf Dolzer & Margrete Stevens, Bilateral Investment Treaties (1995); G. Sacerdoti, *Bilateral Treaties and Multilateral Instruments on Investment Protection,* 269 Recueil des Cours de l'Académie de Droit International, 251(1997). *But cf.* E.Gaillard, 126 Journal du Droit International 273 (1999). *See also* I.F.I. Shihata & A.R. Parra, *The Experience of the International Centre for Settlement of Investment Disputes,* 14 ICSID Rev. — FILJ 299, 303,306 (1999). Concerning the impact of the growing role of multilateral and bilateral investment treaties on the requirement of consent in ICSID arbitrations, *see* J. Paulsson, *Arbitration Without Privity,* 10 ICSID Rev. — FILJ 232 (1995).

and the foreign investor is entirely or partly subject to the domestic law of the host State, the existence of a BIT raises the question of compliance with the rights and obligations contained therein to the level of a matter under international law, with respect not only to relations between the States parties to the treaty but also to relations between the host State and the investor. Inasmuch as BITs usually shun recourse to classic diplomatic protection in favor of a direct ICSID-style dispute settlement mechanism to give effect to the rights and obligations enunciated in the BIT, effect is to be given, in the final analysis, to rules of international law. As already indicated, even those authors who opposed the denationalization and internationalization of investment relations most vehemently consistently regarded umbrella agreements as an exception. With the proliferation of bilateral investment treaties, what was long the exception is becoming the rule.

But there is more to the story. An increasing number of BITs go beyond referring to a dispute settlement mechanism and determine the applicable law themselves. Typically, they refer simultaneously to the domestic law of the State party to the dispute, to the provisions of the treaty itself, and to the principles and rules of international law. The *AAPL v. Republic of Sri Lanka* (1990)[20] and *Antoine Goetz and Associates v. Republic of Burundi* (1998)[21] cases are noteworthy illustrations of the trend — which can only grow stronger — toward ICSID arbitration governed by international law by virtue of the fact that the BIT implicitly or explicitly provides that disputes must be settled not only on the basis of the provisions of the treaty itself, but also, and more generally, on the basis of the principles and rules of international law.

Considered not very long ago in some quarters to be a theoretical fantasy, the theory of the internationalization of investment relations can no longer be questioned: not only must disputes arising out of foreign private investments be settled by international arbitration; they must also be resolved on the basis of international law. No distinction is to be drawn in this regard between

---

20 ARB/87/3, 4 ICSID REPORTS 250; 6 ICSID REV. — FILJ 514 (1991), with observations by N.G. Ziadé; 119 JOURNAL DU DROIT INTERNATIONAL 216 (1992), with observations by E. Gaillard.

21 ARB/95/3 (to be published).

investments under a contract and investments based on a unilateral act of the host State. The law of State contracts is now to be considered as a component of investment law,[22] and it is with good reason that recognition has been given to the emergence of a "new international law of foreign investment"[23] which encompasses but also goes beyond the international law of State contracts.

The arguments once advanced against the theory of the internationalization of State contracts have thus lost any semblance of credibility. This is particularly true for the argument of practicability. As mentioned earlier, it was often argued that international law does not include enough rules on investments to warrant its application. Such criticism was always excessive, for the basic elements of an international law of contracts had been identified long ago.[24] Applied more broadly to foreign private investment, this criticism is entirely groundless today.

The new international law of foreign investment is evolving on two levels.[25] First, it is developing investment by investment, in that each investment operation is governed by norms of international law set out in the relevant bilateral or multilateral treaty. Such is the case for the obligation to ensure the investor "fair and equitable treatment" or "full protection and security." So, too, for treaty provisions guaranteeing the investor national treatment or prohibiting any action prejudicial to the investment other than for reasons of public policy and with an assurance of adequate compensation; provisions ensuring the unimpeded transfer of profits; provisions exempting the investor from changes in national legislation in a given matter; provisions prohibiting discriminatory or confiscatory measures, and the like.

However, the effort to define the norms of international law governing foreign private investment is not limited to particular provisions of treaty instruments. As Antonio Parra notes, "[a]lthough there are many important differences among these instruments,

---

22 Leben, *supra* note 12, at 279.

23 Shihata & Parra, *supra* note 10, at 211; Parra, *supra* note 17, at 361.

24 P. Weil, *Problèmes relatifs . . .*, *supra* note 7, at 189.

25 *See* P. Juillard, *L'évolution des sources du droit des investissements,* 250 Recueil des Cours de l'Académie de Droit International 9 (1994).

they are remarkably homogeneous in their approach to key issues."[26] By sheer repetition, certain clauses of bilateral investment treaties may thus become customary law. Arbitral tribunals, especially ICSID tribunals, already apply rules of customary international law or general principles of law[27] together with treaty provisions. By interpreting treaty norms and identifying specific customary rules or general principles, arbitral tribunals have themselves become a source of what has now become a veritable *corpus juris* of international investment law.[28]

The Guidelines on the Treatment of Foreign Direct Investment laid down by the World Bank in 1992 on the basis of detailed background studies are to play a major role in defining the content of this new branch of international law.[29] In theory, the normative role of the Guidelines is limited since they claim to be no more than a "set of guidelines embodying commendable approaches which would not be legally binding as such but which could greatly influence the development of international law in this area."[30] Drafted after a review of "existing legal instruments and literature, as well as best available practice," the Guidelines therefore should, in their own words, be viewed solely as "representing a framework which embodies essential principles . . . without prejudice to the binding rules of international law at this stage of its development." However, as Ibrahim Shihata observes:

> Through their possible influence on future national legislation, bilateral treaties, judicial decisions, and arbitral awards as well as their potential impact on the day to day behavior of States towards

---

26 Parra, *supra* note 17, at 357.

27 Schreuer, *supra* note 9, at 464 *ff. See also* J.A. Westberg & B.P. Marchais, *General Principles Governing Foreign Investment as Articulated in Recent Arbitral Awards and Writings of Publicists,* 7 ICSID Rev. — FILJ 453 (1992).

28 *See,* for example, the award *in AAPL v. Sri Lanka* (*supra* note 19), which states that the obligation to guarantee the investor "full protection and security" means only that the State must exercise "all due diligence" to this end but is not obligated to guarantee the outcome.

29 IBRAHIM F.I.SHIHATA, LEGAL TREATMENT OF FOREIGN INVESTMENT, THE WORLD BANK GUIDELINES (1993). The text of the Guidelines and of reports clarifying them was also published in 7 ICSID Rev. — FILJ 297 (1992) and 31 I.L.M 1363 (1992). *See also* P. Juillard, *Investissements,* 38 ANNUAIRE FRANÇAIS DE DROIT INTERNATIONAL 779 (1992).

30 SHIHATA, *supra* note 29, at 295.

foreign investors, the Guidelines could influence the evolution of customary international law in this area.[31]

Looking beyond their limited objective and ostensibly low profile, the Guidelines may already be considered to constitute the written expression of rules of customary law. They are, therefore, to serve as a substitute for the major international convention which it has not been possible to elaborate thus far.

Some uncertainties doubtless persist regarding the form and content of the new international investment law. Some of its norms are more in the nature of flexible standards than clear-cut rules, but this is true for all systems of law. The standard of "fair and equitable treatment" is certainly no less operative than was the standard of "due process of law," and it will be for future practice, jurisprudence, and commentary to impart specific content to it. As has been noted, "[a]rbitrators in future cases will undoubtedly have the task of further elucidating . . . international standards. . . ."[32]

It no longer makes sense today to assert that international law lacks norms applicable to foreign private investment. In fact, given the ever-increasing number of arbitral awards, especially ICSID awards, the complaint may soon well be that there are too many such norms.

Even more than the practicability argument, the political argument so often invoked against the internationalization of investment relations is collapsing in light of new developments.

It can no longer be argued that the theory of the internationalization of investment relations advances a hidden agenda aimed at subjecting the Governments and economies of the Third World to the discretion of Western multinational corporations. Quite the contrary, this theory aims at establishing a balance between the interests of the host State and those of the foreign investor. While it shields investors to a certain extent from the political and economic hazards of investing in a foreign country, it also protects States from the excessive demands of overly-powerful multinationals. In the final analysis, there is no conflict between the inter-

31 *Ibid.* at 151–152.

32 *Ibid.* at 212.

ests of the host State and those of the foreign investor. Both parties wish the investment to succeed: the State, from the standpoint of its economic and technological development, and the investor, from the standpoint of the profits it stands to earn.

Another factor is the new pattern of investment flows. For some time, the problem was mainly one of North-South relations — that is, of relations between Western developed countries and developing countries of the Third World. In this context, as noted earlier, support for the application of the domestic law of the host State was often interpreted as a sign of generosity toward poor countries and respect for their newly-acquired sovereignty and still fragile economies, while support for the internationalization of investment relations was viewed as conferring on investors the dignity of a partner having virtual State status. With the globalization of the world economy, private investment has now branched out beyond the narrow North-South axis and includes investments from one country of the South to another and from one country of the North to another. In the wake of the entry on the world economic scene of China and countries from the former Soviet bloc, the distinction between North and South and between developed countries and developing countries has become somewhat blurred. Given this multidirectional pattern of investment flows, only international law is in a position to supply balanced solutions capable of taking into account the variety of individual situations. It was not a jurist's fantasy that led to the development of international investment law; rather, it is a realistic understanding of the contemporary political and economic environment that explains and legitimizes the success of the concept. The ICSID system, to the development of which Ibrahim Shihata has contributed so much, is better equipped than any other mechanism to respect the "balance of the interests of investors and host States,"[33] indispensable to the smooth functioning of foreign private investment.

In an article which he co-authored, the scholar to whom this collection of writings is dedicated underscored "[t]he growing role of international law" in this field and noted that arbitrators "will have before them tremendous new opportunities to contribute to

33 *Ibid.* at 187, 193.

the progressive development of international law in this important area of equal importance to developed and developing countries."[34] The presence of international law in the relations between investors and host States is no longer a matter of dispute. Long contentious, the *ménage à trois* has now settled down and can look ahead to a bright future.

[34] *See* Ibrahim F. I. Shihata & Antonio R. Parra, *Applicable Substantive Law in Disputes Between States and Private Foreign Parties: The Case of Arbitration under the ICSID Convention,* 9 ICSID REV.-FILJ 183, 208, 213 (1994).

LIST OF ABBREVIATIONS

ADB — Asian Development Bank
ADF — African Development Fund
ADR — Alternative Dispute Resolution
AfDB — African Development Bank
AFESD — Arab Fund for Economic and Social Development
AGBM — *Ad Hoc* Group on the Berlin Mandate
AIDS — Acquired Immuno-Deficiency Syndrome
AIJ — Activities Implemented Jointly
APEC — Asia Pacific Economic Cooperation
ATARS — Association for Relations Across the Taiwan Straits

BADEA — Banque Arabe de Développement en Afrique
BCCI — Bank of Credit and Commerce International
BIP — Baltic Investment Program
BITs — Bilateral Investment Treaties
BMZ — *Bundesministerium für Wirtschaftliche Zusammenarbeit und Entwicklung* (German Ministry for Economic Cooperation and Development)
BOO — Build-Operate-Own
BOOT — Build-Operate-Own-Transfer
BOT — Build-Operate-Transfer
BSE — mad cow disease

CACIF — Committee of Agricultural, Commercial, Industrial and Financial Associations
CAS — Country Assistance Strategy
CCPOQ — Consultative Committee on Program and Operational Questions
CDCJ — European Committee on Legal Cooperation
CDF — Comprehensive Development Framework
CDM — Clean Development Mechanism

CDPC — Committee of the Council of Europe, the European Committee on Crime Problems
CERs — Certified Emission Reductions
CESCE — *Compañia Española de Sequros de Crèdit a la Exportacion*
CGIAR — Consultative Group on International Agricultural Research
CIETAC-China International Economic & Trade Arbitration Commission
CIS — Commonwealth of Independent States
CNRT — Counsel for East Timorese Resistance Questions
COFACE — *Compagnie Française d'Assurance Crédit*
CoP — Conference on the Parties
CPC — Committee for Program and Coordinations
CRT — Claims Resolution Tribunal
CUP — Cooperative Underwriting Program

DAC — Development Assistance Committee
DGF — Development Grant Facility
DIS — *Deutsche Institution für Schiedsgerichtsbarkeit* (German Institution for Arbitration)

EAS — Executive Agreement Series
EBRD — European Bank for Reconstruction and Development
ECGD — Export Credit Guarantee Department
EC — European Community
ECJ — European Court of Justice
ECOSOC — Economic and Social Council
EFTA — European Free Trade Area
EIB — European Investment Bank
EIT — Economies in Transition
ELSI — Case concerning Electronica Sicula
EMBL — European Molecular Biology Laboratory
ERUs — Emission Reduction Units
ESA — European Space Agency
ESAF — Enhanced Structural Adjustment Facility
EU — European Union

FAO — Food and Agricultural Organization
FATF — Financial Action Task Force

FDI — Foreign Direct Investment
FI — Financial Intermediary
FIAS — Foreign Investment Advisory Service
FILJ — Fordham International Law Journal
FMLN — Farabundo Marti Front for National Liberation
FSIA-Foreign Sovereign Immunities Act
FT — Fast Track
FY — Fiscal Year

GAOR — United Nations General Asssembly Official Record
GATT — General Agreement on Tariffs and Trade
GCI — General Capital Increase
GDP — Gross Domestic Product
GDR — German Democratic Republic
GEF — Global Environment Facility
GHG — Greenhouse Gases
GI — Government Issue
GMC — Multidisciplinary Group on Corruption
GMOs — Genetically Modified Organisms
GREGO — Group of States Against Corruption
GWP — Global Water Partnership

HIPC — Heavily Indebted Poor Countries
HIV — Human Immuno-Deficiency Virus

IADB — Inter-American Development Bank
IAEA — International Atomic Energy Association
IBRD — International Bank for Reconstruction and Development
ICAO — International Civil Aviation Organization
ICC — International Chamber of Commerce
ICCA — International Council for Commercial Arbitration
ICEP — Independent Committee of Eminent Persons
ICJ — International Court of Justice
ICPO-Interpol
ICSID — International Centre for Settlement of Investment Disputes
IDA — International Development Association
IDB-Inter-American Development Bank
IDF — Institutional Development Fund
IDLI — International Development Law Institute

IEF — International Environmental Facility
IFAD — International Fund for Agricultural Development
IFC — International Finance Corporation
IFIs — International Financial Institutions
IFMS — Integrated Financial Management Systems
IGTFs — Investment Guarantee Trust Funds
IIC — Inter-American Investment Corporation
ILC — International Law Commission
ILM — International Legal Materials
ILO — International Labor Organization
ILOAT — International Labor Organization's Administrative Tribunal
IMF — International Monetary Fund
IMS — Investment Marketing Services
IOIA — International Organizations Immunities Act
IPAs — Investment Promotion Agencies
IPCC — International Panel on Climate Change
IPF — Indicative Planning Figure
IPrax-*Praxis des Internationalen Privat — und Verfahrensrechts* (German periodical)
IRA — Irish Republican Army
IRO — International Refugee Organization
IS — Initial Screening
IsDB-Islamic Development Bank
ITC — International Tin Council
ITO — International Trade Organization
ITU — International Telecommunications Union

JA — Joint Authority
JI — Joint Implementation
JIU — Joint Inspection Unit

LCIA — London Court of International Justice
LDCs — Least Developed Countries

MAI-Multilateral Agreement on Investment
MENA — Middle East & North Africa
MC — Ministerial Council
MDB — Multinational Development Bank
MIGA — Multilateral Investment Guarantee Agency

MIT — Massachusetts Institute of Technology
MITI — Ministry of Trade and Industry
MoP — Memorandum of the President
MSACs — Most Seriously Affected Countries

NATO — North-Atlantic Treaty Organization
NAFTA — North-American Free Trade Area
NGO — Non-Governmental Organization
NIEO-New International Economic Order
NIB — Nordic Investment Bank
NORAD — Norwegian Agency for International Development
NPRI — National Pollutant Release Inventory
NPC — National People's Congress

OAS — Organization of American States
OD — Operational Directive
OECD — Organization for Economic Co-operation and Development
OMS — Operational Manual Statement
OP — Operational Policy
OP — Ordinary Procedure
OPEC — Organization for Petroleum Exporting Countries
OPIC — Overseas Private Investment Corporation
OPN — Operational Policy Note
OPS — Office of Personnel Services
OPS — Office for Project Services
OSF — Opec Special Fund
OSCE — Organization for Security and Cooperation in Europe

PAS — Policy and Advisory Service
PCF — Prototype Carbon Fund
PCIJ — Permanent Court of International Justice
PFI — Privately Financed Infrastructure
PFP — Policy Framework Paper
PIL — Project Investment Loan
PMC — Petroleum Mining Code
PRC — People's Republic of China
PREM — Poverty Reduction and Economic Management Network
PRGF — Poverty Reduction and Growth Facility

PRSP — Poverty Reduction Strategy Paper
PSCs — Production Sharing Contracts
PTT — *Postes, Télégraphes et Téléphones*

QELROs — Quantified Limitation and Reduction Objectives

RIW — *Recht der Internationalen Wirtschaft*
ROC — Republic of China

SACE — *L'Istituto per i servizi assicurativi del commercio estero*
SBAA — Standard Basic Assistance Agreement
SBI — Subsidiary Body for Implementation
SBSTA — Subsidiary Body for Scientific and Technological Advice
SDR — Special Drawing Rights
SEC — Securities Exchange Commission
SECO — Straight Economic Cooperation for International Development
SEF — Straight Exchange Foundation
SoEs — State Owned Enterprises
SSRs — Social and Structural Reviews
STFs — Sponsorship Trust Funds
SWAPP — Swiss AIK Pilot Program

TAB — Technical Assistance Board
TAC — Technical Assistance Committee
TC — Tax Code
TF — Trust Fund
TIAS — Treaties and International Agreements Series
TRI — Toxics Release Inventory
TRIMS — Trade Related Investment Measures

UBS — United Bank of Switzerland
UK — United Kingdom
UN — United Nations
UNCC — United Nations Compensation Committee
UNCED — United Nations Conference on Environment and Development
UNCTAD — United Nations Conference on Trade and Development

UNCITRAL — United Nations Commission on International Trade Law
UNDP — United Nations Development Program
UNEP — United Nations Environmental Program
UNESCO — United Nations Educational, Scientific and Cultural Organization
UNFCCC — United Nations Framework Convention on Climate Change
UNICEF — United Nations Children's Fund
UNIDO — United Nations Industrial Development Organization
UNIDROIT — International Institute for the Unification of Private Law
UNOPS — United Nations Office for Project Services
UNPROFOR — United Nations Protection Force in Bosnia-Herzegovina
UNTAET — United Nations Transitional Administration in East Timor
UNTS — United Nations Treaty Series
UPU — Universal Postal Union
US — United States
USAID — United States Agency for International Development
USSR-Union of Soviet Socialist Republics

WHO — World Health Organization
WIPO — World Intellectual Property Organization
WMO — World Meteorological Organization
WRI — World Resources Institute
WTO — World Trade Organization
WWF — World Wildlife Fund

ZEF — *Zentrum für Entwicklungsforschung* (Center for Development Research)

LIST OF PUBLICATIONS BY IBRAHIM F. I. SHIHATA

BOOKS

In English

THE POWER OF THE INTERNATIONAL COURT TO DETERMINE ITS OWN JURISDICTION: COMPÉTENCE DE LA COMPÉTENCE (Martinus Nijhoff, The Hague, 1965)

THE KUWAIT FUND FOR ARAB ECONOMIC DEVELOPMENT: A LEGAL ANALYSIS (Kuwait Fund for Arab Economic Development, 1968) *also published as* Chapter XII *in* FOREIGN DEVELOPMENT LENDING — A LEGAL ANALYSIS (S.J. Rubin ed., Sijthoff/Oceana, Leiden/New York, 1971)

THE ARAB OIL EMBARGO (Institute of Palestinian Studies, Beirut, 1975)

THE OTHER FACE OF OPEC: FINANCIAL ASSISTANCE TO THE THIRD WORLD (Longman, London, 1982)

THE OPEC FUND FOR INTERNATIONAL DEVELOPMENT — THE FORMATIVE YEARS (Croom Helm, London, 1983) (with others)

MIGA AND FOREIGN INVESTMENT: ORIGINS, OPERATIONS, POLICIES AND BASIC DOCUMENTS OF THE MULTILATERAL INVESTMENT GUARANTEE AGENCY (Martinus Nijhoff, Dordrecht/Boston/Lancaster, 1987)

THE EUROPEAN BANK FOR RECONSTRUCTION AND DEVELOPMENT: A COMPARATIVE ANALYSIS OF THE CONSTITUENT AGREEMENT (Graham & Trotman/Martinus Nijhoff, London/ Boston, 1991)

THE WORLD BANK IN A CHANGING WORLD — SELECTED ESSAYS (F. Tschofen & A. R. Parra eds., Martinus Nijhoff, London/Dordrecht/ Boston, 1991)

LEGAL TREATMENT OF FOREIGN INVESTMENT — "THE WORLD BANK GUIDELINES" (Martinus Nijhoff, 1993).

THE WORLD BANK INSPECTION PANEL (Oxford University Press, 1994)

THE WORLD BANK IN A CHANGING WORLD — SELECTED ESSAYS AND LECTURES, Vol. II (Martinus Nijhoff, The Hague/London/Boston, 1995)

COMPLEMENTARY REFORM — ESSAYS ON LEGAL, JUDICIAL AND OTHER INSTITUTIONAL REFORMS SUPPORTED BY THE WORLD BANK (Kluwer Law International, The Hague/London/Boston, 1997)

THE WORLD BANK INSPECTION PANEL: IN PRACTICE (Oxford University Press, 2000)

THE WORLD BANK IN A CHANGING WORLD — VOL. III (Kluwer Law International 2000)

THE WORLD BANK LEGAL PAPERS (Martinus Nijhoff Publishers 2000)

In Arabic

INTERNATIONAL AIR AND SPACE LAW (Dar Al Nahda Al-Arabia, Cairo, 1966)

INTERNATIONAL ECONOMIC JOINT VENTURES (Ain Shams University Press, Cairo, 1969)

INTERNATIONAL GUARANTEE FOR FOREIGN INVESTMENTS (Dar Al Nahda Al-Arabia, Cairo, 1971)

TREATMENT OF FOREIGN INVESTMENTS IN EGYPT (Dar Al Nahda Al-Arabia, Cairo, 1972)

SECURE AND RECOGNIZED BOUNDARIES (Institute of Palistinian Studies, Beirut, 1974)

A PROGRAM FOR TOMORROW — CHALLENGES AND PROSPECTS OF THE EGYPTIAN ECONOMY IN A CHANGING WORLD (Dar Al-Shorouk, Cairo, 1987)

THE WORLD BANK AND THE ARAB WORLD (Dar Al-Hilal, Cairo 1990)

TOWARDS COMPREHENSIVE REFORM (Dar Suad Al-Sabah, Cairo, Kuwait 1993)

MY WILL FOR MY COUNTRY, VOL. I; INTRODUCTION: OPTIONS AVAILABLE TO EGYPT; REORGANIZING GOVERNMENT (Dar Ibn Khaldun, Dar Al-Amin, 1995)

MY WILL FOR MY COUNTRY, VOL. II; THE GREATER CHALLENGES: POPULATION, EDUCATION AND PRIVATE SECTOR DEVELOPMENT (Dar-Ibn Khaldun; Dar Al-Amin, 1995)

MY WILL FOR MY COUNTRY, VOL. III; TOWARDS A NEW CONSTITUTION FOR EGYPT (Dar-Ibn Khaldun; Dar Al-Amin, 1996)

MY WILL FOR MY COUNTRY, VOL. IV; FIGHTING CORRUPTION (Dar-Ibn Khaldun; Dar Al-Amin, 1997)

MY WILL FOR MY COUNTRY — THE COMPLETE TEXT (Dar Al-Amin, 2nd ed., with additions, 1999)

In French

LE FONDS OPEP POUR LE DÉVELOPPEMENT INTERNATIONAL: LES CINQ PREMIÈRES ANNÉES, 1976–1981 (Longman, London, 1982)

UN AUTRE VISAGE DE L'OPEP: ASSISTANCE FINANCIÈRE AU TIERS-MONDE (Longman, London, 1982)

In Spanish

EL EMBARGO PETROLERO ARABE (Editorial Tres Continentes, Buenos Aires 1980)

LA OTRA CARA DE LA OPEP: ASISTENCIA FINANCIERA AL TERCER MUNDO (Longman, London, 1982)

In Chinese

MIGA AND FOREIGN INVESTMENT (Chinese translation, 1998)

THE WORLD BANK IN A CHANGING WORLD, VOL. I (Chinese translation, 1996)

In Russian

LEGAL REFORM (MOSCOW, 1998)

THE WORLD BANK IN A CHANGING WORLD, VOL. I (Russian translation, MOSCOW, 1999)

ARTICLES

In English

Islamic Law and the World Community, 4 Harvard Journal of International Law 101 (1962)

Toward Absolute Liability in Space Law, *in* PROCEEDINGS OF CONFERENCE ON SPACE LAW, AMERICAN ROCKET SOCIETY, NEW YORK (April 24, 1962)

International Conferences and the Declaration of General Rules of International Law, 5 Revue des Sciences Juridiques et Economiques 13 (Cairo, 1963)

Some Observations on American Legal Positivism, 7 Revue des Sciences Juridiques et Economiques 1 (1965)

The Attitude of New States Toward the International Court of Justice, 19 International Organization 203 (1965)

The Contribution of Judge Badawi to the Jurisprudence of the International Court of Justice, 21 Revue Egyptienne de Droit International 6 (1965)

The Treaty as a Law-Declaring and Custom-Making Instrument, 22 Revue Egyptienne de Droit International 51 (1966)

Some Legal Aspects to the Work of the Kuwait Fund for Arab Economic Development, 24 Revue Egyptienne de Droit International 19 (1968)

Role of Law in Economic Development: The Legal Problems of International Public Ventures, 25 Revue Egyptienne de Droit International 119 (1969); *also published in* WORLD PEACE THROUGH LAW, PROCEEDINGS OF THE BANGKOK CONFERENCE (World Peace Through Law Center, 1969)

Legal Problems of International Public Ventures, *in* WORLD PEACE THROUGH LAW, PROCEEDINGS OF THE BANGKOK CONFERENCE (1969)

On the Extent of Application of Egyptian Law to Foreign Companies Having Their Principal Activity in Egypt, 27 Revue Egyptienne de Droit International 121-128 (1971)

Kuwait Fund for Arab Economic Development, *in* FOREIGN DEVELOPMENT LENDING: LEGAL ASPECTS 121 (S.J. Rubin ed., 1971) (paper presented at a conference of legal advisors of national and international development lending and assistance agencies, sponsored by The American Society of International Law). Also published separately by the Kuwait Fund, 1971.

Arab Investment Guarantee Corporation — A Regional Investment Insurance Project, 6 Journal of World Trade Law 185 (1972)

International Responses for Investment Problems — Some Basic Comments, 64 L'Egypte Contemporaine 169 (1973)

Destination Embargo of Arab Oil — Its Legality under International Law, 68 American Journal of International Law 591–627 (October 1974)

Inter-Arab Equity Joint Ventures, UNCTAD Doc. TD/B/AC.19/R.5 (October 21, 1975) (detailed study prepared in September 1975 for the United Nations Conference on Trade and Development)

Arab Oil Policies and the New International Economic Order, 16 Virginia Journal of International Law 591 (1976)

The OPEC Special Fund — A New Approach to International Financial Assistance, OPEC Fund Publication (1976)

The OPEC Special Fund: Some Basic Features of the Fund and its Operation, 1 OPEC Review 6 (1976)

Egypt, *in* INDIVIDUAL RIGHTS AND THE STATE IN FOREIGN AFFAIRS 204 (E. Lauterpacht & J. Collier eds., 1977)

OPEC Aid, the OPEC Fund and Cooperation with Commercial Sources of Development Finance (4 Journal of Energy and Development 291 (1979), also published separately by the OPEC Special Fund, Vienna, Austria, 1978)

The OPEC Aid Record, 7(2) World Development 161 (1979) (with R. Mabro); *also published as* an OPEC Fund Publication (1979)

OPEC Aid, the OPEC Fund, and Cooperation with Commercial Development Finance Sources, 4 Journal of Energy and Development 291–303 (1979)

The OPEC Special Fund and the North-South Dialogue, 1(4) Third World Quarterly 28-38 (1979); *also published by* the OPEC Fund (April, 1979)

Co-financing and the OPEC Special Fund, XVII(4) Development Digest 55–62 (October, 1979)

Food Production in Developing Countries: Major Constraints and Possible Solutions, 3 OPEC Review 27 (1979)

Cooperation among Developing Countries with Respect to Development Financing and The Role of OPEC Resources in Development Financing, *in* PROCEEDINGS OF THE SECOND WORLD SCIENTIFIC BANKING MEETING: INTERNATIONAL FINANCING OF ECONOMIC DEVELOPMENT (N. Ostojic, M. Cirovic & F. Perroux eds., 1980)

OPEC as a Donor Group (OPEC Fund Publication, 1980); *also published* in German by the German Society for Foreign Policy (December, 1980)

On World Hunger, 4 OPEC Review 21 (1980)

The Future of Arab Aid (OPEC Fund Publication, 1980)

The OPEC Fund for International Development, 3(2) Third World Quarterly 251–68 (1981)

The OPEC Fund for International Development — The First Five Years, 5 OPEC Review 1 (1981); *also published by* the OPEC Fund (November, 1981)

The Emerging Economic Situation in Developing Countries and the Role of the OPEC Group, address before the 16th Conference of the Governors of South-East Asian Central Banks 16-35 (Conference Proceedings, Sri Lanka, 1981)

OPEC and the Third World, 241FA Dossier 1–14 (July/August, 1981)

The Role of Donor Agencies in Facilitating Non-Concessional Transfers to the LDC's, 6 OPEC Review 260–67 (Autumn 1982)

Aid Strategy for Sub-Saharan Africa, 13 OPEC Bulletin 1-5 (April 1982)

The Unique Experience of the OPEC Fund (OPEC Fund for International Development, Vienna, Austria, 1983)

The North-South Dialogue Revisited: Some Personal Reflections, 5(3) Third World Quarterly 569–85 (July 1983)

OPEC Fund for International Development, 5 ENCYCLOPEDIA OF PUBLIC INTERNATIONAL LAW 211–14 (R. Bernhardt ed., 1983) (with A. R. Parra)

Organization of Petroleum Exporting Countries, 5 ENCYCLOPEDIA OF PUBLIC INTERNATIONAL LAW 224–28 (R. Bernhardt ed., 1983) (with A. R. Parra)

Innovations in Multilateral Financial Institutions: The Case of the OPEC Fund for International Development , *in* CONTEMPORARY ISSUES IN INTERNATIONAL LAW: ESSAYS IN HONOR OF LOUIS B. SOHN (T. Buergenthal ed., 1984)

Increasing Private Capital Flows to LDCs, 21(4) Finance & Development 6–9 (December 1984)

Improving the Investment Climate in Developing Countries: The Growing Importance of ICSID, *in* The Nonaligned World (Jul.–Sept. 1984)

The New Proposal for Establishing a Multilateral Investment Guarantee Agency, 7 Third World Quarterly 365-89 (April 1985); also *published* as Chapter 18 *in* POLITICAL RISKS IN INTERNATIONAL BUSINESS: NEW DIRECTION FOR RESEARCH, MANAGEMENT, AND PUBLIC POLICY 309 (T.L. Brewer ed., 1985)

MIGA: A Fresh Instrument for Cooperation, 4 EFTA Bulletin 6–7 (April 1985)

Bringing MIGA to Birth, Euromoney 14–15 (November 1985)

The OPEC Aid Phenomenon in Perspective, 9 OPEC Review 323–50 (Winter 1985) (with N. A. Sherbiny)

The Multilateral Investment Guarantee Agency (MIGA) and its role in the Promotion of Foreign Investment, *in* PRIVATE INVESTMENTS ABROAD 1–17 (Southwestern Legal Foundation/International and Comparative Law Center, 1985)

World Bank's MIGA: A New Instrument for Co-operation, 5 Arab Banker 9–10 (November/December, 1985)

New Agency Aims to Lift International Investment Levels, 16 OPEC Bulletin 19–23 (1986)

Towards a Greater Depoliticization of Investment Disputes: The Roles of ICSID and MIGA, 1(1) ICSID Review 1–25 (Spring 1986)

Obstacles Facing ICSID Proceedings and International Arbitration in General, 3(1) News from ICSID 8 (1986)

The Multilateral Investment Guarantee Agency, 20 International Lawyer 485–98 (Spring 1986)

The Multilateral Investment Guarantee Agency (MIGA) and its Role in the Promotion of Foreign Investment, *in* PRIVATE INVESTORS ABROAD — PROBLEMS AND SOLUTIONS IN INTERNATIONAL BUSINESS IN 1985, Chapter 11 (J. Moss ed., Southwestern Legal Foundation/ International and Comparative Law Center, 1986)

The Role of ICSID and the Projected Multilateral Investment Guarantee Agency (MIGA), 41(1) Aussenwirtschaft 105–22 (April 1986)

A Review of OPEC Aid Efforts, 23(1) Finance & Development 17 (1986)

MIGA and the Standards Applicable to Foreign Investments, 1 ICSID Review 327 (1986)

The Role of ICSID and the Projected Multilateral Investment Guarantee Agency (MIGA), *in* PROMOTION OF DIRECT INVESTMENT IN DEVELOPING COUNTRIES 105 (H. Hauser ed., 1986)

The Settlement of Disputes Regarding Foreign Investments: The Role of the World Bank, with Particular Reference to ICSID and MIGA, 1 Arab Law Quarterly 265-79 (1986); *also published in* 1 American University Journal of International Law & Policy 97 (1986)

The Multilateral Investment Guarantee Agency, 80 American Society of International Law Proceedings 21–27 (1986)

Obstacles Facing International Arbitration, 4 International Tax and Business Lawyer 209 (1986)

Factors Influencing the Flow of Foreign Investment and the Relevance of a Multilateral Investment Guarantee Scheme, 21 International Lawyer 671 (1987); *also published in* ESSAYS ON INTERNATIONAL LAW: THIRTEENTH ANNIVERSARY COMMEMORATIVE VOLUME, Asian-African Legal Consultative Committee 76–94 (1987)

The Multilateral Investment Guarantee Agency (MIGA), *in* 2 FOREIGN INVESTMENT IN THE PRESENT AND A NEW INTERNATIONAL ECONOMIC ORDER 137–152 (D.Chr. Dicke ed., 1987); an earlier version of this article was *published in* 20 International Lawyer 485 (1986)

The Multilateral Investment Guarantee Agency in Perspective, *in* Journal of the Management Professional Association 1–10 (Madras, India, May 1987)

The Multilateral Investment Guarantee Agency (MIGA) and the Legal Treatment of Foreign Investment (five lectures), 203 Recueil des Cours 95-320 (1987); *also published as* 203 Hague Academy of International Law 95-320 (Martinus Nijhof, 1987)

Eligibility Requirements for MIGA's Guarantees, 2 ICSID Review 373–401 (1987)

MIGA: A Timely Initiative for Latin America, 6 Bank's World 14–15 (December 1987)

Environment, Economic Development and Human Rights: A Triangular Relationship? 82 American Society of International Law Proceedings 40–63 (1988)

Encouraging International Corporate Investment: The Role of the Multilateral Investment Guarantee Agency, 23(1) Columbia Journal of World Business 11–18 (1988)

The Role of Arbitration in the Contemporary World, XXVIII(3-4) Rassegna dell' Arbitrato 75–79 (1988)

World Bank and Human Rights, 7 Bank's World 12–15 (February 1988)

The Multilateral Investment Guarantee Agency (MIGA) and the Settlement of Disputes, *in* INTERNATIONAL COMMERCIAL ARBITRATION: RECENT DEVELOPMENTS 345 (Practicing Law Institute, 1988)

International Investment Guarantee Agency (MIGA), *in* PROSPECTS FOR INTERNATIONAL LENDING AND RESCHEDULING, Chapter Twelve (Southern Methodist University, Institute of International Finance, 1988)

Oil Prices and Third World Indebtedness — Is There a Linkage? Paper submitted to the Bergen Conference on Oil and Economics (Bergen, Norway, 1988)

The "Gold Dollar" as a Measure of Capital Valuation After Termination of the Par Value System — The Case of the IBRD Capital, 32 German Yearbook of International Law 55–86 (1989)

Multilateral Investment Guarantee Agency, *in* ENCYCLOPEDIA OF PUBLIC INTERNATIONAL LAW (R. Bernhardt ed., 1989) (with A. Parra)

The World Bank and Human Rights: An Analysis of the Legal Issues and the Record of Achievements, 17 Denver Journal of International Law & Policy 39 (1989)

The Experience of ICSID in the Selection of Arbitrators, 6(1) News from ICSID 4 (1989)

MIGA and the Settlement of Disputes, 1(2) International Quarterly 178 (1989); *also published* as MIGA and Dispute Settlement, *in* 12(4) Middle East Executive Reports 8 (1989)

Law and the Development Process, 9 Bank's World 12–14 (March, 1990)

Earlier Oil Price Rises and Third World Indebtedness, 5(3) Foreign Relations Journal 16 (1990)

The Institute of International Law's Resolution on Arbitration between States and Foreign Enterprises — A Comment, 5 ICSID Review 65 (1990)

The Role of the European Bank for Reconstruction and Development in the Promotion and Financing of Investment in Central and Eastern Europe: A Legal Analysis, 5(2) ICSID Review 207–31 (Fall 1990)

Promotion of Arab and Foreign Investment — General Remarks, *in* INVESTMENT POLICIES IN THE ARAB COUNTRIES 127–142 (Said El-Naggar ed., International Monetary Fund 1990) (paper presented at a Seminar held in Kuwait, December 11–13, 1989)

Promotion of Foreign Direct Investment — A General Account, with Particular Reference to the Role of the World Bank Group, 6 ICSID Review 484 (1991)

Involuntary Resettlement in World Bank Financed Projects, *in* ANTHROPOLOGICAL APPROACHES IN INVOLUNTARY RESETTLEMENT: POLICY AND THEORY (M. Cernea & S. Guggenheim editors, 1991)

International Financing Mechanisms and Institutional Responses, *in* THE ROLE OF LAW IN THE 1992 UNITED NATIONS CONFERENCE ON ENVIRONMENT AND DEVELOPMENT (American Bar Association, May 1991, Virginia)

Towards a Greater Depoliticization of Investment Disputes: The Roles of ICSID and MIGA (ICSID Publication, 1992)

ICSID and Paths to Institutional Cooperation, 9(1) News from ICSID 6 (1992)

The World Bank Legal Framework for the Treatment of Foreign Investment, paper submitted to the European Institute Seminar on Transatlantic Foreign Investment (1992)

The World Bank and the Environment: Legal Perspective, 16(1) Maryland Journal of International Law & Trade 1–42 (Spring 1992)

The World Bank and Non-Governmental Organizations, 25(3) Cornell International Law Journal 623–41 (1992)

Human Rights, Development and International Financial Institutions, American University Journal of International Law & Policy 35–45 (Fall 1992)

Administrative Reform in the Arab Countries — General Observations and Comparative Solutions (1993)

ICSID Arbitration: The Institution's Point of View, *in* PRIVATE INVESTMENTS ABROAD — PROBLEMS AND SOLUTIONS IN INTERNATIONAL BUSINESS IN 1993, Chapter 16 (1–25) (C.J. Holgren ed., Southwestern Legal Foundation/International and Comparative Law Center, 1993)

Civil Service Reform in Developing Countries, 12 Bank's World 11–13 (July–August 1993)

Judicial reform in Developing Countries and the Role of the World Bank, paper submitted to the Seminar on Justice in Latin America and the Caribbean in the 1990s, organized by the Inter-American Development Bank, San José, Costa Rica, February 4–6, 1993 (Inter-American Development Bank, 1993)

The World Bank Group's New "Guidelines on the Treatment of Foreign Direct Investment", 10(1) News from ICSID 4 (1993)

Applicable Substantive Law in Disputes Between States and Private Foreign Parties: The Case of Arbitration Under the ICSID Convention, 9 ICSID Rev. 183 (1994) (with A. Parra)

Recent Trends Relating to Entry of Foreign Direct Investment, 9 ICSID Rev. 47 (1994)

Development Policies and Strategies — With Emphasis on the World Bank Group, *in* THE UNITED NATIONS AT AGE FIFTY (Christian Tomuschat ed., 1995)

Legal Aspects of the World Bank's Assistance to the West Bank and the Gaza Strip, 7 Palestine Yearbook of International Law 101–125 (1995) (with H. Abushakra and H.-J. Gruss)

The World Bank, Human Rights and the Environment, 1 European Law Students Association (ELSA) Law Review 1–11 (1995)

The Joint Development of International Petroleum Resources in Undefined and Disputed Areas, 11 ICSID Rev. 299 (1996) (with W.T. Onorato)

Implementation, Enforcement and Compliance with International Environmental Agreements — Practical Suggestions in Light of the World Bank's Experience, 9 Georgetown International Environmental Law Review 37 (1996)

Some Recent Trends in Banking Law and Their Relevance to the GCC States, paper presented at the Third Banking Conference, Bahrain, October 28-29, 1996, published as Some Recent trends in Banking Law, 13 Arab Law Quarterly 129 (1998)

Matters of State Succession in the Practice of the World Bank, 12 Development and International Cooperation 7–28 (1996)

The World Bank's Protection and Promotion of Children's Rights, 4 The International Journal of Children's Rights 383 (1996)

Corruption — A General Review with an Emphasis on the Role of the World Bank, paper presented at Jesus College, Cambridge, England, September 9, 1996, *published in* 15 Dickinson Journal of International Law 451 (1997); *also published in* CORRUPTION: THE ENEMY WITHIN 255 (B. Rider ed., 1997),

Democracy and Development, 46 International and Comparative Law Quarterly 635–43 (July 1997)

The Role of Law in Business Development, 20 Fordham International Law Journal 1577 (1997)

The Role of the World Bank's General Counsel, *in* PROCEEDINGS OF THE 91ST ANNUAL MEETING OF THE AMERICAN SOCIETY OF INTERNATIONAL LAW, ROUNDTABLE OF INTERNATIONAL FINANCIAL INSTITUTIONS GENERAL COUNSELS 214 (1997)

The World Bank Inspection Panel: A Background Paper on its Historical, Legal and Operational Aspects, paper submitted to the Expert Meeting on the Inspection Panel, Lund, Sweden, October 23–25, 1997

The World Bank, *in* JUSTICE DELAYED — JUDICIAL REFORM IN LATIN AMERICA 119 (E. Jarquín & F. Carrillo eds., Inter-American Development Bank, 1998)

The World Bank in the Nineties, *in* CURRENT LEGAL ISSUES AFFECTING CENTRAL BANKS, Ch. 2 (International Monetary Fund, 1997)

Resolution on the Establishment of the Heavily Indebted Poor Countries (HIPC) Debt Initiative Trust Fund — Introductory Note, 36 International Legal Materials 990 (1997)

Multilateral Investment Guarantee Agency, *in* 3 ENCYCLOPEDIA OF PUBLIC INTERNATIONAL LAW 473–80 (1997) (with A. Parra)

Matters of State Succession in the Practice of the World Bank, *in* LIBER AMICORUM G.E. D. NASCIMENTO E SILVA (P. Casella ed., 1998)

Recent Developments in ICSID, Remarks at the Fourteenth ICSID/Arbitration Association/ICC International Court of Arbitration Colloquium on International Arbitration "Institutional Arbitration: Uniformity and Diversity," 13 ICSID Review 10 (1998)

Some Recent Trends in Banking Law, 13 Arab Law Quarterly 129 (1998)

The World Bank's Contribution to the Development of International Environmental Law, *in* LIBER AMICORUM IGNAZ SEIDL-HOHENVELDERN 631 (1998)

The World Bank Guidelines on the Treatment of Foreign Direct Investment, *in* FESTSCHRIFT ZUM VIERZIGJÄHRIGEN BESTEHEN DER GESELLSCHAFT ZUR FÖRDERUNG DES SCHUTZES VON AUSLANDSINVESTIONEN E.V. KÖLN 1956 BIS 1996 (1998)

Some Observations on the Question of *Riba* and the Challenges Facing "Islamic Banking," *in* ISLAMIC LAW AND ITS RECEPTION BY THE COURTS IN THE WEST (C. Von Bar ed., 1999)

Avoidance and Settlement of Disputes — The World Bank's Approach and Experience, 1(2) International Forum du Droit International 90–98 (June 1999)

The World Bank and the World Debt Problem, *in* LIBER AMICORUM MOHAMMED BEDJAOUI 615–27 (E. Yakpo & T. Boumedra eds., 1999)

The Environment, Arms Control, Human Rights and the World Bank, *in* ADMINISTRATIVE AND EXPERT MONITORING ON INTERNATIONAL TREATIES (P. Szasz ed., 1999)

The Dynamic Evolution of International Organizations — The Case of the World Bank, *in* HISTORY OF INTERNATIONAL LAW (Macdonald ed., forthcoming 2000)

Techniques to Avoid Proliferation of International Organizations — The Experience of the World Bank, *in* PROLIFERATION OF INTERNATIONAL ORGANIZATIONS (C.H.G. Schermers and N.M. Blokker, forthcoming 2000)

The Changing Role of the State and Some Related Governance Issues, European Law Review 1999.

In Arabic

Positive Effects of Judicial Decisions of Annulment of Promotion Decisions, 8–9 Conseil d'Etat Review 59 (Cairo, 1985)

On the Creative Role of the Judge — A Comparative Perspective, 2 Revue des Sciences Juridiques et Economiques 415–31 (Cairo, 1962)

Attitude of New states Towards the International Court of Justice, 20 Egyptian Review of International Law 37–77 (1964)

Arab Economic Cooperation (Annex of Al-Ahram Al-Iqtisadi, Cairo, December 1965). With Dr. Hazem El-Beblawi

State Sovereignty or Jurisdiction in Air Space, 7 Revue des Sciences Juridiques et Economiques 232–306 (1965)

Extent of Subjecting Disputes of International Character to National Judicial Jurisdiction, 9 Review of Government Claims Authority 1–24 (1965)

The South-West African Problem at the UN, 1 International Politics 47-71 (Boutros — Boutros Ghali ed., Cairo, Egypt, 1965)

The League of Arab States and Arab Civil Aviation, 2 International Politics 130–150 (Cairo, 1965)

On the International Civil Aviation Organization, 8 Revue des Sciences Juridiques et Economiques (1966)

The Disarmament Issue, 3 International Politics 239–302 (1966)

The UAR and International Adjudication, 5 International Politics 661–68 (1966)

The UN Charter Between the Text and Its Application, 6 International Pololitics 130–37 (1966)

The UN Fund for Capital Development, 8 International Politics 106–13 (1967)

Economic Cooperation in the Arab Region — The Arab Common Market and Lebanon, *in* COMMON MARKETS 83-169 (Beirut, 1967). With Dr. Hazem El-Beblawi

The International Law Commission Project on the Law of Treaties, 23 Egyptian Review of International Law 77–113 (1967)

Arab Investments in Arab Countries, 12 International Politics 80–92 (1968)

Political Limitations on External Finance, 334 L'Egypte Contemporaine 55–73 (1968)

Legal Framework for the Encouragement and Supervision of Private Foreign Investment, 24 Egyptian Review of International Law 139–58 (1968)

Arab Joint Economic Ventures, 15 International Politics 56–75 (1969)

An International System for Foreign Investment Guarantee — Its Evaluation and Rationale, 25 Egyptian Review of International Law 63–83 (1969)

The First Arbitration Case on Foreign Investment Guarantee, 26 Egyptian Review of International Law 193–217 (1970)

Important Controversial Issues in the Establishment of an International Agency for Investment Guarantees, 12 Revue des Sciences Juridiques et Economiques 521–77 (1970)

International Organizations and Development Finance in the Third World, 23 International Politics 66–85 (1971) *also published by* the National Institute for Management and Development (Beirut, 1971)

The Issue of Secure Boundaries and Israeli Expansion, 25 International Politics 20–57 (1971)

The International Court of Justice — Prerequisites for Developing Its Role, 31 International Politics 38–66 (1972)

The Inter-Arab Investment Guarantee Corporation and Its Role in the Direction of Arab Investment, 353 L'Egypte Contemporaine (1973) *also published by* The Kuwait Fund, 1973)

Petro Wealth in the Face of Arab Development Problems, 36 International Politics (1974)

International Economic Agreements (Ministry of Foreign Affairs, Fourth Diplomatic Round for 1973, Kuwait, 1974)

Nationalization of Chilean Copper before European Courts, 31 Egyptian Review of International Law 205–35 (1974)

Institutional and Administrative Arrangements for Agencies Responsible for the Investment of Arab Funds — Their Efficiency and Reliability, a paper submitted to the "Seminar on Investment Policies of Arab Oil Producing Countries, Kuwait, 1974

Arab Development Finance Agencies, 42 International Politics (1975)

International Organizations and Development Finance, a paper presented to the World Bank Seminar on Project Evaluation, Kuwait, 1975

Joint Ventures in the Context of Arab Cooperation, 39 International Politics (1975)

Different Formulas for the Establishment of Arab Joint Ventures (Kuwait Fund Publication, January, 1975)

OPEC Countries' Aid — An Analytical Study, 4(1) Oil & Arab Cooperation 100–25 (OPEC, 1978) (with R. Mabro)

Arab Joint Ventures (Kuwait Fund Publication, May, 1976)

The OPEC Special Fund — A New Approach to International Financial Assistance (OPEC Fund Publication, presented to "the Business in the Pacific Basin," conference organized by the Financial Times, held in Manila, October, 1976)

Future of Arab Aid, The Arab Future (June 1980). *Also separately published by* the OPEC Fund, 1980

OPEC Countries as a Donor Group (OPEC Fund Publication, 1980)

The Role of the World Bank in the Settlement of Foreign Investment Disputes, 41 Egyptian Review of International Law 1–24 (1985)

Commentary on the Agreement Establishing the Multilateral Investment Guarantee Agency, 41 Egyptian Review of International Law 187–215 (1985)

Multilateral Investment Guarantee Agency (MIGA), 76 L'Egypte Contemporaine 261–77 (October 1985)

A New Instrument for Developing Countries — The Multilateral Investment Guarantee Agency, 1 Dinar 21–24 (Kuwait, 1986)

International Trade and Investment Arbitration, with particular reference to ICSID Arbitration — An Overview, 80 L'Egypte Contemporaine 5–21 (June–October 1989)

Oil Prices and Third World Indebtedness — Is There a Linkage?, 15 Oil and Arab Cooperation 13–47 (Winter, 1989)

Issues Related to Governance in World Bank Borrowing Countries, 425 L'Egypte Contemporaine 17–58 (1991)

Administrative Reform in Arab Countries — General Remarks and Comparative Solutions in (Arab Administrative Development Organization, 1998)

Some Recent Trends In Banking Law with Comparison in the Gulf Cooperation Council Countries, 1(2) Al-Amwal 53–57 (1997)

Bank Restructuring and Merger — Individual Cases and Systemic Failures, 3 Al-Amwal 26–34 (January 1999)

Bank Mergers and Acquisitions — Universal Developments and Outcomes *in* Proceedings of the 1999 Annual Meeting of the Union of Arab Banks, Beirut, 1999

In French

Les Entreprises Communes Arabes: Analyse Critique, 68 L'Egypte Contemporaine 5 (1977)

Le CIRDI et Les Pays en Voie de Développement, Entwicklung/ Développement 48 (October 1984)

L'Agence Multilatérale de Garantie des Investissements (AMGI), 33 Annuaire Français de Droit International 601–13 (1987)

Le CIRDI et les Pays en Voie de Développement et Plus Particulièrement les Pays Arabes, *in* PROCEEDINGS OF THE FIRST EURO-ARAB ARBITRATION CONFERENCE 1–94 (F. Kemicha ed., 1987)

Démocratie et Développement — A Propos de la Notion de Démocratie Durable, *in* PAIX, DÉVELOPPEMENT, DÉMOCRATIE — BOUTROS BOUTROS-GHALI AMICORUM DISCIPULORUMQUE LIBER (1999)

La Banque Mondiale et les Droits de l'Homme, *in* PROCEEDINGS OF THE ABIDJAN SEMINAR ON ECONOMIC, SOCIAL AND CULTURAL RIGHTS, Sponsored by the International Commission of Jurists (1998 forthcoming)

La Banque Mondiale et les Droits de l'Homme, *in* Revue Belge de Droit International (2000)

In Italian

Diritto Allo Sviluppo un Obbligo Giuridico non solo Morale, 84 Cooperazione 74–77 (Maggio 1989)

In Portuguese

A MIGA como Amortecedor Contra a Intervenção Diplomática e a Politização (Anais do Congresso Internacional Sobre Arbitragem Comercial (Rio de Janeiro, 29/31 de Julho de 1985)

In Spanish

Hacia una Mayor Despolitizacion de las Diferencias Relativas a Inversiones: El Papel del CIADI y del OMGI, (ICSID Publication 1991)

Reforma Judicial en los Países en Desarrollo y la Funcion del Banco Mundial (Inter-American Development Bank, 1993)

La Reforma Judicial los Países en Desarrollo y el Papel del Banco Mundial, paper submitted to the Seminar on Justice in Latin America and the Carribean in the 1990s, organized by the Inter-American Development Bank, San José, Costa Rica, February 4–6, 1993

La Experiencia del Banco Mundial, *in* LA ECONOMÍA POLÍTICA DE LA REFORMA JUDICIAL 407 (E. Jarquín & F. Carrillo eds., Inter-American Development Bank, 1997).

CONTRIBUTOR OF THE FOREWORD

JAMES D. WOLFENSOHN

James D. Wolfensohn, the World Bank Group's ninth president since 1946, established his career as an international investment banker with a parallel involvement in development issues and the global environment. Since becoming president on June 1, 1995, he has traveled to more than 100 countries to gain first-hand experience of the challenges facing the World Bank, and its 182 member countries.

On September 27, 1999, Mr. Wolfensohn was unanimously reappointed by the Bank's Board of Executive Directors to a second five-year term as president beginning June 1, 2000. This will make him the third president in World Bank history to serve a second term. During his travels, Mr. Wolfensohn has not only visited development projects supported by the World Bank, but he has also met with the Bank's government clients as well as with representatives from business, labor, media, Non-Governmental Organizations (NGOs), religious and women's groups, students and teachers. In the process, he has taken the initiative in forming new strategic partnerships between the Bank and the governments it serves, the private sector, civil society, regional development banks and the UN.

In 1996, together with the International Monetary Fund (IMF), Mr. Wolfensohn initiated the Heavily Indebted Poor Countries Initiative (HIPC) as the first comprehensive debt reduction program to address the needs of the world's poorest, most heavily indebted countries. In January 1999, Mr. Wolfensohn introduced the Comprehensive Development Framework (CDF), drawing on the lessons of development experience and putting into action the key concepts laid out in his Annual Meetings speeches of 1997 and 1998. Together with the Bank's partners, the CDF is now being piloted in 12 countries, and CDF principles are the basis for Poverty Reduction Strategy Papers (PRSPs) being prepared in low-income countries.

Mr. Wolfensohn has been a strong proponent of designing a digital development architecture to harness knowledge and connectivity to leverage development, and to close the digital and knowledge divides. The Bank is now integrating Information Communications Technologies (ICTs) into the development dialogue, agenda and action, while implementing a series of ICT-based grant and distance learning programs to link developing communities as a means for increased participation, inclusion and opportunity.

Prior to joining the Bank, Mr. Wolfensohn was an international investment banker. His last position was as President and Chief Executive Officer of James D. Wolfensohn Inc., his own investment firm set up in 1981 to advise major U.S. and international corporations. He relinquished his interests in the firm upon joining the World Bank. Before setting up his own company, Mr. Wolfensohn held a series of senior positions in finance. He was Executive Partner of Salomon Brothers in New York and head of its investment banking department. He was Executive Deputy Chairman and Managing Director of Schroders Ltd. in London, President of J. Henry Schroders Banking Corporation in New York, and Managing Director, Darling & Co. of Australia.

Throughout his career, Mr. Wolfensohn has also closely involved himself in a wide range of cultural and volunteer activities, especially in the performing arts. Currently, in addition to serving as President of the World Bank Group, he is Chairman of the Board of the Institute for Advanced Study at Princeton University. In 1970, Mr. Wolfensohn became involved in New York's Carnegie Hall, first as a board member and later, from 1980 to 1991, as Chairman of the Board, during which time he led its successful effort to restore the landmark New York building. He is now Chairman Emeritus of

Carnegie Hall. In 1990, Mr. Wolfensohn became Chairman of the Board of Trustees of the John F. Kennedy Center for the Performing Arts in Washington, D.C. On January 1, 1996, he was elected Chairman Emeritus.

Mr. Wolfensohn has been President of the International Federation of Multiple Sclerosis Societies, Director of the Business Council for Sustainable Development, and served both as Chairman of the Finance Committee and as Director of the Rockefeller Foundation and of the Population Council, and as member of the Board of Rockefeller University. He is an Honorary Trustee of the Brookings Institution and a member of the Council on Foreign Relations and the Century Association in New York. Mr. Wolfensohn is also a Fellow of the American Academy of Arts and Sciences and a Fellow of the American Philosophical Society. In 2000, he was the recipient of the Foreign Policy Association Medal, an Honorary Doctor of Public Service Degree from George Washington University, an Honorary Degree from Ben-Gurion University of the Negev, Israel, and Michigan State University, the Africare Bishop John T. Walker Distinguished Humanitarian Award and the 2000 Global Leadership Award from the UN Association of the USA.

He has been the recipient of many awards for his volunteer work, including the first David Rockefeller Prize of the Museum of Modern Art in New York for his work for culture and the arts. In May 1995 he was awarded an Honorary Knighthood by Queen Elizabeth II for his contribution to the arts. Mr. Wolfensohn has also been decorated by the Governments of Australia, France, Germany, Morocco, and Norway.

Born in Australia in December 1933, Mr. Wolfensohn is a naturalized U.S. citizen. He holds B.A. and LL.B. degrees from the University of Sydney and an M.B.A. from the Harvard Graduate School of Business. Before attending Harvard, he was a lawyer in the Australian law firm of Allen, Allen & Hemsley.

Mr. Wolfensohn served as an Officer in the Royal Australian Air Force, and was a member of the 1956 Australian Olympic Fencing Team.

He and his wife, Elaine, an education specialist and a graduate of Wellesley, B.A., and Columbia University, M.A. and M.Ed., have three children — Sara, Naomi, and Adam.

LIST OF CONTRIBUTORS*

Y. Seyyid Abdulai

Dr. Abdulai is the Director-General of the OPEC Fund for International Development. Previous positions: Executive Director, World Bank; Managing Director, Federal Mortgage Bank of Nigeria.

Mohamed I.M. Aboul-Enein

Dr. Aboul-Enein is the Director of the Cairo Regional Centre for International Commercial Arbitration (CRCICA), Secretary-General of the Arab Union of International Arbitration, Vice-President of the International Federation of Commercial Arbitration Institutions (IFCAI), Chairman of the Cairo Branch of the Chartered Institute of Arbitrators (CIArb), Constitutional Counsel of the People's Assembly of Egypt, and Vice-President of the Egyptian Branch of the International Law Association (ILA). Previous positions: Senior Vice President of the Supreme Constitutional Court of Egypt.

* The editors would like to bring to the attention of the readers of this LIBER AMICORUM that it was impossible to pay full respect to the long list of achievements of everyone who contributed a chapter to this book in the short biographical sketches reprinted here. The editors have therefore tried to focus on the more important achievements of the contributors, trusting that the well-known standing of the overwhelming majority of contributors in the international law and development community is a better guarantee for recognition than any ill-designed attempt by the editors to fully capture and reflect the contributors' true role in and advances to the field of international law and development. In this vein, the editors apologize for any omissions and shortcomings in the above reproduced short profiles of the contributors.

Abdlatif Y. Al-Hamad

Mr. Abdlatif Y. Al-Hamad has been the Director-General/Chairman of the Board of the Arab Fund for Economic and Social Development since 1985. Abdlatif Y. Al-Hamad is a trustee and member of the board of directors of several international development organizations. Previous positions: Minister of Finance from 1981 to 1983; Director General of the Kuwait Fund for Arab Economic Development from 1963 to 1981; Chairman of a Task Force on Multilateral Development Banks.

Fawzi Hamad Al-Sultan

Mr. Al-Sultan is the President of the International Fund for Agricultural Development (IFAD). Previous positions: Executive Director, World Bank; Director, Kuwait Emergency and Recovery Program; Managing Director, Bank of Kuwait and the Middle East; Chairman and Managing Director, International Financial Advisers, KSC; Director of Research, Kuwait Fund for Arab Economic Development.

Karl-Heinz Böckstiegel

Prof. Dr. Böckstiegel is the Holder of the Chair for International Business Law at the University of Cologne, Germany; President of the German Institution of Arbitration (DIS) and the German Association of International Law. Previous positions: President, London Court of International Arbitration (LCIA); President, Iran-United States Claims Tribunal.

Charles N. Brower

Mr. Brower is a partner in the law firm White & Case, Washington, DC, and is a member of the Register of Experts of the United Nations Compensation Commission, as well as on the Panels of Arbitrators and Conciliators of the International Centre for Settlement of Investment Disputes (ICSID). Previous positions: general commercial litigator with White & Case in New York; Acting Legal Adviser Department of State; Judge, Iran-United States Claims Tribunal in The Hague; Deputy Special Counselor to the President of the United States; Judge *Ad Hoc* of the Inter-American Court of Human Rights.

Thomas Buergenthal

Dr. Buergenthal is a Judge of the International Court of Justice. Previous positions: Lobingier Professor of International and Comparative Law, George Washington University Law School; Judge and President, Inter-American Court of Human Rights; Member, UN Human Rights Committee; Member, UN Truth Commission for El Salvador; Vice-Chairman, Claims Resolution Tribunal for Dormant Accounts in Switzerland.

Hungdah Chiu

Dr. Chiu is Professor of Law at the University of Maryland School of Law and Ambassador-at-Large to the United States, Republic of China/Taiwan. Previous positions: President, International Law Association.

Luis Dodero

Mr. Dodero is the Vice President and General Counsel of the Multilateral Investment Guarantee Agency (MIGA) and a Member of the Spanish Court of Arbitration. Previous positions: Deputy General Manager and General Counsel, Compañia Española de Seguros de Crédito a la Exportación, S.A. (CESCE); Legal Advisor, Claims Department, Compañia Española de Seguros de Crédito y Caució; Legal Adviser, INDEIN, a Spanish company with an international clientele. He practiced for several years in his own law firm, specializing in international commercial law, shipping and labor law.

Rudolf Dolzer

Prof. Dr. Dolzer is Professor of Law and pro-Rector at the University of Mannheim, Professor of Law and Director of the Institute of International Law, University of Bonn, Member of the Enquête-Commission "Protection of the Atmosphere" of the 11th and 12th German Bundestag and Member, Commission of Inquiry "Globalization of Economy" of the German Bundestag. Previous positions: Member, Scientific and Technical Advisory Panel of the Global Environment Facility; Director-General in the Office of the Federal Chancellor, Germany.

Christian Dominicé

Dr. Dominicé is honorary Professor of Law of the Faculté de droit of Geneva, Switzerland, Secretary-General of the *Institut de Droit International*, and Member of the Court of Conciliation and Arbitration within OSCE. Previous positions: Dean, Director, and Professor of Law, Graduate Institute of International Studies in Geneva, Switzerland.

Ahmed Sadek El-Kosheri

Dr. El-Kosheri is a partner in the law firm Kosheri, Rashed & Riad, Cairo, Egypt; Judge at the Administrative Tribunal of the African Development Bank, Vice-Chairman of the International Chamber of Commerce (ICC) and the International Court of Arbitration, Ad hoc Judge at the International Court of Justice, and Member of the *Institut de Droit International*. Previous positions: Secretary-General of the Islamic Development Bank; Founding General Counsel of the Arab Fund for Economic and Social Development.

Tom J. Farer

Dr. Farer is Professor of Law and Dean of the Graduate School of International Studies and Director of the Center for China-United States Cooperation, University of Denver. He has published 11 books and numerous articles. Previous positions: President, University of New Mexico; Chairman, Inter-American Commission on Human Rights; Senior Fellow, Carnegie Endowment and Council on Foreign Relations; Fellow, Wilson Center at the Smithsonian.

Florentino P. Feliciano

Dr. Feliciano is the Chairman of the Appellate Body, World Trade Organization. Previous positions: Chairman, Philippine Senate Electoral Tribunal; Member, Asian Development Bank Administrative Tribunal; Member, Philippine House of Representatives Electoral Tribunal; Associate Justice, Supreme Court of the Philippines; and partner in the Philippine law firm, SyCip Salazar Feliciano & Hernandez.

Louis Forget

Dr. Forget is Legal Adviser, Institutional Affairs, Legal Department, World Bank. He holds an LL.M. from the University of Michigan and a Docteur en droit from the University of Paris, France. He joined the Bank in 1972 as operational lawyer. Since 1981, he advised on various aspects of international law, e.g. the law of treaties, state succession, the Bank's relationship with the UN, and human rights. Dr. Forget participated as an observer, representing the Bank, in the preparation of the OECD Convention on Combating Bribery of Foreign Public Officials in International Business Transactions and the Council of Europe's Criminal Law Convention on Corruption.

David Freestone

Dr. Freestone is Chief Counsel, Environmentally and Socially Sustainable Development (ESSD) and International Law Practice Group, Legal Department, World Bank. Previous positions: Professor of International Law at the University of Hull, England.

Ahmed Galal

Dr. Galal is the Executive Director of the Egyptian Center for Economic Studies (ECES). Previous positions: Director of Research, ECES; Advisor, World Bank Private Sector Development Department.

L. Michael Hager

Mr. Hager heads the development law consulting firm, Resolve-Consult International, Inc. Previous positions: Co-founder and Director of the International Development Law Institute (IDLI), Rome, Italy.

Mohamed El-Fatih Hamid

Dr. Hamid is the General Counsel of the Islamic Development Bank. Previous positions: Associate Professor of Law and Dean, Faculty of Law, University of Khartoum, Sudan.

Siv Carlie Jacqueline Hellén

Ms. Hellén is Senior Vice President and General Counsel of the Nordic Investment Bank; Member, Board of Directors, Lithuanian Development Bank; Member, Board of Directors, Investment Bank of Latvia, and Adviser to the

President, Estonian Investment Bank. Previous positions: Bank of Helsinki; Finnish Lawyers' Confederation.

Raul R. Herrera

Mr. Herrera is the General Counsel of the Inter-American Investment Corporation (IIC). Previous positions: Senior Counsel, and Attorney, IIC; Counsel, Federal Deposit Insurance Corporation (FDIC); Attorney, Federal Home Loan Bank Board (FHLBB).

Rosalyn Higgins

Dr. Higgins is a Judge at the International Court of Justice and member of the *Institut de Droit International.* Previous positions: Professor of International Law, London School of Economics; Member, United Nations Human Rights Committee.

Patrick Juillard

Dr. Juillard is Professor of Law at the University of Paris I–Panthéon-Sorbonne. Previous positions include consulting and arbitration work; Visiting Professor, University of Michigan and other foreign universities.

Carol F. Lee

Ms. Lee is Vice President and General Counsel of the International Finance Corporation. Previous positions: General Counsel, Export-Import Bank of the United States; Partner at the law firm Wilmer, Cutler & Pickering; Law Clerk to Justice John Paul Stevens, United States Supreme Court.

Barry Metzger

Mr. Metzger is senior partner of the international law firm Coudert Brothers, New York, New York, USA. Previous positions: General Counsel, Asian Development Bank.

John M. Niehuss

Mr. Niehuss is the General Counsel of the Export-Import Bank of the United States. Previous positions: General Counsel, Inter-American Development Bank; Legal Adviser, Legal Department, World Bank; United States Treasury Department; Merrill Lynch; private law practice.

Francisco Orrego Vicuña

Dr. Orrego Vicuña is Professor of International Law at the Law School and the Institute of International Studies of the University of Chile, and Judge and Vice President of the World Bank Administrative Tribunal. He is also a Member of the Panels of Arbitrators and Conciliators of ICSID, and President of the Panel F-2 of the United Nations Compensation Commission, and Member of the *Institut de Droit International.*

William T. Onorato

Dr. Onorato is Legal Adviser, Energy and Mining, World Bank. Previous positions: Chief Counsel, International E & P for Getty Oil Company; Assistant to the General Counsel, Chevron Corporation.

Maurizio Ragazzi

Dr. Ragazzi is Senior Counsel, Environmentally and Socially Sustainable Development (ESSD) and International Law Practice Group, Legal Department, World Bank. He holds an LL.M. from

Columbia University, New York, New York, and a Ph.D from Oxford University, England. Previous positions: International arbitrator for an international law firm in New York and Paris; principal draftsman of the FIDIC Conditions of Subcontract.

W. Michael Reisman

Dr. Reisman is the Myres S. McDougal Professor of Law, Yale Law School; Member of the Advisory Committee on International Law of the US Department of State; Vice-Chairman of the Policy Sciences Center, Inc.; Member of the Board of the Foreign Policy Association; Member, Institute of World Business Law of the International Chamber of Commerce, and Member, *Institut de Droit International*. Previous positions: Vice-President, then President of the Inter-American Commission on Human Rights of the Organization of American States (OAS); Vice-President and Honorary Vice-President of the American Society of International Law.

Barry A.K. Rider

Dr. Rider is a Professor of Law at the University of London and Director of the Institute of Advanced Legal Studies, London, United Kingdom; Fellow of the Jesus College, Cambridge, and Honorary Professor of Commercial Law at the University of the Orange Free State. Previous positions: Founder and Head, Commonwealth Secretariat's Commercial Crime Unit; Consultant to governments and organizations, including the IMF.

Jeswald W. Salacuse

Dr. Salacuse is the Braker Professor of Law, Fletcher School of Law and Diplomacy, Tufts University, Massachusetts, USA. Previous positions: Dean, Fletcher School of Law and Diplomacy, Tufts University, and Dean, Southern Methodist University Law School; Fulbright Chair in Comparative Law, Italy.

Peter H. Sand

Dr. Sand is Lecturer in International Environmental Law, University of Munich, Germany. Previous positions: Environmental Claims Commissioner, United Nations Compensation Commission; Legal Adviser for Environmental Affairs, Legal Department, World Bank.

Sabine Schlemmer-Schulte

Dr. Sabine Schlemmer-Schulte is Senior Counsel, Operations Front Office, Legal Department, World Bank. She was Personal Assistant to Dr. Ibrahim F.I. Shihata, Senior Vice President and General Counsel, World Bank, from 1995 until his retirement from the World Bank. Adjunct Professor for European Union Law at the Washington College of Law, American University, Washington, D.C., USA; Adjunct Professor for International Trade, Finance and Development Law at the John Marshall School of Law, Chicago, Illinois, USA; Member, Committee on Accountability of International Organizations of the International Law Association; Secretary, Washington Foreign Law Society. Previous positions: Assistant Professor for Public International Law and European Union Law, Europa-Institut, Saarland University, Saarbrücken, Germany; Associate, Deringer, Tessin, Herrmann & Sedemund (now Freshfields-Deringer), Cologne, Germany.

Ignaz Seidl-Hohenveldern

Prof. Dr. Seidl-Hohenveldern is a member of the *Institut de Droit International* and of the Austrian Academy of Sciences. Previous positions: Professor of Law, Saarbrücken, Cologne, both Germany, Vienna, Austria, and Paris, France; Service in the Austrian Federal Chancellory Foreign Affairs; OEEC; Austrian Federal Chancellory Constitutional Service.

Louis Bruno Sohn

Dr. Sohn is the Director of the International Rule of Law Institute, George Washington University, and Distinguished Research Professor, George Washington University, Washington, D.C., USA. Previous positions: Head of U.S. Delegation, Athens Conference on the International Settlement of Disputes; U.S. Delegate, UN Law of the Sea Conference; Counselor on International Law, US Department of State; Legal Officer, United Nations; with delegation of Permanent Court of International Justice and UN Conference in San Francisco.

Francis M. Ssekandi and Peri Lynne Johnson

Mr. Ssekandi is the Special Counsel to the President of the African Development Bank on Good Governance. Previous positions: General Counsel, African Development Bank; Deputy Director General, General Legal Division, Office of Legal Affairs, United Nations, assigned as Principal Counsel for UNDP, UNICEF and other UN Subsidiary Organs.

Ms. Johnson is a Legal Officer, General Legal Division, Office of Legal Affairs, United Nations in New York.

Paul C. Szasz

Mr. Szasz is Adjunct Professor, New York University School of Law and Consultant to the World Health Organization, the UN Environment Program and others. Previous positions: Director and Deputy to the Legal Counsel, United Nations in New York; Secretary, International Centre for the Settlement of Investment Disputes; Attorney, World Bank; Legal and Safeguards Officer, International Atomic Energy Agency, Vienna, Austria.

John L. Taylor

Mr. Taylor is Managing Director and General Counsel, Emerging Markets Partnership (Europe) Limited. Previous positions: General Counsel, European Bank for Reconstruction and Development; senior management positions, Banque Paribas Capital Markets Limited, London; Legal Counsel, Conzinc Riotinto of Australia, Ltd.; Associate, Cleary, Gottlieb, Steen & Hamilton, Washington, D.C., USA, and Stephen, Jaques & Stephen, Adelaide, Sydney, Australia.

Don Wallace, Jr.

Mr. Wallace is the Chairman, International Law Institute, and Professor of Law, Georgetown University Law Center; Of Counsel, Morgan, Lewis & Bockius; delegate to UNCITRAL; and former Chairman, Section of International Law and Practice, American Bar Association.

Prosper Weil

Dr. Weil is Professor of Law emeritus, University of Paris Panthéon-Assas (Paris- 2); Member of the *Institut de Droit International*; Member of the Institut de France, Académie des Sciences Morales et Politiques. Previous positions: Member and President, World Bank Administrative Tribunal.

LIST OF EDITORS

Sabine Schlemmer-Schulte

Dr. Schlemmer-Schulte, a German national, is Senior Counsel, Legal Vice Presidency, Operations Front Office, World Bank. She joined the World Bank's Legal Department in November 1995 as Personal Assistant of Dr. Ibrahim F.I. Shihata, Senior Vice President and General Counsel, working with him until his resignation from the position of General Counsel in October 1998. She continued working with Dr. Shihata, who kept advising the Bank's President, but worked also with the Acting Vice President and General Counsel, Dr. Andrés Rigo Sureda, until Ko-Yung Tung was appointed Vice President and General Counsel in December 1999. Since then, she has been working in the Legal Department's Operations Front Office as well as with Ko-Yung Tung.

Dr. Schlemmer-Schulte's portfolio in the Bank covers a broad range of institutional and policy matters. She was particularly involved in matters concerning the Bank's Inspection Panel (an independent forum created in 1994 to receive complaints of people adversely affected by Bank-financed projects) and the formulation of the Bank's approach to corruption and child labor in its borrowing member countries. Further areas of her work at the Bank include trade and labor law, human rights, state succession, participation by NGOs and civil society in the Bank's work, the Bank's relationship with the IMF, developments in international banking, foreign investment, and, more recently, an initiative to establish an international commodities intermediary to offer hedging instruments to commodities producers in developing countries whose products are subject to price volatility on the global market.

Dr. Schlemmer-Schulte is also Adjunct Professor for European Union Law at the Washington College of Law (WCL), American University. She taught this subject at the Paul H. Nitze School of Advanced International Studies (SAIS), Johns Hopkins University, in Washington, DC, in 1998 and 1999. Since Spring 2000, she is an Adjunct Professor of the John Marshall School of Law, Chicago, Illinois, where she teaches International Trade, Finance and Development Law.

Dr. Schlemmer-Schulte is a Member of the International Law Association's (ILA) Committee on Accountability of International Organizations. She has been a Board Member of the Washington Foreign Law Society (WFLS) since 1998. She was WFLS Program Co-Chair in 1998/99 and is WFLS Secretary since July 2000.

Prior experience to her work in the World Bank includes the position of an Associate with Deringer, Tessin, Hermann & Sedemund (now Freshfields-Deringer) in Cologne, Germany, where she focused on European trade and anti-trust issues in cases before the European Court of Justice (ECJ). She was Assistant Professor at the Institute for European Studies of the University of Saarbrücken, Germany, where she taught public international law and European Union law, specializing in European corporate and banking law matters as well as advising private business. She joined the World Bank Group in 1994, working with the International Centre for Settlement of Investment Disputes (ICSID).

Dr. Schlemmer-Schulte received her initial law degrees, a Licence en Droit and an LL.B. respectively, in France and Germany. She subsequently received a postgraduate degree (LL.M.) in European Union law, a specialized LL.M. in European banking law, and a Doctor of Law (Dr.jur., Ph.D. equivalent) from the University of Saarbrücken, Germany. She also holds an LL.M. in international business and finance law from American University in Washington, DC. She is admitted to the German bar.

Ko-Yung Tung

Mr. Tung, a U.S. citizen, was appointed Vice-President and General Counsel of the World Bank in December 1999. He was elected to serve as Secretary-General of the International Centre for Settlement of Investment Disputes (ICSID), commencing August 2000.

Before joining the World Bank, Mr. Tung was senior partner in the international law firm of O'Melveny and Myers, where he was the Chairman of the Global Practice Group and a member of the firm's management committee. His practice was concentrated on cross-border corporate transactions.

Mr. Tung was born in Beijing, China, and grew up in Japan. He studied physics at Harvard College, graduating magna cum laude, and received his J.D. from Harvard Law School in 1973. He spent a year during his legal studies studying Japanese law at the University of Tokyo, Japan. While in private practice, he taught courses in international business transactions and Japanese law as an adjunct professor at New York University.

His principal outside activities have included serving as Chairman of the East-West Center in Hawaii, on the Advisory Council of Human Rights Watch/Asia and in the Board of the Asian-American Legal and Education Fund. He was a member of the Presidential Commission on International Trade and Investment and the Trilateral Commission. He is a member of the Council on Foreign Relations.

ASSISTANTS TO THE EDITORS

Rowena Margaret S. Gorospe,
Senior Editorial Assistant

Ms. Gorospe, a national of the Philippines, is a consultant with Sabine Schlemmer-Schulte at the World Bank. A recipient of the Hubert Humphrey Fellowship, Ms. Gorospe earned her LL.M. in International Legal Studies at the Washington College of Law, American University, Washington, DC. She received her LL.B from the University of the Philippines. Previous Positions: Legal Assistant, Linklaters and Alliance, Washington, DC; Foreign Service Officer and Acting Director, Division on Economics and Trade, Office of United Nations and International Organizations, Department of Foreign Affairs, Philippines; University Legal Counsel, University of the Philippines; Assistant Attorney, Bito, Lozada, Ortega & Castillo.

Nara Beginyan, Editorial Assistant

Ms. Nara Beginyan, an Armenian national, is a consultant with Sabine Schlemmer-Schulte at the World Bank and an LL.M candidate at the Washington College of Law (WCL), American University (AU), Washington, D.C. Prior to her joining the Bank she was an Open Society Institute (OSI) fellow at the WCL, AU, Washington, DC. She is also a fellow of the Network of East-West Women (NEWW). She received her LL.B. from Yerevan Hrachia Acharian University, Armenia.

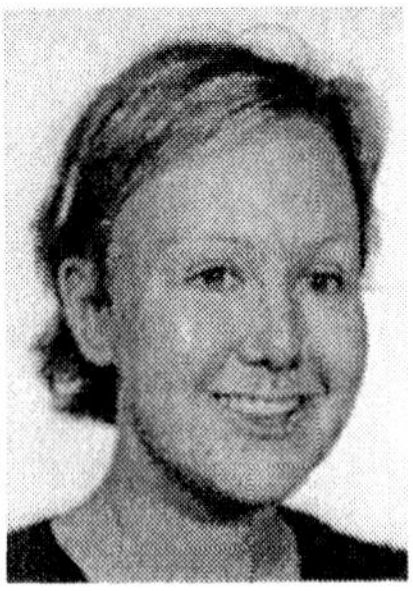

Hege Elisabeth Kjos,
Editorial Assistant

Ms. Kjos, a Norwegian national, is currently studying for her Ph.D. degree at Amsterdam University in the Netherlands. She received her J.D. from Loyola University Chicago School of Law, Chicago, Illinois. She worked as a consultant with Sabine Schlemmer-Schulte at the World Bank. Her J.D. studies included a stage at the University of Leiden, the Netherlands. Previous positions: Research Assistant at the University of Leiden, the Netherlands, and Loyola University Chicago School of Law; and high school teacher in Leirvik, Norway.

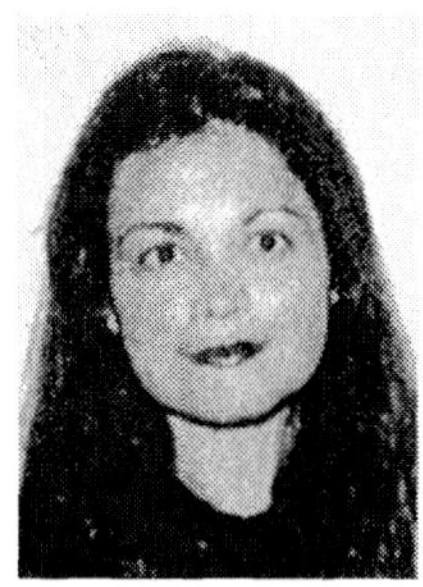

Maria Fernanda Pérez Solla,
Editorial Assistant

Ms. Perez Solla, a national from Argentina, is currently Ph.D. candidate at the University of Buenos Aires, School of Law, Buenos Aires, Argentina. She worked as a consultant with Ibrahim Shihata and Sabine Schlemmer-Schulte at the World Bank. She received her LL.M. in International Legal Studies from the Washington College of Law, American University, Washington, D.C. She received her LL.B. from the University of Buenos Aires, Buenos Aires, Argentina. Previous positions: Research Assistant, Washington College of Law, American University, University Austral, Law School, Buenos Aires, Argentina; Instructor for Legal Studies, University of Buenos Aires, School of Law and Social Sciences.

Johanna Rinceanu, Editorial Assistant

Ms. Rinceanu, a German national, is currently Rechtsreferendarin at the court (Landgericht) Frankenthal, Rheinland-Pfalz, Germany. Recipient of a Fulbright Scholarship, Ms. Rinceanu earned her LL.M. in International and Comparative International Law from George Washington University, School of Law, Washington, DC. She received her LL.B. from the University of Freiberg Baden–Württemberg, Germany. Previously, Ms. Rinceanu worked as a consultant with Ibrahim Shihata and Sabine Schlemmer-Schulte at the World Bank.

Michelle Lemaire, Executive Assistant

Ms. Lemaire, a French national, is currently on secondment with UNDP in Geneva. Ms. Lemaire joined the General Counsel's office in 1998, working with Ibrahim Shihata and Sabine Schlemmer-Schulte. Ms. Lemaire was Ibrahim Shihata's Executive Assistant when he retired from the World Bank. Previously, she worked with the World Bank Legal Department's Africa Division and for different top executives in Banque Paribas in Paris, France.

Meenadchi K. Pillai, Senior Staff Assistant

Ms. Pillai, a national of Malaysia, while retired from the World Bank, continues to make her services available to the Bank. She currently works with the Bank's Administrative Tribunal. She worked with Sabine-Schlemmer-Schulte from January to July 2000. Previous positions before retirement: Legal Department Finance Unit, and Financial Operations Department, World Bank; Malaysian Foreign Service in Moscow, Soviet Union, and Permanent Mission of Malaysia to the UN in New York, New York, USA; Ministry of Finance, Kuala Lumpur, Malaysia, and Prudential Assurance Co., Singapore.